820.

THE OXFORD ENGLISH
LITERARY HISTORY

Volume 8. 1830–1880

THE OXFORD ENGLISH LITERARY HISTORY

General Editor: Jonathan Bate

* already published

This series was conceived and commissioned by Kim Walwyn (1956–2002), to whose memory it is dedicated.

THE OXFORD ENGLISH
LITERARY HISTORY

Volume 8. 1830–1880

The Victorians

PHILIP DAVIS

OXFORD
UNIVERSITY PRESS

OXFORD
UNIVERSITY PRESS

Great Clarendon Street, Oxford OX2 6DP

Oxford University Press is a department of the University of Oxford.
It furthers the University's objective of excellence in research, scholarship,
and education by publishing worldwide in

Oxford New York

Auckland Bangkok Buenos Aires Cape Town Chennai
Dar es Salaam Delhi Hong Kong Istanbul Karachi Kolkata
Kuala Lumpur Madrid Melbourne Mexico City Mumbai Nairobi
São Paulo Shanghai Taipei Tokyo Toronto

Oxford is a registered trade mark of Oxford University Press
in the UK and in certain other countries

Published in the United States
by Oxford University Press Inc., New York

First published 2002
First published in paperback 2004

British Library Cataloguing in Publication Data
Data available

Library of Congress Cataloging in Publication Data
The Oxford English history.
p. cm.
Includes bibliographical references (p.) and indexes.
Contents: – v. 8. 1830–1880: the Victorians / Philip Davis
1. English literature–History and criticism.
PR85 .O96 2002 820.9–dc21 2002025038

ISBN 0-19-818447-6
ISBN 0-19-926920-3 (Pbk.)

10 9 8 7 6 5 4 3 2 1

Typeset in Adobe Sabon
by Regent Typesetting, London
Printed in Great Britain
on acid-free paper by
Biddles Ltd,
Guildford and King's Lynn

For the Friday Night Club:
Jane, Ben, and Brian

Acknowledgements

'We are not sent into this world to do any thing into which we cannot put our hearts' (Ruskin, *The Seven Lamps of Architecture*). But in any individual work such as this there are many debts, conscious and unconscious, owed to scholars, critics, and writers, past and present, which selective bibliographies are barely able to record. I can only mention here my clearest, greatest, and most heartfelt debts: to the generosity of the Leverhulme Trust, for a research fellowship without which I could not have completed this work; to the general editor of the OELH series, Jonathan Bate, with admiration and gratitude; to my best friend and dear colleague Brian Nellist, for those invaluable discussions every week, with the rest of the Friday Night Club—my wife Jane and son Ben; to Frances Whistler in Oxford and Angie Macmillan in Liverpool for kind and expert help in assembling the illustrations; to Rowena Anketell for her meticulous copy-editing; and, finally, to Sophie Goldsworthy commissioning editor at Oxford University Press. I note, with cheer, what a contemporary said of Mr Gladstone, 'Liverpool below, Oxford on top'. Thanks to both.

P. D.

University of Liverpool
August 2001

General Editor's Preface

The Oxford English Literary History is the twenty-first-century successor to the Oxford History of English Literature, which appeared in fifteen volumes between 1945 and 1997. As in the previous series, each volume offers an individual scholar's vision of a discrete period of literary history.[1] Each has a distinctive emphasis and structure, determined by its author's considered view of the principal contours of the period. But all the volumes are written in the belief that literary history is a discipline necessary for the revelation of the power of imaginative writing to serve as a means of human understanding, past, present, and future.

Our primary aim is to explore the diverse purposes of literary activity and the varied mental worlds of writers and readers in the past. Particular attention is given to the institutions in which literary acts take place (educated communities, publishing networks, and so forth), the forms in which literary works are presented (traditions, genres, structural conventions), and the relationship between literature and broader historical continuities and transformations. Literary history is distinct from political history, but a historical understanding of literature cannot be divorced from cultural and intellectual revolutions or the effects of social change and the upheaval of war.

We do not seek to offer a comprehensive survey of the works of all 'major', let alone 'minor', writers of the last thousand years. All literary histories are inevitably incomplete—as was seen from the rediscovery in the late twentieth century of many long-forgotten women writers of earlier eras. Every literary history has to select: in so doing, it reconfigures the 'canon'. We cast our nets very widely and make claims for many works not previously regarded as canonical, but we are fully conscious of our partiality. Detailed case studies are preferred to summary listings.

---

[1] Since Volume 1, *to 1350*, covers many centuries, it is co-written by two scholars.

viii   *General Editor's Preface*

A further aim is to undertake a critical investigation of the very notion of a national literary heritage. The word 'literature' is often taken to refer to poems, plays, and novels, but historically a much wider range of writing may properly be considered as 'literary' or as belonging within the realm of what used to be called 'letters'. The boundaries of the literary in general and of *English* literary history in particular have changed through the centuries. Each volume maps those boundaries in the terms of its own period.

For the sake of consistency and feasibility, however, two broad definitions of 'English Literary History' have been applied. First, save in the polyglot culture of the earliest era, we have confined ourselves to the English language—a body of important work written in Latin between the fourteenth and the seventeenth centuries has been excluded. And secondly, we have concentrated on works that come from, or bear upon, England. Most of the writing of other English-speaking countries, notably the United States of America, is excluded. We are not offering a world history of writing in the English language. Those Americans who lived and worked in England are, however, included.

So too with Scottish, Irish, Welsh writers, and those from countries that were once part of the British Empire: where their work was produced or significantly disseminated in England, they are included. Indeed, such figures are of special importance in many volumes, exactly because their non-English origins often placed them in an ambivalent relationship with England. Throughout the series, particular attention is paid to encounters between English and other traditions. But we have also recognized that Scottish, Welsh, Irish, African, Asian, Australasian, Canadian, and Caribbean literatures all have their own histories, which we have not sought to colonize.

It would be possible to argue endlessly about periodization. The arrangement of the Oxford English Literary History is both traditional and innovative. For instance, the period around the beginning of the nineteenth century has long been thought of as the 'Romantic' one; however we may wish to modify the nomenclature, people will go on reading and studying the Lake Poets and the 'Shelley circle' in relation to each other, so it would have been factitious to introduce a volume division at, say, 1810. On the other hand, it is still too soon for there to be broad agreement on the literary-historical shape of the twentieth century: to propose a single break at, say, 1945 would be to fall in with the false assumption that literature moves strictly in tandem with events. Each volume argues the case for its own period as a period, but at the same time beginning and ending dates are treated flexibly, and in many cases—especially with respect to the twentieth century—there is deliberate and considerable overlap between the temporal boundaries of adjacent volumes.

The voices of the last millennium are so various and vital that English literary history is always in the process of being rewritten. We seek both to chart and to contribute to that rewriting, for the benefit not just of students and scholars but of all serious readers.

Jonathan Bate

Contents

xii *Contents*

List of Figures

A Note on References

Brief biographical information on selected authors will be found at the end of the volume, together with bibliographies covering their major works and some of the most notable modern scholarship concerning them. In addition, there are suggestions for more general reading relevant to the literary history of the period. The bibliographies are intended as starting points for further study, not comprehensive listings of the kind found in the Cambridge Bibliography of English Literature and other sources (the majority of which are now published in electronic form). Whenever possible, the Author Bibliographies include recommended modern editions. An asterisk indicates the edition that has been used in the main body of the book.

Quotations in the text from works written in the period are usually followed by a reference in parentheses. Where possible, these are given in a form that does not depend on access to a particular edition (e.g. chapter, or book and line number), but for works without convenient subdivision, the citation is of the page number of the edition asterisked in the relevant Author Bibliography. Where there is no modern edition, references are to the first edition, unless otherwise stated. Longer references, e.g. to secondary sources, are given in footnotes, but if a source is referred to more than once in a chapter, subsequent references appear in the text in parentheses.

Introduction

Lytton Strachey's *Eminent Victorians* (1918) shows a dazzling irreverence of wit and irony in refusing to take its subjects as seriously as they took themselves. It is no surprise to Strachey that the poet Arthur Hugh Clough, having lost his faith, 'went on looking for it everywhere as long as he lived; but somehow he never could find it'; or that after all his unorthodox struggles 'he should have eventually succumbed, conscientiously doing up brown paper parcels for Florence Nightingale'. Indeed, that formidable woman, denied public office on the grounds of her sex, not only exhausted poor Clough and drove the politician Sidney Herbert to his death, in the effort to carry out her sanitary reforms by proxy; Miss Nightingale, says Strachey, also wrote as if she had got the Almighty Himself into her clutches—and in His case too, 'if He is not careful, she will kill Him with overwork'.

Like Cardinal Manning, Thomas Arnold of Rugby School, and General Gordon, Florence Nightingale constantly took the name of God as a means of guiltlessly fulfilling her own heroic ambitions. None of these people could believe they should merely serve their own secular desires; they were all dutifully serving the call of Providence. 'Ah! it was God's will . . . Clearly, that was the explanation.'

Together with Samuel Butler's *The Way of All Flesh* (1903), *Eminent Victorians* is one of the major works from the generation immediately succeeding the Victorians that helped to give the word 'Victorian' that heavy sinking feeling which so often still accompanies it. We might perhaps speak of a 'Renaissance' cast of mind or say that some phenomenon was essentially 'Romantic', but neither of these descriptors has the derogatory force that 'typically Victorian' has carried from at least 1918. Indeed, for all its amused intelligence, *Eminent Victorians* is in that sense finally a rather depressing book:

it makes the reader feel alternately scornful, embarrassed, appalled, even slightly ashamed in so clearly seeing through the human beings described in its chapters. That is to say, it is depressing in comparison with what a Victorian writer would have done with the same material, with what George Eliot did do in *Middlemarch* (1872) when she had equivalently under her pen the scholarly failure Casaubon, the religious hypocrite Bulstrode, and took them—poor, self-deceptive human specimens that they were—*more* seriously even than they could bear to take themselves. The reader returning to *Middlemarch* is no longer appalled or ashamed or just amused. It is not that George Eliot and Lytton Strachey were looking at entirely different things; any more than you can argue that Victorian literature is *not* about Humanity, Duty, Vocation, Work, Marriage, Family—all those old words, so close to what Strachey would dismiss as humbug, which sound like cracked voices played out on worn-out records from great-grandfather's wind-up gramophone. Rather, it is that the great realist novelist takes those concerns to such a depth of living particularity that they no longer feel the same, whatever their public name. That is the sort of *inner* originality mostly on offer in Victorian literature: it is not entirely different from what you thought it was going to be about, it is just utterly redeemed from cliché, by being in its true reality much more serious, much more important, much more complex and specific than you had ever supposed such ordinary things could be.

In that sense, this book too may hold no surprises, as such. The Victorian story set out here is not offered as radically different from that which has been told before, and indeed there are recognizable key dates which provide a basic, simplified orientation. Most significantly, of course, the reign of Victoria, the longest reign in the history of the country, began in 1837 and ended with her death in 1901. It was itself a substantial part of the long period of relative peace from 1815, and the end of the Napoleonic Wars, until 1914 and the great crash of nineteenth-century humane values in the First World War. This current volume in the Oxford English Literary History begins, however, in 1830 some years before the beginning of Victoria's reign and ends in 1880. Why? Some explanation about these and other dates is in order.

'Men can do nothing without the make-believe of a beginning', wrote George Eliot at the very commencement of her last great novel *Daniel Deronda* (1876). It is important that this volume begins at some point just before the formal accession of 1837: for, however approximately, by this means it says something about the informal, unstructured background to all that follows. In a sense the period begins with endings: with the premature death of the second generation of Romantics—Keats in 1821, Shelley in 1822, Byron in 1824, and Hazlitt in 1830—followed by the loss of Scott in 1832 and of Coleridge in 1834. Thus when Tennyson publishes his *Poems, Chiefly Lyrical* in 1830, he is writing in a consciously *post*-Romantic age, as his friend Arthur Hallam made clear in a famous early review. It is an age that thus inherits a Romantic model of individualistic lyric feeling in a world of Nature which was increasingly difficult to align with the radically changed social circumstances of the early decades of the nineteenth century—in particular, the shift of population from rural to new urban centres, with all the harsh attendant realities of the developing Industrial Revolution. It is strange to think that the year of Keats's death was also the year in which James Mill published his Utilitarian *Elements of Political Economy*, as though symbolic of that tension between the poetic and the materialistic which was to dominate the years to come; or that John Keble, poet of *The Christian Year* (1827) and one of the leaders of the religious revival called the Oxford Movement, though only three years older than Keats, died forty-five years after him; or that 1850 saw the publication of both Tennyson's *In Memoriam* and also, posthumously, Wordsworth's *The Prelude*. That is to say: in an age which may be said almost to have invented the subject of history, the time lags, questionable clarifications by hindsight, alternative possibilities, and temporal overlaps betray both the uncertainties of the times and the problems of historical understanding itself.

Almost literally underlying everything, moreover, was the shift that took place long before 1837 at a crucial turning point in the history of industrial development during the late eighteenth century: the change in heat-energy sources from wood and charcoal to the mining of coal and the use of coke, resulting in radically increased economic growth through new mass processes of iron and steel production. As E. A. Wrigley has argued in his significantly entitled *Continuity, Chance and Change: The Character of the Industrial*

Revolution in England (1988), this was an economy no longer tied to the availability of organic raw materials, dependent upon the annual flow of agricultural production. It was now a mineral-based economy, freed from its roots in a traditional geographical and social world order based upon the land, and capable instead of effecting massive transformations upon nature itself without clear natural limits to growth. It was the chemistry of a whole new capacity for almost autonomous human reordering, with a new power to transform the basic elements of life, new capacities for production and invention, new factories, new finance, new mobility of transport, new locations, and the new self-made men of Samuel Smiles's *Self-Help* (1859). This capacity for transformation within the melting pot of nineteenth-century history was industry's version of the power of art, made real. But what, besides wealth (and poverty), was being created? From the 1840s Karl Marx is in London, Frederick Engels in Manchester, the pair of them like hidden symbols of the underlying fear that economic forces were enforcing uncontrollable change at all levels of human existence.

The very form of experience had changed: hence, the massive sense of disorientation, uprooting, and displacement in the first half of the century; hence the increased sense of a fundamental division between inside and out in the experience of human beings, with the force of reality operating ever more powerfully from without; hence the release of certain values from their origins—in Evangelicalism, in gender, or in class—and the transformation of old traditions within new contexts. The social results of change, the incorporation of the new within the old, are the subject of Chapter 1 of this volume, whilst the political and class modifications are the introductory background to Chapter 7. The changes in the world order, in respect of the sense of what was natural and its place, are the subject of Chapter 2, with reference also to the development of science and, above all, Darwinism. But this is not a book about the Industrial Revolution; it is a book about a process of semi-secularization in which the experience of the Industrial Revolution is but one important part. For Strachey the Victorians had already outgrown religion without being able to bear to realize it: to him, that was what made them almost instantly old-fashioned, both emotionally strained and ponderous, in their unconscious awareness of the gap between a religious morality and their real desires. I want to argue that, on the contrary, the serious relation between belief and unbelief in the period makes unbelief itself a religious phenomenon, in its unwillingness to *be* unbelief, in its intensity, its need, and its search. The spiritual and mental implications of this powerful uncertainty are discussed in Chapters 3 and 4 respectively, in the very test of inner or higher resources in relation to material realities.

The publication of Darwin's *Origin of Species* in 1859 and of *Essays and Reviews*, that controversial work of sceptical theology, in 1860 only gives dates to tendencies, in evolutionary theory and biblical criticism respectively, which were already in evidence. Yet quasi-symbolic dates do provide usefully simple guides, at least to the more visible realities. The process of electoral democracy, begun in the extension of the franchise in the Reform Act of 1832, was virtually completed for adult urban males by the Act of 1867 and for their rural equivalent in 1884. The harsh new Poor Law Amendment Act was passed in 1834, and, for all the railway boom, the subsequent late 1830s and hungry 1840s mark a period of civil unrest, characterized in the Chartist protests of the working classes, amidst economic depression, bad harvests, and outbursts of cholera. That unrest culminates not in the revolutions that went on in Europe in 1848, as had been feared, but in the beginnings of state-enforced improvement of conditions in the Factory Acts and municipal health legislation and, above all, in the Repeal of the protectionist Corn Laws, against the old landed interest, in 1846, allowing imported corn and thus cheaper bread. The Great Exhibition of the Industry of All Nations, in Joseph Paxton's glass-and-iron Crystal Palace in 1851, is the giant symbol, inspired by Prince Albert, to show the world's technological achievements—and the lead taken by Britain —during the first half of the century. On display in this celebration of trade confidence was the visible progress in mechanization, meteorology, optics, electricity, engineering, sanitation, transport and communications, and photography. Yet the question for observers such as Carlyle was whether this was to be a century of invention rather than creativity, of matter more than spirit, of mechanical rather than dynamic thinking. This is the challenge to literature in an age of increasing secularization which forms a backdrop to the literary chapters in this volume, in particular from

Chapter 5 onwards: on drama, on the novel, and on non-fictional prose, and on poetry.

But it is those dates—1846, 1848, or 1851—which begin to mark the achievement of that greater internal stability and increased humanitarianism which characterize 'mid-' or 'high' Victorian England in the third quarter of the century. It is the period of the great social reforming governments of both Disraeli's Conservatives and Gladstone's Liberals, of Forster's landmark Education Act of 1870 with its commitment to education as a national public service—for all the sporadic anxiety generated, for example, by the administrative chaos of the Crimean War (1854–6) or the Indian Mutiny (1857–8).

The conclusion to this volume offers an account of why it is right to end at around 1880, the year that saw the tired demise of the great Metaphysical Society, founded in 1869 to draw on all strains of Victorian thought in the great debate on the purposes of human life. Above all, 1880 was the year in which George Eliot died. Increasingly thereafter—for all the religious effort of writers as diverse as Christina Rossetti, Margaret Oliphant, or George MacDonald—the moral seriousness for which George Eliot stood, in the name of high realism, had to give way either to a quite different late Victorian aesthetic of the 1890s or, alternatively, to the terrible challenge to Victorian humanism reluctantly and painfully embodied in the work of Thomas Hardy—a darkening view already anticipated in the late works of both Dickens in *Our Mutual Friend* (1865) and George Eliot herself in *Daniel Deronda* (1876). Just as Marx lives obscure and hidden in the very midst of the period, so the spirit of Nietzsche threatens its end—in the death of God, of truth, of meaning, all together. In *Twilight of the Idols*, first published in 1889, Nietzsche complains of the timorous compromise of the English Victorians, in particular George Eliot, 'They have got rid of the Christian God, and now feel obliged to cling all the more firmly to Christian morality' ('Expeditions of an Untimely Man'). What was needed instead, he claimed, was a modern thoroughgoing revaluation of all values.

But something in the period, between 1830 and 1880, will not give way, forward or back, and makes it a holding ground for all the great questionings of human meaning and direction. It is the essential period for all those in the modern world who live between heaven and earth, unsure of the former and unsatisfied by the latter. In the chapters that follow this introduction, my aim, structurally, has been to turn the problems involved in the writing of this volume of literary history into the very subject matter of the book: that is to say, *The Victorians 1830–1880* seeks an overview of an age constantly seeking and constantly failing to find an adequate overview or framework for itself. The superabundant production and reckless diversity of writing between 1830 and 1880 involves problems of inclusion, generic definition, and categorization which were themselves part of the anxious, voracious, and unwieldy experimentation of an age often searching for stable frameworks of understanding. That is why a useful image is that provided by the composite photographs of Francis Galton, in the attempt to build up through the superimposition of individual characteristics, one upon another, a more general idea of the original human type. Galton himself, while thinking about analogies with the mental formation of general impressions and blended memories, had specific eugenic and hereditary questions in mind, which are genuinely disturbing in relation to questions about criminality and about family determinism. But these photographs also serve to pose the larger question: how does the human picture take form? They not only involve problems of the formation of human character, of the mix of elements in the chemistry of personality, they also point to the experiments and overlaps that went on between and across all categories and genres in the intermixed complexity of this period.

'Englishness' itself was one of those composites. In the midst of contemporary confusion, there was a powerful Victorian anxiety involved in the effort to trace clear points of origin and conjunction in the historical formation of both language and race. To the imaginative story of the initial blending of the Norman and Saxon elements in the creation of the English character after the Norman Conquest, Matthew Arnold, for example, in *On the Study of Celtic Literature* (1867), added the Celtic power of the Scots, Welsh, and Irish, the 'style' and 'magic' of a passionate imaginative resource still available within the national heritage. But Arnold also went on to include in the mix the rival influences of the ancient civilizations of Athens, Rome, and Jerusalem as well as the modern cultures of Germany and France, until even within his prose-writings he is like a

Composites of the Members of a Family.

Fig. 1. Francis Galton (1822–1911), *Composites of Members of a Family.*
From research in the mid-1860s, Galton's discovery of the composite image,
made by taking very short multiple shots, offered a method of synthesizing
the characteristic physiognomies of a particular class, race, or family.

poet-artist seeking to create the fullest, most well-balanced human being out of the range of dispositions and traditions available. Yet for all his attempts to widen the English mind, there is still in Arnold the desire to bring these varying tendencies and possibilities to a modern, unified, progressive, and urbane centre, both intellectual and geographical. Ever-increasingly, for all the regional diversity, that dominant centre seemed to lie in England and, above all, in London. Despite the continuing superiority of the Scottish universities of the eighteenth-century Enlightenment, in their teaching of philosophy, literature, and science, Edinburgh lost much of its old literary pre-eminence during the century, while the rise of Glasgow was that of an essentially industrial city: hence the arrival in London of writers such as Carlyle, George MacDonald, and David Masson, drawn there amidst a massive wave of Scottish emigration both south and overseas. By 1840 over 80 per cent of Britain's population lived in England. Even for Gladstone, with his Scottish background, 'English' was the name commonly used for all those living on the mainland.

There is of course no composite Victorian, no one definitive picture of Victorian England. Rather, in the light of all the complexities, contradictions, overlaps, and influences, my method has less to do with sequential survey and more with debates, quarrels, disputes, and questionings amongst what are otherwise identified too homogeneously as 'the Victorians'. The very differences and disagreements help to form between them the picture of all that is involved in the great Victorian crisis of belief.

What follows is thus a *literary* history—to do with the closest we can get to individually experienced thoughts and feelings and beliefs—and not a social or cultural history as such, however much literature in this period necessarily extends itself on every front, into every area of discourse and concern: social, economic, political, epistemological, moral, religious, and cosmological. For the very status of historical understanding is itself one of the issues under question in the literature examined in this book. Carlyle, for example, repeatedly warns of how the Victorians' consciousness of their own historical position—their fear of social and historical determinism—was at least as great a threat as was determinism itself, by already doing determinism's work for it. A major theme in this

volume is the phenomenon of a potentially false secondary consciousness within the individual, in particular a historical consciousness, itself resulting from the history of an anxious social need to
'place' the contemporary situation. But literature often gets its
writers to depths below that consciousness even in the expression of
it. For the discipline of history, alone, cannot tell the inner story of
the age in all its resonance of meaning, cannot give the individual
experience of what is invisible, in close imaginative relation to complex and primary linguistic sources. Only a literary language can do
what Carlyle sought within what he called the otherwise 'mechanical' mentality of his age: that is, locate the struggles from below
upwards of a hidden 'dynamic' or a 'buried life' or 'implicit reason',
whatever the poverty or incoherence of the intellectual or cosmological framework encasing it. That is why I try to offer, instead of
mere survey or explanation by paraphrase, as extensive an amount
of direct quotation as space has permitted: 'to make you *feel*'
through specific human examples, as Arnold said of his own specific
literary touchstones, 'that what I say is true'. Or, if not true, exactly,
at least real in the direct imaginative experience of deep meaning that
reading constitutes for serious Victorians.

   And what of that word 'Victorian' after all? In *Portrait of an Age*
(1936)—one of the great correctives to Strachey—G. M. Young says
that the word 'Victorian' first appeared in the 1850s to register the
securing of a new self-consciousness; the *Oxford English Dictionary*
cites E. C. Stedman's *Victorian Poets* (1875). But, as you might
expect, 'Victorian' is not really a Victorian word. Many of the leading Victorian writers were of course, in some sense, anti-Victorian—
or alternatively could be said to be *most* Victorian—in being deeply
critical of the so-called Victorian attitudes of their own age: witness,
most obviously, Matthew Arnold against complacent materialist
philistinism, or Charles Dickens in exposure of religious hypocrisy,
or Ruskin on the unfeelingness and uncreativeness of his times. But
the adverse reaction against the 'Victorians', which begins after
Victoria's death, goes on to include within the term figures such as
Arnold, Dickens, and Ruskin themselves. As Edmund Gosse put it in
an article on 'the Agony of the Victorian Age' in *The Edinburgh
Review* in 1918, 'for a considerable time past everybody must have
noticed, especially in private conversation, a growing tendency to

disparagement and even ridicule of all men and things, which can be defined as "Victorian"'.

In fact, the history of the term since the death of Victoria has been subject to the process described by John Stuart Mill, in his essay on Coleridge in 1840, as all too typical of the history of ideas—'the noisy conflict of half-truths angrily denying one another', every 'excess' in one direction provoking a 'corresponding reaction' in the other, leaving the history of opinion as 'generally an oscillation between these extremes'. Victorianism's own struggle between old and new has become replicated in the history of its reception— between modernists and traditionalists, between the politics of left and right. 'Realism' is *the* Marxist literary mode, or it is a form of bourgeois falsification; Modernism is anti-Victorian, or Victorianism is proto-modern; 'Victorian society' is a study in oppression or the story of developing democracy. 'Victorian Values', Victorian sexuality, morality, class, and imperialism (though the story of this last really belongs to the last quarter of the century)—all these at the least continue to provide the ground for vibrant controversy. As I write, it is not now religion or morality but politics, in the broadest sense, which has become the key framework through which to judge the period, even though the period itself is sceptically troubled about the predominance of any one category of human understanding.

Precisely because a complex intermixture of different meanings, beliefs, categories, and genres is held in solution within the period I describe, there is a grand linking narrative which, I believe, holds together the chapters that follow. Nonetheless, each chapter is designed so that it may be read separately from the others—the relation between the novel's realism and poetry's own alternative version left, for example, in mostly tacit contrast. It is hard to hold together not only the huge variety of Victorian writing but also the varying levels of necessary argument in relation to it: with some regret, for instance, I have mainly had to leave biographical information, which so often can humanize knowledge, to the Author Bibliographies at the back of the book. Equally, when thinking of space, it should be noted that, according to estimate, between 1837 and 1901 over 40,000 novels alone were published. In the face of such plenitude, I did not want to provide lists of titles or to force books into thematic pigeonholes, to be narrowly selective or merely

indiscriminate; but in truth the result of the omissions and trunca-
tions I have found necessary gives me quite as much rueful pain at
the end of the endeavour as the fear of my ignorance had done
continually.

1

Rural to Urban 1830–1850

I. A New World

The census of 1851 showed that for the first time in English history England was predominantly an urban nation, just over half its population living in the cities. Nor was this a gradual change. A mere twenty years earlier, in 1831, three-quarters of the nation had still lived in the countryside. Moreover, the suddenly crowded cities in which the population was coalescing were such as English towns had never been before. At the beginning of the century there was only one English city with more than 100,000 inhabitants, London with a million people; by 1851 there were nine. The new steam-powered industrial organization created social problems which there was as yet no corresponding civic organization designed to remedy: problems of housing and the use of space; problems of public health, sanitation, sewerage, ventilation, paving, and water supply, in the face of cholera, typhus, and consumption; problems concerning working conditions, the regulation of commerce and education. By 1851 about four million people were employed in trade and manufacture and mining, compared to one and a half million in agriculture. It was a whole new order or disorder, a vortex which pulled into the cities' factories and workshops the surrounding population for both labour and consumption. As William Cooke Taylor put it in his *Notes of a Tour in the Manufacturing Districts of Lancashire* (1842), 'The steam-engine had no precedent, the spinning-jenny is without ancestry, the mule and the power-loom entered on no pre-pared heritage: they sprang into sudden existence like Minerva from the head of Jupiter.'[1] The greatest change in English social history took place, within decades, in a society that itself lacked any approved pattern of behaviour with which to accommodate the phenomenon of change.

A defender of the Industrial Revolution, Cooke Taylor nonetheless found himself admitting in his *Natural History of Society in the Barbarous and Civilized State* (1840) that the northern industrial towns were symptomatic of 'a system of social life constructed on a wholly new principle, a principle vague and indefinite but developing itself by its own spontaneous force and daily producing effects which no human foresight had anticipated'.[2] The invention of machinery offered men new power over matter, beyond all previous limits of nature itself. And yet this man-made world seemed to be gaining power over the men and women within it, like a machine that had developed beyond the control of its own inventors. In the very structure of industrial economy, both traditionally personal social relations, as between landowner and tenant, and visible direct causes, as between weather and harvest, were increasingly becoming the simple things of a past often viewed with nostalgia. The new economic system worked through secondary causes, indirect consequences, cogs and wheels within wheels. What Cooke Taylor describes is the sensation of living in the midst of history itself—a history which, seemingly undirected by either divine purpose or human control, did not preserve the past but was creating its own future. What was it that was working itself out within the apparently unstoppable progress of the Industrial Revolution? 'Men understand not what is among their hands', wrote Carlyle in his essay 'On History' (*Fraser's Magazine*, November 1830).

What was confronting England, Carlyle concluded in his 1839 essay *Chartism*, was the second stage of its great task in world history. The first stage had been 'the grand Industrial task' of conquering half or more of the planet for the use of man. What had thus taken place in the later eighteenth century was no spiritual

---

[1] *Notes of a Tour in the Manufacturing Districts of Lancashire* (1842), ed. W. H. Chaloner (Frank Cass, 1968), 4.

[2] Quoted in H. J. Dyos and Michael Wolff, *The Victorian City: Images and Realities*, 2 vols. (Routledge and Kegan Paul, 1973), vol. 1, p. 5. I am also indebted to A. S. Wohl, *Endangered Lives: Public Health in Victorian Britain* (Methuen, 1983).

renaissance, as in the Elizabethan England of Shakespeare, Bacon, and Sidney; it was the physical and material revolution of Watt, Arkwright, and Brindley, the new self-made men of steam, factory, and canal: 'cotton-spinning, cloth-cropping, iron-forging, steam-engining, railwaying, commercing and careering' (ch. 8). Now in the nineteenth century, in the inevitable time lag following the sudden fait accompli of technological development, society had to come to terms with what had happened, as in the domestic peace that succeeded dramatic conquest. This was part of what Herbert Spencer was later to describe in *Man versus the State* (1884) as the evolution from a military to an industrial model of social organization: from a fixed world of commands and conquests to a more fluid world of negotiation and consent. For Carlyle, this second stage consisted of 'the grand Constitutional task of sharing, in some pacific endurable manner, the fruit of said conquest, and showing all people how it might be done' (*Chartism*, ch. 8). In the hidden battles of peacetime, between twenty and thirty thousand people every year in the 1840s in England and Wales were slaughtered by typhus, annually double the amount lost in the battle of Waterloo. In this uncharted second phase of modern development, England, with nothing equivalent behind it in its history, had somehow to catch up in social and human terms with what it had achieved in material ones. The sheer force of the industrial earthquake made itself felt in the continuing waves of social consciousness from which there was no escape at any level of society.

Statistics might help an understanding. The great change might be summarized in the tale of two cities, one of industry, the other of commerce, in particular in the decades between 1820 and 1850. In the industrial cotton-based north, the population of Manchester had risen from 75,000 in 1801 to 202,000 in 1831, and by 1851 had increased to 303,000 bodies. In the south, London had become the largest city in the world: a population of nearly a million in 1801 rose to nearly two million in 1841 and was not far off three million by 1861. These figures were the result of both natural increase and worker-migration from an impoverished countryside: in 1851, 40 per cent of Londoners had been born elsewhere; in the newer phenomenon of Manchester only just over a quarter of the population was native-born. The Victorian age virtually invented the gathering

Fig. 2. Gustave Doré (1833–83), *Under the Viaduct, London* (1872). Over 100,000 people were moved out of their London homes to make way for railway building, resulting in even greater inner-city crowding.

of such statistics (the Statistical Society of London being founded, for example, in 1834). In the midst of rapid and uncertain change, many Victorians loved the collectable certainty of quantifiable facts and tables that measured the changes—sometimes simply for the sake of encyclopaedic accumulation, but also, as in the case of William Farr in the annual reports of the registrar-general, with the aim of obtaining some overall sense of the age and its social patterns. But there were others, such as Carlyle, who were anxiously sceptical of the language of mathematical calculation and of the relevance of abstracted statistics to personally felt existence. The Cambridge philosopher and scientist Whewell deprecated the extension of statistical inquiries into regions where they would touch upon feelings and passions. Ever-shifting from the desire for a bird's-eye view to a need for a view from the ground, it was an age continually asking itself what such abstracts really meant in relation to individual human experience.

Investigative travel literature offered a non-statistical form of report. Harriet Martineau, writing in *Retrospect of Western Travel* (1838), said that, in order to avoid 'confusion of vision' whenever she visited a strange town, she went to the highest point in the vicinity to take a view from above of the 'living map' below her. The popular love of the balloon's eye view of the city—'to grasp it in the eye, in all its incongruous integrity, at a single glance' in the words of Henry Mayhew in the *Illustrated London News* (18 September 1852)—is a caricature of the want of intellectual overview. Down below, by the informal segregation of urban housing along class lines, people could live in virtually separate worlds, strangers to what was happening in other parts of their locality. In *Punch* (March 1850), Thackeray confessed that reading Henry Mayhew's London street journalism had opened a veritable new world to him, a lower-class underworld life of 'strange adventures' that 'exceed anything that any of us could imagine' and yet 'had been lying by your door and mine'. 'We had but to go a hundred yards off and see for ourselves, but we never did.' It was often those who were visiting England for the first time, who best registered the strangeness of the scene, as from outside it.

Hugh Miller approached the outskirts of Manchester, like a man from an older world. Scottish Highlander and self-taught geologist, he saw the river Irwell tracing the story of the abrupt shift from a rural to an urban economy:

The hapless river—a pretty enough stream a few miles higher up, with trees overhanging its banks, and fringes of green sedge set thick along its edges—loses caste as it gets among the mills and the print-works. There are myriads of dirty things given it to wash, and whole waggon-loads of poisons from dye-houses and bleach-yards thrown into it to carry away; steam-boilers discharge into it their seething contents, and drains and sewers their fetid impurities; till at length it rolls on—here between tall dingy walls, there under precipices of red sandstone—considerably less a river than a flood of liquid manure, in which all life dies, whether animal or vegetable, and which resembles nothing in nature, except, perhaps, the stream thrown out in eruption by some mud-volcano. In passing along where the river sweeps by the old Collegiate Church, I met a party of town-police dragging a female culprit—delirious, dirty, and in drink—to the police-office; and I bethought me of the well-known comparison of Cowper, beginning,

> 'Sweet stream, that winds through yonder glade,
> Apt emblem of a virtuous maid,—'

of the maudlin woman not virtuous—and of the Irwell.

Such is Miller's *First Impressions of England and its People* (1847, ch. 3), witnessing a brutal change in the very *nature* of England. On entering the city, loaded with industrial waste and human excrement, the river 'loses caste'. The shift from rural to urban involves a change of class: unable to wash the dirty things clean, the river becomes instead as sullied as the new industrial lower class beside its banks. The late eighteenth-century rural poetry of William Cowper is cancelled by a harsh factual prose. Twelve years before Miller's visit, another outsider, Alexis de Tocqueville, had traced much the same course through Manchester in his *Journey to England*: 'From this foul drain the greatest stream of human industry flows out to fertilise the whole world. From this filthy sewer pure gold flows. Here humanity attains its most complete development and its most brutish; here civilization works its miracles, and civilized man is turned back almost into a savage.'[3] In an age of new and oddly related extremes, the manure was the price of the gold, and people

---

[3] *Journeys to England and Ireland* (1835), trans. G. Lawrence and K. P. Mayer, ed. J. P. Mayer (Faber, 1958), 107–8.

themselves could become, almost literally, the waste products of the system.

Or again, here is London in 1862, seen afresh as though at the moment of its formation by Hippolyte Taine, French man of letters, sailing into sight of the docks and beyond:

> Every quarter of an hour, the mark and presence of man, the power with which he has transformed nature, become more obvious. Docks, warehouses, ship-building and repairing yards, workshops, dwelling houses, part-processed materials, accumulations of goods; to the right, we pass the iron carcase of a church, being made here for assembly in India. Astonishment at last gives way to indifference; it is too much. Above Greenwich the river becomes no more than a street, a mile and more wide, with an endless traffic of ships going up and down stream between two rows of buildings . . . To the west of us a forest of masts and rigging grows out of the river: ships coming, going, waiting, in groups, in long files, then in one continuous mass, at moorings, in among the chimneys of houses and the cranes of warehouses—a vast apparatus of unceasing, regular and gigantic labour. They are enveloped in a fog of smoke irradiated by light. . . . The atmosphere seems like the heavy, steamy air of a great hot-house. Nothing here is natural: everything is transformed, violently changed, from the earth and man himself, to the very light and air. But the hugeness of the accumulation of man-made things takes off the attention from this deformity and this artifice: in default of a wholesome and noble beauty, there is life, teeming and grandiose. The gleam of brown river water, the diffusion of light trapped in vapour, the white and rosy luminosity playing over all these colossal objects, spreads a kind of grace over the monstrous city—like a smile on the face of some dark and bristling Cyclops.[4]

In Taine's original French as in English, the syntax of urban description characteristically had to be that of lists, phenomenal increase without coherent connectives, miming what Taine here twice calls sheer 'accumulation'. For despite Taine's sense of the enormous, unceasing human power involved in the scene, the overwhelming impression is of a build-up of commercial life without overall coherent planning and even beyond human control. As de Tocqueville had put it in 1835 when first confronted by the natural waterways and man-made canals of an energetically ramshackle Manchester: 'On this watery land, which nature and art have contributed to keep

---

[4] *Notes on England* (1871), trans. W. F. Rae (1872), ch. 1 ('Appearances').

damp, are scattered palaces and hovels. Everything in the exterior appearance of the city attests the individual powers of man: nothing the directing power of society. At every turn human liberty shows its capricious creative force. There is no trace of the slow continuous action of government' (*Journeys*, p. 105).

Such observers could see contemporary history in the cityscape itself: the recent individualist origins, its current social consequences, and the urgent need for future remedial planning, almost at one glance. Alexis de Tocqueville had travelled to England in 1835 in search of clarification. He wanted to *see* the formations of history, spread out as in almost geological layers: 'I should like to get a clear picture of the movements of peoples spreading over on top of each other and getting continually mixed up, but each still keeping something that it had from the beginning' (*Journeys*, p. 21).

So much of this uncoordinated creative energy swiftly crowds together in Taine's account: the felt increase in this new world's size, pace, and growth; the reach and scope available to the capital city of 'the Workshop of the World'; and, above all, the transforming mastery of human artifice creating a steam-heated world of its own, evolving beyond the old given world of nature, even at the expense of the original elements of earth, water, air, light, and temperature. There are so many varying stimuli and uninterrupted demands from without upon the visitor's internal nervous system, that a continuous or consistent inner reaction cannot be steadily maintained: 'Astonishment at last gives way to indifference; it is too much.' Because *it*—the sheer mechanical system—does not stop, a human being has to. And then he or she has to start again. Massed particulars, the crowding of sheer phenomenal detail overwhelmed any clear framework of understanding. 'Nothing here is natural.'

The effect of the rise of industry and its towns upon human experience, in terms of the structures of thought and the combinations of sentiment, is the subject matter of this chapter. Much of that story is compressed in shorthand into Taine's first impression, above all in the unresolved human ambivalence in the face of such a scene— 'monstrous deformity', 'a kind of grace'—expressed above all in the language of the grotesque or incongruous: 'a smile on the face of some dark and bristling Cyclops'. Likewise, the street observer Henry Mayhew saw the beautiful play of light upon the cesspools of

Jacob's Island, 'prismatic with grease', and a child dangling her tin drinking cup 'as gently as possible into the stream' whilst 'a bucket of night-soil was poured down from the next gallery' (*The Morning Chronicle*, 24 September 1849). It was as though all that was good and beautiful had existed so long ago that its memory was suppressed save among the instincts of the innocent, incongruously stranded in the midst of squalor. The memories which peaceful country scenes call up, concluded Dickens in *Oliver Twist* (1838), are 'a vague and half-formed consciousness of having held such feelings long before, in some remote and distant time' (ch. 32).

Dickens walked along London streets as though along his own thoughts. The sketches in *The Uncommercial Traveller* (1861)—that essential experimental companion to any study of Dickens's imaginative principles—show a Dickens making use of night-walking for the purposes of urban meditation, or using running water as a kind of underlying 'tune' for the raising of mental daydreams. In Dickens above all, the grotesque is the reaction that results from the failure of traditional categories of response in the face of the unassimilable incongruity of this urban life-energy. Earlier accounts of metropolitan life were picaresque and jolly in their relish of disorder as spectacle—witness Pierce Egan's *Life in London* (1820–1) or Dickens's own *Pickwick Papers* (1836–7). But even in George Sala's *Twice around the Clock* (1858) with its author chummily half-grimacing at his style of 'throwing somersaults over grave-stones' (preface), there is underlying all the self-consciously incongruous playfulness a confused and undismissable terror which the writer either does not know how to express or cannot quite bear to take straight and seriously. As Ruskin put it, in writing of the grotesque in the third volume of *The Stones of Venice* (1853), the group of writers headed in particular by Dickens can only register the disorienting loss of a sense of the natural and habitual by nervily and uncomfortably '*playing* with *terror*' (ch. 3, para. 45).

'Unreadable confusion' is the phrase that Carlyle used in *Chartism* (ch. 3) to describe a situation that did not seem to have found for itself as yet a truthful, articulate language. The situation had to keep taking different expressive 'shapes', said Carlyle, one of which was the frightening development of the Chartist riots. Chartism was a working-class movement for reform which resulted from two major economic causes. First, there was the high unemployment and high bread prices which characterized trade depressions and harvest failures before the Repeal of the Corn Laws in 1846. Second, there was the change in the economy which destroyed the occupations of handworkers. Mostly working from home, numbering together with their families 800,000, handloom weavers found themselves doomed to extinction by steam power. In addition, the danger of mass violence was increased by the tight concentration of huge numbers of the poor in the manifest squalor of the new crowded industrial cities. Cooke Taylor reported anxiously from the factories of Manchester:

Had our ancestors witnessed the assemblage of such a multitude as it is poured forth every evening from the mills of Union-street, magistrates would have assembled, special constables would have been sworn, the riot act read, the military called out, and most probably some fatal collision would have taken place. The crowd now scarcely attracts the notice of a passing policeman, but it is, nevertheless, a crowd, and therefore susceptible of the passions which may animate a multitude. (*The Handbook of Silk, Cotton, and Woollen Manufacturers* (1843), p. 201)

Chartism itself sought permanent political remedies through fulfilment of the People's Charter of 1836. The Charter, which resulted from disappointment with the very limited (middle-class) extension of the franchise in the Reform Act of 1832, contained six major constitutional demands: universal male suffrage, annual parliaments, vote by ballot, payment of Members of Parliament and the end of the property qualification, and equal electoral districts. But for commentators such as Carlyle, working-class agitation from 1838 to 1848, be it in the 'shape' of industrial action or in demands for parliamentary reform, was not simply a direct practical response to hardship, by either physical or moral force: it was, rather, a sort of muffled and distorted language, exhibited as much in deeds as in words, thrashing about to express the heated distress and feverish confusion that resulted from the sudden new system. 'For the last five-and-twenty years,' wrote Carlyle in 1839, 'it was curious to note how the internal discontent of England struggled to find vent for itself through any orifice: the poor patient, all sick from centre to surface, complains now of this member, now of that;—corn-laws, currency-laws, free-trade, protection, want of free-trade: the poor patient tossing from side to side, seeking a sound side to lie on, finds none' (*Chartism*, ch. 9). These were symptoms, in the revolt of the workers, that stood in for thoughts. But there was not as yet, Carlyle lamented, what he himself was temperamentally ill-equipped to offer: an accurate, neutral, explanatory language that offered 'a clear interpretation of the thought which at heart torments these wild inarticulate souls, struggling there, with inarticulate uproar, like dumb creatures in pain, unable to speak what is in them' (ch. 1). Paradoxically, 'the *thing*', as Carlyle had to call the unnamed new reality, is *in* them, though they themselves do not know and cannot say what it is. That is what Karl Marx meant by 'alienation'. Writing in the reading room of the British Museum from 1849 until his death in 1883, Marx—and all that he and Engels together represented— was like a secret background presence on the English scene, undermining the security of individual autonomy in the face of social forces.

It is not of course true that the working classes were as inarticulate as Carlyle judged them to be. Whatever its political limitations, Chartism under William Lovett began to give new confident expression to the radical working-class voice—in its newspapers and political speeches, in poetry and in memoirs. Gerald Massey, Ernest Jones, Thomas Cooper, Ebenezer Elliott, J. B. Leno, Joseph Robson, and Ben Brierley are now recognized as genuine poetic voices offering a powerful sense of communal identity, while research has uncovered artisan women poets such as Glasgow power-loom weaver Ellen Johnson, Mary Colling (a servant), Louisa Horsfield (a factory worker), and Charlotte Richardson (a cook).

To Carlyle, nonetheless, it was the responsibility of the educated class to find the voice that the underclasses lacked. Increasingly it was the middle class which was the new centre of consciousness, the go-betweens who were neither aristocratically aloof from the forces of economic change nor utterly crushed by them. Yet as Matthew Arnold constantly lamented, there seemed to be as yet no 'steady and whole' higher view available to the thinking sections of the middle classes. And correspondingly, despite the best efforts of the Chartists, it remained true that for the mass of the labouring classes within the system, silent and unconscious habituation was a necessary mechanism of accommodation and survival. The Rev Whitwell Elwin gave the following evidence on circumstantial habits to Edwin Chadwick's committee:

Those who think that labourers will work for themselves a reform in their habitations very much underrate the effects of habit. A person accustomed to fresh air, and all the comforts of civilized life, goes into a miserable room, dirty, bare, and, above all, sickening from the smell. Judging from his own sensations, he conceives that nothing but the most abject poverty could have produced this state of things, and he can imagine nothing necessary to a cure but a way of escape. A very simple experiment will correct these erroneous impressions. Let him remain a short time in the room, and the perception of closeness will so entirely vanish that he will almost fancy that the atmosphere has been purified since his entrance. There are few who are not familiar with this fact; and if such are the effects of an hour in blunting our refined sensations, and rendering them insensible to noxious exhalations, what must be the influence of years in the coarser perceptions of the working-man?[5]

A species of sensory deprivation, barely imaginable to the middle classes, was necessary to the working classes. Nor was it just the loss of one sense. A speaker to the Social Science Association in 1862 subtly suggested how the habituation of 'the sense of smell to impure air' 'gradually *blinded* its delicacy' (quoted in Wohl, p. 286). The people in Birmingham, said Hugh Miller in his *First Impressions of England and its People*, live in an atmosphere continually vibrating with clamour: a man who has slept soundly in the vicinity of a foundry night after night awakens disturbed if by some accident the continual hammering ceases; birds kept as pets begin to imitate in their music the screeching of a knife-grinder's wheel or the din of a coppersmith's shop. By this damaged adaptability of the life instinct, the noise was 'inwrought into the very staple of their lives', till popular sports and recreations become like the bird-song, unconsciously rivalling the clang of hammers and engines: 'no town of its size in the empire spends more time and money in concerts and musical festivals than Birmingham' (ch. 13).

'The manufacturing population is not new in its formation alone,' wrote Cooke Taylor in his *Notes of a Tour*; 'it is new in its habits of

[5] *Report on the Sanitary Conditions of the Labouring Population of Great Britain* (1842), ed. M. W. Finn (Edinburgh University Press, 1965), 203.

thought and action, which have been formed by the circumstances of its condition' (ed. Chaloner, p. 7). In his careful testimony to the *First Report of the Commissioners for Inquiring into the State of Large Towns and Populous Districts* (2 vols., 1844), Dr Southwood Smith, one of the principal figures in R. H. Horne's *A New Spirit of the Age* (1844), was disturbed by the poor's sheer lack of response: 'The want of complaint under such circumstances appears to me to constitute a very melancholy part of this condition. It shows that physical wretchedness has done its worst on the human sufferer, for it has destroyed his mind. The wretchedness being greater than humanity can bear, annihilates the mental faculties—the faculties distinctive of the human being.' He concluded grimly, 'There is a kind of satisfaction in the thought, for it sets a limit to the capacity of suffering which would otherwise be without bound' (vol. 1, p. 11). That is the two-sidedness of habituation that fascinated Dickens in characters such as Dorrit, Dombey, and Doctor Manette: a sort of natural unnaturalness by which life is kept going but kept going in twisted and tainted forms. It is like the institutionalized prisoner who tells Dorrit when he first enters the Marshalsea, 'We are quiet here; we don't get badgered here; there's no knocker here, sir, to be hammered at by creditors and bring a man's heart into his mouth. . . . It's freedom, sir, it's freedom!' (*Little Dorrit* (1857), bk. 1, ch. 6).

The demon of Mechanism, wrote Carlyle, 'changes his *shape* like a very Proteus'—at every change of shape hurling the people this way and that (*Chartism*, ch. 4). The very nature and configuration of the common family had changed, with women and children often forced into factory work as cheap labour, and the nominal head of the house frequently left redundant and displaced at home. 'I've waked my little bairns', said one father, denied poor relief because his children were old enough to work in the mill, 'to be at work at five o'clock in the morning!—there to labour to nine at night!—Whilst I was idle all day long—My only work was now, to take them there, and then to fetch them back'.[6] Little children had to become as mothers and fathers to their own smaller brothers and sisters—even, as so often in Dickens, to their own parents. Yet when their own

---

[6] *Richard Oastler: King of Factory Children: Six Pamphlets 1835–1861* (British Labour Struggles: Contemporary Pamphlets 1727–1850; Arno Press, 1972), 23 ('Eight Letters to Duke of Wellington', 1835).

parents could not find work, the greater temptation was for the younger people to desert rather than support them.

In his best-selling manuals *Self-Help* (1859) and *Character* (1871), Samuel Smiles sought to generate, in particular amongst working men, an independence of character, a self-made individualism, sufficient to resist those external encroachments and distortions. The possession of inner resources constituted a sort of moral capital or psychological property—an ideal of strong will and hard work, for those without any other advantages, which was intended to unite artisan and middle class alike. At its centre was a belief in the necessity that individuals should seek to stand their ground, and create and defend their own spatial enclave in both work and home.

It is important to imagine what such an ideal was fighting against. Without that independent space, in the depths of the London underclass, Nancy in *Oliver Twist* is hard pressed to rescue Oliver from the influence of thieves she herself has long since accepted as family. As she formulates her secret rescue-attempt, her thoughts 'were occupied with matters very different and distant from those in course of discussion by her companions', yet they remain thoughts of 'a mind unable wholly to detach itself from old companions and associations' (ch. 44). For her the good can be done only by deceiving those she feels to be no worse than she has been. Thinking splits her in two: the best part of her she can only save in the person of Oliver. 'Character' cannot maintain the integrity that Smiles sought; it struggles instead with its 'story'.

The predominant fear of the social commentators, culminating in Ruskin's *Unto This Last* (1862), was that the age was producing a new, more unfeeling and less human, kind of being, among both the sunken poor and the new self-made rich. The physical desensitization at the lower end of society was matched by its moral equivalent in the new tough ethos of the entrepreneurial ideal. In such a climate, the self-same system that in the first place affected the lower classes physically was also affecting literature mentally. The very structures of thought were being altered.

Of course, not all commentators were automatically pessimistic about the growth of the cities or the future of the Industrial Revolution. Nor were all those who were not pessimistic simply apologists for the triumph of economic motives—like Andrew Ure in his

Philosophy of Manufactures (1835). In *The Age of Great Cities* (1843) a Unitarian minister Robert Vaughan carefully began a theological and philosophical defence of the new challenge by confronting the famous and much-quoted line of the poet Cowper in the first book of *The Task* (1785):

God made the country, and man made the town

To take the country to be simply innocent and natural and the city inherently guilty and artifical was, argued Vaughan, a distortion of human history, a sentimental half-truth. For one thing, from the beginning man also had made the country: 'in the absence of what man has done upon it, the surface of the earth must have remained barren, or have degenerated into a monstrous wilderness'. Nor equally, on the other hand, should it be forgotten, said Vaughan, 'that it was as much a part of the purpose of the Creator with regard to man, that he should build towns, as that he should till the land' (p. 101). For towns were homes. When Jehovah placed the Hebrew tribes in possession of the cities of Canaan, 'he recognised man as a citizen, as an improvement upon man as a wanderer' (p. 103). In the past the great cities—Rome, Athens, Jerusalem—had been centres of civilization and future progression. If in the name of modern progress Manchester now seemed a place of evil and destruction, nonetheless 'the man who is placed in possession of a new power to do wrong, is placed under the influence of new motives to do right. In the moral world, as in the physical, the true equilibrium of things is realized by the action of opposite forces' (p. 255). In that balance, if there is one nation is to be 'lost or saved' by the character of its great cities, Vaughan dramatically concluded, 'our own is that nation' (p. 93). It was a real question: was it beyond human inventiveness that the urban developments of the nineteenth century should not become in the long term a part of that great civilizing movement of Providence?

Vaughan was at least right in this: that what was at stake could not be described simply in terms of 'social problems'. The problems were hardly categorizable: as Carlyle had recognised, they were mental, spiritual, emotional, cosmological even, as well as economic or political. A whole new world order was developing. It was not only that the basic elements of life—air and light and water and weather and sky—were changed, as Ruskin was to show in *The Storm-Cloud of the Nineteenth Century* (1884). The very shapes of experience—the dimensions of both space and time—were distorted.

Although few perhaps could bear to realize what it was they were entering, the city, roofed-in and smoked over, became almost literally a huge separate world of its own, sealed-off spatially and historically. Another foreign observer, Frederick Engels, Manchester agent of his father's business interests in England, described it thus in 1845:

A town, such as London, where a man may wander for hours together without reaching the beginning of the end, without meeting the slightest hint which could lead to the inference that there is open country within reach, is a strange thing. (*The Condition of the Working Class in England*, 'The Great Towns')

This is that characteristic Victorian sense of being immersed, geographically and historically, in the very midst and middle of things, without a strong narrative sense of beginning and end. In *The Old Curiosity Shop* (1841), it is only in chapter 15 when Little Nell and her grandfather are 'clear of London' and in the countryside that they can begin to see what their life was like there.

The sense of space was radically altered in the new world. Butler Williams, who conducted ordnance surveys with a view to seeking conformity between the contours of the land and the street-planning of the city, told the 1844 Inquiry into the State of Large Towns and Populous Districts that the disaster for London had occurred long ago in the rejection of Sir Christopher Wren's plan for re-building after the fire of 1666. Wren's proposed shaping combined logic, proportion, beauty, and health in a city opening directly on the surrounding countryside. To secure ventilation the streets were to be straight, radiating diagonally, as in a polygon, from a series of open centres, 'free breathing places', to be made into gardens or ornamental fountains. Instead in Manchester in the 1830s up to 50,000 people lived underground in dark and airless cellars, in rooms occupied by several families, in beds occupied often promiscuously and incestuously by several bodies; over 13,000 children died in seven years. It was no coincidence that it was the *Manchester* School of Economics, headed by Richard Cobden and

John Bright, that was the major proponent of free trade and laissez faire.

In 1798 Malthus had warned of the dangers of overpopulation, maintaining that population increases more rapidly than food supplies unless or until checked by war and poverty. The population had not only risen dramatically since then, doubling in fifty to sixty years, but had been packed tighter and tighter within the poorer parts of the cities. *The First Report of the Inquiry into the State of Large Towns and Populous Districts* estimated that in the worst districts of Liverpool, the density of population was equivalent to packing nearly half a million people into one square mile of space, 'a picture in miniature of the Black Hole of Calcutta' as one local professional, Dr Duncan, called it.

No wonder if in turn the middle classes sometimes felt themselves living in a surrounded island. However much he campaigned against the hardships of the poor, even Dickens himself, a social hybrid, showed fear of the miasma of social influences, as invisible as unsuspected germs. There were moments when harder, harsher thoughts could not be banished from the softer feelings: Little Dorrit's fear of the Marshalsea taint turning even the family she loved into manipulators and parasites; the contamination of Chancery upon Richard Carstone in *Bleak House* (1853), creating a self-delusion unbearable to witness; the raw fear and shame of the child David Copperfield, forced into Murdstone and Grinby's warehouse and afraid of being dragged down 'little by little' to the level of the labouring youths around him—that whole sense of humans turning into something terrible.

In 'The Great Cities and their Influence for Good and Evil', a lecture given in 1857 and published in *Sanitary and Social Lectures and Essays* (1880), Charles Kingsley said that 'if you cannot bring the country into the city, the city must go to the country'. He envisioned what he called 'a complete interpenetration of city and of country, a complete fusion of their different modes of life, and a combination of the advantages of both', by making the city solely the workshop and the outlying countryside the suburban dwelling house of the people. But the earlier piecemeal attempts to bring the countryside into the towns were more like the 'highly disproportionate' efforts of Mrs Plornish in *Little Dorrit*, having the outside of Happy Cottage painted on the inside wall of the shop, which led into the home-quarters in the back. The comedy and the pathos of such an arrangement was itself a combination of sentiments befitting the incongruity of the times.

In the mud and dust of streets the sheer physical closeness of one thing to another, however qualitatively different, produced dislocated sensations of incongruous kinship, or moral blankness, or vertiginous excitement. In *London Labour and the London Poor* (4 vols., 1851–62), Mayhew describes poor youths sweeping a way across the street for a penny from the affluent, or a prostitute persuading her gentleman to give a coin to a decent old beggar-woman and feeling ashamed of the older woman's thanks. So much seemed momentary and atomized. It was a sensation shaped into questioning by the very form of *Bleak House*: *how* in the jumble of city life was one thing both separable from and yet also connected with another?

With the changes in space, there was also a massive acceleration in the sheer pace of life. The railway, itself a major market for iron, steel, and coal, opened up England, reaching far into it for new markets. Between 1830, after the laying of the Liverpool to Manchester line, and 1850, 6,000 miles of rail were laid, giving employment to 200,000 people: it was called 'railway mania'. To travel from London to Manchester took three days in 1750: in 1830 the new railway meant that it took twenty hours and by 1850 it was down to six. Not until the late 1840s did the railway companies manage to impose Greenwich Standard Time upon the network as a national whole, local time having meant that there was a difference of twenty minutes between Newcastle and London. The railway was like a literal image of the new pace of change. New travellers reported on the effect of speed upon perception. To look at the ground at the speed of ten miles an hour made you feel giddy, as though the passage of time itself had accelerated; objects in the foreground looked dim and indistinct as if, by some strange turnaround, *they* were in motion, swimming or flying past in strange patterns. A commission on the influence of rail travel on public health reported that 'The rapidity and variety of the impressions necessarily fatigue both eye and brain. The constantly varying distance at which the objects are placed involves an incessant shifting of the adaptive apparatus by which they are focused upon the retina; and the mental effort by which the brain takes cognizance of them is scarcely less productive of cerebral wear because it is unconscious' (*Lancet*, 11 January 1862). To Dickens's Dombey, it half felt like a phantasmagoria of Death, making life pass you by more swiftly than you could think, wrenching objects out of your perceptual grasp. To a young man following the track of his seduced sister in Mrs Oliphant's *Salem Chapel* (1863), the sheer speed was like his anxiety itself. Meanwhile, the electric telegraph exchanged thoughts by a kind of 'moral electricity' which conquered physical space: thoughts, said Alexander Somerville, which never took note of the geographical space they had to pass over.

Accompanying all this innovation was a near-frenzy of share-investment, culminating in the abolition of the Usury Laws (which had fixed maximum interest rates, at around 5 per cent) in 1854 and the legalization of limited liability in 1855–6. Investment poured into ventures, often fraudulent schemes as in the crash of George Hudson, the railway king, in 1847: Dickens's portrait of Merdle in *Little Dorrit*, Thackeray's satiric account of the rise of a footman by speculation in 'The Diary of C. Jeames De La Pluche' (1845–6), Douglas Jerrold's literal representation of *A Man Made of Money* (1848), Charles Reade's *Hard Cash* (1863), Mrs Oliphant's *Hester* (1883), Trollope's *The Three Clerks* (1857) and *The Way We Live Now* (1875) all testify to a high-risk England of fevered gambling in which the capital finance, necessary for the support of large manufacturing undertakings, was assuming a separate predatory life of its own. Hugh Miller noted that, for all the growth of the size of industry, in another sense England had actually become smaller by dint of faster transport slicing through the country. 'The same change which has abridged the area of the country', he added, 'has given condensation to its history' ('To the Reader', *First Impressions of England*): as space contracted, time was compressed, and the social and economic practices of whole centuries had been transformed within years.

In one sense of course, time now opened up. Robert Vaughan in *The Age of Great Cities* argued that the leading idea of 'the mechanic' was progressive 'onwardness' whereas the peasant, 'whatever he may see of change in the nature of his implements, is disposed to look on the processes about him as doomed to be in the main as they have been' (p. 160). But in another way time closed in. A new distinctly urban *rhythm* belonged to the machine rather than the seasons. As soon as it was the case that time was felt in terms of economic and personal demands, people had to work, in the significant phrase of the factory-reformer Richard Oastler, '*against time*'.[7] Dr James Kay, writing of the condition of the working classes in cotton manufacture in Manchester in 1832, spoke of the animal machine 'chained fast to the iron machine, which knows no suffering and no weariness': 'the persevering labour of the operative must rival the mathematical precision, the incessant motion, and the exhaustless power of the machine'.[8] Mental muscles harden or retract. 'Senseless and purposeless were wood and iron and steam in their endless labours', said Mrs Gaskell in *North and South* (1855, ch. 50), but the persistence of the machines was rivalled by the tireless endurance of the crowds of workers 'who, *with* sense and purpose, were busy and restless in seeking after—What?' The sheer speed and energy of life implied an increased sense of an urgent goal. But 'all your lives seem to be spent in gathering together the materials for life . . . You are all striving for money. What do you want it for?' (ch. 40). Secondary means seemed to be becoming an end in themselves, onward and onward. Mechanical repetition, said Engels, meant loss of human consciousness, feeling, and purposiveness.

Internally, the function of memory itself was altered, through the very loss of continuities. 'I remember, I remember | The house where I was born', wrote the poet Thomas Hood. The fact that increasingly people no longer lived the whole of their lives in the house where they were born was a new and fundamentally disorienting experience. Most northern industrial towns contained a high proportion of first-generation immigrants: between 1841 and 1851, the proportion of the population of Bradford that came from areas outside Yorkshire itself rose from 10 to 20 per cent, though for some the move out of rural deprivation represented opportunity rather than homesickness. Yet the story of the move of adults from the home and the ways

---

[7] See Cecil Driver, *Tory Radical: The Life of Richard Oastler* (Octagon, 1970), 136.

[8] James Phillips Kay, *The Moral and Physical Condition of the Working Classes Employed in the Cotton Manufacture in Manchester* (2nd edn. 1832; E. J. Morten, 1969), 24–65.

of their childhood goes deeper even than the shift from countryside to town which so often accompanied it. If it is for the most part an untold story, it is because inarticulate silence, in particular among the lower classes, was itself one of the symptoms of, as well as one of the ways of coping with, the experience of displacement. In the city itself Dickens made an attempt at the impossible: at finding an articulate language for the essentially inarticulate experience of the illiterate and blankly lost Jo, always told he had no business here, and yet 'perplexed by the consideration that I *am* here somehow, too' (*Bleak House*, ch. 16).

In the impoverished countryside of the 1830s there was a man who did combine in himself both worker in the fields, born of illiterate stock, and yet also poet. In 1832 the Earl of Fitzwilliam offered an almost destitute John Clare a cottage just over three miles away from his native Helpston in Northborough. He had been living in the tenement in which he had been born, with his mother and father, his wife and their six children: a man of poor health, unable to find work in the agricultural depression that followed bad harvests, acts of enclosure, and the Corn Laws. The prospect of a roomier cottage, with a small amount of land on which to grow vegetables, delighted him and his wife. Yet at the last moment Clare found he could hardly bear the thought of moving. When he did finally give in, he wrote:

> I've left my own old home of homes
> Green fields and every pleasant place
> The summer like a stranger comes
> I pause and hardly know her face
>
> ('The Flitting')
>
> The stream it is a naked stream
> Where we on Sundays used to ramble
> The sky hangs oer a broken dream
> The brambles dwindled to a bramble
>
> ('Decay')

Written with such frightening lucidity, the basic words remain almost the same (home, summer, stream, bramble), but somewhere something in the sense of them is terrifyingly different. The move of three miles, to a poet rooted in a tradition of childhood memories informed by love of Nature, broke John Clare's sense of absolutes and left him insane, till he was forced to leave Northborough too for an asylum. It is an extreme example of the effects of the displacement of memory, in which the particular balance of general determining factors—psychological and personal, cultural and poetic, historical, social, and economic—is radically unclear. But a modern world produced in Clare a deeply primitive reaction: take him away from the place of memory and he began to die, inside. 'A second thought tells me that I am a fool,' Clare had written in a letter of 1821, 'was people all to think & feel as I do, the world could not be carried on— a—green would not be ploughd a tree or bush would not be cut for firing or furniture & every thing they found when boys would remain in that state till they dyd' (*Letters of John Clare*, ed. Mark Story (OUP, 1985), 161). His second thought was the sort of sane second-order rationalization which the century had to learn. But still his first thought—never to leave home, never to accept loss and change as normal—remained like a birthright, older and deeper, the source of both his pain and his poetry.

Other views from ground level were urban and prosaic. In the melting pot of London, Henry Mayhew worked as a sociologist before the category was invented. He did not offer formal overviews or conceptual frameworks—the very things that were missing in common encounters with this new world—but the sheer facts of confused experience. He provided what he called 'a natural history' of street phenomena, nominally assembled under classification by trade or class, but really as jumbled as the streets themselves. Thus he noted the tendency of street people, in particular the costermongers who sold their wares in the open, 'to lapse from a civilized into a nomad state—to pass from a settler into a wanderer' (*London Labour*, vol. 1 'Of the Street-Sellers of Stationary, Literature and Fine Arts'). This recidivist wandering was like a symptom of resistance against the city's modern demands. To many who had been drawn out of the neighbouring countryside into an urban life, the city had seemed to promise increased freedom, economic emancipation from the land, more chance of 'seeing life'. The abolition of the Old Poor Law had at least meant that people were no longer tied to their 'settlement', to the parish of residence in which alone relief of poverty could be given. The resulting *mobility* of labour destroyed the remnants of the old static feudal system of the land in which, in the words of Vaughan, 'society is broken up into castes, and each man comes into the world to fill the narrow space appointed him, and a space the boundary of which he dares not attempt to pass over' (*Age of Great Cities*, p. 309). The great transition into a modern world, argued the pioneering anthropologist Henry Maine, in *Ancient Law* (1861), was the shift from 'status to contract'. Relations were not founded on shared memories and the associated fixed traditions of place but on so-called free bargaining. And yet the freedom of the conditions of hire were not the conditions of subsequent employment.

At the end of *Sybil* (1845) Disraeli complained of the persistent use of false names and single-word slogans in the new language of public affairs: 'all thoughts and things have assumed an aspect and a title contrary to their real quality and style'. Thus, in physical reality, the so-called liberalism of free trade or the so-called mobility and freedom of labour could seem a contradiction, a falsification of language, as Mayhew bears witness:

After a girl has once grown accustomed to a street-life, it is almost impossible to wean her from it. The muscular irritability begotten by continued wandering makes her unable to rest for any time in one place, and she soon, if put to any *settled* occupation, gets to crave for the severe exercise she formerly enjoyed. The least restraint will make her sigh after the perfect liberty of the coster's 'roving life'. As an instance of this I may relate a fact that has occurred within the last six months. A gentleman of high literary repute, struck with the heroic strugglings of a coster Irish girl to maintain her mother, took her to his house, with a view of teaching her the duties of a servant. At first the transition was a painful one to the poor thing. Having travelled barefoot through the streets since a mere child, the pressure of shoes was intolerable to her, and in the evening or whenever a few minutes' rest could be obtained, the boots were taken off, for with them on she could enjoy no ease. The perfect change of life, and the novelty of being in a new place, reconciled her for some time to the loss of her liberty. But no sooner did she hear from her friends, that sprats were again in the market, than as if there were some magical influence in the fish, she at once requested to be freed from the confinement, and permitted to return to her old calling. (*London Labour*, vol. 1: 'Of the Coster-Girls')

Once the novelty of change had worn off, it was not simply the love of a roving life that motivated such apparently stubborn reversions and regressions in the face of routine.[9] Mayhew, staring into the loopholes of urban society, argues that there was also 'indomitable self-will or hatred of restraint or control', 'aversion to every species of law of government, whether political, moral or domestic', 'incapability of continuous labour, or remaining long in the same place occupied with the same object', and 'an unusual predilection for amusements' such as tricks, jokes, and frauds (*London Labour*, vol. 1: 'Of the Street-Sellers of Stationery, Literature and the Fine Arts').

With the erosion of the firm boundary between vagrancy and employment, wandering was the way in and out of a new more fluid system of labour. As Vaughan himself admitted, 'Uncertainty, with regard to social relationship, is more or less everywhere' (*Age of Great Cities*, p. 289). Men, no longer tied to the land and owning nothing but the work of their hands, more frequently changed masters than in the old feudal system; in the violently experienced transitions from boom to slump they moved from job to job or from place to place in search of the job that would take them back into the system. This series of experiences 'does not fall into fixed classes', said Engels, concluding his discussion of 'The Great Towns': 'The condition of the workers in each branch is subject to such great fluctuations that a single working-man may be placed so as to pass through the whole range from comparative comfort to the extremest need.' Indeed one behavioural form of coping with such insecurity was to re-create the extremes as if of one's own accord. Thus a stipendiary magistrate of Thames Police Office gave evidence to the *First Report of the Royal Commission on the Poor Laws* (1834): 'This woman was a fish-hawker, a business by which, in all probability, she gained enough to make her extremely comfortable, but she preferred an alternation of great privation and profligate enjoyment' (quoted in *Report on Sanitary Conditions* (1965 edn.), p. 202). To the magistrate the so-called preference was that of immoral improvidence; to Engels, the apparently perverse behaviour was an externalized form of thinking, symptomatically miming at its own level the speculative risk and gamble of the wider economic world itself.

---

[9] On George Borrow and the gypsies, see below, pp. 429–32.

In the ever-shifting shapes of urban life, nothing so much characterized the early Victorian age as the sensation that too much was going on at the same time, one thing confused within another, in all the indiscriminateness of transitional disorder. By 1871 it was left to Lewis Carroll's through-the-looking-glass view of the consumer world, to recapture how words and things had become so bizarrely mobile:

The shop seemed to be full of all manner of curious things—but the oddest part of it all was, that whenever she looked hard at any shelf, to make out exactly what it had on it, that particular shelf was always quite empty: though the others round it were crowded as full as they could hold. 'Things flow about so here!' she said at last in a plaintive tone, after she had spent a minute or so in vainly pursuing a bright thing, that looked sometimes like a doll and sometimes like a work-box, and was always in the shelf next above the one she was looking at. (*Through the Looking-Glass and What Alice Found There*, ch. 5)

The attainment of a steady view from above, a hierarchical language of clear explanation, was the conscious object of much early Victorian enquiry. But actually it was the pained and energetic bewilderment of the 1830s and 1840s, as registered from below—a force of which Dickens is above all the representative—that most accurately described the new state of things in their unknown newness, before the attempted normalizations of the 1840s and 1850s began to stabilize subject matter into matters of distinct 'social concern'. 'Things flow about so here!' The teeming world that began in *Oliver Twist* (1837) and *The Old Curiosity Shop* (1841) is full of thoughts not yet quite separable from the presence of material objects and struggling within the almost overwhelming force of physical circumstances; ideas crowding upon the mind as thickly as the crowd of people and things around the body; the very principle of mind insecurely located somewhere in between dream on the one hand and external reality on the other. Thus Little Nell on her journey away from London:

How every circumstance of her short, eventful life, came thronging into her mind as they travelled on! Slight incidents, never thought of or remembered till now; faces, seen once and never since forgotten; words scarcely heeded at the time; scenes, of a year ago and those of yesterday, mixing up and linking themselves together; thoughts shaping themselves out in the darkness from things which, when approached, were, of all others, the most remote and unlike them; sometimes a strange confusion in her mind relative to the occasion of her being there, and the place to which she was going, and the people she was with; and imagination suggesting remarks and questions which sounded so plainly in her ears, that she would start, and turn, and be almost tempted to reply (*The Old Curiosity Shop*, ch. 43)

The fact that these thoughts are not in synchronization with time or strictly coordinated with place but begin to find a reality of their own, albeit belatedly, makes thinking finally an act of strange and courageous separation of a life from its surroundings. In the second half of her life, in the great cities of Venice, Florence, and Pisa, Little Dorrit still finds herself thinking of her earlier life in the prison home of London:

Old as these cities are, their age itself is hardly so curious, to my reflections, as that they should have been in their places all through those days when I did not even know of the existence of more than two or three of them, and when I scarcely knew of anything outside our old walls. . . . I thought, 'O how many times when the shadow of the wall was falling on our room, and when that weary tread of feet was going up and down the yard—O how many times this place was just as quiet and lovely as it is to-day!' (*Little Dorrit* (1857), bk. 2 ch. 11)

The sense of a possible separation between thought and place still retains some of its primitive horror for Little Dorrit. But that strangely recovered capacity for thought is the metaphysical product of the physical uprooting of the first decades of the nineteenth century.

II. The Challenge to Thinking

At its most exciting, this was an age which had to relearn, from within a new world of time and space, how to think—how to locate, amidst vertiginous and displaced experience, what Matthew Arnold called a steadying idea. Otherwise it was just a world of facts and sequences. It was as though, in the melting pot of the Industrial Revolution, the whole nature of things had somehow to be thought out again, even as the whole process went on, seemingly faster and faster. 'We are so much in the habit of allowing impressions to be made upon us by external objects, which should be produced by reflection alone, but which, without such visible aids, often escape us' (*The Old Curiosity Shop*, ch. 1).

What was 'society', asked Herbert Spencer at the opening of his *Principles of Sociology* (1876): did it exist as something more than an abstract collective name for the individual units that comprised it? Was the system of modern industry compatible with the principles of the Gospel? asked the young Gladstone. So much early Victorian literature concerns the threat of 'society' becoming a mass process with a mechanism of its own, without room for individual responsibility. And increasingly, as the century wore on, what initially had been confusedly encountered as existential phenomena were broken down and thematized into specialized issues and practical measures: overcrowding, for example, was treated as a problem of democracy and the franchise in its political aspect, but in its physical manifestations was formalized into a problem of public health. Moreover, as with Spencer's word 'society', these differing aspects, names, and categories—the political, the economic, the individual, the social, the moral, the religious, and so on—were subject to questions as to their reality in their own right, the bounds that defined their separate spheres of operation, and the interrelation of one with another. Both Carlyle and John Stuart Mill argued that, in the midst of confusion and uncertainty, the greatest danger was to resort to treating 'half-truths' as though they were whole ones. Where widely differing thoughts seemed each to hold their own partial truths, the task was how to fit those thoughts properly together, and by what overall authority to adjudicate between the overlapping claims of different priorities.

It was often doctors such as James Kay who recognized the need to find what, as Mrs Gaskell put it in *Mary Barton* (1848), Archimedes had sought: the point of leverage from which to move the earth, even as he stood upon it. For Kay, social thinking—thinking about society whilst being in the midst of it—was not like ordinary individual thinking:

The sensorium of the animal structure, to which converge the sensibilities of each organ, is endowed with a consciousness of every change in the sensations to which each member is liable; and few diseases are so subtle as to escape its delicate perceptive power. Pain thus reveals to us the existence of evils, which, unless arrested in their progress, might insidiously invade the sources of vital action.

Society were well preserved, did a similar faculty preside, with an equal sensibility, over its construction; making every order immediately conscious of the evils affecting any portion of the general mass, and thus rendering their removal equally necessary for the immediate ease, as it is for the ultimate welfare of the whole social system. The mutual dependence of the individual members of society and of its various orders, for the supply of their necessities and the gratification of their desires, is acknowledged, and it imperfectly compensates for the want of a faculty, resembling that pervading consciousness which presides over the animal economy. But a knowledge of the moral and physical evils oppressing one order of the community, is by these means slowly communicated to those which are remote; and general efforts are seldom made for the relief of partial ills, until they threaten to convulse the whole social constitution. (Kay, pp. 17–18)

Political economists, the Manchester School who fought for the abolition of the Corn Laws which had protected landowners from the cheap importation of foreign corn, believed in the long-term benefit of trusting natural market forces and free competition, even at the cost of short-term transitional miseries. To them the growth of capitalism was not so much the establishment of a new system but simply the flourishing that naturally followed the release from traditional restraints. To Kay, however, the nation could not be left to run on like a machine. Some artificial social organ of thought had to be established that could act in relation to the more remote parts of the social body, and respond to short-term pains, even as the brain swiftly did in the nervous system of the individual organism. It was the progressive doctors, treating the physical ills of society at first hand, who were among the first to realize that the situation could not be cured simply by individual effort or purely medical intervention. That is why later, as Sir James Kay-Shuttleworth, Kay turned his reforming endeavours from the field of medicine to that of education.

When in their evidence before governmental committees of inquiry they spoke of the social or the human structure, the reformist doctors did not need to employ political rhetoric, they offered the language of a humane professionalism which frequently combined

surgical precision with aesthetic specificity, as thus Samuel Smith, of
the Leeds Infirmary:

There is a beautiful arch of bone formed in the foot, on the middle of which
the main bone of the leg is planted; in walking, the heel and ball of the great
toe touch the ground: the bridge of bones is of a wedge-like form (the same
as the stones which form the arch of a bridge); this bridge receives the
weight of the body; and by its elastic spring, prevents any shock being felt
in leaping, &c. The weight of the body being too long sustained in factory
working, this wedge-like form is lost; the bones give way, fall in, and the
elastic spring of the foot is for ever gone; the inside of the sole of the foot
touches the ground, constituting the deformity which is called the splay
foot.[10]

Even if escaping the more dramatic industrial accidents, the very
body of a worker began to change. Height loss starting from sheer
damage to ankles could be between six and twelve inches. Neither
God nor Nature, said Samuel Smith, intended young children to
stand on their legs twelve, fourteen, sixteen hours a day. In his
evidence to the *First Report of the Commissioners for Inquiring into
the State of Large Towns and Populous Districts* (2 vols., 1844) Dr
Thomas Southwood Smith deplored the transgression of laws as
fundamentally natural and as beautifully balanced as the reciprocal
relation between plant life and animal life, each giving out into the
air what the other needed to take in. He was asked, 'Your medical
attendance never can have the influence you would desire under
these circumstances?' and he replied, 'It cannot; and therefore it is
that I have said, you cannot treat the diseases that are produced in
these localities; for the very same causes that produce the diseases
render the application of the proper remedies impracticable' (vol. 1,
p. 33). To break that vicious circle, isolated individual efforts could
not be sufficient, given the sheer size and scale of the problem. It was
the fundamental mass problem of vast amounts of human, animal,
and industrial excrement that almost literally underlay Victorian
England's conceptual grasp of the determining influence of social
conditions. Between 1858 and 1865 a network of over eighty miles
of sewers was created beneath London, thanks to the civil engineer

---

[10] William Dodd, *The Factory System Illustrated—In a Series of Letters to Rt Hon
Lord Ashley* (1842), ed. W. H. Chaloner (Frank Cass, 1968), 7–8.

Joseph Bazalgette. But its meaning was never merely literal and physical. John Hollingshead's *Underground London* (1862) was full of similes and metaphors: beneath the strata of high civilization, there were the sewers, like the arteries of the city's body, clogged with the discarded yet threatening dregs of human life—a black invisible hell, a hidden low-class animal level, a criminal underworld that nonetheless supported the society above it.[11] The need for a system of interconnecting fast-flowing drains and sewers was a version of the necessity for the large-scale social engineering, beneath the surface level of urban society. If the railways connected the exterior of England, underneath there was to be what Edwin Chadwick, the greatest of early Victorian civil servants, called 'the venous, or arterial system of town drainage'.

Society now worked on a more complicated, more indirect basis than that offered by either the individual model or the model of nature. Kay avoided moralizing—the situation was not simply the fault of wicked factory-owners:

The increase of the manufacturing establishments, and the consequent colonization of the district, have been exceedingly more rapid than the growth of its civic institutions. The eager antagonization of commercial enterprise, has absorbed the attention, and concentrated the energies of every member of the community. In this strife, the remote influence of arrangements has sometimes been neglected, not from the want of humanity, but from the pressure of occupation, and the deficiency of time. (Kay, pp. 79–80)

By 'remote' Kay means that, as by-product, the river pollution, physically so *near* the factories of Manchester, was itself *far* from being the immediate aim or direct positive intention of the manufacturers, and the further secondary effect on public health even less so. The links between cause and effects were, like vitiated air itself, often not directly visible. Although working within the language of physical space, 'remote influence' is emphatically a mental phrase here, seeking what Kay called mental 'dominion *over* matter'—an 'extension of knowledge' beyond man's currently 'limited resources'.

[11] See Peter Stallybrass and Allon White, *The Politics and Poetics of Transgression* (Methuen, 1986) and Kate Flint, *The Victorians and the Visual Imagination* (Cambridge University Press, 2000), esp. 153–61.

In what de Tocqueville had characterized as essentially an individualistic nation, Kay and Southwood Smith thus belonged with
Edwin Chadwick, in defending the need for state intervention, as
from the a new brain centre of society. 'Centralization'—the creation
of national laws on public health and town planning, and the use of
an inspectorate to ensure their implementation—was the century's
most practical version of the long-desired need for a view from
outside and above. It came out of the single most coherent secular
philosophy of the times—the one overall modernizing system of
thought coherently flexible enough to be susceptible to application under many, varying circumstances—namely, Benthamite Utilitarianism.

For Bentham and for his closest follower James Mill, the Archi-
medean lever by which to lift society was the impersonally rational
principle of utility, cutting a path through the individualistic thickets
of short-sighted sentiment and blind self-interest: the usefulness of
any measure was to be calculated at the micro-level in terms of the
measurable balance between the basics of pleasure and pain, at the
macro-level as to whether it served the greater happiness of the greatest possible number. As progressivist professionals, new middle-
class reformers opposing aristocratic dominance and administrative
muddle, Kay, Smith, and Chadwick were effectively Benthamites.

Yet such were the confused cross-currents of early Victorian
England, that Dickens himself could hardly believe that out of the
very Utilitarianism which he had satirized in *Hard Times* as the
enemy of the poor, there came the organization of social welfare
which was the poor's salvation. For perhaps the greatest seeming
incongruity of all was that Edwin Chadwick, author of the *First
Report of the Commissioners for Inquiring into the State of Large
Towns and Populous Districts* of 1844, had also been the main
administrator of the New Poor Law of 1834.

Where the 1844 *Report* was a humane landmark in urging the
necessity for statutory improvement in public health, the New Poor
Law had insisted that no able-bodied man would receive assistance
unless he entered a workhouse—a deliberately not to say punitively
'uninviting place of wholesome restraint' where he would be separated from his wife and children and forced to live under conditions
deliberately designed to be lower ('less eligible') than the lowest wage

obtainable outside. The difference between 1844 and 1834 not only seemed to be one between humane and inhumane intent, it also looked like a difference in principle between the creation of intervention and its removal. In the case of the New Poor Law it had been argued that the statutory payment of outdoor relief under the old welfare system, offered as an automatic right that could always be counted on, had undermined the poor's capacity for independence, by making the defence against poverty economically unnecessary. What was centralization in matters of public health but just such artificial interference?

For Chadwick there was no contradiction. It was the application of the same rational principle, the principle of Utilitarian efficiency for the sake of the greatest possible number, in differing contextual circumstances. If individuals could control their own situation, then they should be left to do so; but if they could not, then it was a matter for public intervention. The trick was to know where to place the difference. What Chadwick sought in both 1834 and 1844 was a beautifully efficient social machinery. Less eligibility was to be a 'self-acting test of the claim of the applicant', a mechanism constantly adjusting itself between the lowest wage rates and the thus tested necessity of the genuinely poor to accept less. Similarly, the rotation of water into the house for consumption and back out of the house in waste disposal, and the use of the city's waste products for fertilization of the surrounding land, was the completion of a circle. Chadwick's opponents complained of the centralization of public works on the grounds of what they took to be Chadwick's own principle: the utility of both competition and the division of labour. But, again, Chadwick made careful and specific distinctions. Competition often meant the unnecessary duplication of expensive equipment across uncoordinated activities. To put the whole work out to tender offered 'Competition *for* the field' as against 'Competition *in* the field'. What appeared to be 'division of labour' in local administration was in fact, argued Chadwick, 'an insubordinate separation': 'Were pins and machines made as sewers or roads are constructed, shafts of pins would be made without reference to heads—in machines screws would be made without sockets.' The principle for Chadwick was not free competition or division of labour for their own sake but sheer Utilitarian efficiency.

Yet there were those to whom it mattered if Chadwick achieved his efficient outcomes not on the basis of Christian morality or humane pity, but as a species of planned social engineering. Richard Oastler, the so-called King of Factory Children, spent the last thirty years of his life from 1830 championing the reform of factory conditions for workers, and yet, such are the cross-currents of the time, was himself one of the reforming Chadwick's most virulent opponents. For Oastler, the mere steward of an estate near Huddersfield, was with the cotton barons John Fielden and Michael Sadler, a Tory-radical revivalist of the aristocratic ideal against both the decayed aristocratic betrayal of the paternal system and the new entrepreneurial ethos. In Carlyle's England of protean change, even those, like the Tories, 'whose principles require them to be still', Vaughan had noted, find themselves required by circumstances 'to be in motion', if only to seek to defend their beliefs (*Age of Great Cities*, p. 149). It was characteristic of the shifting nature of the age that Oastler, like so many of the leaders of the time, did not belong to the class for which he spoke. Malthus, a clergyman, supported the landed interest which the landed economist Ricardo himself opposed; Feargus O'Connor, leader of the Chartists, was an Irish gentleman-journalist; James Mill, a civil servant, defended the capitalist class.

To Oastler, a long-time defender of the northern poor against the New Poor Law, Chadwick was still of a piece with the free-trading, Liberal employers he occasionally opposed. For Chadwick was a new man, where Oastler was emotionally an old one. Oastler did not believe in what in 1849 James Mill's son, John Stuart Mill was to call 'economic man', but in what Bishop Latimer in 1548, in his 'Sermon of the Plough', had called 'the whole man'. A whole man did not split himself into two, did not separate moneymaking activities from other drives and duties, did not take practical endeavour to be an end in itself but part of a spiritual medium on earth. Oastler conceived of himself as involved in that long-established web of interwoven customs, loyalties, ties, memories, and services called the Christian commonweal. 'The factory question is indeed', he wrote in a letter to the Archbishop of York, 'a soul question: it is souls against pounds, shillings and pence' (quoted in Driver, p. 306). Liberalism spoke of working men as 'free agents'; in practice they were really slaves—

wage slaves. 'Money and Machinery' drove a wedge between the nation's old landed and labouring interests. Offered in response to the Chartist protest, the 'one nation' novels of Benjamin Disraeli—*Coningsby* (1844), *Sybil* (1845), and *Tancred* (1847)—derive their celebration of an earlier Young England from the feudal vision sustained by the likes of Oastler. 'Society' now was no longer a form of human unity, said Disraeli, in cities where 'a density of population implies a severer struggle for existence, and a consequent repulsion of elements brought into too close contact' (*Sybil*, ch. 5). Drawn into intense physical proximity, nineteenth-century human beings had increasingly to define themselves in largely private and personal terms, set over *against* the social, shielding their independence from social threats whilst also still yearning for a lost sense of social belonging.

What is more, it is further evidence of the complex and fluid shifts of the developing age that this conservative critique of the new society should shed its class origins and, transformed into the intellectual radicalism of John Ruskin, become by way of William Morris the inspiration of socialist thinkers before the century's end.

Oastler believed he was witnessing not the development of 'society' but the destruction of the deeper unifying meaning of that word. 'Our forefathers' protested Oastler, 'knew nothing about "centralization"—nothing about "unity of plan"'. The constitution of England was 'a paternal constitution—assimilating itself to the local wants of the people', opposed to centralization 'because the happiness of the people is dependent on a diversity of rule, accommodating itself to the local habits and prejudices of the inhabitants of the different parties' (*Oastler*, p. 95). Chadwick had argued that centralization had itself created local government. But it was not what Oastler meant by 'local'. For the impersonal machinery of indirect means had replaced direct personal relations instinct with a traditional sense of the rights of the poor and the duties of the rich.

At the individual and personal level of direct and immediate feeling, 'Who would dare', asked de Tocqueville in his *Memoir on Pauperism* (1835), part 2, 'to let a poor man die of hunger because it's his own fault that he is dying? Who will hear his cries and reason about his vices?' But this was no longer a small manageable world of individual relations, primary necessities, and natural needs, noted de

Tocqueville; once an economic society had rapidly developed beyond the terms of individual understanding and control, there were wider levels of consideration beyond the immediately personal. De Tocqueville was an aristocrat who, significantly, had turned historian, and saw the old aristocratic ideals inevitably giving way to the collective planning of an industrial democracy. On his trip to England he had met Nassau Senior, Chadwick's co-author in the framing of the New Poor Law. And it was Senior, in a retrospective article in *The Edinburgh Review* (October 1841), who frankly admitted that there was no institution 'so eminently artificial' as the proper administration of a vigilant poor law—'none which attempts to overrule or modify so many of the propensities given to us by nature', both in the propensities to idleness in the claimant and in the soft-heartedness of the charitable provider. But such an institution had to be established precisely to begin to restore the natural laws. Those who did not understand the true nature of the social evil of a culture of dependence, the necessity of an overall remedy, or what it meant to be cruel in order to be kind, were 'sentimentalists who estimate a law solely by its apparent harshness when applied to extreme cases'.

But in 1845 Engels had argued that the human content of a system should never be at the mercy of its form. The basic human needs, feelings, and instincts of the workers made them feel bound to proclaim that they 'shall not be made to bow to social circumstances, but social conditions ought to yield to them as human beings' (*The Condition of the Working Class in England*, 'Labour Movements'). In his critique of James Mill's *Elements of Political Economy* in 1844, Marx argued that it was only an alienated or estranged version of 'the social' that could separate itself off not only from the personal and individual but also from the human and humane. Nonetheless, the sympathetic humanism of the 'Condition of England' novel, in the hands of writers such as the Christian socialist Charles Kingsley, too often only ended up trying to *add on* to the industrial scene the estranged idea of the missing elements of human feeling, in apologetic compensation. Structurally, as far as Marx and Engels were concerned, such a response was not sufficiently thoroughgoing. The attempt to build bridges across the dualities of new and old, rural and urban, economic and humane, master and men was, in Marxist eyes, no more than a bourgeois compromise. Quoting Carlyle on 'the completeness of limited men', John Stuart Mill argued in his essays on Bentham (1838) and on Coleridge (1840) that in a war of ideas, 'the noisy conflict of half-truths, angrily denying one another' (*Collected Works*, vol. 10, p. 122), produced only 'half thinkers', 'one-eyed men' on either side (vol. 10, p. 94). But Engels believed in the conflict: there was no way of simply combining the two halves of each pair of opposing ideas in an eclectic synthesis. The apparent crudeness of dialectical oppositions was not, in the eyes of Marx and Engels, a fault in the very structure of nineteenth-century thinking, as John Stuart Mill believed, but thought's genuine reflection of the underlying rupture in the relationship between individual and society. Certain conflicting differences, as between men of the old world and men of the new, were untranslatable, ideologically irreconcilable.

Yet even among the Chartists themselves, those who wished to defeat a market-led society by physical force were in a minority. In 1848 there were revolutions throughout Europe but not in England. Only discontent with the limited extension of the franchise in 1832 had ever united the Chartists as a whole. The mass demonstration on Kennington Common in April 1848 which might have steered Chartism into the international working-class movement of Marx and Engels was far smaller than envisaged and instead of marching on the Houses of Parliament dispersed peaceably. By the late 1840s economic conditions, though not good, were not at starvation level, and government measures in that decade, regarding health, working conditions, and the price of corn, were sufficiently responsive to form a contrast with the hated New Poor Law legislation of the 1830s. In what was increasingly recognised as a time of uncertain transition, there was a licence for practical piecemeal responses.

Correspondingly, an increasingly characteristic experience for many social commentators was not so much a sense of conflict as a disturbing recognition of difficulty and anomaly in the failures of intellectual synthesis. Thus, for example, political economists could speak confidently of the necessity of short-term sacrifices for the sake of long-term gains, and Nassau Senior could define capital by the word 'abstinence': the provision of saved resources for a remote end, through the tough moral discipline of postponing present consumption for the sake of investment in the future. But, as the journalist Robert Williams was to argue in a famous culminating article on 'Laissez-Faire' in *Fraser's Magazine* (1870), there was still for many people a real sense in which the theoretical economists in their demonstrations practically 'disregarded the element of *time* altogether'. Those short-term sacrifices for the sake of a better national future were, he insisted, the actual, piecemeal lives of a whole generation. Even so, it would have made things simpler if the Poor Law commissioners could have been dismissed as 'tigers in men's shape'. As Carlyle had first argued, they were, rather, men 'filled with an idea of a theory'. Their New Poor Law was not simply 'a monstrosity and horror' but, 'heretical and damnable as a whole truth', was 'laudable as a *half*-truth' (*Chartism*, ch. 3). In the struggle to map the structures of thought onto the shapes of reality, what was right and necessary in one context or in one system or at one time could become wrong and damaging in another: there was no rule of relative translation, no clear sign of the generic limit of applicability.

It was out of these grave difficulties in drawing clear lines, in marking the right relation of theory and practice, and balancing the claims of social and individual—indeed, out of the whole felt impossibility of synthesizing different discourses—that the realist novel emerged. Where the language of argument too often encouraged the completeness of limited men, where the explicitness of non-fictional prose had difficulty in formally signalling limits to and omissions from its own case, the realist novel at its greatest was able to shape itself into a holding ground for perplexity.

In Mrs Gaskell's *North and South* (1855) the Hale family in chapter 20 is torn between helping an individual striker in his need and not helping to prolong the strike itself by assisting the turnouts. There would not be such felt conflict between the immediate particular case and the longer-term overall rule, were there not amongst people like the Hales a remaining belief that there should still be some deep reconciling connection between the two levels, somehow making for unified sense.

But if individual ways could not be simply reapplied to social problems, no more could rural ways be transferred into an urban context. In 1821 the Rev Thomas Chalmers had argued in his

Christian and Civic Economy of Large Towns that the situation in the towns should be personalized by turning them back into smaller local districts, each with its own minister, on the Scottish Presbyterian model of the country parish. The minister was to occupy with 'the kindly influence of the mere presence of a human being' the 'mighty and unfilled space interposed between the high and the low'. The original essay-length version of the book had been reviewed sympathetically in *Blackwood's Magazine* (October–November 1819), but still the reviewer argued that, although the principle was right and honourable, a system could not be built which depended on the extraordinary efforts of a few exceptional persons, and that there was no simple way 'to transfer the quiet innocence of the country to the fevered and guilty combinations of a large city' (October 1819). Again in *North and South*, in chapter 8, Margaret Hale finds her relationship to the poor quite altered by the shift from rural Helstone to northern industrial Milton. The old could not be easily translated into the new.

What *North and South* does is show the structural complexity and the human importance of what is otherwise too easily dismissed as Victorian muddle. One commentator, looking back in 1871 on 'The Revolution of the Last Quarter of a Century', diagnosed the times in terms of confused cross-currents rather than clear conflicts: 'The social sorrow of our times is that men do not know their places; no man knows surely either his neighbour's or his own. There is no sort of fixity in any of the institutions of society, no sort of continuance in any of its orders. No order keeps to itself; they all interlock and interpenetrate' (J. Baldwin Brown, *First Principles of Ecclesiastical Truth* (1871), p. 278). A novel such as *North and South*, far more than its predecessors in the 'Condition of England' series, was the vehicle for that interpenetration of one thing and another.

In the city Margaret Hale finds that what had been natural and customary to her in the country has now become institutionalized into 'District Visiting':

'And your name? I must not forget that.'

'I'm none ashamed o' my name. It's Nicholas Higgins. Hoo's called Bessy Higgins. Whatten yo' asking for?'

Margaret was surprised at the question, for at Helstone it would have been an understood thing, after the inquiries she had made, that she intended to come and call upon any poor neighbour whose name and habitation she had asked for. (ch. 8)

Higgins concludes, 'I'm none so fond of having *strange* folk in my house'. But then, immediately, something happens that is typical of Mrs Gaskell's wry sense of both subtle connections in the very midst of apparent distinctions and human contradictions in the midst of avowed consistency. A second later Higgins intensifies that 'strange folk', but precisely in order to relent—'Yo're a *foreigner*, as one may say, and maybe don't know many folk here, and yo've given my wench here flowers out of yo'r own hand:—yo' may come if you like.' If Margaret is 'half-amused, half-nettled at this answer', it is because across the class-divide Higgins is half nettled and half grateful himself. The fact is that the structure is untidily more than that of conflict: there is a subtlety of *tone* that goes deeper than the ostensibly ungracious content, and a sense of interpenetrating levels in which social antagonism also contains the dynamics of personal attraction.

It is as though 'incongruity' has become the unpredictably and involuntarily 'human', defined and valued as such precisely in so far as it will not conform to any premeditated mode of thought or encounter. Margaret's relation with Thornton, the tough yet straight young factory-owner whom Higgins half respects and half dislikes, seems based on an antagonism itself ironically not dissimilar to that she herself experienced with Higgins. For again at moments she 'cannot help' admiring in Thornton, as in Higgins, something she 'had missed before'. What at the level of ideas would be a sign of contradiction is here a sign of life.

Thornton is emphatically the type of new factory man whom Richard Oastler attacked for seeking to destroy the paternal system. Margaret urges him to communicate more with his workers, to show more consciousness of shared relations, even to take more responsibility for the life and education of his people outside their factory lives, as Robert Owen had done, programmatically, in the new model villages and experimental communities of New Lanark in the late 1820s and early 1830s. Thornton replies by asking her to 'tell me' this:

If you are ever conscious of being influenced by others, and not just circumstances, have those others being working directly or indirectly? Have they been labouring to exhort, to enjoin, to act rightly for the sake of example, or have they been simple, true men, taking up their duty, and doing it unflinchingly, without a thought of how their actions were to make this man industrious, that man saving? Why, if I were a workman, I should be twenty times more impressed by the knowledge that my master was honest, punctual, quick, resolute in all his doings (and hands are keener spies than valets), than by any amount of interference, however kindly meant, with my ways of going on out of work-hours. I do not choose to think too closely on what I am myself. (ch. 15)

What he is himself may sound here, as it does to Margaret, like the bull-necked epitome of the Manchester free trader. And yet inextricably mixed with it is what Oastler might recognize as an old-world resistance to conscious interference, to overconsciousness of artificial effect. For Thornton speaks in defence of a living influence, here called 'indirect', but really meaning direct but implicit. The old-fashioned new factory-man provides an ambivalence that Dickens would have recognized, and which Ruskin in a letter to Charles Norton, 19 June 1870, half-recognized in Dickens himself, when he called Dickens, for all his defence of the poor, a 'modernist', 'a leader of the steam-whistle party', whose hero was 'essentially the iron-master'.

There are layers upon layers interpenetrating in novels such as *North and South*: the love story going on within the novel of social concern, but simultaneously the novel of social concern also going on within the love story. In Thornton himself, the old goes on with-in the new, the new within the old, in that viable fluidity which was the alternative to revolution in the dynamics of nineteenth-century England.

For if old pre-industrial pieties were conserved, their preservation was often achieved in unplanned ways and unexpected forms, even as the love of Margaret Hale and John Thornton was disguised within their mutual irritation. In chapter 44 of Dickens's *The Old Cursiosity Shop* an anonymous man watches the fire in the Birming-ham iron foundry. His father had first had the job of fire-watcher years earlier, and was allowed to leave his baby to lie and crawl and fall asleep before the fire, because the mother had died and there was no one with whom to leave the child. 'So the fire nursed me', says the man, and so after the death of his father it has supported his loneliness ever since:

'It's like a book to me,' he said—'the only book I ever learned to read; and many an old story it tells me. It's music, for I should know its voice among a thousand, and there are other voices in its roar. It has its pictures too. You don't know how many strange faces and different scenes I trace in the red-hot coals. It's my memory, that fire, and shows me all my life.'

This is a version of an alternative transforming culture offered, not *against* the ironworks but *inside* them. 'I think', Dickens says in *Bleak House*, 'the best side of such people is almost hidden from us' (ch. 8). But through the intimacy of silent private reading, the realist novel finds more space for that hidden inner reality than the forces of social reality normally allowed. Like the man's fire, it is a book that keeps alive 'my memory . . . my life'. That is why, were it not so incongruous and so vulnerable and underprivileged, the furnace-man's vision might be called subversive—though not as Engels would have wanted it. To Engels the family was an internalized version of the state, an institution for preserving property-owning; anger was the only strong emotion to give realistic dignity to labour. But that vision of the furnace-man, being at once weak and tenacious, needy and creative, pathetic and wonderful, is part of that new interpenetrating combination of almost incongruous sentiments which characterizes the literature of the earlier decades of the period. So it is too when Nancy plots the escape of Oliver and yet refuses to escape with him, saying instead, 'I must go home': it is with a complicated mix of feelings that her middle-class auditors can hardly believe the word 'home' in that underworld context (*Oliver Twist*, ch. 46).

If this was fiction, it was not just literature's fiction. In *Low Life and Moral Improvement in Mid-Victorian England* the journalist Hugh Shimmin reported that in the slums of Oriel Street in Liverpool in 1863 the women still spoke of the love of home. Such sentiments always risk dismissal as the opiate of the self-accommodating masses. 'The demand upon men to sacrifice illusion about their state of life', said Marx, 'is the demand upon them to sacrifice the state of life which requires the illusion' ('Contribution to the Critique of Hegel's Philosophy of Right' (1844), introduction). But what Marx calls illusion is in people such as the furnace-watcher a residual capacity for the creative uses of habituation in making a life and a home, still, within the world—preserving for themselves something of the deeper, half-lost meanings of human society. Consciously or unconsciously, that effort to make a little world, both within the larger world and against it, is the radical inner meaning of an emotional belief in home and family which might otherwise be all too unthinkingly dismissed as conventionally 'Victorian'.

2

Nature

I. Darwin and the Impact of Science

Analogous to the physical shift in population from rural to urban areas, suggested the Cambridge Idealist philosopher James Ward in 1895, was an equivalent shift in the mental map from religious to secular ways of seeing the natural world. In the first of his Gifford lectures, *Naturalism and Agnosticism*, Ward argued that science, with its increasingly autonomous professional language, was like a well-planned town steadily encroaching upon the countryside. Its materialistic inhabitants, safely enclosed within town limits, had shops to supply bread and beef but knew nothing of the herds in the meadows or the wheat in the fields. The very origins of our goods—their sources not only in the countryside but in the divine Creator Himself—were being forgotten or denied. Even James Ward's own sometime mentor, the philosopher Henry Sidgwick, remarked in a letter that 'as he grew older his interest in what or who made the world was altered into interest in what kind of world it is anyway'.[1] *How* things happened—the man-made scientific explanation of phenomena and their laws—was becoming increasingly closed off from any metaphysical or supernatural account of *why* things were as they were in the world.

The Wordsworthian meaning of 'Nature'—as something more than 'the material world', as, indeed, the very language of God—was increasingly both banished and relegated to the backwaters of 'the

---

[1] Quoted in John Dewey, *The Influence of Darwin on Philosophy* (Henry Holt, 1910), 15.

countryside'. Wordsworth's model of memory and feeling—the growth of the human mind from childhood onwards in an ennobling interchange with a sacredly natural world—was displaced and damaged, if not lost.

Yet Wordsworth had hoped that science would offer the poet new vision. And indeed throughout the nineteenth century, the way that scientific discoveries and theories were removing the old barriers of time and space could seem genuinely awe-inspiring: 'What space is to the astronomer, time is to the geologist,' wrote Henry Holland in *The Quarterly Review* for December 1849, '—vast beyond human comprehension, yet seen and comprized by the conclusions of the science.' Yet the case of Hugh Miller (1802–56) is instructive. In his *First Impressions of England and its People* (1847), Miller had defined geology as an expansion of view in the direction of 'the eternity that has been' (ch. 17), compared to which even the eternity of the theologians was flat and abstract. Hugh Miller began as a stonemason but became a rock geologist: the study of geology increased his belief in divine creation and his commitment to the Church of Scotland instead of leading him into materialism. But the age itself, he lamented, was increasingly committed to a secular theory of evolution: 'The infidel substitutes progression for Deity,' he wrote in *The Old Red Sandstone* (1841); 'Geology robs him of God.'[2] Hugh Miller committed suicide in a fit of depression in 1856, aged 54, ostensibly through exhaustion over mere page-proofs. Soon after, John Ruskin wrote consolingly to his widow that people are 'too apt to think everything has been right if a man lives to be old, and everything lost if he dies young': 'God gave the mind to do certain work and withdrew it when that work was done' (quoted in Rosey (ed.), p. 85). Yet arguably Miller's work felt 'done', not in the sense of being complete but in being well-nigh superseded.

The subduing of natural forces by the work of science and the industrial revolution was, argued H. T. Buckle in his overweening *History of Civilization in England* (1857–61), the triumph of the rationality of European civilization. As the century went on, convinced of its own intellectual progress, it was left to men vulnerable to being seen as throwbacks—men such as Hugh Miller and John

---

[2] Quoted in G. Rosey (ed.), *Hugh Miller: Outrage and Order* (Mainstream Publishing, 1981), 73.

Ruskin—to occupy what James Ward called 'the open country', where previously poets, philosophers, and prophets had expatiated freely. To Ward, for all the expansion of the known universe, there was during the course of the second half of the nineteenth century less space in the intellectual world for non-scientific, non-materialistic accounts. The cooperation between science and religion had reached its peak in the 1830s with the publication of the Bridgewater treatises, when the eighth Earl of Bridgewater had commissioned separate treatises on astronomy, physics, geology, and on animal, vegetable, and human physiology—all in relation to the goodness of God as their connecting origin. Ever since then, philosophy and theology were being forced out of science's city. Within the bounds of science, said Ward, the existence of serious gaps—such as gaps in the fossil record—was like *rus in urbe*, oases of countryside, within the city, which science could not leave be. The modernizing city state of science sought to contain within its bounds the whole universe.

Thus James Ward noted that the science that for centuries had been known as 'natural philosophy' and 'natural history' had now become separated from 'philosophy' and divorced from 'natural theology', and incorporated instead into professional 'Science' and its discrete branches. William Whewell coined the specialist term 'Scientist' in 1840, in his *Philosophy of Inductive Sciences*, and the *Oxford English Dictionary* offers the mid-to-late nineteenth century as the starting point for the 'modern' secularized meaning of science, citing the Oxford theologian W. G. Ward in the *Dublin Review* (April 1867): 'We shall . . . use the word "science" in the sense which Englishmen so commonly give to it; as expressing physical and experimental science, to the exclusion of theological and metaphysical.'

For Charles Lyell and Charles Darwin, burdened with anxieties about the reception of their ideas in orthodox religious circles, the new specialization was the scientists' modest attempt to create and defend a neutral space defined by the limits of knowledge. The world of nature was handed over to the natural sciences, without necessary or immediate implications for what may or may not lie beyond. Hence the coining of the protective term 'Agnosticism' by T. H. Huxley in 1869 at the inaugural meeting of the Metaphysical

Society. Agnosticism confined knowledge to the world of material phenomena: beyond that the First Cause was unknown—perhaps unknowable, perhaps non-existent. Agnosticism began as the name for a method in scientific discipline: there could be no compulsion to believe anything without adequate reasons or proofs. But in the slippery uncertainties of the century it also became a position midway between belief and disbelief or, more aggressively, a statement of scepticism.

At its most neutral the best name for the position of the scientists, suggested James Ward, was naturalism. Though, like the city, science might seem part of a modern denaturalized world-view, in its own terms it was offering a far more, not a far less, naturalistic view, in which the world and its inhabitants, including the minds of human beings, was explicable in terms of constant laws of nature. This understanding of nature belonged to science, not to theology or cosmology, and it was offered as inductive, not deductive. The French sociologist Auguste Comte (1798–1857) had divided the history of human intelligence into three chronological developments: first, the theological, committed to first and final causes; next, the metaphysical, in which supernatural agencies were replaced by abstract forces; finally, the positive state, when the human mind gives up its search for absolutes respecting the origin and destiny of the world and confines itself to the discovery of real facts and the actual laws that govern them. It was as though the Victorian period, beginning to quit the first, was still lurching in transition between the metaphysical and the scientific.

There was, after all, a historical and economic logic which seemed to be behind this development. The increased specialization of the various branches of human knowledge—separated not only from each other but from reference to a First and Absolute Cause—was an application, to the whole intellectual universe, of the principle of the division of labour that Adam Smith had brought to bear upon political economy. To observers such as James Ward, nineteenth-century science appeared to be the product of the same social, economic, and secularizing conditions that also produced the development of the city.

For certainly, the most important scientific thinking in the age took its starting point from a sense of the pressures acting within and upon the social and economic development of human beings: above all, the pressures of population. By what is otherwise a remarkable coincidence, each of the three major proponents of a theory of evolution in Victorian England—Herbert Spencer, Charles Darwin, and Alfred Wallace—independently found a single essay from the recent past taking a decisively clinching place in the formation of their thinking. It was T. R. Malthus's *Essay on the Principle of Population*, first published in its full pessimism in 1798 and modified in 1803.

Malthus's hard law of nature was that population always tended to increase in geometric ratio (2, 4, 8, 16) whereas the means of subsistence could only be increased in arithmetic ratio (2, 4, 6, 8). Thus population would always threaten to outstrip resources. But if the potential increase in population was great, and yet the actual increase was extremely slow, then the difference must be due to the invisible but necessary existence of the remorselessly self-acting law of a 'great and constant check to population'. The great natural check to the increase of plants and animals must be 'want of room and nourishment', creating premature death for all those who were too many. And there were always too many. The role of humans in this terrible natural wastage was not to try, at peril of our future, to ignore those checks: on the contrary, the influence of Malthus lay behind the creation of the New Poor Law of 1834 and the workhouse principle, since it was argued that giving extra financial relief to the poor only meant artificially encouraging them to breed more. The only room for manoeuvre was, as the 1803 revision tried to emphasize, to channel those bleak checks into as beneficial a social form as possible—by substituting for the threat of famine, for example, the strategy of delayed marriage. There was no harmony between man and the planet; the planet did not provide a natural home but was like a crowded city; poverty and suffering were natural. Yet with that Hobbes-like view of the war of nature, Malthus was no infidel theoretician; he was a Christian minister who saw a deeply fallen world of nature as an arena of struggling probation.

The revised compensatory emphasis upon the human capacity to turn the very pressure of disaster into a spur for alternative solutions was what attracted Herbert Spencer to Malthus. As a result, it was the self-educated Spencer, more philosopher of science than scientist, who coined the famous phrase 'survival of the fittest'—the phrase Wallace urged upon Darwin—in an essay of 1852, 'A Theory of Population, Deduced from the General Law of Animal Fertility':

> Nature secures each step in advance by a succession of trials, which are perpetually repeated, until success is achieved. All mankind in turn subject themselves more or less to the discipline described; they either may or may not advance under it. . . . For as those prematurely carried off must, in the average of cases, be those in whom the power of self-preservation is least, it unavoidably follows, that those left behind to continue the race are those in whom the power of self-preservation is the greatest—are the select of their generation.

In those repeated trials, pressure of population is the proximate cause of progress: 'it forced men into the social state', 'it is daily pressing us into closer contact and more mutually-dependent relationships'. The very pressure produced new progressive forms: 'Were it not for the competition this entails, more thought would not daily be brought to bear upon the business of life; greater activity of mind would not be called for; and the development of mental power would not take place'.[3]

To Spencer evolution meant progress. To Darwin and Wallace it retained more of the original Malthusian grimness. Malthus's law and the sort of vocabulary that Malthus brought to mind in Spencer ('check', 'competition', 'perpetual repetition', 'trial', 'select') constituted for both Darwin and Wallace, quite independently, the groundwork for the theory of the struggle for existence and natural selection—the mechanism of *how* evolution proceeded that distinguished theirs from any other preceding theory of evolution.

Science for Darwin and Wallace had not begun in the study room but in the hard real-life laboratories, the natural worlds in miniature, of the plains and archipelagos of the imperial colonies. It was during a fit of malaria in 1858, in the wild near New Guinea, that Wallace suddenly found himself remembering with personal force the account he had read in Malthus over ten years before concerning the 'positive checks'—disease, famine, war, accidents—that kept savage

---

[3] In James R. Moore (ed.), *Religion in Victorian Britain, 3. Sources* (Manchester University Press, 1991), 405–7.

populations stationary. Darwin first happened upon Malthus whilst reading for amusement in October 1838, but as ship's naturalist, he had already been given an emphatically physical idea of checks and extinction in the voyage of HMS *Beagle* to the desolate coast of Patagonia in 1834. The barren plains were bafflingly memorable to Darwin at the time, for they seemed so eternally wretched and useless. Yet they were an image of the early world. These geographic voyages were, Darwin realized, also simultaneously journeys into Europe's past. On the voyage of the *Beagle*, an earthquake had brought a book—Lyell's *Principles of Geology*—to life: 'A bad earthquake at once destroys our oldest associations: the earth, the very emblem of solidity, has moved beneath our feet like a thin crust over a fluid—one second of time has created in the mind a strange idea of insecurity, which hours of reflection would not have produced' (*The Voyage of the Beagle*, 20 February 1835). Later, when likewise turned into books, the journeys of Darwin and Wallace themselves shook the apparently solid ground that lay beneath European civilization.

There were three basic principles involved in the Darwin–Wallace theory. Two seemed to celebrate life's liberal generosity and the world's ever-growing fullness: the principle of massive *productivity* amidst all life forms, and the creative richness of their chance *variability* even from their own parent types. But the third factor, the wedge as Darwin was to see it, was the Malthusian check upon such potential and leisurely infinitude: the finite limitation of resources that demanded for survival the necessity of the struggle of competition and adjustment and selection. As Darwin wrote in his 1838 notebook: 'One may say there is a force like a hundred thousand wedges trying [to] force every kind of adapted structure into the gaps in the oeconomy of nature, or rather forming gaps by thrusting out weaker ones'.[4]

On the Origin of Species by Means of Natural Selection (1859), subtitled *The Preservation of Favoured Races in the Struggle for Life*, might have been better represented as simply *The Struggle for Life*. For evolutionary theory abolished the very idea of 'favoured

---

[4] Quoted in Robert Young, *Darwin's Metaphor: Nature's Place in Victorian Culture* (Cambridge University Press, 1985), 42. I am indebted to this work which with Gillian Beer's *Darwin's Plots* (Routledge, 1983) has proved seminal.

origins' wrought by acts of separate divine fiat. The one aboriginal life form out of which all other forms of life on earth derive is lost and overtaken in the very process of its own evolution. Only retrospectively, after a long unretraceable process of the gradual accumulation of slight differences, do we find that a distinct species has come into being. Nor is natural selection itself the origin of the chance variations upon which it works; it is simply the origin of the fixing of these in definite paths and grooves and channels. But its operation was beyond anything human beings could plan or calculate, and almost beyond anything they could imagine. We can only understand its infinitesimally slow and gradual workings, says Darwin, by analogy with the *artificial* selection carried out by pigeon-fanciers. The man who first selected a pigeon with a slightly larger tail 'never dreamed what the descendants of that pigeon would become': 'a breed, like a dialect of a language, can hardly be said to have had a definite origin' (*Origin of Species*, ch. 1).

It is always too late to go back to discover an origin which, paradoxically, never *became* an origin until long after it had been absorbed into complex modifications of itself. For Darwin's is the story of life only ever partially recovered from the very middle of itself. As the scientist Darwin most admired, Charles Lyell, had put it in his *Principles of Geology* (3 vols., 1830–3), in paraphrasing his own predecessor James Hutton: 'In the economy of the world I can find no traces of a beginning, no prospect of an end' (vol. 1, ch. 4). What was involved in Darwinism was not a fixed beginning-to-end sequence of distinct, static, taxonomically definable essences but a whole continuous *life process*, without impassable dividing lines, which as it went along was always making itself up out of itself, from the very midst of existence. There is, argued Darwin, 'no clear line of demarcation' between species and subspecies, or between subspecies and well-marked varieties, or between lesser varieties and individual differences: 'These differences blend into each other in an insensible series' (ch. 2).

For the Greeks, for Plato and Aristotle in particular, said the American pragmatist John Dewey, 'Species, a fixed form and final cause, was the central principle of knowledge as well as of nature'. Otherwise, how was it that, while all the individual creatures came and went, the basic form in which they were shaped remained the same? In its lack of clear lines, change to the classical Greeks would seem 'mere flux and lapse; it insults intelligence'. Genuinely to know was classically 'to grasp a permanent end that realizes itself through changes' (Dewey, p. 6), a general law or original form lay above or behind the apparently various flux. But Darwin said of species what Galileo had said of the earth: *it moves*. The forms were not fixedly imposed upon matter from above, but evolved from below. Any chance possibility might be realized, bottom-up as it were, and established to a greater or lesser degree.

This was the radical causal inversion of thinking, the Copernican Revolution carried out on the earth itself, that Darwin brought to the old idea of nature bearing everywhere the marks of God's design. As a Cambridge undergraduate Darwin had read, and admired, Paley's *Natural Theology* (1802), for five decades the great text for the argument from design, the deduction of God the creator from the evidences in His creation. But what Darwin saw was that it was not that God fitted each vegetable and each creature happily into its appropriate place by design. On the contrary, out of the mass of forms unhappily struggling to fill it, each place was occupied by those that adapted better to its demands and opportunities than did their competitors. Turn round the apparent happy and beautiful fittingness of all surviving forms, and on the other side of that picture lay the ruthless elimination of the far vaster number of forms that had tried to fit in and failed the competition. Repeated key terms within the central fourth chapter of the *Origin of Species* concern the competition for allied forms to find a niche within the same 'place', or to 'fill up' an unoccupied place, in what Darwin called the 'economy' or 'polity' of nature. Natural selection only preserved some, by destroying many: it was arguably first of all a destructive force.

The triumph of evolutionary theory has often been dated at the meeting of the British Association for the Advancement of Science in 1860. There Samuel Wilberforce, Bishop of Oxford, sarcastically asked Darwin's great propagandist T. H. Huxley whether it was through his grandfather or his grandmother that he claimed descent from a monkey: Huxley had retorted that he had rather have an ape for an ancestor than a bishop misusing his faculties. Yet even before Darwin, evolutionary theory had always been 'economical' as a form of explanation. *Vestiges of the Natural History of Creation* (1844)

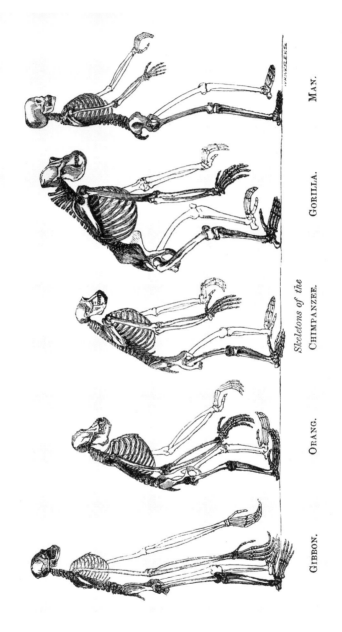

GIBBON.   ORANG.   CHIMPANZEE.   GORILLA.   MAN.

Skeletons of the

Fig. 3. Man and evolution from the apes: *Skeletons*, a drawing by Waterhouse Hawkins from specimens in the Museum of the Royal College of Surgeons, reproduced in T. H. Huxley's *Man's Place in Nature* (1863).

was a speculative work which, though Darwin despised its lack of solid science, helped to create the conditions for the reception of Darwin's theory.

The cosmology of *Vestiges* sought to reconcile evolution with theology by seeing evolution in terms of a self-developing blueprint created by God. This made the argument not so much one between science and religion as between two competing versions of natural theology: one embodying God's plans in evolving nature, the other demanding His continual intervention. For Robert Chambers, the anonymous author of *Vestiges*, evolution was 'an idea more marked by simplicity than perhaps any other of those which explained the great secrets of nature' (ch. 14). Its economy lay first in the fact that it did not require of the Almighty a separate exertion for the creation of each life form. Secondly, all the labours of the taxonomists in seeking minutely to define the essence of a species in contrast to a subspecies, or a subspecies in contrast to a variety, were likewise unnecessary if, in time, species were only varieties that had become strongly established, and varieties no less than potential or nascent species. Thirdly, and most economical of all, the creation of a new function in a life form did not require the development of an entirely new organ but the modification of an existing one, opportunistically adapted to its new purpose. In seizing such chances, natural selection, as Darwin was to say, 'is continually trying to economise in every part of the organisation' (*Origin of Species*, ch. 5).

Although he did not choose to make it explicit for fear of the consequences, where Darwin differed from Chambers was, of course, that Darwin's economy allowed precisely for what Paley had declared impossible: a design without a designer. Without an intended origin or a teleological end, there need be no shaping intelligence: intelligence itself was evolved from within the system. To R. B. Mackenzie, attacking Darwin in *The Darwinian Theory of the Transmutation of Species Examined* (published anonymously in 1868), the tacit but fundamental principle of the whole Darwinian system seemed a ridiculously illogical 'inversion of reasoning': 'that, in order to make a perfect and beautiful machine, it is not requisite to know how to make it'.[5] But with Darwinism a thing could come into

[5] Quoted in Daniel Dennett, *Darwin's Dangerous Idea* (Allen Lane, The Penguin

being by emergence, higgledy-piggledy, through trial and error: if it seemed a chance in a million that it should finally come to be, then it was feasible that over aeons all the other 999,999 possibilities did have their chance and happened to fail. Malthus's law, when converted into natural selection, was not a positive thing in itself, and certainly not an intelligence, but a part of the long self-acting process of life on earth. It was the idea of 'self-acting' mechanisms—the phrase Wallace used of natural selection in his autobiography *My Life: A Record of Events and Opinions* (1905)—that so often fascinated the Victorians, be the idea appalling or amazing. The grand theory of natural selection found room for accident within necessity, for diversity within uniformity, for optimism and pessimism alike. It brought together life's sheer variety, detail, and process within a single constant law that itself was a law not of constancy but of change: remarkably, conservation of the system itself acted as a trigger for transformations within it.

For if in this economy of nature, *space* was at a premium, *time* was not. Lyell's geology had claimed its status as a science by arguing for 'uniformity' in the development of the earth rather than a series of abrupt catastrophes. The Catastrophists, such as Adam Sedgwick and Hugh Miller, saw in the geological record evidence of a series of distinct eras ended by seismological calamities. Such catastrophes, they believed, required fresh acts of Divine intervention to follow in order to produce new creations. But Lyell argued that, without proof to the contrary, the state of the world must be the result in ages past of the same basic processes, operating gradually and continuously upon the earth's surface, as were operating on it now. Thus he turned the human mind to the contemplation of the great age of the earth that existed before human existence itself and beyond anything calculable from the five books of Moses in the Bible. This was the pre-human perspective that human thinking, like Tennyson's, was belatedly to inhabit:

> There rolls the deep where grew the tree.
>   O earth, what changes hast thou seen!
> There where the long street roars, hath been
> The stillness of the central sea.

Press, 1995), 65. On *Vestiges of the Natural History of Creation*, see James A. Secord, *Victorian Sensation* (Chicago University Press, 2000).

> The hills are shadows, and they flow
> From form to form, and nothing stands;
> They melt like mist, the solid lands,
> Like clouds they shape themselves and go.

(*In Memoriam* (1850), 123)

Hills flow and solids melt as in a speeded-up film, wound backwards not forward. In the course of time, mountains had eroded, beds deepened, deposits were buried. Geologists could locate within the depths of the earth itself a pre-human memory

Moreover, what was happening in geology was mirrored not only in biology but also in the world of physics. The sheer economy of the natural system was further emphasized in thermodynamics by the acceptance of the law of the conservation of energy that in 1847 was extended by Helmholtz to the sphere of organic life. 'The energy that would animate a crime', wrote George Eliot in chapter 42 of *Middlemarch* (1872) at a crucial turning point for Dorothea, 'is not more than is wanted to inspire a resolved submission.' The amount of the sheer raw stuff of life remained the same, for energy could not be created or destroyed: it was in its use that it was transformed. The popularizing physicist John Tyndall in 'Science and Man' summarized the findings of the scientist J. P. Joule, in his work on heat-loss and heat-gain, with characteristic imaginative force:

This doctrine recognises in the material universe a constant sum of power made up of items among which the Protean fluctuations are incessantly going on. It is as if the body of Nature were alive, the thrill and interchange of its energies resembling those of an organism. The parts of the 'stupendous whole' shift and change, augment and diminish, appear and disappear, while the total of which they are the parts remain quantitatively immutable. Immutable, because when change occurs it is always polar—plus accompanies minus, gain accompanies loss, no item varying in the slightest degree without an absolutely equal change of some other item in the opposite direction. (*Fragments of Science for Unscientific People*, 2 vols. (1871), vol. 2, pp. 342–3)

Faraday, in his researches into magneto-electricity and electrochemistry, had likewise argued that the various forms under which the force of matter are made manifest have 'one common origin' and 'are convertible one into another' (*Fragments of Science*, vol. 2,

p. 341). Helmholtz, Faraday, James Clerk Maxwell, William Thomson (later Lord Kelvin)—in their different ways these were scientists seeking a single explanation of cosmic processes. Together with 'Darwin's bulldog' Thomas Huxley, the mathematician W. K. Clifford, and the astronomer Richard Proctor, Tyndall was one of the great Victorian popularizers of those scientific ambitions. In an attempt to return specialized studies to the general culture, these writers sought a language within the popular literary and political journals of the time by which to bring science to a public without a formal scientific education. Huxley could deliver a popular lecture on the universe by starting from 'a piece of chalk'. The first issue of the specifically scientific periodical *Nature* (4 November 1869) insisted that it was 'impossible to separate science from other knowledge and from daily life: all new discoveries especially must have ties with every part of our nature'. The impact of Darwinism, in particular, could not be confined.

It is a mark of the movement of ideas that at one point Karl Marx had wanted to dedicate the second volume of *Das Kapital* to Darwin—though Darwin himself, wary as ever of extrapolated meanings outside his field, declined the honour. For Marx at his most admiring, Darwin offered vital confirmation that life had a sheerly materialistic basis and was above all a process that as such denied permanent distinctions of type or of class. Despite Darwin's own caution, he provided within the wider scheme of things, said Marx, a death blow to teleology—dissolving the idea of a fixed end to life inscribed from the very beginning of time.

At another level, it also seemed to both Marx and Engels that Darwin's 'economy' was unconsciously a view of Nature made in the very image of the economics of the society which discovered it. Social Darwinism, as advocated by Sumner and practised by Carnegie and Rockefeller in America, was the explicit name of the movement that enthusiastically turned 'the survival of the fittest' into a ruthless defence of competitive capitalism and of colonial imperialism, sanctioned by nature itself. Social Darwinism saw nature as not just like a city but, as Hardy put it in *The Woodlanders* (1887), like 'a city slum' (ch. 7).

Inadvertently, said Engels, Darwinism showed how high capitalism was really animal behaviour. In the *Condition of the Working*

Class in England (1845) Engels had seized upon the habit of calling factory workers mere 'hands'. Thirty years later in 1875 he wrote an essay on 'The Part Played by Labour in the Transition from Ape to Man', in which he argued that it was man's upright posture that freed the hand for using tools, which in turn demanded the evolution of further degrees of perfected dexterity. It was intelligence embodied in the practical work of the hand, not in the separate abstractions of the head alone, that gave man his major evolutionary development. The downgrading of manual labour into mere 'hands', ruled by the separate calculating brain of the capitalist, was the Industrial Revolution's divisive distortion of the biological revolution, of both the body physical and the body politic.

There is a view which continues to reduce the Victorian achievement to Victorian times. Thus, for example, two of Darwin's leading modern biographers, Adrian Desmond and James Moore, argue in *Darwin* (1991) that Darwin's ideas have essentially political roots and are a metaphoric extension of the ideology arising out of the socio-economic condition of Victorian England. And even a book entitled *The Victorian World Picture* (by David Newsome, 1997) opens with the disclaimer that, in contrast to claims once made for the Elizabethan age, there is no Victorian world-picture: there is social history rather than cosmology.

In truth, Darwin's own fears partly colluded in this restriction of meaning. We know that he delayed publication for over twenty years, before being suddenly forced into it by Wallace's remarkable finding of the same theory. But he did say that in publishing he secretly felt as if he were committing a murder—and it was presumably the murder of God's Nature he had in mind. Even so the *Origin* does not read like a radical work: the cumulative profusion of facts convinces by almost submerging the very form of thought—eliding proof of the theory by the facts, into explanation of the facts by the theory. Notoriously, it contains just one reticent sentence concerning the possible future extension of the theory into 'the origin of man and his history'. After all, the initial task of Lyell and Darwin was to try to limit their work to the realm of an inductive science rather than trespass into premature deductions about cosmology, and even in his later writings on man himself in *The Descent of Man* (1871) and *The Expression of the Emotions in Man and Animals* (1872) Darwin was muted. He continued publicly to make his cautious, conventional nod towards the idea of a Creator, and was relieved to hear from Charles Kingsley that he could read the *Origin of Species* as if it were, like Chambers's *Vestiges*, still compatible with religious belief: 'I have gradually learnt to see that it is just as noble a conception of Deity, to believe that he created primal forms capable of self-development into all forms needful *pro tempore* and *pro loco*, as to believe that he required a fresh act of intervention to supply the *lacunas* which He Himself had made' (quoted in Young, p. 106).

Even so, the human, philosophical, and theological implications of Darwin's work were, though thoroughly various and ambiguous, irresistibly uncontainable. The finally unavoidable challenge was how to take a pre-human, non-human system in human terms, supported or unsupported by grounding in God. Science-city could not restrain itself: it had to have cosmological ambitions that went beyond its social history. The *Oxford English Dictionary* takes most of its citations for the words 'cosmos' and 'cosmology' not from the Elizabethan age but from Victorian writers of the second half of the century. The key figure here was Herbert Spencer, who took the evolutionary system as far as it could possibly go.

II. Cosmologies and Anthropomorphisms: Darwin, Spencer, and Ruskin

It was left to Herbert Spencer (1820–1903) to make it clear that the universe of the evolutionists was not made in the light of nineteenth-century society but, on the contrary, that nineteenth-century society was being seen in the light of the evolving universe. Evolution is definable, says Spencer in *First Principles* (1862), as a change from simple to complex: 'from an indefinite, incoherent homogeneity to a definite, coherent heterogeneity' (pt. 2, ch. 16). The specialization of science itself was one part of the evolutionary process of differentiation:

The advance from the homogeneous to the heterogeneous is displayed not only in the separation of these parts from each other and from religion, but also in the multiplied differentiation which each of them afterwards undergoes. ('Progress: Its Law and Cause' (1857), in *Essays: Scientific, Political and Speculative*, 1858)

But separation at one level was followed by reintegration at a higher level. The more the whole becomes individuated into different parts, the more a relation between those parts becomes necessary. We see this 'cosmical equilibration' at every level, argued Spencer: in astronomy, in the formation of planets and their revolving satellites; in geology, in the multiplication of related differences across the earth's crust and in its atmosphere; in biology, in the growth of independent and yet cooperating organs within separate organisms; and in sociology, in the rise of special industrial centres of organization.

In all this Spencer was not the static system-builder he is often dismissed as being. It was precisely the dynamic unexpectedness of the analogies which for Spencer confirmed the universality of his law of life, the connections surprising him in the very act of thinking. It was spontaneously unexpected that the opening of new roads and railways throughout the country should feel analogous to the opening of new channels of nervous communication within the brain. It felt paradoxical that in each separate field of specialization and differentiation, the same common process was being repeated: 'We see at once that there are not several kinds of Evolution having certain traits in common , but one Evolution going on everywhere after the same manner' (*First Principles*, pt. 2, ch. 24).

That sense of a whole world operating at different yet related levels is what in Spencer excited George Eliot as a young woman. For the novelist, syntax itself was a version of evolution in the development of mind from simple to complex sentences. To Spencer mentality had to be largely serial—because men had to spell out their thoughts in sequence—but Nature itself was not serial. Increasingly, in the crowdedness of the world's fecundity, more than one thing was happening at a time, more than one phenomenon was claiming its place in consciousness. Out of this came the necessity for the mind to hold some things in unconsciousness, to banish them into automatic habit, or to try to pursue two or three different yet related trains of thoughts, simultaneously, through a successive syntactic medium. George Eliot's long self-modifying sentences of mind, working their way backwards and forwards through subordinate clauses, are a product of that dense simultaneous process of differentiation and connection. So too, John Tyndall admired the involved and inverted sentences of Milton's *Paradise Lost*: the distant relation of one part of speech to another was part of a developed mental awareness of relations in space (*Fragments of Science*, vol. 2, p. 92). Syntax was a growth of organization analogous to the evolutionary shift in music from simple harmony to Bach's counterpoint, or to the development from primitive tribes to the complex interrelationships of modern societies.

What is more, the book that traced such movements—in particular, the second part of Spencer's own *First Principles*—could be created precisely by its mimetically describing, stage by stage in chapter after chapter, the building blocks of the evolution of life itself. Spencer recapitulates near the end of chapter 14:

Such propositions as those set forth in preceding chapters, 'The Persistance of Force', 'The Transformation and Equivalence of Forces', 'The Direction of Motion', and 'The Rhythm of Motion' unite within single bonds phenomena belonging to all orders of existence. And if there is such a thing as that which we here understand by Philosophy, there must eventually be reached a universal integration.

What builds up together, law by law, in the world outside assembles itself, analogously, chapter by chapter within Spencer's model world of thought. 'It explains everything!' as Lady Constance is slyly made to say of the *Vestiges* in Disraeli's *Tancred* (1847). There is no mistaking the grand scale of ambition here: Spencer's is the boldest representative of the great Victorian search for a model of synthesis connecting all aspects of existence.

When books try to be world-views, when thoughts and chapters seek each to represent the different parts of the world, then the very form and syntax of the work result from the struggle to get its thoughts and parts into right hierarchical order. The big Victorian questions are connected with that dense formal struggle. Was evolution containable within theology, as Robert Chambers and Charles Kingsley believed? Or was religion itself explained within and superseded by evolutionary theories, as Spencer and Comte would argue? Was Darwinism explicable within the terms of Marx, or was the history of human society still tied to the wider environmental and biological processes of evolution? At the heart of all high Victorian controversy, however clumsily, was that sort of last-ditch conflict between huge competing overviews, each claiming a more comprehensive grasp of the whole order of things than any other. In the most interesting of these clashes—as between the language of biology and the language of economics—the two were not so much mutually incompatible as competitively overlapping, each claiming to be that larger-level explanation which thus included and drove the other. So it was that Alice in *Through the Looking-Glass* (1871) asked 'who was it that dreamed it all?': the Red King was part of her dream, yet within it he claimed she was part of his (ch. 8). ' "The question is," said Humpty Dumpty, "which is to be master—that's all" ' (ch. 6).

Shying away from the big words of philosophical controversy, Darwin's language was very different from Spencer's, in part a result of the difference between the scientist and the philosopher of science. But if man as subject matter was not present in the *Origin of Species*, man's language was unavoidably omnipresent. In the act of writing the book, the question of man's place in nature was inextricably and pre-voluntarily implicit in the very language Darwin found himself having to use.

Consider Darwin's definition of two of his key terms. First, in his account of natural selection, the Malthusian idea of a 'check' operating daily has become reified if not personified into the idea of a constantly checking presence:

It may metaphorically be said that natural selection is daily and hourly scrutinising, throughout the world, every variation, even the slightest; rejecting that which is bad, preserving and adding up all that is good; silently and insensibly working, whenever and wherever opportunity offers, at the improvement of each organic being in relation to its organic and inorganic conditions of life. (ch. 4)

This is not simply a written record of Darwin's particular thoughts; rather, we are in at the very formation of the linguistic ability to do human thinking in essentially pre-human and non-human realms. It is on such occasions, at the very bounds of sense, that the *Origins of Species* as an act of writing is, almost involuntarily, at its most philosophically interesting.

There is a similar problem of an almost unavoidable anthropomorphism, arising out of the very origin of the race's language, in a
second example—Darwin's description of the struggle for existence:

I use the term Struggle for Existence in a large and metaphorical sense,
including dependence of one being on another, and including (which is
more important) not only the life of the individual, but success in leaving
progeny. Two canine animals in a time of dearth, may be truly said to
struggle with each other which shall get food and live. But a plant on the
edge of a desert is said to struggle for life against the drought, though more
properly it should be said to be dependent on the moisture. . . . In these
several senses, which pass into each other, I use for convenience' sake the
general term of struggle for existence. (ch. 3)

'[C]onvenience' shows that a more neutral and literal scientific language, and its concomitant way of thinking, had not yet been fully
evolved or accepted, though its necessity has been half-reluctantly
glimpsed. Darwin's response to criticisms of his metaphors reveals
his frustration: 'Every one knows what is meant and implied by
such metaphorical expressions; and they are almost necessary for
brevity.'[6] But much of the half-inadvertent value of the *Origin* is the
presence within it of a language still in transition from the old human
to the new scientific world-view. Here, the fact that the differing
senses of 'struggle for existence' were said to 'pass into each other'
meant that for once at least Darwin's language found itself suddenly
close to the spirit of evolution itself, blurring the demarcation lines
between varieties and subspecies, and subspecies and species. At
times, even in Darwin, metaphors are very close to being traces in
language of what were real, physically evolved affinities in nature.

Herbert Spencer had no doubt that human language and thought
could map themselves onto the non-human world which had produced them. For the most part, however, Darwin's language, like his
argument, had to work tentatively backwards. In Darwin, human
terms struggle to turn round upon their own anthropomorphism,
lodged as it is deep in the subject-verb-object grammar of intent.
Natural selection is not really Nature acting intentionally like God:
back to front, the language describes as 'selected' all that is merely

⁶ See Morse Peckham's Variorum text of *The Origin of Species* (University of Penn-
sylvania Press, 1959), 165.

left surviving after elimination. Primarily it destroys—and it isn't really even an 'it'. Indeed, even the word 'Nature', in the work of this the greatest nineteenth-century naturalist, might finally have to go. 'It is difficult to avoid personifying the word Nature,' Darwin conceded: 'but I mean by Nature, only the aggregate action and product of many natural laws, and by laws the sequence of events as ascertained by us' (Variorum text, p. 165). It is no wonder that Dewey was to speak of Darwinism as 'the greatest dissolvent in contemporary thought of old questions' (Dewey, p. 19): it was not only that it would not solve the old human questions, but it threatened to dissolve them, making the old nouns and indeed the very grammar of the old human ways of thinking evaporate and disappear in the verbs of process.

Thus when Darwin writes of natural selection 'rejecting that which is bad, preserving and adding up all that is good', it is clear that 'bad' is circularly defined by its being rejected, and 'good' likewise simply by the reality of its being preserved. There are no absolute criteria external to the economy of what merely happens. In each environment 'natural selection will not necessarily produce absolute perfection', warns Darwin at the end of chapter 6: it will produce only what is relative 'to the standard of that country'. There is not a 'right' word, nor a naturally sanctioned human language any more, when natural processes are both anterior and indifferent to the human valuations sunk deep in our very capacity for articulation. We are not masters of the circumstances that create the make-up of our own wishes and motives: 'my physical and intellectual textures', said John Tyndall, 'were woven *for* me not *by* me' (*Fragments of Science*, vol. 2, p. 362). Thus, this sense that the world was inexpressible and almost unthinkable in the human terms which human beings could not escape employing was the implicit denial of the progress that evolutionary theory often seemed to imply: man, ostensibly at the top of the tree, found his very language gifts virtually disinherited. That is how, as we shall see, Darwin could lead not to a renewal of Spencer's confidence but to the bleakness of Thomas Hardy.

That is also why, near the very beginning of the controversy, Revd Adam Sedgwick, professor of geology at Cambridge, reviewing *Vestiges* in *The Edinburgh Review* (July 1845), wrote with far-seeing horror that its author 'has annulled all distinction between physical and moral'. Sedgwick had long urged that we continue to trust our language as itself naturally given us:

> In speaking of the laws of nature and of the harmonious changes resulting from their action, in spite of ourselves we fall into language in which we describe the operations of intelligence . . . [It] bears the image of such things as rise up of necessity in the mind, from our relation to the things around us. If we forget him in our thoughts, with our lips at least we must do homage to the God of nature.[7]

But to Darwin even the word 'accident' was tendentious, as he indicates when describing the dispersal of seeds by wind, sea, bird, and iceberg: 'These means of transport are sometimes accidental, but this is not strictly correct: the currents of the sea are not accidental, nor is the direction of prevalent gales of wind' (*Origins*, ch. 11). The word which 'more properly' should be used, says Darwin correcting himself, is not 'accidental' but 'occasional'. The word 'accident', or rather the feelings associated with it, became a means of placing and dating its user. Those who felt horror at the thought that man himself was accidental belonged to the old world of God's Nature: to them the word 'accident' was the opposite of the idea of 'design'. But those to whom the word 'accident' had no meaning belonged to what they took to be a modern world-view, in which everything was simply the result of the universality of physical causation. Thus, a Darwinist who refused to employ Chambers's strategy of making evolution theological might find austerely that he had *less* to say of the meaning of the world than ever had been said before.

There were many late nineteenth-century literary works directly influenced by Darwin, in particular by George Meredith and Thomas Hardy.[8] But perhaps the closest literary version of a pure Darwinist rejection of meaning—not in strict ideas but in essential human predicament—is found in Matthew Arnold's ancient analogue *Empedocles on Etna* published in 1852, seven years before the *Origin of Species*.

Empedocles believes that amidst the flow of atoms we are only

---

[7] Adam Sedgwick, *A Discourse on the Studies of the University* (1833; Leicester University Press, 1969), 14.

[8] See below, pp. 534–48.

'strangers here', and what he offers to disinherited man is this terrible conclusion: 'Because thou must not dream, thou need'st not then despair' (1. 1. 426). That is a negative second-order 'because' (a sort of 'just because', or 'because of *x* it doesn't necessarily follow that *y*'), the 'because' of a man who no longer lives in a universe that provides man with reason for his life. Both word and syntax are turned around in those double negatives because of the inversions demanded of human thought itself in such a world:

> Man errs not that he deems
> His welfare his true aim,
> He errs because he dreams
> The world does but exist that welfare to bestow.

> (1. 1. 173–6)

'Born into life!—'tis we, | And not the world, are new' (1. 1. 207–8). In that life and that world, even the worst that can happen to us is, despite the report of our feelings, utterly and blankly natural:

> Like us, the lightning fires
> Love to have scope and play;
> The stream, like us, desires
> An unimpeded way;
> Like us the Libyan wind delights to roam at large.

> Streams will not curb their pride
> The just man not to entomb,
> Nor lightnings go aside
> To give his virtues room;
> Nor is that wind less rough which blows a good man's barge.

> Nature, with equal mind,
> Sees all her sons at play;
> Sees man control the wind,
> The wind sweep man away;
> Allows the proudly-riding and the foundering bark.

> (1. 2. 247–61)

The terrible paradox of this struggle for existence lies in that 'like us', which undermines in us the very power of protest. For the non-human forces that would oppose humans, in the very pressure for place in the universe, come out of the same life-force as do the humans. It is likewise intolerably paradoxical that it is through an anthropomorphic language ('Nature, with equal mind, | Sees all her sons at play') that this non-anthropomorphic account of an indifferent world is so shockingly registered.

That Darwin was reluctantly aware of this threat to human status, and that he feared it as a bleak and silencing negation, is clear from a conversation that the Duke of Argyll recorded with Darwin in the last year of his life,

in which Argyll remarked that when he contemplated the remarkable contrivances recorded in Darwin's books on earthworms and orchids, he found it impossible to do so 'without seeing that they were the effect and expression of mind. I shall never forget Mr Darwin's answer. He looked at me very hard and said, "Well, that often comes over me with overwhelming force; but at other times," and he shook his head vaguely, adding, "it seems to go away."' (quoted in Young, p. 112)

So much for Darwin seemed to go away. In his brief *Autobiography* (1887) he noted how over the years he had somehow, and to his regret, simply given up reading poetry, stopped listening to music or looking at landscapes, losing all feeling for and pleasure in aesthetic tastes. He blamed his all-consuming work for this atrophy of the emotional part of his brain, claiming that his mind had 'become a kind of machine for grinding general laws out of large collections of facts'.[9] Yet, as with the breakdown of the young John Stuart Mill, it was not just the sheer intense amount of work, but the implications of its content, that accounted for this blank human loss.

John Ruskin had long predicted that the loss of human imaginative power was the inevitable consequence of a new professionalism that left man and the world only half of what they were. 'When I want to know why a leaf is green,' he complained in lecture 2 of *The Queen of the Air* (1869), 'they tell me it is coloured by "chlorophyll"' (para. 57). The science sounded instructive, 'but if they would only say plainly that a leaf is coloured green by a thing which is called "green leaf", we should see more precisely how far we had got'. In *Deucalion* (1875–83) in the years of his long final desperation at the

---

[9] Charles Darwin and Thomas Henry Huxley, *Autobiographies*, ed. G. de Beer (Oxford University Press, 1974), 84.

secular education of his times, he went so far as to dare, crankily, to lament the very use of the microscope:

And still, with increasingly evil results to all of us, the separation is every day widening between the man of science and the artist—in that, whether painter, sculptor, or musician, the latter is pre-eminently a person who sees with his Eyes, hears with his Ears, and labours with his Body, as God constructed them; and who, in using instruments, limits himself to those which convey or communicate his human power, while he rejects all that increase it. (*Works*, vol. 26, p. 116)

In *Modern Painters*, Ruskin had criticized the Wordsworth who wrote 'we murder to dissect' for failing to understand 'that to break a rock with a hammer in search of crystal may sometimes be an act not disgraceful to human nature, and that to dissect a flower may sometimes be as proper as to dream over it' (vol. 3, pt. 4, ch. 17, para. 7). By 1851, with science increasingly separating itself from natural theology, Ruskin, thinking of Lyell, wrote: 'If only the Geologists would let me alone, I could do very well, but those dreadful Hammers! I hear the chink of them at the end of every cadence of the Bible verses' (*Works*, vol. 36, p. 115). To the man who listened with human ears, the very sound of the world was changing, unbearably. 'I take,' he said defiantly, 'Wordsworth's single line'

We live by admiration, hope, and love

'for my literal guide, in all education' (*Works*, vol. 28, p. 255). Yet when in 1872 Darwin published *The Expression of the Emotions in Man and Animals*, he wrote as a scientist staying on the outside of his subject, looking at photographs of faces of children and of zoo animals, and offering the dispassionate argument that emotions were learnt and acquired, had a survival value, and were part of the physiological continuum from animals to man. To Ruskin, however, the human feeling that naturally accompanied our thoughts and our sights was not an anthropomorphic fiction, an illegitimate intrusion upon the non-human blankness of the world, but an irreducible experience of inner reality. That the sight and smell of a rose was beautiful was a *fact*. 'In these books of mine, their distinctive character, as essays on art, is their bringing everything to a root in human passion or human hope' (*Modern Painters*, vol. 5, pt. 9, ch. 1, para. 7). In contrast, Darwin was convinced that what he admired in the tail feathers of the Argus pheasant was what attracted the female Argus pheasant: in the cause of sexual selection, beauty was a physical and not a spiritual factor (*The Descent of Man* (1871), ch. 13).

It was not that Ruskin was unaware of the dangers of illegitimate emotional projection operating falsely upon the objects of perception. 'The pathetic fallacy' was Ruskin's own name for the unwarranted linguistic tendency in the nineteenth century for the ascription of human feelings to non-human objects in the landscape (*Modern Painters*, vol. 3, ch. 12). It resulted from the need of a disinherited generation to find, all too literally, a *place* for human emotion in the universe. Hence the adjectival weakness of writers such as Charles Kingsley:

> They rowed her in across the rolling foam—
> The cruel, crawling foam

Second-rate poets see wrongly, said Ruskin, because they feel strongly and love the primrose for more than just itself. On the other hand, there are those, like scientists, who can see a primrose accurately, only because they feel nothing about it except that it is a primrose. But the first-rate poets and the best artists are they who, feeling strongly, still can think strongly and see truly.

Nonetheless, the puritan in Ruskin never took the existence of art for granted, never believed in it as a self-sufficient specialism. Consequently, he was never afraid of asking fundamental questions about the very origin and purpose of art in the world. One of those questions was directed in particular towards the realist or naturalist school of art: Why should Nature need our Art? In the great tenth chapter 'Of the Use of Pictures' in *Modern Painters*, volume 3 (1856) he puts the fundamental objection against artificiality, however realistically deployed: isn't a painting always inferior to a view from a window—let alone to the experience of actually being in the reality it depicts? 'Is there, then, nothing to be done by man's art? Have we only to copy, and again copy, for ever, the imagery of the universe?' 'Not so,' he replied in the first volume of *The Stones of Venice* (1851); 'We have work to do upon it':

This infinite universe is unfathomable, inconceivable, in its whole; every human creature must slowly spell out, and long contemplate, such part of it as may be possible for him to reach; then set forth what he has learned of it for those beneath him; extricating it from infinity, as one gathers a violet out of grass; one does not improve either violet or grass in gathering it, but one makes the flower visible; and then the human being has to make its power upon his own heart visible also, and to give it the honour of the good thoughts it has raised up in him, and to write upon it the history of his own soul. (ch. 35, para. 5)

This is not the pathetic fallacy: emotions here feel received, not projected; the human response feels called for rather than gratuitous. Nor is this anthropomorphic arrogance: there is no pretence that a single human being can do anything more than selectively attest to one small part of the universe, and no claim that human witness improves the flower. But human emotion honours and fulfils that which calls its good thoughts into being. And art, the highest development of human responsiveness, to Ruskin marks the necessity of human consciousness to see and value the universe and by that gratitude complete it. At the foot of the cross in Tintoretto's *Crucifixion*, Mary 'has cast her mantle over her head, and her face is lost in its shade, and her whole figure veiled in folds of gray': the difference 'between that gray woof, that gathers round her as she falls, and the same folds cast in a heap upon the ground' is life itself (*Modern Painters*, vol. 5, pt. 9, ch. 1, para. 8).

Why then, asks Ruskin, is the nineteenth century an age in which painting seems to have less and less human interest and more and more concentration on what in previous times had been merely the natural background? A medieval knight or monk looking at modern painting would ask: why do these people now spend the whole of their lives making pictures of tress and clouds and bits of stone and runlets of water, instead of gods and saints and heroes?

In the struggle to get into right relation with the universe, there are for Ruskin two opposite and yet related errors: the first, 'that of caring for man only; and for the rest of the universe, little or not at all'; the other, 'that of caring for the universe only;—for man, not at all'. It is the second, he says, which 'in a measure, is the error of modern science' (*Modern Painters*, vol. 5, pt. 9, ch. 1, para. 9). It is the error of modern art too, if we lose trust in ourselves and our place in the universe.

To steer between those two errors of caring too much or too little for man and to locate man's proper relation, Ruskin does not employ

Fig. 4. J. M. W. Turner (1775–1851), *Rouen from St. Catherine's Hill*, c.1832.
To John Ruskin, this was a painting notable for its expression of natural infinity in all the fluctuating hues and shades of sky.

abstract argument. Instead, like a painter, he makes his reader humanly see and feel, in space, what it is he means. Look at Turner's *Rouen from St Catherine's Hill* in his Rivers of France series:

> The whole sky is one ocean of alternate waves of cloud and light, so blended together that the eye cannot rest on any one without being guided to the next, and so to a hundred more, till it is lost over and over again in every wreath—that if it divides the sky into quarters of inches, and tries to count and comprehend the component parts of any single one of those divisions, it is still as utterly defied and defeated by the part as by the whole—that there is not one line out of the millions there which repeats another, not one which is unconnected with another, not one which does not in itself convey histories of distance and space, and suggest new and changeful form. (*Modern Painters*, vol. 1, pt. 2, sect. 3, ch. 3, para. 23)

In the all-too-controlled art of seventeenth-century Dutch realism, said Ruskin, you can count the bricks in a wall. Not so here, as the picture keeps reshaping itself as an indivisible whole before the spectator's eyes. Yet, although there are indeed no humans in the picture, modern painting of this order tests the role and the place of the human element in the universe. It shows how art at its greatest is the one form of human thinking which takes humans *beyond* their capacity for simple projection, conscious planning, or easy measurement.

Where a painting is an expression not of repetition but of infinity, then human beings have gone beyond themselves, by creating something *more* than they can easily cope with

> for this simple reason, that it is impossible for mortal mind to compose an infinity of any kind for itself, or to form an idea of perpetual variation, and to avoid all repetition, merely by its own combining resources. The moment that we trust to ourselves, we repeat ourselves, and therefore the moment that we see in a work of any kind whatsoever the expression of infinity, we may be certain that the workman has gone to nature for it. (*Modern Painters*, vol. 1, pt. 2, sect. 3, ch. 3 para. 22).

In the end, to Ruskin 'nature' does no more and no less than offer humans a language of creative discovery—a deeper, more validated, more mysterious, unpredictable, and sacred language, he believed, than any offered by contemporary science, economics, or politics.

But the law is that nature can rightly serve human beings only when it makes them feel that they are serving it.

What the natural creation offered was what Ruskin called 'mystery', but a mystery of ordinary life. In everyday perception you never see everything but you never see nothing, says Ruskin (*Modern Painters*, vol. 4, pt. 5, ch. 4, para. 4): there is always something which you cannot see and always something which you can (vol. 1, pt. 2, sect. 2, ch. 5, para. 4). *There*, between those two points of seeing all and seeing nothing—in the very range of the human visual field—lies man's place in nature. And that is what the poet Keats had said philosophy should be: not axioms, but felt on the pulses.

Yet Ruskin can offer axioms too. His constant aim 'of bringing everything to root in human passion' and his oft-repeated belief 'that all great art is the expression of man's delight in God's work not his own' are not, he insists, finally incompatible. For observe, he says, bringing the two together in his final great turn of thought: '[man] is not himself his own work: he is himself the most wonderful piece of God's workmanship extant' (*Modern Painters*, vol. 5, pt. 9, ch. 2, para. 1). The mystery that was beyond the human was still to be seen and felt within human terms.

To Herbert Spencer the equivalent to 'mystery' in evolutionary theory was called 'the unknowable'. It was a vital distinction.

'Matter, however conceived by us, cannot be matter as it actually is.' Thus, Spencer argued, we always have a residual sense of reality 'dissociated as far as possible from those special forms under which it was represented in thought' (*First Principles*, pt. 1, ch. 4, para. 26). That sense of reality is the deduction of something beyond our conceptions, towards which our conceptions are always partially gesturing. This was Spencer's version of agnosticism, more positive than anything Huxley had first meant by the word. For to Spencer if science is the realm of *knowledge*, knowledge is also always establishing ahead of itself an ever more definite sense of what is *unknown*: 'we cannot conceive of any explanation profound enough to exclude the question—What is the explanation of that explanation?' (pt. 1, ch. 1, para. 4). Spencer took from the Kantians Sir William Hamilton and H. L. Mansel the recognition that the unknown is part of knowing: 'as on conceiving any bounded space, there arises a nascent consciousness of space outside the bounds; so when we think of any definite cause, there arises a nascent consciousness of a cause behind it' (pt. 1, ch. 4, para. 26). 'Religion' is the name Spencer gives to the final incapacity of knowledge in the face of that progressively ever-retreating unknown. Conventional religion in contrast is really irreligious to him, because its claims to know the truth are inevitably anthropomorphic. Its secret fear, he claims, is that one day science will explain away all its man-made mysteries.

Spencer thus sees science as a movement towards the formation of ever more abstract laws that lead human beings beyond the field of everyday concrete experience beloved by such as Ruskin. 'The most abstract conception, to which Science is slowly approaching, is one that merges into the inconceivable or unthinkable, by the dropping of all concrete elements of thought' (*First Principles*, pt. 1, ch. 5, para. 29). In his *Autobiography* (2 vols., 1904) Spencer gives an instance of how inconceivable to the imagination even very familiar scientific 'facts' become, as, far from home, he looks over the country stretching beyond the River Hudson and finds it

interesting, and a little difficult to think of it as some three thousand miles from the island on the other side of the Atlantic whence we had come. Not easy was it either, and indeed impossible in any true sense, to conceive the real position of this island on that vast surface which slowly curves downward beyond the horizon: the impossibility being one which I have vividly felt when gazing sea-ward at the masts of a vessel below the horizon, and trying to conceive the actual surface of the Earth, as slowly bending round till its meridians met eight thousand miles beneath my feet: the attempt producing what may be figuratively called a kind of mental choking, from the endeavour to put into the intellectual structure a conception immensely too large for it. (vol. 2, p. 390)

This mental choking, so unlike Ruskin's love of infinity, comes out of a world defamiliarized. True religion, for Spencer, is the point at which these abstractions of science, which defeat anthropomorphism, shade into the finally unknowable—that last conception of the unconceptualizable that bursts our intellectual frameworks:

By continually seeking to know and being continually thrown back with a deepened conviction of the impossibility of knowing, we may keep alive

the consciousness that it is alike our highest wisdom and our highest duty
to regard that through which all things exist as The Unknowable (*First
Principles*, pt. 1, ch. 5, para. 31)

Spencer's grand cosmic synthesis was celebrated in John Tyndall's
famous Belfast Address before the British Association in 1874. Yet,
although Spencer's agnosticism is not as austere a vision as that of
Arnold's solitary Empedocles, it is nonetheless a vision which, in
positing as the ultimate reality an abstractly sensed 'it', beyond
human terms or feelings, is absolutely opposed to humanizing the
world. Morley in his *Voltaire* of 1879 protests about the abstractions
of eighteenth-century deism, 'It was not by a cold, a cheerless . . .
conception such as this, that the church became the refuge of humanity in the dark times', and Seeley in his *Natural Religion* of 1882
argues that the affections die 'in a world where everything great and
enduring is cold'.[10] It is a coldness that threatens Gwendolen in
Daniel Deronda (1876) as a terrible objectification of life: 'Solitude
in any wide scene impressed her with an undefined feeling of im-
measurable existence aloof from her, in the midst of which she was
helplessly incapable of asserting herself. The little astronomy taught
her at school used sometimes to set her imagination at work in a way
that made her tremble' (ch. 6). Scientific concerns about entropy, the
ageing of the sun, and the instability of nebulae were part of that
climate. It is the coldness that at every level Hardy feared.

In heated opposition to both Darwinism and Agnosticism, Ruskin
thus unashamedly insisted that it is the child's conception of God as
a 'He' and not an 'It' which is 'the only one which *for us* can be true'
(*Modern Painters*, vol. 4, pt. 5, ch. 6, para. 7). Ruskin's God grants
that allowance as natural to us, where Spencer's austere Unknowable Abstraction is silent. To the question 'But this poor miserable
Me! Is this, then, all the book I have got to read about God in?'
Ruskin replies, 'Yes, truly so.' When we compare nature's architecture with man's, rocks are always stronger, mountains always
larger, all natural objects more finished; yet, says Ruskin, the extra
dimension of effort that man's imperfection and inferiority call forth
in him is the expression of a soul. 'For through thyself only canst

---

[10]   John Morley, *Voltaire* (1879; 1893 edn.), 280; Sir John Seeley, *Natural Religion*
(1882), quoted by F. W. H. Myers, *Essays: Modern* (1885), 305.

thou know God' (*Modern Painters*, vol. 5, pt. 9, ch. 1, para. 14), however flawed that self: 'through the glass darkly. But except through the glass nowise' (para. 15). Otherwise, Ruskin prophesies, the moment that we desire that God, 'instead of stooping to hold our hands', should arise and be understood through a more adult and scientific understanding, will be the moment when 'God takes us at our word': 'He rises, into His own invisible and inconceivable mystery; He goes forth upon the ways that are not our ways, and retires into the thoughts which are not our thoughts; and we are left alone. And presently we say in our vain hearts, "There is no God"' (vol. 4, pt. 5, ch. 6, para. 7). Taking things humanly is not something we as humans should seek to transcend or, says Ruskin, we shall only destroy ourselves in the process.

III. Beyond Nature and After Religion: The Future in J. S. Mill and T. H. Huxley

For forty years, from the first publication of his *Discourse on the Studies of the University* in 1833 to his adverse reception to the *Origin of Species*, Adam Sedgwick, professor of geology at Cambridge and ordained minister of the Church of England, fought against what he took to be a two-pronged reduction of the nature of man. To Sedgwick (1785–1873), both evolutionism and Utilitarianism were alike in rooting man within the primitive biological drives of pleasure and pain. 'The principle of utility and the principle of natural selection', argued J. G. Schurman in *The Ethical Import of Darwinism* (1888) 'have such strong elective affinities' (p. 126). Pleasure and pain were animal life's basic indicators, the gauges of repulsion and attraction: does it hurt? is it desirable? Via Malthusian struggle, utility itself was—initially to Huxley's horror—a principle within the theory of natural selection: the survival of a species depended upon its concentration upon what worked as needful and useful for its preservation. In Darwin's *Descent of Man* even the higher aesthetic sense descended from the advantages that beauty offered in the sexual selection of mates. Man had originated out of animals; thought and mind had originated out of sensation and body. In his *Principles of Psychology* (1855) Herbert Spencer argued that passions came in 'bursts' and thoughts felt like 'blows' because our whole life was originally physical, developing inwardly from a long series of external shocks to the nerves. Even individual conscience gradually evolved as an internalization of the tribe's approval or disapproval.

To the opponents of the Darwinian world-view this was reductive. Darwin, Ruskin conceded, may be right: all forms may evolve out of the same force and process. Yet in the living present, the forms do *not* pass into each other but have their own evolved reality. Nor does the purpose of life always revert to mere continuance: 'The reason for seeds is that flowers may be; not the reason of flowers that seeds may be' (*The Queen of the Air* (1869), lecture 2, para. 60). Relations, said Ruskin, are 'independent of their origin' (para. 62).

This was also the position of the Catholic biologist St George Mivart (1827–1900). Mivart warned against 'the widespread tendency now existing to sacrifice other and more important considerations to considerations as to origin' (*Essays and Criticisms*, 2 vols. (1892), vol. 2, p. 271). Argument should be based on 'a true knowledge of what man is *now*' (p. 314). He cited John Morley's *On Compromise* (1874) on the age's historicizing and relativizing tendencies. For Morley had argued that increasingly in the present age there was more concern with 'the pedigree and genealogical connections of an idea, than with its own proper goodness or badness, its strength or its weakness'. It was a tendency that makes men shrink 'from importing anything like absolute quality into their propositions'. Morley concluded thus on the historicization of thought and belief: 'In the last century, men asked of a belief or a story, Is it true? We now ask, How did men come to take it for true?' (quoted in Mivart, *Essays and Criticisms*, vol. 2, p. 271).

Within evolutionary theory the modernizers' future, argued Mivart, was based on reducing the present to the terms of the past. But where we are going to is not the same as where we have come from. It was true that in the various natural and instinctive processes performed by creatures devoid of self-conscious intellect, there was 'somehow and somewhere a latent rationality', but the rationality belonged to that higher source which was 'the ultimate and common cause of them all': 'it is *in* them, but it is not *of* them' (*Essays and Criticisms*, vol. 2, pp. 348, 350). Mivart believed that the truths of evolutionary biology could be brought into right relation with that higher source, in the divine truth of Catholicism. Yet for all his pains, the net result for Mivart was that on one side he was denounced by Huxley, his former mentor, and on the other finally excommunicated by the Catholic Church.

To John Henry Newman, in contrast, it had been a mistake from the very first for Paley to couple religion with natural theology. It was a linkage that left religious beliefs at the fickle mercy of science's latest and ever-changing discoveries. In 1841 in his pamphlet 'The Tamworth Reading Room' (reprinted in *Discussions and Arguments on Various Subjects*, 1872), Newman had opposed Sir Robert Peel's proposal for the establishment of mechanics' institutes and reading rooms to provide 'Useful Knowledge' of natural history, chemistry, and astronomy for the working classes. To Newman's astonishment Peel—though himself a religious man—wanted to omit politics and religion from the syllabus, because they offered grounds for dissension and dispute; instead he offered science as a 'neutral ground' for all to start from and meet upon. The age's leading Conservative used an essentially Utilitarian language, to argue that the study of science, like all education, led to a general moral improvement.

Newman retorted that the study of Nature as a separate system always tends to atheism. Science only gives us facts, not their meaning. It too easily assumes that there is only one answer to the question, 'Does the sun shine to warm the earth, or is the earth warmed because the sun shines?' For science offers a model of thought in which 'first comes knowledge, then a view, then reasoning, and then belief'. Yet such conclusions are only like (more or less confirmed) opinions: they have no root in them. Logicians, says Newman to the Mills and the Darwins of the world, 'are more set on concluding rightly than on right conclusions': 'they cannot see the end for the process'. Religion believes in a wholly different order of thought— which cannot simply start from knowledge because nothing can: 'we shall never have done beginning, if we determine to begin with proof'. Human beings always begin, however riskily, from some belief.

But for others, the progress of science and the new scientific worldview did not seem to need the old religious beliefs. Both Utilitarianism and Darwinism were so economical and so apparently complete as forms of explanation. Looking back in 1900, in his study *The English Utilitarians*, Leslie Stephen argued that much of the Utilitarians' mastery of explanation lay in the way that associationist psychology[11] combined a basic simplicity with the capacity for the evolution of complexity within it. By a sort of chemistry—equivalent to Darwin's biological economy—it was a natural law of associationism that the elements of human consciousness were fixed and finite, in relation to basic pleasure and pain, but that their combination was infinitely variable and plastic. Although Utilitarianism declared the fundamental primacy of pleasure, in the course of human education and development some *kinds* of pleasure, argued John Stuart Mill, became more desirable than others, the sheer *quantity* of a lower kind giving way to the greater *quality* of a higher kind. Hence his classic formulation in his revisionist *Utilitarianism* (1863), 'It is better to be Socrates dissatisfied than a fool satisfied' (ch. 2).

However, it was also crucial to progressivist Utilitarianism that the state of nature out of which man originated was no necessary guide to, or even limit upon, his future development. Or, if there was a founding and continuing limit within human nature, it could only be proven to be so in the light not of past theologies but of those future experiments that human beings carried out upon themselves in the search for further improvement. John Stuart Mill believed in the theoretical possibility of a future science which could eventually explain and predict human behaviour. In the mean time, there had to be the liberalism of opportunity and experiment. Thus, the social and political goal of Utilitarianism was emphatically the opposite of Darwin's rawly selective Nature: it was not the survival of the fittest but the greatest happiness of the greatest possible number.

Effectively, therefore, Utilitarianism sought to abolish the very idea of 'Nature' or, at the very least, the human colonizing of that word as some sort of static standard. 'So true is it', said John Stuart Mill near the opening of *The Subjection of Women* (1869), 'that unnatural generally means only uncustomary, and that everything which is usual appears natural.' For Mill this linguistic reorientation was nothing less than the opening of the human mind to social and

---

[11] See below, pp. 175–6.

political opportunities to begin to create new kinds of human being. It sought to rise above what an opponent, Sir Henry Taylor, writing in *Fraser's Magazine* (February 1870) called the physical, biological, natural 'ground-work' for the different roles and treatment of men and women. To a Darwinist these were mere 'survivals' lasting on from a state of society in which physical force was supreme. Modern history, in order to be modern, had now to catch up with itself through rational political intervention. For what Mill sought was a new human nature which was no longer that of unthinking social custom. He sought a mental 'cultivation' through which, beyond the merely physical,

the most elevated sentiments of which humanity is capable become a second nature, stronger than the first, and not so much subduing the original nature as merging it into itself. . . . This artificially created or at least artificially perfected nature of the best and noblest human beings, is the only nature which it is ever commendable to follow. (*Collected Works*, vol. 10, p. 51)

This was what T. H. Huxley was to call in *Evolution and Ethics* the horticultural process rather than the cosmic one: culture seeking to progress beyond biology. For in Mill's late essay 'Nature', published posthumously in 1874 but written in the 1850s, the logician had sought to clarify the whole issue for a modern world by distinguishing the meanings of the word 'Nature'.

Mill had argued that 'Nature' had two primary and distinct senses, too often confused and entangled in ordinary people's thinking. 'It either denotes the entire system of things, with the aggregate of all their properties, or it denotes things as they would be, apart from human intervention' (*Collected Works*, vol. 10, p. 401). In the first and more inclusive sense of the term, said Mill, 'there is no need of any recommendation to act according to nature, since it is what nobody can possibly help doing, and equally whether he acts well or ill' (p. 379). But in the second more restricted sense of the word, 'in which Nature stands for that which takes place without human intervention, the very aim and object of action is to alter and improve Nature in the other meaning' (p. 380). We humans make changes, and hence it is we who may make a difference between Nature 2 and Nature 1.

In *The Subjection of Women* Mill argued that people too often ignored that capacity for improvement, speaking vaguely but fanatically instead of 'the intention of Nature and the ordinance of God' (the two significantly offered together as though virtual synonyms). It was part of the reaction against progressive eighteenth-century rational enlightenment that in the nineteenth century, said Mill, whenever an old opinion was strongly rooted in feeling, 'the worse it fares in argumentative contest, the more persuaded its adherents are that their feeling must have some deeper ground' (ch. 1)—an intuitive ground in some deep unchangeable 'nature'. But Nature itself is neither rational nor moral; bad actions, for example, are themselves perfectly natural.

Whether human beings had consciously acknowledged it or not, their task throughout history had always been not to follow Nature obediently but instead, interveningly, to create Art—in a sense of that word that was wider if not deeper than Ruskin's. To dig, to plough, to build, to wear clothes—these are art, culture, civilization in direct infringement of the injunction to follow nature:

Everybody professes to approve and admire many great triumphs of Art over Nature . . . But to commend these and similar feats, is to acknowledge that the ways of Nature are to be conquered, not obeyed: that her powers are often towards man in the position of enemies, from whom he must wrest, by force and ingenuity, what little he can for his own use, and deserves to be applauded when that little is rather more than might be expected from his physical weakness in comparison to those gigantic powers. All praise of Civilization, or Art, or Contrivance, is so much dispraise of Nature; an admission of imperfection, which it is man's business, and merit, to be always endeavouring to correct or mitigate. (*Collected Works*, vol. 10, p. 381)

In that sense, our human nature *is* to be artificial: to thwart, modify, and improve the spontaneous ways of nature that exist without us. Indeed, such artifice in human beings 'is as much Nature as anything else': 'everything which is artificial is natural—Art has no independent powers of its own: Art is but the employment of the powers of Nature for an end' (p. 375).

Man, said Darwin, 'can never act by selection, excepting on variations which are first given to him in some slight degree by nature' (*Origins*, ch. 1). So too with Mill, we are only adapters and modifiers in life's second, not its first, place. But within that second and subsequent rank on earth, we literally find *room* for manoeuvre:

The united powers of the whole human race could not create a new property of matter in general, or of any one of its species. We can only take advantage for our purposes of the properties which we find. A ship floats by the same laws of specific gravity and equilibrium, as a tree uprooted by the wind and blown into the water. The corn which men raise for food, grows and produces its grain by the same laws of vegetation by which the wild rose and the mountain strawberry bring forth their flowers and fruit. A house stands and holds together by the natural properties, the weight and cohesion of the materials which compose it: a steam engine works by the natural expansive force of steam, exerting a pressure upon one part of a system of arrangements, which pressure, by the mechanical properties of the lever, is transferred from that to another part where it raises the weight or removes the obstacle brought into connexion with it. In these and other artificial operations the office of man is, as has been often remarked, a very limited one; it consists in moving things into certain places. We move objects, and by doing this, bring some things into contact which were separate, or separate others which were in contact: and by this simple change of place, natural forces previously dormant are called into action, and produce the desired effect. (*Collected Works*, vol. 10, p. 375)

By the manipulation of the uniform conditions in which we find ourselves, Man can turn knowledge of the laws of necessity into a capacity for freedom and change. We escape being determined by antecedent circumstances by using our very knowledge of that determinism to create some of those circumstances themselves. Again it is an act of economy: human art is not a creation of new forces but a use of old forces in new places. 'Though we can do nothing except through laws of nature, we can use one law to counteract another. According to Bacon's maxim, we can obey nature in such a manner as to command it' (p. 379).

What this meant was that nothing need have or keep its so-called 'natural' place in the world. The novelist Mrs Oliphant, reviewing *The Subjection of Women* in *The Edinburgh Review* for October 1869, recognized how the argument that women were no longer to have or know their 'place' was based on a denial of 'nature' in the very form of the woman's body and its procreative function. In the nineteenth century, she said with bitter irony, everything must be resolvable, nothing must be irremediable: the problems associated with the body and its instincts—of the relation of childbirth and childcare to the lives and careers of women—must be solved by the mind, and nature's original burdens ameliorated by utopian reason's artifical invention of alternative social structures. For Mill such responses resulted from fear of modern liberty. The very basis of society could and should be thought out again; there were no longer natural grounds which could be securely taken for granted or left unexamined. But, said his opponents, on what basis, on what principle or underlying reason, was this second nature to be created? Mill's modern human beings were naturally artificial and rationally self-inventing.

The story of the schools of evolution and of Utilitarianism, and their complex joint relation concerning humankind's place in nature, culminates in a grand, summarizing synthesis in 1893, in T. H. Huxley's Romanes lecture *Evolution and Ethics*. There the evolutionary process to which Darwinist Huxley was committed now finally includes within it, despite Huxley's long resistance to Utilitarianism, the emergence of a Millite part of Huxley as a liberal progressive. But in the process Huxley is led into a final break, within evolutionary theory, from Herbert Spencer.

Spencer argued for the ethics of evolution: the struggle for existence and the survival of the fittest were laws that applied equally to men in society as to plants and animals in a state of nature. Now Huxley spoke rather of the evolution of ethics: the history of civilization recorded how step by step human beings had succeeded in kicking away the ladder by which they had climbed, until they began to create a civilized world increasingly separate from the natural cosmos. The bleakest possible Darwinist implication was here simply accepted: that there was no sanction for morality in the ways of the cosmos.

There is no mistaking Huxley's sense of fundamental paradox in what follows: that the conscience of man should revolt against the moral indifference of nature which itself produced him, and seek to establish its own state within a state instead, was as if the 'microcosmic human atom' had turned round upon 'the illimitable macrocosm' that was its own origin: 'The influence of the cosmic process on the evolution of society is the greater the more rudimentary its civilization. Social progress means a checking of the cosmic process at every step and the substitution for it of another, which may be called the ethical process' (*Evolution and Ethics*, p. 33). To Herbert Spencer responding in a letter to J. A. Skilton, 29 July 1893, Huxley was putting an end to evolutionary process and to the naturalistic synthesis: it was virtually 'a surrender of the general doctrine of evolution in so far as its higher applications are concerned', offering nothing for the development of social organizations; it was practically 'a going-back to the old theological notions which put Man and Nature in antithesis' (*The Life and Letters of Herbert Spencer*, ed. D. Duncan (1908), p. 336).

It was this fissure between man and the cosmos, finally acknowledged by Huxley, that let in the pained presence of Thomas Hardy. The creature that was a product of evolution had evolved to a point of consciousness and feeling which unconscious and indifferent evolution itself could not satisfy. It would have been better

never to have begun doing than to have *over*done so indecisively, that is, than to have created so far beyond all apparent first intention (on the emotional side), without mending matters by a second intent and execution, to eliminate the blunders of overdoing. The emotions have no place in a world of defect, and it is a cruel injustice that they should have developed in it.

If Law itself had consciousness, how the aspect of its creatures would terrify it, fill it with remorse![12]

Jude the Obscure (1895) marked the failure of the Millite project. The efforts of Jude and Sue, to create a second nature for themselves in a society for the future, were utterly defeated. The ancient biological drives of sex—as if by nature's revenge—still undermined all rationalized modern attempts to sustain the independent value of human love. As the Utilitarian Henry Sidgwick had said of himself at the end of his *Methods of Ethics* (1874), Jude had looked for Cosmos and found only Chaos. There was none of Huxley's optimism for Hardy. The universe that the young astronomer looked out into in *Two on a Tower* (1882) was too immense, too impersonal, too sheerly void for human beings. 'It may be questioned', Hardy con-

[12] F. E. Hardy, *The Life of Thomas Hardy*, 9 May 1881.

cluded in a notebook entry for 7 April 1889, 'if Nature, or'—mindful of the Darwinist disinheritance of human language—'what may be called Nature'

so far back as when she crossed the line from invertebrates to vertebrates, did not exceed her mission. This planet does not provide the materials for happiness to higher existences. Other planets may, though one can hardly see how. (F. E. Hardy, *The Life of Thomas Hardy*)

If human beings were morally superior to the physical world, it was a world which nonetheless, unjustly, remained more powerful than they, both within and without.

Thus, like so many Victorian histories, this one ends with the question as to whether anything or anyone could withstand the forces that went ultimately into the making of Thomas Hardy. One resistant attempt at an answer deserves brief final mention.

In a review essay on Huxley in 1893, the Idealist philosopher Adam Seth (also known as Pringle-Pattison) criticized Hardy's views on nature and linked them, perceptively, to the despair of Arnold's Empedocles, quoting from Act 1 scene 2:

> No, we are strangers here, the world is from of old . . .
> .   .   .   .
> To tunes we did not call, our being must keep chime.

Significantly both the review essay and the book in which it finally appeared were entitled *Man's Place in the Cosmos* (1897). Seth's argument goes like this: Huxley's *Evolution and Ethics* serves to remind us that the non-human nature which is the blind selective force behind Darwinism is not sufficient to hold that cosmos together once human beings are evolved. Thus cosmically, man is left in a middle state, which Hardy too easily assumed to be a limbo. In fact, the implicit message of the human position is that human beings cannot return to their Origin but must discover and pursue their End, to help complete the cosmic narrative. The Idealist, said Seth, believes with the evolutionist in the unity of the cosmos. But refusing to accept that the sole principle of explanation is to carry back facts or events or existences to the antecedent conditions from which they arose, the Idealist differs from evolutionists in believing that the true nature of explanation must be forward and not back: 'the true nature of the cause only becomes apparent in the effect' (*Man's Place in the Cosmos*, p. 11). What Seth urged was that the very gap between the ways of the non-human world and the aspirations of its human products should be seen not as a depressing fact of disinheritance but as a sign for a future. It was a sign that man was not accidental but necessary, necessary to be the creature that not only finds but then bridges that gap. It is a conviction, not a demonstration, says Seth, but if the race is successfully to fight against the premature despair of Arnold and Hardy, it needs the sustaining belief that it is sanctioned with a mission. The gap that man creates between man and nature, said Seth, is itself a result of the further promptings of the cosmos at a new level.

How far that belief could be sustained, however, is a question that takes us to the next two chapters—on religion and on mind.

3

Religion

On Sunday 30 March 1851, for the first and only time in English history, an official census was conducted of attendance at all places of religious worship. It showed that roughly seven million of the eighteen million inhabitants of England and Wales attended public worship. With the Roman Catholic congregation numbering less than 400,000, those in religious attendance were split almost equally between Church of England services and the main Protestant Dissenting or Nonconformist chapels (Methodist, Congregationalist, Baptist, Presbyterian, and Unitarian). It was a shock. Only half the nation was attending religious services; only a quarter was attending the services of the established national Church. In his official report on the census, Horace Mann, the statistician in charge, concluded that 'a sadly formidable portion of the English people are habitual neglecters of the public ordinances of religion'.

What is more, the regional breakdown of the figures showed that the Church of England, or Anglican Church, had become a largely rural, middle-class institution, strongest in the villages and country towns of the south, weakest in the northern manufacturing districts. In the great industrial towns of the north such as Leeds, the Dissenting or Nonconformist chapels were twice as popular as the Church of England, and yet still only about half as successful as the overall national average. On the other hand, as people rose in the social scale, it became the norm for them to change from Dissent to Anglicanism, the Church of the establishment. It was a sign of the end of a nation, said J. A. Froude in the preface to *The Nemesis of Faith* (1849), when an old faith was preserved only 'in false show of reverence either from cowardice, or indolence, or miserable social convenience'.

The statistics themselves make it an even bet as to whether by the middle of the century Victorian England was best described as still a fundamentally religious age or as a period of growing secularization. Yet this was an age in which between 1836 and 1863 over a third of all books published were of a religious nature. Amidst the general rise of the press, religious newspapers appeared and flourished such as the (Church of England) *Record* (1828) and *Guardian* (1846), the (Low Church) *Christian World* (1857), the (High Church) *Church Times* (1863), *The Nonconformist* (1841), *The Wesleyan Times* (1849) and *The Methodist Recorder* (1861), and the (Catholic) *Tablet* (1843) and *Universe* (1860)—many of which as the century went on began regularly to print sermons. Millions of copies of tracts and sermons were published each year by religious societies. The popular Baptist preacher Charles Spurgeon published a sermon every week from 1854 until 1917. What is more, where before in the Church of England there had been the Psalms alone, this was the new age of the Anglican communal hymn—over 400 collections were published in the 1850s and 1860s, with the wonderfully inclusive *Hymns Ancient and Modern* appearing in 1861. The great hymn-writers included Francis Lyte ('Abide with me') and John Mason Neale ('Jerusalem the golden') and there were a number of newly important women writers: Sarah Flower Adams ('Nearer my God to Thee'), Mrs Alexander ('All things bright and beautiful'), Dora Greenwell, Frances Ridley Havergal, and Anna Laetitia Waring.[1] 'Onward, Christian soldiers', 'Dear Lord and Father of mankind', 'Lead, kindly light', 'The King of love my Shepherd is', 'The day Thou gavest, Lord, is ended': all these are the products of an age that hardly seems godless.

And yet even so devout a figure as John Henry Newman describes himself in his autobiography as looking out into the nineteenth-century world of material independence and hectic business, and seeing there no sign that God could possibly exist: 'If I looked into a mirror, and did not see my face, I should have the sort of feeling which actually comes upon me, when I look into this living busy world, and see no reflexion of its Creator' (*Apologia Pro Vita Sua*

[1] See J. R. Watson, *The English Hymn* (Clarendon Press, 1997), chs. 13–16.

(1864), pt. 7). Arguably the most thoroughgoing religious poetry of the age, that of the Catholic Gerard Manley Hopkins, existed in complete and virtually unpublished isolation from such a world. For within that world, as Carlyle said in *Sartor Resartus* (1834), the inner cry of the human heart could no longer be an unequivocally affirmative 'Yes': instead there was the threat of 'the Everlasting No', the sense of void at the centre of a material, meaningless existence. For Newman there remained a last choice: either there was no Creator or, by some terrible aboriginal calamity, the human race had become discarded and separated from His presence. The Victorian world was to Newman a sort of Dickensian orphan: 'a boy of good make and mind, with the tokens on him of a refined nature, cast upon the world without provision, unable to say whence he came, his birthplace or his family connections' (*Apologia Pro Vita Sua*, pt. 7).

Would the boy try to reclaim his lost inheritance as a child of God or, like Edmund Gosse and Samuel Butler by the century's end, reject all fathers, earthly and heavenly, in the movement towards secular adult autonomy? Newman, at any rate, positively welcomed the final embattled decisiveness that the nineteenth-century predicament demanded: 'It is one great advantage of an age in which unbelief speaks out, that Faith can speak out too; that, if falsehood assails truth, truth can assail falsehood' (*The Idea of a University* (1852; rev. 1859, 1873), pt. 2 'University Subjects', ch. 5, sects. 1–2). The Church, he concluded, now gains in intensity what she has lost in extent.

Yet crucially there was a third possibility not countenanced by Newman: the anguished position of those agnostics or honest doubters symptomatically torn between 'yes' and 'no'—suspended, like the age itself it seemed, in between belief and disbelief. In his *Autobiography* John Stuart Mill recognized he was part of a very tiny, unrepresentative minority when he admitted having had no difficulty in throwing off religious belief, because he had never been brought up to have any. Those who had been raised with a belief which they could now neither wholly follow nor simply quit were a mid-century generation who found themselves—in the famous words of Matthew Arnold—'Wandering between two worlds, one dead | The other powerless to be born' ('Stanzas from the Grande Chartreuse'). In need of some sort of modern translation of

Christianity, could these troubled children of the mid-nineteenth century grow up to find a new form of faith? Paradoxically, perhaps the most powerful religious phenomenon of the age was religious doubt, the sheer life-seriousness with which the threat of unbelief was experienced by those who could live in ease neither with nor without religion.

For the sake of those with just such difficulties, said Carlyle, writers were to be the world's new priests, a literary faith replacing a dogmatic one. In an age of mechanical materialism, it was writers who insisted on the world's spiritual reality, with or without the formal support of religion as such. In *Sartor Resartus* Carlyle quoted Goethe's dictum that 'the Philosopher must station himself in the middle' (bk. 1, ch. 10), in the very midst of the life and struggles of the nation. Yet with the Church of England losing its authority as the traditional *via media* (or middle way), that middle position in Victorian England was all too often a place of limbo or uncertain compromise, rather than integration or renewal. Between north and south, urban and rural, secular radicalism and religious traditionalism, to the intellectual middle class in particular the whole difficult situation of contemporary belief must have seemed historically poised. This was the class from which Coleridge in *On the Constitution of Church and State* (1829) had most hoped to draw 'the *Clerisy* of the nation': 'the learned of all denominations', of all arts and sciences, who were to act as resident guides and educational agents in each parish of England and serve the spiritual and cultural needs of the country. Instead for many there was the uncomfortably in-between position of agnosticism. To use a distinction offered by the Scottish divine Thomas Chalmers (1780–1847), at the very opening of his posthumously published 'Prelections on Butler's Analogy' (1849), the most characteristic form of Victorian agnosticism was not that of sceptical 'disbelief', affirming the falsehood of any given doctrine, but 'unbelief', the want of a positive reason for affirming its truth. Whether it was a habitable place at all or an intolerable no man's land, 'unbelief', asserted Chalmers, was 'the intermediate line' between the regions of belief and disbelief.

The very existence of that wavering line could cause panic. Looking back at the end of the century, the Anglican theologian Henry Scott Holland (1847–1918) concluded that in the face of both new social needs and new scientific methods, a people had talked themselves into a fear of doubt. The external world appeared so materially solid, in both social effects and scientific evidences; the inner world, in contrast, so invisible, so unsupported as perhaps to be really non-existent. 'Men in a panic are frightened at finding themselves afraid.' Precisely because their faith was troubled, they first distrusted and then abandoned it. By a bitter irony, concluded Scott Holland, the very fact that their faith was 'in distress' became 'an argument against it' (*Lux Mundi*, ed. Charles Gore (1889), essay 1).

Moreover, this was an age of change and fluctuation, not eternity. Since the Great Reform Bill of 1832, enlarging the franchise, 'reform' of one sort or another had been in the air—with the possibility of a reforming parliament even disestablishing the Church of England. To those caught in the middle of the religious uncertainty the issue was expressed in the language not only of reform but of the Reformation: the sixteenth-century movement against the universal authority of the Church of Rome that had created the rise of Protestantism in Europe and the establishment of the Anglican Church in England. It is no surprise to find the first great history of the English Reformation—J. A. Froude's *The History of England from the Fall of Wolsey to the Death of Elizabeth* (12 vols., 1856–70)—appearing at this time. It was as though the old conflicts and compromises of the Reformation itself were being played out to the last in the conditions of nineteenth-century England, for the sake of the very future of faith. What had been more or less held together amidst the schisms of the Reformation was now perhaps finally coming apart. Parties as fundamentally opposed as Roman Catholics, Church of England reformers, and the humanist radicals who called for a new more secular religion, all used at times the phrase 'a new Reformation', agreeing at least in this: that the period 1830–80 marked a second great, and perhaps final, crisis for the Western conscience.

The period can be divided into two, almost chronologically, even though some authors writing in the second half may 'belong' by temperament or belief more to the first, and vice versa. But the early part of the period was an age still dominated by the theology of the Fall, whilst from about 1850 there is a sense of a people feeling more easily at home on the earth.[2]

[2] I am indebted here to Boyd Hilton, *The Age of Atonement: The Influence of*

I. 1830–1850: Evangelicalism, the Broad Church, and Tractarianism

In a famous article 'Church Parties' in *The Edinburgh Review* (October 1853), W. J. Conybeare claimed that by mid-century the Church of England consisted of three main groups: the Low Church Evangelicals who believed in Bible-centred literalism, enthusiastic individual conversion experiences, and plain services; the Anglican High Churchmen who believed in the Church, its formal traditions, liturgies, and sacraments; and in between the two the Broad Churchmen who, committed to a truly wide national establishment, responded to developments in contemporary biblical and scientific studies by being liberal in theology. Conybeare estimated that out of 17,000 clergymen in 1851, 38 per cent were Evangelical, 41 per cent High, and 21 per cent Broad.

The Evangelical Movement had its origin in the second half of the eighteenth century as a religion of the heart in reaction against the formalizing effects of the Age of Reason upon the Church. Taking its name from its commitment to spreading the Evangel or the Gospel, Evangelicalism claimed to stand for a puritan renewal of the 'vital simplicities' of the old Reformation, purifying the faith of all ceremony and sacrament, the last formal traces of Roman Catholicism. Evangelicalism was a fundamentalist Protestant movement that crossed the sectarian bounds between the Church of England and the Dissenting Churches, where it also drew upon the strength of John Wesley's eighteenth-century Methodist revival.

It had four fundamental doctrines. It assigned absolute supremacy to the Word of Holy Scripture, prior to all institutionalized religious structures. It emphasized the corruption of human nature, through the Fall into original sin: hence the inability of human beings, born into suffering and liable to damnation, to bring about their own salvation. It thus preached justification by direct faith in the work of Christ's cross and God's grace rather than salvation by individual efforts of reason or good works. Finally, it laid stress upon the inward experience of individual adult conversion rather than the formal sacrament of infant baptism.

In its emotional insistence upon individual inner seriousness, the broad populist influence of Evangelicalism upon the Victorian character can hardly be overestimated. It is true that Evangelicalism was notoriously anti-intellectual and anti-literary: Carlyle at the opening of his *Reminiscences* (1881) recalls his Evangelical father considering poetry and fiction in general to be 'not only idle, but *false* and criminal'. And yet even former Evangelicals who went on to become writers, such as Ruskin and George Eliot, retained within their writing that extra-literary anxiety and concern which gave their works their tense realist seriousness. It was not only that such figures, including Newman, were Evangelical in their early lives. What Evangelicalism gave the Victorians—even those who would never or no longer have called themselves evangelical—was a base for an extraordinarily energetic sense of individual conscience and moral earnestness. This need for the individual to be consciously 'serious', to be earnestly responsible and disciplined, to 'recollect himself', arose directly from a lingering belief in the perils of the Fall. Evangelicalism's God was a hard God. The Scottish Evangelical Thomas Chalmers at the commencement of his *Bridgewater Treatise* (1833) castigated those merely 'poetical' believers in a 'mild and easy religion' who 'in the mere force of their own wishfulness, would resolve the whole character of the Deity into but one attribute—that of a placid undistinguishing tenderness'.

Evangelicalism affected social policy as well as religious life. The tough non-interventionist approach, favoured by Thomas Chalmers, insisted that the hard world of economic suffering was part of man's probation on earth. Charity was an individual and spontaneous offering of humanity; it was not a matter for state laws which made men only charitable by proxy. State intervention destroyed the fallen necessity for individual self-help: that voluntary struggle in moral effort which was the individual's salvation on earth and in heaven. 'Physical Evil', as James Stevens put it in 1831, 'is necessary for the promotion of moral good' (*The Poor Laws an Interference with the Divine Laws*, p. 65).

Yet in its earlier days Evangelicalism had also contained an humanitarian strain. The so-called Clapham Sect, who lived around

London's Clapham Common, stressed the individual's personal accountability for his or her fellow souls and the consequent necessity in this unhappy world for redemptive social and charitable work, most notably in William Wilberforce's campaign against the slave trade. That first heroic, missionary generation died out in the 1830s but from the 1840s the philanthropic emphasis, in relation to factory legislation and the relief of poverty, was carried forward through the paternalistic leadership of Lord Shaftesbury (1801–85). Perhaps only the primitive Christian power of Evangelicalism could have forced Shaftesbury, a man of intense pride and almost ungovernable passion, into that war with his own character which transformed its strength into a force for good. One of the characteristic biblical texts he chose for his tombstone was the warning, against himself: 'Let him that thinketh he standeth take heed lest he fall.'

As with any form of revival, it was always going to be hard for Evangelicalism to retain its force through a second and a third generation. The movement did still manage to maintain its wide-ranging influence throughout the 1850s. In the emotional intensity of his appeal to the individual conscience, the most celebrated Evangelical preacher was the Baptist minister Charles Spurgeon (1834–92). During the Indian Mutiny of 1857 when Indian soldiers rose against their British officers and captured Delhi, he drew a huge crowd of nearly 25,000 on the Day of National Humiliation. He regularly attracted mass open-air audiences of up to 8,000, particularly amongst the lower-middle and working classes, and raised £31,000 to build for himself the Metropolitan Tabernacle, holding 5,000 worshippers. Revivalism retained its power through the British tour of the American Evangelists Moody and Sankey between 1873 and 1875 and in the rise of William Booth's Salvation Army from 1878.

And yet already by the mid-1830s Evangelicalism was becoming a victim of its own initial success, a rigidified force whose spiritual dynamic was becoming increasingly absorbed into those worldly practices of frugal economy, paternalistic discipline, and industrious self-help which were to become known as the puritan work ethic. As an essentially anti-intellectual movement, moreover, Evangelicalism was never going to find within itself fresh sources of inner develop-

Fig. 5. J. Buckley, *Revd C. H. Spurgeon*, 1858. In October that year, Spurgeon preached to ten thousand people inside the Music Hall in Surrey Gardens, when a cry of 'Fire' produced a stampede, resulting in seven fatalities.

ment and ideological renewal. By April 1839, in an article on 'The State of Religious Parties' in *The British Critic*, John Henry Newman was claiming that Evangelicalism had no intellectual weaponry with which to encounter the advance of secular rationalism. As R. W. Dale, himself a Nonconformist Evangelical, was to put it in his lecture *The Old Evangelicalism and the New* (1889), the movement was increasingly found 'wanting in a disinterested love of truth for its own sake, otherwise than as an instrument for converting men'. Its sermons had become increasingly stereotyped in their earnest repetition of its few key themes: 'the corruption of human nature, the utter inability of man to co-operate in the work of salvation, the all-sufficiency of faith, unconditional salvation, the wonders of grace, the ardour of divine love'. Moderate Evangelicals such as Charles Simeon (1759–1836), for over fifty years the highly influential incumbent at Holy Trinity Cambridge, had tried to soften the movement's harshness. Yet it remained the religion of sin and suffering, of fear and guilt and damnation, which nearly crippled Dickens's Arthur Clennam in *Little Dorrit* (1857). Listening to an Evangelical sermon in a theatre which the night before had been the scene of vulgar life, Dickens wrote in 1860, 'Is it necessary or advisable to address such an audience continually as "fellow-sinners"? Is it not enough to be fellow-creatures, born yesterday, suffering and thriving to-day, dying to-morrow?' (*The Uncommerical Traveller*, ch. 4). Hence Dickens's satire against the inhumane cant of Chadband in *Bleak House* (1853) or Trollope's exposure of the zealous this-worldly ambition of the Bishop's chaplain Mr Slope in *Barchester Towers* (1857).

It could seem humanly vital thus to defeat the Evangelical grip. George MacDonald spent most of his religious life resisting his early experience of the unloving harshness of Scottish Calvinism. In *David Elginbrod* (1863), the obsessive young Harry is found pacing about the diamond-patterned carpet in his room. He makes sudden, strange divergences from his regular movement of stepping upon every third diamond, as if to test the apparently predestined shape of his life: 'How *can* God know on which of those diamonds I am going to set my foot next?' (vol. 2, ch. 4). He is rescued by the help of a new tutor. Through a physical exercise which is also a psychological one, Hugh Sutherland shows the boy how to create within a mass of straw the space for a cave, not by building the form from outside but by hollowing it out from within.

Yet to other writers, who had less faith than Dickens or Mac-Donald in any alternative, the failure of Evangelicalism stood for something equivocally more regrettable. J. A. Froude concluded that 'the pale shadow called Evangelical religion' had merely 'clothed itself' second-hand in the language of the great sixteenth-century reformers Luther and Calvin ('Conditions and Prospects of Protestantism', in *Short Studies on Great Subjects*, 4 vols. (1867–83), vol. 2). The Lutheran Reformation had staked salvation not upon man's works but upon faith in God's grace, and Calvinism was the strongest possible expression of that utter dependence, in holding a doctrine of predestination. In the tradition of St Paul, Luther and Calvin had represented man 'as born unable to keep the commandments, yet as justly liable to everlasting punishment for breaking them' ('Calvinism', in *Short Studies*, vol. 2). That conflict spoke of what life still felt like to Froude, however much secular philosophers asserted freedom of will. Calvinism, he said, had represented in a religious language what were now seen to be the scientific laws of determinism: despite the individual's repentance or punishment, the consequences of the wrongs of the past remain, and the laws of nature, being general and no respecter of persons, allow the innocent to suffer those consequences alongside the guilty. Yet Calvinism, argued Froude, belonged to a tougher world than nineteenth-century people would allow their own to be: 'For hard times hard men are needed.' The nineteenth century was increasingly, he believed, a softer time; an age when inside and outside the churches, people were becoming less truly afraid of what would come to those who did not believe in Christ.

Froude was representative of so many stranded mid-Victorians. Another such, William Hale White, looking back in 1885 from within his experience of Dissent, lamented that the hard puritan spirit which Evangelicalism had tried to represent was increasingly lost to the generation which reached adulthood in the period 1850–80. Modern enlightened philosophy, he wrote, 'proclaims the unity of our nature', seeking to bring together 'all that is apparently contrary in man, and to show how it proceeds really from one centre'; but primitive Christianity laid awful stress on the duality in us, and the stress laid on that duality is the world's salvation. The words right and wrong are not felt now as they were felt by Paul. They shade off into the other. Nevertheless, if mankind is not to be lost, the ancient antagonism must be maintained. The shallowest of mortals is able now to laugh at the notion of a personal devil. No doubt there is no such thing existent; but the horror at evil which could find no other expression than in the creation of a devil is no subject for laughter, and if it do not in some shape or other survive, the race itself will not survive. (*Mark Rutherford's Deliverance* (1885), ch. 6)

In 1832 it had still been possible for Bulwer-Lytton to write a novel of guilt and damnation such as *Eugene Aram*, after the Romantic neo-Calvinist model of Byron and William Godwin. To the outrage of some of the novel's critics, Bulwer had turned his subject from the consistently bad man he was historically supposed to be, into the far more disturbingly split portrait of a scholar whose one sudden evil act of murder was at variance with the whole of his life, before and after. Whilst still trying to continue undetected in his normal life, Eugene Aram secretly experiences the Fall, the duality or bisection of man, within his own person.

By 1860 that language of stark duality was being reformulated or 'shaded off', as Hale White put it, within the Broad Church movement. For in that year appeared *Essays and Reviews*, a collection of essays by six clergyman and one devout layman, which caused more immediate controversy than had Darwin's *Origin of Species* the year before. The group came out of an Oxford in liberal reaction after the conversion of Newman to the Church of Rome, and included Frederick Temple, a successor to Thomas Arnold as headmaster of Rugby; Mark Pattison, historian of ideas and rector of Lincoln College; Baden Powell, Oxford professor of geometry and a supporter of the theory of evolution; and Benjamin Jowett, professor of Greek and master of Balliol College.

Dubbed by their opponents 'the seven against Christ', they were accused of reducing religion to the terms of a progressively enlightened human history. They rendered merely human and provisional, it was said, the Word of God: putting in doubt the belief in eternal punishment and a Day of Judgement, the truth of miracles, the accuracy of the Jewish history and of the Gospel narrative. These were the charges made by Frederic Harrison in the progressivist *Westminster Review* of October 1860.

In fact as a secularist Harrison welcomed the volume's liberalism. What he could not make out, he said, was how this 'Neo-Christianity' was compatible with the writers' remaining within the Church of England. Yet it was precisely the Church's ancient language of exaggerated duality that Jowett, for one, was seeking to reform—'the opposition, not only of words, but of ideas, which is found in the Scriptures generally, and almost seems to be inherent in human language itself':

The law is opposed to faith, good to evil, the spirit to the flesh, light to darkness, the world to the believer; the sheep are set 'on his right hand, but the goats on the left' . . . The opposition is one of ideas only which is not realized in fact. Experience shows us not that there are two classes of men animated by two opposing principles, but an infinite number of classes or individuals from the lowest depth of misery and sin to the highest perfection of which human nature is capable, the best not wholly good, the worst not entirely evil. (*Essays and Reviews* (1860), ch. 7 'On the interpretation of Scripture')

In his reformulation of a subtler middle way, Jowett took as his watchword: 'Interpret the Scripture like any other book'.[3] In this he believed he was actually completing the work of the old Protestant Reformers, by going back to the Gospels to recover, through historical and textual criticism, the direct Word itself which the Catholic Church had subsequently made into abstract theological creeds. According to Jowett, textual criticism of the Bible was not a betrayal of the Reformation but the Reformation's second stage. For Jowett the task was to recognize the permanent underlying spirit within the letter of the historical forms of utterance. And that spirit was progressively revealed: what was appropriate to the childhood of the race was no longer appropriate to the race in its nineteenth-century adulthood. The present age marked the completion of a change from the half-civilized to the civilized world, correspondent to the change from Old Testament Law to New Testament Gospel: 'a change from

[3] As a classical textual scholar, Jowett brought to the Bible the tools he used in his translations of Plato, Aristotle, and Thucydides. On the role of Hellenism in Victorian culture see Richard Jenkyns, *The Victorians and Ancient Greece* (Clarendon Press, 1980).

fear to love, from power to wisdom, from the justice of God to the mercy of God' (*Essays and Reviews*, ch. 7).

Like evolutionary theory, biblical textual studies cast doubt on the historical truth of the five books of Moses, including Genesis. The Tübingen school under F. C. Baur in Germany interpreted the New Testament as the product of a historical conflict between Peter and Paul, or Gentile and Jewish Christianity, and dated the Gospel of St John at 150 years *after* the birth of Christ. This was no mere matter of dry scholarship: in 1865 the studies of Bishop Colenso, in questioning the horrific punishments described in the Old Testament, resulted in his dismissal from the bishopric of Natal for alleged heresy. The Gospel story itself was being fundamentally rewritten. D. F. Strauss in *Das Leben Jesu* (1835), Renan in *La Vie de Jésus* (1863), and John Seeley in *Ecce Homo* (1865) offered apparently naturalistic, historically factual accounts of the life of Christ, shorn of myths and miracles. To Strauss, the 'myth' of the life of Jesus was a poetic fiction arising out of earlier Jewish accounts of the Messiah and modified by the impression of Jesus upon the ideas of his earliest followers. Marian Evans (later to become George Eliot) translated Strauss in 1846 as part of her move away from her early Evangelicalism, but said in a letter to Sara Hennell, 14 February 1846, that 'dissecting the beautiful story of the crucifixion' made her 'Strauss-sick'.

Yet Jowett insisted that the thrust of dispassionate biblical criticism was not merely negative. The purpose of modern criticism was to resist the alleged tendency that, ever since the Reformation, 'all intellect has gone the other way'—away from religion. The claim that religion was simply the truth could all too easily leave believers unthinking and thinkers unbelieving. Too often and too quickly, argued Baden Powell, epistemological questions of truth and error had been turned into moral matters of right and wrong, without sufficient attention given to the distinction between the alleged truth of a position and the arguments by which it was supported. Above all, concluded Jowett, modern criticism was to have a liberal, broadening effect, destroying false lines of distinction not only in the language of religion but also between the religious sects themselves: 'It places us, in some respects (though it be deemed a paradox to say so), more nearly in the position of the first Christians to whom the

New Testament was not yet given, in whom the Gospel was a living word, not yet embodied in forms or supported by ancient institutions' (*Essays and Reviews*, ch. 7). This then was the attitude of that movement within the Church of England which, in opposition to the doctrinal literalness and narrowness of Evangelicalism, became known as the 'Broad Church'. Its aim was to restore the Church of England to being the Broad Church of the whole undivided nation: neither High nor Low, neither wholly sacramental nor wholly Evangelical, but able broadly to include within its Christianity opposite and contradictory opinions.

Behind the Broad Church movement lay the influence first of Samuel Taylor Coleridge (1772–1834) and then of Thomas Arnold (1795–1842). In 1829 in *The Constitution of Church and State* Coleridge had argued that if the nation's landed interest represented the idea of permanence and its mercantile and manufacturing classes the idea of progression, then the idea that a National Church embodied was the spiritual wealth of the nation, counterbalancing the country's merely material improvement. In the light of that ideal, Thomas Arnold, headmaster of Rugby school, dedicated his life to trying to reinstitute the Reformation ideal of a truly inclusive National Church, bringing back into its fold the Dissenting or Nonconformist sects which had stubbornly refused to join it throughout the subsequent centuries. Without that reconciliation, he believed, the Church of England was in danger of occupying a lost middle position. As the Jesuit priest in Elizabeth Missing Sewell's *Margaret Percival* (1847) puts it, Anglicans are disconcerted once they see that the case that the Dissenters make against the Church of England is just like the case that the Anglicans had made against the Church of Rome.

National religion was being torn apart by internal controversies. The Hampden case featured a liberal theologian under attack from the High Church Oxford Movement when proposed as Oxford professor of divinity in 1836 and, again, as bishop of Hereford in 1847. The Gorham judgement of 1850 dragged the civil courts into an extremist dispute between neo-Calvinists and neo-Catholics as to whether baptismal regeneration, the belief that the sacrament washed away the guilt of original sin, was or was not an essential doctrine of the Church of England. The Reformation was alive again in these splits. In his inaugural lecture as professor of modern history at Oxford in 1841, Thomas Arnold had argued against fanaticism, by claiming that 'belief in the desirableness of an act differs widely from belief in the truth of a proposition'. Hence practical human societies which intended to be both collectively stable and liberally inclusive, should ensure that, even whilst leaving room for the pursuit of truth by many different means, 'their end should be good rather than truth'.

It was that liberal spirit of pragmatic moral accommodation, seeking to sink all oppositions and differences in the common good of a Christian nation, that only served to infuriate traditional, conservative High Churchmen. Reviewing *Essays and Reviews* in the conservative *Quarterly Review* (January 1861), Samuel Wilberforce, Bishop of Oxford, detected in the collection a general belief in intellectual progress which was in implicit denial of the Fall. For once in agreement with the *Westminster Review* and Frederic Harrison, albeit from the opposite point of view, Wilberforce argued that the authors of *Essays and Reviews* were Victorian middlemen, not so much Broad as caught between two stools: 'They believe too much not to believe more, and they disbelieve too much not to disbelieve everything.' Jowett in particular was 'dissolving into a general halo of goodness all distinct doctrinal truth' precisely because he tried to abolish differences. But as John Henry Newman had first put it in 'The Tamworth Reading Room' (1841), 'Differences, then, are the natural attendants on Christianity, and you cannot have Christianity and not have differences.' '*Is* Thomas Arnold a Christian?' Newman is said to have asked, with bitter irony. Samuel Wilberforce, son of William Wilberforce and a second-generation consolidator, remained a traditionalist within the Church of England, famous not least for his attack on Huxley and Darwinism. But it was the Oxford Movement, led by three fellows of Oriel College, Oxford—John Keble, Edward Bouverie Pusey, and Newman himself—that sought to shake the Church of England itself, in so far as its traditional *via media* seemed to them no longer robust or tenable.

The Oxford Movement, or Tractarianism as it was also known, took its origin from Keble's Assize Sermon in 1833 against a secularized parliament's interference in matters spiritual in the Church of

Ireland. The series of circulated *Tracts for the Times* that followed were intended to alert the clergy to the current critical state of the Church of England and restore its relation to the primitive Christianity of the Ancient Church. 'There was need', Newman was to write in his autobiography, 'of a second Reformation' (*Apologia Pro Vita Sua*, pt. 3). Another leading member of the Oxford Movement, Hurrell Froude—the elder brother of J. A. Froude—put it more violently: 'The Reformation was a limb badly set—it must be broken again in order to be righted' (*Remains*, 2 vols. (1838), vol. 1, p. 433). In apparently freeing itself from the Church of Rome, Protestantism, he believed, had enslaved Church to State even as Israel had been in bondage to Egypt.

Under Jowett, the Broad Church party in Oxford wanted to make clear that creeds and dogmas came not from Christ but from the Catholic Church. In contrast, Newman's Tractarian Oxford demanded a new counter-reformation which restored the necessity for both dogma and the Church as essential to the developed understanding of Christian meaning. In his novel *Callista: A Sketch of the Third Century* (1855), Newman imagines the conversion of a pagan young woman in the early days of the primitive Church. The convert feels she needs something more than her own personal intuitions: she senses a whole unknown order of meaning surrounding the fragments she does grasp. Drawn to Christianity,

if she had been asked, what was Christianity? she would have been puzzled to give an answer. She would have been able to mention some particular truths which it taught, but neither to give their definite and distinct shape, nor to describe the mode in which they were realized. (ch. 26)

Just as even the most moral of persons can find written moral injunctions at first either objectionable or inexplicable, when set down coldly and formally, so, admitted Newman, even religious people may find theological definition unfamiliar and jarring—as though wrenched out of its living context within them and put into a foreign and external medium. Yet Callista feels she needs the theology that lies behind her immediate sense of religion, like the complete thought behind her dim feeling, in order to know how to *take* that religion in its full implicit meaning, in the whole shape of its interconnected relationships. Dogma to her is not Jowett's institutionalized series of abstract rules and detached sentences; rather, as Newman argued first in *The Arians of the Fourth Century* (1833) and then in his great *Essay on the Development of Christian Doctrine* (1845, rev. 1878), dogma is the history of Christianity explicitly spelling out, part by part, over centuries of dispute, what was already whole, implicit, and incarnate in the original spirit of the words of Christ: 'And this world of thought is the expansion of a few words, uttered, as if casually, by the fishermen of Galilee' (*University Sermons*, Sermon 15, first preached 1843). It was the religious version of the doctrine of evolution.

The Gospel's 'half sentences, its overflowings of language, admit of development; they have a life in them' (*University Sermons*, Sermon 15). This belief in the life resonantly latent in Christ's original utterances was different from Evangelicalism's simple belief in biblical literalism. For John Keble and Isaac Williams were, together with Newman, the poets of the Oxford Movement, and the Movement read Scripture as though closer to poetry than to a set of regulations. In contrast to the enthusiastic, literal-minded directness of the individualistic Evangelical preacher, the Tractarians believed in 'reserve'—in spiritual meanings that could not simply be materialized and paraphrased but needed metaphor and imagination. In his *Lectures on Poetry* (1832–41) and in Tract 89 (1840), Keble—a major influence upon the poetry of Christina Rossetti—reminded his audience that God Himself spoke a spiritual or symbolical language, as through a veil of reserve. Thus, in the words of Isaac Williams, 'whatever He makes known opens to view far more which we know not' (Tract 87, 1840). A doctrine is *hid* in language: a thought which was to come close to the heart and practice of the poet Hopkins.

The Evangelicals, argued Isaac Williams, tended to take the doctrine of Atonement—that Christ's sacrifice on the cross paid for our sins—as a simple, literal, sacrificial bargain which guaranteed salvation. But teachings are best conveyed not by explicitly stating a theology, 'any more than our Lord does in His own teaching', but rather 'by the tone of a person's whole thoughts, by the silent instruction of his penitent and merciful demeanour' (Tract 87, 1840). 'Tone' here is the literary-religious word that marks the whole subtle, inner working of the *spirit* of a real person, hidden deep within both his language and his silence. To the Tractarians, an individual is never right merely on the ground of holding a general opinion which happens to be true, unless he holds it in a particular manner of being. What one most really and deeply *means*, as Newman insisted in his *Apologia*, is always autobiographical.

Yet the Oxford Movement still went on within the confines of a strict theology. Like Evangelicalism, Tractarianism did not believe in the primacy of human reason and did believe in the primacy of the Fall. In these two areas, the fundamental similarity of the two movements, underlying even their very differences, bears a close examination.

First, as to fallenness: what J. A. Froude said of Newman was as true of the Oxford Movement as it had been of Newman's own youthful Evangelicalism: 'sin with Newman was real' (*The Nemesis of Faith* (1849), p. 160) and 'real' was a vital word for the Tractarians. In his University Sermon 'On Justice, as a Principle of Divine Governance' (Sermon 6, 1832), Newman argued that in times of political peace and national safety, people are induced to the unreal belief that human nature is better than it is, that 'evil is but remedial and temporary' and 'repentance is a sufficient atonement for it'. But *Callista* tells of the tougher days of persecution rather than peace.

For in those days a young Christian, Agellius, is genuinely afraid of making the awful final commitment of being baptized. It was then no mere convention. 'Sin after baptism is so awful a matter,' he laments, 'There is no *second* laver for sin; and then again to sin against baptism is so *great* a sin.' Yet the priest Caecilius is merciless towards evasion and delay: 'You are, then, of the number of those who would cheat their Maker of His claim on their life, if they could (as it is said) in their last moment cheat the devil' (ch. 13). In the mean time, while you gamble on a final deathbed repentance, chides the priest, 'Would you live without God in the world?' But the emphasis here is on baptism rather than conversion, because this is Tractarianism's High Church sacramental world, not Evangelicalism's individualistic one.

As to the status of human reason, Tractarianism remained as opposed to the autonomous primacy of rationalism as Evangelicalism had ever been. When Newman first joined the dons' common room in Oriel College, he said it *stank* of logic. As Newman insists in his *Essay in Aid of a Grammar of Assent* (1870), man is *not* fundamentally a reasoning animal, but a seeing, feeling, contemplating, acting animal who cannot wait to prove everything by paper logic but, in order to begin a life, must start from where and from what he actually is, with all the risks of belief:

> I am what I am, or I am nothing. I cannot think, reflect, or judge about my being, without starting from the very point which I aim at concluding. My ideas are all assumptions, and I am ever moving in a circle. I cannot avoid being sufficient for myself, for I cannot make myself anything else, and to change me is to destroy me. If I do not use myself, I have no other self to use. My only business is to ascertain what I am, in order to put it to use. (ch. 9, sect. 1)

That reality, that ancient rooted sense of a given self, existed prior to all second-order reasoning. Yet though man cannot change what he is born with, he can make progress with it. 'Each of us', concludes Newman, 'has the prerogative of completing his inchoate and rudimental nature, and of developing his own perfection out of the living elements with which his mind began to be' (ch. 9, sect. 1).

It was as part of this developing and completing that reasoning had a role. As Newman says in *Loss and Gain*, his 1847 novel of Oxford life, a man 'might not realise his own belief till questions had been put to him' (pt. 2, ch. 6): the right question could reveal retrospectively what had been implicitly forming itself inside him all the while, without his knowing it. The difference from Evangelicalism was that Tractarianism still did put questions to itself—*using* the very gift of reason precisely in order to argue against the certainty of reason and on behalf of the subordinate relation of reason to faith. The aim with Newman in particular is always, thus scrupulously, 'to put ourselves on the guard as to our proceeding' and 'protest against it' even 'while we do it' notwithstanding: 'We can only set right one error of expression by another. By this method of antagonism we steady our minds . . . by *saying and unsaying to a positive result*.'[4] Opposed to the transcribed repetition of stock positions, Newman's complex syntax is constantly working with and against itself, in a dense self-modifying way quite unknown to Evangelicalism's narrow anti-literary, anti-rational style. Hence, in the great turning

---

[4] Quoted in John Coulson's important book *Religion and Imagination* (Clarendon Press, 1981), 66.

sentences of the *University Sermons*, Newman's writing always feels like the act of thinking everything out afresh *through* language: 'Faith cannot exist without grounds or without an object; but it does not follow that all who have faith should recognize, and be able to state what they believe, and why'; 'True faith then, admits, but does not require, the exercise of what is commonly understood by Reason' (Sermon 13); 'It is no proof that persons are not possessed, because they are not conscious, of an idea' (Sermon 15).

A rationalistic age, complained Newman, assumed there were no problems that could not be solved or seen through by human reason; it did not believe in inexplicable or inexhaustible meanings, and had no notion of 'half views and partial knowledge, of guesses, surmises, hopes and fears, of truths faintly apprehended and not understood' (Tract 73, 1836). The literary critic R. H. Hutton was an admirer of Newman precisely because of this deeper sense of meaning, inseparable from a profoundly religious state of mind. Increasingly when the deepest thinkers of the age seemed to be the poets and the novelists, in particular Wordsworth and George Eliot, it was only Newman who seemed to Hutton to preserve within the religious realm an equivalent creative depth. Yet Newman represented a mentality in marked contrast to that possessed by what Hutton called the ordinary 'Hard Church' mind of Victorian England. By this Hutton meant, in particular, those conventional Broad Churchmen who stuck to a few unexamined articles of popular belief; but the dangers of a decline into rigid and complacent 'common sense', which Hutton outlines, applied equally to Evangelicals. The general Hard Church mind, said Hutton, ignores the more delicate laws of growth and change, treating 'the stalk, the leaf, the bud, the flower' as distinctly separate things, not as various aspects of the same thing: 'to the hard understanding,' he concludes, 'a great number of disconnected fixed notions take the place of insight into the gradual and complex growth of slowly maturing life' (*Theological Essays* (1871), ch. 11).

In his *Apologia*[5] Newman himself scorned the puritan conversion-memoir which retrospectively fixed and divided life into separate and definite stages. When (what turned out to be) his journey to

⁵ See below pp. 432–4.

Rome was most deeply in process, Newman could neither say at the time nor recall afterwards where he really was:

Pass a number of years, and I find my mind in a new place; how? The whole man moves; paper logic is but the record of it. All the logic in the world would not have made me move faster to Rome than I did; as well might you say that I have arrived at the end of my journey because I see the village church before me, as venture to assert that the miles, over which my soul had to pass before it got to Rome, could be annihilated, even though I had had some far clearer view than I then had, that Rome was my ultimate destination. Great acts take time. (pt. 6)

From 1841 to 1845, it was logically predictable to a rationalizing outsider that Newman would convert from the Anglican High Church to Roman Catholicism itself. But what Newman offers, in contrast to such knowingness in advance, is that organic auto-biographical process of thought which is struggling to *discover* its own implicit reasoning by remaining within the route and the tempo that its thinker finds himself blindly following. In the words of R. H. Hutton, Newman's is not the perspective obtained by those who feel 'able to look down' as if from some height of reason condescendingly above the human realm, but a view 'for those who felt themselves looked down upon'—fallen creatures struggling within the world (*The Spectator* (7 Dec. 1895), p. 815).

The essential connection between or behind the Evangelical and Oxford movements was nonetheless obscured in the controversy that followed Newman's publication of Tract 90, in 1841, leading as it did to his eventual conversion to Roman Catholicism in 1845. For Pusey, the Reformation had been the providential means of England's remaining true to the Ancient Church: the Anglican Church was the Catholic Church in England, despite what had happened to the Church of Rome. But when Newman left the Church of England, the reform from within lost its momentum. In another age, more welcoming to belief, Newman might not have needed to have become a Roman Catholic, finding there in the authority of Rome the strongest, most systematic defence of the faith at a time when personal belief was most vulnerably under attack. As it was, as a result of Newman's defection, it came to seem as though the whole Oxford Movement had been Catholics in Anglican clothing. Newman himself became for the rest of his life a figure relatively isolated from the mainstream, though out of that isolation came his most significant writings.

And yet, for all the differences, from 1833 to 1841 High Tractarianism was ultimately a way of correctively reinventing Low Evangelicalism, with stronger resources and defences. Pusey himself, professor of Hebrew at Oxford and the austere hermit-like figurehead of the Oxford Movement, respected Evangelicals for their ancient zeal for souls. 'So rare is thoughtfulness,' he preached in a sermon entitled 'Review of Life', that in an increasingly secular world 'if any look thoughtful, men think he must have some sorrow. To be what Scripture calls "grave" is to have some hidden anxiety or grief. To be a "serious" person is a name of reproach.'

In such a world, theology was liable to be treated as if it were a matter for psychology, and seriousness interpreted as pathology. But Pusey's sermons are more than anything else about the old-fashioned, austere discipline of penitence and vigilance necessary to sustain a serious inner life, in the face of the awfulness of post-baptismal sin. As he sternly puts it in a sermon 'Re-Creation of the Penitent': 'God does not take away trials, or carry us *over* them, but strengthens us *through* them.'[6] The Fall was the breaking of the link, the union between God and man, such that humans no longer will what He wills. What mattered, across the divide between Evangelical and Tractarian, was the revival of a religious spirit strong enough to combat both that old fallenness and the new rationalistic challenges that discounted it.

The connection between the Oxford and the Evangelical movements did continue to be recognized, if only by the most sensitive and troubled of their opponents. The poet Arthur Hugh Clough experienced at first hand both the Broad Church movement as a pupil at Thomas Arnold's Rugby from 1829 and then the Oxford Movement under the tutelage of W. G. Ward from 1837. Torn between the two, he attributed his subsequent lapse into anguished unbelief to the 'over-excitation' of the religious sense resulting (as he

---

[6] For Pusey, see Owen Chadwick (ed.), *The Mind of the Oxford Movement* (A & C Black, 1960) which reprints excerpts from his *Parochial Sermons* (3 vols., 1852–73), *Sermons Preached before the University of Oxford* (1859–72), and *Lenten Sermons* (1858–74).

puts it in the wry epilogue to *Dipsychus*, 1850) from 'the religious movement of the last century, beginning with Wesleyanism, and culminating at last in Puseyism'—the low and high movements together.

Clough's friend and Thomas Arnold's own most famous son offered one name for the whole theological tendency that connected Wesley with Pusey: Hebraism. The religion descended from the Hebrews, wrote Matthew Arnold in *Culture and Anarchy* (1869), 'has always been severely preoccupied with an awful sense of the impossibility of being at ease . . . when there is something which thwarts and spoils all our efforts'. This something is sin 'which I heard Dr. Pusey the other day, in one of his impressive sermons, compare to a hideous hunch-back seated on our shoulders' (ch. 4).

Matthew Arnold it is, above all, who seeks to make the story of the second half of the nineteenth century a turning-away from the Hebraism of St Paul to what Arnold calls the Hellenism of Plato, from the human being as 'an unhappy chained captive, labouring with groanings that cannot be uttered to free himself from the body of this death' to 'a gentle and simple being, showing the traces of a noble and divine nature'. It is to that alternative emphasis that we shall turn, shortly, in Section II.

Yet art was made out of the Hebraic spirit, and the great Victorian novel of the Fall which, defiantly valuing pain, best characterizes the religious seriousness of the period 1830–45 appeared in 1853. It serves to illustrate, finally, much of what is at stake in this section.

Charlotte Yonge's *The Heir of Redclyffe* rivalled *Jane Eyre* (1847) and *David Copperfield* (1850) in sales, but the latter two established their contemporary liberal credentials with attacks on Evangelicalism in the persons of Mr Brocklehurst and the Murdstones. *The Heir of Redclyffe* belongs to a different and earlier age: though set in the nineteenth rather than the third century, it is as surely as *Callista* a work of primitive Christianity.

Charlotte Yonge was a Tractarian; her parish priest was the good and gentle John Keble. Yet like Bulwer-Lytton, Charlotte Yonge takes as her protagonist a dark Byronic figure, Guy Morville. The inheritance motif which dominates this novel is almost Calvinistic in its deeper meaning: Guy fears that he is heir not only to the seat of

Redclyffe but to the violent psychological demon of the Morville family. He cannot trust his own character, with its sudden violent bursts of temper.

It is a view of himself that is shared by his cousin, the severe moralist Philip Edmonstone. There is an inherited history here too, a backlog of rivalry between the two branches of the family. Moreover, Philip's own personal history also predisposes him to a bitter lack of trust in fallen human nature. Philip gave up his future as academic and clergyman for the sake of his dependent sister, only to find his sister almost immediately marrying for rank, despite him.

But Guy's distrust of himself and Philip's distrust of Guy are not the same thing. Like Hurrell Froude on whom he was partly modelled, Guy uses his self-distrust as a discipline by which to fight against and overcome himself. Philip, much more confident of the truth of his own views, is like a more intelligent version of R. H. Hutton's Hard Churchman. He remains stuck with a static view of an unreliable Guy, whereas with Guy it is the very fear of his own unreliability that leads him gradually and carefully beyond it. Indeed, Philip's version of Guy is left to become increasingly more indicative of Philip himself than of Guy. Terrifyingly, Philip simply does not see the serpent of obsessional psychological malice concealed within his own ostensible moral rectitude.

And then suddenly, just when he seems to have established his life, Guy dies, on a honeymoon tour abroad with his loving bride, as a result of an infection caught whilst nursing his enemy Philip. If the sceptical modern reader finds such a death almost literally incredible, the fact is that, inside the novel, Philip himself can hardly believe it either. Yet Guy's is a classically good death. The absolute belief lodged inside this book leaves Guy celebrating this prematurely wasted life of his as a completed achievement in self-reformation. The acts of control and forgiveness which had begun in him as effort, in the end have ceased to be so. There is a sort of ruthlessness, even, in his refusal to let his deathbed be harassed by anxiety for the future of his pregnant young wife, Amy: 'There was something in his perfect happiness that would not let her grieve' (ch. 35).

Yet the future well-being of Amy is secured by a similar refusal of the temptation of natural, this-worldly feelings. Instead of always mourning, she tells a friend: 'I can get happy very often when I am by

myself, or at church, with him; it is only when I miss his bright outside and can't think myself into the inner part, that it is so forlorn and
dreary' (ch. 42). In many different ways Guy's life continues in Amy.
As Philip looks at her he sees 'there was a likeness to that peculiar and
beautiful expression of her husband's, so as, in spite of the great
difference of feature and colouring, to give her a resemblance to him'
(ch. 36).

But the novel is most deeply concerned with how Philip has to live
with the spirit of Guy thereafter. He knows now that he has consistently wronged Guy as well as inadvertently brought about his
death. And now, like Guy before, he is 'afraid of himself' (ch. 42)—
in all the damned and paradoxical duality of his inability either to get
out of, or to remain simply being, that self. When he hears his own
sister still talking of Guy in unjust terms, so reminiscent of himself
before, it is like an adult's nightmare version of the old nursery tales
in which 'a naughty child, under the care of a fairy is chained to an
exaggeration of himself and his own faults, and rendered a slave
to this hateful self' (ch. 38). Even forgiveness—from Guy, from Amy,
from the bereaved family—feels like punishment. Months after
Guy's death Amy gives birth to a girl-child who cannot inherit
Redclyffe; in consequence, worst punishment of all, the estate must
come to Philip himself, in Guy's place. Philip would prefer now to
waive the claim he had always secretly coveted, but the novel is
austere in its insistence on the necessity of returning to the world
rather than escaping from it: 'He kept the possessions which he
abhorred, and gave up the renunciation he had longed to make; and
in this lay the true sacrifice, the greater because the world would
think him the gainer' (ch. 40). Philip can now afford to do what he
had long wanted to—marry Laura, Amy's sister—as easily as the
once-envied Guy had been able to marry Amy herself, despite
Philip's own objections at the time. It is a saddened, chastened, yet
not unsuccessful marriage and life that he has to live out.

Yet what makes this a novel of the Fall is not only its commitment
to what has to go on inside unhappiness. Part of the experience of the
Fall also lies in half-unattained glimpses of a transcendent vision, the
memory of which accompanies a life that must still doggedly continue without the full, transcendent completion. In Guy even before
his marriage there were his good angels: certain high places and

scenes of sea and sky, books, melodies, words from the Bible. In Philip that transcendence is the memory of Guy contained within his guilt, whilst in Amy it is the memory of Guy contained within her sorrow. Amy's maid says she would never forget how her lady looked as she knelt by Guy's deathbed: 'It was not grief: it was as if she had been a little way with her husband, and was just called back' (ch. 35). So Amy continually speaks of Guy to her little baby, long before she can possibly understand, 'saying "papa", so that his child might never recollect a time when he had not been a familiar and beloved idea' (ch. 44). With that 'idea' living through her, Amy never remarries; in an earthly sense, her life must seem over at 21.

That such a vision was already a challenge to mid-nineteenth-century views is clear from R. H. Hutton's article 'Ethical and Dogmatic Fiction' in *The National Review* (January 1861). As an admirer of Newman, Hutton also admires Charlotte Yonge's ethical idealism in comparison with the 'superficial' versions of truth that he claims are offered in the mere copyist social realism of a Trollope or a Thackeray. But as a Broad Church modern man Hutton also speaks of Miss Yonge's 'archaic narrowness', her feudal dogmatism, her opposition to the liberal free play of individualism, and, above all, the already old-fashioned representation of her characters 'as perfectly content under repressions which would, by any mind of more speculative faculty than her own, be felt as intolerable'. Yet what Hutton is rejecting as archaic and narrow is nonetheless a whole world-view offered by the century's most formidable religious novel, in conscious opposition to more modern accounts of range and freedom in a life.

In 1849 in his preface to *The Nemesis of Faith*, J. A. Froude claimed that 'religion of late years has been so much a matter of word controversy, it has suffered so complete a divorce from life, that life is the last place we look for it'. But the achievement of *The Heir of Redclyffe* is to re-create the vision of existence in which religion is not so much part of life, as life a part of religion. In *Essays and Reviews*, Mark Pattison had charted the tendency, inherited by the nineteenth century from the preceding Age of Reason, to reduce religion to practical morality: 'The keeping in the back-ground the transcendental objects of faith, and the restriction of our faculties to the regulation of our conduct, seem indeed to be placing man in the foreground of the picture, to make human nature the centre round which all things revolve' (ch. 6). In contrast, by making its beliefs neither easily acceptable nor easily dismissable but disturbing and ancient and genuinely metaphysical, *The Heir of Redclyffe* re-imagines a religious vision of life manifestly opposed to what Nietzsche was to call the nineteenth century's increasingly 'human, all too human' world-view.

In George MacDonald's *David Elginbrod* a character complains of narrow-minded people who treat theology like a map 'with plenty of lines on it', all of them 'lines of division'. Asked, 'Does God draw no lines then?' he replies, 'When he does they are pure lines, without breadth, and consequently invisible to mortal eyes; not Chinese walls of separation, such as these definers would construct' (bk. 3, ch. 12). It is true that the party lines dividing one sect from another—in particular Tractarianism from Evangelicalism—became in the inner workings of certain individuals less firm, less clear, or more unpredictably emergent than might have been supposed. Nonetheless, Newman opposed the Broad Church on the grounds that there were lines that did really exist, lines that human beings crossed in their thoughts and their actions and even in the very syntax of their writings, albeit lines that were invisible to them. The period from 1830 to about 1845, it may be concluded, stands in memory and defence of those pure lines, of which human distinctions are imperfectly approximative; it represents the necessity for those fixed beliefs, ideas, and positions which in Newman and in Charlotte Yonge stay firm because inevitably recurrent rather than because wilfully reasserted. The subsequent crossing of apparently fixed lines, the partial adoption of one position within the ostensible terms of another, is ever increasingly the story of the period from 1850.

II. The Mid-Victorian Change

The creed of a race, said Leslie Stephen, is not just a rationally agreed philosophical system, nor simply the expression of its industrial activities and social functions. It also has to do with the place it offers for imagination and the emotions. At the beginning of *English*

Thought in the Eighteenth Century (2 vols., 1871), a book inspired by Mark Pattison's contribution to the history of ideas in *Essays and Reviews*, Leslie Stephen talks about what happens in the modern world when a new secular order of understanding begins to succeed an old sacred one (vol. 1, ch. 1). Initially the new order has not had time to become the expression of anything more than the logic that banishes its predecessor. Emotional experience that found expression within the old symbols now seems silenced. The new way seems to offer less meaning than before, because it has not yet worked its way into becoming conceivable to the general mind as a form of life. Thus, the old ways have to linger, and have to be banished, alternately, until a new language of symbols and associations can serve as a replacement.

That is what so many novels after 1850 do: recreate the old era, the Hebraic world-view, inside one of its characters, in order to see how to work through and move beyond it. 'I have often thought it is part of the inner system of this earth', says the protagonist of J. A. Froude's *The Nemesis of Faith* (1849), 'that each one of us should repeat over again in his own experience the spiritual condition of each of its antecedent eras' (p. 113). So it is with Arthur Clennam in Dickens's *Little Dorrit* (1857), slowly putting his Calvinist upbringing behind him. George Eliot's *Adam Bede* (1859) is likewise the story of a movement from an old Adam to a new. Yet at the same time Adam must not simply sacrifice the memory of his early fallen love, Hetty, for the sake of gaining a new life with Dinah instead: 'Evil's evil and sorrow's sorrow . . . Other folk were not created for my sake, that I should think all square when things turn out well for me' (ch. 54). If within a single lifetime a major character moves from an old dispensation to a new, there is often someone else in the novel who remains left behind: so it is in the double structure of Dickens's *Bleak House* (1852–3) with Esther Summerson on the one hand and her secret mother, Lady Dedlock, on the other; or in George Eliot's *Silas Marner* (1861), with Silas escaping the hard world of evangelical damnation through the love of a child, whilst the child's secret father, Godfrey Cass, has finally to confront a moral reality more inexorably unforgiving than his previous gambling upon chance.

It was a characteristic Victorian intuition that in certain representative individuals the experience of previous ages was being recapitulated at the level of personal histories. In *Vestiges of the Natural History of Creation* (1844), Robert Chambers argued that embryos passed through the same stages of development as had the species itself, rising through the forms of the lower animals by following the same laws in an abbreviated and accelerated fashion. Ontogeny (the history of the individual) recapitulates phylogeny (evolutionary genealogy). As it was in biology, so it was in human history: Auguste Comte argued that 'the phases of the mind of a man correspond to the epochs of the mind of the race' (*The Positive Philosophy*, trans. Harriet Martineau, 2 vols. (1853), vol. 2, p. 3).

The story of three families serves to illustrate, in brief, the theological change that took place from early to middle Victorianism: the Newmans, the Froudes, and the Arnolds. Indeed, the story of the two younger Newman and Froude brothers, each modifying the Tractarian position of their elder siblings, helps to place that change as coming into full acknowledgement at around 1850.

Francis William Newman (1805–97) was four years younger than John Henry (1801–90). To the horror of his brother who severed all relations with him, Francis Newman went through almost every possible form of religious experience the nineteenth century had to offer. His *Phases of Faith* (1850) tells the story: Evangelicalism, the Plymouth Brethren, missionary work in Baghdad, rejection of Calvinism, involvement in biblical criticism—almost everything except his brother's route from Tractarianism back to Rome. Finally, rejecting all mere *forms* of 'faith at second-hand', he asserted the necessity of a direct personal spirituality, an individualism which John Henry Newman considered clear proof that Protestantism led to infidelity.

But Francis Newman belongs to a gentler and more flexible worldview. In his work on what he called 'the natural history' of the soul, he claimed that the dark views of 'Paul and Luther and Bunyan' on sin and the Fall were the result of their desperate intolerance of their own imperfection. They split themselves into two, and turned upon and magnified their imperfection as though it were an enemy within them. Instead Francis Newman offers an adjusted language that can bear to tolerate the pain of repeated failure: 'what is popularly called, "the total depravity of human nature" is more correctly, the essen-

tial, eternal imperfection of every created existence' (*The Soul*
(1849), p. 81). It is not in outright villainy that the Fall is most felt but
in the predicament of one who is already keenly penitent:

> He resolves to speak with meekness, but he finds himself excited and
> bitter, if not in word, yet in heart. He resolves to be chaste, and his
> thoughts become impure. He resolves to worship God in spirit; but his
> mind wanders into countless imaginations. He resolves to be contented,
> and his heart swells with a foolish ambition. He resolves to be humble, but
> he is mortified that somebody gave him too little honour. He resolves to
> be simple; yet he said something to make himself admired. And so all
> through, 'when he would do good, evil is present with him'. (p. 82)

In this revised version of the Fall, Francis Newman works towards
a sense of compassionate forgiveness and an appreciation of flawed
goodness in unexpected places and people. Possibilities are individual, not predictable. Sin is not so damnably habituating that we
cannot suddenly make a change—and renew that change even after
we have lapsed again. Passion should be trusted even through its
mistakes, because its sheer 'depth and power of life' takes a person
into those direct experiences where alone genuine change can
happen. The only possible way is that of the new individual journey
in which, by breaking up the old second-hand religious forms that
have grown over the nineteenth century, 'each soul will assume its
own *character*' (*The Soul*, p. 180).

James Anthony Froude's relation to his rigidly Tractarian brother
Richard Hurrell Froude went further; like an extreme representation
of the relation of secularization to religion, it was violent and reactive. At Oxford the younger Froude (1818–94) turned to John
Henry Newman in place of his own elder brother who died of tuberculosis in 1836, aged 33; but he then needed Carlyle to fend off the
influence of the Tractarians, becoming Carlyle's disciple and later his
(by then not uncritical) biographer. His admiration for Reformation
Protestantism freed him from Newman but he also needed freedom
from Protestantism. The young Froude was the classic Victorian
doubter, the man always reactively caught in between positions,
without being able to maintain himself independently. In *The
Nemesis of Faith* (1849), equivocally and characteristically half-

novel, half-autobiography, Froude's protagonist Markham Sutherland, losing all orthodox religious faith, uses a naturalistic argument to claim that human beings cannot help what they do but are the evolved products of Nature's laws: 'men had to grow as we grew. Their passions developed rapidly, their minds slowly; but fast enough to allow them, in the interval of passion, to reflect upon themselves' (p. 94).

Thus, 'our failures are errors, not crimes' (p. 96). To Froude, as later to Thomas Hardy, Nature is 'like the miserable Frankenstein': 'experimenting among the elements of humanity', it sends us into the world as ill-designed creatures (p. 78). We are not saints or sinners, because the world is neither as high nor as low as Christianity had had it: 'it is a world of men and women, not all good, but better far than bad', and a world we must both love and yet die in (p. 154).

Markham's new life becomes a secular experiment by one of Frankenstein's creatures in the relation of happiness and morality. In refuge from his loss of God, he finds himself instead in love with a married woman whose husband, as she herself begins to realize, has never really loved her. She loves Markham but if she runs off with him she will lose her beloved child. Then suddenly the child dies. The woman, at once bereft and free, simply turns in the midst of her pain to Markham. But he is shocked by her; he does not understand how she can make the transition from the death of the child to the making of a new sexual life. The apparent expediency feels like sin again. Markham cannot find the belief in himself to create, consolidate, and morally justify the sort of secular future proposed, and he falls back upon a figure very like J. H. Newman to return him to a religious retreat. As Karl Marx argued in 1852, at the beginning of *The Eighteenth Brumaire of Louis Bonaparte*, it was precisely at crisis points when people seemed to be revolutionizing themselves, creating something previously non-existent, that they anxiously fell back for a time upon the reassuring terms and precedents of the past: 'Just so does the beginner, having learnt a new language, always re-translate it into his mother-tongue; he has not assimilated the spirit of the new language, nor learnt to manipulate it freely, until he uses it without reference to the old and forgets his native language in using the new one.' Though defended by Marian Evans and Arthur Hugh Clough, *The Nemesis of Faith* was publicly burnt by William

Sewell, sub-rector of Froude's old college in Oxford and a man as virulently anti-Catholic as he was anti-secularist.

Nowhere is this complicated process of learning a new language better shown than in Mrs Humphry Ward's *Robert Elsmere*. Published in 1888, it stands as the great, culminating, recapitulatory novel of the century's religious experience. It is also *the* novel of a third representative family, the Arnolds, the family most committed to take upon themselves collectively the role of Coleridge's national clerisy. Mary Ward herself was the product of a mixed marriage between a woman of stern French Protestant stock and the second son of Arnold of Rugby. Tom Arnold (1823–1900) destroyed his academic career in Oxford by converting to Roman Catholicism, only to turn away from J. H. Newman and then finally reconvert, to the despair of his wife and the ruin of their marriage. Mary Arnold, later Mrs Humphry Ward, was left for ever torn between her two parents.

Robert Elsmere takes what George MacDonald called the religious blueprint of the Victorian age and makes the way that its lines do *not* map onto individual realities the very subject matter and problem of the novel. For like Mary Ward's other major novel *Helbeck of Bannisdale* (1898) which investigates the love between a devout Catholic and the daughter of a secular sceptic, *Robert Elsmere* is a story of what becomes increasingly a mixed marriage, of deep mutual love trying to hold together what religious differences are involuntarily pushing asunder.

Robert Elsmere is a 'modern' man moving—with an almost ironically religious earnestness—from Anglican clergyman to biblical critic, from intellectual doubter of Christianity's truth to missionary social worker. Through all these changes, he still believes in a God and honours the human and historical Jesus. Moreover, he still loves and needs Catherine, who married him in his first faith and remains in her simple, fundamental, and unchanging old belief at the opposite end of the nineteenth century. 'You are going to devote your life to attacking the few remnants of faith that still remain in the world?' she cries, burying her face in her hands, confessing herself 'unable to understand': ' "And rather than try," he insisted, "you will go on believing that I am a man without faith, seeking only to destroy." "I know you think you have faith," she answered, "but how can it seem faith to me?"' (ch. 39). 'Very few women of the present day', claims Mary Ward, 'could feel this particular calamity as Catherine Elsmere must feel it' (ch. 29). For to Catherine 'marriage makes two one': 'And if husband and wife are only one in body and estate, not one in soul, why, who that believes in the soul would . . . endure such a miserable second-best' (ch. 20). Mary Ward admired Charlotte Yonge, one of the other women of the century who could feel as Catherine felt. Indeed, as an 18-year-old Mary Arnold had had one of her first stories rejected by Charlotte Yonge's magazine, *The Monthly Packet.* In *Robert Elsmere,* accordingly, Catherine's Protestant faith is like an Evangelical rerun of the Tractarianism behind *The Heir of Redclyffe,* now brought into contact with a husband's equally sincere but clashingly new convictions.

In fact, Catherine eventually does make the secondary liberal concessions the modern world supposes to be so easy: overcoming in herself her late father's puritan resistance to her younger sister's musical talent; trying to tolerate her husband with the strange, reluctant thought that God has many languages and not just one. Yet still 'each phrase she had spoken had seemed to take with it a piece of her life': ' "You were right—I *would* not understand. But in a sense I shall never understand. I cannot change," and her voice broke into piteousness. "My Lord is my Lord always: but He is yours too . . . say what you will." ' (ch. 43). To Catherine her God is not just hers, subjectively, as Robert supposes: to her He abides, outside her own idea of Him and even through Robert's denial of Him.

The prime minister himself, W. E. Gladstone, in a long review of *Robert Elsemere* in *The Nineteenth Century* (May 1888), shrewdly complained that, as an Evangelical, Catherine—and the religious spirit she represented—was left intellectually defenceless. But the emotional force of the book is that her ancient faith is not so much unintelligent as helpless. Behind Catherine is a fanatically devout father, now deceased, a Church of England clergyman who survived the Oxford of the 1840s unscathed by Tractarianism, through a mixture of Evangelicalism and Quakerism. Behind Robert, however, is the Oxford of the Liberal reaction which followed Tractarianism, led first by Jowett and then revived in the 1870s by T. H. Green. It is the Idealist philosopher T. H. Green who says, in the person of

Elsmere's benign mentor Mr Grey, 'All religions are true, and all are false'—true in the spirit of what they seek to represent, false in the letter or form of so doing (ch. 19).

Against this historical background, Robert's mind remains equivocally 'full of that intense spiritual life of Catherine's which in its wonderful self-containedness and strength was always a marvel, sometimes a reproach, to him. Beside her, he seemed to himself a light creature'. Yet he also knows that in the modern world there are those like Squire Wendover, a scholar of the Mark Pattison type, who would now describe Christianity as a myth or a fairy story. In Robert's mind, how can the thought of Wendover fit alongside the thought of his wife: 'Could any reasonable man watch a life like Catherine's and believe that nothing but a delusion lay at the heart of it?' (ch. 19). Yet increasingly, other thoughts—of evolutionary theory, of historical evidences, of comparative religion—begin 'to press, to encroach, to intermeddle with the mind's other furniture' (ch. 20)—thoughts he cannot think within the old framework.

Elsmere does not want to lose his wife, yet like her he does not want their marriage to be no more than a sort of secondary compromise. He wants to believe that the human love they have for each other has a sufficient primacy, despite their religious differences. Yet at the same time, to the Churchmen and to Catherine herself, even the sympathetic admiration he continues to have for orthodox religion (because of the human goodness contained within it) is more dangerous than an outright opposition would be. Just as the couple's relationship places their distance from each other within such chafing intimacy, so at the book's other level, the very nearness of one form of belief to another makes ever clearer the crucial distinctions that keep them apart. Mary Ward was in some ways still a loyal granddaughter of Arnold of Rugby, yet, at those moments when each partner fears losing the other, her novel is necessarily closer to John Henry Newman's insistence on the important of differences than it is to the accommodations of Broad Churchmen.

For what makes *Robert Elsmere* a *novel* is not only that it gives a human dimension to the theological map. It is also that the lack of fit between the two levels, human and religious, creates an intermediate realm of pained confusion which the nineteenth-century novel itself comes into existence to mark and to explore. There are sides here,

however reluctantly, and no simple marriage or easy synthesis—
because the assumption of liberal human integration is one of the
very points at issue. Catherine's sister, Rose, who grew up in conflict
between her own commitment to a violinist's art and her father's
and elder sister's forbidding religion, is well placed to realize 'the
profound change which had passed over the Elsmeres' life':

> As much tenderness between husband and wife as ever—perhaps more
> expression of it even than before, as though from an instinctive craving to
> hide the separateness below from each other. But Robert went his way,
> Catherine hers. . . . All sorts of fresh invading silences were always coming
> in to limit talk, and increase the number of sore points which each
> avoided. (ch. 37)

This personal fracture contains in its silence the whole more-
than-personal history of nineteenth-century belief. For the story of
Victorian faith is most clearly and deeply registered in the representative contrast, across thirty years, between *The Heir of Redclyffe*
and *Robert Elsmere*. What is more, *Robert Elsmere* contains as it
were both novels within itself, for there Mary Ward finds in herself a
version of the Hebraism of Charlotte Yonge meeting the counter-
influence of her own uncle, Matthew Arnold.

'My uncle was a Modernist long before the time. In "Literature and
Dogma",' claimed Mrs Humphry Ward, 'he threw out in detail
much of the argument suggested in "Robert Elsmere"' (*A Writer's
Recollections* (1918), p. 235). In *St. Paul and Protestantism* (1870)
and *Literature and Dogma* (1873) Matthew Arnold had tried to cast
off the burden of English puritanism he had castigated in *Culture and
Anarchy* in 1869.

This was done in the name of the 'literary' as opposed to the
'literal', the 'cultural' as opposed to the 'dogmatic'. For where
Hebraism was fixed and strict and tied to the letter of the law, what
Arnold called Hellenism—the very essence of culture as derived from
the Greeks—was subtle and fluid and alert to the tone of the spirit.
Following his father and Jowett, Matthew Arnold deployed 'criticism' to recover the essential spirit of the Bible from the letter of an
outworn theology long imposed upon it. But it was increasingly
literary rather than textual criticism. It operated in the service of a
literary religion which saw the outward literal truths of the past, such

as 'the Kingdom of God' or 'the Resurrection of Christ', as neither more nor less than deep spiritual metaphors for the inner life. The aim was to free 'literature' from the 'dogma' surrounding it; to liberate the Bible's deepest 'poetry' of meaning from the theologians' language of 'science'. This was Arnold's spiritual-aesthetic counter to Newman, in finally completing the emancipation from Evangelicalism.

In Arnold the literary critic is the good, deep, experienced reader who understands 'that the language of the Bible is fluid, passing, and literary, not rigid, fixed, and scientific', who knows nuance, senses subtlety, hears what is distinct and particular. He exists to recognize in Scripture those moments that 'make for life'—not mechanically taking any book whole, but finding out its 'best self'. The Bible's best self, its closest relation to Christ, is manifest when it is shorn of its secondary layers of historical superstition and interpretative dogma: then it works, against the striving of the Scribes and Pharisees, through Jesus's own mild 'inward mode of working'.

How does Arnold presume to know where the Bible is most itself? In the introduction to *Literature and Dogma*, Arnold himself quoted Frederic Harrison's complaint that 'we seek in vain in Mr Arnold a system of philosophy with principles coherent, interdependent and derivative'. But for Arnold the critic does not work by systems of philosophy or dogmas of belief. Literary judgment emerges not through assertion or argument, it

comes almost of itself; and what it displaces it displaces easily and naturally, and without any turmoil of controversial reasonings. The thing comes to look differently to us, as we look at it by the light of fresh knowledge. We are not beaten from our old opinion by logic, we are not driven off our ground—our ground itself changes with us. (*Literature and Dogma*, introduction)

This is one of the age's deepest accounts of the distinctive nature, risk, and tact of literary thinking. It draws upon Coleridge when in *Aids to Reflection* (1825) he speaks of having faith in whatever in the Bible '*finds*' me'. A practice rather than a theory, a finding rather than a striving, it gradually accumulates, like the mysterious process of experience itself, into a form of implicit and intuitive wisdom which is the relaxed opposite of Hebraic 'pressing'.

In the same spirit, God is the experience of a '*not ourselves*', said Arnold quoting the seventeenth-century Platonist Henry More; a 'something about us that knew better, often, what we would be at than we ourselves'.

We did not make ourselves and our nature, we did not provide that happiness should follow conduct, as it inevitably does; that the sense of succeeding, going right, hitting the mark, in conduct, should give satisfaction, and a very high satisfaction, just as really as the sense of doing well in his work gives pleasure to a poet or a painter, or accomplishing what he tries gives pleasure to man who is learning to ride or to shoot; or as satisfying his hunger, also, gives pleasure to a man who is hungry. (*Literature and Dogma*, ch. 1.3)

Against the puritanism of work as a fallen, gloomy struggle, Arnold offers from the Hellenism of Aristotle and Plato a sense of natural pleasure, of artistic delight even, intrinsic to the achievement of morality. For that is what makes Arnold's religion more than the morality of willed rule and practical injunction: religion adds to such morality of command and prudence the feel or touch of emotion—'the gratitude, devotion, and awe, the sense of joy and peace' that the first man felt in doing right (ch. 1.4). It is an experience of getting into closer and happier touch with a sense of perfection.

The greatest example of that embodied perfection is Jesus, in whom, as by a miracle, the old grimly Hebraic duality of conflict between body and spirit simply and graciously did not appear to exist. That is why Paul, so much in conflict, loved and followed Jesus. For what Arnold saw in Paul was what he felt should have been the final release from the laws and tensions of of Hebraism:

Most men have the defects, as the saying is, of their qualities. Because they are ardent and severe, they have no sense for gentleness and sweetness; because they are sweet and gentle they have no sense for severity and ardour. A Puritan is a Puritan, and a man of feeling is a man of feeling. But with Paul the very same fulness of moral nature which made him a Pharisee, 'as concerning zeal, persecuting the church, touching the righteousness which is in the law, blameless' [Philippians 3: 6], was so large that it carried him out of Pharisaism and beyond it, when once he found how much needed doing in him which Pharisaism could not do. (*St. Paul and Protestantism*, ch. 1)

'He is driven for the very sake of righteousness to put the law of righteousness in the second place, and to seek outside the law itself for a power to fulfil the law' (ch. 1). This was the origin of Arnold's second Reformation: to understand that the true inward meaning of losing life in order to gain it was to let the strained effort of anguished ego give way to the gracious, joyously enlarging sense of the 'not ourselves'. It made for the possibility of a greater wholeness of being, in place of what before had been so painfully dual.

For the old dualism—the schism between the way of religion and the way of the world, and the correspondent split between the life of the inward self and the life in society outside—had always been the Arnold clan's deepest fear and enemy. So it is in *Oakfield* (1853), a novel by Matthew's younger brother W. D. (William) Arnold. For there the earnest young Oakfield finds himself imagining how in the old religious days of the Reformation or even of the Wesleyan revival, a man might find courage to stand as a prophet in the world boldly rebuking vice and speaking truth. But people who in these times sought to return to the first principles of earlier ages, to gain eternal reasons for what should be done in time, found themselves left with a vulnerable earnestness which was mocked and redundant. In the mid-nineteenth century, in a fallen world made all too normal through the process of its own history, there seem to Oakfield 'only two courses open,—either to quit society altogether, or to mix in it on its own terms' (vol. 1, ch. 2).

What Oakfield decides to do is take himself away from Oxford, where he could have taken orders and gained a fellowship, into a different society, enlisting in the army in Imperial India. It was not until 1858 that, following the Indian Mutiny, control of India was transferred from the East India Company directly to the British Government. But from 1818 India had been a practical testing ground for theories of government and economic and social reform—in particular those of progressive Westernizers, such as James Mill (author of the influential *History of India*, 1819) and Thomas Macaulay, striving to create a Western-educated elite in the face of an Oriental traditionalism dismissed as 'backwardness'. Later it was his experience of the administration of India that led James Fitzjames Stephen (in *Liberty, Equality, Fraternity*, 1873) to oppose John Stuart Mill's belief in the primacy of social liberty, by insisting that the Raj was founded upon conquest rather than consent, and that in all societies power, not freedom, remained the major, underlying political reality.[7]

Ironically for Oakfield, however, India only offers him the same difficulties he has always had, in a different form. The great problem of his essential homelessness in the world is only exacerbated. A believer in the liberal Christian values of the West, Oakfield is nonetheless horrified by the grossness of European society in India. Yet he steers away from priggishly becoming a latter-day hermit, only to feel the corresponding danger of becoming a mere machine, 'a "first-rate officer", as it is called, and ceasing to be a man' (vol. 2, ch. 7). To be alone or to go into society: 'Is all truth a see-saw?' (vol. 2, ch. 3). If not a see-saw, then 'how to hit the mean between the two is the great problem' (vol. 1, ch. 3).

More than any of his brothers, William Arnold had inherited his father's fierce earnestness. It was Thomas Arnold who, like an old prophet, had sought to bring Christianity everywhere, and most of all into those areas of practical life which seemed most resistant to it. The Church existed primarily 'for the purpose of making men like Christ—earth like heaven—the kingdoms of the world the kingdom of Christ', but now it had lost that universal purpose and become a mere secondary institution (A. P. Stanley, *Life and Correspondence of Thomas Arnold* (1844), ch. 8, 18 November 1835). The world was at once the enemy of Christianity and the place in which Christianity was to work. Arnold's Rugby school became a microcosmic version of the attempt to reform such a world even by creating an alternative society within it. Oakfield's is the resultant effort to create a undivided life with a narrative force, and to be a lay member of the clerisy within the world. Yet looking at the whole Arnold family and its influence, R. H. Hutton diagnosed ironic failure: the very intensity of the desire for unity had only exacerbated the pained sense of dualism ('Dr. Arnold after Fifty Years', *The Spectator*, 18 June 1892).

---

[7] See Andrew Porter (ed.), *The Oxford History of the British Empire*, 3. *The Nineteenth Century* (Oxford University Press, 1999), chs. 18 and 19; and Javed Majeed, *Ungoverned Imaginings: James Mill's 'History of India' and Orientalism* (Clarendon Press, 1992).

But the problem of committing religion *to* the world without losing religion *in* the world was not just a problem for the Arnold family. These families—the Arnolds, the Froudes, the Newmans—are no more or less than intimate genetic representatives of the great Victorian religious debate: lines which at one moment divide brother from brother, at the next cross and recross in different patterns within the mental formation of the self-same individual. With the religious problem climactically poised in suspended solution, it was as though for almost every position that there had been in human history or that there could be in the imaginable future, there was in the confused and disturbed variety of Victorian England some human representative—for each thought a person partially embodying it.

Newman had described what happens when a powerful idea *first* begins to gain possession of a people; in the melting pot of Victorian England it was rather to do with what was happening to all the old accepted ideas when immersed within the solvent of doubt:

At first men will not fully realize what it is that moves them, and will express and explain themselves inadequately. There will be a general agitation of thought, and an action of mind upon mind. There will be a time of confusion, when conceptions and misconceptions are in conflict, and it is uncertain whether anything is to come of the idea at all, or which view of it is to get the start of the others. . . . After a while some definite teaching emerges; and as time proceeds, one view will be modified or expanded by another, and then combined with a third; till the idea in which they centre, will be to each mind what at first it was only to all together. (*An Essay on the Development of Christian Doctrine* (1846 edn.), p. 36)

It was as though amidst the Victorians something was struggling to work itself out to a conclusion through the opposing thoughts lodged in different conflicting individuals. Although it has sometimes been said that the Victorian age produced outside the realm of science no truly innovative thinkers, the originality of the period exists in its ability to return to the origin of any given position and think it out again through the controversies that went on both between and within widely differing individuals.

That is why, in addition to the family quarrels, it is in the great Victorian debates and disputes—rather than in the several different positions taken singly in isolation—that the deepest issues of the period are most powerfully gathered. Looking back in 1889, as a contributor to *Lux Mundi*, a collection of 'studies in the religion of the incarnation' by Oxford's leading High Church Anglicans, Aubrey Moore suggested that throughout the ages the emphasis in the religious temper had oscillated between two doctrines of God— God as transcendent, the Creator separate from the world; and God as immanent within His Creation. The second half of the nineteenth century was, he said, the age of the Incarnation rather than of the Fall, and, especially with the rise of evolutionary theory, an age of immanence rather than of transcendence.

It was F. D. Maurice's dispute with H. L. Mansel that representatively confirmed this direction to religious thought in the second half of the century.

The early-century theologians of the Fall, such of Chalmers, had characteristically taken the line that economic ills could only be cured by bearing the suffering that resulted from them. In contrast, F. D. Maurice (1805–72) sought to anticipate economic disasters and prevent them before they happened, through the establishment of workers' associations and cooperatives. In his Christian Socialism, Maurice stands as a powerful summary of all that was humanitarianly involved in the ever-increasing shift to a theology centred upon the love offered in the Incarnation, rather than the pain suffered in the Atonement.

Brought up as a Unitarian rejecting the divinity of Christ, Maurice was converted to an orthodox belief in the Incarnation. He came to see that the Incarnation of Christ was the means of overcoming man's incapacity to draw closer to God, by God's drawing closer to man instead. Maurice's *Theological Essays* (1853), dedicated to his friend Tennyson, included an attack on the doctrine of hell and everlasting punishment which cost Maurice his chair in divinity at King's College, London. 'Mr Maurice's most emphatic teaching', said R. H. Hutton, who followed Maurice out of Unitarianism, 'was, that to be immured in self,—to have no vision of the source of life and redemption—*is* hell, the worst conceivable hell' (*Aspects of Religious and Scientific Thoughts*, ed. E. M. Roscoe (1899), p. 273), for hell was the self without God. Conversely Maurice also believed that human beings could find God in themselves, directly, in immediate personal relation. 'Theology', as an external and notional view of things divine, actually got in the way of 'religion'—when by religion Maurice meant not an 'idea' of God but the 'knowing' of Him as a living God within.

H. L. Mansel (1820–71) began like Maurice from a scepticism about philosophical theology. But Mansel's Bampton lectures of 1858, *The Limits of Religious Thought*, insisted on the doctrine of a fundamentally *un*knowable God. Mansel discounted the belief in direct human knowledge of God, which he associated above all with Francis Newman, and started instead from Kant's distinction between phenomena, things as they are known to us, and noumena, things as they are in themselves. We cannot know absolute reality, as it is apart from ourselves, just as we cannot know from the finite what is infinite. The problems of theology are thus no different from the problems of philosophy—both have to do with the constitutional limits of the human mind.

Yet what fascinates Mansel is not just that things-as-we-see-them and things-as-they-really-are-in-themselves are separate. For though indeed absolutely separate, phenomena and noumena are related paradoxically, within consciousness itself, even as reciprocally independent. That is to say: by what is an act of self-sacrifice in Mansel, it is precisely the awareness of the inevitable limitation of our conceptions which austerely creates that sense of a reality absolutely separate from them—a truth beyond us of which our way of knowing 'indicates the existence, but does not make known the substance' (lecture 5). Says Mansel, magnificently, 'The existence of a limit to our powers of thought is manifested by the consciousness of contradiction, which implies at the same time an attempt to think *and* an inability to accomplish that attempt' (lecture 3). Thus in this world we can never do without ourselves, and yet we cannot see ourselves separately. We can only glimpse ourselves in the act of seeing what is not ourselves; we can only imagine, in austere abstraction, ourselves apart from what we see, or things apart from our seeing them. Moreover, we have to recognize that how we think of God is not what God is, but what Mansel, after Kant, calls a 'regulative' not a 'speculative' idea. 'If we know not the Absolute and Infinite at all, we cannot say how far it is or is not capable of likeness or unlikeness to the Relative and Finite' (lecture 5). All attempts to conceive God are anthropomorphic: philosophic reason is simply the most proud form of seeing God in human terms.

Not for Mansel then John Stuart Mill's famous battle-cry against worship of a cruel God in his *Examination of Sir William Hamilton's Philosophy* (1865): 'I will call no being good, who is not what I mean when I apply that epithet to my fellow-creatures.' For Mansel used reason to defeat reason, to show its limitations and self-contradictions—leaving faith, in an age of religious decline, austerely in the unnameable realm of the immeasurably non-human beyond. In all this, Mansel's was the last great nineteenth-century effort at a theology of transcendence: a God who, again in Nietzsche's phrase, was not to be taken as 'human, all too human' but who was rather, in the bare words found by Tennyson, at one point in the process of *In Memoriam*, 'What is, and no man understands' (124).

Nonetheless, as R. H. Hutton put it in chapter 5 of his *Theological Essays* (1871), 'so closely twinned are the threads of human faith and scepticism' in Mansel, that to many believers the claim that God could not be known did not look like a defence of faith but a victory for doubt. A senior Oxford cleric was heard to remark after Mansel's lectures that he never expected to hear atheism preached from the University pulpit. Leslie Stephen claimed triumphantly that Mansel had played into the hands of the agnostics, and Herbert Spencer took over from Mansel for his own purposes the idea of a negative absolute.

But the fiercest attack upon Mansel was Maurice's in *What is Revelation?* (1859). In truth, Maurice's book is best read via Hutton's review of it in his *Theological Essays*—partly because Hutton is clearer than Maurice, partly because in a companion volume, *Literary Essays* published in the same year (1871), Hutton brings the implications of Maurice's thought into the world of literary as well as religious history. In his writings on Tennyson, Arnold, and George Eliot in particular, Hutton is constantly exploring the presence of belief in the experience of unbelief, of God inside human ways of thinking, of religion within apparently secular novels. And this was legitimate in the eyes of Maurice as it could not have been to Mansel in his austerity.

To Maurice, notes Hutton, Mansel was a believer 'in the

irremoveable veil which covers the face of God'. He leaves us only with regulative ideas, adapted 'notions' of a very distant, disappearing God, rather than those direct spiritual realities which Maurice believed alone could change us. Mansel's claim is that because our knowing capacity is limited and God inexhaustible, we can never know directly more than a distorted fraction of His Nature. But this, counters Hutton on behalf of Maurice, is a misunderstanding of the meaning of 'the infinite' by taking the term in quasi-physical terms:

In short, righteousness and love are qualities which, if we are competent to know them really in any single act, we know to be the same in all acts; and all that we mean by calling them infinite is, that we have more and more to learn about them for ever, which will not change and weaken, but confirm and deepen, the truth gained in every previous act of knowledge. (*Theological Essays*, ch. 5)

For Hutton and Maurice, human experience holds good incarnate, knows something of the essential truth of the holy even within its own doubts and limitations.

In the battle between Maurice and Mansel it was the liberal humane spirit of the Broad Church which seemed to have won the victory. But the looming, critical question for the Broad Church was whether its victory was not really that of a disguised yet advancing secularism, surreptitiously arising within the Broad Church itself.

It was a sign of the times, when in 1896 Frederick Temple (1821–1902), one of the maligned contributors to the Broad Church's *Essays and Reviews*, finally became archbishop of Canterbury and head of the Church of England. But only the previous year in his *Lectures on Disendowment* (1895) Temple had voiced what he took to be the central problem of his lifetime—the problem of keeping the doctrine of incarnation in balance, as between the socialization of religion and the spiritualization of society:

There is always a considerable difficulty in defining with any precision the relation between the things of this world and the things of the other, because on the one side there is a very serious danger that, if these two things are allowed to come into too close a contact, the things of the other may seem to be absorbed into the cares of the world, and on the other hand there is a very great danger, perhaps the more serious danger of the two, that, if the demarcation between them be made too strong, the result will be that the principles of religion will be altogether excluded from their proper influence on our conduct in this life.[8]

The more the Broad Church sought to break down separate lines of demarcations, the more the work of one realm went on within the terms of another. There was religious work to be done within the terms of social amelioration or scientific enquiry. But as the greatest of the *Lux Mundi* group, Scott Holland put it, Faith had regularly to recall itself from the very midst of its temporal incarnations:

It has no more right to identify itself with any intellectual situation than it has to pin its fortunes to those of any political dynasty. Its eternal task lies in rapid readjustment to each fresh situation, which the motion of time may disclose to it. It has that in it which can apply to all, and learn from all. Its identity is not lost, because its expressions vary and shift: for its identity lies deep in personality; and personality is that which testifies to its own identity by the variety and the rapidity of its self-adaptation to the changes of circumstance. So with faith. . . . Each situation forces a new aspect to the front. But ever it is God and the soul, which recognise each other under every disguise. (*Lux Mundi*, essay 1)

The old scriptural paradox of losing oneself to find oneself takes on further meaning in the molten fluidities of the later nineteenth century.

Even so, the very desire to bring religion and social concern into ever-closer contact produced novels such as *Robert Elsmere* or Eliza Lynn Linton's *Joshua Davidson, Christian and Communist* (1872). Implicitly such works posed Marx's question about the creation of a wholly new language: as the end of the century approached, how far was the religious novel from turning itself into becoming the political novel instead? Elsmere resigns from the Church of England and attempts to establish instead a new secular religion. His 'New Brotherhood' is dedicated to bringing the human example of Christ back to life upon earth in the poorest parts of London. To prevent practical Christianity becoming impossible, says Joshua Davidson, son of a carpenter, 'The modern Christ would be a politician' (*Joshua Davidson*, ch. 4). It was but a step to the position of John

[8] Quoted in E. R. Norman, *Church and Society in England 1770–1970* (Clarendon Press, 1976), 14.

Stuart Mill, as disclosed in his late essay 'Utility of Religion', where he argued that it was 'perfectly conceivable that religion may be morally useful without being intellectually sustainable'. The essay was published only after Mill's death, for Mill's father had always cautioned him against impolitic avowals of infidelity in public. John Stuart Mill was the age's undercover alien within the religious world: he worked within current structures and forms as long as they were progressive or at least remediable, seeking reform from within. Whilst religion carried forward the improvement of morality within it, all was well; but increasingly the situation was reversing itself and 'one of the hardest burdens laid upon the other good influences of human nature has been that of improving religion itself' (*Collected Works*, vol. 10, p. 406).

Thus, in an age of immanence and incarnation, the great question was whether, with Maurice or Scott Holland, religion was going on within the concerns of secularization or whether, on the contrary with Mill or Marx, secularization was working its way to emancipation even within the very thinking of religion.

Remarkably, it was the realist novel that was the home for, as well as partly the product of, such considerations. For the realist novel was the holding ground, the meeting point, for the overlapping claims of secularization and belief held together in a version of common life.

Its most characteristic form is not that of *Oakfield*, which is trying to *become* a realist novel just as urgently as its protagonist is trying to make a real life for himself. The achieved realist novel is rather as it is in the norms offered by Trollope or Elizabeth Gaskell: an apparently agnostic humanist form, written within the framework of ordinary daily life, without recourse, it seems, to explicit ends or purposes transcending the common world. Thoroughly embodied in the world, it seems quietly sceptical of theoretical positions, in comparison with the complications of reality in practice.

And yet with both these authors, the realist novel stands to a kind of natural theology implicit within it, even as Trollope describes the honest man in relation to his own honesty: 'The really honest man can never say a word to make those who don't know of his honesty believe that it is there'; 'The honest man almost doubts whether his honesty be honest, unless it be kept hidden' (*The Eustace Diamonds*

(1872), ch. 53). The novel in Trollope, as in Mrs Gaskell, is written by so deeply implicit a believer as not to impose, reveal, or even find quite statable the belief, except as hidden in some sense of bafflingly mundane mystery. It involves what Elizabeth Missing Sewell calls 'taking what is given' in *The Experience of Life* (1853)—and, for a devout spinster, includes taking what is *not* given too, as if it were so. The novel in such hands is content to be normalizing, at home in the world of secondary considerations. Yet within the normal, characters can find and lose their lives with a strangeness known to barely anyone else in the world, perhaps hardly even to themselves.

A lonely old man, rejected in love in his youth, turns to a young woman in his care whose own lover has disappeared abroad; she accepts the old man's offer of marriage, only for the younger man to return the very next day. The old man can hardly bear the pain of the act of chivalry, of generous abnegation, which he knows he eventually will have to perform:

It was the one day in advance which had given him the strength of his position. But it was the one day also which had made him weak . . . Had John Gordon come in time, the past misery would only have been prolonged, and none would have been the wiser. . . . As it was, all the world of Alresford would know how it had been with him, and all the world of Alresford as they looked at him would tell themselves that this was the man who had attempted to marry Mary Lawrie, and had failed. (Trollope, *An Old Man's Love* (1884), ch. 11)

Of his softness in letting Mary go, 'he feared it of himself, was sure of it of himself, and hated himself because it was so'. Yet for all his desire to be, for once, stern and cruel and selfish in acquiring some final happiness in life, 'he could not alter his own self' (ch. 11). When he thinks of taking in his arms a girl who really loves elsewhere, 'it was not that he feared her for himself, but that he feared himself for her sake' (ch. 19). At such moments when goodness mingled with shame and fear is almost an act of self-cancellation, the realist novel is like Trollope's man in the right, innocently walking apparently unarmed within the world: 'his very strength is his weakness' (*Barchester Towers* (1857), ch. 37). For, as Scott Holland was to put it, the doctrine of immanence means that 'faith lies *behind* our secular life, secreted within it: and the secular life, therefore, can go on as if no faith was wanted'. But it is only 'as if' in Trollope: faith is wanted, is implicit. For again, as Scott Holland says of ordinary secular life, our common starting point: 'Its own practical activity is complete and free, whether it discover its hidden principle or not.' That hidden principle of 'Religion' only means 'the coming forward into the foreground of that which is the universal background of all existence' (*Lux Mundi*, essay 1). But Trollope's old man has to keep the strength of his better motivation, like himself, in the background of life, hidden behind the pain of his felt weakness in having to surrender the woman.

Readers did not have to know that they themselves were religious or the book was religious, in order to be moved. The natural life proffered in such novels of Trollope and Mrs Gaskell was often life which had not yet arrived at the recognition of its own implicit religious grounding and perhaps never would. These novels were the common repositories of life; they offered an initial assent—the life within them seemingly an uncompleted beginning, to be accepted nonetheless as perhaps all we have. How readers went on to interpret that life, whether there was anything more behind or beyond it, was left—as in life itself—to them.

In this way the realist novel offered a human holding ground equally hospitable to the non-believer, coming from a quite opposite direction. So it is with George Eliot in her portrayal of Silas Marner: that inarticulate man cannot describe and does not need consciously to know the essentially religious change that has come over him in the course of bringing up a deserted baby girl as his own. Long after the disillusionment he suffered with the harsh formal religion of his early life, Marner relearns trust—a trust so deep that he cannot specify whence or in what, only that it comes through the child without her even knowing it and is confirmed in the peasant voice of Dolly Winthrop. To George Eliot at least, it simply does not matter if such trust is called a religious or a human phenomenon: the two are one. *Adam Bede* is similarly the great Methodist novel written by a non-believer: George Eliot admires Dinah Morris for the human goodness which she expresses through the form of Methodism, without George Eliot caring too much about the form itself. The intervention of George Eliot as narrator is itself a writer's version of Dinah's moral interventionism, in action.

For George Eliot is the one Victorian novelist to have an explicit philosophy which turns old forms into modern contents and, thus, religion itself into humanist realism. Behind *Silas Marner* (1861) is her own translation, in 1854 as Marian Evans, of Ludwig Feuerbach's *Essence of Christianity* (1841). This book was a vital contribution to the century's ever-increasing humanization of religion as something naturally present in human life without formal dogmas. It was also part of the process that converted Marian Evans, Evangelical turned non-believer, into George Eliot, realist novelist, instead.

What Feuerbach offered was a rule of religious translation. God did not make man in His own image: it was the other way round, we created God out of human qualities and human needs. Human beings unconsciously projected upon their God their own fragile ideals, to give Justice and Mercy and Love a surer form and a more permanent reality, *outside* those selves. It was this idea of alienation—the projecting upon another of what really belonged to ourselves—which so attracted Marx to Feuerbach.

'The Greeks and Romans', says Feuerbach, 'deified accidents as substances: virtues, states of mind, passions, as independent beings' (ch. 1, pt. 2). They turned adjectival qualities, such as 'war-like', into substantive gods, like Mars, worshipping their statues. Elements *within* the human situation were dramatized into being independent forces and personified powers presiding *over* it. The Christians likewise made 'mental phenomena into independent beings' in the shape of the Holy Trinity, of angels and devils. Yet nineteenth-century realism, in its widest sense, dissolved these forms back down into that intervolved mass of complex human ordinariness which the dense language of prose characteristically represented. In the prosaic secular grammar of the modern world, said Feuerbach, what used to be seen as divine powers were no longer to be the subjects of sentences. Instead, translated from above to within the human condition, those powers were manifested now as smaller undeified 'accidents', qualities, trying to find a place for themselves within the crowded context and syntax of modern life. It marked a shift from the age of religious fictions to an age of prosaic realism.

So, at the end of chapter 4 of George Eliot's own *Adam Bede* (1859), Adam feels on the sudden death of his father an equally sudden regret at his own harshness to his father in the old man's latter days, and George Eliot closes the chapter by saying, formally: 'When death, the great reconciler has come, it is never our tenderness that we repent of, but our severity.' That vain hindsight is in tacit contrast with the scene, a chapter later, in which Mr Irwine, an easy-going Anglican clergyman, goes upstairs to pay his habitual visit to the tiresome invalid, his sister:

Anne's eyes were closed, and her brow contracted as if from intense pain. Mr Irwine went to the bed-side, and took up one of the delicate hands and kissed it; a slight pressure from the small fingers told him that it was worth while to come up-stairs for the sake of doing that. He lingered a moment, looking at her, and then turned away and left the room, treading very gently—he had taken off his boots and put on slippers before he came up-stairs. Whoever remembers how many things he has declined to do even for himself, rather than have the trouble of putting on or taking off his boots, will not think the last detail insignificant. (ch. 5)

There Irwine does for his sister something equivalent to what Adam now vainly regrets not doing for his father. But it was only in the light of death that Adam sees, too late, the value of what otherwise might seem small, sentimental, and insignificant. Only the very end of life, in the abstract form of Death, gives belated importance to the medium of life in which such little unremembered and barely appreciated acts of kindness go on without any proud or obtrusive claim as to their importance. It is as though Feuerbach said: if only we could translate what all too belatedly is seen as important at the very end of life, back into the unheroic ordinariness of life's middle. What the realist novel aspires to is just such a substitution of apparently mundane content for a merely dramatic form.

And Feuerbach would claim that this translation was not merely the secularization of what used to be religion but rather the spiritualization of secularization itself: 'Thus do things change. What yesterday was still religion, is no longer such to-day; and what to-day is atheism, to-morrow will be religion' (*The Essence of Christianity*, ch. 1, pt. 2). That human content, whatever the form it takes, is for George Eliot the true spirit of religion, and to her it made little difference what name anyone gave that content which the novel held in solution. 'Please not to call it by any name,' says Dorothea to Will Ladislaw when he praises her personal belief; 'You will say it is Persian, or something else geographical. It is my life. I have found it out, and cannot part with it. I have always been finding out my religion since I was a little girl' (*Middlemarch* (1872), ch. 39).

Yet to think that the form of a belief is less important than what it humanly and morally results in seemed to some of George Eliot's orthodox religious critics the kind of Utilitarian pragmatism practised by Mill. To W. H. Mallock in *Is Life Worth Living?* (1879), George Eliot's was a second-hand, parasitic belief about the value of beliefs, in an age which was using a vague spiritualized version of personal morality as a means of transition from a religious to a post-religious era. Where George Eliot argued that Christianity was unconsciously a product of human values, Mallock argued that those human values were on the contrary a historical product of Christianity: take away the supporting Christian framework and they would not last for long in the face of secular temptations. Which way round it really was, insisted Mallock, *did* matter. Charlotte Yonge herself, reviewing J. W. Cross's *George Eliot's Life* in *The Monthly Packet* (May 1885), quoted George Eliot's own dictum: 'Heaven help us! said the old religion; the new one from its very lack of that faith will teach us all the more to help one another.' Yonge had admired *Adam Bede* and *Silas Marner* because they remained fully human stories, but thought the later work to be gloomily suffering from what George Eliot herself described as 'the severe effort of trying to make certain ideas incarnate'. George Eliot, she concludes, had untutored 'religious *sentiments*', 'frustrated beliefs' which, 'cramped by her Atheism', could only come out as the tortuously laboured didacticism of an essentially secular morality. Thirty years earlier, *The Heir of Redclyffe* had been Charlotte Yonge's last-ditch attempt to avoid such a future for the novel.

By way of conclusion to this tangle of considerations, there is a novel published in 1853—the same year that saw the publication of novels as diverse as *The Heir of Redclyffe*, *The Experience of Life*, and *Villette*, all of them written by women writers—which may serve as a final test case of all that stands in tense balance within the Victorian religious crisis. It was a novel in favour of which Charlotte Brontë deliberately and generously delayed the publication of *Villette* because, as she told its author in a letter of 12 January, it had 'a philanthropic purpose, a social use' which Charlotte Brontë felt her own work had not. For, compassionately, it told the story of an infatuated young woman who has borne a child out of wedlock, offering as Charlotte Brontë put it, 'hope and energy to many who thought they had forfeited their right to both'. And yet Mrs Gaskell's *Ruth*—one more example of the sensitiveness of the Victorian woman-writer at crucial phases of spiritual sensibility—is also historically a religious as well as a social novel, a product of Elizabeth Gaskell's mid-century Unitarianism. As religious outsiders because of their opposition to the doctrine of the Holy Trinity, Unitarians were notably charitable and forgiving towards outcasts, believing in a merciful God who did not damn sinners to everlasting punishment. Yet what makes *Ruth* a characteristically *creative* Victorian realist novel in that all these exterior categories—the social, the religious, the ethical, the psychological, the humanitarian, the feminine—are thrown inside a human melting pot, and all the boundary lines between them shift and reform, until we see what vision of the world is implicit in the act of particular reconfiguration.

In contrast, when they discover an unmarried mother in their midst, the Pharisees in this novel want to draw firm and unmoving lines. Mr Bradshaw, the businessman who is the chief financial supporter of the local Nonconformist chapel, has no doubts: 'He drew a clear line of partition, which separated mankind into two great groups, to one of which, by the grace of God, he and his belonged' (ch. 25).

In her opposition to such Hard Church fixities, what makes Mrs Gaskell a novelist is also what makes her, not just a sympathetic liberal social reformer, but a deeper and subtler Christian than Mr Bradshaw. Clear lines give way to surprises, shifts, and paradoxes. For what spoils and damages Ruth is also what rehabilitates her. However it has arisen, the bond between mother and child remains, in Wordsworthian terms, autonomously natural. Ruth becomes a serious woman because, suddenly, a pretty orphaned child of 16, seduced by a well-to-do young man who then deserts her, has become a mother, unable to hide her sheer joy in giving birth to her baby. Here she is just afterwards, in the house of the Bensons, the Nonconformist minister and his sister who have taken her in:

'Now go to sleep, Ruth,' said Miss Benson, kissing her, and darkening the room. But Ruth could not sleep; if her heavy eyes closed, she opened them again with a start, for sleep seemed to be an enemy stealing from her the consciousness of being a mother. That one thought excluded all remembrance and all anticipation, in those first hours of delight.

But soon remembrance and anticipation came. Then was the natural want of the person, who alone could take an interest similar in kind, though not in amount, to the mother's. And sadness grew like a giant in the still watches of the night, when she remembered that there would be no father to guide and strengthen the child. (ch. 15)

It is both paragraphs, both halves of the nineteenth-century experience which Mrs Gaskell preserves, the humane and yet the fallen. I am a mother; he has no father.

Earlier Miss Benson had told her brother what had happened when Ruth overheard the doctor say that she was pregnant: 'she whispered quite eagerly, "Did he say I should have a baby?" Of course, I could not keep it from her; but I thought it my duty to look as cold and severe as I could. She did not seem to understand how it ought to be viewed, but took it just as if she had a right to have a baby' (ch. 11). As in the joy of the birth of the child, there is something *more* in this book than 'seeing the thing in a moral light' and true religion is not blind to it. Benson himself, thinking of Mary Magdalene, says later of his attempt to help save this life, 'I take my stand with Christ against the world' (ch. 27). But his sister is, as he well knows, not really just another of the world's Mr Bradshaws, and her moral light changes. Initially she was only good to Ruth in deference to her brother rather than for Ruth's own sake. But not knowing 'how to thank you for all you are doing', Ruth had surprised her after a while by asking very quietly one night, whether 'you will *let* me pray for you'. It took Miss Benson aback—we are both sinners, she replied:

'Let us pray for each other. Don't speak so again, my dear; at least, not to me.'

Miss Benson was actually crying. She had always looked upon herself as so inferior to her brother in real goodness; had seen such heights above her, that she was distressed by Ruth's humility. (ch. 12)

This is what goodness is in this novel: a surprising shift of the novel's perspective that feels like a small human version of Christian repentance and conversion in the living change of heart; across those invisible lines of which George MacDonald spoke, a felt realignment of theoretic principles in the light of real felt human practice. And it is as though for the most part it has to be that way in this fallen world: mistakes, conventions, and prejudices first; only then reality in the second place, felt as such by its coming through like a powerful emotional corrective. What is more, the goodness is immanently inseparable from, deeply incarnate within, emotions which are felt at the time as if they were only those of distress or sorrow or humility. It is like the face of sorrowful feeling that Ruth sees upon a stone carving hidden away in a dark corner of a church:

> There was a half-open mouth, not in any way distorted out of its exquisite beauty by the intense expression of suffering it conveyed . . . the eyes looked onward and upward to the 'Hills from whence cometh our help'. And though the parted lips seemed ready to quiver with agony, yet the expression of the whole face, owing to these strange, stony, and yet spiritual eyes, was high and consoling. If mortal gaze had never sought its meaning before, in the deep shadow where it had been placed long centuries ago, yet Ruth's did now. Who could have imagined such a look? Who could have witnessed—perhaps felt—such infinite sorrow, and dared to lift it up by Faith into a peace so pure? (ch. 23)

This figure dares to show its face, as Ruth herself hardly can at the time: the faith it has in exposing its feelings is itself revealed within those feelings. Close to the spirit of Gothic admired by Ruskin in the second volume of *The Stones of Venice* (1853)—the anonymous individual worker putting his whole soul into some little piece of work that nobody save God might ever see—it is this religious apprehension in *Ruth* that makes life so intense, allowing nothing to be dismissed, emotionally, as merely ordinary. Where John Stuart Mill looked forward to a world of social justice and human happiness, there is something in this novel that, without seeking such things, needs individual human beings, once started, to go through their own sadness and pain, rather than avoid or reform them at some different level.

A modern reader may well regret this novel's remaining commitment to an acknowledgement of fallenness even after 1850—and on two counts. First, as a single mother, Ruth, though treated with sympathy, is not saved from shame or pain as a part of her experience.

When Ruth finally has to tell her boy the secret of his parentage, she says that one terrible thing is that the hard words people will use of her will be 'partly true' (ch. 27)—not wholly true, yet not wholly untrue; if now untrue, made so only because she herself has long since accepted whatever of painful truth there was in them. However much social stigmatizing is condemned as a cruelty which only hardens the heart of those it damns, the novel becomes increasingly more interested in Ruth herself than in social reform. It is offered as a complicated achievement that Ruth can say to her son, 'Never get confused by your love for me, into thinking that what I did was right' (ch. 27): there is something *other* than love in this novel, which love itself can acknowledge without perishing. Secondly moreover, the humane attempt made by the Bensons, to save Ruth and her innocent child from their neighbours' hardness by claiming she is a widow, is condemned even in its good intentions, and proves a failure besides when the truth finally leaks out.

These are apparently 'modern' objections to the residual strictness of the book and yet, as so often, they have their origin in the period itself. In the liberal *Westminster Review* (April 1853), G. H. Lewes had wanted the Bensons, instead of shielding Ruth, to have been more progressively defiant of outside opinion: 'what they could believe in for *themselves*, they could not believe in for *others*'. W. R. Greg, Unitarian opponent of the Calvinist God and friend of Mrs Gaskell, criticized *Ruth* in *The National Review* of January 1859, because its author had imagined a pure child-creature whose downfall was through no real fault of her own, only then to backtrack by affirming 'that the sin committed was of so deep a dye that only a life of atoning and enduring persistence could wipe it out'. Charlotte Brontë complained that to be redeemed Ruth should not have had to die in the end.

But when the Bensons lied about Ruth's situation and helped keep the boy's origins a secret even to himself, they effectively took John Stuart Mill's Utilitarian view, putting consequences before principles. For that was Mill's point—that people did not have to be consciously committed believers in Utilitarianism in order to do what was most useful; it was humanly natural to waive general principles when in particular cases they proved harmful, for the sake of a greater good that followed. It seems to go with so many changes of focus characteristic of this novel in particular and the Victorian novel in general.

And yet in retrospect Benson believes that in looking to consequences 'we have dreaded men too much, and God too little'. A different line should have been taken, a line closer, we might say, to those which were so hard drawn within the world of Charlotte Yonge. 'Formerly,' Benson goes on, 'if I believed that such or such an action was according to the will of God, I went and did it, or at least I tried to do it, without thinking of consequences. Now I reason and weigh what will happen if I do so and so—I grope where formerly I saw' (ch. 27). Now he has lost his clear instincts of conscience. For faith in this novel is not just a separate, higher part of life; it is a blind venture in this world, whose way becomes clear only in retrospect. The vision of life in this novel insists that finally, blindly, Ruth should work through the consequences of the whole of her story, rather than half-evasively begin a new one.

This is faith having at last to be true to itself as faith, regardless of where it might lead. 'If Ruth began low down to find her place in the world, at any rate there was no flaw in the foundation'—for now, once her past is revealed to all, her place is founded at least on the basis of the truth (ch. 28). It is the very spirit of the Hebraism of Bunyan's *Pilgrim's Progress* to which Mrs Gaskell refers: 'He that is low need fear no fall' (ch. 29). On that basis the thought that even to tell a lie finally does no good is raised into the greater belief that 'truth and goodness' are 'one and the same' (ch. 23).

So it proves, even as truths come to light which seem initially to offer neither goodness nor happiness. Mr Bradshaw not only finds out about Ruth, he also discovers a fraud perpetrated in his firm by his own son. Just as he vowed never to set foot again in Benson's house or chapel and will not go back upon his word in the name of dogged consistency, so Bradshaw virtually breaks himself in trying not to forgive his son—because 'I have not one standard for myself and those I love . . . and another for the rest of the world' (ch. 30).

What is more, Ruth has to develop her own kind of internal hardness. In contrast to the fate of Hardy's Tess of the d'Urbervilles who loses her baby and is pursued by her seducer until she must murder him, it is the remembrance of being a mother that saves Ruth from falling into the hands of her own seducer a second time, when he returns years later and desires her afresh. For the truth is that he is no longer simply a young lover, but the father of her child who deserted not just her but his own son. It is a moral difference of view that makes her *see* him differently, for the sake of the innocent child's protection, even while his voice recalls past feelings from which, she is shocked to find, she hardly wants to protect herself. When, moreover, Ruth has to tell her innocent son her guilty truth, the one thing that overcomes her last-minute fear is her sudden catching of his look of 'absolute terror' at the sight of her ominous delaying (ch. 27). That look makes her change into being the responsible mother again, responsible even for having to tell him what that mother has been and has done.

In the end, through her very disgrace, Ruth is at least free to devote herself to serving as a nurse, during a local epidemic of typhoid when help is needed from anyone who dare offer it. It is part of the book's law, first, that 'she did not talk about religion; but those who noticed her knew that it was the unseen banner which she was carrying'; and second, that the more she is now admired, the more 'she felt just as faulty—as far from being what she wanted to be, as ever' (ch. 30). But Ruth dies, as a result of nursing her former lover. Why so? asks the modern secular reader. Yet it is as though the whole of the book exists in the end for these last paragraphs, when Leonard, the bereft son, meets Bradshaw, the broken father, by the grave in the chapel-yard:

His face was swollen with weeping; but when he saw Mr Bradshaw he calmed himself, and checked his sobs, and, as an explanation of being where he was when thus surprised, he could find nothing to say but the simple words:
'My mother is dead, sir.'
His eyes sought Mr Bradshaw with a wild look of agony, as if to find comfort for that great loss in human sympathy; and at the first word—the first touch of Mr Bradshaw's hand on his shoulder—he burst out afresh. (ch. 36)

Bradshaw says, 'Let me take you home, my poor fellow' and for 'the first time, for years', he enters Benson's house with 'her son'. 'My mother is dead, sir' was not just a fact or an explanation. The words burst out, the eyes sought the man, according to the book's law of real need—for both parties.

That all this should come out of Ruth's seduction is not to say that this ending was simply its purpose or justification: the sequence is too long and subtly changing for that. Cause and effect, complained Carlyle in 'Signs of the Times', is becoming the only category under which we look at life. But in the very middle of the book, as in the very midst of life, it is said of the Bensons that if they could have seen the future, 'though they might have shrunk fearfully at first, they would have smiled and thanked God when all was done and said' (ch. 18). For those who believe in history, *Ruth* is a mid-century novel pulled between the tendencies of each half of the age. But for those who imagine believing as Mrs Gaskell does, *Ruth* is a vision of both religion and ordinary existence working upon each other in one life.

Where Mr Bradshaw 'drew a clear line of partition', *Ruth* is closer to Ruskin's account of 'naturalism', which refuses the presumption of pre-emptive selection:

It is only by the habit of representing faithfully all things, that we can truly learn what is beautiful, and what is not. The ugliest objects contain some element of beauty; and in all, it is an element peculiar to themselves, which cannot be separated from their ugliness, but must either be enjoyed together with it, or not at all. The more a painter accepts nature as he finds it, the more unexpected beauty he discovers in what he at first despised; but once let him arrogate the right of rejection, and he will gradually contract his circle of enjoyment, until what he supposes to be nobleness of selection ends in narrowness of perception. (*Modern Painters*, vol. 3 (1856), pt. 4, ch. 3, para. 15)

The art of pure idealism chooses the good and ignores evil; the art of degraded sensuality chooses evil and leaves the good. But sited steadfastly in between, realism is, in Mrs Gaskell as in Ruskin, implicitly religious: it is 'faithful' in not prematurely drawing lines but in taking good and evil, tough and tender together, thereby creating what is always 'unexpected'.

Such realism, be it avowedly religious or secular, finds good in the very heart of sorrow, value in the midst of degradation, and something religious in the terms of common life. But it does so most powerfully when it has weighed the fallen alternatives, so present in the portrayal of Philip in *The Heir of Redclyffe*: sorrow at the heart of good, degradation in the midst of value, psychological needs under cover of religion. Where it was without that test or balance, and thus without sufficient substance to its faith, the humanitarianism of the second half of the nineteenth century was to find nemesis in the reluctantly bleak testimony of the post-religious novels of Thomas Hardy.

4

Mind

In a predominantly physical and materialist age the danger, Thomas Carlyle warned, was that a people would not only adopt mechanical procedures of thought but come to believe that the mind itself was a machine. In 'Signs of the Times' (*The Edinburgh Review*, June 1829) Carlyle spoke of an insidiously growing assumption that 'to the inward world (if there be any) our only conceivable road is through the outward' and that 'what cannot be investigated and understood mechanically, cannot be investigated and understood at all'. The inner life was in danger of being denied its own real existence, dismissed as a place of merely subjective retreat.

To the French literary man Hippolyte Taine, mechanicalism was the English way. In his *Notes on England* (1871) Taine took the engineer George Stephenson as a brilliantly representative example of 'The English Mind'. Stephenson's mind resembled an inventor's workshop, in which he mentally fitted together various mechanical parts, piece by piece, until he arrived, by a process of trial and error, at a working combination. This was 'the very shape' of the English mind, in contrast to the more speculative and aesthetic French mentality. Concerned with building inductively upon facts and details, the English, said Taine, were characteristically practical rather than theoretical; they were devoted to utility rather than beauty, to improvised adjustment rather than thoroughgoing rational radicalism. 'In all that they do here they can make progress only by trial and error and groping their way: they learn their business, whatever it may be, by persistent attention to it, by work and sheer technical grind: they are purely empirical.'[1] For the empiricist, knowledge came solely

---

[1] *Notes on England* (1871), trans. W. F. Rae (1872), ch. 8.

from experience and experiment, and experience was conceived as predominantly the impression of the external world by means of the senses.

Symptomatically, the very meaning of the word 'materialism' was extended during the century. Materialism became a socio-economic term—to do with a concern with material needs to the neglect of spiritual matters—as much as a philosophical one—the belief that nothing exists except matter. The general power of materialism was established in Victorian England through four interconnected developments which served to fulfil Carlyle's nightmare. There was first of all, of course, the sheer driving force of the Industrial Revolution. There was also in the socio-political realm the quintessentially practical theory of Utilitarianism which aggressively sought to clarify the complexity of human mind in terms of a calculation of its basic drives in seeking pleasure and avoiding pain. Under Utilitarianism the self was characterized in terms of a fundamental self-interest which was to be engineered towards the general benefit by the corrective use of reward and punishment through the agencies of institutionalized law and social approbation. Thirdly, the Scientific Revolution offered a view of Nature as a single vast mechanism, of which the engine was the blind processes of Darwinian evolution. Finally, the established psychological theory of associationism offered a model of the human mind as an inner product of repeated outward impressions combined within a passive memory. This materialist theory of mentality was further strengthened by mid-century biologists and physiologists, for whom mind and its inner experience was often no more than the result of molecular changes in the working of the brain. It is not that we are *not* automata, it is simply that we are *conscious* automata, insisted T. H. Huxley at his most extreme. The feeling of free, conscious volition that we believe initiates an action, he argued, really only *accompanies* it, like 'the steam whistle which signals but does not cause the starting of the locomotive' ('On the Hypothesis that Animals are Automata', 1874).

By the end of the century, F. W. H. Myers was left arguing that just as in the 1830s, 1840s, and 1850s 'the old orthodoxy of religion' might have seemed 'too narrow to contain men's knowledge' so in turn by the 1870s and 1880s 'the new orthodoxy of materialistic science' was now 'too narrow to contain their feelings and aspirations'. Thus, 'just as the fabric of religious orthodoxy used to be strained in order to admit the discoveries of geology or astronomy, so now also the obvious deductions of materialistic science are strained or overpassed in order to give sanction to feelings and aspirations which it is found impossible to ignore' (*Phantasms of the Living* (1886), introduction). What is 'soul' that is not just mind? What is 'mind' that is more than brain? As so often in Victorian England, the categories, the very distinctions between them, were up for grabs. 'The unity of our first instinctive faith has been broken', concluded the philosopher Edward Caird in 'The Problem of Philosophy at the Present Time' (1881; reprinted in his *Essays on Literature*, 1892). The age of simple unconsciousness was long past, said Caird, and in its place educated men stood now in ever-increasing need of strenuous acts of conscious rethinking: 'Bacon said that in the last period of ancient civilization philosophy took the place of religion, and the same is to some extent true now'.

Hence George MacDonald's portrait in *Wilfrid Cumbermede* (1872), of Charley, the doubting son of a stern Evangelical father, who, characteristically of his generation, can accept nothing on trust or at second-hand: 'The more likely a thing looked to be true, the more anxious was he that it should be unassailable; and his fertile mind would in as many moments throw a score of objections at it, looking after each with eager eyes as if pleading for a refutation. It was the very love of what was good that generated in him doubt and anxiety' (ch. 21). Turning round upon himself, Charley dare not even *wish* to believe, lest 'for what I know, that might be to wish to be deceived'. But a friend says to him that perhaps it would be better to be deceived and never find out that religion was a fiction. To which Charley cries fiercely: 'Never to find out would be the hell of all hells' (ch. 35). If religion is no more than mere psychology—the unconscious projection of his own needs—then it is the last remnant of a true religious impulse in him that itself will reject such religion. Whereas earlier ages had been marked by bitter feuds between opposing camps, single-minded and wholehearted in their fundamental opposition to each other, the characteristic thinkers of the nineteenth century, argued A. N. Whitehead in *Science and the Modern World* (1926, ch. 5), were in two minds, divided not so much against each other as within *themselves*. 'Unhappy Consciousness' was the name Hegel gave in the *Phenomenology of Mind* (1807) for the mind which has become aware of its own divisions and was only held together by that tense awareness.

If not instinct, then reflection; if not religion, then philosophy. Yet those who turned to philosophy did so only to find no clear uniformity amongst the philosophers. There was rather what the Idealist philosopher J. F. Ferrier (1808–64) described as a series of incongruous contests without the possibility of a common resolution:

> All the captains are sailing on different tacks, under different orders, and under different winds; and each is railing at the others because they will not keep the same course with himself. There is not a single controversy in philosophy in which the antagonists are playing at the same game. The one man is playing at chess, his adversary is playing against him at billiards; and whenever a victory is achieved, it is always such a victory as a billiard-player might be supposed to gain over a chess-player, or such a defeat as a billiard-player might be supposed to sustain at the hands of a chess-player. (*Institutes of Metaphysics* (1854), introduction, para. 15)

There was no one game or agreed set of rules, in a century in which, even so, pluralism seemed vertiginously painful and utterly paradoxical. The very boundaries—between sensation and cognition, man and animal, male and female, civilized and primitive, character and environment—were ever-shifting sites of controversy. In this Babel of voices, each language—of the Utilitarian or the Idealist, of the body or of the mind, of individual freedom or social determinism—was in danger of offering a synthesis of the others only by translating them into its own terms.

Yet symptomatically the Metaphysical Society, which brought together so much of the whole range of thought and belief in Victorian England, managed to maintain itself powerfully for ten years from 1869. Including in its midst Utilitarians, Positivists, Unitarians, Anglicans, Catholics, agnostics, scientists, politicians, and poets, it numbered amongst its members figures as distinguished and distinct as Prime Minister Gladstone, Christian Socialist F. D. Maurice, the Catholic Archbishop Manning, scientists Huxley and John Tyndall, the Comtean Frederic Harrison, the Unitarian James Martineau, and literary figures as various as Tennyson, Ruskin, R. H. Hutton,

Walter Bagehot, J. A. Froude, John Morley, A. P. Stanley, and the brothers James Fitzjames and Leslie Stephen. For all the symptomatic irresolvability of the debates, the meetings of this society symbolized the broad Victorian commitment to philosophy—to philosophy not as a wholly professionalized specialism but as the common meeting ground for urgent articulation of the final implications of the age's intellectual diversity.

But, as many commentators recognized, the philosophic conflict of beliefs and ideas was no more and no less than a formalization of a process going on, less consciously, within the very structure of the modern world itself. Thus, for example, in an essay on 'Religious Uncertainty' (reprinted in his *Aspects of Religious and Scientific Thought*, 1899), R. H. Hutton noted how the specialized division of labour in the modern world meant that a large part of the permanent mind of good people—the mathematician, the scientist, the economist, the geographer, the musician, and above all the practical wage earner—had become quite normally absorbed in new secular concerns, interests, and necessities. These were demanding activities which simply consumed most of the energy devoted in earlier ages, Hutton claimed, to the ultimate spiritual issues of time and eternity. 'The world of finite interests and objects', Edward Caird likewise concluded, 'has rounded itself, as it were, into a separate world, within which the mind of man can fortify itself.' The fullness, variety, and rapidity of such a world meant that, without premeditation or design, the individual in the middle of things could unconsciously forget questions of beginning and end and find instead, said Caird, 'ample occupation for his existence, without ever feeling the need of any return upon himself, or seeing any reason to ask himself whether this endless striving has any meaning or object beyond itself' ('The Problem of Philosophy at the Present Time'). There are now, claimed the Cambridge philosopher Henry Sidgwick in 1864, more 'symmetrical people' than there have ever been—people who 'seem so really fitted for this world as it is' and 'live to the full, the natural life, and never seem to wish for more'. There remains only death to frighten them.[2]

---

[2] Cited in Frank Miller Turner, *Between Science and Religion* (Yale University Press, 1974), 42, to which I am generally indebted.

Against the background of a socially pragmatic and unphilosophic drift towards modern secularization, this chapter concerns psychology—defined broadly as the study of the human mind—and the more or less conscious frameworks of thought and models of self which, outside formal theology, were available to intellectual life within the period. In particular, it treats of the vision and scope of human life implicit within both the formalized and informal philosophies of the time, and the fate of tacit thoughts or inner needs that did not fit easily into the dominant materialistic structures. Though expressed in abstract terms, this is not an abstract matter: at the very least, what people thought their minds could do affected the very nature of their thinking. Section I begins with the materialistic frameworks of thinking and the modifications that went on inside them.

I. 'The New Psychology': Psychology as a Branch of Science

It is extraordinary that so much of the physiological science of mind in the nineteenth century originates from phrenology, the study of bumps on the outside of the human head.

Developed by the Austrian anatomist Franz Joseph Gall (1758–1826) and his disciple J. G. Spurzheim, phrenology had three basic principles: that the brain was the organ of the mind; that it was itself composed of more than thirty particular and independent organs, like multiple mini-brains, each of which served separately to provide task-specific functions and emotions; and that by natural endowment the size of the different parts of the brain, assessed through examination of the cranium, determined the relative power of their different faculties. Instead of an artificial list of separate abstract personifications introspectively drawn up by philosophers of the mind (the so-called faculties of free will, memory, instinct, etc.), phrenology claimed to offer specifically locatable cerebral functions.

Included amongst those who took an interest in what was a vastly popular pseudo-science were no lesser figures than George Eliot and Harriet Martineau. The serious appeal of phrenology lay in the possibility it offered the mind of turning itself inside out and thereby laying objective hold upon itself. Speaking autobiographically,

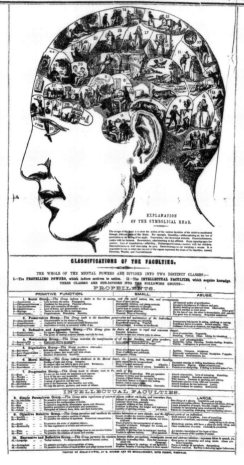

Fig. 6.　Multiple mini-brains and the world within: the classification of the mind's faculties in F. Bridges, 'Symbolical Chart of Phrenology', c.1848.

George Combe (1788–1858), the principal proponent of phrenology in Britain, described what mental mapping could do for what had previously seemed blindly subjective dilemmas:

I can well recollect the painful conflicts which I experienced in my own childhood and the difficulty which I felt in determining which feeling was right. For example: Having a large Self-esteem, and tolerably good Combativeness and Destructiveness, I was easily offended, and I often burned to gratify my feelings of revenge; but Benevolence and Conscientiousness would whisper that this was wrong. I felt instinctively the opposition between these feelings, but I knew not their relative values. . . . Phrenology conferred on me the first internal peace of mind that I experienced.[3]

From the midst of confusion there was a deep Victorian impulse first to map the objective existence of separate faculties and separate disciplines, and then to find some way of locating the bounds within which each came appropriately into play. With Combe, although the underlying dispositions were physiologically innate, an understanding of their relative strength offered the possibility of genuine self-help, particularly when the gratification sought by one sentiment threatened the bounds of another. One could seek to arbitrate over the organization, compensating for weaker dispositions and modifying stronger ones. This was ever the crucial mitigating factor within Victorian materialism: namely, the possibility of mind, thus conscious of its own brain, being able on the basis of that very consciousness to override or rebalance its inherent structuring. The pre-Darwinian belief in the active role of the *will* in the adaptation of species, favoured by the French naturalist Lamarck, remained residually strong throughout the century.

Phrenological doctrine also held that the mind had two symmetrical hemispheres. This seemed to offer the possibility that one side of the brain could act as sentinel and security for the other. A different variation was envisaged by Hewett Watson, writing in 1836 in the *Phrenological Journal* of which he was to become editor: contemplating the coexistence of one's own ideas or feelings *and* the

---

[3] 'An Address Delivered at the Anniversary of Spurzheim' (1840). See the valuable anthology of psychological texts 1838–90, Jenny Bourne Taylor and Sally Shuttleworth (eds.), *Embodied Selves* (Oxford University Press, 1998), 42. I am also indebted to Rick Rylance, *Psychological Theory and British Culture 1850–1880* (Clarendon Press, 2000).

presumed wishes or ideas of others, he argued that each impulse was centered in a different half of the brain, creating the possibility of conflict or cooperation between them. Yet the degree of possible asymmetrical independence available to either of the two halves also had pathological implications. Works such as R. L. Stevenson's classic account of extreme duality, *The Strange Case of Dr. Jekyll and Mr. Hyde* (1886), imaginatively explored the implications: 'if I could rightly be said to be either, it was only because I was radically both'. In Tennyson's 'Cephalis', there is the extraordinary idea

> I have got two wives, both fair, and they dwell with me under a dome
> .   .   .   .
> One lives in a room to the left and one in a room to the right,
>   And I sit between them and hear them call to me day and night.

It was not clear exactly how the two hemispheres interrelated or whether a third force, such as intelligent free will, could act as an overriding commander. But a common image throughout the century was that of a piano-player trying to get the skill of both right and left hand working independently and yet in synchronization.

The surgeon Sir William Lawrence (1783–1867) compared Gall and Spurzheim to the old man in the fable who assured his sons, on his deathbed, that a treasure was hidden in his vineyard. They began immediately to dig over the whole ground in search of it, but found no treasure at all. Yet the loosening of the soil, the destruction of the weeds, the admission of light and air, were so beneficial to the vines, that the quality and excellence of the ensuing crop were unprecedented. Their treasure was not miraculous but entirely natural: this was a parable of scientific secularization.

The natural treasure buried in phrenology and harvested in the second half of the century was summarized by G. H. Lewes in his *Biographical History of Philosophy* (1845–6): Gall had taken the problem of mental functions out of its traditional place in the abstract realms of metaphysics and philosophy and re-established it within the world of physical science, in biology and physiology. Thus the theory of brain as the organ of mind and the theory of the cerebral localization of mental functions within the two hemispheres bore riches in the middle years of the century—but only once the examination of the brain was undertaken not via the skull, but directly and internally through neurological research and brain dissection. These are the first steps towards modern neuroscience and the location of particular parts of our humanness in particular cortexes of the brain.

Sensory-motor analysis, for example, revealed two distinct sets of nerves—one for sensation, the other for movement—located in the automatic reflexes of the spinal nerve roots. Analogous reflex functions in the brain itself, as if it were a developed continuation of the spinal cord, were noted by Thomas Laycock (1812–76) and named by William Benjamin Carpenter (1813–85) as 'unconscious cerebration'. A form of 'thinking' was arising from within the body itself. By mid-century the physicians Henry Holland (1788–1843) and A. L.Wigan (1785–1847) were arguing a scientific case for 'the double brain' or even a 'duality of mind' on the basis of the two hemispheres: hence the possibility of divisions even to the point of madness. The way was paved for a more humane and scientific understanding of the insane in the latter half of the century. Amidst a wide variety of research and hypothesis, 'The New Psychology', declared *The Fortnightly Review*, 'may be summed up in one word—the study of biology' (September 1879). A number of new medical journals specializing in mental science were part of this development, including the *Journal of Psychological Medicine and Mental Pathology* (1848) which was the first British journal devoted to psychiatry, *Asylum Journal* (1853) becoming the *Journal of Mental Science* (1858), and finally, above all, *Brain* (1878) edited by the leading British neurologists David Ferrier (1843–1928) and John Hughlings Jackson (1835–1911). It is characteristic of the story here recounted that at the beginning of his career in 1859, when first a lecturer in pathology at London Hospital Medical College, Hughlings Jackson considered abandoning medicine to study philosophy—as if those were the two major alternatives for a thinker about mind. He chose medicine.

In the first series of *Problems of Life and Mind: The Foundations of a Creed* (2 vols., 1874–5), G. H. Lewes summarized the shock of the revolutionary change:

Who that had ever looked upon the pulpy mass of brain substance, and the nervous cords connecting it with the organs, could resist the shock of incredulity on hearing that all he knew of passion, intellect, and will was nothing more than molecular change in this pulpy mass? Who that had ever seen a nerve-cell could be patient on being told that Thought was a property of such cells, as Gravitation was a property of Matter? (vol. 1, p. 128)

Yet there was a mitigating factor within what otherwise might have looked like the dehumanizing story of biological determinism. For however much with evolutionists such as Lewes and Herbert Spencer, mind was reduced to the workings of material nature, that material nature in which mind was immersed was itself conceived as containing vitalist signs of mentality in the first place. Crucially, to Lewes, the brain was not the sole but only the most important organ of mind, for the body itself had many other cellular and nervous centres of sensation and volition which were nascent forms of thought and consciousness. The brain is the commander-in-chief of the whole army but if it be killed, the army has still its substitute generals and colonels, even its corporals to take charge of life: 'a part of an organ may be destroyed without the function of the organ disappearing' (*The Physiology of Common Life*, 2 vols. (1859–60), vol. 2, p. 428). The cells can of themselves regroup.

In *The Foundations of a Creed* Lewes argued that in science the role of explanation is necessarily limited. We have no knowledge of anything but phenomena, as registered by the experience of the senses. Nor do we know the separate essence of any fact or object as it is in itself; we only know it *relative* to other facts and objects in the way of succession or similitude. Science is thus concerned with the laws of sequences, with the constant relations of antecedents to consequents, but not with any further causal explanations as to *why* those sequences take place. It only knows *how*. Science is post-metaphysical.

Influenced by the seventeenth-century Dutch philosopher Spinoza, Lewes offered a vision of Nature as one whole living process in which nothing was truly separate. Thus, said Lewes, 'in cause and effect there are not two things, one preceding the other, but two aspects of one phenomenon successively viewed'. Metaphysical philosophy only taught us to step out of time and 'personify the distinction': to make 'cause' something static, different, and apart from 'effect', 'creating the effect by a mysterious legerdemain' (*The Foundations of a Creed*, vol. 2, p. 362). That creation of an atemporal mystery Lewes calls 'fetishism'. Thus, myself as distinct from my thoughts and sensations, or the substance of things-in-themselves separate from their attributes and relations, or the forces and causes supposedly behind the ongoing sequence of events—all these so-called essences were either unknowable or non-existent. They were like the creation of God according to Feuerbach: the projection of a mysterious, false, and static objectification.

This was the empirical attitude of secular translation shared by John Stuart Mill and the whole group of progressive writers associated with *The Westminster Review*, which Marian Evans (later George Eliot) effectively edited after Mill. Lewes encouraged Marian Evans to render into English the work of Feuerbach and Spinoza, even as they were beginning their common-law partnership. It was that work which enabled George Eliot to summarize the secular rationalist position as a radical modern translation from the old language of mysterious metaphysical entities. 'The language of all peoples soon attains to the expressions *all, universal, necessary*', she wrote, yet this serves only 'to isolate such expressions, to operate within them apart from experience, to exalt their relative value into an absolute value'.[4] Hippocrates, said Lewes, was a true scientist when long ago he saw 'mental maladies' as related to 'abnormal brain-action' rather than absolute sin: 'But during the reign of theologians and metaphysicians this scientific standpoint was deserted, and mental maladies passed from the hands of physicians into the hands of priests: exorcism and prayers took the place of hygiene and prescriptions' (*Study of Psychology*, ch. 1).

In this George Henry Lewes was a follower of the Positive philosophy of the French thinker Auguste Comte (1798–1857). Comte's *Cours de Philosophie positive*, an abridgement of which was translated into English by Harriet Martineau in 1853, was founded on two major ideas. The first was that of the Three Chronological Stages in the developing demystification of human thought: initially, the Theological Stage, where God or gods provided the language of ultimate explanation; then the Metaphysical, in which supernatural

<hr>

[4] 'The Future of German Philosophy', *The Leader* (28 July 1855), repr. in *Essays of George Eliot*, ed. Thomas Pinney (Routledge and Kegan Paul, 1963), 148–53.

powers were replaced by the language of abstract forces; and finally the Positive (or Scientific) viewpoint which dismisses the absolute mysteries of origin and end in the universe and confines itself to the narrative sequence of scientific laws discoverable in the midst of this world. At this point it becomes clear that men and women are not abstract or universal but historical beings, the product first of their biological conditions and then of the social conditions interacting with them. If time was the medium for the evolution of biological life, history was the equivalent for man's social life. Once morality lost the authority of God and the rewards of the afterlife, it became a series of psychological, social, and political problems.

But to Comte the nineteenth century was stalled anachronistically in a transitional state of mental incoherence, because those three incompatible frameworks of mind were still locked into existence at one and the same time. Hence Comte's second great idea was to accelerate the progress towards modern mental coherence by an encyclopaedic system of education. Students were not just taken through a range of arbitrarily divided specialized subjects, each with its own rationale, but through a comprehensive account of the development of each subject out of the one preceding it, and founding the one to follow. 'Sociology', the study of humans in society, was to be the culminating and most complex science. Then, over all, there was to be a new class of meta-scientists concerning themselves with the present state of each of the sciences, discovering their interrelations, and reducing their particular principles to a lesser number of common generalizations.

As with the work of Herbert Spencer in England, the Comtean Course thus descended sequentially—from the simple overall generality of astronomy, to physics, to chemistry, to biology, down finally to the final complications of human sociology—in a way that replicated in the individual mind the successive universal story of the unfolding, evolutionary logic of human thought. By creating a clear sense of the progress into modern consciousness, the course was to remove the experience of dislocation which individuals suffer when the old framework within which they think and feel seems somehow no longer to *fit* with what was going on in the modern world around them.

As John Stuart Mill indicated in *Auguste Comte and Positivism*

(1865), this attempt at a single grand system of thought, in place of an incompatible diversity of individual points of view, had social as well as intellectual ambitions. To combat both the individualistic muddle and the specialized division of labour in the nineteenth century, Comte believed that the more that thoughts fitted into one whole rationally agreed framework, the more the individuals who held them might fit into a genuinely uniform society.

Mill shared Comte's fascination with the unconscious history of ideas—in particular, ideas which survived as though they were intuitively natural and foundational only because their origin was not remembered by those who inherited them as part of their make-up. To Mill, these sacramental catchwords, such as the so-called 'laws of nature', disguised the working of material self-interest in history; they created an anachronistic language that prevented thought just when it seemed to be expressing it. Assumptions about women's permanent 'nature', for example, hampered their future development. Yet much as Mill, like Lewes, embraced the positivist commitment to a post-theological, post-metaphysical age of empirical realism, the Mill of *On Liberty* (1859) had to part company with Comte's systematization. Mill's liberalism insisted on the necessity of personal freedom and individual diversity in an age of mass society. He admitted that the liberal belief in the individual's freedom to hold and express any creed, could not itself *be* a creed but only a second-order social doctrine. Yet Mill prized variety not simply out of English pragmatism, but because he believed pluralism offered the maximum opportunities for the open-ended development of a future world. He wanted room left for individual manoeuvre, free from both modern systematization and the old-world refusal of any alternative between duty and sin.

Comte offered his own revisions of his position. For him, the scientific materialism of the *Philosophie positive* had been the engine of change. It had reversed the tendency of the theological and metaphysical systems to explain the external world in terms of human feelings, by explaining man in terms of the external world. Yet the sign of true rational emancipation was not to hate the mistakes of the past but to redeem them. Thus, the new level of consciousness released by a course in Positivism had, in turn, to break free of the course that had led to it. The next human task was to rise above materialism and find some room in the world for what in the past had been humanity's higher considerations. Accordingly Comte's *Philosophie positive*, translated by Harriet Martineau in 1853, was succeeded by his *Politique positive*, translated by J. H. Bridges in 1865. In the latter the feelings, ousted by intellect from their central role in the universe, had now to seek from the intellect a role for themselves in a new ordering that went beyond materialism. Thus, now that the material world was safely established through the self-preserving efforts of the males, the females as the traditional guardians of feeling would spread private emotions into the public sphere. A new poetry was to show the people how emotionally to inhabit what philosophy had laid bare at the level of idea. There was to be a new religion in celebratory defence of common humanity. Whereas syntheses in the sciences were the inevitable result of logic, human beings were to be held together as the result of freely chosen sympathy and love: 'In other organisms the parts have no existence when severed from the whole; but this, the greatest of all organisms, is made up of lives which can really be separated' (*A General View of Positivism* trans. J. H. Bridges (1865), ch. 6). The very word 'altruism' was coined by Comte.

The supporters of the *Philosophie positive* went one way, usually with Mill and the Utilitarians. The more emotional and vitalist followers of the *Politique positive* belonged to the ambience surrounding George Eliot and took a different route. For this latter group, Comte's later work offered a shift from the blankness of scientific explanation to the religion of an altruistic, collective, creative humanity. It was that utopia which George Eliot in turn taught Lewes to value—not indeed as a formal philosophy, since its weaknesses were apparent—but as a vision of the development of wholly new human emotions, through which to create the future.

But in likewise modifying a basically materialist philosophy John Stuart Mill took a different route from Comte. The really substantial division in the mid-nineteenth century was pointed out by Mill himself in his essay 'Coleridge' (1840): 'Coleridge used to say that every one is born either a Platonist or an Aristotelian: it may be similarly affirmed, that every Englishman of the present day is by implication either a Benthamite or a Coleridgean' (*Collected Works*, vol. 10, p. 121). James Mill had made sure that his son, John Stuart, was born an Aristotelian in the form of a Benthamite Utilitarian. But the alternative to this scientific and socio-political mindset lay in a rival transcendental tradition—in the countervailing effort made by the heirs of the Idealist Coleridge to reclaim psychology for philosophy. That the younger Mill felt the need to take cognizance of that alternative made his personal and intellectual history deeply symptomatic of the needs of the age. It is to that anti-materialist alternative that we now turn.

II. 'Psychology is pre-eminently a *philosophical* science'[5]

In retrospect, the great Victorian crisis concerning the very frameworks of mental understanding was most powerfully represented in the extremity of John Stuart Mill's secret breakdown in 1826, aged 20. It seemed the breakdown of the Benthamite mind itself:

> It occurred to me to put the question directly to myself, 'Suppose that all your objects in life were realized; that all the changes in institutions and opinions which you are looking forward to, could be completely effected at this very instant: would this be a great joy and happiness to you?' And an irrepressible self-consciousness distinctly answered, 'No!' At this my heart sank within me: the whole foundation on which my life was constructed feel down. All my happiness was to have been found in the continual pursuit of this end. The end had ceased to charm, and how could there ever again be any interest in the means? I seemed to have nothing left to live for. (*Autobiography* (1873), ch. 5)

So much of the very shape of Mill's thinking had been based upon linear sequence: laws were no more than knowledge of the constant, predictable sequences of certain phenomena; progress consisted in the forward march of time as a result of using that knowledge to follow the logic of rational modifications. Now suddenly, as by a question that took Mill out of linear time, the 'end' itself had already ended, 'ceased' prematurely. The life of the radical social reformer had previously consisted in unconsciously 'placing my happiness in

---

[5] Sir William Hamilton, *Lectures on Metaphysics and Logic*, 4 vols. (Edinburgh, 1859–60), vol. 1, lecture 3.

something durable and distant, in which some progress might be always making, while it could never be exhausted by complete attainment'. But now by a single inadmissible thought, the framework had broken down and Mill in his intellectual integrity had broken down with it. Left hanging depressively in the unshaped middle of things, Mill was stranded within an abandoned life that was no longer philosophic and purposive but psychological and lonely. Benthamism was essentially a social programme: without the public mission, the person seemed to be nothing in himself, since Benthamism itself left nothing in the realm of the personal.

When later, in 1838, Mill came to write his essay on Bentham, he noted that the most disturbing aspect of the case was that when Bentham was wrong it was not because the Utilitarian considerations he urged were of themselves demonstrably not rational and valid, 'but because some more important principle, which he did not perceive, supersedes those considerations, and turns the scale'. That was what Carlyle called 'the completeness of limited men' to which all men were frighteningly liable.

That was why Mill needed Coleridge: to remind the Bentham in him of the aspect his thoughts presented to a mind opposite to his own, and to offer another sense of meaning which might serve as challenge and modification. In the most important philosophical controversies, one observer sees one thing, a second sees another, and often, said Mill, both sides are right in what they affirm and wrong in what they deny. The excess of one half-truth in one direction creates a corresponding reaction of the other half-truth in another. What Mill sought in 'Coleridge' was to halt the history of mutually damaging exaggeration that beset these dialectical splits. He wanted, instead, to bring the half-truths together in his own mind, 'like mutually checking powers in a political constitution', and out of this dialogue between two persons in one head create within himself a new synthetic combination of mental person which he could then become. That was how the philosophical mind could overcome the limitedness of the personal mind.

The empirical assumption here was that a philosophic whole could always be made out of the combination and recombination of different parts; the liberal assumption that went with it was that whatever was partly true in one camp could be assimilated into the terms of the opposing camp, thereby transforming both. Empiricist philosophy insisted that all knowledge arises from induction, by generalizing from the observation of particulars. To Bentham complexity itself was no more than a combination of simple elements. For the purpose of analysis the complex wholes of human society and human mind could thus be broken down into the sum of their parts. Even our senses, argued Mill, were not adapted by nature to let in perception of a whole object all at once, but only one attribute at a time, in rapid succession. The mind was an essentially serial process. It was only by the laws of repeated association that the rapid succession of parts became condensed into the impression of a whole.

Associationism was a physical and passive theory of mind developed from Locke and Hume by David Hartley in the mid-eighteenth century and further refined by the late eighteenth-century Edinburgh philosophers Dugald Stewart and Thomas Brown. It described a mechanism by which one thought automatically called up another close to it, on the basis of the impressions left in the mind by the force of external events working upon the senses. Establishing physical channels along the nerves and brain, the memory of sensory experience would set going a train of thought as of its own accord. These connections might be chronological, following a recalled order of events, or might be spatial, when grouped according to degrees of similarity, but in any case the mind was at its most rational when the order of thoughts within consciousness corresponded to the ordering of events in the external world. As Mill puts it in a paraphrase of *Analysis of the Phenomena of the Human Mind* (1829) by his father, James Mill:

When two phaenomena have been very often experienced in conjunction, and have not, in any single instance, occurred separately either in experience or in thought, there is produced between them what has been called Inseparable, or less correctly, Indissoluble Association. (*An Examination of Sir William Hamilton's Philosophy* (1865), ch. 11)

What John Stuart Mill in his *System of Logic* called the Law of Obliviscence followed upon that sense of automatic amalgamation: when a number of ideas suggest one another by association with such certainty and rapidity as to coalesce together in a group, then the separate parts have a tendency to drop out of consciousness and become unconscious or forgotten links. Association proceeded by passive memory without the necessity of conscious, voluntary recollection.

In his *Lectures on the Philosophy of the Human Mind* (1820) Thomas Brown crucially extended the range of associationism by adding that the connections might be emotional and psychological as well as temporal, spatial, and logical. Moreover, the sequences of association were susceptible both to checks and to creative transformation by a later, more active intervention of mind. Mill found modified support for this refinement in Alexander Bain, the founder in 1876 of *Mind*, the first specialist psychological journal ever produced in any country. In Bain's highly influential *The Senses and the Intellect* (1855), and *The Emotions and the Will* (1859), associationism was given the hard-wiring of the nervous system as its organic support. Bain recognized that minds of sufficient motor energy were not content to remain within their old paths of repeated association or the fixed channels of their habitual organization, but, as Herbert Spencer and G. H. Lewes also argued, sought to cut new pathways and make new links and shapes of thought in the brain, through fresh metaphorical connections or more complex syntactical formulations.

Nonetheless, after his breakdown, Mill himself merely patched up his ruined mental framework. He had bravely acknowledged that Coleridge and Wordsworth stood for a range and depth of cultural human meaning—historical, social, personal, emotional, artistic— which Bentham in his concentration upon the single principle of self-interest had omitted. But he still believed that what Wordsworth and Coleridge stood for could be added onto the Benthamite framework, as fresh associations and new pathways, without making a fundamental political or philosophical difference. Thus Mill did not abolish the Benthamite principle that pleasure was the primary good but only grafted onto it a distinction between 'higher' and 'lower' pleasures. He still resisted as untrue any theory of knowledge and the human mind that could fundamentally threaten his empiricist philosophy. Ironically, he thereby rejected the epistemology that Coleridge himself derived from Kant.

In chapter 9 of *Biographia Literaria* (1817) Coleridge had argued that we are not merely passive sense-instruments but actively carry into the world with us antecedent frameworks, categories such as consciousness of time and of space, which, like mental spectacles, enable us to bring the world to focal life, as 'phenomena' relative to ourselves. But we can no more separately see what we bring to the world than we can see what the world of objects would be like in themselves ('noumena') without us. This was the Kantian 'a priori'— or Idealist or intuitionalist—philosophy, consisting of those innate anterior forms of human consciousness claimed as necessary to the very existence of the world of experience. These forms or frameworks were precisely what factual and empirical realists such as Mill, Lewes, W. K. Clifford, and Huxley rejected as metaphysical abstractions.

After Coleridge there was a second wave of mid-century Idealism which John Stuart Mill himself still felt obliged to challenge in the philosophy of Sir William Hamilton (1788–1856). As professor of logic and metaphysics at Edinburgh University, Hamilton took consciousness out of its place as a product of the associationist world of his predecessors, Thomas Brown and Dugald Stewart, and into the constructive role it possessed within German Idealism.

For Hamilton the condition for the beginning of intelligence is *difference*. The simplest act of perception begins with an irresistible conviction of two facts: that I am, and that something different from me exists. This antithesis, between the ego on the one hand and the external world of the non-ego on the other, may be experienced as a form of opposition or dualism. But truly, argues Hamilton, it is not that the one precedes and opposes the other, but that the two, subject and object, are created *together* at the same time in the self-same act of perceiving their very difference: 'The two terms of correlation stand in mutual counterpoise and equal independence; they are given as connected in the synthesis of knowledge, but as contrasted in the antithesis of existence' ('Philosophy of the Unconditioned', *The Edinburgh Review* (October 1829)). There is, behind the narrow, isolated ego which seems to exist over and against the outside world, a wider and more foundational form of consciousness in the human self which offers a complex unity of existence. This 'a priori' or 'universal' consciousness cannot point to itself, cannot be seen.

But it can be deduced relative to, and invisibly implicit in, the act of knowledge of self *and* other that it makes possible. It is a tacit third presence, and it makes a difference.

For if on the one hand a human being is no more than an individual object among many other such objects in the world, he is also capable of regarding all objects, himself included, in relation to a whole to which they belong. Idealist philosophy begins, as Mill's empiricism does not, from this sense of a prior whole.

What is at stake here, in human terms? For the philosophically experimental poet Tennyson, in empiricist mood, the growth of self-consciousness in a child was precisely linked to its loss of a primordial sense of undivided being. The baby has never yet thought that 'this is I', has never paid attention to its own mental states *as* its own:

> But as he grows he gathers much,
>   And learns the use of 'I' and 'me',
>   And finds 'I am not what I see,
> And other than the things I touch.'
>
> So rounds he to a separate mind
>   From whence clear memory may begin,
>   As thro' the frame that binds him in
> His isolation grows defined.

(In Memoriam 45)

The birth of consciousness was, wrote Tennyson here, like a 'second birth of Death'. The very creation of identity seemed both a separating and a narrowing, a sad fallen realization of the breaking of a link. But for the Idealist such as Hamilton there is something more within the creation of the personal self than loss, loneliness, and the fracturing of the universe of experience into the antithesis between self and others. *In Memoriam* was in search of that something more.

There is still, say the Idealists, a tacit universal consciousness in each person, a more-than-egoistic consciousness which is involved in the very existence of our world. In a contribution to *Essays in Philosophical Criticism* edited by Andrew Seth and R. B. Haldane in 1883, the Idealist T. B. Kilpatrick argued that nineteenth-century pessimism—beginning with the philosophy of Schopenhauer and ending in the writings of Thomas Hardy—was the inevitable result of confining consciousness to the merely personal self. For the Idealist, consciousness is not merely self-consciousness and not just a passive product of existence: there is something irreducibly mysterious and creative about its the way it comes into being. Thus Hamilton on the workings of the mind:

I do not hesitate to maintain, that what we are conscious of is constructed out of what we are not conscious of—that our whole knowledge, in fact, is made up of the unknown and the incognisable. (*Lectures on Metaphysics and Logic*, 4 vols. (1859–60), vol. 1, lecture 18)

There is always something latently beyond or beneath our knowledge that paradoxically makes our very knowledge possible—movements of mind too swift, deep, or implicit to be detected, 'but which manifest their existence indirectly through the medium of their effects' (lecture 18). The conscious mind begins to discover the concepts that it has unconsciously brought with itself, only in the very act of using them. It makes assumptions, it takes leaps, without being aware of what is behind those assumptions or between those leaps. Consciousness is not separate from the unconscious; rather, it arises out of the unconscious, exists precisely by realizing that, and cannot operate without the unconscious as its enabling background.

In a series of articles in *Blackwood's Magazine* (1838–9), one of Hamilton's pupils, J. F. Ferrier, made it clear that, for all the attempts of the physiologists, the mind could never be to itself a mere object of scientific enquiry:

I can attribute no consciousness to this object. The consciousness is in myself. But suppose I vest myself in this object. I thus identify myself with mind, and realize consciousness as a fact of mind, but in the meantime what becomes of mind as an object? It has vanished in the process. . . . What can mind become an object to? Not to me, for I am it. (*Blackwood's Magazine*, February 1838)

We divest mind of its vital characteristic of consciousness, in order to view it as an object; if we try to put that consciousness back in, then like some strange object out of *Alice in Wonderland*, it becomes us or we become it again. We cannot know ourselves.

In his massive *Examination of Sir William Hamilton's Philosophy* (1865), John Stuart Mill at his most Positivist sought finally to destroy the threat of what he took to be this metaphysical mystification of experience. Where, for example, Hamilton used the term 'mental latency' to explain how knowledge could exist even when it was not being used, to Mill 'the law of obliviscence' offered a better account. Instead of there being the Hamiltonian chimera of a mystical unconscious, there was simply below consciousness and comprising it a physical nervous system, automatically holding together associations for the mind to recall. Likewise, instead of Hamilton's ideal construction of ego and non-ego, there were in the beginning, said Mill, simply our sensations. Only later did we extrapolate consciousness out of the stream of sensation and make it into a separate faculty; only later did we create the idea of an external reality existing separably from those sensations. Mill's attack on Hamilton was like his earlier attack on the Cambridge philosopher William Whewell (1794–1866) over the heuristic method of induction. Whewell had argued that 'particular facts are not merely brought together': 'there is a new element added to the combination by the very act of thought by which they are combined' (*The Philosophy of the Inductive Sciences*, 2 vols. (1840), vol. 2, p. 213). To Whewell it was as though in acts of discovery, the mind and the world were in some mutually creative relation. But in a review of Whewell and again in his *Logic*, Mill retorted that a mental conception implies correspondence to something conceived: if what was conceived was indeed proved factually true, then the mind had *added* nothing but simply found something which was already externally existent without it. The 'idea' really belongs to the 'facts' of objective nature. As another Cambridge Idealist John Grote put it, the world described by the Positivists is one to which 'we ourselves are accidental', where mind follows 'desultorily and accidentally after fact' (*Exploratio Philosophica*, pt. 1 (1865), chs. 1 and 4). Mill, as rationalist, spent his life sacrificing 'mind' to what it thought of.

There is no doubt that Hamilton's reputation suffered through Mill's dismissal of intuition as unjustified mystification. But Mill's critique could not prevent a third wave of Idealist philosophy arising in the 1870s and 1880s, from men mostly taught by the Platonist Jowett in Oxford—in particular, Edward Caird (1835–1908), T. H. Green (1836–82), Bernard Bosanquet (1848–1923), and F. H. Bradley (1846–1924). These men were the so-called 'neo-Hegelians' in so far as they opposed what they took to be Hamilton's rigid overemphasis on the Kantian unknowability of noumena, of things as they were in themselves. Pushed too far, they argued, it led to the sceptical position—namely, that the human consciousness which made the world of phenomena objectively knowable was really only a fiction-making subjectivity. What the neo-Hegelians concentrated on was that moment of double realization when the thought that all we have is things-as-they-appear-to-us simultaneously gives us the *idea* of things-as-they-are-in-themselves, even though we cannot reach them. Even the earliest of notions is not single: we no sooner feel ourselves to exist than we feel something to exist *besides* ourselves. We think on both sides of the boundary.

Given the manifest limitation of human powers, it might have seemed that the epistemology of the followers of Comte was reasonable: it urged a drawing back and confining of ourselves to phenomena, leaving aside all speculation about a world beyond. Yet, as Edward Caird put it in 'The Problem of Philosophy at the Present Time', 'the two terms thus separated by abstraction are essentially united'. The very act of defining and limiting anything irresistibly presupposes something beyond it. It is the same as if we tried to withdraw from the world and concentrate on our individual lives alone: 'our experience of the world *is* our experience of ourselves' and to the extent that we 'succeed in withdrawing from the world without' so we 'narrow the world within'. 'It is impossible', concluded Caird, 'to solve the problem of the inner life without solving the apparently wider problem of the outer life' ('The Problem of Philosophy at the Present Time'). Likewise, in 'Popular Philosophy in its Relation to Life', T. H. Green claimed that empiricism provided a false and divisive language which misled people as to human nature and its possibilities.[6] If we limit self and self-realization to selfishness, said Green, we are the victims of the current psychology derived from Locke and Hobbes and Hume, for people exist in a world which is not simply *outside* them. The individual and the social modes could not be fundamentally separate; they were no more than different aspects of the same search for self-realization.

[6] *Works of Thomas Hill Green*, ed. R. L. Nettleship, 3 vols. (1888), 3. 92–125. See also Melvin Richter, *The Politics of Conscience: T. H. Green and his Age* (Weidenfeld and Nicholson, 1964), esp. ch. 7.

Again, what is humanly at stake here? The character of Cynthia in Mrs Gaskell's *Wives and Daughters* (1866) shows what it might mean to evade or misuse the power of human consciousness. A witty and beautiful young woman on the surface, neglected and damaged beneath, she is also both manipulative and self-abusive, as here in conversation with her half-sister:

'I am not good, and I told you so. Somehow I cannot forgive [Mamma] for her neglect of me as a child, when I would have clung to her . . . Don't you see I have grown up outside the pale of "oughts". Love me as I am, sweet one, for I shall never be better.' (ch. 19)

'Would you be my friend if—if it turned out ever that I had done wrong things? Would you remember how very difficult it has been to me to act rightly' (she took hold of Molly's hand as she spoke). . . . 'Oh, Molly, you don't know how I was neglected just at a time when I needed friends most. Mamma does not know it; it is not in her to know what I might have been if I had fallen into wise, good hands. But I know it; and what's more,' continued she, suddenly ashamed of her unusual exhibition of feeling, 'I try not to care, which I daresay is really the worst of all; but I could worry myself to death if I once took to serious thinking.' (ch. 40)

It would be simpler if these were merely excuses, but they are also true. Even so, Cynthia's consciousness of her own past circumstances does not help her to distinguish herself from them, but *creates* nothing more in her than a redoubled passivity. She remains within a sheerly psychological world, impervious to other claims. Just as her life keeps on going within time's succession, so these sentences always carry on past the point of moral consciousness which should given them pause. Followers of the socialist and philanthropist mill-owner Robert Owen (1771–1858) would claim that human beings were wholly the products of their social environment. But to Idealists such as T. H. Green, the act of reflection upon ourselves offered a point from which we cannot and need not simply be identical with our histories, the amoral sum of our experiences and inheritances. To Green, the thoughts and influences that pass through our passive minds are not yet *ours*, and are never wholly *us*, until and unless the consciousness that presents us to ourselves accepts them as such.

Tennyson himself read J. F. Ferrier and owned his *Institutes of Metaphysics* (1854). Yet the honest doubt of *In Memoriam* was due not least to Tennyson's incredulous fear at the Idealist thought that the human mind might be greater than anything it witnessed, including its own fear and pain and sorrow. The bereaved man half thinks that to dwell in his 'spirit' is only to live in a 'dream', yet when he tries to say 'adieu' to the dead, 'I cannot think the thing farewell' (123). To the Idealists, the consciousness that can think things is by that measure *more* than the things it thinks, even though its existence is only implied—half revealed and half concealed—in what it does.

For the Idealists then, human consciousness is not an illusion, as it was for Huxley: rather it constitutes the possibility, and can create the realization, of something more than the acceptance of determinism. For, crucially, morality in T. H. Green is not merely obedient, as with Evangelicalism, or calculative, as in Utilitarianism, but actually creative. It is not a mere act of will or character or conscience. Moral being is the free 'expression or utterance' of the human being in a single, whole self-realization that takes *every other part* of the person up into its achievement (*Prolegomena to Ethics* (1883), bk. 2, ch. 2, para. 144).

On the basis of this account of moral freedom, and of the need for the individual to take his place in the wider social world in order to fulfil his true nature, Green's political version of Idealism was a liberalism which, as compared to Mill *On Liberty*, offered something more than merely doing what one likes, without harming others. For Idealism, the chief good and goal in life is not simply happiness, individual or collective, but 'an idea of something absolutely desirable, which we cannot identify with any particular object of desire without soon discovering our mistake in the dissatisfaction which ensues upon the attainment of the particular object' (*Prolegomena to Ethics*, bk. 3, ch. 3, para. 199). That sense of an unattainable and inexplicable absolute end may seem indefinite even to the point of self-extinction, because finally it exists in lieu of the use of the word 'God'. But against the charge of vagueness Green argued that 'we cannot fully know what any capability is till we know its ultimate realisation' (ch. 1, para. 172). 'We all recognize, and perhaps in some fragmentary way practise, virtues which both carry in themselves unfulfilled possibilities, and at the same time plainly point out the direction in which their own future development is to be sought for' (bk. 4, ch. 4, para. 353).

Thus, the individual self-denial which was registered in the conduct of a useful social life was just such a future indicator, having in it the spiritual potentiality for development. A Utilitarian might well have applauded the fact that generations of Oxford undergraduates were inspired by Green to become in one way or another public servants and useful citizens. But to Mill, unlike Green, self-sacrifice was not a relative intimation of an absolute virtue, it was not even a value in itself: if it served as a practical, consequential means to the greater happiness of a greater number, then it was justifiable simply in terms of external usefulness. To Green self-sacrificing work was, though a very literal and very practical form of action, also a spiritually metaphorical act: 'It is not the renunciation, as such, but the spiritual state it represents that constitutes the value of the life spent in self-devoted service to mankind' (bk 3, ch. 5, para. 273). Thus it is not society alone with which Green is concerned, but the social dimension within the individual, and the individual effort within the social world, alike. And for Green, just as the spiritual may go on incarnate within the sphere of social life, so religion now carries on non-dogmatically within the realm of philosophy.

In Green and in Caird, Idealism offered the Victorian mind a form of human possibility which was neither dogmatic theology nor materialistic science. That was why both men admired Wordsworth for the unparaphrasable language of his faith, adding something new to the English mind:

> the soul
> Remembering how she felt, but what she felt
> Remembering not, retains an obscure sense
> Of possible sublimity, whereto
> With growing faculties she doth aspire,
> With faculties still growing, feeling still
> That whatsoever point they gain, they still
> Have something to pursue.
>
> (*The Prelude* (1850), 2. 315–22)

It was a poetry that itself offered 'an idea of something absolutely desirable, which we cannot identify with any particular object'.

III. Psychology, the Unconscious, and Literature

In 'The Problem of Philosophy at the Present Time' Edward Caird acknowledged that, for all its benefits, there was risk involved in the philosophic process. Philosophy must start by making things worse for the thinking mind: it meant a long and often professional haul through formal analytic consciousness, before what must be taken apart could ever be put back together again in a living unity. In this Caird was remembering in 1881 the warnings of Carlyle in an essay entitled 'Characteristics', published fifty years earlier.

In 1831 Carlyle had said that philosophy arose not so much as a remedy for, but as itself a symptom of, the loss of instinctive faith. In 'Characteristics' (*The Edinburgh Review*, December 1831), one of the great prophetic essays of the century, he had claimed that 'the mere existence and necessity of a Philosophy is an evil' and had foreseen that it could only struggle to heal its own existence like 'a disease expelling a disease'. To Carlyle something had gone fundamentally wrong when an age like his own could no longer be a time of primary, dynamic faith but had to turn round upon itself and become a period of self-conscious reflection, of second-order critical philosophy instead:

The sign of health is Unconsciousness. In our inward, as in our outward world, what is mechanical lies open to us: not what is dynamical and has vitality. Of our Thinking, we might say, it is but the mere upper surface that we shape into articulate Thoughts;—underneath the region of argument and conscious discourse, lies the region of meditation; here, in its quiet mysterious depths, dwells what vital force is in us; here if aught is to be created, and not merely manufactured and communicated, must the work go on. Manufacture is intelligible, but trivial; Creation is great, and cannot be understood.

Creative thinking came from sources below the arrangements of normal consciousness: it was an act of faith. Self-consciousness, in Carlyle's sense, arose precisely out of our losing touch with that deeper self: ironically this new *self* was a secondary *social* product. Nineteenth-century people were peering too much into that mirror of themselves which their minds seemed to provide. It was a consciousness that did not so much arise out of existence as seek to 'explain' it instead. Yet only a small fraction of the domain of man, said Carlyle, is available to conscious explanation or fore-thought.

It was not that Carlyle had believed that there could be a simple romantic return to pure, natural, dynamic unconsciousness: he knew that the very desire for such a return would be an ironic and contra-dictory product of self-consciousness itself. What he was trying to do, instead, was at least hold onto what he took to be an innate psychological truth: that, beneath all the demands of modern-day consciousness, creative and dynamic thinking remained the natural goal 'towards which our actual state of being strives'.

Carlyle was prophetic: with all the strange, new forces of the Industrial Revolution bearing down upon it, the half-stunned human world of the 1830s did indeed have to struggle and strive for expressive access to alternative forms and sources of inner mentality. It was a generation that caught its thinking at the very borderland of pre-consciousness:

Although Oliver has roused himself from sleep, he was not thoroughly awake. There is a drowsy state, between sleeping and waking, when you dream more in five minutes with your eyes half open, and yourself half conscious of everything that is passing around you, than you would in five nights with your eyes fast closed, and your senses wrapt in perfect unconsciousness. At such times a mortal knows just enough of what his mind is doing, to form some glimmering conception of its mighty powers, its bounding from earth and spurning time and space, when freed from the restraint of its corporeal associate. (Charles Dickens, *Oliver Twist* (1838), ch. 9)

Looking back in *The Fortnightly Review* of February 1872, George Henry Lewes saw in Dickens, instead of formal rationality, what he called an animal intelligence and an hallucinatory energy. It was as though by such strange indirections as that in *Oliver Twist* Dickens had had to *recall*, nascently out of the realms of childhood and from under all the physical restraints which dominated it, the almost forgotten existence of mind itself. In *The Physiology of Common Life* (1860) Lewes said that as the presence of the external world became more and more obtrusive, 'we need the aid of philosophy to reinstate the vanished conception of our inner life' (vol. 2, ch. 10). But formal philosophy could not work for Dickens, and it is no coincidence that it was to Carlyle that he had dedicated *Hard Times* (1854), that novel against mechanical thinking. What restored to Dickens a glimpse of the existence of a dynamic inner life was experience like Oliver's of pre-perception.

That vertiginous sense of being caught in the very shift between worlds, between faculties, between different realities inside and out was characteristic of early Victorian England. The categories did not seem to fit together—neither mind with body nor, equivalently, human spirit with material society. The most powerful language of the early years was not that of conscious moralization or politicization; it was more like the language of sensation, in the shock of physical thought. To Walter Bagehot looking back in 'First Edinburgh Reviewers' (1855), it had seemed an absurd universe, 'How can a soul be a merchant? What relation to an immortal being have the price of linseed, the fall of butter? . . . The soul ties its shoe; the mind washes its hands in a basin. All is incongruous.'[7]

Throughout the 1830s and 1840s there is this sense of a world waking up, confusedly, as from a strange dream. The contemporary fascination at the trances induced by what was called 'animal magnetism' or 'mesmerism', after its eighteenth-century discoverer F. A. Mesmer, fitted well with this sensation. Harriet Martineau, Tennyson, Wilkie Collins, and Dickens himself were among the literary people who saw in mesmerism an alternative way of catching 'some glimmering conception' of the unseen mind. By a series of passes of the hand the mesmerist would create fits, visions, trances, and acts of somnambulism in his patient—as a result, it was claimed, of communicating some invisible electromagnetic fluid across the atmosphere. Public demonstrations were like early experimental brain-research in the form of high theatre. The mesmerist seemed to become the will and mind to the patient's body, as though the two were halves of a single person. To devotees such as Harriet Martineau, mesmerism offered a new form of medical healing, on the very boundary between mind and body.

Like the phrenologists, the main English proponents of mesmerism were no mere quacks: John Elliotson (1791–1868), for example, a close friend of Dickens, was professor of medicine at University

---

[7] *Collected Works of Walter Bagehot*, ed. N. St John Stevas, 9 vols. (*The Economist*, 1965–78), vol. 1, p. 338.

College until his commitment to mesmerism forced his resignation in 1838. Indeed, like phrenology, mesmerism paved the way, however inadvertently, for later psychological advance. In the 1840s as a result of the work of James Braid (1795–1860), a Scottish physician practising in Manchester, and of Carpenter and Laycock, mesmerism was redescribed in psychological terms, as 'hypnotism'. From being initially explained as the effect of the stare of the operator upon the ocular nervous system of the subject, hypnotism was now redescribed in terms of the suggestible power of the patient's own unconscious. Both Carpenter and Laycock, though rivals, quoted Hamilton's great saying: 'What we are conscious of is constructed out of what we are not conscious of'. By 1880, in Paris, Charcot was applying hypnosis to the study of nervous disorders, in particular hysteria, to the immense interest of the young Freud. Thus, as so often in this period, what had felt disturbing and abnormal in the 1830s—the primitive phenomena of dreams, illusions, childhood fears, hysteria, delirium, and mental derangement—had become by 1880 reformalized into a professional investigation of what lay behind the functioning of *normal* mental life.

So it is in the writings from the 1870s to the 1890s of the philosopher and psychologist James Sully (1842–1925), a follower of George Henry Lewes and George Eliot, and in turn an acknowledged influence upon Freud. What in the insane became a dislocation of reality, argued Sully, was in the sane a state of emotion resulting from the associations of memory—the difference was one of degree, not kind:

In passing from place to place, in talking with others, and in reading, we are liable to the sudden return by hidden paths of association of images of incidents that had long seemed forgotten . . . An idea of memory seems sometimes to lose its proper moorings, so to speak; to drift about helplessly among other ideas. (*Illusions: A Psychological Study* (1881), ch. 10)

Similarly, Sully wrote of what he called 'the process of filling in' that goes on mentally within any normal act of physical perception: 'To say where the line should be drawn here between perception and observation on the one hand, and inference on the other is clearly impossible' (ch. 3). Evolutionary theory meant not expecting absolute boundary lines between thinking and seeing, or between memory and hallucination. In *The Fortnightly Review* (March 1893), in an essay on 'The Dream as Revelation' later cited by Freud in *The Interpretation of Dreams* (1900), Sully described how in sleep, evolution is reversed and adults go back to the groundwork of their life, in a primitive animal immersion in bodily sensation. In so doing he summarized the research led by the century's great brain-neurologist John Hughlings Jackson into the three-tiered evolution of the mind itself—high-, middle-, and low-level centres governing, respectively, complex thought and will, the movements of voluntary muscles, and the automatic processes of respiration and circulation necessary to maintain life:

The newest conception of the brain is of a hierarchy of organs, the higher and later evolved seeming to control, and in a measure to repress, the functional activities of the lower and earlier. Translated into psychological language, this means that what is instinctive, primitive, elemental, in our mental life, is being continually overborne by the fruit of experience, by the regulative process of reflection. (*Fortnightly Review* (March 1893))

But the highest and most lately developed functions of the nervous system, said Hughlings Jackson, were precisely those that were the most vulnerable to the first signs of disturbance, decay, and disease.

In this way, the last decades of the century are frequently shadowed by cumulatively pessimistic anxieties, voiced by the psychiatrists (or alienists as they were known) James Crichton-Browne and Henry Maudsley, the zoologist Edwin Ray Lankester, and by the eugenicist Francis Galton.[8] It was feared that the primitive unconscious might be more a threat than a support to rational consciousness and that the higher levels of self-control and moral responsibility might be rendered ineffective as a result; that mental disorder might be inheritable; that racial degeneration or individual regression were real alternative possibilities to evolutionary progression.

Yet from Carlyle's 'Characteristics' via Hamilton even to D. H. Lawrence's *Psychoanalysis and the Unconscious* (1921), there was a

[8] For a wider view of Galton, otherwise masked by his notoriety in eugenics, see A. S. Byatt, *The Biographer's Tale* (Chatto and Windus, 2000) and D. W. Forrest, *Francis Galton: The Life and Work of a Victorian Genius* (Paul Elek, 1974), both of which offer accounts of his wide-ranging mental experiments as statistician and observer of himself and others.

recurrent counter-affirmation in the nineteenth century: the unconscious discovered and affirmed, not as Freud's agency of repression, created by consciousness's denial of dangerous material, but as a genuinely original creative force in its own right. No one did more in the 1880s to try to defend that existence from the encroachments of the age's commitment to consciousness than F. W. H. Myers (1843–1901).

Myers's argument was that during our long evolutionary adaptation to new environments there has been a continual displacement of the 'threshold' of consciousness. There were certain faculties that natural selection had lifted above that threshold, for the working purposes of everyday material existence; other powers, which were not called into consciousness as immediately useful, were stored subliminally below consciousness, in a kind of dynamic memory. It was these latter unseen powers of which we consciously knew little that emerged as by a 'subliminal uprush' in the creative discovery of suddenly recalled potential. In ways that are reminiscent of the language of George Eliot in *Middlemarch*, Myers, like Hamilton, speaks of microscopic levels of consciousness, like invisible ultra-violet rays beyond the end of the conscious spectrum. 'The man of genius is what he is by virtue of possessing a readier communication than most men possess between his supraliminal and his subliminal self'. Hence 'that sudden creation of new cerebral connections or pathways which is implied in an inspiration of genius' (*Human Personality and its Survival of Bodily Death* (1903), ch. 3). These are informal powers of human thought unrecognized by philosophy yet vital to the race's deeper continuance.

Moreover, if these subliminal forces did not belong with this material world, ventured Myers, it might even be because they were in close touch with a more spiritual dimension. The intermixture of religious, spiritualist, psychological, and physiological elements might seem weird, but it was precisely the broad area of research proposed by Sheridan Le Fanu's 'philosophic physician' Dr Hesselius, in the collection of fictional case studies entitled *In a Glass Darkly* (1872). In the study of people who claim to see ghosts, there were, claimed the doctor, three basic possibilities: they may simply be visionaries whose illusions are created either by guilt or by nerve-damage; or, they may really have what the eighteenth-century mystic

Swedenborg called the internal sight, which sees more clearly the things of the other life than the outer eye does the things of the world; or, most interestingly between the two, through trauma or disease they may have lost a layer of mental skin, as it were, and become affected by a terrible confusion of influences—from inside, outside, and beyond—'against which we were intended to be guarded' ('The Familiar', prologue).

Myers himself was one of the founding members in 1882 of the Society for Psychical Research, together with his former tutor, the philosopher Henry Sidgwick, and Edmund Gurney, an investigator into the dynamics of hypnotism. Telepathy, the power of prayer, the possibility of the existence of the personality after death and of the visionary reality of ghosts—these were the proposed topics for research, in the belief that the science of psychology should be tentatively extended into a serious reconsideration of mental intuitions which previously had been banished to the realm of religious crankiness or primitive superstition. It is not surprising that Tennyson was an early associate since *In Memoriam* had been just such an attempt to explore any possible language or world-view, old or new, spiritualist or physiological, in response to death and loss. But other associates of the Society were to include Charles Dodgson (Lewis Carroll), Gladstone, Ruskin, the artist Frederic Leighton, the physicist J. J. Thomson, the philosophers William James and Henri Bergson, and Carl Jung. Indeed it was William James who first recognized that Myers's theory of the subliminal self was what he called a momentous discovery in the history of psychology—a vision of the unconscious as innocent and creative rather than dangerous or unhealthy.

It was a pupil of Sir William Hamilton who applied a similar conception of the unconscious to the world of art. In *Poetics: An Essay on Poetry* (1852) and *The Gay Science* (2 vols., 1866), *The Times*'s leading reviewer E. S. Dallas argued that if we want to know the real if hidden history of human thought we should not consult philosophy which 'is the result of conscious effort' so much as art which 'comes unconsciously, and is the spontaneous growth of the time' (*Gay Science*, vol. 1, ch. 3).

It is not that the artist romantically eschews consciousness. To Dallas, he makes *use* of the known 'but his use of knowledge is ever to suggest something beyond knowledge'. Through knowledge and consciousness, 'the artist appeals to the unconscious part of us', seeking 'to establish a connection with the unconscious hemisphere of the mind, and to make us feel a mysterious energy there in the hidden soul':

The poet's words, the artist's touches, are electric; and we feel those words, and the shock of those touches, going through us in a way we cannot define. Art is poetical in proportion as it has this power of appealing to what I may call the absent mind, as distinct from the present mind, on which falls the great glare of consciousness, and to which alone science appeals. (*Gay Science*, vol. 1, ch. 9)

It was as Matthew Arnold had it in 'The Buried Life'—that the poetic feeling is what happens when sometimes

> A bolt is shot back somewhere in our breast,
> And a lost pulse of feeling stirs again.

To Dallas there was some hidden indefinable extra in poetry, over and above its conscious translatable content. This effect was achieved by acts of what we call 'imagination' and 'memory': imagination being the name we give to the qualitative change to a faculty or combination of faculties when dynamically charged; memory that strange, contradictory creative process involved in somehow unconsciously knowing what is being searched for, even whilst in genuine search. But both are not so much separate faculties as functions of the same mysterious process of non-mechanical thought:

Trains of thought are continually passing to and fro, from the light into the dark, and back from the dark into the light. When the current of thought flows from within our ken to beyond our ken, it is gone, we forget it, we know not what has become of it. After a time it comes back to us changed and grown, as if it were a new thought, and we know not whence it comes. (*Gay Science*, vol. 1, ch. 7)

Opposed to both puritanism and Utilitarianism, Dallas characterized the unconscious powers and effects of poetry in terms of non-moralistic and non-utilitarian 'pleasure'. To the Evangelical and the Benthamite alike, the pursuit of pleasure through poetry was no more than an escapist retreat into a Tennysonian world of lotos-eating. But Dallas is not talking about pleasure-seeking: he says, Seek and ye shall *not* find it—for pleasure does not obey the command of consciousness. Nor does it accept the necessity of the grim moral world of conscience and conflict; for it is the object of art, as of the gospel itself, to set us free, says Dallas 'from this fierce struggle, from this life of conscious endeavour' (*Gay Science*, vol. 2, ch. 15). Against art's moralists and the damage he thought was done to poets of the 1850s and 1860s by overconsciousness of self and society, Dallas offers the creative beauty and delight of art. For art, and in particular poetry, recalls for Dallas the naturalness of a pre-lapsarian world and serves as a form of love or grace.

Yet if art kept alive a form of human thinking which was otherwise in danger of being overpowered by the very consciousness of the age, it was still necessary—to a humane and democratic age in need of creativity—that such thinking should not be left solely within the domain of the artists. It should be recognized as belonging to the human psyche in general. As Comte had said of the process of formalization, the establishment of any new subject depended upon its ability to establish its own necessary space within the field of human inquiry by breaking free of the encroachments of the studies preceding and surrounding it. Thus, even though the opposing camps of brain research and metaphysical philosophy had each contributed to an appreciation of unconscious forces, the establishment of 'Psychology' depended upon its release from both disciplines, whilst applying concerns formerly categorized as artistic to the cause of common humanity. This development was signalled in that final great Victorian achievement of scholarship, the ninth edition of the *Encyclopaedia Britannica* in which there appeared for the first time in 1886 a separate article on 'Psychology'.

Previously, psychology had been covered in the article on 'Metaphysics' by H. L. Mansel; now there was formal emphasis on the value of a non-physiological psychology in representing a distinct area of human being. The author, a former pupil of Henry Sidgwick who went on to become Sidgwick's successor as professor of mental philosophy and logic at Cambridge, was James Ward (1843–1925). It was Ward who argued that the true subject matter of psychology and what distinguished it from physiology and philosophy alike was the characteristically *individual* standpoint of psychological experience. Where previously the word 'subjective' had been taken as that which was epistemologically inferior to what was true (because 'objective'), Ward insisted on the reality of the subjective as meaning the living viewpoint of an experiencing subject. William James claimed that it was this statement which confirmed a new era in English thought, and in an address to the Society for Psychical Research in 1896 he defended what he called 'the personal and romantic view of life'. This involved experiences which, often capricious, discontinuous, and not easily controlled, required particular persons, living through complex life histories, for their production—and thus neither could be known nor should be discounted by the impersonal forms of thought (*The Will to Believe and Other Essays in Popular Philosophy* (1915), 'What Psychical Research Research has Accomplished'). It was as though the brother of Henry James was taking all that the psychological realism of the Victorian novel had offered and turning it back again into the real-life experiments of individuals in the world.

Like the genre of realism itself, 'psychology' was becoming ever-increasingly a holding ground for raw individual reality, amidst the competing and overlapping claims of philosophy, science, theology, sociology, and so on. It was (to change metaphor) a way of holding, in individual solution, the human mix before it crystallized out into definite conscious forms and disciplines. 'Character too is a process and an unfolding', wrote George Eliot in *Middlemarch* (ch. 15). And it is the work of George Eliot that emerges as the culminating meeting place of all the concerns that have gathered in this chapter.

In an article in *The Nineteenth Century* (1886), Myers pictured the human brain as a vast manufactory with thousands of interconnected looms at work. He was trying to imagine the mental struggle to superimpose new requirements upon archaic structures and take the mind out of its old machinery and onto a new stage of moral development:

The class of orders received has changed very rapidly during the last few hundred years. I have now to try to turn out altruistic emotions and intelligent reasoning with machinery adapted to self-preserving fierceness or manual toil. I am hindered not only by the old-fashioned type of the looms, but by the inconvenient disposition of the driving gear. I cannot start one useful loom without starting a dozen others that are merely in the way. (vol. 20, p. 656)

The great mental negotiator between the claims of old ways and new ways, judgement and mercy, belief and secularization, self-development and altruism, art and life, was not Myers—or Comte or Herbert Spencer in their systematizations—but George Eliot in the very process of her novel-writing. It was Myers who in 1873 had welcomed George Eliot on a visit to Cambridge when famously she spoke to him, at dusk in the garden of Trinity College, Cambridge, of God, Immortality, and Duty: how inconceivable the first, unbelievable the second, yet how peremptory and absolute the last. In place of God, it was the brain of George Eliot which, in its movements up and down, right and left, had felt bound to undertake the duty to encompass in the novel both psychology and philosophy, art and science, individual and society, life and thought, in lieu of the unity previously offered by orthodox religion.[9] It was that dexterity of combination which George Henry Lewes said had surprised him most of all: he had always known that Marian Evans was a formidable abstract thinker but, for all his encouragement of her as a writer, he had not realized that she would also have the spontaneous dramatizing power to create specific concrete life—using both cerebral hemispheres, both hands in synchronization. For Lewes in his biography of Goethe (1855) had laid particular emphasis on the attraction of the German poet towards the philosopher Spinoza, as if the one were the opposite counterpart of the other, quoting from Goethe as follows:

The all-equalising peace of Spinoza was in striking contrast with my all-disturbing activity; his mathematical method was the direct opposite of my poetic style of thought and feeling . . . Mind and heart, understanding and sense, sought each other with eager affinity, binding together the most different natures. (*Life and Works of Goethe*, bk. 3, ch. 6)

Secularization meant that no century was more concerned than the nineteenth century with the possibility of salvation by translation: religion translated into science or ethics or poetry, ethics translated into politics, poetry translated into philosophy, mind translated into brain or heart into mind—these were characteristic concerns on every side. 'Mind and heart, understanding and sense, sought each other'. Emotions were cognitive, the unconscious and the conscious

[9] See below, pp. 384–96.

needed each other, character and context were interrelated. In all this George Eliot as novelist is the great mediator and translator, finding thoughts within feelings, feelings about thoughts—'with that distinctness which is no longer reflection but . . . an idea wrought back to the directness of sense, like the solidity of objects' (*Middlemarch* (1872), ch. 21). It is George Eliot above all who sets herself to do her writing in constant movement between consciousness and unconsciousness, working at both the macro- and microscopic levels of life: like her scientific researcher Dr Lydgate, she 'wanted to pierce the obscurity of those minute processes which prepare human misery and joy, those invisible thoroughfares which are the first lurking-places of anguish, mania, and crime' (*Middlemarch*, ch. 16).

   In short, the realist novel itself became the form for dealing with the problems of consciousness which Carlyle had described. For as Trollope wrote in *The Bertrams* (1859, ch. 19), the people in novels are all 'turned inside out'. That is to say, in the novel self-consciousness is no longer depicted self-consciously from within, but narrated instead as if from outside itself and related to less conscious levels of inner being. Above all, it was panoramically viewed—in a way that it cannot be within the particular personal life—as coexisting alongside other innerly sealed and yet emotionally overlapping individuals in the world. The novel turned, as George Eliot put it, from outside estimates of a man 'to wonder, with keener interest, what is the report of his own consciousness' and then turned back out again to other simultaneously existing 'human lots', 'seeing how they were woven and interwoven' (*Middlemarch*, chs. 10, 15).

5

Conditions of
Literary Production

In 1859, at the age of 31, the novelist Mrs Margaret Oliphant (1828–97) became a widow. The family had left England for Italy in the hope of improving the health of her husband, Frank. An impecunious painter and stained-glass-window artist, he had not told his wife that he had already been diagnosed in England as having a fatal tuberculosis. The family income abroad was sustained only by Mrs Oliphant's regular contributions to *Blackwood's Magazine*, one article per month earning her £20. At Frank's death Mrs Oliphant was left in Italy, £1,000 in debt, with two young children and pregnant with another. She had wholly to take on the traditionally male role of breadwinner.

In 1860 she returned to England, staying at first with her brother, also named Frank, and his family in Birkenhead, and then moving to Edinburgh. There, as she recalled near the very end of the second volume of her *Annals of a Publishing House* (1897), she paid a desperate call on the publishers William and John Blackwood. She offered them a proposal for a serial story, but reluctantly they declined. The widow took leave of them as if it didn't matter. She went home to her three children, playing with them 'in a sort of cheerful despair'—'which they say is part of a woman's natural duplicity and dissimulation'.

When the children were in bed, however, Mrs Oliphant stayed up most of the night writing a story which turned out to be the first of her successful series of provincial life, *Chronicles of Carlingford*—seven tales from *The Executor* in 1861 to *Phoebe Junior* in 1876.

Between those dates she also wrote more than twenty other novels. By 1864 she was receiving as much as £1,500 for *The Perpetual Curate* which was printed in three volumes, accordingly to customary practice, immediately after its serialization in the magazine. The usual rate for popular authors in mid-career was between £100 and £500. Writing *The Perpetual Curate* very much hand-to-mouth, in the midst of family life, Mrs Oliphant regularly stayed at best only one or two instalments ahead of magazine publication. She missed just one issue, through grief at the death of her eldest daughter Maggie, in January 1864, aged 10. This was to be the height of her success.

It was not long before a further crisis befell her. From 1850 her eldest brother Willie, a drunkard and debtor, had been a financial burden on her and he remained so for more than twenty years. But in 1868 her other brother Frank in turn suffered financial ruin. Mrs Oliphant took in his two eldest children, sending Frank junior to Eton along with her own two sons, whilst the parents went abroad. In 1870 brother Frank returned, a widower, in a state of nervous collapse. Mrs Oliphant now took him in, along with his two youngest girls. The whole family—her own two boys, an increasingly feckless Frank and his four children—were wholly dependent upon her and her writing.

Astonishingly for such a burdened and stalwart matriarch, she added to her own difficulties by extravagant spending on entertainment, travel, and dress, as well as on the boys' expensive and ambitious education. It was as though, in order to survive psychologically as well as financially, she needed to convert the continuous heavy weight of domestic responsibility into the nervous fun of a kind of gambling. As she admits in her posthumously published *Autobiography*, 'The alternations of anxiety and deliverance were more congenial than the steady monotony of self-denial.' Whether this way of managing was best described as 'trusting in God' or as 'tempting Providence' she herself did not know (ed. Elisabeth Jay, pp. 135–6). But this was the same woman who, in 'natural duplicity', had cheerfully played with her children whilst fearing financial ruin. In such ways the life of Mrs Oliphant had shaken down into something not easily categorizable, even by herself. That is what made it a *life*— indeed, one very like the lives of the struggling characters in her own novels. For by another act of natural duplicity she was often using her anxieties, family and financial, as the very subject matter of the writing which was intended to help allay them. Out of this came such powerful but still underrated achievements as *Salem Chapel* (1863), *Agnes* (1865), *Harry Joscelyn* (1881), *Hester* (1883), and *Kirsteen* (1890).

Sharply intelligent, she saw herself as continuing the tradition of witty scepticism that began with Jane Austen, a robust feminine cynicism which she considered far subtler than the masculine variety. Yet she envied the financial success of more popular, sentimental novelists such as Dinah Craik (1826–87). It was not that Mrs Oliphant was ever poor: by 1873 she was earning about £2,000 a year and, according to the statistician Dudley Baxter in his *National Income* (1868), less than o.3 per cent of the income-bearing population of England and Wales earned between £1,000 and £5,000. Yet, with the insecurity of being at the lower end of the high earners, Mrs Oliphant envied her rivals. Trollope in his *Autobiography* (1883) claimed he had earned £70,000 in total over twenty years, and he had received over twice as much for his most highly paid novel, *Can You Forgive Her?* in 1864 as had Mrs Oliphant for *The Perpetual Curate*. In the years just before his death in 1863 Thackeray was earning £7,200 a year; in 1863 George Eliot received £10,000 for *Romola*. The cost of housing gives some idea of the purchasing power of such sums: in mid-century, a large country house cost between £7,000 and £10,000; £2,000 secured a very large town house (Mrs Oliphant purchased a large house at Windsor for £1,600 in 1878); £300 a modest suburban villa. Mrs Oliphant complained in a letter to Blackwood in 1885 that the highest-paid doctor was said to be able to earn £15,000 a year, a great barrister £20,000, the painter Millais £25,000: 'It will be a long time before an author makes half so much.'

Yet what really harassed Mrs Oliphant was the uncertainty of her annual earnings, exacerbated by her burdens and her extravagance alike. Male writers, where they did not have private means, usually had alternative livelihoods—in particular in teaching, the civil service, the Church, or journalism. Charles Kingsley and J. H. Newman were clergymen, Wilkie Collins and Charles Reade at least trained as barristers, Walter Bagehot was a banker, and Coventry Patmore a librarian at the British Museum. William Ainsworth turned from lawyer to publisher, John Stuart Mill was in government service at the India Office. Trollope did not resign his £800 per annum position at the Post Office until 1867 when he had published nineteen novels. Obtaining the editorship of a major periodical secured a career, but though Thackeray earned up to £600 a month as editor of the *Cornhill*, Mrs Oliphant was denied any such opportunity. Never in the assured first rank with Thackeray or George Eliot or Trollope, Mrs Oliphant faced periodic crises, the more so as her brand of provincial realism seemed to be going out of fashion in her later years. By the 1870s and 1880s Mrs Oliphant found herself using her publishers, Blackwoods and Macmillans, as bankers, drawing advances for novels which were not yet even written whilst dashing off articles to ward off ever-rising debts. Her mortgaged life was tied to the ongoing *successiveness* of book after book, article upon article, of one dependent trouble after another, bereavement upon bereavement, with the demands of serial instalments and financial arrears alike catching up on her. That successiveness—in a career lasting fifty years, comprising a hundred novels and many hundreds of articles—is central to the story to be told in this chapter.

Amidst these difficulties Mrs Oliphant had always to keep her writing, like her financial worries, in the background, while she struggled with a brave face to maintain a normal happy family home for her dependents. Like realism itself, the woman writer was caught between the claims of art and life. Elizabeth Gaskell describes how after the writing of *Jane Eyre* Charlotte Brontë's existence was 'divided into two parallel currents'—her life as Currer Bell, the author; her life as Charlotte Brontë, the woman, sister, and daughter:

There were separate duties belonging to each character—not opposing each other; not impossible, but difficult to be reconciled. When a man becomes an author, it is probably merely a change of employment to him. He takes a portion of that time which has hitherto been devoted to some other study or pursuit; he gives up something of the legal or medical profession . . . and another merchant or lawyer, or doctor, steps into his vacant place, and probably does as well as he. But no other can take up the quiet, regular duties of the daughter, the wife, or the mother, as well as she whom God has appointed to fill that particular place. (*The Life of Charlotte Brontë* (1857), vol. 2 ch. 2)

In the case of Mrs Oliphant it was not only that she feared she had sacrificed her gifts to the demands of the market but that, after all that, she had still failed as a mother as well as an artist. At the end, after her sons had predeceased her, she thought that perhaps her very attempts to make desperately light of her work and of her troubles, for their sake, had only succeeded in inadvertently teaching her boys not to take their own lives seriously enough. Both sons had simply sponged upon her, between them showing various symptoms of the male family traits of depression, alcoholism, extravagance, and ill health.

This chapter concerns the effect upon literature of a developing mass market and its material forces. Mrs Oliphant's was a life that fully embodied that business, giving a living force to three inter-related themes in the sections that follow. They are: the position, importance, and anxiety of the middle classes within the new economic ordering; the new cultural dominance of prose and prose fiction, as the realist novel grew closer to the ordinary matter-of-fact material world than literature had ever been before; and the increased place given to the woman's voice in the unparalleled development of women writers.

Nothing typifies the Victorian age more than the committed but anxious position of the world of literature in relation to the wider world. In writers such as Mrs Oliphant it was registered most power-fully at the personal level, in terms of the relation between writing and living, and at the generic level, in terms of the development of the novel as a form constantly making inroads upon real life.

I. The Literary Profession, the Book Trade, and Culture

'This', said John Stuart Mill, writing 'On Civilization' in *The Westminster Review* (April 1836), 'is a reading age.' Whereas between 1800 and 1825 only about 580 books appeared each year, by mid-century the figure had risen to over 2,600 titles and by 1900 it was over 6,000.[1] In the 1830s steam had replaced operation by hand in

---

[1] All writers on reading and publishing in Victorian England are deeply indebted,

the printing trade. Paper, the scarcity of which had forced up the price of books earlier in the century, was in abundant supply once no longer handmade but machine-produced.

'When books were few,' wrote Mill, 'to get through one was a work of time and labour.' Now everything was speeded up, and reading matter itself became more ephemeral. Once newspaper tax had been reduced to a penny stamp in 1836, it was the production of newspapers and periodicals that drove the presses faster and faster. In 1864, with stamp duty now repealed, there were 1,764 periodical titles listed in *Mitchell's Newspaper Press Directory*; by 1887 there were 3,597. The mass entertainment industry in general began to boom: day trips by rail, theatre and music hall, pubs and pleasure gardens. The consumption of newspapers, periodicals, and books was part of that increase in leisure pursuits. The percentage of fiction amidst major books published rose from 16 per cent in the period from 1814 to 1846 to nearly 25 per cent in the 1870s and 1880s. By 1880 approximately 380 new novels were appearing each year.

The expanding market for reading matter lay in what may be all too loosely described as the middle class, earning at least £100 per annum, more comfortably £300, and comprising about 20 per cent of the nation. Between the old-established middle class (of merchants and bankers, large employers of labour, and the higher professions such as law) and the ranks of working-class unskilled labour, there arose a particular section of the newer middle class which doubled over thirty years. The categories are imprecise, but in the new social structures of England, the professions—physicians, teachers, civil servants, and other professional or commercial white-collar workers—which numbered over 300,000 in the census of 1851 were estimated at well over 650,000 by 1881. The largest increases were among those engaged in education, literature, and science (in particular, writers); in commerce; and (at the lower end of this fluid and amorphous middle class) in trade. Some estimates indicate that during the second half of the century the average lower middle-class income may have risen in real terms by over 70 per cent. Skilled

as here, to the pioneering work of R. D. Altick, in particular *The English Common Reader* (University of Chicago, 1957) and John Sutherland, in particular *Victorian Novelists and Publishers* (Athlone, 1976), and, more recently, to Simon Eliot, *Some Patterns and Trends in British Publishing* (The Bibliographical Society, 1994).

workers, small shopkeepers, and domestic servants added to the growth of the demand for reading matter. More disposable income, extended leisure, a rising population, and increased literacy meant a larger market. A national report of 1840, based simply on the ability to sign the marriage register, declared that 67 per cent of males and 51 per cent of females were literate: the percentage rose slowly but steadily throughout the century, whilst the differential between the sexes also closed, and by 1871 the figures were 81 per cent and 73 per cent respectively. Even in 1825 the publisher Archibald Constable had spoken of his vision of 'literature for the millions': overreaching himself in his excitement, he was bankrupt within a few months, to the ruin of Walter Scott. Nonetheless, between 1840 and 1870, whilst the British population rose by 40 per cent, the number of books published annually rose by 400 per cent. The Bible remained the best-seller: over 4,500,000 copies of the Bible and the New Testament being printed between 1848 and 1850 alone.

In the 1850s and 1860s in particular, the pace of circulation increased ever more rapidly, with the development of printing factories and high-speed presses from America. A mechanized foundry could produce five times more type a day than the old hand-setting process. Reprinting itself became easier in the 1850s with the advent of easily stored paper-mould stereotyping, into which molten metal was poured, making it possible for new impressions to be produced without complete resetting. The time gap between the publication of an expensive first edition and a cheap reprint grew smaller and smaller, dipping beneath a year. The very cost of reprints was lowered by the abolition in 1852 of resale price maintenance, the fixed price agreed by all booksellers, resulting in increased competitive possibilities for a free trade in books.

Yet compared to the newspaper side of the industry, book publishers remained relatively conservative. The great stabilizing factor for publishers was the steady profit to be made from comparatively small runs (500 to 1,000 copies) of expensive three-volume novels, priced at half a guinea per volume for a period of 70 years from Scott to the 1890s. The great Victorian triple-decker thus still cost thirty-one shillings and sixpence in 1867 when a respectable family might earn forty-eight shillings a week and (according to Dudley Baxter) the average weekly wage of the most skilled and highly paid workmen, such as instrument workers and cabinetmakers, was between twenty-eight and thirty-five shillings. Even if there was a later cheap one-volume reissue in five- or six-shilling editions, five shillings in the 1830s bought five pounds of butter or ten pounds of meat.

But the new mass development that enlarged the market, or provided a second market, was the sale of the three-decker novel initially either in monthly shilling parts or serialized in the periodicals of the 1850s and 1860s.

Issued in monthly parts, Dickens's *Pickwick Papers* famously burst upon the scene in 1836–7, winning 40,000 subscribers per issue for a 300,000-word novel which cost £1 in easy instalments over twenty months. The go-ahead publishers Chapman and Hall commissioned Dickens to write a prose commentary merely to accompany a series of Cockney sporting pictures in shilling numbers illustrated by Seymour and then Phiz: it was Dickens's idea to make the prose into a picaresque continuity from number to number and wrest the initiative from illustration to text, making of it all something very different from the comic sporting novel of R. S. Surtees (*Jorrocks' Jaunts and Jollities*, 1831–4 or *Handley Cross*, 1843).

The shortage of type during the first stages of the boom in English novel production meant that the necessity of printing serially encouraged the practice of serial publication. Once established, serial composition, rapid piecemeal proof-reading in sheets, and publication in parts increased the pressure on authors to be part of a strict industry. The very nature of the book had changed: throughout the various phases of publication and reprinting, the authorial revision of a succession of proofs became another stage in the history of the text, almost as significant as the state of the original manuscript.

Nonetheless, the method of publication in paper-covered monthly numbers, which enabled novels to be sold like newspapers independently of bookshops, was never as successful for other authors as it was for Dickens. Bulwer-Lytton and Dickens's own protégé Wilkie Collins were two further exceptions who did notably well, as did the Dickensian imitator of comic picaresque Albert Smith (1816–60). But bestriding the market, Dickens alone made £10,000 for *Our Mutual Friend* (1864) from a print run of 28,000 per monthly issue. Chapman and Hall had 2,290,000 parts of various Dickens novels for sale in 1847. Although George Eliot's *Middlemarch* and *Daniel Deronda* were successfully issued in bimonthly and monthly part-numbers in 1871–2 and 1876 respectively, the practice of publishing in numbers died out by 1880 and was declining throughout the 1860s in favour of magazine serialization.

It was largely as a result of the new practice of incorporating serialized new fiction that the first number of the *Cornhill* in 1860 sold nearly 120,000 copies, offering the opening chapters of work by Trollope (*Framley Parsonage*) and essays by Thackeray (*Roundabout Papers*) as well as contributions from Ruskin and Elizabeth Barrett Browning. It is an indication of the new pressure of market forces upon writers that Trollope had originally submitted his Irish novel *Castle Richmond* to the *Cornhill* but was urged to write a more popular classical story of English provincial life instead: it became *Framley Parsonage*. Dickens's *Household Words* began at sales of 100,000 and *All the Year Round* at 120,000, rising to 180,000–250,000 for the Christmas issues 1862–5: these were the magazines people had to buy if they wanted a first sight of *Hard Times* in 1854, *A Tale of Two Cities* in 1859, or *Great Expectations* in 1860. Moreover, as magazines were passed around and read aloud amongst families, or bought for communal enjoyment in clubs, the overall readership was wider than sales: it was estimated that the total actual readership of weekly and monthly magazines was 250,000 in 1831 rising to 6,094,950 in 1864.[2]

With sales of that magnitude, Dickens was reaching further down and further across the social scale than any of his contemporaries in his effort virtually to reinvent the national culture in his own terms. Yet amongst the working classes it was more often plagiarized versions of Dickens, than Dickens himself, that made an impact. Dickens at his most successful could sell 100,000 copies of a one-shilling monthly issue of *The Old Curiosity Shop* (1840–1), but a popular broadsheet—giving on a single long page an account of some horrific or exciting event at a cost of up to a penny—could sell over a million copies. The new popular working-class reading material of the 1830s and 1840s was a development of the broadsheet, arising out of increased literacy: the melodramatic serial story

---

[2] Tedder, 'Periodicals', *Encyclopaedia Britannica* (9th edn.), vol. 18, p. 538.

was issued in penny parts by writers such as G. W. M. Reynolds (1814–79), who with his mixture of sensationalist romance combined with social protest was capable of selling between 60,000 and 100,000 copies of his work on the first day of publication. It is estimated that his serial *The Mysteries of London* sold nearly a million copies between 1845 and 1855.[3]

Meanwhile, the opportunistic publisher Richard Bentley began the practice of cheap six-shilling reprints, with his 'Standard Novels' in 1832. By 1847 he was offering a new edition of 109 titles, the price of which he reduced by up to a half in 1849. In 1852 he further established his 'Shilling Series' and his 'Railway Library' again at one shilling. In 1858 Chapman and Hall cooperated with W. H. Smith in issuing 'yellowbacks', two-shilling reprints of popular novels. The yellowback series also included adventure and detective stories, more risqué and sensationalist, for the increasing market formed by the literate working class. Cheap collected editions of authors such as G. P. R. James, William Ainsworth, and Bulwer-Lytton who had become popular classics in their own lifetime also began to appear— the 'Cheap Edition' of Dickens appeared at one and a half pence a part, forming an average price of three shillings and sixpence per novel. Cheap foreign reprints appeared from Harper Brothers in America and Tauchnitz in Germany. *Chambers's Edinburgh Journal*, launched in 1832, was dedicated to bringing a wide range of 'useful knowledge' to the working class, including a knowledge of literature and the classics. In the same year Charles Knight published his *Penny Magazine* in the belief that knowledge was the common property of the human family—the only property that could be equally divided without any diminution of the whole. In 1852, amidst flourishing sales of encyclopaedias, dictionaries, and grammars, John Cassell began to introduce his encyclopaedic self-instruction course, *Cassell's Popular Educator* in one-penny numbers, selling 1,000,000 by 1885. Mrs Beeton's *Book of Household Management* (1861) sold 60,000 copies in its first year.

As to poetry and the poets, only Tennyson the Poet Laureate could

---

[3] See esp. Louis James, *Fiction for the Working Man* (Oxford University Press, 1963) and his *Print and the People 1819–1851* (Allen Lane, Penguin, 1976) which was also published as *English Popular Literature 1819–1851* (Columbia University Press, 1976).

Fig. 7. 'Frontispiece for *The Penny Magazine*', 1832, established by Charles Knight for Henry Brougham's Society for the Diffusion of Useful Knowledge, a secular movement for the propagation of reading among the masses.

match the success of the great novelists: *In Memoriam* (1850) sold about 25,000 in its first year and a half, *Idylls of the Kings* (1859) sold 10,000 in its first week and earned him £11,500 in five years. In 1865 Tennyson made £12,000 from literature. But the original edition of Browning's *The Ring and the Book*, volumes 1 and 2 (1868–9) was of 3,000 volumes and lasted until 1882, and by 1871 Browning considered a sale of 2,500 in a year good by his standards. For most poets, the writing of poetry offered status but little money.

But the general reading market prospered, as the mere statistics show. What *The Times* had called the 'taxes on knowledge' were reduced and then abolished: the stamp tax on newspapers in 1855 and the government duty on paper in 1861. The window tax was also ended in 1851, increasing light and thus the opportunities for reading, in up to one-seventh of the houses in the country. National markets developed from London as a result of improvements in roads, railways, and the development of the penny post. By the later 1870s W. H. Smith, with a network of newsagent stalls on every main railway line in the country, could deliver the 5 a.m. edition of London-printed papers to Bristol by 9 a.m. and Newcastle by noon. Free public libraries were just beginning to multiply following the passing of the Ewart Act in 1850, and by 1850 there were 610 mechanics' institute libraries holding almost 700,000 volumes, circulating 1,820,000 a year. In addition, for one guinea a year Mudie's circulating library would allow subscribers to take out one volume at a time without limit. Charles Edward Mudie had opened his Great Hall, the headquarters of his circulating library, in New Oxford Street in 1852 and proceeded to amass there 960,000 volumes in ten years, of which nearly half were novels. The business brought in up to £40,000 per annum in the 1860s and acquired as many as 120,000 volumes a year. With sufficient bulk purchasing power to demand a 60 per cent discount on the retail price from the publishers, with a market of up to 25,000 subscribers, it was Mudie (and W. H. Smith with his 15,000 subscribers) who could dictate the success of a novel, could censor content from his Evangelical perspective, and insist upon the three-decker format, necessitating as it did the continuing return of the one-volume subscriber to complete the novel as a whole.

A further great new market opened up in children's literature, first, with Evangelical tales such as those written by ALOE ('A Lady of England', Charlotte Maria Tucker, 1821–93), but then with secular adventures for boys in Frederick Marryat's nautical stories and the works of W. H. G. Kingston, Captain Mayne Reid, and later of George Henty, culminating in R. M. Ballantyne's *Coral Island* (1858). A market for schoolboy tales followed the success of Thomas Hughes's *Tom Brown's Schooldays* (1857). Children themselves became buyers as well as recipients. Mayne Reid's *The Scalp Hunters* (1851) is thought to have sold a million copies, though his greatest success was perhaps *The Headless Horseman* (1866), a prototype story of the Wild West. Correspondingly, stories for girls, often concerned with growing up in families, were written by authors as talented as Harriet Mozley, Elizabeth Sewell, and Charlotte Yonge. Anna Sewell's *Black Beauty* (1878) was a best-selling animal story. In the work of some of these writers, including the fantasies of George MacDonald, the very boundaries between adult and child, or between male and female, became exploratively blurred. Charlotte Yonge said that she did not know whether *The Daisy Chain* (1856) was written for adults or for children, and in the novel itself what is most impressive is the way in which the children form a family between themselves, taking adult responsibility for each other at different times and in subtly differing ways.

Everywhere the dominant tendency was one of enormous cumulative expansion, even in the language itself. While from 1730 to 1739 it is estimated that only 577 new words came into the language, between 1830 and 1839 the number had risen to 2,521, in particular through an increase in scientific, technological, and sociological terms. At the same time, Victorian philology was taking a new turn, away from antiquarianism, in the direction taken by history, archaeology, geology, and Darwinism itself. Arising out of the work of the Philological Society founded in 1842, the *Oxford English Dictionary* was in the early stages of preparation in the 1860s. It was part of an age of great amassing enterprises in scholarship and in publishing, just as surely as in industry or government: the *Oxford English Dictionary*, the *Dictionary of National Biography*, the monumental ninth edition of the *Encyclopaedia Britannica*. Knowledge itself seemed to be burgeoning, even as the nation grew. Just as Leslie Stephen's *Dictionary of National Biography* was concerned with the biography of persons, 40 per cent of whom belonged to the nineteenth century, so James Murray's *Oxford English Dictionary* (originally *A New English Dictionary*) was concerned with the biography of the nation's words, in two dimensions: historical as well as current usage. Moreover, with the growth of the Empire and the development of the United States, Canada, Australia, and New Zealand, English itself had become the world language by the close of the nineteenth century. From America, Harriet Beecher Stowe's *Uncle Tom's Cabin* (1852) sold 1,500,000 copies around the world in its first year. The number for whom English was the mother tongue rose from about 26 million in 1800 to 126 million in 1900.

The world was changing and expanding for authors too. Traditionally the writer, said Thomas Carlyle in 'The Hero as Man of Letters', was an anomaly or 'accident in society' (*Heroes and Hero-Worship* (1841), lecture 5). In writing he has to find his own way without rule or necessity, overcoming the sense of the arbitrary from sentence to sentence, from one work to the next, in the act of establishing himself. Once he had finished, there was still the risk of going unrecognized and unrewarded, morally and financially. Our writers are our informal prophets, our modern preachers, said Carlyle, and yet, he lamented, they have been left gratuitously 'at the mercy of blind Chance', 'one of the thousand arriving saved, nine-hundred-and-ninety-nine lost by the way'. Carlyle believed that individual struggle was a vital part of what he called the writer's ordeal, but that some form of social assistance, of institutional organization was necessary and was on its way. 'For so soon as men get to discern the importance of a thing, they do infallibly set about arranging it, facilitating it, forwarding it.'

By 1847 George Henry Lewes could claim in an article on 'The Condition of Authors' that 'literature has become a profession': 'It is a means of subsistence, almost as certain as the bar or the church' (*Fraser's Magazine*, March 1847). Although the attempt to set up a society of authors largely failed, writers gradually secured sounder legal contracts and copyrights. Instead of accepting a lump sum for an edition of unlimited size, authors began to follow the example of George Eliot and take regular royalties, a small amount paid for each copy sold. From a sample of 600 literary writers in the nineteenth century, whose fathers' occupations can be identified, 77 per cent came from the middle class.[4] By 1888 over 14,000 people in London alone made a living from writing, albeit mainly through periodic journalism.

Opportunities for fresh independent-minded provincials, often from a strong Nonconformist educational tradition, had increased. It became possible for thinkers such as Lewes or the self-educated Herbert Spencer to maintain themselves as freelance writers through the periodical press without being dependent upon allegiance to any institution or patron. The periodicals brought together literature, philosophy, history, sociology, and politics—without fixed lines of demarcation. Serialized fiction existed alongside the world of social policy, current affairs, and science. The spacious non-specialist review-essay characteristically moved to and fro between the book reviewed and the subject matter that arose out of it.

Matthew Arnold complained in *Culture and Anarchy* (1869), with some justification, that political and religious sectarianism lay behind the original founding of the periodicals, leaving each with its own party line, at the expense of true critical disinterestedness. *The Quarterly Review*, founded in 1809, and *Blackwood's Edinburgh Magazine* from 1817 were both Tory, as was *Fraser's Magazine* (1830–82). *The Edinburgh Review* (1802) was Whig, as was Bagehot's and R. H. Hutton's *National Review* (1855–64). Whig, said Bagehot, meant not so much a creed as a character: a character heedless of large theories or great imaginative speculations, with a clear view of the next step and a strong conviction that the present world could be quietly and moderately improved. Alternatively, under the editorship of John Stuart Mill (1836–40), *The Westminster Review* was radical and utilitarian, and always thereafter liberal-progressivist under John Chapman and Marian Evans, as was *The Leader* (1850–60) under G. H. Lewes and *The Fortnightly* under John Morley from 1867 to 1882. *The Monthly Repository* under W. J. Fox (1827–37) turned from unitarian religion to radical liberal politics.

Nevertheless increasingly, from the 1860s onwards, in conditions of generally increased economic and political stability, periodicals

---

[4] Richard Altick, 'The Sociology of British Authorship: The Social Origins, Education and Occupations of 1,100 British Authors, 1800–1935', *Bulletin of the New York Public Library* (June 1962), 401.

became less rigidly partisan under genuinely literary editors. In the period 1859–69 a large number of important new publications was launched (115 in 1859 alone). As well as *The Fortnightly Review* (from 1865 under Lewes and Trollope, before Morley), these included *Macmillan's Magazine* (from the publisher Alexander Macmillan in 1859, as a showcase for his goods, edited by David Masson and later John Morley), Dickens's weekly *All the Year Round* in 1859 (in succession to his *Household Words*, 1850), and *The Cornhill Magazine* (from that most enterprising publisher George Smith in 1860, and edited in turn by Thackeray, Lewes, and Leslie Stephen). In addition from 1856 the weekly *Saturday Review* began publishing influential review articles of the latest novels. During the 1860s too the literary world responded to the growing female market: Emily Faithfull launched the women's Victoria Press, Mrs Henry Wood and Mrs Braddon edited *The Argosy* and *The Belgravia* respectively. With the accent on criticism rather than prejudice, and with an increased literary emphasis in response to the widening range of market across the sexes, the new periodicals allowed for a broader range of views. Under the editorship of R. H. Hutton, perhaps the best regular critic of the century, *The Spectator* developed from 1861 what was virtually a school of literary criticism committed to careful discriminations, supported by illustrative evidence rather than descriptive adjectives. At *The Times* E. S. Dallas maintained a high standard of reviewing as literary editor throughout the fifties, until he left the paper in 1865. By the late 1870s the practice of using signed or at least initialled contributors began to replace the practice of anonymity, and articles were seen to represent their author and not necessarily the journal.

What all this meant was the development of a vigorous, nonspecialized, polymathic freedom of thinking in Victorian England, working within a definition of 'literature' or 'letters' wide enough to allow speculative linguistic movement across and between several disciplines. In 1858 J. H. Newman argued that any writing in which words tried to express thoughts and not just stand for things—where language was employed 'in its full compass, as including phraseology, idiom, style, composition, rhythm, eloquence'—was itself 'a sort of Literature' (*The Idea of a University*, pt. 2 'University Subjects', ch. 2, sect. 3). At a different level, in *Ranthorpe* (1847) his novel of literary life, George Henry Lewes specifically dismissed the idea of romantic genius as something utterly special and apart: it was not that genius differed from common humanity in suffering more, it differed only in being able to give that suffering greater expression (bk. 4 ch. 8). Art was not to be separated off from the full range of common, contemporary life.

Amidst all this burgeoning growth, there remained a sense that nonetheless it was not an unqualified good. To John Stuart Mill writing 'On Civilization' in 1836, the world was already bolting its intellectual food in an act of consumption that made books less solid, more like newspapers. Over 25,000 different journals of all kinds were produced during the reign of Victoria.[5] Symptomatically, the word 'to scan' changed its very meaning over the period, from examining minutely to skimming or getting the gist. 'The world reads too much and too quickly to read well', Mill had concluded.

A hurried sequential style was, according to Henry H. Breen, 'peculiar to the nineteenth century', changing the very shape of experience and syntax of thought. In its emphasis on successive linear time, he said, it might be called 'the *railway* style':

It is alike remarkable for the rapidity of its transitions from thought to thought, and for the length of theme the writer may go over without drawing breath. It has no time for colons or semicolons, and bestows but a passing notice on the commas. As to full stops, it admits of only one, and that it calls a *terminus*. Stops were well enough in the steady, stately, coach-horse phraseology of the Johnsons, but they are unsuited to our days of electricity and steam. (*Modern English Literature: Its Blemishes and Defects* (1857), p. 141)

As the machine-operated printing presses rolled, English grammar itself was becoming more linear, more speedy. One hundred years earlier in 1750, Samuel Johnson could write thus, for example, on the metaphysical poet Cowley's fantasy of retreat from the world:

He forgot, in the vehemence of desire, that solitude and quiet owe their pleasures to those miseries, which he was so solicitous to obviate; for such

[5] Estimated by Walter Houghton in 'Periodical Literature and the Articulate Classes', in J. Shattock and M. Wolff (eds.), *The Victorian Periodical Press: Samplings and Soundings* (Leicester University Press, 1982), 3–28.

are the vicissitudes of the world, through all its parts, that day and night, labour and rest, hurry and retirement, endear each other; such are the changes that keep the mind in action. (*Rambler*, 6 (7 Apr. 1750))

In contrast Breen must have had in mind the age's most emphatically serial writer, Charles Dickens, in the railway journey of Dombey in chapter 20 of *Dombey and Son* (1848) where the only terminus is 'Death', or in the phantasmagorial flight of Carker in chapter 55:

The clatter and commotion echoed to the hurry and discordance of the fugitive's ideas. Nothing clear without, and nothing clear within. Objects flitting past, merging into one another, dimly descried, confusedly lost sight of, gone!

This is serial prose, registered as much in the precipitate syntax of the driven sentences as in the larger fact of publication in urgent monthly parts. It flashes past: 'He could not separate one subject of reflection from another, sufficiently to dwell upon it, by itself, for a minute at a time.'

Arising out of the review format, it was the essay, said Walter Bagehot, that most symptomatically marked the transition 'from ancient writing to modern'. In 'The First Edinburgh Reviewers' in *The National Review* for October 1855, Bagehot agreed with Mill that review-writing 'exemplifies the casual character of modern literature': temporary, fragmentary, wide-rangingly suggestive and provisional, rather than complete and definitive. But for all the risks of superficiality, the essay form was meeting the challenge that democracy offered to the contemporary reality of intellectual thought. Compared with the slowly winding professorial lecture, the modern essay, said Bagehot, is more linear, more swift and ranging, more alive in time, more intimately conversational. It was forcing serious subject matter out of the study and taking it, with the renewed energy of urgent relevance, into the common world. In such ways, if literature was becoming a profession, it was to be *the* profession that operated against the rise of specialized professionalism itself.[6]

---

[6] See Stefan Collini's important work *Public Moralists: Political Thought and Intellectual Life in Britain 1850–1930* (Clarendon Press, 1991), in particular on the rise of specialization in the late 19th and early 20th cents. Also see John Gross, *The Rise and Fall of the Man of Letters: Aspects of English Literary Life since 1800*

There were many such ways in which Victorian literature was fighting against the world out of which it arose and to which it remained committed. For within that literature, democracy was often struggling with itself, the middle-class readership made to confront and resist some of the very tendencies related to its success. This tension was inevitable when there were such strong relations between the extension of literary communication and the development of democracy. Before 1800 the English language, said Carlyle in 'The Hero as Man of Letters', was for most people something heard and not seen. But printing was a natural development of writing, and, said Carlyle, democracy was the further natural development of wide-scale printing. By widening the access to books, the invention of print had helped to create the individual who could begin to think alone and independently: increasingly throughout the nineteenth century that access and the sheer amount of print proliferated. Yet the difficulty for democracy, concluded Matthew Arnold, 'is how to find and keep high ideals' ('Democracy' (1861), in *Complete Prose Works*, vol. 2, pp. 3–29). The working-class hero of George Eliot's *Felix Holt, the Radical* (1866) is concerned that the extension of the franchise should not take the place of the extension of education. What was important, insisted Arnold, was not only that people could read but what they did read. Democracy would be undermined, and the working classes betrayed by their own lack of education, without a proper schooling and a high level of culture for all. But in the great expansive boom of the Victorian period, it was the middle class, in particular, that became the initial focus of both extended opportunities and increased anxieties.

It is the middle class which is the great reader; that immense literature of the day which we see surging up all round us—literature the absolute value of which it is almost impossible to rate too humbly, literature hardly a word of which will reach, or deserves to reach, the future—it is the middle class which calls it forth, and its evocation is at least a sign of the widespread mental movement in the class. Will this movement go on and be fruitful: will it conduct the middle class to a high and commanding pitch of culture and intelligence? (Matthew Arnold, 'A French Eton' (1863–4), in *Complete Prose Works*, vol. 2, pp. 262–325)

(Weidenfeld and Nicholson, 1969) and Harold Perkin, *The Rise of Professional Society: England since 1880* (Routledge, 1989).

'Widespread' was played off against 'high', the one to be converted into the other, in the effort to save the raw energy of the middle classes from being consumed in that crude, over-literal, and material sense of meaning which Arnold in *Culture and Anarchy* called the philistinism of the bourgeois world of business.

Arnold saw the rise of a new threefold class system, each class-mentality bound within its own narrow vested interests, rigidly dividing and deforming society into three. If the lower classes were crudely brutalized and the aristocracy effetely materialized, the best chance for the immediate moral future of the nation, Arnold believed, lay with the education of the rising class in between. Arnold accepted that the primary effort of existence was first '*to affirm one's essence*' ('Democracy'). But, once achieved, the second challenge for a society was that it should not just affirm but '*transform itself*' turning existence into civilization, material values into spiritual ones ('A French Eton'). Having already secured a reliable level of subsistence, it was the middle classes that constituted the Victorian testing ground for the possibilities of ordinary human development beyond the material stage. For the middle class, poised in the midst of the new historical situation—'with so many correspondence, communications, and openings into the lower class'—was the vanguard for all that lay both below and before it ('Ecce, Convertimur ad Gentes' (1879), in *Complete Prose Works*, vol. 9, pp. 1–19).

If the education of the middle class fails, argued Arnold, the education of the working classes will go down with it. In *Culture and Anarchy* he argued that 'Plenty of people will try to give the masses, as they call them, an intellectual food prepared and adapted in a way they think proper': 'ordinary popular literature' offers just such fare, merely re-enforcing what it claims the working classes really want, while 'our religious and political organisations' are ever ready to provide well-meaning indoctrination. But culture, says Arnold, does not try to 'teach down' to the level of the lower classes, does not have the ulterior purposes of premeditating how to 'win them for this or that sect of its own, with ready-made judgments and watchwords'. Instead culture seeks to 'do away with classes', to make universally available 'the best that has been known and thought in the world'; for genuine literature, unlike dogma or ideology, seeks to find its way freely into the minds of what are thus individuals and not target-groups. This is the true 'social idea', he concludes, 'and the men of culture are the true apostles of equality' (ch. 1). Evangelicals, Utilitarians, and radical journalists in the first half of the century were often suspicious of literature. But it was the Arnoldian idea of liberal self-education that became ever-increasingly throughout the later nineteenth and early twentieth centuries the inspiration of working-class efforts at cultural betterment and mental independence.

Beginning, nonetheless, with the education of the middle classes, what Arnold offered above all was a more literary way of thinking, even for those who were not themselves creative writers. 'Criticism' in his hands was not mere belletrist appreciation, but an alternative to the tunnel vision of the religious or political party line. The critic did not rigidly adhere to just one book, one class, one party, one country, or one thought, but was a comparative thinker, able to take thoughts from anywhere. As Arnold put it in his preface to *Literature and Dogma* (1873), culture means '*getting the power, through reading, to estimate the proportion and relation in what we read.* If we read but very little, we naturally want to press it all; if we read a great deal, we are willing not to press the whole of what we read.' Culture here is not Carlyle's single-minded hero-worship; it is instead, in its sheer width and flexibility of experience, the subtler capacity for what Arnold called 'returning upon oneself'. In other words, a critical mind could bear to turn round upon itself and see limitations in the midst of what it admires, as well as possibilities within what it might otherwise instinctively reject.

By steadily 'refusing to lend itself' to 'ulterior, political, practical considerations', said Arnold, a genuinely 'disinterested' intelligence was thus to emancipate itself from the deformed cerebral machinery by which ugly vested interests automatically produced set thoughts in the human mind ('The Function of Criticism at the Present Time' (1864), in *Complete Prose Works*, vol. 3, pp. 258–85). This is what Mill in 'Civilization' had called a 'counter-tendency', to get the modern world out from within itself, to look at itself, and to turn round upon itself.

Yet if Arnold's critical work existed for the sake of the middle class, his working life was spent—very much in practical terms—amongst the school-children of the working classes. For thirty-five years, from 1851, Matthew Arnold was one of Her Majesty's

Inspectors of Schools, struggling inside the grinding inadequacies of the English education system. John Stuart Mill feared the potentially coercive power of the democratic state if allowed to set the agenda for education. But the parlous state of the nation's schooling made Arnold advocate the necessity for unified state action, in the teeth of the resistance to centralized control that came from differing religious denominations, from local self-government, and from the employers of cheap young labour.

Middle- and upper-class parents were free to educate their children in any way they wished: at home, through governess or tutor; or in private schools, day or boarding. Secondary schools, taking education beyond the elementary stage and leading onto university level for a small minority, were for the fee-paying middle and upper classes and were without state aid or regulation. They included everything from the great 'public' schools such as Eton and Harrow and Rugby, to the charitably endowed grammar schools in Leeds and Liverpool, to private ventures as terrible as Dotheboys Hall in Dickens's *Nicholas Nickleby*. But the only state-aided schools in the nineteenth century were 'elementary' schools, offering bare training in the basic skills of reading, writing, and arithmetic to the children of the labouring poor for at most six years, before they commenced work at an age between 10 and 13. Rudimentary institutions for teacher-training were established in the 1830s. But school attendance only became universally compulsory after Forster's national Education Act of 1870. It was the second Reform Act of 1867 with its increased momentum towards universal democracy that finally prompted the national educational reforms of the 1870s, either in support of the democratic movement or to ameliorate its threat.

In 1851, there were nearly five million children of school age (between 3 and 15 years) and of these 600,000 were officially at work, over two million at school, and the rest at neither. In the state schools, mechanical rote learning was demanded by Robert Lowe's Revised Code of 1862 which insisted, in the narrow Utilitarian spirit satirized by Dickens in *Hard Times*, on 'payment by results'. This, said Arnold, was to put 'information' in place of 'culture'. As he argued in a lecture on 'Literature and Science' (1882), there was more to human nature than the desire for pure knowledge, and what literature did—as science could not—was to put knowledge 'into relation with our sense of conduct, our sense for beauty, and touched with emotion by being so put' (*Complete Prose Works*, vol. 10, pp. 53–73). This, as he wrote in *Culture and Anarchy*, is what *humanizes* knowledge.

As part of this process, the inspectorate by 1871 had helped see to it that 'English Literature' was formally made part of the elementary syllabus. It meant no more at first than that a passage of poetry, between 100 and 300 lines, was to be memorized and its meanings and allusions learnt. But even at elementary level, insisted Arnold in his General Report of 1880, the passages of poetry should be chosen not as an introduction to something else ostensibly more practical but in their own right and for their own sake as 'centres of interest'. What needs protecting, argued Arnold 'is best described by the word *interesting*', innocent of ulterior purposes: 'I do but take note, in the word *interesting*, of a requirement, a cry of aspiration' ('Civilisation in the United States' (1888), in *Complete Prose Works*, vol. 11, pp. 350–69).

E. A. Abbott, clergyman-headmaster of the City of London school, gave examples from Shakespeare's *Richard II* of what he thought a middle-class schoolboy could be expected to understand:

> That which in mean men we entitle patience
> Is pale cold cowardice in noble breasts.

Give reasons for justifying or condemning this maxim. . . . 'Yet can I not of such tame patience boast?'—What is the difference between 'patience' and 'tameness', 'tameness' and 'cowardice'?[7]

In his influential *Study of Words* (1851) R. C. Trench spoke of the positive enriching of a language when 'two or more words which were once promiscuously used, are felt to have had each its own peculiar domain assigned to it, which it shall not itself overstep, upon which the others shall not encroach' (lecture 5). This sort of study— from the schools to the universities—made of language a matter not merely of words and sounds but of *thoughts* in their mental domains. But more than that, Archbishop Trench wrote that the first discovery that words are 'living powers' was like 'the acquiring of another sense, or the introduction into a new world' (lecture 1). Charlotte

---

[7] See Alan Bacon (ed.), *The Nineteenth-Century History of English Studies* (Ashgate, 1998), 177.

Brontë told Mrs Gaskell that it was Trench who helped open her eyes to the need to take time in 'patiently searching for the right term' (*Life of Charlotte Brontë*, vol. 2, ch. 2).

To get at the real meaning of a carefully written sentence was complicated: 'It is only because English is our mother tongue, and we therefore understand its utterances for the most part intuitively, and without the laborious process of formal analysis, that this fact has been so long overlooked.'[8] But the analysis of the ancient languages, of Latin and Greek, had long been the staple diet of the public schools and the great universities, and the formal study of English literature and language only began to 'come in accidentally, as it were,' noted F. W. Maurice, 'to illustrate the books which the pupil is reading for another purpose, not as separate subjects'.[9] The formal organization of what before had been instinctive or accidental was the price of democracy, where democracy was defined by Arnold as 'a force in which the concert of a great number of men makes up for the weakness of each man taken by himself' ('Democracy'). It was a price that several contributors to a symposium in the *Pall Mall Gazette* (1886–7) were unwilling to pay: asked whether English literature should become a subject taught at a modern university, Walter Pater replied, 'Why transform into a difficult exercise what is natural virtue?' (quoted in Bacon, p. 242). Yet in the teeth of accusations of being an 'easy' school, in comparison with mathematics, the classics, or philology, 'English' entered the list of subjects for degrees offered by the University of London in 1859, more than fifty years ahead of the ancient universities of Oxford and Cambridge. This then is the period that marks the beginning of the study of English Literature as a formal discipline, for one crucial and ambitious purpose. To the worried defenders of culture it was organized education, in teaching what to read and how, that was to support the rescue of human meaning.

Thus, at the very onset of the processes of institutionalization, Victorian intellectual writers worked, paradoxically, within the institution to get beyond institutions, within the hurried successive-

---

[8] The anonymous author of an article on 'The Study of English Classics' in the *Museum and English Journal of Education* (March 1867), repr. in Bacon (ed.), 126.

[9] *Has the Church, or the State, the Power to Educate the Nation?* (1839), repr. in Bacon (ed.), 55.

ness of time in search of meanings beyond mere transience, within the form of books to get to that real life outside them which was the books' own subject matter, and within the middle class to get beyond the confines of class. Within each class, said Arnold, 'there are a certain number of *aliens*, if we may so call them,—persons who are mainly led, not by their class spirit, but by a general *humane* spirit' (*Culture and Anarchy*, ch. 3). Yet these aliens, which Coleridge in an earlier generation had called the clerisy, were not alienated: they worked within the structures they sought to change, without being of them. Where in *The German Ideology* (1845–6) Marx had complained that doctors too often spoke only as doctors and lawyers thought only as lawyers, and never now as human beings separate from their professions, the implicit claim of Victorian writers and intellectuals was to be a humane profession that worked against mere professionalism itself, a non-capitalist agency lodged in the middle of the market society it sought to modify, with access to the whole range and depth of the English language unfettered by specialist interests.

So it was that in *Unto This Last*, serialized in *The Cornhill Magazine* in 1860, Ruskin sought to redeem the word 'value' from the contemporary place to which political economy assigned it within the terms of exchange, and to restore in its stead the memory of the ancient meaning from the Latin verb *valere*: to be well or strong in life. What was involved in Ruskin's diagnosis was a prophetic use of etymology, of what he called in *Sesame and Lilies* 'the peerage of words' in a debased age. 'Rich' is only a relative second-order word, dependent for its meaning upon 'poor'. The extra diachronic dimension—the time, experience, and thought offered within the history of the language as it comes back to life under the pen of the attentive writer—offered an alternative to synchronic enclosure within the world of contemporary social pressures. The language tells us more truly, says Ruskin, that 'There is no wealth but life' (essay 4).

Speaking in the town hall, Bradford in 1864 on the proposed opening of a new exchange, Ruskin declined what he called the role of 'a respectable architectural man-milliner' and spoke instead like one of Arnold's aliens in defence of life itself:

My good Yorkshire friends, you asked me down here among your hills that I might talk to you about this Exchange you are going to build: but, earnestly and seriously asking you to pardon me, I am going to do nothing of the kind. . . . I do *not* care about this Exchange of yours. . . . I do not care about this Exchange—because *you* don't. . . . The first, and last, and closest trial question to any living creature is, 'What do you like?' Tell me what you like, and I'll tell you what you are. ('Traffic', in *Works*, vol. 18, pp. 433–5)

This, in Ruskin's own inimitable style as guest speaker, is what Carlyle called anomaly, Mill counter-tendency, and Arnold a turning round.

II. The Rise of Prose

'We think that, as civilisation advances, poetry almost necessarily declines.' In 1825 in his essay 'Milton' (*Edinburgh Review*, August 1825) Thomas Babington Macaulay (1800–59), historian and man of letters, signalled what he took to be the inevitable rise of an age of prose: non-fictional and even anti-fictional.

In science, argued Macaulay, progress means that the first speculators get left behind. But in poetry the first practitioners are never surpassed: it is poetry itself that gets left behind. Poetry belongs to the darker ages of magic; as enlightenment breaks through, its mystery is exposed as illusion. There are two distinct worlds of human consciousness—poetry and prose, one ancient, one modern: 'We cannot unite the incompatible advantages of reality and deception, the clear discernment of truth and the exquisite enjoyment of fiction.' The inevitable modern movement is towards the gains and losses involved in prosaic understanding and demystification. If Shakespeare had been asked to write a book *about* the complex motives of human action, he could not have done it; what he could do was bring into being the motives themselves, in the creation of his plays. Now we know more and create less. 'In proportion as men know more and think more, they look less at individuals and more at classes.' Thinking has become more general, more consciously explanatory and philosophical.

Though right about the essential direction, in one sense Macaulay could hardly have been more wrong. It was *fictional* prose that was about to explode upon the age, albeit a fiction claiming increasingly to be as close as possible to common reality. From 1837 to 1901 over 40,000 novels were published. Between 1846 and 1848 alone, for example, the reader of new novels could find *Dombey and Son, Jane Eyre, Wuthering Heights, Tancred, Vanity Fair, The Tenant of Wildfell Hall, Mary Barton, Yeast,* and *Loss and Gain.* Between 1860 and 1863 among the new novels on offer were *Great Expectations, Mill on the Floss, The Woman in White, Evan Harrington, Silas Marner, Romola, Framley Parsonage, Orley Farm, East Lynne, Lady Audley's Secret, No Name, The Water Babies, Sylvia's Lovers,* and *Salem Chapel.* In a letter to the American publisher J. T. Fields in 1855, Charles Reade, author of sensational and historical novels such as *The Cloister and the Hearth* (1861), spoke of the novel as the 'great prose epic' in place of the epic poetry of the ancients.

The premature death of the second generation of great Romantic poets—Keats in 1821, Shelley in 1822, Byron in 1824—only helped to produce such a situation. The immediately post-Romantic years through the 1820s and 1830s became a near hiatus in English literature. It was a period which was bequeathed a Romantic model of feeling—in particular, the childhood love of nature rooted in the countryside—increasingly inappropriate to the changed social, industrial, and urban conditions of the later nineteenth century.

Whilst the poet Wordsworth lived on until 1850, an almost symbolically anachronistic Lake District recluse, second-generation Romantic prose writers such as Thomas De Quincey, William Hazlitt, and Charles Lamb confronted in the London of the 1820s the loss of the naturally supportive Wordsworthian background to memory provided by the countryside. What the medium of prose offered the displaced writer, in lieu of a sense of feeling naturally at home in the world, was the alternative background of a lower, more indirect, and, above all, more circumstantial language which could spell out the predicament of emotional experience amidst new contexts and changing conditions. What, in turn, these writers brought to prose was a new capacity for personal voice, confessional and conversational, for which in the past only poetry had seemed to offer expression. Together these two attributes—voice and context—were to make for the dual language of the novel.

In the hands of George Eliot, a few spoken words—like those of the exasperated Lydgate in the face of his wife's passive resistance to domestic economies, 'Understand, then, that it is what *I like to do*'—generate twice as many words around them, in place of a direct reply:

> There was a tone in the last sentence which was equivalent to the clutch of his strong hand on Rosamond's delicate arm. But for all that his will was not a whit stronger than hers. She immediately walked out of the room in silence, with an intense determination to hinder what Lydgate liked to do. (*Middlemarch* (1872), ch. 64)

Such sub-vocal words provide—like the nineteenth-century realist novel as a whole—the human context, filling in the tonal circumstances and bringing *forward* the background story to human meaning. 'To think is to speak low', said Max Muller, Professor of Comparative Philology at Oxford, in a 'lecture on Mr Darwin's Philosophy of Language' reprinted in *Fraser's Magazine* (May 1873). A low-voiced under-prose speaks of what George Eliot calls 'that roar which lies on the other side of silence' (*Middlemarch*, ch. 20), putting in what poetry would leave out or leave implicit. For the aftermath of that failed marital conversation carries over into a further paragraph of nearly 300 words, as Lydgate takes with him out of the house a

> deposit of dread within him at the idea of ever opening with his wife in future subjects which might again urge him to violent speech. . . . In marriage, the certainty, 'She will never love me much', is easier to bear than the fear, 'I shall love her no more.'

For all their explicitness these painfully suppressed thoughts *about* the situation have to remain silently and helplessly *within* it, without recourse to escape or transcendence, as the situation simply goes on and on, unresolved.

The novel about one's fellow creatures, read in private yet with a sense of shared relation not only to the characters but to the tacit community of other readers, was the main alternative to more immediate forms of cultural unity. Reading aloud to the family or in a group made the links and resonances more explicit. Indeed, as though within a giant family setting, Dickens's public readings of his works were an attempt to close the gap between public and private, for it was Dickens who most wanted popular drama to succeed as a national democratic form of culture.[10] In an age of expanded audiences for political debate, political speeches were an alternative dramatic medium for creating direct and immediate shared feeling— the aim of orators as powerful as Gladstone, John Bright, or Ernest Jones—with writing turned back out into speech, and belief and feeling extending over whole crowds. Yet in the attempt to obliterate the distinction between inside and out, the slippage into demagoguery was, nonetheless, well-nigh inevitable.

Poetry retained its high status. The career of Matthew Arnold as both poet and critic is one long campaign for the nobility of poetry— 'the grand style'—in what nonetheless Arnold recognized as the unpoetic age of the democratic realist novel. One social index of that continuing high status is that it was Tennyson, the Poet Laureate— not Dickens or Trollope—who was given a peerage. Yet increasingly throughout the nineteenth century, whatever the actual achievements of the poets, the name 'Poetry' too often became a vague shorthand term for a lost lyrical directness of first-person feeling, an ideal of Romantic transcendentalism that was seemingly no more, alongside other religious and spiritual losses.

In its place appeared an ostensibly smaller, more domesticated bourgeois world. The close relation between the world of the realistic novel and the circumstances of its middle-class readers, the authorial reassurance offered by the detailed sense of an automatically placeable context, seemed to some reviewers, even in the 1860s, to be a poor replacement for the leap of connective imagination necessary to the reading of poetry. In the hands of such as Trollope, complained *The Saturday Review* (21 September 1867), the ostensible normality of the overly literalistic novel was 'essentially the literature of the moral and respectable middle-class mind, of people too realistic to be bothered by sentiment, too moral to countenance the sensationalism of crime, and too little spiritual to accept preachments or rhapsody for their daily use'. Trollope called himself a craftsman or artisan, not an artist.

Thus, even at the moment of its great rise, the realist novel could be dismissed as unimaginative second-rate art and unthinking popular entertainment. In an article 'False Morality of Lady Moralists' in

[10] See below, pp. 257–80.

The National Review (January 1859), W. R. Greg complained that the novel induced a comparative passivity of the brain by the addictive surrender to an ever ongoing mass of material. The long novel offered a world of its own sufficiently close to the real world as to be, almost unthinkingly, a replacement for it. Reading time got increasingly close to the time depicted in the novels themselves: as Trollope put it in his *Autobiography* (1883), 'On the last day of each month recorded, every person in his novel should be a month older than on the first . . . It is so that I have lived with my characters, and thence has come whatever success I have attained' (ch. 12). The rise of Evangelicalism had revived the old puritan doubts about fictions: here was the realist novel hiding its fictionality in a way that poetry did not. Young readers and women readers, significantly conjoined, were seen as emotionally susceptible to fiction as fantasy.[11] Resistance was further lowered when the fantasy was so thoroughly concealed within everyday appearances.

'We have become a novel-reading people,' proclaimed Trollope famously in 1870 ('On English Prose Fiction as a Rational Amusement').[12] But in the first decades of the century no second-generation Romantic could have imagined that, within a few further decades, prose was to become for the first time in the history of English literature the dominant mode of literary expression. Nonetheless, some sense of the magnitude of the shock may be retrospectively reconstructed from a reading of Hazlitt's essays comparing poetry and prose.

To Hazlitt, in 'On Poetry in General' (1818), prose was a lower, demotic medium compared to the writing of poetry. For poetry was not just a specialized literary activity: a contempt for poetry was, he wrote, a lack of respect for everything in the *world* that partook of beauty, power, harmony, and passion. Poetry opens up the world, reveals its greatest heights and lowest depths; it has something creatively divine in it. In explicit contrast to prose, 'it describes the flowing not the fixed. It does not define the limits of sense, or analyze the distinctions of understanding, but signifies the excess of the

---

[11] See Kate Flint, *The Woman Reader 1837–1914* (Oxford University Press, 1993).

[12] In *Four Lectures*, ed. M. L. Parrish (Constable, 1938; repr. 1976).

imagination beyond the actual or ordinary impression of any object or feeling.' Above and beyond the prosaically ordinary, poetry is thus to 'common language' what wings are to feet, and poets are 'winged animals' whose inspiration lifts them above the mere ground of prose. Poetry flows like 'the music of language' releasing the secrets of harmonious beauty; whereas 'the jerks, the breaks, the inequalities, and harshnesses of prose' fatally disrupt 'the flow of a poetical imagination'.

Common prose differs from poetry, as treating for the most part either of such trite, familiar, and irksome matters of fact, as convey no extraordinary impulse to the imagination, or else of such difficult and laborious processes of the understanding, as do not admit of the wayward or violent movements either of the imagination or the passions.

The rise of a prose world thus threatened to constitute in Hazlitt's eyes a veritable fall into a reduced sense of reality.

From the solitary passionate mountain heights of Romanticism's individual lyric elitism, literature passed to the novel's common ground of social language and shared dialogue. It was like Biddy's riposte to Pip in *Great Expectations*, when he prates of how Joe Gargery would only feel uncomfortable were he to mix with Pip's higher-class friends—'And don't you think he knows that?' (ch. 19). It was a bringing down to earth.

Thus it was that the great German Romantic philosopher G. W. F. Hegel in his *Lectures on Aesthetics*, delivered in the 1820s, concluded that the novel was the quintessential product of a prose world order which no longer believed the universe to be poetic at its core. In the novel such poetry as remained within the human heart was subject increasingly to the prosaic reality of the external realm. It was an art that seemed already to have given in to the impress of an increasingly material world, enmeshed in the mere particular narrative of its ordinary contingencies.

To Hazlitt, moreover, prose was not only a demotic but also an indiscriminate medium—well suited, as it turned out, to the hurriedly incongruous intermingling of high and low in the jostling city streets of the 1820s–1840s. In his essay 'On the Prose Style of Poets' (1822), Hazlitt notes that prose, unlike poetry, has no innate order or decorum: no rhyme, no measure, no time or space of its own by which formally to separate itself from ordinary discourse. The prose writer 'always mingles clay with his gold': 'he rises with the lofty, descends with the mean, luxuriates in beauty, gloats over deformity' as his subject demands, as he goes along in headlong pursuit of it. 'It is all the same to him', sentence after sentence poured out in the successive mass jumble of prolific linear prose. So, De Quincey's 'The English Mail-Coach', written nostalgically in 1849, turns characteristically from jovial remembrances to thoughts about sudden death, with hardly a transition.

It is this apparent indiscriminateness that Dickens exploits, suddenly mixing comic and serious together in a new combination of sentiments.[13] 'I don't eat babies,' says the monstrous dwarf Quilp in *The Old Curiosity Shop*; 'I don't like 'em' (ch. 50). 'What is to be done with him?', cries Miss Trotwood at the sight of her poor, dirty, runaway young nephew: 'Why if I was you,' replies Mr Dick, one of Dickens' holy idiots, 'I should—. . . I should wash him!' (*David Copperfield*, ch. 13). Whispering through the door in ludicrous urgent bursts to the young boy locked in his room, Peggotty says to David, 'What I want to say is. That you must never forget me. For I'll never forget you' (*David Copperfield*, ch. 4). And a sentence that might have been too easily passed over, now read in slow-motion telegraphese, becomes an achievement. Dickens knows full well the hidden shifts of level within prose's ongoing line, when suddenly even comic incongruities become serious and moving.

It was precisely prose's evolved capacity for such quick, improvised, and unsignalled inner changes that by 1848 was being celebrated by Charles Kingsley as a mature creative freedom:

For indeed, as elocution is the highest melody, so is true prose the highest poetry. Consider how in an air, the melody is limited to a few arbitrary notes, and recurs at arbitrary periods, while the more scientific the melody becomes, the more numerous and nearly allied are the notes employed, and the more complex and uncertain is their recurrence, in short, the nearer does the melody of the air approach to the melody of elocution, in which the notes of the voice ought continually to be passing into each other, by imperceptible gradations, and their recurrence to depend entirely on the emotions conveyed in the subject words. Just so, poetry employs a

---

[13] On Dickens, with particular relation to Thackeray, see below pp. 296–317.

confined and arbitrary metre, and a periodic recurrence of sounds which disappear gradually in its higher forms of the ode and the drama, till the poetry at last passes into prose, a free and ever-shifting flow of every imaginable rhythm and metre, determined by no arbitrary rules, but only by the spiritual intent of the subject. ('On English Composition', *Introductory Lectures delivered at Queen's College, London* (1849), in Bacon (ed.), pp. 85–6)

It is that repeated phrase 'passing into' which is crucial in describing the very movement of prose itself, a linear process containing within the world's time subtly half-hidden fluctuations of level and direction.

That is why serialization could become a natural if challenging mode for prose. 'One cannot always stop to see how it all looks', said Kingsley himself in the midst of his hard-pressed writing of *Westward Ho!* (1855) in serial numbers, one issue passing into another. In what Trollope called the rushing mode of publication, it was often the case that the first time an author could see his work as a whole was only at the end of the proofing process or, much later, when the instalments were prepared for a new edition in volume form. Even as they went along, authors had to seek some form other than that of sheer successiveness, for which nonetheless successiveness might still be the vehicle.

As so often, it is Dickens above all who relishes turning problems into opportunities. Manuscript was submitted to the printers who then provided the author with galley proofs for revision, if time permitted. In such circumstances it was necessary for the author to become a careful calculator of the relation of the number of hand-written pages to the number of pages that appeared finally in print. When Dickens received back the proofs for the first number (chs. 1–3) of *David Copperfield* in April 1849 he found that for once he had miscalculated and had more space at his disposal. He never liked to be seen to give short measure or to be providing padding either, and he therefore added a long passage—not to the end of chapter 3 but in its midst, concerning Little Em'ly's flirting with danger on 'a jagged timber' which 'overhung the deep water at some height':

The light, bold, fluttering little figure turned and came back safe to me, and I soon laughed at my fears, and at the cry I had uttered; fruitlessly in any case, for there was no one near. But there have been times since, in my manhood, many times there have been, when I have thought, Is it possible, among the possibilities of hidden things, that in the sudden rashness of the child and her wild look so far off, there was any merciful attraction of her into danger, any tempting her towards him permitted on the part of her dead father, that her life might have a chance of ending that day? There has been a time since when I have wondered whether, if the life before her could have been revealed to me at a glance, and so revealed as that a child could fully comprehend it, and if her preservation could have depended on a motion of my hand, I ought to have held it up to save her. There has been a time since—I do not say it lasted long, but it has been—when I have asked myself the question, would it have been better for little Em'ly to have had the waters close above her head that morning in my sight; and when I have answered, Yes, it would have been.

This may be premature. I have set it down too soon, perhaps. But let it stand.

David Copperfield was published monthly. When five years later he came to write *Hard Times* as a *weekly* serial, Dickens complained that 'the difficulty of the space is CRUSHING', without the 'elbow-room' and 'open places in perspective' of his usual 'patient fiction-writing' in monthly parts. Here in *David Copperfield* a space in the proofs is transformed into a sort of time-out, an open place in perspective. It is not that the passage simply adds a dramatic sense of foreboding. Dickens is never just a popular sensationalist. But suddenly, as the temporarily stationing effect of the paragraphing stops the work being simply at the mercy of time, Dickens's technical problem of finding another few pages is turned into metaphysics. The future hidden from the narrative present is itself by now a memory to its narrator, Copperfield himself. What if David had known in advance what he knows now only in retrospect? Perhaps wisely, linear life denies human beings the place or time for that terrible but impossible choice. But in the light of what was to become of her life, 'would it have been better for little Em'ly to have had the waters close above her head that morning'? If it had happened and Em'ly had drowned, the knowledge of that terrible future, which alone might have justified the accident, would never have been possible when that future would have been rendered non-existent by the very act. It is as though in the midst of both narrative and retrospect David is asking: What is the right way, when is the right time to give a truthful account of a life? His very sense of its being too late to think such things 'may be premature' here, but 'let it stand'. The narrator has to leave these strange unplaceable thoughts standing in print behind him, and go on with his sequential narrative.

In Dickens the endings of his paragraphs, his chapters, and especially his part-numbers are not mere 'cliff-hangers': as ever his art is to transmute low into high, making them also ideas in process, rhythmic punctuations, temporary forms of stationing. Even as Dickens goes along in the midst of *Great Expectations*, for example, the movement is constantly marked by farewells and returns at the end of the weekly part-numbers: temporary endings and attempted rebeginnings, little deaths and the continuance of life despite them. In fact, serialization now seems like a slower and more orchestrated way of reading a novel compared with the form in which we have the same novel nowadays as a ready whole, to be read in any size chunks the reader likes. For Dickens used serialization not simply for individual expression or market excitement but to try to make a secure family out of the whole nation. He was being characteristically only half humorous when, in an advertisement in the *Athenaeum* of March 1847 for a cheap edition, he spoke of his becoming a 'familiar piece of household stuff', 'a permanent inmate of many English homes where, in his old shape he was only known as a guest'. It was family feeling that Dickens the visionary was seeking to re-create, disdainful of the anxieties of a Mill or an Arnold in the face of a new democracy. Read aloud throughout the homes of England, each issue aimed to produce, however temporarily, an emotional state in which all the people felt the same thing at the same time.

The writers who most successfully went along with the monster force of serial mass production were those who thus sought to harness its energy to their own purposes. But serialization, said *The Saturday Review* of 21 September 1867, was only fine for Dickens and Wilkie Collins, because they were sensationalist writers, trading upon suspense and curiosity. 'Make them laugh, make them cry, make them *wait*' was Dickens's famous advice to Collins. It was not so good for the 'non-sensational writer, who does not rest his interest on playing bopeep with a secret'.

This was not quite fairly put. But there were anti-sensational authors who hated the push into serialization and knew it was wrong for them, in particular George Eliot and Mrs Gaskell. Writing *North and South* for *Household Words* in 1854–5, Mrs Gaskell found herself cajoled by the editor, no other than Dickens himself, for failing to end each episode at a point of tension. 'Compelled to hurry on events with an improbable rapidity', especially towards the end of her story, Mrs Gaskell decided in the book edition to insert five further chapters (44–8).

What these chapters do is offer the protagonist, Margaret Hale, a change of *place*, in order to slow down *time*. A stay in London 'gave her time to comprehend the sudden change which had taken place in her circumstances within the last two months' (ch. 44). Then, in chapter 46, a physical journey back to Helstone replays the story of the whole novel, now within her own mind. Returning to her late father's parsonage, only to see the alterations made by the new occupant, Margaret is left with a further inner conviction of slight but continual change that destroys her belief in the very stability of individual significance:

I am so tired—so tired of being whirled on through all these phases of my life, in which nothing abides by me, no creature, no place . . . And I too change perpetually—now this, now that—now disappointed and peevish because all is not exactly as I had pictured it, and now suddenly discovering that the reality is far more beautiful than I had imagined it.

It is through Margaret that Mrs Gaskell herself is able to slow down the physical whirling of story. For here human character is the (nonlinear) result of story coming to terms with itself: character is the extra time and the extra dimension that follows from stopping the story at the ongoing physical level, and replaying it instead at the mental one. It is for Margaret here almost as in the dream-world described in chapter 45: 'Time and space were not, though all things seemed real. Every event was measured by the emotions of the mind.' The adding of those extra chapters turns sequential story round upon itself into memory, self-consciousness, and character.

In between the writers who thrived on serialization and those who resisted it lies the case of Trollope who modified the pressures to his own terms. Trollope only felt really secure in serializing his fiction *after* he had completed the novel as a whole; he loved having at least one future work complete in manuscript while the present one was being printed. Yet as a result of the rejection of *Castle Richmond*,

Framley Parsonage was not half complete by the time serialization in the *Cornhill* commenced in January 1860. Nonetheless it is a good example of the characteristic spirit of compromise in Trollope, in the way it both is and is not a work dependent for its effects upon immediate serialization.

At the close of its fifth number (ch. 15), for example, the young vicar Mark Robarts is reduced to tears by his elder colleague, Mr Crawley, for his falling off as a parish clergyman. The last paragraph begins: 'It was some hours before Mr Robarts left his room. As soon as he found that Crawley was really gone, and that he should see him no more, he turned the lock of his door, and sat himself down to think over his present life'. This could have marked a mental and spiritual epoch in Robarts's existence. Yet it doesn't with Trollope. A reviewer in *Bentley's Quarterly Review* had already complained in July 1859 that in Trollope man is the unheroic creature of external circumstances 'led by temporary aims, rather than in the attitude of defying and controlling them'. And so the potentially decisive interview with Crawley is remembered only once, briefly, in the midst of chapter 19 when, still in the midst of financial entanglements which his earlier tears and thoughts have done nothing to assuage, Robarts desperately acknowledges to himself—yet still only in passing—that 'Mr Crawley had been right when he told him that he was a castaway.' As R. H. Hutton was to put it in *The Spectator* (September 1867), in a review characteristic of Victorian criticism at its best:

Mr. Trollope's power is not concentrated but extensive and gradual in its approaches. The skill with which he gives us view after view of his different characters, each looking, at first, as if it were only the old view over again, but proving before long to have a something added, which gives you a sense of a completer knowledge of the characters, reminds us of nothing so much as the zigzags of a road terraced up to a steep hill-side from which you are constantly getting the same view of a valley repeated again and again. But each time with some novelty of aspect and additional command of its relation to other neighbouring valleys, in consequence of the added height.

The reader is involved in the gradual *process* of such reading—concerned as much with what turns out in the silent discontinuities *not* to happen as with what actually does. The slight but not monumental change, the potential unrealized, the subliminal possibility half-forgotten in its non-occurrence, the central issue displaced and zigzagging, the implicitly chastening effect of this view of life—all these are Trollope's non-sensationalist uses of a possible sensationalism.

Thus, resisted, embraced, or modified, what was at stake in serialization as in the very syntax of prose-writing was the Victorian obsession with what to do with the force of onward-driving time: how, formally, to find room or place within it for all that could not simply go along with transience.

A final example from *David Copperfield* may serve to show this ambivalent relation to the passage of life in time. For in the midst of busily establishing his career, David makes secret admission to himself that his youthful marriage to Dora is not as he had dreamed of it being. This is, he thinks, part of the general adjustment to reality that all adults must have to endure; and yet, equally, there are specific things wrong with this particular marriage:

> Between these two irreconcileable conclusions: the one, that what I felt was general and unavoidable; the other, that it was particular to me, and might have been different: I balanced curiously, with no distinct sense of their opposition to each other. (ch. 48)

Macaulay said that the modern age was to be one of increasingly generalized knowledge and explanation. But much of the realist novel occupies, as here, an exploratory area of existence—in a moment of retrospective time-out, as it were, between the particular and the general, in a sub-vocal language on the very borderline between the private and the public. It is that rich, uncertain, unnamed, but emphatically human area that above all characterizes Victorian literature.

III. New Voices

It is of course Dickens who most acutely imagines what it would be like to be an illiterate creature in a world full of letters, signs and advertisements:

> It must be a strange thing to be like Jo! To shuffle through the streets, unfamiliar with the shapes, and in utter darkness to the meaning, of those

mysterious symbols, so abundant over the shops, and at the corners of streets, and on the doors, and in the windows! To see people read, and to see people write, and to see the postmen deliver letters, and not to have the least idea of all that language—to be, to every scrap of it, stone blind and dumb! It must be very puzzling to see the good company going to the churches on Sundays, with their books in their hands, and to think (for perhaps Jo does think, at odd times) what does it all mean, and if it means anything to anybody, how comes it that it means nothing to me? (*Bleak House* (1853), ch. 16)

It is equally characteristic of Dickens's vertiginous turn of mind that the imagination of being without words should go on within them. Literature was opening up.

Moreover, by means of Sunday schools and friendly societies, literacy itself continued to spread among the working classes throughout the century. In the rural night school in chapter 21 of George Eliot's *Adam Bede* (1859): 'It was touching to see these three big men, with the marks of their hard labour about them, anxiously bending over the worn books, and painfully making out, "The grass is green", "The sticks are dry", "The corn is ripe".' For self-taught enthusiasts such as Francis Place (1771–1854), tailor and radical, with a personal library of 1,000 volumes, the improvement of the working classes was a package—material, political, moral, and, not least of all, educational. It was Place who drafted the People's Charter of 1838, on behalf of universal male suffrage, and it was the example offered by those Chartists who believed in the power of knowledge—in particular the great autodidacts Samuel Bamford, Thomas Cooper, and William Lovett—that inspired the capacity for 'self-help' which Samuel Smiles so wanted the working classes to discover.

The great staple works were of course the Bible and Shakespeare, and those two models of Protestant individualism, Bunyan's *The Pilgrim's Progress* (1678, 1684) and Defoe's *Robinson Crusoe* (1719). But in the reading of more recent books, beyond the eighteenth century, it was like the extension of the franchise: there was always a time lag, often of a generation, between the reading habits of the working classes and those of the middle class, until cheap or second-hand copies of high-quality works became available on the book-stalls. Then it was, above all, the works of Dickens, Carlyle, and Ruskin, together with F. T. Palgrave's great poetry anthology,

Palgrave's Golden Treasury, first published in 1861, which created generations nurtured in the Victorian ethic of educational self-improvement. For before working-class education was finally formalized, said one enthusiast, reading was an adventure, opening up new worlds, offering 'the freedom of the universe', giving a new voice and identity to previously silenced minds.[14] The very boundaries between life and literature, between fact and fiction, were thrillingly thrown open. By the end of the century, the young daughter of an impoverished bookkeeper could find her life changed by coming upon Carlyle's *Sartor Resartus*:

Suddenly, blazing from the printed page, there are the words, the true resounding words that we couldn't find . . . 'Who am I? The thing that can say I. Who am I, what is this ME?' I had been groping to know that since I was three. (quoted in Rose, p. 46)

Or a Lancashire woman-weaver gains an education at the Nelson Women's Co-operative Guild, amazed to find in the very poetry of Tennyson that 'anyone had an experience like mine' (quoted in Rose, p. 78):

> Break, break, break
> On thy cold grey stones, oh Sea!
> And I would that my tongue could utter
> The thoughts that arise in me!

Yet Hardy's *Jude the Obscure* (1895) is the story of the young autodidact who develops just sufficiently to encounter, with pain, all the obstacles to a fuller development in the modern world.

Even so, the borderline between the literary and what apparently had to be left outside literature was shifting. Charles Kingsley's *Alton Locke* (1850) describes the growth of a working-class tailor-poet who begins, in imitation of Byron and Tennyson, by writing about pirates landing on the Pacific Islands. He is told by his Scottish mentor, Mackaye, that true poetry, like true charity, begins at home. For realism here is offered as part of the class issue: the rise of the middle-class writer in defence of realism was only the beginning of a story which would continue through to the reality of the working classes. But again there was a time lag involved. As Hugh Miller

---

[14] Quoted in Jonathan Rose's highly instructive *The Intellectual Life of the British Working Classes* (Yale University Press, 2001), 67.

pointed out in 'Literature of the People' (*Essays*, 1862), the rise of realism meant that the lower classes were no longer portrayed in literature as buffoons but were now treated with imaginative sympathy. Nonetheless, it would require, said Miller, the development of more genuinely working-class writers to reveal the full potential of intelligent inner life hidden within the lot of the poor. But at least the realism of the Victorian novel had begun the process, creating, in the very spirit of democratic education, an assimilable tradition that brought high literature into new contact with ordinary subject matter.

Nonetheless, for the present, argued Mrs Oliphant, it was the middle classes, not the working classes themselves, who were most interested in reading of an Alton Locke: 'he is no hero for the semptress, who makes her romance out of quite different materials' ('The Byways of Literature: Reading for the Million', *Blackwood's Magazine* (August 1858)). For all the Chartist-inspired achievements not only in autobiography and poetry but also in the political journalism of men such as Julian Harney (1817–97), editor of the mid-century *Red Republican* and *Friend of the People*; for all the rise of the self-taught enthusiast such as John Clare or Hugh Miller, it is true that the nascent voice of the lower classes was heard most powerfully via the new literary dominance of the middle class: in Dickens, or Kingsley, or the street journalism of Mayhew.

It was for the most part through their political consciousness that the rebel writers of the working class first found a voice. The great defence of the writing that came out of poverty was written by one of the models for Alton Locke as for George Eliot's Felix Holt: Gerald Massey (1828–1907) in his 'Preface to the Third Edition of *Babe Christabel*' (1854). In the conditions in which the poor exist, where the poor man has no time for the peace of mind out of which poetry should best proceed, said Massey, 'humanity must be either rebel or slave': better to be a rebel and at least speak out.

Yet such writing had an uncomfortable and disturbing status in Victorian England—especially for those fortunate enough *not* to have to forge an identity for themselves out of an initially political consciousness. In the reviews, in particular with regard to industrial and factory novels such as Frances Trollope's *Michael Armstrong* (1840) or Charlotte Elizabeth Tonna's *Helen Fleetwood* (1841), the issue was all too forcefully polemicized into a basic split between those who favoured literary detachment and those who supported political engagement. When John Bright (1811–89), the forceful Liberal radical, argued that culture meant no more than an affected smattering of outworn Latin and Greek and that nothing was more important at the present time than practical politics, it was in the same spirit of polar opposition that Matthew Arnold wrote *Culture and Anarchy* in literature's defence.

But as so often in the period it was the uneasy, shifting area in between the opposite camps which marked what was really at stake. Hence the compromise achieved in many novels by setting the action at a distance of twenty, thirty, or forty years earlier. For two opposite but mutually linked tendencies were going on at the same time, as though struggling to belong together: on the one hand, the establishment of literature as a distinct and defended area, also a separate profession and even an industry; on the other, within those forms, a counter-tendency which internally recommitted art—in its content, in its urgency—to the service of the world outside. The dual responsibilities of art both to what it stood for in itself and to its external subject matter left Victorian writing in conscience-ridden occupation of an indeterminate area where the competing claims of life were held in tension.

That tension found expression in a continuous variety of competing languages, of which the class issue was but one. Another, in which the issue could be rearticulated, lay in the defence of the provincial and the regional as against the central and cosmopolitan.

Until his death in 1835 the journalist William Cobbett acted as a popular tribune railing against what he called 'the System'. The centralizing system, said Cobbett, replaced primary, visible realities such as the harvest with the abstract falsifications of economic theory and paper money. *Rural Rides* appeared in 1830, a provincial travel journal of first-hand experience in defence of the land. In the same spirit, Cobbett's much-reprinted *Grammar of the English Language* (1818) did not exist to offer a crash course in standard English, as was increasingly insisted upon in the bourgeois manuals of 'correct' usage later in the century, but to further the cause of truth and honesty, through the exposure of bad grammar and poor logic, and the provision of the right means of articulating inner thought. His *Advice to Young Men* (1830) fought at the personal level for the traditional functions of husband, father, and citizen. To Matthew Arnold, however, Cobbett even in his strengths was the representative narrow Englishman, the robust and practical philistine coarsened by engagement in reactive political conflict: 'England's dog' ('Heinrich Heine').

Whether it was the combative Englishman or the passionate Celt, what was always lacking in the provincial type was what Arnold called 'urbanity', the tone of the city, of the intellectual centre to the nation, such as was offered by the French Academy ('The Literary Influence of Academies', in *Essays in Criticism*, series 1, 1865). There is no measure, balance or patience, no clarity of form, no dignity of style, says Arnold, without the ease of centrality. Hence the strain of the political poet, such as Massey, when his thoughts are filled with one reactive idea—the thought that society had not given him his rights—however just it might be: 'Be it true, be it false, it is equally a woe to believe it; to have to live on a negation' (*Alton Locke*, ch. 4). Hence too, as Arnold saw it, the vain struggles of the Dorchester poet William Barnes (1801–86) and all dialect-speakers, Scots, Welsh, and Irish, diminished in the remote rural backwaters of Britain, trying to ignore the current of history.[15]

Yet Barnes's Wessex protégé, Thomas Hardy, retorted in a note to himself: 'Arnold is wrong about provincialism, if he means anything more than a provincialism of style and manner in exposition. A certain provincialism of feeling is invaluable. It is of the essence of individuality, and is largely made up of that crude enthusiasm without which no great thoughts are thought, no great deeds done.'[16] This is from a man who had not been to university, and there is a similar defiant force in Dickens, always feeling that he was fighting against the odds. There is a similar story too behind the delay in the commencement of the writing careers of a whole series of writers who lacked the status and confidence of a formal higher education—in particular of course women writers. Notoriously in a letter of 1837 the Poet Laureate Robert Southey had dismissed the youthful poems sent him by Charlotte Brontë as an indulgence in a literary day-

[15] See below p. 475.
[16] F. E. Hardy, *Life of Thomas Hardy*, 20 Nov. 1880.

dreaming which, he wrote, unfitted a young woman for the ordinary uses of the world without fitting her for anything else. No wonder Charlotte Brontë and Marian Evans first published under masculine pseudonyms: Currer Bell and George Eliot. But even Anthony Trollope did not publish his first novel until he was 32 and after a series of failures, only established himself with *The Warden* in 1855 when he was 40. Trollope had not been able to go on from Harrow to Oxford or Cambridge, partly because of the collapsed state of family finances (particularly as he was the younger son) and partly because his teachers and his family simply thought him slow and stupid.

Yet when Hardy speaks in defence of provincial feeling, it is above all an expression of everything that went into the formation of the regional novel of the nineteenth century. Whereas George Eliot subtitled her great epic *Middlemarch* as no more and no less *A Study of Provincial Life*, and Hardy himself in the 'General Preface to his Wessex Edition' (1912) argued that 'the domestic emotions have throbbed in Wessex nooks with as much intensity as in the palaces of Europe' and that 'anyhow, there was quite enough human nature in Wessex for one man's literary purpose', Matthew Arnold still insisted that 'A great human action of a thousand years ago is more interesting than a smaller human action of to-day' ('Preface to the First Edition' of *Poems*, 1853).

Within the realm of those smaller human actions of today the most genuinely new voice was not that of the worker-poet nor even perhaps that of the regional novelist but the voice of the woman writer. 'Millions are in silent revolt against their lot. Nobody knows', cries Charlotte Brontë's protagonist, 'how many rebellions besides political rebellions ferment in the masses of life which people earth' (*Jane Eyre* (1847), ch. 12). To break that silence was inevitably a private act, easily slighted in comparison with ostensibly larger public events. Yet again and again Jane Eyre finds her voice— first, as a 10-year-old orphan girl unjustly treated by her aunt, 'forced by the agonizing stimulus into precocious though transitory power' (ch. 2) because she has no one else to protect her but herself:

Speak I must. . . . Shaking from head to foot, thrilled with ungovernable excitement, I continued—

'I am glad you are no relation of mine. I will never call you aunt again as long as I live. I will never come to see you when I am grown up; and if any one asks me how I liked you, and how you treated me, I will say the very thought of you makes me sick, and that you treated me with miserable cruelty.' (ch. 4)

The rawness sent shock-waves through literature. 'Something spoke out of me over which I had no control': gradually that 'something' became recognized by Jane as indeed her deepest self. Years later, as she stands, a mere governess, before her employer Mr Rochester, there is another of those transitory outbursts of a latently underlying passion—but now it is in the name not of outraged justice but of vulnerable love:

'Do you think, because I am poor, obscure, plain, and little, I am soulless and heartless? You think wrong!—I have as much soul as you—and full as much heart! And if God had gifted me with some beauty and much wealth, I should have made it as hard for you to leave me, as it is now for me to leave you. I am not talking to you now through the medium of custom, conventionalities, nor even of mortal flesh: it is my spirit that addresses your spirit; just as if both had passed through the grave, and we stood at God's feet, equal—as we are!' (ch. 23)

There is no mistaking the real size of a personal rebellion by the end of that speech. It is that voice, in that medium, beyond social conventionalities, that constitutes a breakthrough for Charlotte Brontë.

So much that had gone on within the private life of the race, the ordinary life of individual feeling, had passed unrecorded. 'The advent of female literature promises a woman's view of life, woman's experience,' declared G. H. Lewes; 'In other words, a new element' ('The Lady Novelists', *Westminster Review*, July 1852). Suddenly there were female voices, as here, talking of the deep secret of first love:

'The first strange thing is, that every woman approaches this crisis of her life as unawares as if she were the first that ever loved.'

'And yet all girls are brought up to think of marriage as almost the only event in life. Their minds are stuffed with thoughts of it almost before they have had time to gain any other ideas.'

'Merely as means to ends low enough for their comprehension . . . connection with somebody or something which will give them money, and ease, and station, and independence of their parents. This has nothing to do with love.' (Harriet Martineau, *Deerbrook* (1839), ch. 15)

First love here is like the secret loss of emotional virginity, whether anything subsequently comes of the relationship or not. In *Deerbrook* Harriet Martineau, an outspoken pioneering feminist, used the novel-form to give a still private rather than public language to the silence of her gender.

What is more, her speakers do not stop short in speaking at last of this secret history:

'How strange if this process really awaits women—if it is a region through which their path of life must stretch—and no one gives warning, or preparation, or help!'

'It is not so strange as at first sight it seems. Every mother and friend hopes that no one else suffered as she did—that her particular charge may escape entirely, or get off more easily. Then there is the shame of confession which is involved: some conclude, at a distance of time, that they must have exaggerated their own sufferings, or have been singularly rebellious and unreasonable. Some lose the sense of the anguish in the subsequent happiness; and there are not a few who, from constitution of mind, forget altogether "the things that are behind". When you remember, too, that it is the law of nature and providence that each should bear his and her own burden, and that no warning would be of any avail, it seems no longer so strange that while girls hear endlessly of marriage, they are kept wholly in the dark about love.' (*Deerbrook*, ch. 15)

This is how, in the language and voice of the novel, the private could be made public and general without ceasing to be private and specific and vulnerable. Indeed it is, rather, the public world that is here privatized. E. S. Dallas said in *The Gay Science* (2 vols., 1866) that as the formal boundary between public and private was becoming ever less clear in the modern world, 'We dwell far more than we used on the private side of human life': 'Woman peculiarly represents the private life of the race' (vol. 2, ch. 17).

Thus, reviewing *Jane Eyre* Mrs Oliphant had concluded, 'This, which is the age of so many things—of enlightenment, of science, of progress—is quite as distinctly the age of female novelists' ('Modern Novelists—Great and Small', *Blackwood's Magazine*, May 1855). Commentators in the 1850s such as W. R. Greg believed that the supply of the fiction market had fallen increasingly into the hands of women writers. It was also popularly accepted from the 1840s onwards that women, and in particular young women, formed a majority of novel-readers. In fact, though manuscripts sent to publishing houses were increasingly from female aspirants, it seems that the overall proportion of female authors remained relatively static at around 20 per cent: it was their qualitative importance that was growing.

The equivalent movement in poetry saw the rise of the Victorian 'poetess'. L.E.L (Letitia Elizabeth Landon, 1802–38) in 'Calypso Watching the Ocean' and Augusta Webster (1837–94) in 'Circe' mount lyric defences of redundant feeling outside the realms of Odyssean male epic. Where Jean Ingelow (1820–97) works mainly within a language of nature, Dora Greenwell (1821–82) and Adelaide Anne Proctor (1823–1910) find a language of pity that extends to social issues, as though one mark of the advance of Christian civilization was that it made a gentle female voice more audible.

But the expressive movement reaches its culmination in Christina Rossetti's 'Monna Innominata' (1880), a sonnet sequence modelled on the Renaissance love lyric written in unavailing passion to 'unnamed ladies', in the sexual-religious tradition of Dante's adoration of Beatrice and Petrarch's love for Laura. Only now it is the woman who speaks for herself, and the man who is the unattainable, possibly married, object of her love. Moreover, as the preface makes clear, it is a sequence written as the single woman's alternative to Elizabeth Barrett Browning's *Sonnets from the Portuguese* published thirty years before in 1850—the sonnet sequence which, based on the poet's courtship by Robert Browning, ended in an overcoming of the traditional sorrow of the Renaissance models of despised love, through the achievement of the happiness of marriage. But Christina Rossetti returned to that tradition, where passion for the unattainable showed human love at its most powerfully characteristic. In 'Monna Innominata', although the man belongs to another, the love itself is not wrong; yet though the love is not wrong, it cannot be consummated. In its impossibility of satisfaction it must be taken up into the only form left for it, for which indeed its yearning dimly stood: religious love. Yet, in another of Rossetti's fine twists, while the love of God is always higher, it could never have come into being as

Fig. 8. Pencil portrait of Christina Rossetti, aged 17, by
her brother Dante Gabriel Rossetti, 1847—the year in
which she published her first slender volume of verse,
through the private press of her grandfather.

love—rather than fear or duty—without the experience of the human example:

> love is such
> I cannot love you if I love not Him,
> I cannot love Him, if I love not you.

(Sonnet 6)

The market wanted domesticated love poetry, whilst society identified women as the guardians of human feeling. But while still following love through to the very end of its course, 'Monna Innominata' is written in troubled and austere defiance of those priorities.

The distinction between married and unmarried women writers was of particular concern to Mrs Oliphant. As she argues in a piece on the art of autobiography in *Blackwood's Magazine* (August 1881), those who had kept themselves intact had intense personal memories, were emotionally single-minded. But the woman who has married and has children finds her experience overtaken, confused, and yet also made dense by the successive variety of claims, the unceasing busyness of a life which is no longer simply one's own. Perhaps, Mrs Oliphant tried to persuade herself, that was why Charlotte Brontë's work seemed much more powerful than her own: it had the intense yearning and frustration of the single woman, on the verge of fantasy. And yet, she added, 'I have had far more experience and, I think, a fuller conception of life' (*Autobiography*, p. 10). As Mrs Gaskell, another of the great married realist novelists, put it in a letter of 25 September 1862 to a young aspirant: 'When you are forty, and if you have a gift for being an authoress you will write ten times as good a novel as you could do now, just because you will have gone through so much more of the interests of a wife and a mother.' That was why it was *Mrs* Gaskell, *Mrs* Oliphant: the realist novel came out of their being wives and mothers. It was domestic realism, in its compromise and its untidiness, in its privileging of experience over abstract reason, that was the characteristic mode for the woman writer who had found and made a home in the world. For Mrs Gaskell the advantage was that by the age of 40, in contrast to the widowed Mrs Oliphant, she could write as she wanted, free from the necessity of having to earn money.

Yet there remained a problem, which was partly statistical. In the

1840s there were 1,050 women to every 1,000 men. By 1851 over one million women remained unmarried. Because of the statistical imbalance of males to females—the result of higher child mortality among boys; of losses by war and emigration (which last carried off three times as many men as women); and also of a trend towards delayed male marriage—there were more than 400,000 'excess women' over the age of 20 in 1851, and most important of all they were largely in the upper, articulate, and educated sections of society. They could not marry, at a time when marriage was the most and often the only respectable estate and career for the middle-class female. These statistics alone made the writing of something like Charlotte Brontë's *Villette* (1853) virtually inevitable. They lie behind Dora Greenwell's fine essay 'Our Single Women' (*Essays*, 1866), with its cry that woman should 'attain, in print, to the fearless, uncompromising sincerity she misses in real life'.

'Give us back our suffering, we cry to Heaven in our hearts—suffering rather than indifferentism', cries Cassandra in a novel of that name written by Florence Nightingale in 1852 but unpublished in her own lifetime. The low health from which, notoriously, so many Victorian ladies suffered was not, said that most intelligent of feminists Frances Power Cobbe (1822–1904), the positive suffering of disease: 'They were obliged . . . to remain very frequently in bed at breakfast-time, and later in the day to lie on the sofa with darkened blinds and a considerable exhibition of Eau-de-Cologne.'[17] This was suffering in denial of itself, a psychosomatic indifferentism that existed for want of 'Hope—something to live for, something which she may look to accomplish' (Cobbe, p. 115). Thus Cassandra cries out for positive suffering, at least: 'For out of nothing comes nothing. But out of suffering may come the cure. Better have pain than paralysis.'

So much of *Villette*, in its account of a plain single woman faced with the shame of needing love, vacillates between those alternatives, pain or paralysis, before finally daring the pain of hope. Lucy Snowe admits that she has tried to do a deal with life: 'I had wanted to compromise with Fate: to escape occasional great agonies by submitting to a whole life of privation and small pain' (ch. 4). Where for

---

[17] Cobbe, 'The Little Health of Ladies', *The Contemporary Review*, 31 (1878), repr. in *Gender and Science*, ed. K. Rowold (Thoemmes Press, 1996), 113.

Tennyson it was 'better to have loved and lost | Than never to have loved at all' (*In Memoriam*, 27), the temptation for Lucy Snowe is to accept the condition of a plain spinster as a fixed and determined destiny, in never loving or being loved at all, rather than suffer the uncertainties of recurrent hope. Yet the voices of Charlotte Brontë's women are strong precisely because, however involuntarily, they cannot thus give up on the life within them. The bravest cry in Victorian fiction comes near the close of *Villette* when Lucy Snowe suddenly says to Paul Emanuel at the very moment of his departure, 'My heart will break!'—with no guarantee of any response whatsoever (ch. 41).

'I *will* be happy', cries Jane Eyre (ch. 34), after the seemingly irrevocable loss of a life of love with Rochester, as she struggles against the conventional temptation to surrender herself to the clergyman St John Rivers. Whatever the damage to her feelings, it is an instinctive emotional intelligence that saves her from St John, distinguishing 'the man' from 'the Christian', and detecting in him precisely that half-corrupted, compensatory spirituality of which she herself is in danger. It is that refusal of false substitutes which releases, once again, her true voice.

As Mrs Oliphant admits, the voices of Charlotte Brontë's Jane Eyre, Shirley, and Lucy Snowe were the first to speak for those 'extra half-million' who felt, and were also ashamed to feel, that 'nobody was coming to marry us, nobody coming to woo':

It was life they wanted . . . They wanted their life, their place in the world, the rightful share of women in the scheme of nature. Why did it not come to them? The old patience in which women have lived for all the centuries fails now and again in a keen moment of energy when some one arises who sees no reason why she should endure this forced inaction, or why she should invent for herself inferior ways of working and give up her birthright, which is to carry on the world.

The reader was horrified with these sentiments from the lips of young women. The women were half ashamed, yet more than half stirred and excited by the outcry, which was true enough if indelicate. ('The Sisters Brontë', *Women Novelists of Queen Victoria's Reign* (1897), p. 46)

In Mrs Oliphant's eyes, what Charlotte Brontë's young women wanted was no more than their natural, biological birthright in marriage and procreation.

Traditionally there had been a role—a sacred place—for women denied that function. In Elizabeth Missing Sewell's *The Experience of Life* (1853), young Sarah complains of her feelings of redundancy and purposelessness to her deeply devout maiden aunt, after whom she has been named. The aunt turns the pages of her Bible and reads, 'The unmarried woman careth for the things of the Lord, that she may be holy both in body and in spirit; but she that is married careth for the things of the world, how she may please her husband' (ch. 13). There are some people who have definite, fixed work to do in the world, and there are others, mainly spinsters like herself, says the aunt, whose work as spare souls is indefinite and scattered, giving help as occasion arises. 'But there's a mistake of words in the matter,' says the aunt, as she seeks to find function in what seems the very lack of one, 'All work—work for God that is—is definite' (ch. 41).

In contrast, it seemed to Mrs Oliphant that the young women of a later generation who 'took their first inspiration' from the cry of Charlotte Brontë, 'have quite forgotten what it was she wanted, not emancipation but extended duty' (*Women Novelists of Queen Victoria's Reign*, p. 50). Jane Eyre herself clarifies that issue, when, near the end of the novel, the crippled Rochester, now a widower, asks her whether she is marrying him simply because she delights in sacrifice. It is the question asked by every emancipated reader of a later generation, but Jane replies, 'What do I sacrifice? Famine for food, expectation for content.' If that is sacrifice, she insists, wittily, 'then certainly I delight in sacrifice' (ch. 37). It is the same as when the scarred and blinded man had asked, 'Am I hideous, Jane?': he hears in reply, 'Very, sir; you always were, you know.' Though Charlotte Brontë rejected Mrs Oliphant's admired Jane Austen, for an alleged want of human passion, the happy and intelligent wit here is as lightly sane as anything in the great woman novelist of the preceding generation.

But, in truth, Mrs Oliphant felt *herself* increasingly left behind, in particular through the rise in the 1870s and 1880s of a relatively new, more confident and disturbing group of women—young, unmarried, and increasingly outspoken, for whom, constituting as they did almost half of all women published, literature seemed to provide an alternative existence. The women writers of sensationalist fiction in the 1860s—Rhoda Broughton, Mary Braddon, Ellen Wood, the latter two working under the respectable guises of 'Mrs Braddon' and 'Mrs Henry Wood'—saw themselves as the emancipated daughters of Charlotte Brontë. George Eliot, the alternative role model for the woman writer, they judged to be passionless, in writing within the allegedly more masculine mode of moral realism. But in place of the traditional female language of the heart, the sensationalist women writers sought to substitute the shock of passion, playing upon the nerves. It is this that shocks the husband in Florence Wilford's *Nigel Bartram's Ideal* (1871), the remarkable story of a wife who tries to keep secret her authorship of a sensationalist novel.

Yet Mrs Oliphant was right about a younger generation forgetting what Charlotte Brontë's women wanted. When in the middle of the novel, Jane Eyre discovers that Rochester is already married, the bigamy that was to characterize the sensation novel is a temptation which is firmly rejected:[18]

I will hold to the principles received by me when I was sane, and not mad— as I am now. Laws and principles are not for times when there is no temptation: they are for such moments as this . . . Preconceived opinions, foregone determinations are all I have at this hour to stand by; there I plant my foot. (ch. 27)

What is more, the moral voice that there confirms the rejection is still, and still passionately, Jane's own. Finding a voice in *Jane Eyre* is not just a triumph of literary expression or a matter of psychological relief; it is part of the protagonist's own search within the book to locate a deep personal reality.

And yet the sensation writers were not wholly wrong in detecting in Charlotte Brontë unresolved elements of desire. *Jane Eyre* and *Villette* struggle for their identity in an area in between realism and fantasy. Lucy Snowe never wants to be defined or analysed: until almost the end of the novel, in a characteristic mixture of defiance and fear, she keeps something always hidden behind whatever it is that people think her to be. That inner refusal—in effect a refusal by the inner life of a total commitment to realism—is part of what disturbs Mrs Oliphant, in something of the same way as Emily

[18] See below pp. 321–35 on the sensation novel.

Brontë's *Wuthering Heights* (1848) disturbed Charlotte herself by its autonomous power of uncontrolled imagination.[19]

For Mrs Oliphant, realism was a way of holding things together. That was why the depiction of a conflict between being a mother and being a wife left Mrs Oliphant so equivocal about Anne Brontë's *The Tenant of Wildfell Hall* (1848). What makes that book a great realist novel is the fact that the protagonist, for once in a Brontë fiction, is a mother—but a mother who has made the terrible mistake of marrying a figure based upon the Brontës' own ruined brother, a corrupt drunkard. Helen Huntingdon gradually discovers, to her lonely horror, 'how much of my higher and better self is indeed unmarried' (ch. 29). Even so, in the very effort to excuse her husband, she begins to find that 'things that formerly shocked and disgusted me, now seem only natural. . . . I am gradually losing that instinctive horror and repulsion' (ch. 30). That must not happen to their son. An iron force of anxious responsibility enters the novel as the mother-in-her realizes that she dare not leave her son to his father's influence and example. With lonely intelligence, she writes in her diary of the vicious circle in which her anxieties ironically confine her:

Often his bursts of gleeful merriment trouble and alarm me; I see in them his father's spirit and temperament, and I tremble for the consequences; and, too often, damp the innocent mirth I ought to share. That father on the contrary has no weight of sadness on his mind—is troubled with no fears, no scruples concerning his son's future welfare . . . therefore, of course, the child dotes upon his seemingly joyous, amusing, ever indulgent papa, and will at any time exchange my company for his. (ch. 37)

'This disturbs me greatly,' she says, painfully knowing just how much is owing to an involuntary selfishness: 'It is hard that my little darling should love him more than me . . . If I, for his good, deny him some trifling indulgence, he goes to his father' (ch. 36). Yet at the same time, she feels it

not so much for the sake of my son's affection (though I do prize that highly, and though I feel it is my right, and know I have done much to earn it) as for that influence over him which, for his own advantage, I would

---

[19] See below pp. 318–21, 363–4.

strive to purchase and retain, and which for very spite his father delights to rob me of, and, from motives of mere egotism, is pleased to win to himself; making no use of it but to torment me, and ruin the child. (ch. 37)

The very complexity of the thinking, clause by clause, is proportional to the tightness of the trap in which it is so helplessly lodged. That is the paradox so often involved in domestic realism, and Mrs Oliphant for one felt herself able to bear and sustain it in her writing as in her life. What troubled her about *The Tenant of Wildfell Hall*, however, was that, in order to save her son, the woman felt obliged to leave her husband, take the boy away with her, and become single again.

In such ways, therefore, the nineteenth-century 'Woman Question' was also a question about the place, value, and size of personal experience, and the forms it could legitimately endure or create. It concerned all that was contained, hidden, or confined within those personal relationships and personal feelings which formed the very basis of human society in the Victorian world.

It did not just concern women. The emotional capacity in all human beings, male *and* female, said Ruskin in *Sesame and Lilies* (1864), was under threat in the industrial nineteenth century. Literature offered an alternative society, and in that inner world a reader who read well would enter not only into the thoughts of the great authors but the very feeling of those thoughts, sharing their passion in order to know them fully: 'Passion or "sensation". I am not afraid of the word; still less of the thing. You have heard many outcries against sensation lately; but, I can tell you, it is not less sensation we want, but more' (*Sesame and Lilies*, 'Of Kings' Treasuries', para. 27). What was needed, said Ruskin, was not less of the thing, just because of sensationalist writers such as Mrs Braddon, but the better version of what was distorted within false semblance: 'Having no true emotion, we must have false emotions dressed up for us to play with . . . The justice we do not execute, we mimic in the novel and on stage' (para. 39). At their best, novels 'have serious use, being nothing less than treatises on moral anatomy and chemistry; studies of human nature in the elements of it', but 'they are hardly ever read with earnestness enough to permit them to fulfil it' (*Sesame and Lilies*, 'Of Queens' Gardens', para. 77).

Yet it was not just a matter of the society of books. It was women, said Ruskin, as the traditional biological guardians of human care, who were to bring the reality of human feeling back into England. Within the alternative inner society of their marriages, they were to act as agents of humanity, in critical relation to husbands all too often entangled in the ways of the world of business. The distinct but complementary characteristics of the sexes existed not just for the matching of two persons but to marry together the different sides of human nature itself in an ever revitalized whole.

Yet to Ruskin's insistence that it was upon women that the human instincts of the nation now largely depended, John Stuart Mill retorted acidly, 'They are declared to be better than men; an empty compliment, which must provoke a bitter smile from every woman of spirit, since there is no other situation in life in which it is the established order, and considered quite natural and suitable, that the better should obey the worse' (*The Subjection of Women* (1869), ch. 3). To Mill it seemed that women were being asked to carry the burden of men's feelings, not their own. Literature itself shows Victorian women struggling with their so-called 'natural' guardianship of love, in all the anxiety of either feeling too much or feeling too little.

It is part of the story of the nineteenth century that traditionally ascribed roles and functions should begin to give way to the idea of free and individual persons, and the debate between Ruskin and Mill offers the distinction at its starkest. For what was at stake, as Mrs Oliphant herself saw, was the question of the very nature of human nature itself, in the rivalry between the language of religious biology in Ruskin and the language of progressive politics in Mill.

Reviewing Mill's *Subjection of Women* in *The Edinburgh Review* (October 1869), Mrs Oliphant granted what she well knew from her own life, that the sacrifices of self, time, and career which both biology and society demanded of women could logically unjust. But the restlessness of the nineteenth century, she claimed, was a result of its belief that somehow every disadvantage could or should be remedied. A puzzled logician from outer space, looking down upon the planet

would find many things expedient that are not altogether just. He would find necessities which nature imposed, but which abstract equity turned against. He would find indeed a great troubled confused uncertain world, ruled by anything but logic, not even ruled by justice, in which century after century had over again demonstrated the impossibility not only of perfection in action or agreement in thought, but even of any infallible code of right and wrong as applied to the most intimate relations of life.

To the realist novelist, the law of the universe was not simply logic or justice.

Indeed it was precisely by staying within the ostensible smallness of the female's situation, in all its vulnerability, that a determinedly realist writer could often get *below* the level of large conceptual definitions, into uncharted areas. So it is with Trollope's *Miss Mackenzie* (1865), where the protagonist, a plain unmarried woman, comes into money in her mid-thirties. With the belated chance to begin life, she feels like some mariner launching out 'alone to sea in a small boat' (ch. 2). The fine sense of scale that makes of this a pluckiness, rather than a heroic courage, does not finally diminish or patronize her situation. On the contrary, there develops in small, unexpected ways and areas a sort of defiant wit in Miss Mackenzie which becomes a real life-force. 'It is not as if you two were young people, and wanted to be billing and cooing,' says one potential mother-in-law to her. To which she thinks: 'Why should she not want billing and cooing as well as another? . . . She had had none of it yet' (ch. 9). That it would be new to her is what makes it new again for the reader, as though large 'themes' (love, the single woman) were somehow less important than the small lives that embodied them in their own way. If the prosaic world-view of the Victorian age threatened a reduction in the size of human life and art, it was often the voice of women that kept the big life questions indefinitely alive—alive even in their indefiniteness—precisely *within* the struggles of ostensibly small and ordinary existence.

Above all, then, the very voice of the woman—the difficulties, needs and questionings she represented—could not be confined simply to women writers but had a powerful widening presence within the writings of virtually all male authors too—among the poets, perhaps Tennyson most of all. But here, as a final clinching example, is Trollope's Alice Vavasour who, having broken one engagement of marriage to a bad man whom she passionately loved, is now contemplating breaking another to a better and gentler man, for reasons she cannot quite articulate:

That Alice Vavasour had thought too much about it, I feel quite sure. She had gone on thinking of it till she had filled herself with a cloud of doubts which even the sunshine of love was unable to drive from her heavens. That a girl should really love the man she intends to marry,—that, at any rate, may be admitted. But love generally comes easily enough. With all her doubts Alice never doubted her love for Mr Grey. Nor did she doubt his character, nor his temper, nor his means. But she had gone on thinking of the matter till her mind had become filled with some undefined idea of the importance to her of her own life. What should a woman do with her life? There had arisen around her a flock of learned ladies asking that question, to whom it seems that the proper answer has never yet occurred. Fall in love, marry the man, have two children, and live happy ever afterwards. I maintain that answer has as much wisdom in it as any other that can be given;—or perhaps more. (Anthony Trollope, *Can You Forgive Her?* (1864–5), ch. 11)

And yet the passage continues despite the attempt of the male narrator to cut it short:

Alice Vavasour was ever asking herself that question, and had by degrees filled herself with a vague idea that there was a something to be done; a something over and beyond, or perhaps altogether beside that marrying and having two children;—if only she knew what it was.

It is as though Trollope has intuitively worked his novel into a place from which the part of himself represented by the bluff male narrator cannot extricate it. The more aggressively the rationalizing narrator tries to enforce the prosaic way against modern self-consciousness ('Fall in love, marry the man, have two children, and live happy ever afterwards'), the more the language within that exaggerated male framework turns its rebellious force to reimagining Alice's question in Alice's own tone of voice: 'What *should* a woman do with her life?' As the linear prose gradually begins to stumble upon the woman's problem—'But she had *gone on* thinking of the matter *till* her mind had become *filled* with some *undefined* idea of the importance to her of her own life'—suddenly the woman's problem becomes itself an urgent version of a general human anxiety, implicit and undefined in

Trollope and officially repressed as a misplaced Romanticism, but made explicit in George Eliot. It is a question not just egotistically about 'the importance of her own life' but, as with everyone, 'the importance *to her* of her own life'. And at that smaller and yet also deeper level, it raises the context-disrupting possibility of '*a something* over and beyond, or perhaps altogether beside' the ordinary prescribed course of life. It is that apparently impractical and formless 'undefined idea' for which *Can You Forgive Her?* still finds uneasy room. For indeed, the nineteenth-century novel itself, with all its specificities, is nonetheless the great 'undefined' genre—in its capacity to contain all indefinites within its holding ground. 'There is no species of art which is so free from rigid requirements,' said George Eliot of the novel in 'Silly Novels by Lady Novelists' (*The Westminster Review*, October 1856); 'Like crystalline masses, it may take any form.'

With such openings and questionings, the Victorian age is of course the golden age, the renaissance, of the woman writer: to match Dickens, Trollope, Thackeray, Tennyson, and Robert Browning, there are George Eliot, Mrs Gaskell, and the Brontës, as well as Christina Rossetti and Elizabeth Barrett Browning. Paradoxically, it was the newly increased consciousness of the disadvantages of educated middle-class women that placed such women, as writers, in the very vanguard of Victorian literature. This was precisely because for women the general nineteenth-century problems of feeling and purpose and redundancy were all the more freshly and intimately acute, and because the novel, the new literary form for their expression, was both appropriate and available to the woman writer. A single woman who, disappointed in love, had moved from the Manchester literary scene to become a publisher's reader in London, writes of her life to her friend Jane Carlyle, the underrated wife of Thomas Carlyle, whose own literary skill was expressed only in her personal correspondence:

I do not feel that either you or I are to be called failures. We are indications of a development of womanhood which as yet is not recognized. It has, so far, no ready-made channels to run in, but still we have looked, and tried, and found that the present rules for women will not hold us—that something better and stronger is needed . . . There are women to come after us, who will approach nearer the fulness of the measure of the stature of a woman's nature. I regard myself as a mere faint indication, a rudiment of the idea, of certain higher qualities and possibilities that lie in women, and all the eccentricities and mistakes and miseries and absurdities I have made are only the consequences of an imperfect formation, an immature growth. (*Selections from the Letters of Geraldine Endsor Jewsbury to Jane Welsh Carlyle*, ed. Mrs Alexander Ireland (Longmans, Green and Co., 1892), pp. 348–9)

This was Geraldine Jewsbury (1812–80) whose all too underrated novels *Zoe: A History of Two Lives* (1845) and *The Half Sisters* (1848) have a sexual life-force that is 'a constant striving after something not set down' (*The Half Sisters*, ch. 5). Women like her, books like hers—and characters like George Eliot's idealistic young Dorothea Brooke struggling within the mundane context of *Middlemarch*—by embodying thoughts and aspirations they could not bring to completion were at the very least 'the rudiment of an idea' or what Trollope called 'a something' working itself out in need.

   Virginia Woolf, herself the daughter of a characteristically troubled Victorian man of letters Leslie Stephen, writing of George Eliot's female protagonists concluded thus: 'The ancient consciousness of woman, charged with suffering and sensibility, and for so many ages dumb, seems in them to have brimmed and overflowed and uttered a demand for something—they scarcely knew what—for something that is perhaps incompatible with the facts of human existence' ('George Eliot', *The Common Reader* (1925)). What began with Maggie Tulliver in *The Mill on the Floss* (1860) was not just a social problem: the position of women in Victorian society. For even to solve the social problem was no more than to begin upon the problem as a whole: the search for the purpose of a human life. With Gwendolen Harleth in *Daniel Deronda* (1876) the 'Woman Question' had become an existential problem equivalent to that of seeking a religious life-purpose.

6

The Drama

'In England,' concluded Matthew Arnold in an article in *The Nineteenth Century* (August 1879), 'we have no modern drama at all.' Drama was a more social form of art than was involved in the private act of reading. And 'our vast society', explained Arnold, 'is not homogeneous enough, not sufficiently united, even any large portion of it, in a common view of life, a common ideal capable of serving as a basis for a modern English drama.'

The variegated nature of Victorian theatre was the product of a definite social history. The Theatre Regulation Act of 1737 had restricted the performance of spoken drama to the two 'legitimate' patent theatres, Covent Garden and Drury Lane. Until the replacement of the Act in 1843, following the recommendation of Bulwer-Lytton's select committee on the state of drama in 1832, the other minor theatres had to combine dialogue with the diverse forms of music and song, dance and mime, scenery, pageantry, circus, and spectacle. By then the popular taste for such 'illegitimate' theatre was firmly established, and the demand for such entertainment was greatly increased by the huge growth in the working-class population of London and by an accompanying improvement in ease of public transport. With the rise of new theatres not only in the West End but also in the poorer East End of London, and the increase of theatres royal and touring companies in the provinces, there were more theatres in existence in Britain than ever before.

Characteristically Dickens, celebrant of the Crummles travelling theatre troupe in *Nicholas Nickleby* (1839), was alive to the secret reasons for the popularity of low comic fiction—in particular, burlesque and pantomime 'where there is no affliction or calamity that

leaves the least impression'. The unconscious secret of the success of
such common entertainment lay in the 'temporary superiority to the
common hazards and mischances of life' offered by means of 'a very
rough kind of poetry' to 'an audience of vulnerable spectators' all too
liable to suffer pain and sorrow in their daily lives ('A Curious Dance
Round a Curious Tree', *Household Words*, 17 January 1852). To
Dickens drama was, to the common people at least, all that Matthew
Arnold wanted it to be to the nation as a whole: a natural collective
imaginative outlet and a form of communal cultural cohesion.[1]

In his novels—in the theatre inside his head where he heard so
many distinct voices—Dickens puts in that realist consciousness of
sorrow and pain which gives value to the very attempt to escape
them: through laughter, through play, and through the everyday use
of acting itself. But Joe Whelks of Lambeth, a working-class arche-
type, 'is not much of a reader, has no great store of books, no very
commodious room to read in, no very decided inclination to read,
and no power at all of presenting vividly before his mind's eye what
he reads about'. 'With the help of live men and women', however,
confiding to him in the theatre 'their innermost secrets, in voices
audible half a mile off', the story was exteriorized and imagination
itself was made almost physical ('The Amusements of the People',
Household Words, 30 March 1850). 'It is probable that nothing will
ever root out from amongst the common people an innate love they
have for dramatic entertainment in some form or other.'

Yet the cohesion of high and low, in terms of both social class and
literary genre, failed in the world of theatre. It is true that the social
mix in individual establishments was always varied and, if anything,
was eased by segregation through pricing—the lower classes cus-
tomarily taking up the pit and the gallery, as opposed to the stalls and
dress circle. But, roughly speaking, after 1843 the situation divided
along class lines. The music halls took up much of the lower popular
market, from the seedy singing and drinking saloons called 'penny
gaffs' to the large luxurious halls which numbered almost 400
throughout the country by 1870. On the other hand, encouraged by
the enthusiastic attendance of the Queen herself, so-called genuine
theatre sought to become more respectable, both socially and artis-

[1] I am indebted here to Juliet John, *Dickens's Villains: Melodrama, Character,
Popular Culture* (Oxford University Press, 2001).

tically. Charles Kean and Macready were seeking to raise the standards of Shakespearean production. Madame Vestris established the physical elegance of theatre—first at the Olympic with the classical extravaganzas and revues of J. R. Planché (1796–1880) (higher and genuinely witty versions of pantomime and burlesque); then in partnership with her actor-husband Charles Mathews at the Lyceum. Pictorial effects were powerful because scene-painters and set-designers included Clarkson Stanfield, David Cox, David Roberts, Edward Burne-Jones, and Lawrence Alma-Tadema, later to become illustrious artists in their own right. Geraldine Jewsbury's novel *The Half Sisters* (1848) depicts the struggle of an actress to rescue her profession from the old imputations of sexual laxness and to achieve standards recognizably those of an artist. New standards made the Victorian period, though not a fine age for drama, a great age of theatre.

Yet for all such efforts, Tom Taylor (1817–80), looking back from 1871 over the previous twenty years, wrote that many people from *all* classes had ceased to frequent the theatre because, compared with the state of literature as a whole, a general lowliness of standard still prevailed:

they have ceased to find what they want there,—comedy which will amuse without disgusting by excess or offending by indecency; tragedy which will move and elate without repelling by imperfectness and bad taste of impersonation; drama which will thrill and enthral without condescending to vulgar claptrap, crawling realism, or the mere physical excitement now christened sensation. (*The Theatre in England: Some of its Shortcomings and Possibilities* (1871), pp. 7–8)

To Taylor, himself a dramatist, drama had become the secondary imitation of vulgarly degenerated forms.

Most Victorian drama remained melodrama—originally meaning drama accompanied by music, but now with the musical element subsumed by the romance of strong emotions, violently shifting from comedy to pathos, within exciting plots. Like a higher, more sorrowfully sentimental version of all that Dickens had seen at work in pantomime, domestic melodrama offered the middle classes the explosive relief of intense emotional simplification amidst moral clarity. Dickens himself may have used the father–daughter plots of *The Hunchback* (1832) and *The Daughter* (1837) by the popular dramatist James Sheridan Knowles (1784–1862), when working on *Our Mutual Friend* (1865). Throughout the period, scenes such as the famous last farewell of a wrongfully condemned sailor and his wife, in Douglas Jerrold's nautical melodrama *Black-Ey'd Susan* (1829), continued to have a strong appeal:

WILLIAM.   Susan! you know the old aspen that grows near to the church porch; you and I, when children, almost before we could speak plainly, have sat and watched, and wondered at its shaking leaves . . . I cut from the tree this little branch. [*Produces it.*] Many a summer's day aboard, I've lain in the top and looked at these few leaves, until I saw green meadows in the salt sea, and heard the bleating of the sheep. When I am dead, Susan, let me be laid under that tree—let me—

(Act 3, scene 5)

Such overt scenes show a representative Victorian sensibility historically far less coolly restrained, and far more unembarrassedly inclined to the relief and refuge of vicarious tears, than society a hundred or more years later. Where poetry and the novel had to find an inner language with which to defend, investigate, and test emotions, the language of drama had to be much more physical, unmediated, and momentary in speaking for itself. Drama was left to be the public outlet that offered, most outwardly and immediately, the direct expression of feeling which the age craved. It was the genre that had to carry, openly in public, the weight of what society thought private feelings *should* be.

Many of the stock melodramas were versions of old Gothic tales such as *The Vampire*; some were taken from French or German models; others were adaptations of English novels—in particular, the Newgate crime series, the novels of Scott and Dickens, and the sensation fiction of Mary Braddon and Charles Reade. It was Dion Boucicault (1822–90), of an Irish-French descent as mixed as the sources of his achievement, who was the greatest showman and moneymaker, with the magnificent scenery of upper-class life in *London Assurance* (1841), the romance of *The Corsican Brothers* (1852) taken from the French, and the Irish dramas of passionate love and spectacular violence, such as *The Colleen Bawn* (1860) which earned him £10,000 in a year. In *English Dramatists of To-Day* (1882), William Archer, a key supporter of Ibsen in the

1880s, dismissed Boucicault as the great representative of an age which had picked up and thrown together anything from the old theatrical lumber-room: 'He knows every papier-mâché property, every paste-board character, every threadbare phrase' (p. 39). But what Archer really wanted to dismiss was melodrama itself in all its crudely overt exposure of inner life. Thus, in C. H. Hazlewood's 1863 adaptation of Mary Braddon's popular sensation novel of the year before, *Lady Audley's Secret*:

LADY AUDLEY. Where can he be now? Still in India no doubt. He is mourning my death perhaps—ha, ha! Why I have only just begun to live—to taste the sweets of wealth and power. If I am dead to George Talboys, he is dead to me. Yes, I am well rid of him, and on this earth we meet no more.
GEORGE [*touching her on the shoulder*]. Yes, we do.
LADY AUDLEY [*turning with a shriek*]. George Talboys!

(Act 1, scene 1)

The transparent use of the aside was symptomatic:

LADY AUDLEY. Ah, here comes Robert Audley, he must not see me with a cloud upon my brow! Let me again resume the mask, which not only imposes on him, but on all the world.

(Act 2, scene 1)

As E. S. Dallas put it *The Gay Science* (2 vols., 1866), 'the dramatist cannot plaster and conceal defects of construction by comment or description' (vol. 1, ch. 8). The realist novel could achieve new depths of psychological realism and with it, in the hands of writers such as George Eliot, new and subtler accounts of ordinary undramatic tragedy. But a melodrama such as Leopold Lewis's *The Bells* (1871), in seeking to depict the protagonist's inner guilt for a secret murder committed long years ago, had to depend upon experiments with mental externalization.

On the eve of his daughter's wedding, Mathias—the character whose portrayal launched the acting career of Henry Irving—has a nightmare-like vision of his being placed before a court of law. He protests to this very court that this is a mere dream. But still within this dream, the court has a mesmerist who sends Mathias to sleep, in order to extract a confession from his unconscious. He wakes to find he has betrayed himself. The crowd in court turns back into the wedding crowd, in the midst of which he stands madly imagining there is still a rope around his neck.

However promiscuous their sense of form, the Victorians took genre seriously. What could or could not be done was not just a sign of the internal condition of literature; to them it meant something about the contemporary state of human possibility out in the world. Genres stood for and held onto possible human realities, within the race's history, which were waiting to be activated and reactivated.

To the question of what nineteenth-century drama could be like, George Henry Lewes led the call for contemporary realism in drama, just as he had commended it in the novel. Born into a theatrical family, a failed actor and dramatist, Lewes insisted in *The Leader* (3 August 1850) that the successful dramatists of the day could only be those who resisted the imitation of Elizabethan forms and the burdens of a great but long-gone past: 'We do wish that the dramatist should not be an archaeologist, that he should not strive to revive defunct forms, but produce a nineteenth-century drama.' That was effectively to condemn the neo-Elizabethan poetic efforts of Westland Marston (1819–90) in *Marie de Meranie* (1856) or R. H. Horne (1803–84) in *The Death of Marlowe* (1837) and *Gregory VII* (1840)—the last of whom went on heroically writing his blank-verse tragedies rather than melodramas, knowing his plays were unlikely to reach the stage. Poeticized historical dramas too, such as Lytton's *Richelieu* (1839), W. G. Wills's *Charles the First* (1872), Robert Browning's *Strafford* (1837), or Tennyson's *Queen Mary* (1875) and *Becket* (1893), were in danger of having more to do with the history of the genre rather than the history of the nation. Like the novelists Dickens, Collins, Reade, and Thackeray, the poets flirted with the stage, but then took the dramatic element back into their own domain, in the development of the dramatic monologue.

It seemed to R. H. Horne, in *A New Spirit of the Age* (1844), that the poets and the novelists were dividing the world of drama between them and taking it away, leaving true dramatists stranded in a stage world of burlesque and farce with a language all too easily exposed as thin. Drama could not imitate the direction taken by the novel as Lewes had urged: to Horne, realist drama was not drama at all. The mid-nineteenth-century life of home and family, he argued, was simply too small and mundane to be truly dramatic.

The story of how drama was being left behind—the neo-mythic story of the nineteenth-century Fall of Dramatic Man—was told in the novels that succeeded the drama. It is the subject of Dickens's *Little Dorrit* (1857), in the actorly decline of the father, painfully pretending to be the patriarch he no longer is. It is repeated in the eclipse of Michael Henchard in Hardy's *The Mayor of Casterbridge* (1886). There Hardy takes the more ancient type of the physical man of action—the large primeval figure, like Emily Brontë's Heathcliff, living from within outwards—and locates the evolutionary point at which, through the growth of conscience and self-consciousness in himself, he begins to die out through the very progress of modern civilization. The death of living drama and the naturally dramatic man is the history that Nietzsche was to tell in *The Birth of Tragedy* (1872) and *The Genealogy of Morals* (1887) and, later, Freud in *Civilization and its Discontents* (1930). It is, for better or worse, the story of the civilized establishment of a smaller, more psychologically internalized world, suited to the realm of the novel that grew up with it. In *On Liberty* (1859) John Stuart Mill had defined the situation in terms of the growth of mass social mediocrity, to the loss of individual character.

There was no dramatist who fully articulated the difficulty for drama in the period, and the realist reform of Victorian drama was modest. Direct concern with contemporary social and religious controversies was not encouraged by the censorship that issued from the Lord Chamberlain's Examiner of Plays, but Douglas Jerrold (1803–57) wrote a number of satiric dramas against the world of money in the early 1830s (*The Rent Day, The Golden Calf, The Factory Girl*), Tom Taylor cautiously defended the plight of the discharged prisoner in *The-Ticket-of-Leave Man* (1863), H. J. Byron (1834–84) included in his comedies—*Cyril's Success, Partners for Life, Married in Haste*—a telling sense of marital difficulty, and George Henry Lewes himself penned an adaptation of Balzac, *The Game of Speculation* in 1851. Yet social awareness often seemed more a product of the age, a setting, rather than a direct source of imaginative vitality. Indeed, an awareness of social setting often served only to reduce characterization to stereotyping.

Nonetheless from 1865 to 1870 the realist playwright Tom Robertson (1829–71) had a formidable run of success at the Prince of Wales's, with a company headed by Squire Bancroft and his wife Marie Wilton. His well-constructed domestic dramas—known as 'cup and saucer comedies'—encouraged in place of melodrama a naturalistic acting of conversation, with attention to physical details, careful juxtaposition of social groups, and fine stage management. *Society* (1865), for example, contains a tiny scene, which became famous for its understated delicacy, wherein an aristocratic suitor, not having a key and unable to join his sweetheart in the garden, looks up to see a nursemaid walking casually with her guardsman-lover. The nursemaid simply lets the gentleman into the square, the guardsman saying not a word and taking no further part in the play. In this quiet new realism, the silent untold story of the nursemaid and the guardsman is a piece of incidental life, which creates *in* the play the sense of a world freely existing around it. In *Essays in Theatrical Criticism* (1882), Mowbray Morris argued that such effects were powerful only in their comparative novelty. Realism was not so much a genre in itself, he believed, but only what was left after Robertson took away the negatives of Victorian theatre: it was not 'the stilted artificial style', not 'the buffooneries of the farce-writers', not 'the witless gods and goddesses of burlesque' (pp. 167, 172).

Even so, plays such as *Society* and *Caste* (1867) were alert to social questions and class tensions, and moreover were genuinely able to use that alertness through the groupings on the stage, such that the play becomes as mobile as the social mobility which is its subject. In Robertson's *Caste*, for example, the Honourable George D'Alroy is in love with Esther, a poor girl he saw in the theatre dancing in a ballet, the daughter of Eccles, a freeloading drunk. George's friend, Captain Hawtree, loftily tells him, 'all those marriages of people with common people are all very well in novels and in plays on the stage, because the real people don't exist, and have no relatives who exist' (Act 1, scene 1). Though George tries wholly to dismiss Hawtree's remarks, he cannot quite ignore the various embarrassments Eccles brings with him, in re-creating stereotypes of response all round: 'Ah, sir, the poor and lowly is often 'ardly used. What chance has the working man'; 'May I hope that you will allow me to offer you this trifling loan?' (Act 1, scene 1). Nor, more importantly, can George ignore Esther herself:

GEORGE. When people love there's no such thing as money—it don't exist.

ESTHER. Yes it does.

For Esther knows: 'father has been out of work a long, long time. I make the bread here, and it's hard to make sometimes. I've been mistress of this place, and forced to think ever since my mother died, and I was eight years old' (Act 1, scene 1). It is a mark of the small but precise and telling turn which Robertson gave to Victorian drama that he tells his actors in a stage direction: '[*This speech is not to be spoken in a tone implying hardship*]'. It is the quiet shifts and movements in Robertson that go some way towards turning themes into realities.

Behind Robertson's *Caste* lies Bulwer-Lytton's *Money* (1840), a play that genuinely does seek to confront the two great obstacles that get in the way of serious direct speech in Victorian drama, made thin by the absence of poetry and unaided by the novelist's sub-vocal support. Those two obstacles were the all-pervading falseness of social stereotyping, threatening to overwhelm individual utterance; and its melodramatic opposite, the self-disauthenticating transparency of overt emotional exclamation.

Money begins by telling the conventional Victorian story of a how a proud but dependent secretary, Alfred Evelyn, suddenly and unexpectedly inherits a fortune. When he was poor, his beloved Clara—an equivalently neglected orphan in the same household—reluctantly rejected his offer of marriage. When he becomes rich, he secretly settles money upon her so that she too may be independent in future. But though he finds he can have the pick of the girls, now he is rich, he still cannot win Clara who, scrupulously, will not be one to accept him after he is wealthy if she rejected him while he was poor. In a world of falsenesses, Evelyn feigns ruin in order to test who are his true friends: it is Clara alone who helps by offering him the money she does not know he had secretly given her in the first place. Only then is she told by a third party that the money was indeed his secret gift even whilst he suffered a second time the bitterness of her rejection. For all the predictable twists and turns that bring it to this point, the play then becomes subtle and dense:

CLARA. While your words were so bitter, your deeds so gentle! Oh, noble Evelyn, this, then, was your revenge!

EVELYN. You owe me no thanks; that revenge was sweet! Think you it was nothing to feel that my presence haunted you, though you knew it not? That in things, the pettiest as the greatest, which that gold could buy . . . I had a part—a share?

(Act 5, scene 3)

Both of the simple contrasting terms—nobility and revenge—become so complicated here that, for once, the meanings begin to be larger than the words that would hold them.

His only consolation, says Evelyn, was the thought that if Clara did go on to become the wife of another, at least this would be in part secretly due to him, due 'to the love that you despised!' She denies she despised his love. So, why then did she reject it, when he was poor? It is Clara's turn to disclose hidden motives—motives that go back to the past but are revealed almost too late: 'My father, like you, was poor—generous; gifted, like you, with genius, ambition; sensitive, like you, to the least breath of insult. He married as you would have done—married one whose dowry was penury and care! Alfred, I saw that genius the curse to itself!' Evelyn responds as might be expected, 'Clara, we should have shared it!':

CLARA. Shared? Never let the woman who really loves, comfort her selfishness with such delusion! In marriages like this the wife cannot share the burden; it is he—the husband—to provide, to scheme, to work, to endure—to grind out his strong heart at the miserable wheel! The wife, also, cannot share the struggle—she can but witness despair! And therefore, Alfred, I rejected you.

(Act 5, scene 3)

Suddenly on the Victorian stage this *is* drama's own generic sense of life's reality. Shorn of the novel's extra language of reassurance and immediately vulnerable to life's passing even as it goes along, drama forms a human arena here in which actions do speak truer than words, if only one could hear their language; in which, equally, motives naturally do go unseen for not being spoken; and in which explanations can happen only after events. Sincere speech is no longer either suspect or thin here. Even as they think themselves to be discovering a past of irrevocable misunderstanding and loss, the couple are—without yet quite knowing it—really creating the basis for their future together, as the characters catch up with their life.

Yet there was an alternative way of making Victorian drama real, even though at some cost to the quality of the reality depicted. The other route to success in Victorian drama was to react against the Victorian demand for feeling, and work by a satiric exploitation of the drama's very deficiencies. The master here, in transforming burlesque into satire, was W. S. Gilbert (1836–1911), best known as Arthur Sullivan's librettist in the Savoy Operas produced between 1875 and 1896. Gilbert was a dramatist in his own right, adroitly using theatre *against* itself in order to show the untrustworthy artificiality of so-called real life.

Thus for example, if the typical melodramatic use of the bare aside seemed a clumsy exposure of a character's inner thinking, then Gilbert adroitly set himself to make it barer and clumsier still. In *The Palace of Truth* (1870), one of his fairy-tale plays, there is a magic that requires all the characters to say openly what they are thinking, but without their knowing that they are doing so. A princess protests to her false lover-prince that he had told her he never loved a women till they met: he replies, unwittingly but with a wonderfully innocent gusto, 'I always say that' (Act 2). A flirt sits down by the prince, exposing her ankle as she does so, and then speaks her own stage directions out loud: 'I now remove my glove | That you may note the whiteness of my hand. | I place it there in order that you may | Be tempted to enclose it in your own.' When immediately he falls to that temptation, she says '[*with affected indignation*]', 'If you had any enterprise, | You'd gently place your arm around my waist | And kiss me' '[*struggling to release herself*]' (Act 2). Such counterpoint between speech and act turns the crudely artificial techniques of conventional theatre into a critique of acting in real life. That is the purpose for which Gilbert uses blank verse.

If to Dickens the kind innocence of pantomime was to make comic to an audience all that was far from comic in life itself, then Gilbert offers a more malign twist of gusto. As he puts it in an introductory note to *Engaged* (1877), the characters inside his plays should not know they are in a comedy, they should say and do the most absurd things in the most serious manner possible: 'It is absolutely essential to the success of this piece that it should be played with the most perfect earnestness and gravity throughout.' Thus, for an audience not to take the characters as seriously as they take themselves, not to trust their reality but to look *at* them, as at a mirror society on stage, was the alternative to the claims so often made in realist Victorian literature for response by sympathy.

Precisely through these techniques of reversal, however, the audience to *The Palace of Truth* begins to think how humanly impressive it would be if people really did mean what they said and could deeply articulate it. The habitual plain-speaker in the court gives away the fact that his very frankness is itself counterfeit 'in hopes my clumsy boorish insolence | Might please you by its very novelty' (Act 2). And the very, very good girl in the play finally admits 'that my morality is all assumed' (Act 3). In *Engaged*, a play that contemporary audiences found tipping over into something genuinely disturbing, no character pursues anything more than his or her self-interest, to the point of a dizzying logical absurdity. A widower-father blithely tells his soon-to-be-wedded daughter to be sure to have entirely her own way in marriage: 'These were your angel mother's principles through life, and she was a happy woman indeed' (Act 2). A young man, baffled by a complex plot that will see one young woman marry his friend and one not, but unsure which is which, addresses both together:

One of you will be claimed by Cheviot, that is very clear. To that one (whichever it may be) I do not address myself—but to the other (whichever it may be) I say I love you (whichever you are) . . . you and you only (whichever it may be) with a single-hearted and devoted passion. (Act 3)

In turning the world itself into a mass acting-place, Gilbert is the virtuoso Thackeray of the theatre, his grotesque comic verses in *Fun* so like those of the satiric Thackeray himself.

Yet William Archer said that Gilbert 'could never quite escape' from the one great theme of Victorian theatre which he had made his own from *The Palace of Truth* onwards: the hypocritically false appearances of Victorian society (*The Old Drama and the New* (1923), p. 276). Thereafter nothing quite surprises Gilbert in the act of creating art.

In contrast, there remains within Victorian drama a lingering tradition that, as with Dickens, still positively believes in 'acting' and sees its function off-stage to be something more than insincerity. It is encapsulated in the lovely little work *Masks and Faces, or Before and*

Behind the Curtain (1852) by Charles Reade and Tom Taylor. The collaboration itself came close to a union of the harder and softer elements in Victorian drama: the violent sensationalism of Reade is tempered by the gentler more sentimental art of Taylor, in much the same way as Taylor, a second-generation editor of *Punch*, the great comic magazine, had mellowed the harsher, more satiric approach of his predecessors, Douglas Jerrold and Thackeray.

Masks and Faces goes back a generation or more to authentic theatrical figures of the previous century, Colley Cibber and Peg Woffington. It starts with an eighteenth-century dose of toughened scepticism, administered during an opening exchange between two male admirers and would-be lovers of the leading actress of the day: 'We all know Peg Woffington; she is a decent actress on the boards, and a great actress off them.' This hardened outer element remains for much of the play, to toughen up Tom Taylor's inner sentimentality. For Peg Woffington is herself formidable: a leading actress of comedy, she is an experienced woman, with a past, who protects herself from the world of falseness around her with her own brand of witty scepticism.

She is at her best when she visits the impoverished family of poor Triplet, a decent man who has failed as an artist three times over—as painter, as poet, and as tragic dramatist—but was kind to the actress when she was just a young girl selling oranges. Peg urges him to try to write a comedy for her, which she will help to put on stage. Yet Triplet finds that the struggle to write comedy painful 'Yes! somehow sorrow comes more natural to me'. Nor can his wife help, he explains to the actress, for she seems to have lost her sense of humour:

WOFFINGTON. What! Because the poor thing can't laugh at your comedy.
TRIPLET. No ma'am, but she laughs at nothing.
WOFFINGTON. Try her with one of your tragedies.

(Act 2)

This is one of those moments when again a genre seems to realize itself and the comic spirit exists not just as a style but as a life-force and a form of belief. It is like the fine comic moment in James Albery's *Two Roses* (1870) when the blind young Caleb Deecie is criticized for being very 'impudent': 'he doesn't seem conscious of his affliction. They say pity the poor blind; but he seems determined not to feel his own suffering, which is most impious; for when tribulation comes we ought to tribulate, and not fly in the face of Providence and be happy' (Act 2).

Peg Woffington, 'a decent actress on the boards, and a great actress off them', is the spirit of comedy who will not tribulate when triulation comes. The Triplet family is poor, miserable, and starving; the actress puts on a great performance in enjoying the disguise of her kindness:

BOY. Mother, will the lady give me a bit of her pie?
MRS TRIPLET. Hush, you rude boy.
WOFFINGTON. She is not much of a lady if she doesn't! . . . Eat away; children, when once I begin the pie will soon end; I do everything so quick . . .
GIRL. Mother! the lady is very funny!
WOFFINGTON. You'll be as funny when you're as well paid for it.

(Act 2)

This is realism—acting itself made real—offered as something more than Mowbray Morris's mere absence of melodrama. It is also as though the actress has to hide the soft Tom Taylor part of her, even from herself.

But it is the same virtue in Peg Woffington that finally leads her to return her infatuated admirer, Mr Vane, to his wife, though this was one man she had momentarily believed in (and thought unmarried). In giving him up she surprises herself, as though she could have been expected to have long since outgrown simple goodness: 'to bring back the husband to his duty—what a strange office for a woman like me': 'There is only one way—but that way is simple. Mr Vane thinks better of me than I deserve—I have only to make him [*with a trembling lip*] believe me worse than I am' (Act 2). Acting is not egoism here but concealed selflessness—achieved by an actress whose lot it is to receive 'admiration, but rarely love, triumph but never tranquillity'. The rather lonely private self behind it all, which both creates and watches the performance, can know her value only as lodged somewhere between those two ill deserts: 'better than I deserve' and 'worse than I am'. That drama could get through to that—albeit, as a critic as severe as Matthew Arnold might say, for moments only, in rather conventional language within a finally sentimental little play—is nonetheless still an achievement.

'We oft confound the actor with the part', the play concludes (Act 2), and not just on the stage itself. What is important in *Masks and Faces* is not its portrayal of the outside or the inside of the protagonist but the play's capacity to find a means of speaking out of the linked difference between them. To put it another way, what is trustworthy is not so much the person conceived of as utterly apart from the role assigned, but a sense of the distinction between the two found within 'the part' itself. At that point this drama seems close to some original truths about how individuality comes into being within the social world.

7

Debatable Lands: Variety of Form and Genre in the Early Victorian Novel

I. Post-Aristocratic: Bulwer-Lytton, Disraeli, and Kingsley

For Edward Bulwer-Lytton (1803–73), a different age had begun with the death of the great poet-aristocrat in 1824:

> When Byron passed away, the feeling he had represented craved utterance no more. With a sigh we turned to the actual and practical career of life: we awoke from the morbid, the passionate, the dreaming, 'the moonlight and the dimness of the mind', and by a natural reaction addressed ourselves to the active and daily objects which lay before us. . . . Hence that strong attachment to the Practical, which became so visible a little time after the death of Byron, and which continues (unabated, or rather increased) to characterize the temper of the time. (*England and the English* (1833), bk. 4, ch. 2)

The intellectual spirit of the thirties, argued Bulwer, had become social, economic, materialistic, and political. In particular, the Great Reform Bill, finally passed in 1832, now dominated the public temper. The rotten boroughs which had been in the pocket of the local aristocracy were abolished and the seats were redistributed to form constituencies in the new towns; the franchise was extended in the boroughs to all householders rated at £10 or more and in the counties to all £50 tenant-farmers. The Reform Act only extended the franchise, cautiously, to the new economically successful and respectable middle classes, forestalling any further unrest from this newly powerful section of the populace. But as the harbinger of democracy, it helped create a volatile new class-consciousness and, in particular, served only to increase the working classes' consciousness of exclusion. A Chartist pamphlet of 1836 claimed that out of six million males of voting age only 840,000 had the franchise and that, in effect, one-fortieth of the adult male population had the power to make laws binding upon the rest.

Bulwer's contemporary and friend Benjamin Disraeli argued in *Coningsby* (1844) that in effect the Act of 1832 had finally destroyed the old society of the three great feudal estates—the nobility, the clergy, and the third estate (so numerous as to be served only via representatives)—by virtually conceding the idea of universal male suffrage, as implemented eventually in 1867 and 1884. Disraeli's aristocrat complains in *Sybil* (1845) that 'society' no longer means the traditional principle of human association, cooperation, or community but stands for the mere numerical system of 'aggregation under circumstances which make it rather a dissociating than a uniting principle' (ch. 5). It was now urged that 'the people' should not be virtually, but actually, represented: 'But who are the people? And where are you to draw a line? And why should there be any?' (*Coningsby*, bk. 1, ch. 7). A middle-class reform of the aristocratic framework of society was under way, with the claim that the progressive middle class represented the future of 'the people' as a whole. Under such conditions of social mobility and reordering, description by rank, function, class, or politics was no longer simply automatic: the very language of ascription became interpretative, seeking to establish an identity across a whole range of differing roles, interests, and influences. Like a sign of these cross-cut times, struggling for clear identity, Bulwer himself, born into an aristocracy which on his father's side dated back to the Norman Conquest of 1066, became in his thirties a reforming Liberal Member of Parliament, from 1832 to 1841. Disraeli's aristocratic but socially conscientious young protagonists were the Tory equivalent. Bulwer turned Conservative only in the 1850s, joining Disraeli in the Cabinet in 1858.

In dismissing Romantic individualism and taking the social sphere as the replacement medium, the public Bulwer was also seeking, at the personal level, to leave behind his own Byronic sexual past. There had been a scandalous affair with Byron's own Lady Caroline Lamb, followed by a disastrous marriage which resulted first in his being cut off by his mother and becoming a social outcast dependent for his income upon writing, and finally in Rosina Bulwer-Lytton's portrayal of her husband as a sexual libertine in her novel *Cheveley* (1839). Post-aristocratic and post-Romantic, the new increasingly democratic age was to be to Bulwer what middle age was to the individual—a state no longer young, no longer dangerously passionate or dreamy, but even in its reforms materialistic, Utilitarian, cautiously practical, and respectably dour:

We were in the situation of a man who, having run a certain career of dreams and extravagance, begins to be prudent and saving, to calculate his conduct, and to look to his estate. Politics thus gradually and commonly absorbed our attention, and we grew to identify ourselves, our feelings and our cause, with statesmen and economists, instead of with poets and refiners. (*England and the English*, bk. 4, ch. 2)

Yet at the same time, Bulwer was a poet, a dramatist, and, above all, a novelist whose restless if flawed experimentation within fictional sub-genres helped bring into existence an intermingled range of future possibilities for the novel in the decades to come.

For Bulwer's career coincided with a time when the situation of 'literature' itself was shifting and mutating, by 'the removal of time-worn landmarks, and the breaking up of hereditary elements' correspondent with analogous changes in society (*England and the English*, bk. 4, ch. 6). His very versatility, suggested the critic David Masson, was the product of his desire to work out self-consciously, through practice, a theory of the Novel which would make it a truly higher form of art than Bulwer had found it (*British Novelists and their Styles* (1859), lecture 4). To Bulwer the novel had to do with novelty, and creative novelty had to do with bringing into the world a new form, a new combination of elements, even if all its elements were individually as old as the earth itself. The young writer, he says, 'multiplies himself in a thousand objects' (*Ernest Maltravers* (1837), bk. 3, ch. 2). Yet as he said himself in an essay 'On certain Principles of Art in Works of Imagination' reprinted in *Caxtoniana* (1863), the hardest achievement in Art was not only to invent new combinations but to give them a life which endured long after the life of their own creator. By that criterion, the interest of Bulwer's work is finally more historical, in respect of the developing *idea* of the Novel, than complete in itself and living. Yet even as such, its inventive range offers one of the best introductions to the variety of genre and sub-genre in the prose writing of the second quarter of the century.

Bulwer's own success began, typically, with the depiction of aristocratic life, in the best-seller *Pelham* (1828) which sold over 200,000 copies throughout the century. It belonged with those novels of the fashionable world of London, published by Henry Colburn, which in his 1827 essay 'The Dandy School' Hazlitt had ridiculed as 'silver fork' fiction, because of Theodore Hook's fascination with the fact that the fashionable 'eat their fish with a silver fork'. The main exponents of such fiction were Hook, Lady Blessington, T. H. Lister, and Mrs Gore—whose *The Hamiltons* (1834) concerned the social effects of the Reform Bill, and whose *Cecil* (1841) depicted the life of a Regency dandy, contemporary with Byron.

To Bulwer the silver-fork novel had grown out of the fact that the moral and spiritual qualities of 'nobility' were becoming finally and totally separated from the traditional structures which should have sustained them in the midst of an increasingly mercantile world. The aristocracy had become merely 'social' and 'fashionable', nobility reduced to a matter of tone and manners and clothes. The middle classes, seeking to bridge the gap through the use of money, 'eagerly sought for representations of the manners which they aspired to imitate, and the circles to which it was not impossible to belong': hence the popularity of silver-fork fiction as a guide to emulation. Yet in a climate of haughty affectation on one side and covert envy on the other, the writers of silver-fork novels could not help giving the game away and 'unconsciously exposed the falsehood, the hypocrisy, the arrogant and vulgar insolence of patrician life' (*England and the English*, bk. 4, ch. 2).

But young Pelham himself is, quite consciously, both upper-class dandy and undercover satirist of all he seemingly colludes in: 'somewhat better than the voluptuary, and somewhat wiser than the coxcomb, which were all that at present it suited me to appear' (*Pelham*, ch. 14). Hidden within those disguises is a proud aristocratic intelligence which wittily despises what the aristocrat has come to: it is the secret spirit of Byronic satire which allows Pelham, according to his philosophy, to be facetious with the serious, serious with the frivolous, because in the decadent society surrounding him 'things which are usually treated with importance are, for the most part, deserving of ridicule; and those which we receive as trifles swell themselves into a consequence we little dreamt of before they depart' (ch. 68). This is a secret and alienated intelligence which, as the novel develops, increasingly has to find a place for itself within, rather than in opposition to, a language of morality. Turning the silver-fork novel against itself, *Pelham* is the prophetic pre-Victorian story of a dandy's progress towards a responsible middle age of authentic seriousness, in both marriage and politics.

This was to do inside the silver-fork novel, within the person of its protagonist, what Thackeray and Dickens were to do more simply outside it: parody it until it could be replaced by something more down-to-earth. Dickens has Kate Nickleby read his parody 'The Lady Flabella' to Mrs Witterley in chapter 28 of *Nicholas Nickleby* (1839). Thackeray's burlesque on Mrs Gore ('Lords and Liveries by the Authoress of "Dukes and Dejeuners", "Hearts and Diamonds", "Marchionesses and Milliners"') appeared in *Punch* in 1847 as one of his *Novels by Eminent Hands*. The satiric parody of one class-genre—aristocratic silver-fork novels—merged into the beginning of an alternative, the creation of middle-class realism.

Thackeray in particular was corrosively alert to the falsities and compromises hidden within generic hybridization. Like his friend Bulwer, Benjamin Disraeli had first attained popularity as a novelist with a silver-fork novel—*Vivian Grey*, published in 1826–7—whilst his *Venetia* (1837) was another fictionalized account of the later life of Lord Byron. Evolving, like the century itself, out of that upper-class starting point, it was Disraeli who then helped create a second-wave silver-fork novel in the 1840s, transformed by social concern: the Young England novels written in aristocratic support of the old feudal society. For this was a radical Toryism which was seeking to expose within its own party the hypocrisy of Conservatism which 'would only embrace as much liberalism as is necessary for the moment'. What *do* Conservatives wish to conserve? They dare not wish, said Disraeli, to preserve the ancient order undone by the Reform Act but, like temporizers, they simply want 'to keep things as they find them as well as they can', whilst going along with the minimum of reform necessary to retain power (*Coningsby*, bk. 7, ch. 2). To Thackeray, however, Disraeli's Young England novels were the false grafting of one genre, one class, and one age upon another. Disraeli's was the fashionable novel seeking to regenerate itself through a misalliance with the novel of social realism; a new young branch of the old aristocratic class was forcing its conscientious fantasies upon the contemporary concerns of the common people of the nation. Thackeray's burlesque 'Codlinsby' appeared in *Punch* in 1847, dismissing *Coningsby* as 'a glorification of dandyism, far beyond all other glories which dandyism has attained. Dandies are here made to regenerate the world—to heal the wounds of the wretched body politic—to infuse new blood into torpid old institutions—to reconcile the ancient world to the modern.'[1]

Within two years of publishing *Pelham*, Bulwer had turned his fictional world upside down in the writing of the low-life criminal novel *Paul Clifford* (1830). *Paul Clifford* was the first of the Newgate novels (1830–47), named after the famous London prison and *The Newgate Calendar*, the popular collections of the lives of criminals which appeared throughout the eighteenth century. The Newgate novels formed a bridge between eighteenth-century crime fiction, such as Fielding's *Jonathan Wild* (1743) or Godwin's *Caleb Williams* (1794) and the Victorian detective story, in particular in the hands of Wilkie Collins. Bulwer's *Paul Clifford* and *Eugene Aram* (1832), the story of a scholar-murderer, and William Harrison Ainsworth's *Rookwood* (1834) and *Jack Sheppard* (1839–40) were sensationally popular.

In Bulwer's hands, the Newgate novel was also sporadically half-turned into a novel of liberal-reformist social concern: the difference in wrongdoing between the underworld and the respectable world, says Bulwer in *Night and Morning* (1841), is often the difference between crimes and sins: but where crimes are dangerous because illegal, sins are safe—especially when practised by the fashionable and powerful (bk. 5, ch. 13). Circumstances create guilt. In contrast, in his prefaces to *Rookwood*, Ainsworth spoke for his work as

---

[1] Thackeray's *Contributions to the Morning Chronicle*, ed. G. N. Ray (University of Illinois, 1955), 39.

self-containedly generic—as pleasurable entertainment in the field of revived romance and drama. When Ainsworth reinvents Dick Turpin's legendary ride on Black Bess from London to York or Jack Sheppard's chronicled series of escapes from the impregnable Newgate, he is re-creating a low-life romance, alternative imaginative histories leaping out of the real-life moral or legal context surrounding them. The absolute technical and physical effort involved in Jack Sheppard's single-handed struggle to overcome the obstacles of imprisonment in Newgate, wall after wall, door after door, together with the psychological force of living up to his reputation as the great escape-artist, is a triumph of the individual—no more and no less than a displaced popular version of the heroic ideal. Yet, in an age of ever-increasing social responsibility, the Newgate novels were indiscriminately criticized by reviewers, particularly in the Tory *Fraser's Magazine*, for supposedly condoning if not endorsing criminal activity.

In Bulwer the great moments come in the final trial speeches of Paul Clifford and Eugene Aram. At the end of Paul's powerful account of the injustices of his outcast life, there is a momentary hiatus before the jury retire to consider its verdict:

> The Jurors looked confusedly at each other, but not one of them spoke even by a whisper; their feelings, which had been roused by the speech of the Prisoner, had not, from its shortness, its singularity, and the haughty impolicy of its tone, been so far guided by its course, as to settle into any state of mind clearly favourable to him, or the reverse; so that each man waited for his neighbour to speak first, in order that he might find, as it were, in another, a kind of clue to the indistinct and excited feelings which wanted utterance in himself. (*Paul Clifford*, ch. 35)

This is what interests Bulwer—this suspended moment of silence, like a hole at the very centre of reality, that holds open a nameless space between the political speech and the resumption of normalized conventionality. So it is with the Roman tribune, struggling between the ways of aristocracy and democracy, at the moment of his brief triumph:

> he turned his sword alternately to the three quarters of the then known globe, and said, in an abstracted voice, as a man in a dream, 'In the right of the Roman people *this* too is mine!'

Low though the voice, the wild boast was heard by all around as distinctly as if borne to them in thunder. And vain it were to describe the various sensations it excited; the extravagance would have moved the derision of his foes, the grief of his friends, but for the manner of the speaker, which, solemn and commanding, hushed for a moment even reason and hatred themselves into awe; afterwards remembered and repeated, void of the spell they had borrowed from the utterer, the words met the cold condemnation of the well-judging; but at that moment all things seemed possible to the hero of the people. (*Rienzi: The Last of the Tribunes* (1835), ch. 6)

It is for the sake of 'spells' like this—before the reactions, rationalizations and realist outcomes of plot that follow upon it—that Bulwer is, even in fragments, an experimental novelist. Not least of all, in *Rienzi* and his spectacular best-seller *The Last Days of Pompeii* (1834), Bulwer also establishes the Victorian interest in Rome as an analogous story of empire.

But again it was Thackeray, the great sceptical purger of false fiction, who sought to destroy the Newgate sub-genre by satiric parody, first in *Catherine* serialized in *Fraser's Magazine* in 1840, and then again, in response to Bulwer's *Lucretia* (1846) and a second wave of Newgate novels, in his *Punch* burlesque 'George De Barnwell'. Indeed, so destructive did Thackeray seem that Bulwer was barely dissuaded from demanding an old-fashioned duel. Yet to Thackeray, melodramatic romance was here illegitimately posing as realism, and the aesthetic confusion created the falsity of much contemporary fiction. What Thackeray criticized most was not so much the alleged immorality of the Newgate novel, its half-hidden love affair with crime and sex and the power of evil, but on the contrary what he took to be its sham morality. The creation of virtuous streetwalkers or brave robbers made charity itself seem untrustworthy. Even Dickens's revisionary incorporation of the Newgate novel in *Oliver Twist* (1837) seemed to Thackeray essentially sentimental.

Bulwer wrote no more crime fiction after Thackeray's attacks. Following the fiasco with *Lucretia* he turned, again apparently at random, to the gentler family feelings of domestic fiction. *The Caxtons* (1849), a great popular success, is the story of a young man who can go on being unashamedly a son even after becoming an adult. In trouble with love, for example, he does not turn away from his father but towards him. If this seems 'typically Victorian', it is because Bulwer helped to make it so: 'Now I know that it is not the custom of lovers to confide in fathers and uncles. Judging by those mirrors of life, plays and novels, they choose better; valets and chambermaids, and friends whom they have picked up in the street' (pt. 8, ch. 2). His young protagonist actually creates that recommitment to the patriarchy, at some personal cost, in defiance of contemporary consciousness in seeming unmanly or immature. It is 'the confidence between son and father' that Dickens's equivalent young narrator, David Copperfield, so keenly feels the want of, a year later in 1850. For in its easy commerce between trusting and confiding, 'confidence' here is a lovely word, to do with a permanent love in the relationship, for all the failures of other kinds of love: 'I pressed my father's hand, and I felt then, that while that hand could reply to mine, even the loss of Fanny Trevanion could not leave the world a blank. How much we have before us in life, while we retain our parents' (*The Caxtons*, pt. 8, ch. 2). By means of this at once formal and informal handshake, the pieties of tradition become instinctively inherited private emotions, and a loyalty which was once feudal and hereditary here becomes not merely bourgeois and domesticated but intuitive, familiar, and felt. This is Ruskin's post-aristocratic vision in *Sesame and Lilies* (1865): that what had been lost in traditional feudal society could now be refound within the private kingdom, and the *moral* if not social nobility, of the ordinary family. It is in the realist family novel that the vision of noble qualities is made ordinary flesh. Hence that touching smoking-room scene in Mrs Gaskell's *Wives and Daughters* (1866), where in the midst of the male ritual of filling the pipe, the younger son stoops over his newly bereaved father, the squire, and 'stroked his cheek', almost unconsciously, even as the dead wife and mother would have done (ch. 23).

Nor is the domestic realism of *The Caxtons* without its thought experiments. The two brothers in the novel, uncle and father, are offered as, respectively, the military man of action and the sedentary man of letters, with a history of some conflict between them. The young son and nephew who loves them both finds himself thinking that if the two had swapped careers, 'if Roland had taken to literature and my father had been forced into action', then 'each would have had greater worldly success': the soldier needed a touch of the scholar's calm detachment to turn him into a wiser counsellor and strategist; the scholar needed something of the warrior's urgent intensity to force him into using his learning, to produce some passionate poem or history. The thought continues at some length:

> But, as it was—with his slow pulse never stimulated by action, and too little stirred by even scholarly ambition—my father's mind went on widening and widening till the circle was lost in the great ocean of contemplation; and Roland's passionate energy, fretted into fever by every let and hindrance, in the struggle with his kind—and narrowed more and more as it was curbed within the channels of active discipline and duty—missed its due career altogether. (pt. 3, ch. 5)

until the vivacious length makes the reader ask harder, What exactly is the thought and the point of it? For often the realist novel gives room to what seem to be life's casually arising thoughts which nonetheless, bearing a strong emotional content, appear in search or want of a formal framework to make their importance clearer.

It becomes evident in the course of the book that this is what might be called a natural symbol—standing for *more* than itself without ever ceasing literally to *be* itself. As Coleridge says of symbol, in preference to allegory, in *The Statesman's Manual* (1830): 'it always partakes of the Reality which it renders intelligible; and while it enunciates the whole, abides itself as a living part in that Unity, of which it is the representative'. Lodged as it is in just one small part of the book, it gradually becomes clear that Bulwer's realist symbol has a wider twofold meaning within the whole. First, it relates to Bulwer's self-interrupting interest in parallel or other worlds, in which the story told in the midst of this book could go quite differently in another. Imagine, he says (in pt. 15, ch. 1), losing contact with a young man who, with a mixture of good and bad qualities, could go either way in the future. Then suppose you hear of him again in later years having done something either extraordinarily good or extraordinarily evil: in *either* eventuality you will find your mind running rapidly back and you will say, with hindsight, 'How natural!—only So-and-so could have done this thing!' By certain changes in the proportions of the compound-mix, the father and the uncle could each, or both, have gone further or done better. The genetic material, as we would call it, was all there, at least between the two of them, if not quite in either separately. And that is the second idea, which relates to Bulwer's concern for form and wholeness within the wide-ranging work of the novel. For the father and uncle are held together both in the mind of their loving son and nephew and in their own love for him—and, more, exist together in another modified version of themselves, in the inherited make-up of this young man of the next generation, who indeed finally completes the family form of the novel by marrying not Fanny but his uncle's daughter, Blanche. As it is in the mix of genres within the hybrid novel, so it is with the chemistry of genes in the family history.

Bulwer's experiments continue with two sequels to the *Caxtons*— *My Novel* (1853) and *What Will He Do With It?* (1859)—in which the young protagonist of that first novel becomes himself the framing author of the subsequent novels. But at the heart of Bulwer's enterprise lies the Faustian wish not only to produce these written experiments but to write about the very process of experimentation itself. This was to be done not by way of digression in the midst of a realist text but by creating an analogical form, concerned with the transformative powers of magic, mysticism, or alchemy. The result was what David Masson called the novel of 'supernatural phantasy' (*British Novelists and their Styles*, lecture 4) and Bulwer himself called 'the metaphysical novel', in particular *Zanoni* (1842) and *A Strange Story* (1862), as well as the ghost story 'The Haunter and the Haunted, or the House and the Brain' (*Blackwood's Magazine*, August 1859) and the science fiction *The Coming Race* (1871).

The first two or three of the seven books of *Zanoni* are one of Bulwer's finest achievements in describing his art's search for a language. For there Bulwer introduces a whole series of interrelated characters, each concerned with some version of art for which, almost allegorically, he or she stands.

Pisani, an unsuccessful composer, works as an orchestral violinist, who, at certain moments, cannot help introducing strange, impromptu variations that throw the collective performance into disarray. His daughter, Viola, sings the leading role in Pisani's own hitherto rejected opera: music passing into her soul becomes, it is said, poetry. After the death of her father, it is a poetry that seeks expression, at a further level of initiation, within the world itself—in the form of love. For there comes into her life an aspiring young painter, Glyndon. But Glyndon is only an incomplete artist: he has only moments of breakthrough in his otherwise conventional paintings. As Zanoni, the book's magical wise man, sees, what disables Glyndon and keeps him conventional is fear—fear of both the world's opinion and his own powers; fear that virtue is not eternal, that God is non-existent. In the end it is Zanoni, not Glyndon, who dares love Viola even though it means Zanoni must sacrifice his superhuman occult powers for involvement with the real, in the form of a mortal.

In *Zanoni* the sister arts—and magic and love and religion—are all versions of each other in the creative attempt to give some exploratory shape and name to the unknown. Yet by the end of the novel, as so often in Bulwer, the outward narrative cannot carry the weight of the inner meaning and turns into routine instead. In the *Dictionary of National Biography*, Leslie Stephen said that Bulwer was a talent who thought he was a genius. The talent often runs out before the completion of the formal plotting of each venture, and ignites itself only by beginning another. Bulwer preached wholeness and harmony of design and yet often writes best in fragments or at beginnings.

But this is not simply Bulwer's personal or artistic failure. In *The Statesman's Manual* (1816) Coleridge wrote, 'It is among the miseries of the present age that it recognizes no medium between *Literal* and *Metaphorical*', as though a statement must be either fact or fiction, with nothing allowed any hold in between. Seeking just such a medium between the two, Bulwer in his 'Introduction' to *Zanoni* has to speak equivocally of producing a work which was a romance and not a romance, an allegory and not an allegory. By 1859, as increasingly the century clarified itself, David Masson was insisting that a definite distinction between Romance and Realism had become central to an understanding of the Victorian novel:

Now, when we speak of a Romance, we generally mean 'a fictitious narrative, in prose or verse, the interest of which turns upon marvellous and uncommon incidents'; and when we speak of a Novel, we generally mean 'a fictitious narrative differing from the Romance, inasmuch as the incidents are accommodated to the ordinary train of events and the modern state of society'. If we adopt this distinction, we make the prose Romance and the Novel the two highest varieties of prose fiction, and we allow in the prose Romance a greater ideality of incident than in the Novel. (*British Novelists and their Styles*, lecture 1)

Yet in the 1840s Bulwer still wanted to work within a mixed mode in which the distinctions between romance and realism, allegory and symbol, were in the very process of coming into being. Romance was the aristocratic, high poetic mode, Realism the new democratic one: it was another of Bulwer's attempts to hold the two ways together. Thus the task—which in the preface to the 1835 edition of *The Disowned*, 'On the Different Kinds of Prose Fiction', he described as 'dim and shadowy allegory'—was to *suggest* a second book, like a second world, behind the realism of the first one, without the second taking it over.

So, for example, a wise old doctor describes to his sceptical young colleague how a young woman in their care has become too much a creature of soul, just as the young man himself is too much a figure of mind. There are disadvantages both ways:

she in whom soul has been led dimly astray, by unheeding the checks and the definite goals which the mind is ordained to prescribe its wanderings while here; the mind taking thoughts from the actual and visible world, and the soul but vague glimpses and hints from the instinct of its ultimate heritage. Each of you two seems to me as yet incomplete, and your destinies yet uncompleted. Through the bonds of the heart, through the trials of time, ye have both to consummate your marriage. I do not—believe me—I do not say this in the fanciful wisdom of allegory and type, save that allegory and type run through all the most commonplace phases of outward and material life. (*A Strange Story* (1862), ch. 79)

'You will need one another': the marriage is necessary at many levels. To gain access to those differing levels, the reader cannot just be the passive spectator of a scene that uninterruptedly passes for real life, but must become a participant in the unfolding mentality of the creative process itself. For Bulwer's novels have to discover from within themselves that they *are* allegorical, and that allegory is itself a representation of something real in the nature of the created universe.

Bulwer loved experiencing the different modes of being that came into his head as he moved from one mode of writing to another. The realist author often works, as Bulwer says in his essay 'On Art in Fiction' (1838), by 'groping his way', content with writing onwards from chapter to chapter, working in time with an emergent meaning that evolves out of the very experience of the story as he goes along— what Trollope was to call 'living with' his characters (*Autobiography* (1883), ch. 13). But the metaphysical novelist is less concerned with going along with what he takes to be the everyday illusion of reality, in fiction and in life. He wants instead to *see through to* the prior and underlying nature of reality itself which, as in Plato, we live out on earth in partial forgetfulness. *A Strange Story*, published by Dickens in *All the Year Round* in 1861–2 (despite his doubts about what he called Bulwer's 'weirdness' in relation to magic), was an attempt to resurrect the mystical novel twenty years after *Zanoni*. In it the young doctor, called Fenwick, is offered by occult magic a kind of X-ray vision of another young man, Margrave, who himself has strange powers. 'The brain now opened on my sight, with all its labyrinth of cells . . . I saw therein a moral world, charred and ruined' (ch. 32). As though in a trance, Fenwick sees in that powerful brain three virtually allegorical lights: one red, working from the brain along the arteries, veins, and nerves, like the principle of animal life; one azure, struggling to enter into and wilfully direct the red, as if it were the principle of intellectual being; and finally one silver, shining clear and independent 'within the ruins of its lodgment'. The doctor senses that the silver light must be the mark of the soul, 'about to carry into eternity the account of its mission in time', because he feels it reflect back upon his own soul 'its ineffable trouble, humiliation, and sorrow'. The mind, he realizes, is storming the soul:

And I could not comprehend the war, nor guess what it was that the mind demanded the soul to yield. Only the distinction between the two was made intelligible by their antagonism. And I saw that the soul, sorely tempted, looked afar for escape from the subjects it had ever so ill controlled, and who sought to reduce to their vassal the power which had lost authority as their king. I could feel its terror in the sympathy of my own terror, the keenness of my own supplicating pity. I knew that it was imploring release from the perils it confessed its want of strength to encounter. And suddenly the starry spark rose from the ruins and the tumult around it,—rose into space and vanished; and where my soul had recognized the presence of soul there was a void. (ch. 32)

The 'sympathy' here is more ancient, mysterious, and visionary than the moralized fellow feeling of liberal humanism. As Fenwick wakes and tries to resume his sceptical position, Margrave comes back to life without his own soul.

There remained one further fictional mode for Bulwer in the 1840s: the historical novel. It was yet another opportunity to explore what that most literary-minded of historians Macaulay called 'the debatable land' of literature which lies, ill-defined and ill-regulated, between 'two distinct territories', with two warring powers— Reason and Imagination—each with its claims for sovereignty ('History', *Edinburgh Review*, May 1828).

The Last of the Barons (1843) is the work of Bulwer's that most deserves to survive as a complete whole. Like *The Last Days of Pompeii* (1834), *Rienzi: The Last of the Tribunes* (1835), and *Harold: The Last of the Saxon Kings* (1848), *The Last of the Barons* concerns the sacrificial failure of the Last Man, the individual representative of an older order, in the progressive march of a larger history. In *The Last of the Barons* the slow, gradual, and imperceptibly tiny movements of time, so characteristic of the realist novel, give way to the larger, historic, and public *drama* involved in the suddenly visible ending of one era and the beginning of another.

Set in the years 1467–71, *The Last of the Barons* is the story of the Earl of Warwick, the last great king-making aristocrat in the reign of Edward IV. What Warwick sees is the change in society which is slowly converting an agricultural into a trading population, with the gradual formation of a middle, trading class between knight and vassal. The King is 'the Man of his Age', who supports the rise of this class against the power of the old barons. Even within his own class Warwick sees a transformation of the aristocracy from a martial to a court order, a change from arms and chivalry to intrigue and politics which he considers to be only another version of the trader spirit— 'the spirit that cheats, and cringes, and haggles' (bk. 11, ch. 1).

The specific attraction of the historical novel for Bulwer is thus that it provides a version of what it feels like to live through a period of historical change, a version moreover which not only is analogous to the experience of change of the nineteenth century but may even be in part its ancestral cause. 'We are passing out of old forms of activity into others new and on their present scale untried,' wrote J. A. Froude, literary man and historian of sixteenth-century England, 'and how to work nobly in them is the one problem for us all': 'Our calling is neither to the hermitage nor to the round table. Our work lies now in those peaceful occupations which, in ages called heroic, were thought unworthy of noble souls' ('Representative Men', in *Short Studies on Great Subjects* (4 vols., 1867–83), vol. 1). What *The Last of the Barons* offers to a post-heroic age is the story of large, heroic, noble drama and how it faded. Yet this is not simply nostalgia. As Bulwer puts it in his preface to *Harold*, his emphasis within the debatable land is not to employ History to aid Romance, but to employ Romance in the aid of History: it means that Bulwer seeks a large emotional and imaginatively near-mythic form for what remains nonetheless a form of thinking about social change.

For there is a third figure in the balance of power in *The Last of the Barons*. Robert Hilyard stands as the people's champion, a revolutionary preparing for wider democratic changes by working first of all through the awakened political interests of the new middle class. Standing on either side of the politic King, Hilyard, the Man Ahead of his Age, and Warwick, the Man Behind the Times, have much strangely in common as men of principle:

both desired to increase liberty; both honestly and ardently loved the masses; but each in the spirit of his order: Warwick defended freedom as against the throne, Hilyard as against the barons. Still, notwithstanding their differences, each was so convinced of the integrity of the other, that it wanted only a foe in the field to unite them as before. (bk. 11, ch. 3)

It is not difficult to see here Bulwer's vision of underlying allegory. It is as though the space between the people becomes as important as the people themselves in defining them, and that space opens and closes and mutates according to the new fluidity of the classes and the political situation. Hence: king and middle classes versus the aristocracy, or, alternatively, aristocracy and populace versus the trading classes, or, just possibly, middle classes and aristocrats against the king, in the shifting of positions, alliances, and conflicts within the debatable land. The large dialectical movements between the three classes and their representatives becomes a form of thinking in Bulwer just as it was in Walter Scott, for these were writers in at the very origins of the great elements of national thought.

The downfall of Warwick lies in his undivided if injudicious simplicity: he is instinctively a whole man, feeling no emotional distinction between public and private life. But there are other newer men
who are specialists. What was no more or less than cunning in
Edward IV has developed into specialized political skill above all in
the person of the coming man, Richard of Gloucester, soon to
become Richard III. The pragmatic politicians in the novel can coolly
separate off from their view of affairs that passion of human meaning which Warwick always wholeheartedly brings to whatever he
is involved in. They can so manipulate Warwick's uncalculating,
consistent, and thus predictable instinct that it may be used against
itself. When Warwick finally has to break with his King and join
those who were formerly his foes, the division of his world breaks his
own heart: 'separated from his old companions in arms . . . alone
amongst men whom the habits of an active life had indissolubly connected, in his mind, with recollections of wrath and wrong' (bk. 11,
ch. 2). It is like the case of the staunch Royalist in J. H. Shorthouse's
John Inglesant (1880) who, amidst the chaos of the English Civil
War, can find no visible form on earth that can contain his transcendent religious faith without betraying it. Hence, in the endeavour to
find authentic forms to incarnate the spirit, and the accompanying
struggle to escape the frameworks that imprison it, Inglesant, that
most loyal of men, appears to be the most changeable of all.

In all this *The Last of the Barons* could easily have remained a
romance about the ending of one representative individual and the
origins of subsequent social and historical developments. In fact, the
historical novel, even in retrospect, is left to remain irresolvably in
the very *middle* of affairs, without conclusive verdict, as soon as
Bulwer asks the question: What would have happened if Warwick
had triumphed over Edward IV at the battle of Barnet? The whole
imagination of the course of English history opens before him, in
another of Bulwer's experiments with form.

Had it been durable and effectual, the system that Warwick represented—'of the whole consequences of which he was unconscious'—
might have changed monarchic into aristocratic government. The
landed Norman aristocracy would have protected through 'broad
and popular institutions' the agricultural populace on which its
strength was founded; and the middle or commercial classes would

have risen much more slowly than when made, first under Edward IV and finally under Henry VIII, 'the instrument for destroying feudal aristocracy' (bk. 11, ch. 2). The absolute monarchy of the Tudors, the subsequent reaction against the Stuarts, even the Civil War itself, might all never have happened.

And yet had these things never happened, there might have been no gathering of 'all the vigour and life of genius into a single and strong government' with 'the graces, the arts, the letters of a polished court'. We should have lost 'the resources of a commercial population destined to rise above the tyranny at which it had first connived, and give to the emancipated Saxon the markets of the world' (bk. 12, ch. 3). The past does not end but is changed, and changed again and again, by what its future makes out of it.

The spirit of the age fought amorally 'for the false Edward and against the honest Earl' (bk. 11, ch. 2). Yet in the unfolding of its huge and long consequences, what came to pass was, disturbingly, something beyond the clarity of immediate moral judgment and not simply as false or limited as the human sources from which it derived. 'Upon the victory of that day, all these contending interests—this vast alternative in the future—swayed and trembled' (bk. 12, ch. 3). That turning point, and with it the momentary vision of two parallel future possibilities, is not seen merely in the light of hindsight but in the light of imagination itself, as an impossible, almost extra-historical vision of what will always remain unclear to creatures immersed in time.

'Without presuming to decide which policy would have been happier for England' (bk. 11, ch. 2), this is a story that, seen from a position outside its world, had in it material which could have developed in many ways and in different forms. History in *The Last of the Barons* becomes awesomely a process, a form, and an epic mystery of life, in its own right.

If Bulwer-Lytton consciously represents the aristocrat in the post-aristocratic world, the new and coming view belonged of course to the middle class, as within the changing shape of the nation, its very position became central and consolidating. Indeed, it is the rise of the progressive middle class which is the subject of Macaulay's best-selling *History of England*, a project originally intended to cover the whole period from 1688 to 1830. But by the beginning of the second half of the nineteenth century, the middle class, like a bridge across the chasm between rich and poor, stood less for reform than for that middle way between aristocracy and radicalism which was the way out of political conflict—its writers often acting as articulators and mediators.

And yet, for all the consolidation, there still remained a problem involved in the loss of the old forms. Looking back, for contrast, at a collection of medieval writings on the lives of the saints, J. A. Froude in 1850 argued that the very point of those ancient lives had been their essential sameness. They sought perpetually to reproduce the single type, the exemplary pattern called Saint, in whom virtue was more important than individuality. The characteristic literary mode for such an age was therefore allegory, wherein the reality of the particular gives way to the understanding of the general abstract truth it represents. But modern life to Froude was manifestly more libertarian, more contingent, and more variously personal, private, and particular, without clear ranks and orders. It was the age not of saints' lives and allegory but of individual biography and literary realism, of a wider variety of particular people, possessing even so less knowledge of what they were *for*. Too often either they had no models of devotion or heroism or the models they did have—'the shopkeeper type, the manufacturer type, the lawyer type'—were such as sacrificed the human to the economic ('The Lives of the Saints', in *Short Studies on Great Subjects*, vol. 1).

In such a context, Froude's friend and brother-in-law Charles Kingsley (1819–75)—clergyman, poet, essayist, novelist, naturalist, socialist, social reformer, historian—may be said to represent, in his energy and conscientiousness, one characteristically middle-class version of Bulwer's versatility in the pursuit of form. Looking at England in 1851, Kingsley saw the problems of his time in terms of a fermenting mass of rich, confused content in search of a proper framework for itself: 'What a chaos of noble materials is here—all confused, it is true—polarized, jarring, and chaotic—here bigotry, there self-will, superstition, sheer Atheism often, but only waiting for the one inspiring Spirit to organize, and unite, and consecrate this chaos into the noblest polity the world ever saw realised' (*Yeast* (1851), ch. 17). In the mean time, what Kingsley's realist social novels unashamedly offered was the honest, second-best strategy of a fragmentary form appropriate to the very subject matter: 'jumbling religion and politics—the human and the divine—the theories of the pulpit with the facts of the exchange', till the order and the relationships within it began to come right (ch. 14). Yet with that there was a deeper nightmare side to Kingsley that emerges at strange moments within his writing. Nothing is more powerful in his work than the almost literal break-down of radical political consciousness in the eponymous working-class hero of *Alton Locke* (1850)—when, in brain fever, he finds himself degenerating into a crowd of dividing and multiplying polypi and has mentally to fight his way back up the evolutionary scale, through the ape whose 'fruitless strugglings to think' are periodically overtaken 'by wild frenzies, agonies of lust and aimless ferocity', until he can remake himself afresh in the struggle through to renewed sanity (ch. 36). At that level Kingsley understood something genuinely deep about the unstable nature of form in all areas of thought and action in the second quarter of the nineteenth century, and the weird configurations of shapes and categories that had accompanied it.

In his habitual stance, however, Kingsley turned his energies into the sort of almost brutally single-minded assertiveness which Matthew Arnold dismissed as the mark of the middle-class philistine. For certainly Kingsley did want to lay vigorous hold of the chaos: however confused and distorted the current mix of spiritual and material, it was for him the very essence and relish of life that the two were one. Kingsley's was an emphatically Protestant vision of an incarnate animal world, of urgent Christian socialist action in the world as it was; a world of consummated marriage not celibacy, of downright realism not allegory.

By 1859 what worried David Masson about the future of the novel was a loss of the experimentation of its early years, and, increasingly in its place, a narrow concentration upon the relevance of the social present. The novel was becoming, he believed, the novel of 'Purpose', of social reality, of transient but recurrently absorbing crises. This social-realist emphasis, said Masson, was due above all to the down-to-earth practical Christianity of Charles Kingsley—the loud 'muscular Christianity' dismissed by his critics as the philistine religion of 'John Bull', the great national stereotype. What Kingsley had done, claimed Masson, was what 'in a simpler walk of fiction' Thomas Hughes had also done in his public-school novel for boys, *Tom Brown's Schooldays* (1857), a commemoration of Dr Arnold's Rugby. Hughes claimed that Tom Brown was even down to his very name a type of the English middle classes, and 'here in the study of the education of an English schoolboy,' said Masson, 'there is the same argument as in Mr. Kingsley's works for the supreme competency of Christian principle in the formation of character' (*British Novelists and their Styles*, lecture 4). Such books 'of the right Saxon sort', in Masson's phrase, sought to provide the model of character that Froude had claimed to be lacking in the post-aristocratic, post-heroic modern age. It was a middle-class model offering a set of secondary background virtues—individual self-reliance, general trustworthiness, energy in the service of duty, and moral courage— which, as one modern commentator has put it, 'would provide the best chance of first-order virtues being upheld in unknown circumstances'.[2] To Masson, this was no more and no less than the middle-class, common-sense alternative to the problems set by Bulwer's metaphysical and experimental fictions.

Yet the work of Kingsley's that Masson singled out for praise was the historical novel *Hypatia* (1853), for being closer to his ideal of extending the modern novel to 'epic breadth of interest'. For, as Disraeli's Sybil had found, the historical novel arose from within the social novel:

She had seen enough to suspect that the world was a more complicated system than she had preconceived. There was not that strong and rude simplicity in its organization which she had supposed. The characters were more various, the motives more mixed, the classes more blended, the elements of each more subtle and diversified, than she had imagined. . . . The consequences had outlived the causes, as customs survive opinions. (*Sybil*, bk. 5, ch. 2)

It is the existence of the history novel that makes the nineteenth-century social novel take on a deeper dimension and a deeper language, beneath the level of current opinion. For its relevance lay not just in the way that the past informs the situation of the present, and

---

[2] Stefan Collini, *Public Moralists: Political Thought and Intellectual Life in Britain 1850–1930* (Clarendon Press, 1991), 114.

only partly in the Victorian need to trace origins and traditions in the midst of present uncertainties. Most valuable of all was the capacity of the historical novel to offer a model of social complexity unfolding over the course of long periods of time that eschewed the tempting simplicity of immediate reactions.

Kingsley believed Disraeli's social vision to be well meaning yet aristocratic and nostalgic and therefore fundamentally misplaced. But just as Disraeli's next novel after Sybil, *Tancred* (1847), went east to the Holy Land beyond the world of England and Europe, so *Hypatia* (1853) takes Kingsley's reader out of contemporary England into fifth-century Alexandria. Cardinal Wiseman's *Fabiola* (1854) and J. H. Newman's *Callista* (1855), the Catholic novels written in direct reply to *Hypatia*, portrayed the age of the Fathers as possessing the original clarity of conversion and martyrdom. But for Kingsley the early ages of the Church in the East, amidst the decadence of the late Roman Empire, were characterized by an inchoate confusion.

Thus the novel works through a series of overlapping personal journeys: Philammon a young monk leaves the monastery for the city and then leaves Christianity for philosophy; Raphael Aben-Ezra, a clever and cultivated Jew, finds himself on exactly the opposite route, the two being linked by their studying under the beautiful Hypatia, an aristocratic, Neoplatonic pagan priestess. In turn, Hypatia's brand of sexual power is contrasted with both the franker attractions of the courtesan Pelagia and the reluctant growing love of Raphael for a Christian woman, Victoria. It is not only that the big questions are embodied in these people—questions of religion, philosophy, Christianity, paganism, morality, intellectualism, sexuality, love— but the contrasting interplays between the characters become like a form of thought seeking the precise shade of meaning for each of these abstractions within the right balance and proportions of a life. The language of the book is thus at its most characteristic when Philammon contemplates the terrible possibility that Pelagia may be damned, however much she subsequently is penitent: yet even so moral reformation is to be sought, for 'Better virtue with hell, than sin with heaven' (*Hypatia*, ch. 24). That is the book's careful rearrangement of 'a' and 'b', 'x' and 'y'.

Dialogue is the most characteristic means for this working-out, as between two of Philammon's aged seniors in the monastery where Arsenius, who has retired from the world to become a monk, is now desperately thinking of retiring from the monastery to become a hermit. An old man, he remains haunted by guilt for a past life which still tempts him back again 'like a moth to the candle which has already scorched him'. To this Pambo replies,

Many a monk, friend, changes his place, but not the anguish of his soul. I have known those who, driven to feed on their own thoughts in solitude, have desperately cast themselves from cliffs, or ripped up their own bodies, in the longing to escape from thoughts, from which one companion, one kindly voice, might have delivered them. . . . Better to be anxious for others than only for thyself. Better to have something to love— even something to weep over—than to become in some lonely cavern thine own world,—perhaps, as more than one whom I have known, thine own God.

'Do you know what you are saying?' asks Arsenius, 'Do you know whither your argument leads?' 'I am a plain man,' is the reply, 'and know nothing about arguments. If a thing be true, let it lead where it will, for it leads where God wills' (ch. 11).

Do you know whither your argument leads? The easiest answer for a commentator is that it leads straight to a self-confirmation of Kingsley's this-worldly Protestantism, established—at the earliest— a full eleven centuries later. But the opposite is nearer the truth: in *Hypatia* Kingsley creates a form complex enough, with sufficient obstacles, to make him have to rediscover his beliefs as if for the first time again, in a history imaginatively analogous to their original setting. Both voices in this small section are working hard, in fear, to convince each other, and what have since become commonplaces here seem urgent and fundamental truths again. Indeed, in a way the historical novel here de-historicizes thoughts and beliefs: long before they were clothed in categorizations, says the language of Art, these beliefs originally stood for something at the level of discovered thoughts. 'If a thing be true, let it lead where it will': the Victorian historical novel is at its best when it imagines, in the very midst of a historical conflict, the nascent experience of anomaly, the sensing of germs of preconceptual thought in search of a future form through which fully to *be* thought. And if these two old men are also like two elements in Philammon's own mind on the eve of his own departure, it is only because across the book as a whole all the characters are also thoughts weighed against each other within the one great mind of the novel itself. For all Kingsley's rejection of allegory, *Hypatia*, like so much Victorian fiction, has beneath its doubts and conflicts an ancient layer of allegorical meaning informing the personal and particular. What makes it kin to allegory is that the spaces between the people are as important as the people themselves, for across those spaces, by both dialogue and more tacit formal contrasts, is negotiated the whole area between love and lust, religious and pagan thinking. In *Science and the Modern World* (1926), A. N. Whitehead argued that in earlier ages 'there were opposing camps, bitterly at variance on questions which they deemed fundamental' whereas in the more muddled perplexity of the nineteenth century 'each individual was divided against himself' (ch. 5). A historical novel such as *Hypatia* represents both states—the diametric clashes without and the ambivalences within.

Many nineteenth-century historical fictions are entertainments simply offering immersion in a different world: in particular, there are the architectural plots of the Newgate novelist Harrison Ainsworth (*The Tower of London*, 1840; *Old St Paul's*, 1841; and *Windsor Castle*, 1843); the costume romances of G. P. R. James whose reputation Thackeray, once again, destroyed by burlesque; and Charles Reade's epic best-seller *The Cloister and the Hearth* (1861), telling the life of a man who finally turns out to be the father of Erasmus. More seriously, R. D. Blackmore's *Lorna Doone*, set in the late seventeenth century, still retained in a popular regional novel of 1869 elements characteristic of the historical novel after Walter Scott: the stalwart hero-narrator as representative yeoman-farmer of England; the class differences between lover and beloved; the struggle to establish national law and order, with the Doones as Catholic aristocrats-turned-outlaws as a result of the confiscation of their lands; the use of an earlier age of stark civil unrest to depict the necessity of taking sides, amidst the clash between political and personal allegiances. In Blackmore, the mix is, to use Bulwer's terms, finally more history for the sake of romance than vice versa. But what the Victorian history novel offers at its most powerful is the best paradigm for the struggle of the novel itself to meld the different categories which the Victorian age held in solution. For, like the novel in its intermixture of sub-genres and modes, history in these visions combines and recombines the elements of a situation into a form larger, more far-reaching, and more complex than the divided intentions of its several human parts. Thus, finally, Charles Lever's *Tom Burke of Ours* (1844) is the story of a young Irish adventurer who, in revolt against Tory oppression at home, fights for the French revolutionary forces of Napoleon, only to find himself returning to Ireland in disillusionment, to live the private life of a landowner which is neither Tory nor revolutionary. It is a novel that thus ends where most Victorian novels begin, offering the history of the end of the history novel itself.

Ironically, it was only in the later decades of the century when historians ceased to be literary men like Macaulay and Froude and become professional researchers instead, that they actually seem to get closer to the form and vision of the historical novel. In the debatable land, it is an emancipated version of the literary imagination which these historians came to use, to transform the terms of natural science—compounds and elements, grafting and growing, the balancing, shifting, blending, and modifying of forces in time—into the terms of human history. Thus William Stubbs in his great *Constitutional History of England in its Origin and Development* (3 vols., 1873–8) offers a nineteenth-century Darwinist version of Edmund Burke's vision of the inseparable relation of change and continuity. In Stubbs, as in the finest Victorian historical novels, history gets made as it goes along—through adaptations, improvizations, and sudden openings for both nascent and lapsed forces, in a process which intermixes freedom and necessity.

II. Post-Aristocratic: Thackeray versus Dickens

At the beginning of what are supposed to be his memoirs, *The History of Henry Esmond, A Colonel in the Service of Her Majesty Queen Anne, Written By Himself*, Henry Esmond complains that the Muse of History too often busies herself only with the public affairs of kings, like a humble mistress-in-waiting: 'Why shall History go on kneeling to the end of time?' There are other histories besides the official ones with wigs on: 'I would have History familiar rather than heroic: and think that Mr Hogarth and Mr Fielding will give our children a much better idea of the manners of the present age in England, than the Court Gazette and the newspapers which we get thence.' Behind this fictional eighteenth-century autobiographer, in 1852, there is of course his creator William Makepeace Thackeray, would-be successor to the satiric artist William Hogarth and the satiric novelist Henry Fielding.

That is not Thackeray's only disguise. For all his stance as anti-heroic realist and giant-killer, Thackeray is himself an aristocratic writer—in satiric defence of Carlyle's real aristocracy of spirit, if not of birth. In his writing, though not in his life, Thackeray is somewhat like the eponymous protagonist of *The Adventures of Philip* (1862): 'Mr. Phil, theoretically a Radical, and almost a Republican (in opposition, perhaps, to his father, who, of course, held the highly respectable line of politics)—Mr. Sansculotte Phil was personally one of the most aristocratic and overbearing of young gentlemen' (ch. 10). Only, Thackeray is too intelligent, too fly, to be caught in vulnerable reaction against parents or times.

In an essay of 1864 reprinted in his *Literary Studies* (1879) Walter Bagehot said of Thackeray that the footman's view of life was never out of his head, haunting and lowering his thoughts. For Thackeray had begun his satiric career with the *Yellowplush Papers* (1837–8), aristocratic life seen through the eyes, and described through the spelling, of a common footman. 'The Diary of C. Jeames De La Pluche, Esq.' (1845–6) is likewise a satirical account by a cockney footman of the rise of a fraudulent railway entrepreneur, based upon George Hudson, to whose new money the old titled nation bows down with one accord. Yet constantly the comic savagery in these early works turns both ways, high and low, against the snobs who look up to others *and* the snobs who look down upon them, with the footman as both source and object of the ridicule. To the wry Bagehot of *The English Constitution* (1867), if you did not want a fully egalitarian society and could not have the ancient caste system, then what was needed to keep England going was just such a culture of deference. But within what William Roscoe called 'the debateable land between the aristocracy and the middle classes', Thackeray will have nothing to do with what was to become bourgeois compromise in Bagehot or realistic accommodation in Trollope.[3] *The Book of Snobs* (1848) is at once, quite consciously, anti-snobbish *and* itself snobbish in mockery of the pretensions of the aspiring middle classes.

It is an intelligence of lethal mobility. An anxious widowed mother seeks reassurance from her brother-in-law as to her son's sexual behaviour:

'I'll go and thank God that my boy is innocent. He is innocent. Isn't he, sir?'

'Yes, my dearest creature, yes,' said the old fellow, kissing her affectionately, and quite overcome by her tenderness.

Thackeray then characteristically adds this distancing toughness:

He looked after her as she retreated, with a fondness which was rendered more piquant, as it were, by the mixture of a certain scorn which accompanied it. 'Innocent!' he said . . .

And yet how did he manage to see through his nephew when the mother failed to? As the old fellow to the mother, so Thackeray to the old fellow: 'Very likely', adds Thackeray drily, the old gentleman 'judged of Arthur by what he himself would have done' (*Pendennis* (1850), ch. 54).

Nothing and no one escapes the unremitting idea of disillusionment in Thackeray's work, of life always falsifying itself and turning into role-play and theatre. 'What is it? Why does it come to drive all the good thoughts away?', cries Laura to her young husband-to-be, 'What is that wicked *but*? And why are you always calling it up?' Arthur Pendennis, journalist and novelist, replies:

'*But* will come in spite of us. *But* is reflection. *But* is the sceptic's familiar, with whom he has made a compact; and if he forgets it, and indulges in happy day-dreams, or building of air-castles, or listens to sweet music, let us say, or the bells ringing to church, *But* taps at the door, and says, "Master, I am here. You are my master; but I am yours. Go where you will you can't travel without me. I will whisper to you when you are on your knees at church. I will be at your marriage pillow. I will sit down at your table with your children. I will be behind your death-bed curtain." That is what *But* is,' Pen said. (ch. 71)

---

[3] See the excellent G.Tillotson and D. Hawes (eds.), *Thackeray: The Critical Heritage* (Routledge, 1968), 272.

And, he tells her, *But* says to him even now that if she 'had reason as well as love' and 'knew you as you are', 'she would love you no more'.

With Thackeray it is not so much reason as well as love, as reason in place of it. In their very goodness, for example, there is a sort of slave morality in women, as wives and as mothers: 'It is those who injure women who get the most kindness from them' (*Vanity Fair*, ch. 50). And slave morality must end in a twisted revenge: Pendennis facing the misery his mother suffers on his behalf, 'scarcely ventured to return the kiss which the suffering lady gave him'; ' "She persecutes me," he thought to himself, "and comes to me with the air of a martyr" ' (*Pendennis*, ch. 57).

Look at what happens in even the well-intentioned cover-up helplessly recorded in *Henry Esmond*:

In houses where, in place of that sacred, inmost flame of love, there is discord at the centre, the whole household becomes hypocritical, and each lies to his neighbour. The husband (it may be the wife) lies when the visitor comes in, and wears a grin of reconciliation before him. The wife . . . swallows her tears, and lies to her lord and master; lies in bidding little Jacky respect dear papa; lies in assuring grandpapa that she is perfectly happy. (bk. 1, ch. 11)

Lies, lies, lies. Yet it was Thackeray who had movingly and accurately praised Dickens's *Christmas Carol*—that great therapeutic assault upon disbelief in good feelings—as 'a national benefit, and to every man or woman who reads it a personal kindness' ('A Box of Novels', *Fraser's Magazine*, February 1844). But where Scrooge had at his side the Spirits of Christmas Past, Present, and Future, Pendennis has 'the sceptic's familiar' or what is called in chapter 5 of *The Newcomes* (1855) a 'satirical monitor'.

In his study of Thackeray in John Morley's 'English Men of Letters' series (1879), Trollope pointed out that from his very first novel *Barry Lyndon* (1844) Thackeray's procedure was always essentially anti-Dickensian: 'As the central character with Dickens had always been made beautiful with unnatural virtue,—for who was ever so unselfish as *Pickwick*, so manly and modest as *Nicholas*, or so good a boy as *Oliver*?—so should his centre of interest be in every respect abnormally bad' (*Thackeray*, ch. 1). *Barry Lyndon* itself is also written against Charles Lever's Irish novels of military adventure—in particular the best-selling and genuinely interesting *Confessions of Harry Lorrequer* (1839), concerning a lovable outcast chancer who tries to live his life in the accidents of the moment, like the black-sheep emigrant to the colonies in Henry Kingsley's *The Recollection of Geoffrey Hamlyn* (1859). In Thackeray's darker version, told by his own Irish rogue-protagonist, Lyndon's immorality is left silently registered throughout his loud self-justifying moralizing as it gradually and continually disauthenticates itself. The merchant-trader, the speculator on the Stock Exchange cry out against men who engage in gambling, he says, and yet 'though it *seems* all pleasure' gamblers work hard at their business all night—'and I should like to know how much more honourable *their* modes of livelihood are than ours'. 'It is', he concludes, 'a conspiracy of the middle classes against gentlemen' (*Barry Lyndon*, ch. 9). Behind that voice lies Thackeray's true eighteenth-century ancestor, not so much the genial Henry Fielding but the writer Thackeray also most feared: Jonathan Swift, in his constant, bitter satiric ventriloquism.

In Thackeray there is always an initial sense of untamed individual vivacity in the ability to satirize—in Becky Sharp's mimicry or Clive Newcome's cartoons—for to Thackeray no one is quite a hypocrite in his laughter. And there is a real verve in those improvisations of knowing wit that take place in the interstices of moral life—thus Becky Sharp in the face of the good little Amelia's complaints of her conduct with Amelia's husband, George Osborne:

'Why did you come between my love and me? . . . For shame, Rebecca; bad and wicked woman—false friend and false wife.'

'Amelia, I protest before God, I have done my husband no wrong,' Rebecca said, turning from her.

'Have you done me no wrong, Rebecca? You did not succeed, but you tried. Ask your heart if you did not.'

She knows nothing, Rebecca thought. (*Vanity Fair*, ch. 31)

Yet even here the cold brilliance of that secret wit comes from meaning being taken away rather than added. Indeed, in one sense, for all the increased seriousness, Thackeray never left off the work of parody, for Thackeray's is like a second text written in disenchanted revision of the first underneath it. The best ink in Vanity Fair, says

Thackeray, would be ink that disappeared within a couple of days: what is awful is the faded yellow of youthful emotions that were supposed to last for ever. The shift from embarrassingly innocent and romantic youth to wry and unillusioned middle age is like life's satire in Thackeray, and it is something equivalent to that shift—into something terribly *simpler* to the novelist—that the reader always must undergo in reading him.

It gets no more comfortable when Thackeray is more implicated in his own protagonist than he is with Barry Lyndon. One of the strongest things in Thackeray is his account of young Arthur Pendennis's sexual attraction towards Fanny Bolton, the wholly decent daughter of his housekeeper. That Pen does *not* finally seduce her, that he falls desperately ill instead, feels more like an escape than an achievement of genuine innocence, except in the purely nominal sense:

An immense source and comfort it was to Pendennis (though there was something selfish in that feeling, as in most others of our young man), that he had been enabled to resist temptation at the time when the danger was greatest, and had no particular cause of self-reproach as he remembered his conduct towards the young girl. As from a precipice down which he might have fallen, so from the fever from which he had recovered, he reviewed the Fanny Bolton snare, now that he had escaped out of it, but I'm not sure that he was not ashamed of the very satisfaction which he experienced. (ch. 53)

'What could have made him so hot and eager about her but a few weeks back?' If Pen's now having 'no particular cause for self-reproach' here feels more like luck than morality, still people are very glad of such luck. It is what George Osborne wanted at the end of chapter 29 of *Vanity Fair* when, about to leave his young wife and go to war, he regrets that his sexual intrigue with Becky only six months after his wedding does not leave him free to bid his wife farewell with a clear conscience. It is painful to measure the serialization of *Pendennis* (November 1848–December 1850) against Dickens's alternative version, *David Copperfield* (May 1849–November 1850), the two fictional autobiographies of young writers published at much the same time and often reviewed together. As David Masson said, so disarmingly, in the first shock of the contrast, 'Why is Mr. Dickens, on the whole, genial, kindly, and romantic, and Mr. Thackeray, on the whole, caustic, shrewd, and satirical in his fictions?' ('*Pendennis* and *Copperfield*: Thackeray and Dickens', *North British Review*, May 1851).

For where Thackeray has always that nagging 'But', the best Dickensian moments show people struggling to convey their heart's meaning despite the 'Buts', though not in avoidance of them. The common young fisherman Ham asks David Copperfield to try to convey to little Em'ly his continuing feelings for her despite her sexual betrayal of him—he is not crying in the pauses expressed by dashes, says Dickens, but 'collecting himself':

I loved her—and I love the mem'ry of her—too deep—to be able to lead her to believe of my own self as I'm a happy man. I could only be happy—by forgetting of her—and I'm afeerd I couldn't hardly bear as she should be told I done that. But if you, being so full of learning, Mas'r Davy, could think of anything to say as might bring her to believe I wasn't greatly hurt: still loving of her, and mourning for her: anything as might bring her to believe as I was not tired of life, and yet was hoping fur to see her without blame, wheer the wicked cease from troubling and the weary are at rest—anything as would ease her sorrowful mind, and yet not make her think as I could ever marry, or as 'twas possible that anyone could ever be to me what she was—I should ask of you to say that . . . (ch. 51)

As he seeks for 'anything', 'anything' that might serve against the painful truth expressed in the equally repeated 'and yet', Ham's love is in both—in the selfless desire to 'bring her to believe' that he is not greatly hurt, alongside the inability to let her be told that he could ever 'be happy by forgetting of her' for someone else. For Dickens finally does not want truth without feeling or feelings without truth. It is not that Ham's difficulty here is due to the common man being less learned than David, any more than Dickens is either less intelligent or more emotionally self-indulgent than Thackeray. Rather, Ham's is the language of what Carlyle, throughout *On Heroes, Hero-Worship, and the Heroic in History* (1841), called sincerity rather than mere honesty. For honesty is conscious and conscientious in seeking to tell the truth it sees; but sincerity of the heart goes further, releasing without fear a depth of unconscious meaning in people that deepens and enriches their utterances rather than merely betrays or contradicts them. Thackeray is honest but—or precisely because—he could not wholly believe in sincerity. What can be said about Thackeray and his world may be right or wrong but is exhaustible and limited, because in Thackeray human meaning is limited; but the whole world opens up in a sincere saying, and what can be said about Dickens is sudden and resonant and can never be complete.

It was as though at times Thackeray flirted with being Dickens: in *Vanity Fair*, for example, in the depiction of the constant Dobbin or in the love of Rawdon for his son. And even then, 'But taps at the door'. Dobbin's fidelity is also a sort of weak delusive folly. And the one good feeling in Rawdon's life serves only to condemn Becky in the reader's eyes as an uncaring mother, whilst in Rawdon's own eyes 'he felt somehow ashamed of this paternal softness, and hid it from his wife—only indulging in it when alone with the boy' (ch. 37). Or then again, Colonel Newcome, the straightforward embodiment of old military and gentlemanly England, deteriorates, morally, precisely by fighting on their own ground the selfish money values to which he is opposed.

For Masson there was a split within the very formation of the early Victorian novel, that in writing his mid-century *British Novelists and their Styles*, he saw finally consolidating itself in terms of Thackeray's realism versus Dickens's romanticism. The danger for Thackeray lay in realism degenerating into cynicism, for Dickens of romance lapsing into sentimentality, in sheer reaction against each other. What Masson meant by the realist novel, in the hands of what he takes to be the leader of the school, he illustrates at its most dangerous and extreme by means of the following example of relativism:

'The truth, friend!' Arthur said imperturbably; 'where is the truth? Show it me. That is the question between us. I see it on both sides. I see it in the Conservative side of the House, and amongst the Radicals, and even on the ministerial benches.' (*Pendennis*, ch. 61)

'I take things as I find them.' I look at two brothers, he says, John Henry and Francis Newman, arriving at virtually opposite religious positions with equal intensity, and the novelist that Pendennis becomes believes in the sincerity of both, finds each destroying the belief of the other, and so writes about characters, not principles, in second-order detachment rather than conflict: 'If the truth is with all these, why should I take side with any one of them?' 'The sum comes to the same figures, worked either way.' Reviewing *Philip* in *The Spectator* (9 August 1862), Walter Bagehot noted what he called Thackeray's refusal to encumber himself with big ideas: it was as though he did not believe that they were big and could only study the personalities of those who did think so.

Even the historical novel, in Thackeray's hands, is not as it was in Bulwer's or Kingsley's, a form for rethinking deep original conflicts after the model of Walter Scott. *Henry Esmond* is set in the late seventeenth, early eighteenth century, because Thackeray is interested in the point at which the idealizing of feudal, religious, family, and personal responsibilities is replaced by a more individualist and rationalist criterion that destroys the old idols. If Henry Esmond turns from Catholic to Anglican, if he tries to remain a Tory rather than a Whig, it becomes increasingly clear that there is no longer any felt *reason* for doing so, save for his personal attachment to a particular family house and its mistress: 'A strange series of compromises is that English history; compromise of principle, compromise of party, compromise of worship!' (bk. 3, ch. 5).

Thus, if Cromwell and his son, after him, had been crowned and anointed, then it seems to Esmond that they would have assumed the divine right of English kingship as much as any Plantagenet or Tudor or Stuart: 'I am an English man and take my country as I find her' (bk. 3, ch. 1). After all, the Whig lovers of English freedom were compelled to send to Holland and later to Hanover for a king around whom they could rally. And High Church Tories were ready to die for a Papist family, the relics of the deposed Stuarts, that had sold England to France. 'In England you can but belong to one party or t'other, and you take the house you live in with all its encumbrances, its retainers, its antique discomforts, and ruins even; you patch up, but you never build up anew' (bk. 3, ch. 5). And so it is even with love: 'If we had not met Joan, we would have met Kate, and adored her. We know our mistresses are no better than many other women, no prettier, nor no wiser, nor no wittier. 'Tis not for those reasons we love a woman, or for any special quality or charm I know of' (bk. 2, ch. 15).

Yet even through his own and his country's changes, Esmond seeks to maintain an ideal of absolute loyalty, a role for chivalry, service, and sacrifice—even if finally for no reason save that the family took him in when he was an outcast boy, and that he has always loved Rachel the mistress of the house, and that he grows to love the vain Beatrix her daughter. The feeling of Esmond in those differing kinds of love, his feeling for both husband and wife in their unhappy marriage, for both mother and daughter in their increasingly strained relations—these are not dirty modern secrets but are subtly and honourably and even beautifully contained within the idea and language of an albeit melancholic service. It is Henry Esmond, rather than Colonel Newcome, who vulnerably and personally maintains an old-world nobility, not on a historic battlefield but in the last formal refuge of private and domestic virtue. Amidst the destruction of the feudal family, Esmond ends by marrying the widowed mother in the autumn of their lives, turning from son and servant to husband and lover.

It was a risk that Thackeray privately regretted having taken, though the French man of letters Hippolyte Taine thought *The History of Henry Esmond* the only novel Thackeray ever wrote: the others were satires. In the anxiety and the earnestness of mid-Victorian middle-class England, in its need for clear sympathies and definite beliefs, the very elusiveness of satire made readers and critics uneasy. Masson himself tried to say, in his obituary article, that Thackeray was like his own portrayal of Warrington in *Pendennis*: a clever man half-ruined by a bad early marriage, whose very hatred of cant prompted him to 'kick the words art, the ideal, transcendentalism &c. to death', while his more vulnerable inner beliefs came out only in bursts and flashes. Yet satire offered Thackeray the protection of a formal genre, supported by the traditions of the preceding century. 'You call me heartless and cynic, for saying men are false and wicked' (*Philip*, ch. 26). Thackeray retains an absolute, implicit standard together with no expectation that people will live up to it.

Thackeray leaves no secure position for his reader. And that is what he celebrates above all in the brilliant denouement of *Vanity Fair*, where Becky finally destroys the good, slow, little Amelia's long-held sanctification of her dead husband, George, freeing her to marry the long-suffering loyal Dobbin. 'I tried—I tried my best, indeed I did, Rebecca,' says Amelia, 'but I couldn't forget –' and Thackeray slyly has her finish her sentence 'by looking up at the portrait', *the* portrait which has made a frozen idol of a man she was just beginning to find disloyal when he died. Life as a reality is less pious and more mobile:

'He never cared for you. He used to sneer about you to me, time after time; and made love to me the week after he married you.'

'It's false! It's false! Rebecca,' cried out Amelia, starting up.

'Look there, you fool!' Becky said, still with provoking good humour, and taking a little paper out of her belt, she opened it and flung it into Emmy's lap. 'You know his handwriting. He wrote that to me—wanted me to run away with him—gave it me under your nose, the day before he was shot—and served him right!' Becky repeated. . . .

Emmy's head sank down, and for almost the last time in which she shall be called upon to weep in this history, she commenced that work. . . . Was she most grieved, because the idol of her life was tumbled down and shivered at her feet; or indignant that her love had been so despised; or glad because the barrier was removed which modesty had placed between her and a new, a real affection? 'There is nothing to forbid me now,' she thought. 'I may love him with all my heart now. Oh, I will, I will, if he will but let me, and forgive me.' I believe it was this feeling rushed over all the others which agitated that gentle little bosom.

Indeed, she did not cry so much as Becky expected—the other soothed and kissed her—a rare mark of sympathy with Mrs. Becky. She treated Emmy like a child, and patted her head. 'And now let us get pen and ink, and write to him to come this minute,' she said.

'I—I wrote to him this morning,' Emmy said, blushing exceedingly.

Becky screamed with laughter (ch. 67)

It is not just the names that change and move about so; there are the multiple ironies and the shifting versatility of tones. For if Becky has the dexterous pleasure of using her essential contempt for Amelia, in the cause of doing Amelia good for once, Thackeray himself enjoys being even quicker, even more devious and untraceable than Becky herself. As Becky spontaneously laughs—against herself as well as at Amelia—the whole human scene becomes celebratory, against the false seriousness of overdetermined conscience. And yet even here, seeing through everything from above it all, Thackeray remains the unillusioned aristocrat, who refuses permanent uncritical identification with any one human centre of feeling.

Vanity Fair famously ends with his shutting up the box and putting away the puppets. But the conclusion of *Philip* suggests a darker ending for Thackeray, after all, on stage: 'When the boxes have got their nightgowns on, and you are all gone, and I have turned off the gas, and am in the empty theatre alone in the darkness, I promise you I shall not be merry. Never mind! We can make jokes though we are ever so sad. We can jump over head and heels . . .'.

If Masson believed Dickens represented novel as romance rather than novel as realism, to Dickens these distinctions only emerged in the course of novels which combined the two within what in the preface to *Bleak House* (1853) is called 'the romantic side of familiar things'. In Dickens the various modes and genres keep coming and going almost vertiginously within a single work.[4] Thus in *Nicholas Nickleby* (1839)—that great loose apprentice novel during the course of which Dickens first really learnt how to become a novelist—there is Nicholas himself planning how to rescue the beautiful Madeline from being forced into marriage to the old moneylender Arthur Gride. 'To restless and ardent minds', a new morning usually seems the time when hope is strongest in the face of difficulties: 'But when we come, fresh, upon such things in the morning, with that dark and silent gap between us and yesterday; with every link in the brittle chain of hope to rivet afresh; our hot enthusiasm subdued, and cool calm reason substituted in its stead; doubt and misgiving revive' (ch. 53). Now, 'when he thought how things went on, from day to day' in the world outside—'how youth and beauty died', 'how much injustice, misery, and wrong there was, and yet how the world rolled on, year after year'—the romance inside Nicholas is overwhelmed by thoughts as from without and gives way. Suddenly there was little reason why the one case in which he was so greatly concerned 'should not form an atom in the huge aggregate of distress and sorrow'. And yet 'by dint of reflecting on what he had to do, and reviving the train of thought which night had interrupted, Nicholas gradually summoned up his utmost energy'.

Forster in his *Life of Dickens* (3 vols., 1872–4) said that speedy, intuitive, anxiously impatient Dickens could never endure 'the interval between the accomplishment of anything and its "first motion"' (vol. 1, bk. 2, ch. 1). It is in those dark and silent gaps, however, that

---

[4] For Dickens and the city, see above, Ch. 1; on his literary career, Ch. 5.

Fig. 9. 'It was labour that must in time have broken down the strongest man' (John Forster, *The Life of Charles Dickens*): detail from Daniel Maclise's painting *Dickens as a young man* (1839, aged 27) and R. H. Mason's photograph *Charles Dickens* (1864–5, aged 52–3).

Dickens like Nicholas faces the challenges to his sense of rhythmic continuity, and so it is for Dickens formally in the act of writing. For Dickens began in *Sketches by Boz* (1833–6) and *The Pickwick Papers* (1836–7) as a serial producer of loose collections of scenes and characters, unstable, expansive, and picaresque, until an increasingly continuous narrative began to shade into genuine novel-writing even as it went along. Finding or recovering sudden trains of thought, changing from chapter to chapter or character to character as from night to day and back again, using hiatuses and interruptions as opportunities for contrasting and testing different generic modes of thinking—this rhythmic mixture of planning and improvisation became the maze-like Dickensian way of writing.

The *Pickwick Papers* began to take off with the fourth number (ch. 10) when low Sam Weller entered the scene as a centre of cockney experience that was increasingly both to contrast with and to support Pickwick's lofty innocence. Morally and aesthetically the whole of the first movement in *Nicholas Nickleby*, describing the ill-treatment of children at Dotheboys Hall, is crying out for the sudden focusing of Nicholas's final 'Stop', 'Must not go on', 'No!' in chapter 13. What clinches in Dickens the realization of the novel's form in the midst of its own initially apparent looseness, as well as what distinguishes him from Thackeray, is the finding of a human emotional centre, like a suddenly activated magnet for the novel's scattered iron filings.

It is because of this orientating search for its own emotional centres that even the mature Dickens novel still has to have so many new or returning characters, offering differing shades of contrast. The entry of a Miss Wade or a Henry Gowan within *Little Dorrit* is like a shadow altering the moral orientation of this world in which people meet 'to act and react on one another' (bk. 1, ch. 2). Physician does not enter the novel until late in book 2 amongst other satirical representatives of the high society crowding around the wealth of Merdle such as Bar and Bishop. But 'where he was, something real was' (ch. 25). Characters are not brought in simply for their own sake but for their effect on the atmospheric space around them and on those characters hitherto occupying it. In his working notes for *Hard Times* (1854), Dickens can be seen in the very process of introducing the cynical young James Harthouse for the sake of his relation to Utilitarian Mr Gradgrind via Gradgrind's daughter: 'To shew Louisa, how alike in their creeds, her father and Harthouse are?— How the two heartless things come to the same in the end? Yes. But almost imperceptibly.'[5] The sense of juxtaposition began early for Dickens. In *The Old Curiosity Shop* (1841) the narrator pictures a beautiful young girl he has just seen, who lives in the midst of a grotesque junk shop:

I am not sure I should have been so thoroughly possessed by this one subject, but for the heaps of fantastic things I had seen huddled together in the curiosity-dealer's warehouse. These, crowding on my mind, in connection with the child, and gathering round her, as it were, brought her condition palpably before me. I had her image, without any effort of imagination, surrounded and beset by everything that was foreign to her nature (ch. 1)

In his revision of the text for publication in volume form, Dickens went beyond his characteristic 'gathering round her, as it were', adding that Little Nell 'seemed to exist in a kind of allegory'. In this he was influenced by a review in *The Athenaeum* (7 December 1840) in which Tom Hood described *The Old Curiosity Shop* as 'like an Allegory of the peace and innocence of Childhood in the midst of Violence, Superstition, and all the hateful or hurtful Passions of the world'.

'A kind of allegory': 'Yes. But almost imperceptibly.' A kind of allegory in Dickens means that in *Great Expectations* (1861) Pip's Ambition is set alongside Joe Gargery's Innocence in a kind of jarring attraction intuitive to Dickens's way of seeing. For suddenly those abstract nouns burst upon the reader's mind as though with moral capital letters; as though beneath all the psychological realism and despite all Pip's understandable defences and Joe's excuses for him, the space between the two figures becomes charged with the name of something absolute and primal at the level of family betrayal.

Again, a kind of allegory means Tom Pinch playing Holy Fool to Pecksniff's Hypocrite in *Martin Chuzzlewit* (1844). But what is more, having created significant space between the two, Dickens then goes to work his changes within it. Tom's unwavering belief in Pecksniff may be a ridiculous weakness, a back-handed compliment

[5] Most conveniently reprinted in an appendix to the World's Classics edn. of *Hard Times*, ed. Paul Schlicke (406), or see *Dickens's Working Notes for his Novels*, ed. Harry Stone (Chicago University Press, 1987).

to his own simple goodness, but when eventually he is forced to see *through* Pecksniff, the effect of disenchantment is far more painful for him than it would be for a Thackeray. As Tom's best friend puts it, speaking for the inextricably *mixed* feelings of the Dickens reader too: 'I don't know whether to be glad or sorry that you have made the discovery at last' (ch. 36). Similarly when Tom finds the formerly vivacious Mercy, Pecksniff's younger daughter, now so unhappy in her marriage and yet still so unkind in tongue, 'Tom was sorry to hear her speaking in her old manner. He had not expected that. Yet he did not feel it a contradiction that he should be sorry to see her so unlike her old self, and sorry at the same time to hear her speaking in her old manner' (ch. 37). In such saturated spaces, created between different characters and between different times, Dickens can measure emotionally how people both do and do not change and why 'at the same time' you might and might not want them to.

In all this, a Dickens novel is not like a novel by George Eliot or Mrs Gaskell or Trollope. It is harder in Dickens to stop at some point and rest content in the depiction of a character or a scene seemingly equivalent to real life, which thus exists, intrinsically justified, for its own sake. There is a world in Dickens, at once strange *and* familiar, and within that medium it is as though the reader only realizes at a point much closer to the *end* of the process what vision those strange beginnings and modifying transformations have been in search of. It is like the death of Nemo, the fallen and ruined man with no name, early in *Bleak House*: 'If this forlorn man could have been prophetically seen lying here, by the mother at whose breast he nestled a little child, with eyes upraised to her loving face, and soft hand scarcely knowing how to close upon the neck to which it crept, what an impossibility the vision would have seemed' (ch. 11). Always in Dickens you have to go forward before you can go back. Only gradually will it emerge, backwards as it were, that this Nemo was father of the illegitimate Esther through a liaison with a woman who denied the child, married, and is now called Lady Dedlock. But long before that in chapter 22 Liz, one of the battered wives of the brickmakers, unknowingly reinvokes that image of Nemo's imagined mother, in relation to the future of her own new baby:

I have been a thinking . . . of all the many things that'll come his way. My master will be against it, and he'll be beat, and see me beat, and made to fear his home, and perhaps to stray wild. If I work for him ever so much, and ever so hard there's no one to help me; and if he should be turned bad, 'spite of all I could do, and the time should come when I should sit by him in his sleep, made hard and changed, an't it likely I should think of him as he lies in my lap now, and wish he had died as Jenny's child died!

But her friend Jenny says that she wants Liz's baby to live precisely because her own recently died. One mother would sacrifice her child, the other would give anything to have it back, but for all their apparent opposition, says Jenny, 'we mean the same thing, if we knew how to say it'. So too, to fear that the baby boy must turn out badly *and*, on the other side of time, not to believe that a mere baby could have turned into the man who ended so badly: they too are the same thing if we knew how to say it. Nothing could be emotionally further from Thackeray's saying 'the sum comes to the same figures, worked either way'. Thinking in Dickens is very strangely placed, osmotic and phenomenally mobile in its movement between bodies and across boundaries. And it has to go on emotionally within whatever expressive medium or predicament characters have had to find for themselves. That is why, unlike Bulwer or Kingsley, Dickens is the great experimenter who does not need another time or place, in history or imagination, in which to get beneath conventionalism.

Even in its mere social range, Dickens's world is larger and more extensive than Thackeray's: compare *Bleak House* with *The Newcomes*. For, erupting into fame from obscure and secret origins—his father a clerk imprisoned for debt in 1824, the 12-year-old son suddenly separated from his family and sent out into a blacking workshop—Dickens was, as one critic has put it, 'The Man From Nowhere'.[6] And, as such, he went everywhere socially, in the midst of things, physically and metaphysically, breaking down categories.

For there are worlds within worlds in Dickens: little high-class social worlds which 'wrapped up in too much jeweller's cotton and fine wool . . . cannot hear the rushing of the larger worlds, and cannot see them as they circle round the sun' (*Bleak House*, ch. 2); underworlds which, as in the household of Fagin in *Oliver Twist* (1838), frighteningly replicate comforting family structures within

---

[6] Andrew Sanders, *Dickens and the Spirit of the Age* (Clarendon Press, 1999), ch. 1.

nightmare inverted orders; little psychic worlds in which a debtor prisoner like William Dorrit can still pretend amidst the wreckage to be the aristocratic 'Father' of the Marshalsea, or where Doctor Manette, traumatized by his imprisonment in the French Revolution of *A Tale of Two Cities* (1859), holds onto a frail minimal life by constantly returning to the cobbling of shoes.

And yet all these apparently separate small worlds can suddenly give way before a vision of *the one world* in Dickens. So it is with the feeble young aristocrat Lord Frederick Verisopht, who would remain a figure of satire in Thackeray. In Dickens he unexpectedly turns into a mere, sheer human being, when, half-drunk, half-scared on the eve of a duel into which he has been duped, he is all of a sudden faced by the intimation of Death:

> Fields, gardens, hedges, everything looked very beautiful; the young man scarcely seemed to have noticed them before, though he had passed the same objects a thousand times. There was a peace and serenity upon them all, strangely at variance with the bewilderment and confusion of his own half-sobered thoughts, and yet impressive and welcome. (*Nicholas Nickleby*, ch. 50)

When the coach stops, 'he was a little surprised to find himself in the act of smoking; but, on reflection, he remembered when and where he had taken the cigar'. This is what Graham Greene called Dickens's 'secret prose' that presents a mind 'speaking to itself with no one there to listen'.[7] Death in Dickens is not to do with the ritual mourning that informs the customs and writings of so much of Victorian England: his concern, as in *Dombey and Son*, is rather with mortality as the great alternative language to that of the commercial world, until death finally reveals itself as *the* moment of essentially religious conversion.

Again and again in Dickens, something hidden reveals itself, and then the novel gets itself made, its characters come to sudden life and focus, in front of our very eyes, in a way that makes class and category and statistics give way to the reality of the individual. For though Sissy Jupe was told at school that out of a million inhabitants of a town only twenty-five starved to death in the streets in the course

---

[7] 'The Young Dickens', *The Lost Childhood and Other Essays* (1951), in Stephen Wall's excellent critical anthology *Dickens* (Penguin, 1970), 359–63.

of a year, she could not help thinking, 'it must be just as hard upon those who were starved, whether the others were a million or a million million' (*Hard Times*, ch. 9). To the Man from Nowhere, the ever-shifting centre of *Bleak House* can rest for one moment in that battered woman nursing her baby at the brickmaker's house:

when she looked at it she covered her discoloured eye with her hand, as though she wished to separate any association with noise and violence and ill-treatment, from the poor little child. . . . I think the best of such people is almost hidden from us. (ch. 8)

and yet, seven hundred pages later, the centre will have found itself, of all places, in that hitherto absurd effete aristocrat, Sir Leicester Dedlock, rendered near paralysed by his wife's desertion: 'After vainly trying to make himself understood in speech, he makes signs for a pencil. . . Sir Leicester writes upon the slate, "Full forgiveness"' (ch. 56). 'Let it be known . . . I am on unaltered terms with her.' The blow finds in him the still living sufficiency of the old formal language of aristocratic chivalry to speak for love: 'His formal array of words might have at any other time, as it often had, something ludicrous in it' (ch. 58). But *this* time, as if nothing in him had changed but only become more of what it had been originally meant to be, what was ludicrous was no longer so: class stereotypes and allegorical positionings alike give way before a sudden emotionally achieved individual, standing, even so, for more than just himself.

For always in Dickens's world of far-reaching connections and unexpected mutations, the force of a significance must be picked up—'now in one shape, now in another' (*Dombey and Son* (1848), ch. 35)—and taken to heart somewhere by somebody, in the centres and refuges of goodness. The moment these centres are found is like the moment George Henry Lewes describes when meaning and understanding flash into being: 'The words float suspended, soulless, mere sounds' and then suddenly, grouped into significance, 'they start into life, as a supersaturated saline solution crystallizes on being touched by a needle-point' (*Problems of Life and Mind: The Foundations of a Creed*, 2 vols., 1874–5, vol. 2., p. 142). It is like the great little moment of change in chapter 32 of *David Copperfield* when Mr Peggotty is smitten with the loss of little Emily and Mrs Gummidge suddenly, comically, movingly, stops being the moaning widow—or rather uses her moaning widowhood actively in feeling for others. At such points, it is not that Dickens is saying that the reader is to become as simple as Mrs Gummidge, any more than the adult Pip can go back to living with Joe Gargery; but rather that she is a part of the language, a disposition that needs other elements, other characters, including the betrayer Steerforth, alongside it to make a whole; that she is an emotion that needs a thought.

Dickens, the great commoner, does his democratic work within the life of a distorted medium: the high hidden within the low, the inner displaced within the outer; the wise dismissed as the stupid; love inextricable from pain. A ruined suitor at the Court of Chancery, 'who periodically appears from Shropshire, and breaks out into efforts to address the Chancellor at the close of the day's business' was mentioned comically and peripherally in chapter 1 of *Bleak House*. It is not until chapter 15 that we see what all the comedy, the grotesquerie, from which Dickens habitually begins, is really and finally *for*—not just for its own sake, however entertaining; not just for that play of imagination which critics have called, all too predictably, 'anarchic' or 'subversive'; not even for the political satire and social concern of straighter realists; but for this:

'Go into the Court of Chancery yonder, and ask what is one of the standing jokes that brighten up their business sometimes, and they will tell you that the best joke they have, is the man from Shropshire. I,' he said, beating one hand on the other, passionately, 'am the man from Shropshire.'

Grotesques may be figures like Quilp in *The Old Curiosity Shop* who have made themselves so physical, so much an outside without anything within, that all that can be done with them finally is tear them to pieces. But just as often in Dickens they are like Mr Gridley here, or like Newman Noggs in *Nicholas Nickleby*, people who have fallen from a higher station and yet retain within that lowness something morally lofty. Dickensian comedy exists finally for the sake of that turn from laughter to tears, that shift from outsides to insides, which suddenly even in tiny places seems to free, to enlarge, and to change the whole perspective of the surrounding world. As his landlady says of Mr Gridley who was always angry with his slovenly fellow lodger but always kind to his children, 'A person is never known till a person is proved' (ch. 15). Dickens is against knowingness, for these changes, as someone in *Dombey and Son* stumblingly puts it, 'They—they're a metaphysical sort of thing. We—we haven't leisure for it. We—we haven't courage. They're not taught at schools or colleges' (ch. 33).

There is no horror so traumatizing to Dickens as the thought of a world split between outsides and inside. Yet the vision of life without love, of a social world comprised of people apparently without real inwardness and belief, of which Thackeray could write with such satiric gusto in *Vanity Fair*, is something that Dickens wrestles with increasingly from *Dombey and Son* onwards, even as the novels themselves become formally less free and increasingly enclosed by their society. From the first of the Christmas books, *A Christmas Carol* (1843) to the last, 'The Haunted Man' (1848), there is in Dickens an implicitly Christian defence of memory and emotion, of the moral necessity to feel life whatever the content or even the pain of that feeling. Yet constantly in his long, terrible denial of love for his own daughter, Dombey fights to keep inner and outer worlds apart. And always, even in fear, anger, or hatred, something almost primitive in him is reaching across the divide, despite himself, impelling thoughts and feelings back to the person to whom they still relate. 'As if she had the clue to something secret in his breast of which he was hardly informed himself' (ch. 3).

It is the denial of significance, the very absence of inner heart, found in the implacable externality of those false artists, Skimpole in *Bleak House* or Gowan in *Little Dorrit*, that is hardest to deal with, for like an antitype the negation absorbs into silence the very possibility of response, argument, or appeal. What results from the denial of the reality of values emotionally assumed hitherto to be morally universal is their disoriented banishment to frustrated and lonely places within a man such as Arthur Clennam in *Little Dorrit*. When Clennam finds himself in the company of false people such as Gowan, when Little Dorrit finds herself secretly wincing at what morally has become of her father, sister, and brother, the silent inner experience of feelings turned into painfully critical thoughts feels like a sort of implicated banishment. In the words of *Dombey and Son* it is thought which 'could neither struggle into light nor get back into total darkness' (ch. 37). The alternative to such pained sensitiveness lies in the dangerous strategy deployed by Eugene Wrayburn in *Our*

Mutual Friend (1865): a man who defends himself through the adoption of a resistant weariness, until he must either become utterly heartless or be genuinely converted by the experience of something worthwhile. Only occasionally in the later darker novels can humane feelings, weakened and driven inward, find room and scope in the corrupted world outside, by which to establish or restore sane judgement and a state of well-being. But the more that those feelings are denied space within a Dickens novel, the more they are to be felt by the reader outside it instead.

8

Alternative Fictions

'One of the principal facts of civilization is, that it more and more contracts the limits within which the different elements relating to man oscillate.'[1] In the domestic realism of Dickens or Elizabeth Gaskell—in particular in the relations between parents and children, or husband and wife—it was as though the emotional and moral boundary lines of the age were being drawn close. With David Copperfield at the bed of his dying wife, with Ruth confessing her past to her own young son, there is a quasi-physical intuition of what feels natural, of what must go half-unspoken, and where violation begins. The tender sense of a vulnerable piety, an instinctive emotional decorum, was what Thomas Hood was pointing to when he said of Dickens's earliest work that 'the drift is natural, along with the great human currents, and not against them'.[2]

But when, within the same period, a young woman can speak like this to her lover, even on her deathbed, the drift is emphatically *against* the great human currents of mid-nineteenth-century feeling:

'I wish I could hold you,' she continued bitterly, 'till we were both dead! I shouldn't care what you suffered. I care nothing for your sufferings. Why shouldn't you suffer? I do. Will you forget me—will you be happy when I am in the earth?'

Heathcliff replies 'savagely':

'I have not one word of comfort—you deserve this. You have killed

---

[1] Adolphe Quetelet, *Treatise on Man* (1835), conclusion, quoted in Robert Mighall, *A Geography of Victorian Gothic Fiction* (Oxford University Press, 1999), 170.

[2] *Memorials of Thomas Hood*, ed. by his daughter, with preface and notes by his son, 2 vols. (London, 1860), vol. 2, p. 41.

yourself. . . . You loved me—then what right had you to leave me? What right—answer me—for the poor fancy you felt for Linton? . . . I have not broken your heart—you have broken it—and in breaking it, you have broken mine.' (Emily Brontë, *Wuthering Heights* (1847), ch. 15)

Yet when, thus violently, *Wuthering Heights* opposes the language of civilization, it does so paradoxically in the name of love.

It is not the civilized moral love represented by Linton in the world of Thrushcross Grange, with all those qualities that George Eliot might admire:

That insipid, paltry creature attending her from *duty* and *humanity*! From *pity* and *charity*! He might as well plant an oak in a flower-pot, and expect it to thrive, as imagine he can restore her to vigour in the soil of his shallow cares. (ch. 14)

Heathcliff dismisses such moral qualities as weak substitutes for natural primary feeling. Across the space between the two houses, the Heights and the Grange, the oscillations are wide, violent, and well-nigh allegorical. The Romantic passion of Catherine and Heathcliff manifestly lies beyond the terms of the normalizing narrative frameworks of Lockwood and Nelly Dean in which it is set, beyond too the differing Christian interpretations of Linton and Joseph.

There is in Catherine and Heathcliff no second-order moral consideration for the other person. 'Why shouldn't you suffer? I do.' Better instead that the two should be together and feel the same—good or bad. There is only the 'right' of the relationship, to which one partner urgently lays claim when the other betrays it—without room for compunction as to the egoism involved, without the luxury of a spurious offer of impartiality. Separation is only understood as unfaithfulness; egoism is only the distorted effect of rejection and aloneness; the self as an entity is always less real to Heathcliff and Catherine than those passions *within* the self which stand for *more* than it. Only the dangerous dialogue and its ruthless dialectic is trusted. For by that process and its strange logic, the language of love comes *through* the very tone and vocabulary of anger and hate, without need of care or protection. These are two people who are so much one and the same, at a level established ever since childhood, that, in adulthood, they cannot mate and become one. Sympathy here is not George Eliot's belief in imaginatively feeling *for* another, so much as that primal magnetic force which means involuntarily feeling the very same, as by infection.

No ordinary language can express these strange configurations and their deep logic. 'I love *my* murderer—but *yours!*' says Heathcliff, 'How can I?' My murderer and your murderer are the same person here; namely, Catherine herself, who married Linton as the social world's safer, more prestigious second-best, in place of the Heathcliff of an earlier more primal existence. And if there are two Catherines, there are likewise two Heathcliffs, one who is a part of Catherine and one left alone outside her. It is as though for Heathcliff and Catherine an extraordinary spiritual relationship must be expressed frustratedly through physical terms which nonetheless cannot consummate it.

Wuthering Heights has just such a *consistently* strange ontological language pattern of its own, without outward reaching similes or metaphors. Catherine, for example, does not just dreamily seek some transcendental other world—'an existence beyond you'—but, more paradoxically, 'an existence of yours beyond you' (ch. 9). As Virginia Woolf saw in *The Common Reader* (1925), *Wuthering Heights* is a much more difficult work than Charlotte Brontë's *Jane Eyre*. There is no reassuring first-person focus in *Wuthering Heights* but instead, says Woolf, a less personalized and yet more private ambition to say something gigantic, containing within it the whole universe: 'It surges up in the half-articulate words of Catherine Earnshaw, "If all else perished, and he remained, I should still continue to be; and if all else remained, and he were annihilated, the universe would turn to a mighty stranger. I should not seem part of it" (ch. 9)' ('*Jane Eyre* and *Wuthering Heights*'). Something transcendent, and yet not recognizably Christian, seems to support the relationship of Catherine and Heathcliff; but it is something neither extrapolatable from the relationship nor consummated within it. It needs to speak the language of Heaven and Hell—but heaven and hell on earth. It is like the Romantic imprisoned longing of Browning's 'Two in the Campagna':

> Only I discern—
> Infinite passion, and the pain
> Of finite hearts that yearn.

And as Virginia Woolf concluded, Emily Brontë's great, mystic sentence about the universe 'remains unfinished'. All that Catherine and then Heathcliff can do is die with it.

The whole of the second half of the book is civilization's attempt to exorcise the residual, primitive Romantic survival figure, as though Heathcliff were some Gothic monster. By a sort of anticipation of Darwinian evolution, the genetic material is repeated and reworked in different combinations and contexts, reducing the oscillations, until a second Catherine with the eyes of the first can begin to exorcize the presence of Heathcliff, in something momentarily very like the voice of Heathcliff himself: '*Nobody* loves you—*nobody* will cry for you, when you die. I wouldn't be you!' (ch. 29).

Yet even after her death, Heathcliff does not bear the memory of the first Catherine in wounded introspective mourning, but acts it out in angry revenge upon models of the first generation expressed in the persons of their descendants. Against the second, increasingly civilized world—the modern world that more and more contracts the limits within which the different elements relating to man oscillate—Heathcliff still stands out, like a figure from myth. For all the civilized taming of the elements of Heathcliff and Catherine, the almost genetic memory of that alternative first race, now buried in the quiet earth, remains as powerful a challenge to the Victorian liberal-humanist world as Nietzsche's *Genealogy of Morals* (1887) was to be.

In an age in which the realist novel seems both to come out of and to return to the ordinary life external to it, *Wuthering Heights* on the contrary represents something separate in itself, with its own geography, biology, and virtually untranslatable mythology: a quintessentially other world envisioned utterly within its own terms. Alternative worlds are the subject of this chapter.

I. The Sensation Novel

Throughout the period there were persistent attempts to extend the reality of so-called domestic realism. Within the loose overall genre of 'the novel', it was sub-genres that served to protect the creation of possible alternative worlds.

One such was the sensation novel of the 1860s. In her reviews in *Blackwood's Magazine* Mrs Oliphant claimed that it was the Brontës—though in particular, she thought, Charlotte—who were the inspiration of the female sensationalism of Mary Elizabeth Braddon, Rhoda Broughton, and Ellen (Mrs Henry) Wood.[3] Equivalently, behind its main male proponents, Wilkie Collins and Charles Reade—as Mrs Oliphant pointed out in a review of *Great Expectations* in *Blackwood's Magazine* (May 1862)—was Charles Dickens, who supported both Collins and Reade through publication in his periodical *All the Year Round*. They appealed to a side of Dickens—with his murders and madness, his family secrets and hidden ancestries, his lurid scenes of common life transformed into fantastic grotesquerie—that was becoming increasingly less acceptable to the realists of the later nineteenth century, such as Mrs Oliphant herself.

For crime, murder, arson, bigamy, madness, escape and desertion, mistaken identity and false inheritance were the staple elements of sensationalism. In this English version of the racier French fiction of George Sand, Balzac, Flaubert, and Zola, the language of nerves—of irritation or shock, of frightened guilt or frustrated desire—was offered as the alternative to the language of the heart: '"Half-past four," she thought; "it will be dark at six, and I have a long walk home." Home! she shuddered at the simple monosyllable' (Mary Elizabeth Braddon, *The Doctor's Wife* (1864), vol. 2, ch. 9). To Wilkie Collins in *Armadale* (1866), almost anything was better than the homely boredom of the domestic sentimentalists, such as Trollope or Mrs Gaskell: 'In the miserable monotony of the lives led by a large section of the middle classes of England, anything is welcome to the women which offers them any sort of harmless refuge from the established tyranny of the principle that all human happiness begins and ends at home' (Book the Last, ch. 3). In Braddon's novel—a partial imitation of Flaubert's *Madame Bovary*—the fiction-loving wife and her dull but decent doctor-husband have nothing to say to each other; there is between them no 'electric telegraph which unites the widest regions of thought and fancy' (vol. 1, ch. 10).

The 'electrical novel' was another name for the work of the sensa-

---

[3] See above pp. 248–9.

tionalists and the sheer power of the sensations they produced. Helped by the compulsiveness of serial publication, the writing seemed to create an electrical stimulus that short-circuited more intellectual or morally contemplative responses, appealing below the level of mind by jolting the readers' nervous system with feelings of excitement and horror. Braddon herself believed that she owed as much to Dickens as to the Brontës, not least in that hallucinatory depiction of people almost literally taken *out* of themselves at moments of high stress: 'Did not Fagin think about the broken rail while he stood in the dock, and wonder who would mend it?' (*The Doctor's Wife*, vol. 3, ch. 8).

But above all it was the bodily sensations of sexual passion that took the place of domestic pieties—in what Mrs Oliphant called an 'intense appreciation of flesh and blood', an 'eagerness of physical sensation' (*Blackwood's Magazine*, September 1867). In Braddon's *Lady Audley's Secret* (1862) the protagonist feels thought physically: at some points, involuntary and half-suppressed changes come over her face, her pallor, when she fears discovery, as if only her skin is keeping her secret within her; at other times she defies enquiry with a brightness of smile or eye that seems, almost sexually, to share the fact that there is a secret underneath it all and yet outface the attempt at public proof.

What the sensation novel really offered, believed Mrs Oliphant, was a language for sexuality and adultery. In Ellen Wood's *East Lynne* (1861), a best-seller of 400,000 copies, Isabel Vane, convalescing alone abroad, is desperate to get away from the attractive attentions of an old flame, Francis Levison. She is greatly relieved when her husband, Robert Carlyle, joining her for a few days away from business, gives in to her inexplicit yet strangely desperate plea to be taken back with him:

'Nay, Isabel,' said Mr Carlyle; 'if you are so much in earnest as this, you shall certainly go back with me.'
Then she was as a child let loose from school. She laughed; she danced in her excess of content; she showered kisses on her husband, thanking him in her happy gratitude. Mr Carlyle set it down to her love for him; he arrived at the conclusion that, in reiterating that she could not bear to be away from him, she spoke the fond truth.

'Isabel,' he said, smiling tenderly upon her, 'do you remember in the first days of our marriage, you told me you did not love me, but that love would come? I think this is it.'

Her face flushed nearly to tears at the word; a bright, glowing, all too conscious flush. Mr Carlyle mistook its source, and caught her to his heart. (ch. 22)

It is the very paragraphing which betrays the secret emotional infidelity, in the terrifying *proximity* of the distance between the two of them. Wilkie Collins's *The Evil Genius* (1886) is the furthest development of such juxtapositions and substitutions: a wife reaches for her husband through the curtains that separate one room from another only to touch the other woman, the governess, instead. Thereafter, as the man divorced by his wife lives instead with his mistress, the very form of the book takes on a self-entangled doubleness in place of monogamy: 'With equal sincerity of feeling, he reproached himself for his infidelity toward the woman whom he had deserted, and devoted himself to his duty toward the woman whom he had misled' (ch. 36). If duty towards the second relationship tries to atone for the want of duty in the first, guilt says it is also in place of it. As in *Wuthering Heights*, chaos here is not so much the opposite of order as an inverted counter-form of it.

It was not only the content of the novels which shocked. It was widely rumoured that the real home lives of sensationalist novelists such as Wilkie Collins and Mary Elizabeth Braddon were sexually irregular. Rhoda Broughton's *A Beginner* (1894) is an account of a young woman who, like Broughton herself over twenty-five years earlier, brings shame on her family by writing a racy novel. The 'Newspaper novel' was thus yet another name for the sub-genre, precisely because of its relation to gossip. For the sensational novel was connected to the world of journalism and the public disclosure of domestic secrets in the sexual scandals, mental and marital breakdowns, bigamies, and domestic murders relished in the popular press. As such it was in part a popular successor in crime to the Newgate novel of the 1830s and 1840s, poised on the titillating borderline between the private and the public, the secret and the scandalous. Sales themselves were sensational, for this was the novel at its most novel: as news and shock.

Thus the sensation novel was also a new domesticated version of eighteenth-century Gothic, trading in secrecy, sexuality, and violence. Amidst the apparatus of ruined houses, melodramatic confinements and escapes, delicious fears, and superstitious horrors, late eighteenth-century writers such as Mrs Radcliffe, Horace Walpole, and Matthew Lewis had offered to an ostensibly progressive, enlightened, and civilized world the haunting frisson of the encounter with an earlier and darker Gothic age, medieval, barbaric, and irrational. It was Henry James who, reviewing the work of Braddon, famously credited the sensation novel with being the new Gothic—admitting into fiction 'those most mysterious of mysteries, the mysteries that are at our own doors' ('Miss Braddon', *The Nation* (9 November 1865), 594). If writers such as Braddon and Collins did not take their readers out of the house, at any rate they brought unhomely horror and confusion into it. The means of the realist novel were employed upon Gothic fiction, precisely to offer an alternative to domestic realism itself. Thus in *East Lynne*, the sensationalist novel re-enters the novel of domestic realism, like a secret unconsciously present within it, when the adulterous and divorced wife, Lady Isabel Vane, disguised by a disfigurement resulting from a railway accident, returns unrecognized to the home and the children she deserted, to act as humble governess in a house where her former husband has now a new wife and baby.

Indeed, the world offered within the sensational novel was like a strange undermining double to the world of realism. The sensation novel specialized in the use of duplicates, ghosts, borderline states, and transposed identities, to produce mental uncertainties. In Sheridan Le Fanu's *Uncle Silas* (1864), a young woman wakes to find that the hotel to which she was brought for safety, under cover of night, is actually in the light of day the very house from which she was fleeing. The whole story of Wilkie Collins's *The Woman in White* (1860) turns upon two young women, one sane, one escaped from a lunatic asylum, being so much 'the living reflexions of one another' that the sane girl can be buried away in the lunatic asylum instead, until she too is well-nigh out of her wits. Braddon's *Lady Audley's Secret* is itself acute about the indefinite borderline between criminal responsibility and so-called madness. Or again, in Le Fanu's *The Rose and the Key* (1871), Maud Vernon finds that the mansion she is visiting is really a female lunatic asylum in genteel disguise, showerbaths offered as though for hygiene, straitjackets masquerading as corsets and stays.

Sex, madness, and social reform was the melodramatic cocktail offered by Charles Reade in *Hard Cash* (1863). There a father has his son, Alfred, confined to a private lunatic asylum to prevent his exposing him as an embezzler—pained relations between father and son being another of the unruly reactive elements of the sensation novel, as in Collins's *Basil* (1852) and *Hide and Seek* (1854). In Reade's asylum the maltreatment of Alfred is intensified after he rejects the sexual advances of his female keeper.

Sensation novels were in every sense, said Mrs Oliphant, 'feverish productions', and brain fever itself becomes a culminating symptom of all that goes on within them. So at the height of delirious trauma in Wilkie Collins's *Basil* (1852), 'It was as if something were imprisoned in my mind, and moving always to and fro in it, moving, but never getting free' (pt. 3, ch. 1). With a life of its own, a traumatic thought imprisoned within the mind seems to begin to suck the mind into itself, until that thought actually seems to become the whole world: this is the nightmare of the sensational novel itself, in which the patients replay their lives in horribly transmuted forms.

What was offered was thus mental drama. An anonymous reviewer writing in *The Spectator* (3 February 1866) claimed that the nineteenth century does believe 'in love and jealousy, and in a feeble way, even in hate' but rarely does it identify itself with the deeper mental intensity out of which such passions spring. With 'madness in novels', however, the mental territory shifts: 'probability becomes unnecessary', 'everything was possible'. In the realm of everyday realism, 'how many helpless wretches must beat their brains against this hopeless persistency of the orderly outward world, as compared with the storm and tempest, the riot and confusion within' (*Lady Audley's Secret*, vol. 2, ch. 6). Now suddenly with sensationalism the repressed riot and confusion were turned inside out. The apparent unnaturalness from a realist point of view was no obstacle to a subgenre whose self-enclosed world offered a different internal nature of its own. As Wilkie Collins made clear in the dedicatory preface to *Basil*, 'The Novel and the Play are twin-sisters in the family of Fiction': 'the one is a drama narrated, as the other is a drama acted'. Collins and Reade shared with Dickens himself the ambition to be playwrights as well as novelists. But one of the places that drama goes in the Victorian age is into the melodrama of the sensation novel, versions of many of which also appeared on stage. Collins's were known as 'novels with a secret'.

Basil is a good starting point because here, as early Collins, the sensation novel was not yet quite used to itself. It has a protagonist still youthfully open and innocent enough to register the primacy of naïve shock. Basil, the younger son of a family which proudly dates back to the Conquest, falls in love with Margaret Sherwin, a linen-draper's daughter he sees on a London omnibus: 'It was only for a moment—but the sensation of a moment often makes the thought of a life' (pt. 1, ch. 7). Margaret's father allows the marriage on condition that it remains secret and unconsummated for a year while Basil's father can be brought to accept it. In the mean time, Margaret is seduced by her father's clerk, who seems to have been secretly tutoring her that way for a long time, before ever she met Basil. Basil finally traces them to a sordid hotel in one of the worst parts of London. The story that Basil thought he was living, as a young husband, turns out to have been not at all the story he was really leading. Basil's stunned and recoiling mind has now to turn round on itself and rerun within it a narrative that belies the innocence of domestic realism—'I had sensations, I had thoughts, I had visions, now':

In the clinging heat and fierce seething fever, to which neither waking nor sleeping brought a breath of freshness or a dream of change, I began to act my part over again, in the events that had passed, but in a strangely altered character. Now, instead of placing implicit trust in others, as I had done; instead of failing to discover a significance and a warning in each circumstance as it arose, I was suspicious from the first (*Basil*, pt. 3, ch. 1)

Disinherited by his upper-class father, deceived by a lower-class wife with whom he has never had sex, Basil can only fall ill when life's clear narratives and moral structures break down. In their place there is the underclass and the sexual underworld undermining past ideals and certainties. And the fall from a moral world into a sexual world makes for the protagonist's fall into the realm of psychology and psychosis.

For Henry James, it was Wilkie Collins who was the true creator of the sensation novel. Braddon herself said that Collins was her literary father and that she owed *Lady Audley's Secret* (1862) to Collins's *The Woman in White* (1860). Indeed with *The Woman in White*, as Mrs Oliphant herself was acute enough to see in a review in *Blackwood's Magazine* (May 1862), Collins had discovered what would become 'a new school in fiction', a new sub-genre.

Mrs Oliphant saw that Collins had overlaid the domestic history with highly wrought sensation so precisely, so apparently naturally, and with such watertight precision of plot, that the book defended itself in its own terms, in a form of its own. A bluff rationalist in *The Moonstone* (1868) may say, 'Let us look to what we *can* discover in the future, instead of what we can *not* discover in the past' (Third Narrative, ch. 8), but the two directions—progression and reconstruction—are not mutually exclusive in Collins. What holds together *The Woman in White* and *The Moonstone* is the eerie sense that as the book is moving forward on the track of discovery, simultaneously it is also moving backwards towards the secret that had long lain waiting in hiding beneath the façade of secure civilization. As Trollope said of Collins, 'he not only, before writing, plans everything on, down to the minutest detail, from the beginning to the end; but then plots it all back again, to see that there is no piece of necessary dove-tailing which does not dove-tail with absolute accuracy. The construction is most minute and most wonderful' (*Autobiography* (1883), ch. 13). 'But,' Trollope added, 'I can never lose the taste of the construction.' As part of what it meant to be a realist novelist, Trollope prided himself on never having secrets from his readers, on having his readers always going alongside him, living *with* his characters in an unfolding of knowledge close to the movement of everyday linear time.

Trained, like Reade, as a barrister, Collins created his narratives in imitation of the procedures of witnesses in a criminal trial, each contributing a personal fragment to the successive chain of evidence. It was that forensic skill that led Henry James in his review of Braddon to speak of Collins's novels as more the work of science than of art. For as Braddon herself puts it in chapter 15 of *Lady Audley's Secret*, 'A thousand circumstances so slight as to be forgotten by the criminal' become 'links of steel in the wonderful chain forged by the science of the detective-officer'. It is the juxtaposition of the slightness and the steeliness, just *before* one becomes the other, that is

Collins's subject matter. For there the very rationality of the detective figure still has a sort of residual pre-civilized horror about it—its source seen, in retrospect, to be predeterminedly present amidst the casual movements of the criminal.

'Physicians and lawyers are the confessors of this prosaic nineteenth century' (*Lady Audley's Secret*, vol. 3, ch. 5). It was the discourses of medical psychology, of detective forensics, and of law that Collins borrowed and eerily transformed, in memory of past religious and supernatural equivalents. Thus, one side of Collins's work will say, 'Nothing in this world is hidden for ever' (*No Name* (1862), First Scene, ch. 4): 'Sand turns traitor, and betrays the footstep that passed over it . . . hate breaks its prison-secrecy in the thoughts, through the doorway of the eyes.' And yet another side will offer to that modern quasi-Calvinism Count Fosco's enlightenment rejoinder: 'Crimes cause their own detection, do they? And murder will out . . .? If the police win, you generally hear all about it. If the police lose, you generally hear nothing . . . Crime causes its own detection! Yes— all the crime *you* know of. And what of the rest?' (*The Woman in White*, Second Epoch, ch. 3). Collins is a rationalist who by that very token is in love with what escapes or defies reason.

The novels work their way into the irrational parts of the mind. For inside them the dispassionate external chain of factual evidence is anxiously retraced through the subjective, psychological associations of thought: the formal procedures of law transformed into the more secret laws of mind. Thus, for example, in *No Name* Mrs Lecount, Noel Vanstone's vigilant and villainous housekeeper, finds herself baffled by the appearance in her master's home of a Miss Bygrave—in fact Magdalen Vanstone in disguise, trying to win back the family money from her unscrupulous cousin Noel by seducing him into marriage:

There was something vaguely familiar to her in the voice of this Miss Bygrave; and, at the same time, in unaccountable contradiction, something strange to her as well . . .
    She had got no farther than this during the day; she could get no farther now: the chain of thought broke. (The Fourth Scene, ch. 5)

Yet lying awake at night, the darkness seems to help Lecount's thinking. At one point her uneasily wandering thoughts break off and there is a momentary blank. Then 'with electric suddenness', she starts up, thinking, 'Miss Vanstone again!!!':

She was quite incapable of tracing the mental process which had led her to discovery. She could not get sufficiently far from herself to see that her half-formed conclusions on the subject of the Bygraves, had ended in making that family objects of suspicion to her; that the association of ideas had thereupon carried her mind back to that other object of suspicion which was represented by that conspiracy against her master; and that the two ideas of those two separate subjects of distrust, coming suddenly into contact, had struck the light. She was not able to reason back in this way from the effect to the cause. (The Fourth Scene, ch. 5)

Lived forward, this is free, heuristic creativity; but scientifically analysed back again, it is unconsciously determined. That translation—*and* the felt gap—between the two discourses, the two dimensions of mind, is what fascinates Collins.

What interested Collins was thus a kind of blindness in the face of an unknown apparently external reality—as of being kept long in the dark. That is why in *Poor Miss Finch* (1872) the portrayal of a blind girl is not only one of Collins's characteristic defences of the physically handicapped as socially neglected, but an image of a mental sense experiment that Collins was always carrying out in one way or another upon so-called realism, breaking it down into component parts to be found inside as well as outside us:

Remember that, situated as I am, my fancy is peculiarly liable to play me tricks, and that I have no sight to see with, and to show me—as other people's eyes show *them*—when they have taken a false view of persons and things. (Part the First, ch. 20)

'Was it monition or monomania? What if I am wrong after all? What if this chain of evidence which I have constructed link by link is woven out of my own folly?' (*Lady Audley's Secret*, vol. 2, ch. 10). Pure objective seeing comes late in *The Woman in White* and *The Moonstone*, and when it does come, to correct or corroborate the imagination's fears and suspicions, then the achievement of confirmed reality is no more than an end to the novel, offering only a lingering and disturbing sense of disproportionate anticlimax: 'The paltry means by which the fraud had been effected, the magnitude and daring of the crime it represented, the horror of the consequences involved in its discovery, overwhelmed me' (*The Woman in White*, The Third Epoch, ch. 10). A few words of forged writing lay behind it all: what had been so terrible in the dark is now turned oddly trivial again in the light of the solution.

In *The Moonstone* Ezra Jennings, who is writing a secret book on the underlying laws of the brain, finds in the delirious ramblings of Dr Candy fragmentary coded clues which he eventually translates into a clear rational narrative of thought. Despite the loss of the faculty of speaking connectedly, there are still traces of the faculty of thinking connectedly, at the deep unconscious level of the brain's activity. So too in *The Law and the Lady* (1875) the ruined mind of the crippled Dexter is a sort of palimpsest. 'His memory was the least injured of his faculties', and his memory still speaks '(unconsciously to himself)' through the mad metaphorical stories he tells the novel's lady detective, revealing a supposed murder actually to have been a suicide (vol. 3, ch. 41). A reviewer of *The Woman in White* in *The Saturday Review* claimed that no reader could leave a Collins novel unfinished but, solutions discovered and curiosity sated, few would feel inclined to read it a second time. Hence the reader's compulsive urge for another and another instead.

This was why the distinguished Oxford theologian H. L. Mansel, writing in *The Quarterly Review* (April 1862), spoke of sensation novels as a species of decadent drug stimulating the craving which they supplied—a charge that, incidentally, may throw extra light on Collins's own growing dependency on laudanum. 'Excitement, and excitement alone, seems to be the great end at which they aim', said Mansel. To Mansel, the sensation novel made the inner life of both its characters and its readers in thrall to external incident and plot. The sacrifice of characters to story destroyed the belief in the power of individual responsibility and the autonomous integrity of the normal self. It was not that the language of the sensation novel was always emotive and melodramatic. Collins for one deliberately simplified and streamlined his language to the driving pace and luring power of story. He coolly sacrificed the steadier power of language's meaning, within the felt present, to the ability of story to call up *off* the page, within the mind of the reader, the unconsummated possibilities of the future, felt as anxiety and suspense.

What alone can stop the plot of the sensational novel dead in its tracks is the rare ability of its protagonists not to submit to maintaining their secrets or their fears, but to step out of the compulsive chain of events and risk facing possible exposure. In the old language it meant *not* doing further evil in the desperate hope that good might eventually come of it. In *Armadale* (1866), the attractively wicked Lydia Gwilt for a long time keeps her options open. In marrying Midwinter she may be preparing to use him for her long-standing hopes of revenge against his friend, Alan Armadale; or she may be giving up that old life and starting afresh since, to her surprise, she finds herself genuinely falling in love with him. Which way the incipient structure will go is like an image of the sensation novel's own experiment in form.

In *No Name* (1862) Magdalen Vanstone stakes her very life on trying to win back the family fortune: 'She turned to the relentless Purpose which was hurrying her to her ruin, and cried to it with the daring of her despair—Drive me on!' (The Sixth Scene, ch. 1). Yet just out of view beyond sensationalism's self-enclosed maelstrom of excitement, there remains the wider and near-forgotten moral issue that must emerge at the end of the game, when there is nowhere further 'on' to go. For if Magdalen finally does win the wretched Noel, as in the heat of the game we want her to, then she sacrifices herself sexually, losing all possibility of a real emotional life—which emphatically we do not want. On the very eve of her success, Collins for once has his protagonist hesitate:

She stayed out, until the night fell and the stars appeared. . . . The vain hope that accident might defeat the very end for which, of her own free will, she had ceaselessly plotted and toiled, vanished and left her; self-dissipated in its own weakness. She knew the true alternative and faced it. On one side, was the revolting ordeal of the marriage—on the other, the abandonment of her purpose. Was it too late to choose between the sacrifice of the purpose, and the sacrifice of herself? (The Third Scene, ch. 13)

To Mansel the sensation novel was tacitly a form of despair: it made human beings into chess pieces, trusting chance in order to evade consequence in the secular game of life. At the critical moment, character gave way to story—or had even become its own story: 'Yes! too late. The backward path had closed behind her. Time that no wish could change, Time that no prayers could recall, had made her purpose a part of herself: once she governed it; now it governed her.'

Sensation novelists felt the social pressure of such criticism. Mary Elizabeth Braddon herself admitted to Bulwer-Lytton, 'I have thought very much over what you said in your last letter with regard to a novel in which the story arises naturally out of the characters of the actors in it, as contrasted with a novel in which the actors are only marionettes, the slaves of the story' (17 January 1864). In the first volume of the three-volume *John Marchmont's Legacy* (1863) she had achieved her finest creation in the person of Olivia Arundel, a woman steadfastly trying to do good, 'to whom nature had given strength but denied grace'(vol. 1, ch. 7). In Olivia, Braddon had found herself a character who remained somehow separate from her actions, in whom the very will to morality had replaced the spirit of it. Other characters in the novel admire and respect Olivia as though she were the heroine of a High Church novel by Charlotte Yonge, but for all her virtue and her beauty, they too somehow sense that something primary is missing: 'she keeps 'em off—she seems allers to keep 'em off' (ch. 17). What is more, in this alternative version of Victorian goodness, Olivia herself recognizes the fact she cannot be loved in that way as an implicit life judgement. In this she is in telling contrast with the irreverent vitality and erotic grace of Rhoda Broughton's own young heroines in *Cometh Up as a Flower* (1867), *Not Wisely But Too Well* (1867), or *Nancy* (1873), for out of those single young girls grows the emancipated witty woman who can narrate their stories. Yet although Braddon told Bulwer that she thought she had for once here made story subordinate to character, even the kindest reviewers of *John Marchmont's Legacy* said that after the first volume the characters broke down as the story set in.

Nonetheless the sensation novel was not without its defenders. In particular, E. S. Dallas argued that so far from being self-evidently primitive and inferior, the plot-centred novel was actually offering a radically different account of the relation between the world of events and the formation and maintenance of human identities within it. 'The art of fiction, which makes character succumb to the exigencies of plot, is just as defensible as that which breaks down incident before the weight of character' (*The Gay Science*, 2 vols. (1866), vol. 2, ch. 17). At one extreme, in the language of character, the individual was defined as a coherent 'I' set over against the social realm. This was the preferred Victorian world where the responsibility of the self was proven by its making a difference. At the other extreme, there were narratives hinting anxiously at the action of laws outside individual and moral control or even perhaps consciousness. 'In point of fact,' concluded Dallas, 'most novelists attempt to mix up the two extreme views of life, though they cannot help leaning to one side or to the other.'

At the very least then, the existence of the sensationalist sub-genre and its modification in other contexts acted as a testing ground for the development of fundamental novelistic techniques, such as the balance between character and story, demanding a more creative awareness of the beliefs about reality that were implicit within them. What is a new melodramatic sub-genre in its own right in Collins or Reade was in the larger genius of Dickens no more than one strand in a multi-variegated novel, such as *Bleak House* (1853). In *Bleak House*, detection is so far extended and transfigured that the novel becomes an investigation into the very metaphysics of its own form and plot, in the struggling necessity to locate identifiable centres and discover hidden connections. In that way, the sensation novel can seem no more and no less than an example of how in Victorian England sub-genres were experiments which often found their fullest expression in being taken up in work which thereby offered itself as wider, more humane, and virtually uncategorisable: thus, Dickens's use of Collins, or George Eliot's treatment of the 'Woman Question' within *Middlemarch*, or Tennyson's transcendence of elegiac in *In Memoriam*.

Yet it is equally true that to confine sensationalism to being simply a sub-genre is to limit the life of its significance. It bursts into the reality of the realist novel itself whenever realism's secure boundaries are threatened, transforming everything. Indeed, for all Mrs Oliphant's opposition, it happens in her own *Salem Chapel* (1863). At the crisis, the young Nonconformist minister Arthur Vincent pursues his eloped sister, Susan, to London by night-train, frantic to catch up physically with his own worried thoughts of her ahead of him in both space and time: 'He could scarcely endure the slowness of the motion . . . No express train could travel so fast as the thoughts that went before him, dismal pioneers penetrating the most dread abysses' (ch. 19). Meanwhile, at imaginatively much the same time, the widowed Mrs Vincent wakes to find herself still at home, minding the parish in place of her son. The temporal relativism of different people in different places sharing a similar anxiety about the same loved one leaves Mrs Vincent mentally scattered and fragmented, after a desperately disturbed night:

Snatches of momentary sleep more dreadful than wakefulness had fallen upon her during the awful night—moments of unconsciousness which plunged her into a deeper horror still, and from which she started thinking she heard Susan call. Had Susan called, had Susan come, in any dreadful plight of misery, her mother thought she could have borne it; but she could not, yet did, bear this . . . one moment rising up against the intolerable, the next sitting down dumb and steadfast before that terrible necessity which could not be resisted. (ch. 21)

Left as her clergyman-son's local representative, she 'had a sensation that the pew, and indeed the whole chapel, trembled with the trembling that was in her own frame', but knowing 'at the same time that everybody was looking at her, and that Arthur's credit was involved', she 'stood up steadfastly, holding her book firm' (ch. 21). *This* is what sensationalism and realism each mean, no longer as secure and separate literary categories, but set free as conflicting elements within the struggle of a single character.

II. Fairy Tales and Fantasies

When the painter's art was in its infancy, wrote John Ruskin, before the dawn of realism, it consisted merely in simple outlines and pleasant colours 'which were understood to be nothing more than signs of the thing thought of, a sort of pictorial letter for it, no more pretending to represent it than the written characters of its name'. 'Such art', said Ruskin, 'excited the imagination, while it pleased the eye. But it *asserted* nothing, for it could realize nothing.' The reader looked upon it as a symbol, and went on to form truer images for himself: 'This act of the mind may be still seen in daily operation in children, as they look at brightly coloured pictures in their story-books' (*Modern Painters*, vol. 3 (1856), pt. 4, ch. 4, paras. 7–9).

But as soon as art developed in the Renaissance what Ruskin calls 'the power of realization', it began to assert its own literal reality, in its own right. Viewers could now look at paintings, as through a window, almost effortlessly, without their seeing becoming thinking. Ironically, the paintings threatened to replace the reality they were originally meant to stand for, their very finish getting in the way of the imagination of less visible dimensions of meaning.

In an essay 'On Polish' in 1865, one of Ruskin's friends and admirers, George MacDonald, declared that true polish of style was the result not of 'putting on', through the application of more and more layers of rich paint and varnish, but rather 'of taking off'. 'Polish', he wrote, 'is the removal of everything that comes between thought and thinking'. So, at the very end of MacDonald's *St. George and St. Michael* (1876), in the aftermath of the Civil War, the heroine returns to the ancient ancestral home to find the grand staircase open to the elements, chambers reduced to gaps in walls. Even thus she registers, nonetheless, the original underlying 'idea' of the castle all the more for the semi-disappearance of its physical reality. 'Simplicity is the end of all Polish.'[4]

For both Ruskin and MacDonald, one of the simplest, most accessible forms of writing, close to the primal infancy of art, was the fairy tale. Like Ruskin's medieval paintings, the fable could not be confused with the external everyday world but instead offered passage to a realm more ancient and visionary. MacDonald's *Phantastes* (1858) begins as in a dream, with the design of branch and leaves on a bedroom carpet coming magically to life and opening out into a real landscape. As the protagonist sets foot into that landscape he simultaneously enters the world of medieval romance.

Ruskin's own fairy tale, *The King of the Golden River*, written in 1841 but not published until 1850, followed a traditional formula: three brothers (two cruel and greedy, the youngest good but downtrodden) and a task (to find a river of gold by taking a small amount of holy water to the summit of a high mountain and pouring it into a stream). Three times each of the two older brothers refuses to give water to the needy; at journey's end both are turned into a black stone—the fate of those who have brought water which is proved unholy. But Gluck, the younger brother, gives precious drops of his

[4] 'On Polish' is to be found in MacDonald's *A Dish of Orts* (1893), as are 'The Fantastic Imagination', 'Wordsworth's Poetry', and 'The Imagination: Its Functions and Its Culture' cited later below.

water first to an old man, second to a child, and finally to a little dog, until he has none left to pour into the stream. As Ruskin notes, where the two older brothers, thirsty for gold, denied appeals of ever-increasing strength—from dog to child to old man to brother—Gluck responds to three appeals which *diminish* in their claims. Yet in his failure lies Gluck's success, for he has been following out, unbeknownst to himself, a second *moral* story, a secret inner mission, hidden within the outward terms of the *magical* first one. Gluck's is the truly holy water for being given to others in need: accordingly the river turns not into literal gold but into a naturally rich source of irrigation for the whole valley. 'There is', as Ruskin was later to put it in *Unto This Last* (1862), 'no wealth but life.' *The King of the Golden River* represents the childlike primal story that the new, real, adult world of the Industrial Revolution had forgotten or betrayed. 'You cannot get rid of the child's need', said George MacDonald, even if 'you have forgotten what it is the need of' (*Adela Cathcart* (1864), vol. 2, ch. 2).

Ruskin and MacDonald were themselves, as it were, the needy children of the Romantics. In the *Preface to Lyrical Ballads* (1800) Wordsworth had dared to claim that rustics and children and mothers were closer to the elementary laws and primary simplicities of human nature. Coleridge believed that the simplicity and absoluteness of fairy tales habituated the mind to love of the great and the whole. Those adults who laughingly disowned their childhood illusions, existed—ungrateful and hard of heart—in fragments. These thoughts inform the Christianity of Dickens's *A Christmas Carol* (1843), just as surely as the lines from Wordsworth's 'Michael' (1800) which speak of the child as a gift bringing to adults renewed hope and 'forward-looking thoughts' rightly serve as the epigraph to George Eliot's *Silas Marner* (1861). The meaning that children had for adults was not of course something the children consciously provided: on the contrary, what they offered was an *un*consciousness at the very root of human existence—the first heart, the innocence of new life—that must be both gratefully loved and nurturingly protected by older, more damaged souls. For Victorian Romantics, childhood gave access to a realm of feeling and imagination prior to both the jadedness of ageing and the scepticism of the times. It was not just a matter of children appearing as characters within adult or realist forms, and changing them from within: what the children represented found a form of its own in the Victorian fairy tale. It located a realm of lost potential and gave it a formal defence by genre. The translation into English of the tales of the brothers Grimm, of *The Arabian Nights*, and of the works of Hans Christian Andersen in the first half of the century helped create a foundation for the child-writing of the second.

'For my part I do not write for children,' declared George Mac-Donald, 'but for the childlike, whether of five, or fifty, or seventy-five' ('The Fantastic Imagination'). Fantasy-writing thus offered the Victorian writer the chance to find within the fresh world of the apparently little—a fairy story, a child—something actually large or deep, from a wholly other dimension. 'If there's one thing makes me more angry than another, it is the way you humans judge things by their size', says the North Wind in MacDonald's *At the Back of the North Wind* (1871, ch. 5). Complex thoughts come out of apparently tiny simplicities.

Thus in MacDonald's *The Princess and Curdie* (1882) the boy protagonist says to the benign great-great-grandmother figure who magically keeps changing her shape and appearance: 'If you want me to know you again ma'am, for certain sure, could you not give me some sign, or tell me something about you that never changes—or some other way to know you, or thing to know you by?' To his literal-mindedness he hears this in reply, like a great religious law in childlike translation:

No, Curdie; that would be to keep you from knowing me. You must know me in quite another way from that. It would not be the least use to you or me either if I were to make you know me in that way. It would be but to know the sign of me—not to know me myself. (ch. 7)

'That which is inside is the same all the time' is the wisdom-saying behind all this.

Old thoughts are new again, as once before in the beginning. So it is in the argument for the painful fallen necessity of recrimination put by Mrs Bedonebyasyoudid in Charles Kingsley's *The Water Babies* (1863):

'I did not know there was any harm in it . . . You are a little hard on a poor lad,' said Tom.

'Not at all; I am the best friend you ever had in all your life. But I will tell you; I cannot help punishing people when they do wrong. I like it no more than they do; I am often very, very sorry for them, poor things; but I cannot help it . . .'

And there came over the lady's face a very curious expression—very solemn and very sad; and yet very, very sweet. And she looked up and away, as if she were gazing through the sea, and through the sky, at something far off; and as she did so, there came such a quiet, tender, patient, hopeful smile upon her face that Tom thought for a moment that she did not look ugly at all . . .

'I am the ugliest fairy in the world; and I shall be, till people behave themselves as they ought to do. And then I shall grow as handsome as my sister, who is the loveliest fairy in the world; and her name is Mrs. Doasyouwouldbedoneby. So she begins where I end, and I begin where she ends.' (ch. 5)

For a moment, by her own imagination, the figure of punishment has become her more beautiful, forgiving sister, since (as with MacDonald in the changes of the fairy grandmother) all the magical women in *The Water Babies* are actually part of each other and finally, theologically, one.

At such moments the fairy tale gives its Victorian writer access to a wonderful, near-motherly sense of pre-lapsarian peace. So it is when the chimney sweep's boy sheds his dirt and, it seems, his earthly skin, on entering the sleepily purifying waters of Kingsley's Vendale. Or at the end of Jean Ingelow's *Mopsa the Fairy* (1869) when a little boy returns from the fairy world and lays his head gladly on his father's waistcoat, recalling how a short time before he had carried Mopsa in his own waistcoat pocket. Or again, there is the young man in the picaresque *rite de passage* of *Phantastes* who suddenly finds a place of refuge from the wood in the cottage of an old woman:

She held out her hand to me, and the voice of sweetness again greeted me, with the single word, 'Welcome'. She set an old wooden chair for me, near the fire, and went on with her cooking. A wondrous sense of refuge and repose came upon me. I felt like a boy who has got home from school, miles across the hills, through a heavy storm of wind and snow. (ch. 19)

MacDonald took from the German thinker Novalis the thought that 'philosophy is really home-sickness', and that the life of man was thus 'a continual attempt to find his place, his centre of recipiency, and active agency' ('The Fantastic Imagination'). In Kingsley's underwater world or MacDonald's dark wood, there is in the fairy tale a formal attempt to create a whole small world which by an act of moral orientation could eventually become a 'home' or 'centre' for thought, after travels through strange areas of pre-consciousness. So Curdie, a young boy-miner lost somewhere at the top of the king's palace, works out the orientation of his world by turning his mind inside out:

Those who work well in the depths more easily understand the heights, for indeed in their true nature they are one and the same: mines are in mountains; and Curdie, from knowing the ways of the king's mines, and being able to calculate his whereabouts in them, was now able to find his way about the king's house. He knew its outside perfectly, and now his business was to get his notion of the inside right with the outside. So he shut his eyes and made a picture of the outside of it in his mind. Then he came in at the door of the picture, and yet kept the picture before him all the time— for you can do that kind of thing in your mind—and took every turn of the stair over again. (*The Princess and Curdie*, ch. 3)

'Then when he came to himself at the top where he stood, he knew exactly where it was, and walked at once in the right direction.' One of the greatest things that can be done for your fellow man, said Mac-Donald in an essay on 'Wordsworth's Poetry', is to put him into that mood, condition, or imaginative *place* 'in which thoughts come of themselves'. Then he can go on in the right direction.

At his best, accordingly, MacDonald finds a physical and imaginative home in which to restore the big thoughts as necessary again, coming of themselves. In *At the Back of the North Wind*, the boy Diamond tells the North Wind that he will try to be brave in future, adding however that 'trying is not much'. 'Yes it is,' responds the North Wind, '—a very great deal, for it is a beginning. And a beginning is the greatest thing of all. To try to be brave is to be brave' (ch. 7). Or a young princess panics and runs precisely the wrong way: 'That is the way fear serves us: it always sides with the thing we are afraid of.' After she realizes her mistake, she is scared that she will always be like that. No, says her magical great-great-grandmother, you were taken by surprise: it is only 'when people do wrong things wilfully that they are the more likely to do them again' (*The Princess and the Goblin* (1871), chs. 14 and 15). These are not to be dismissed as tacked-on Victorian moralizings but have the original surety of parent thoughts coming of themselves at the right time, from behind the little experiences of beginning. The very tone in which they are uttered is like what MacDonald said about the best songs, where the words and the music somehow appear to be all one thing: 'as if each word could be uttered only in that tone, and was incapable of distinction from it, except in idea, by an acute analysis' (*Phantastes*, ch. 5).

Gradually by such art, the Victorian fairy story stopped having to defend itself by merely appealing to the self-justification of genre:

At all events, we will make believe that there are fairies in the world. It will not be the last time by many a one that we shall have to make believe. And yet, after all, there is no need for that. There must be fairies; for this is a fairy tale: and how can one have a fairy tale if there are no fairies? . . . Am I in earnest? Oh dear no! Don't you know that this is a fairy tale, and all fun and pretence; and that you are not to believe one word of it, even if it is true. (*The Water Babies*, ch. 2)

'[E]ven if it is true': Kingsley's adult tone is arch, satirically playful, and still uncertainly transitional here. It is in the hands of George MacDonald, for all his own maddening unevenness, that the Victorian fairy story begins to turn 'make believe' into an image of true belief—testing how far what had begun in child's form could retain its virtue in adult religious terms, without becoming merely regressively nostalgic.[5] In MacDonald's *The Princess and the Goblin*, the grandmother sets the child-princess the discipline of a task:

'But I must put you to one trial—not a very hard one, I hope. This night week you must come back to me. If you don't, I do not know when you may find me again, and you will soon want me very much.'
'Oh! please, don't let me forget.'
'You shall not forget. The only question is whether you will believe I am anywhere—whether you will believe I am anything but a dream. . . . It will rest with yourself, after all.' (ch. 11)

[5] Cf. Stephen Prickett, *Victorian Fantasy* (Harvester, 1979), 193 on Kingsley and MacDonald: 'To see their similarities in philosophy or literary theory is to understand something about their age and their culture; to see their differences is to guess at what made two very different men.'

Will you *believe* in me after I am not here with you? That is what the older figures are always asking the children in these books, until, by taking away the apparent physical reality, magic becomes transformed into what it is a symbol of: the spirit of religious faith. That is how finally the little Victorian fairy tale can contain within it—as we shall see in the last movement of this chapter—the tradition of Dante's *Divine Comedy*, Spenser's *Fairy Queen*, and Bunyan's *Pilgrim's Progress*.

But it could do so because MacDonald, above all, believed that 'in everything that God has made, there is layer upon layer of ascending significance'. A child's fear, woods, mines, mirrors, dreams, the feeling of being lost—these things do not merely 'convey' or 'describe' a meaning; they *are* a meaning in themselves:

It is God's things, his embodied thoughts, which alone a man has to use, modified and adapted to his own purposes: therefore he cannot help his words and figures falling into such combinations in the mind of another as he had himself not foreseen, so many are the thoughts allied to every other thought, so many are the relations involved in every figure, so many the facts hinted in every symbol. ('The Fantastic Imagination')

That there is always more in a true work of art 'than the producer himself perceived while he produced it' is, says MacDonald, 'a strong reason for attributing to it a larger origin than the man alone'. The artist is dealing with things that embody thoughts beyond his own: he does not create the meanings, he catches them and puts them into form. 'A man is rather *being thought* than *thinking*, when a new thought arises in his mind' ('The Imagination: Its Functions and its Culture'). Genius means 'one who understands things without any other body telling him what they mean' (*At the Back of the North Wind*, ch. 22) and it begins, as did MacDonald himself, with the instinctive creativity of the untaught child.

To the modern post-Freudian reader, the idea of women and children and rustics acting as spiritual agents may appear suspicious or ridiculous, whilst faith in childhood as naturally innocent may seem an irrecoverable and regressive cliché. Yet even in the nineteenth century there were voices expressing equivalent doubts. Not all Victorian stories for or about children followed the Romantic model of feeling which Ruskin and MacDonald, Dickens and George Eliot had inherited from Wordsworth and Coleridge. 'Come children,' Thackeray had said caustically to his adult readers in the last sentence of *Vanity Fair*, 'let us shut up the box and the puppets, for our play is played out.' In an essay on 'Fairy Stories' in 1868, Ruskin argued that literature for children should be innocent of prematurely troubling childhood peace; it should not be a vehicle for 'inculcating' adult doctrines, but should result 'naturally' from the evolution of simple old stories in their accumulated universal experience. But characteristically, Thackeray's own fairy tale for children, *The Rose and the Ring* (1855), is a burlesque of the form. Fairy Backstick's magic rose and magic ring each render their bearer irresistibly lovable, yet Thackeray's satiric point is that charm, attractiveness, and popularity are a form of adult sham and illusion. The world-weary fairy herself learns that, for all the powers of magic, she must give her favourites a little misfortune, in order that they might grow up satisfactorily. The fact that in the end the prince and the princess love each other without need of magic is the positive side of the tale's belief in a disenchanted reality. Yet throughout the tone is knowing and ironic. A dying queen begs her ladies to look after her daughter after her death: 'Of course they said they would. Of course they vowed they would die rather than any harm should happen to the Princess.' And of course they desert the little girl soon after. Or Thackeray will say to his child-audience at another point, 'O remarkable circumstance! O extraordinary coincidence, which I am sure none of you could *by any possibility* have divined!'—the self-mocking irony acknowledging the children as intelligent accomplices in the detecting of fiction. Ruskin said that 'of all writers whatsoever of any people or language', he would most strictly forbid Thackeray to young readers of both sexes. Where in Thackeray the cult of the child raised suspicion or provoked accusations of cliché, for Ruskin and MacDonald, childhood was precisely the realm where for once the sense of suspicion and the consciousness of cliché had not yet come into being.

Yet there was always the potential for a playfulness which was not quite as innocent as it seemed: Christina Rossetti's 'Goblin Market' (1862) is a now classic example of the children's fairy tale turned riddlingly subversive in its range of disguised adult connotations.

Above all, there is one short story, written in 1856, which is crucial in this context of a sceptical counter-tradition.

Its narrator recalls a dream he had one night that the great idea of his life as a poet was about to be fulfilled. The following day he sees in the street a shop sign which seems to bear out the promise of his dream. It simply says: 'Simon Lubkin. Dealer in Romancement'. He asks a man coming out of the shop, what is this Romancement. The man replies, 'It would piece almost anything together' and make it solider than stone. That is the what the poet had wanted—something that would connect the whole of human life, not just on the page but in solid reality. ROMANCEMENT.

Returning the next day, the poet looks again at the sign. And then he sees the delusion of his imagination. 'A hideous gap yawns between the N and the C, making it not one word but two': ROMAN CEMENT. It would piece almost anything together and make it solider than stone. Now the very word divides. 'The dream was over' ('Novelty and Romancement', *The Train*, October 1856).

The tale was written by Lewis Carroll: it is an image of his comically disguised disappointment. It is also an image of how Lewis Carroll could never be George MacDonald, though the children of MacDonald were the first youthful readers of the prototype of the Alice books, *Alice's Adventures Underground*, besides the real-life Alice Liddell herself. Indeed their enthusiastic reception had encouraged the author to go ahead with publication.

In 1802 in 'Resolution and Independence' Wordsworth wrote of a meeting with the old leech-gatherer in all his stoic solidity, as a mystic revelation of bare life: 'My question eagerly did I renew, | "How is it that you live, and what is it you do?"'. But Lewis Carroll writes in *Through the Looking-Glass* (1871):

> So having no reply to give
>   To what the old man said,
> I cried, 'Come tell me how you live!'
>   And thumped him on the head.
>   .   .   .   .   .
> I shook him well from side to side
>   Until his face was blue:
> 'Come tell me how you live,' I cried,
>   'And what it is you do!' . . .

Under cover of the violence of playful parody, this was Lewis Carroll's austere and near-contemptuous protest at the whole Romantic attempt to set up religion in terms of human feelings.

In a nineteenth century caught between two worlds, there was a struggling commitment—in Ruskin if not quite in Carroll—to retain a belief in the sources of natural feeling; a struggling commitment—in MacDonald if not at all in Thackeray—not solely to define adulthood and knowledge, progressively, as the ability to detect and eradicate illusion and cliché. But a reluctant fall out of the realm of romancement is central to the Alice books:

Just then a Fawn came wandering by: it looked at Alice with its large gentle eyes, but didn't seem at all frightened. 'Here then! Here then!' Alice said, as she held out her hand and tried to stroke it; but it only started back a little, and then stood looking at her again.

'What do you call yourself?' the Fawn said at last. Such a soft sweet voice it had!

'I wish I knew!' thought poor Alice. She answered, rather sadly, 'Nothing, just now.'

'Think again,' it said: 'that won't do.'

Alice thought, but nothing came of it. 'Please, would you tell me what you call yourself?' she said timidly. 'I think that might help a little.'

'I'll tell you, if you'll come a little further on,' the Fawn said. 'I can't remember here.'

So they walked on together through the wood, Alice with her hands clasped lovingly round the soft neck of the Fawn, till they came out into another open field, and here the Fawn gave a sudden bound into the air, and shook itself free from Alice's arm. 'I'm a Fawn!' it cried out in a voice of delight. 'And, dear me! you're a human child!' A sudden look of alarm came into its beautiful brown eyes, and in another moment it had darted away at full speed. (*Through the Looking-Glass and What Alice Found There* (1871), ch. 3)

Here in the wood, where there are no names, is one of the few moments of warm connectedness in either of the Alice books. Yet the whole incident is like Thomas Hardy's austerely frail little poem 'The Fallow Deer at the Lonely House', where the deer is like a natural perfection, outside human life, which we cannot ever really meet with and yet suspect we are always missing. For as soon as they leave the wood, names return in place of intimate touch and, with the names, consciousness creates separation. Then even the asking of questions cannot help:

'Would you tell me, please, which way I ought to go from here?
    'That depends a good deal on where you want to get to,' said the Cat.
    'I don't much care where—' said Alice.
    'Then it doesn't matter which way you go,' said the Cat.
    '—so long as I get somewhere,' Alice added as an explanation.
    'Oh, you're sure to do that,' said the Cat, 'if you only walk long enough.' (*Alice in Wonderland* (1865), ch. 6)

Questions get her nowhere, because there is nowhere to go in this world, no purpose. The Victorian attempt to moralize away the resistant elements of the irrational and the grotesque within the tradition of childrens' tales is here defiantly undone. In Carroll's Wonderland the fairy tale's changes of size change nothing else; there is no deep meaning to growing up here. Through Carroll's looking glass, mirrors do not perform the fantasy-magic promised by Mac-Donald in *Phantastes*: 'All mirrors are magic mirrors. The commonest room is a poem when I turn to the glass' (ch. 10). Instead, logic itself being reversed, you run only to stay still, and even the book's marvellous verbal mobility leaves the reader nowhere. There is still a sense that there are strong feelings and powerful thoughts somewhere at work within the Alice books, out of all proportion to the lightness of presentation. But like the Fawn they cannot be confronted. For as Alice says of one the Hatter's remarks, the language, though certainly English, seems autistically separate from human meaning: '"But what *am* I to do?" said Alice. "Anything you like," said the Footman, and began whistling' (*Alice in Wonderland*, ch. 6). The Mock Turtle and the Gryphon do lessons for ten hours the first day, nine the next, and so on: '"And how did you manage on the twelfth?" Alice went on eagerly.' In the face of such questions the subject is merely changed, for the trick is simply to try to avoid or defer the idea of ending—of death: '"But that must happen very often," Alice remarked thoughtfully. "It always happens," said the Gnat' (*Through the Looking-Glass*, ch. 3).

Always upon the apparently comic and zany world of Lewis Carroll falls a bitterly satiric version of what George MacDonald in *Phantastes* called 'the shadow': the disenchantment of the world.

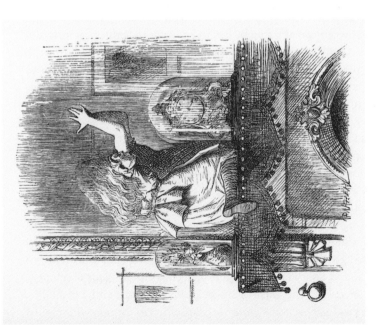

Fig. 10. John Tenniel (1820–1914), 'Alice Through the Looking-Glass', 1871, the two sides: as George MacDonald puts it, 'All mirrors are magic mirrors' (*Phantastes*, 1858).

Once, as I passed by a cottage, there came out a lovely fairy child, with two wondrous toys, one in each hand. The one was the tube through which the fairy-gifted poet looks when he beholds the same thing everywhere; the other that through which he looks when he combines into new forms of loveliness those images of beauty which his own choice has gathered from all regions wherein he has travelled. Round the child's head was an aureole of emanating rays. As I looked at him in wonder and delight, round crept from behind me the something dark, and the child stood in my shadow. Straightway he was a commonplace boy, with a rough broad-brimmed straw hat, through which brim the sun shone from behind. The toys he carried were a multiplying glass and a kaleidoscope. I sighed and departed. (ch. 9)

Charles Dodgson was an ordained High Churchman, an abstract mathematician from Christ Church, Oxford, and a shy and fundamentally disappointed man who relished logic games and seems to have found most of his emotional satisfaction in the company of little girls. But when he wrote under the name of Lewis Carroll, he became his own literary shadow.

In December 1894 in an article in *Mind*, 'What the Tortoise Said to Achilles', Dodgson set up one of his infinite regresses of logic. Just before their race the Tortoise slows down Achilles by insisting that before he can use any rule he has to have another rule that tells him why and how he may apply it, and the Tortoise makes Achilles write them all out: 'Have you got that last step written down? Unless I've lost count, that makes a thousand and one. There are several millions more to come . . .'. This was characteristic of Dodgson's critical use of reason *against* reason: the method playful, the purpose austere. In Lewis Carroll the playfulness can become a farrago of fantasy; but the austerity underneath becomes a bitterly ironic act of cool, intelligent, teasing aggression upon the reader. 'Everything's got a moral,' says Carroll's Duchess—adding, 'if only you can find it'. For all her conviction that she is 'real', Alice does not know if she is a part of the Red King's dream or he a part of hers. All writing is nonsense writing: nothing is ever really signified. Behind Lewis Carroll there is still the stringent High Churchman and critical logician who will not make the category mistake of putting feelings in the place of religion, or this world in the place of the next, or literature in the place of a theological silence very close to Mansel's. No wonder the philosopher Wittgenstein admired Lewis Carroll, not only for his language games but in the spirit of Wittgenstein's own famous dictum: That of which we cannot speak, we must pass over in silence. The creative celebration of what remains a nihilistic state is the art which in an appendix to *Modern Painters*, volume 4 (1856) Ruskin had identified as the bitter spirit of grotesque caricature, of wild humorous ghastliness. It deals with thoughts unapproachable by other more direct means: thoughts of marginalized concerns, or cancelled feelings, and pointless revenge; experiences of wildly oscillating or incongruously mixed feelings, in all the mass-frenzy of Victorian increase and proliferation.

Ruskin gives as an example the zany verse humour of Thomas Hood (1799–1845) who began as a high Romantic poet and ended as a writer of low comic prose. But the straighter, clearer meaning of Hood's life was finally preserved in his children's biographical compilation from his letters, *Memorials of Thomas Hood* (1860).[6] This beautiful, neglected, accidental by-product of a book covers the years 1835 to 1845 when the constant concern in the Hood household was the thought of Hood's imminent death, weakened as he was by financial worries, periodic exile in Germany, and consumption. Yet Hood strove to make that mortal anxiety itself an accommodated and manageable part of the very life of the family. His letters show Hood employing a version of Victorian family-art to ensure that the sadness was enclosed in comedy:

I one day overheard a dispute between Tom and Fanny as to what I was. 'Pa's a literary man,' said Fanny. 'He's not!' said Tom, 'he's not a literary man—he's an invalid.' (*Memorials*, vol. 2, p. 55)

Yet it is a comedy humanized by the underlying shared sadness:

[Tom] was very delighted to see me back, but I suppose I did not romp with him quite equal to his expectations, for after a day or two, as I was sitting reading, he said with an arch look at his mother, 'I do wish my pa would come home.' (vol. 2, pp. 30–1)

No wonder Hood felt close to Dickens. For Hood does not use his childish puns and shifts of register ('he's not a literary man—he's an

---

[6] See below, pp. 420–1.

invalid'), as Lewis Carroll does, to expose the world as an uncaring nonsense game, nullifying feeling by a tacitly satiric intelligence:

'Why do you sit out here all alone?' said Alice, not wishing to begin an argument.
'Why, because there's nobody with me!' cried Humpty Dumpty. 'Did you think I didn't know the answer to *that*? Ask another.' (*Through the Looking-Glass*, ch. 6)

But unlike Hood, Lewis Carroll in his loneliness had no children of his own. 'Human nature is so constituted', he wrote, 'that whatever you write seriously is taken as a joke, and whatever you mean as a joke is taken seriously' (*Sylvie and Bruno Concluded* (1893), ch. 8). All Lewis Carroll could do was to exploit the seriousness as joke, the joke as seriousness, till the difference was impossible to locate. It is always said that the comically shambolic inventor, the White Knight, was Lewis Carroll's parody of Charles Dodgson. 'You didn't cry so much as I thought you would,' he says to Alice, when he has finished his song. In her new-found rationality and independence, she didn't cry at all. Nothing in Carroll can finally heal the split between adult and child, intelligence and sentiment.

Yet in the map of the grotesque in the nineteenth century, it is Edward Lear who occupies the territory between Lewis Carroll and Thomas Hood. In Lear's nonsense verse the austere, marginalized bachelor stance of Lewis Carroll is given the disguised feelings of a Hood, though those feelings are only registered through a further sense of their loss.

> He weeps by the side of the ocean,
>   He weeps on the top of the hill;
> He purchases pancakes and lotion
>   And chocolate shrimps from the mill.
>   ('How pleasant to know Mr Lear!')

The rhymes are childish, the solutions and juxtapositions nonsensical in lieu of growing mad. The frenzied clowning makes smaller what is already humiliated, until the Dong can only invent a luminous nose, as huge as Lear's own, with which to seek his lost beloved through the dark:

> But when the sun was low in the West
> The Dong arose and said,—
> 'What little sense I once possessed
> Has gone quite out of my head!' -
> And since that day he wanders still
> By lake and forest, marsh and hill,
> Singing—'O somewhere, in valley or plain
> Might I find my Jumbly Girl again!
> For ever I'll seek by lake and shore
> Till I find my Jumbly Girl once more!'
>
> ('The Dong with a Luminous Nose')

Like Lear's sly and ironic little limericks ('There was an Old Man in a Barge | Whose nose was exceedingly large | But in fishing by night | It supported a light | Which helped that Old Man in a Barge'), parody at least offers the help of what can be made, however strangely, from misfortune.

Lewis Carroll never believed he could use his mathematical abilities, removed from emotional or existential anxiety, to try to map formal reason onto the nature of reality. But a mathematician in an imaginary two-dimensional world called Flatland begins to do just that.

Flat people cannot see inside a square precisely because they have no third dimension, no sense of above, from which to perceive it. They can only transcend their limitations by abstract calculation. So the mathematician proves to his little grandson that the number of square inches in a square can be found by simply squaring the number of inches on the side.

The child meditates on his grandfather's calculation and then, taking a sort of mental and evolutionary leap, replies: 'But you have been teaching me to raise numbers to the third power: I suppose 3 to the power 3 must mean something in Geometry; what does it mean?' (Edwin A. Abbott, *Flatland: A Romance of Many Dimensions* (1884), ch. 15). Questions are still educative here as they are not in Lewis Carroll's world. Abbott (1837–1926), appointed as head of his old school, the City of London School, in 1865 at the age of 26, was one of the pioneering educators of his time. He introduced into his curriculum the specialist study of both English literature and the sciences, and wrote books on Shakespeare's grammar, on Bacon and on Newman, and on the Broad Church interpretation of Christianity after the example of his friend John Seeley's *Ecce Homo* (1866) in which a personal Christ was portrayed as the breaker of conventions and the tester of assumptions. *Flatland* is Abbott's liberal thought experiment about the frameworks of understanding within which people must live, their determining effect upon the very shape of their thoughts, and the necessity for strenuous open-minded thinking in order to be able to extrapolate beyond them as relative rather than absolute.

To a degree *Flatland* belongs with Victorian dystopian satires and science fictions such as Bulwer-Lytton's *The Coming Race* (1871) and Samuel Butler's *Erewhon* (1872)—themselves in their different ways products of Darwinian ideas of evolution. What a work such as *Erewhon* offers is the view from *outside* the contemporary framework of understanding. A journey to another world, in which sickness is punished but crime is cured, throws light on the partial irrationality of both that world-view and our own. It is a version of the cultural relativism that found expression in E. B. Tylor's landmark work of social anthropology *Primitive Culture* (1871), defining 'culture' not as Matthew Arnold had, but as encompassing the customs, laws, beliefs, traditions, and practices that form the complex whole of the life of a given people. As such it takes a rationalist's view of beliefs, not as they are held internally and individually, but socially and historically, as the mindset within which both consciously and unconsciously individuals must operate. 'So it is with most of us: that which we observe to be taken as a matter of course by those around us, we take as a matter of course ourselves'; the greatest human invention is that 'we can be blind and see at one and the same moment' (*Erewhon*, chs. 12, 13).

What saves *Flatland* from easy satire is the effort of imagination required not only of the protagonists in order to ascend to a higher dimension but also of readers themselves in order to reverse and descend to a lower. Indeed, Abbott's Flatland hero, in shape a square, himself must descend to Lineland, where people live as points in a straight line which they themselves cannot see because it goes straight through their insides. They have no sense of sides, of right or of left, and they communicate and even reproduce by means of sounds. The hero must even go down further to Pointland, where there is but one creature who is to himself his own world and universe.

But, as the heroic square-figure begins to understand the principle of analogy, he must also ascend to the three-dimensional world of Spaceland where he is given a nearly mind-blowing vision of what 'upwards' means, in order to imagine himself as a Cube:

I mean that every Point in you—for you are a Square and will serve the purpose of my illustration—every Point in you, that is to say in what you call your inside, is to pass upwards through Space in such a way that no Point shall pass through the position previously occupied by any other Point; but each Point shall describe a straight Line of its own. (ch. 16)

Yet when the square-figure suggested to the inhabitants of the three-dimensional world that there must be in turn a land of Four Dimensions, they had rejected the idea just as surely as he had previously rejected theirs, and just as blindly as the point-people had had to resist his own version of a higher perspective. And when he returns to Flatland, where all such thinking is outlawed as madly irregular, he himself can barely hold onto his vision of another dimension.

But the greatest visionary works of the Victorian period are those which defy such dismissiveness, by staying loyal to a transformed version of the fairy story, taking the child's form into the very world of adulthood.

One such is Mrs Oliphant's fable *A Beleaguered City* (1880)—the story of the people of a provincial French town, Semur, who are expelled from their own city, from the homes of their fathers, by the city's own dead, because they have betrayed the past meaning of life in living materialistically and forgetting God. It is narrated within realistic conventions, by a number of different inhabitants of the town, even though the subject matter itself defies realistic belief. For the tale is in danger of being dismissed as a fairy story even from within itself—the editor of the several narratives, the town mayor is a self-consciously rationalistic modern man, who equates religion with superstition, particularly among females. Yet, as the people of Semur are made to become as children again and relinquish modern sophistication, even the mayor finds himself praying to God as to a father. A saddened widower Paul Lecamus, known as the feeblest-minded of the inhabitants, is alone allowed to remain in the city and live among the felt but invisible presence of his beloved dead. But even he cannot understand all that he hears: 'It was more beautiful than any of our music, for it was full of desire and longing, yet hope and gladness; whereas among us, where there is longing, it is always sad.' He laboured after the meaning, but 'in the middle of a phrase, in a word half breathed, a sudden barrier would rise'. 'Though I was alone with the unseen, I comprehended it not,' concludes Lecamus, 'only when it touched upon what I knew, then I understood' (ch. 5). As she tries to make what was once important important again and almost literally bring what is dead back to life, Mrs Oliphant herself confronts in Lecamus the extreme imaginative dilemma of the Victorian visionary novelist working within the world of realism: how to give a sense of the unknown, when even *that* can only be registered through what we already know. 'We are made so,' says Lecamus; 'What we desire eludes us at the moment of grasping it.' The people will promise anything in the way of religious observance in order to be allowed to return to their homes. But within hours of their return to normal life, they begin to return also to their previous indifference. Thus the mayor: 'Even in my own case—I say it with sorrow—it did not continue' (ch. 10).

George MacDonald's own greatest effort at continued vision, *Lilith*, did not appear until 1895. Yet, itself years in the writing, it is also the work he was really composing all his life and must be included here as the culmination of its genre.

Lilith is like a serious version of *Through the Looking-Glass*, for it begins by removing a scholarly young man called Vane from his library, taking him through a mirror into an alternative realm. This second world, says his guide, overlaps and interpenetrates with this one, existing in the self-same time and place: 'That tree stands on the hearth of your kitchen, and grows nearly straight up its chimney' (ch. 4). Vane may only be dreaming in his library, for it is as though he is entering a world imagined inside one of his own books. But he feels he has lost his sense of home, forgotten his name, and has nowhere to go: 'I had not yet, by doing anything in it, made *anywhere* into a place!' (ch. 16). 'To go back,' says his guide, in words he can barely follow, 'you must go through yourself, and that way no man can show another' (ch. 4). In this second world Vane feels that even as he is regarding a scene of external activity, he is also somehow studying a metaphysical argument. The guide, who turns out to be old Adam himself, tells Vane that he has only ever thought he understood things because 'your understanding of them is only your being used to them, and therefore not surprised at them' (ch. 30). That is too often the adult way.

A second structural challenge thus emerges when Vane encounters a host of sensitive, orphaned, childlike creatures called the Little Ones or Lovers. They are wise and kind but not fully conscious and, like Peter Pan, they do not want to grow. They say that if they grew, it would only be because they had been greedy, like the race of bad and stupid giants called 'fat' in their world but 'rich' in Vane's. It is by this means that MacDonald incorporates and personifies within his story the very genre of children's fiction, the very ideal of childhood perfection, and makes his immature protagonist ask himself a question about the Little Ones which begins to force the book itself finally beyond fairy tale: 'Surely, I thought, no suppression of their growth can be essential to their loveliness and truth and purity! . . . Life and law cannot be so at variance that perfection must be gained by thwarting development!' But then again: 'Why should they grow? In seeking to improve their conditions, might I not do them harm, and only harm?' (ch. 14).

It is partly the presence of these children that helps the book to a new linguistic vitality. They speak of water as 'the glad of the ground'; of shadow as having 'no thick' to it; of living safely high up in the trees above the heads of the giants and no longer being 'run-creatures' but 'fly-creatures'; of evil ones who 'death it'. Vane himself asks, 'What is behind my *think*?' while Adam, speaking of one of his sleepers in the House of Death, says 'Her wake is not ripe yet, she is busy forgetting'. Yet as Vane also puts it, 'I have heard it said that some words, because they mean more, appear to mean less' (ch. 15) —words such as God or Love. Thus, the other way MacDonald finds for redeeming the old words is by the way of paradox, of losing and gaining at once: 'It is possible to grow by means of not growing'; 'Everybody who is not at home, has to go home'; 'You wish to die because you do not care to live . . . no one can die who does not long to live.'

The fate of the children is connected with Vane's encounter with Lilith herself, the legendary first wife of Adam, wicked mother of the princess of the Little Ones. To Vane, in his own struggle for growth, she stands for both disguised evil and sexual temptation, and he is drawn into her black room as though it were her brain. It is his task to bring Lilith back to the family of Adam where in the House of Bitterness she must be made to see herself, to see what she has done to herself, and then to give up that very self which she still thinks of as her life, when it is really her death. In the course of this inflicted suffering, itself incomprehensible to nineteenth-century humanism and insupportable outside the structures of ancient faith, the reader begins to realize that MacDonald has sought nothing less than to recreate Dante, to renew the whole epic sweep of *The Divine Comedy* from Hell through Purgatory to Paradise, for the Victorian age, even as it was dwindling away. It is a culmination of the great Victorian concern with death, as the final trial of the status of human life in the universe.

For hardly anything in the literature of the period can match the ending of *Lilith* in terms of either structure or belief, the two being stunningly inseparable as MacDonald imposes a last test upon what he, like Mrs Oliphant in *A Beleaguered City*, knows his age will otherwise surely dismiss as a mere belated dream. There are two great end-movements in *Lilith*, as Vane lies down to sleep in the House of the Dead, waiting till he has been through all the wrongs he has ever done and all the further trials required of him, and can at last awaken into a new life.

The first comes in chapter 43 when he awakes to find all the other sleepers gone, the landscape into which he rushes cold and bare. Suddenly he finds Adam again, who tells him: 'You are still in the chamber of death, still upon your couch, asleep and dreaming, with the dead around you.' To Lewis Carroll this would be like the paradox of the liar who says he is telling you the truth in admitting his lies. But though to himself Vane seems wide awake, 'I believed I was in a dream, because he had told me so.' Even in a dream, says Adam, which I tell you *is* a dream, you believe that I am something more than a part of that dream.

If that was not enough, the sleeper awakes again at the end of the penultimate chapter of *Lilith*, and finds himself pushed through a door which becomes 'the board of a large book in the act of closing behind me'. He is back in his library, where he started, as if he had dreamt the whole thing there. Yet in the final chapter, 'The Endless Ending', he does not end, like a modern man, with the thought that it has all been an intricate fiction. Instead Vane asks himself: Can it be that this last waking is also still in the dream, just as before according to Adam? 'That I am still in the chamber of death, asleep and dreaming, not yet ripe enough to wake?' Or, to offer another alternative, 'Can it be that I did not go to sleep outright and heartily, and so have come awake too soon?'

Whatever the status of this life to which he now returns, he must wait: 'asleep or awake, I wait.' Poised thus at the height of intelligent imagination turning itself inside out, backwards and forwards in search of its possession of a final reality, *Lilith* does what Lewis Carroll could not or would not. It offers a last, mind-spinningly serious alternative to the question teasingly posed in *Through the Looking-Glass*—whether the whole thing is Alice's dream of the Red King or the Red King's dream of Alice—and ends closer to Dante and to Bunyan than to Lewis Carroll.

9

High Realism

'Fairies and demons, remote as they are from experience, are not created by a more vigorous effort of imagination than milkmaids and poachers.' In a series of articles in *The Fortnightly Review* (May–November 1865), entitled 'The Principles of Success in Literature', George Henry Lewes mounted a sustained defence of realism in fiction which found its culmination in one definitive sentence: 'The imaginative power' of a work, claimed Lewes, has been 'too frequently estimated according to the extent of *departure* from ordinary experience'. Realism meant that high literature need not depart from ordinary experience but could find a basis within it.

It is the corrective reaction against the work of Dickens in the late 1850s and 1860s, of which Lewes was himself a part, that defines better than can any abstract taxonomy the concerns of later Victorian realism. In part, this was the attempt of a steadier more established period, from the beginning of the second half of the century onwards, to exorcize the Dickensian demon of the early unruly decades. But it was also a campaign to take the novel to new levels of both psychological and philosophical development.

In a review article in *The Westminster Review* (July 1856) 'The Natural History of German Life', George Eliot complained that for all Dickens's gift for powerfully registering external idiom and manners, there was in him an incapacity for the direct portrayal of deep, inner psychological realities. Similarly, Henry James, reviewing *Our Mutual Friend* in *The Nation* (21 December 1865), spoke of Dickens as 'the greatest of superficial novelists'. Dickens had a compelling imaginative energy that made his surfaces appear as depths, but he had insufficient formal intelligence, said James, to know what to do with that particularizing power in relation to man and human life in general. To Lewes himself, writing in *The Fortnightly Review* (February 1872), Dickens's was a hallucinatory animal intelligence creating a delusive hybrid world of its own: Dickens gave the illusion of realism but into realist forms and appearances smuggled myths, fantasies, eccentric and phantasmagorical unrealities made real only by the imaginative conviction of his feelings.

To Lewes, a straighter realism was not merely to do with restricting fiction to everyday persons, events, and minutiae, in opposition to the melodrama of sentimentalism and sensationalism. Even the democratic purpose of presenting an accurate picture of present-day life—making material and social reality the foundation of literature—was only one part of realism's modernizing agenda. To Lewes, as to his partner George Eliot, the primary reason for the existence of realism lay in the wider moral aim of committing imagination first to realizing, and then to rescuing, the inherent value of ordinary human life on earth. For realism there were no categories in the world which were now outside the remit of literature: the novel had to go everywhere, take in everything. The realist novel—however fictively, partially, or hubristically—thus sought to re-create the world. As an inevitable accompaniment, it was bound to question from within itself what if anything, beyond the reality of biological continuance, could support, explain, or justify the human world's own equivalent ongoing existence. It was a questioning that became the more urgent upon reality when the novelist could no longer rely upon the assurance of a religious justification and felt the need for an alternative.

This chapter will consider 'high realism', in terms of the raising of the domestic novel in the 1860s and 1870s to the heights of such serious questioning. By then, the novel offered the most subtle, diversified, and complicated network of shifting interrelationships available to human thinking. But even in the 1830s there had been novels which, though subsequently half-neglected, had in them at source something of that generic existential earnestness, that directness of relation to daily life, which belonged to the history of the development of a realism of high seriousness in the later decades. In particular, there was Harriet Martineau's *Deerbrook* (1839) which was admired by Charlotte Brontë, and Maria Edgeworth's *Helen* (1834) which impressed Elizabeth Gaskell: to examine these works offers a means of beginning to define the nature and direction of later Victorian realism.

I. Two Novels of the 1830s and their Legacy

Both Maria Edgeworth and Harriet Martineau were in their different ways daughters of the eighteenth-century Enlightenment. Maria Edgeworth (1767–1849) was raised by her atheist father to be an exemplary product of the age of reason. Influenced by Rousseau on education and by Adam Smith on economics, Richard Lovell Edgeworth knew James Watt and Matthew Boulton, the great pioneers of the Industrial Revolution, as well as the scientist and radical Dissenter Joseph Priestley. They met for debate at the Birmingham Lunar Society, that rich intellectual mix of Unitarian dissent and progressive secular freethinking. Harriet Martineau (1802–76) herself grew out of early Unitarian influences to become a thoroughgoing secular determinist, influenced by Bentham on public policy, Adam Smith on economics, and Hartley on associationist psychology. The discovery of general laws in the world relieved her, she said, from her childhood insecurities by showing the place of necessities within reality.

Stern feminist advocates of freethinking reason, both women were public-spirited writers of didactic, educative tales in support of political economy and radical Utilitarian reform. They thus brought into their more genuinely fictional writings a continuing sense of severe necessities which in the early decades of the nineteenth century gave a fresh accent to the word 'duty'. In part, this moral and intellectual seriousness was a response to the felt pressure of Utilitarianism demanding what was the *use* of writing mere fictions. In part, it derived from specific Unitarian influences upon both writers, in so far as Unitarians, denying the divinity of Christ, sought relation to God through a correspondingly more urgent emphasis on human morality. In part, too, they took inspiration from all that culminated in Wordsworth's 'Ode to Duty' (1807), in its rich blurring of morality, religion, and reason. For in that poem 'duty' was not the dead weight of conventional social imposition, so easily parodied as merely 'Victorian' by the rebellious sons of the century's end, such as Samuel Butler. It was the call of a law, a reason, a truth, a need in the universe, in opposition to the idea of mere wilful freedom or blind chance.

In both *Helen* and *Deerbrook*, the novel of ideas seeks to work out with the novel of experience a union of general and particular, of contingent and necessary, which remains true to a thoroughgoing exploration of reality. Through their characters these novels think out their own situation even as they go along, in ways that, though easily dismissed as overly explicit or didactic, in fact have lasting implications for the formal development of the nineteenth-century realist novel. Both are concerned not merely with surface verisimilitude but with finding a right relation to the truth. Granted, nothing immediately follows upon either of these novels: *Helen* is Maria Edgeworth's last novel, written when she was already going out of fashion; the writing of *Deerbrook* was inconclusive, leading to no further novel or obvious change in Harriet Martineau, but only renewed ill health. Like so much writing in the hiatus years of the 1820s and 1830s, they are like something truncated, lost, or overtaken by a different age. And yet they also represent something unsure of, and in retrospect awaiting, the possibilities of development.

In her *Autobiography* Harriet Martineau claimed that her decision to turn from her *Illustrations of Political Economy* (1832–4) and *Society in America* (1837) and write a novel instead arose out of her desire to escape 'the constraint to be always correct, and to bear without solicitude the questioning of my correctness' (vol. 2, p. 108). Vitally, for Harriet Martineau the novel begins where the writing of social purpose ends, by letting in unclassified thoughts. For in its sense of life, *Deerbrook* seeks a natural freedom from the constraint of single unequivocal meanings: 'The most cunning allegory that ever was devised is plain and easy', says one character, 'in comparison with the simplest true story,—fully told.' For in the inexhaustibleness of real life, 'You never know that you have come to the end' (ch. 6).

Yet the subject matter of *Deerbrook* is not freedom so much as the rich density of human experience that results, for better and worse, from constraints. As the story of a country doctor, Edward Hope, his wife Hester and her sister Margaret, set in a rural village, *Deerbrook* is nominally a novel of domestic realism and a novel of community, and Harriet Martineau invoked the name of Jane Austen in defence. But within that rough definition its taut orientation of space and scope is very specifically worked out, as in an early dialogue between the two sisters:

'I almost wonder sometimes whether all things are not made at the moment by the mind that sees them, so wonderfully do they change with one's mood, and according to the store of thoughts they lay open in one's mind. If I lived in a desert island (supposing one's intellect could go on to grow there), I should feel sure of this.'

'But not here, where it is quite clear that the village sot (if there be one), and Mr. Hope, and the children, and we ourselves all see the same objects in sunlight and moonlight, and acknowledge them to be the same.' (ch. 2)

The overlapping co-presence of so many people in the same place seems to leave hardly any mental room at all, in the reality of this sort of novel, for the solitary Romantic's sense of absolutely individual experience. Here then, Edward Hope, though initially preferring Margaret to the more beautiful but less stable Hester, finds himself entangled into marrying Hester, while Margaret lives with them in the same house. He knows in his heart of hearts he has made 'a mistake'—'he could scarcely endure the thought; but it was so' (ch. 16)—and it is a mistake which has now to be secretly accommodated. In his own home, 'at my own table, by my own hearth', Hope 'cannot look up into the faces around me, nor say what I am thinking', but must be 'more lonely than ever before—and yet never to be alone with my secret' (ch. 19).

Outside the home, moreover, Hope falls victim to the close pressure of vicious social gossip, first concerning malpractice and grave-robbing, and then concerning his marriage. *The Times*'s literary reviewer E. S. Dallas dismissed the domestic novel as 'gossip etherialized, family talk generalized' (*The Gay Science*, 2 vols. (1866), vol. 2, p. 286). And certainly there is little room in the world of *Deerbrook* to keep the inner story free of its outward, circumstantially partial misrepresentation and prevent its frail truth from being absorbed into social reality. The novel cannot create for its protagonists a freely subjective life on some 'desert island'. Yet by moving *between* within and without, a novel such as *Deerbrook* can stand as a genuine alternative to the social language of gossip. Thus when Hope keeps silent about his previous unfulfilled love for Margaret, it is because 'that which had been truth . . . would become untruth by being first admitted now' (ch. 36). That is why such room as the novel can find for inner thought in character and in novelist alike is not mere leisurely didacticism but part of its formal struggle for 'a true story—fully told': 'A story of the mind you mean . . . not of the mere events of life' (ch. 6). In this, as in its acute sense of the bewildering pressure of a plurality of lives overlapping each other in time and space, *Deerbrook* is like an early intellectual forerunner of George Eliot's *Middlemarch*.

'You never know that you have come to the end.' It is only *after* he has married her, when he thinks he has settled for a life that is merely second-best, that Hope actually begins to fall in love with his wife. This is because, for all her jealous insecurities, Hester is actually strengthened by facing the troubles of her husband and sharing them with him; to Hester it is almost a relief that real external problems were able to take the place of her shadowy inner anxieties. For all Charlotte Brontë's enthusiasm for *Deerbrook*, it is here that the seed of Harriet Martineau's later dislike of the 'subjective misery' of Brontë's *Villette* is already sewn. For Martineau's tough-minded review in *The Daily News* (3 February 1853) was so critical of the restless mental vacuity left in Brontë's female characters by the obsessive Romantic yearning for love that it caused a permanent breach between the two women. Critics often speak of the Brontës collectively, but to understand their differing orientation is to understand something of the map of English fiction by the middle of the century. Between the Brontë who is the most realist of novelists—Anne Brontë in *The Tenant of Wildfell Hall*—and the Brontë who is the most romantic—Emily Brontë in *Wuthering Heights*—Charlotte Brontë exists ambivalently and uneasily, as though between parts of herself. That is why *Shirley* (1849) is split between two women protagonists, Caroline Helstone and Shirley Keeldar, Caroline keeping within her a strong consciousness of 'something wrong somewhere', of the 'want of something of your own' (chs. 22, 10), while Shirley, a version of Emily Brontë, seeks in place of Milton's *Paradise Lost* a new visionary cosmology, centring upon Eve as a Titan (ch. 18).

Charlotte Brontë's 1850 preface to her sister Emily's *Wuthering Heights* (1847) betrays a continuing anxiety about the need for realism and first-person control.

There is no alternative world in *Deerbrook*. Instead, in the face of both distortion without and secrecy within, *Deerbrook* is realism's taut inner story of an accommodation that is nonetheless as much a surprise as an achievement. For in the marriage as in the novel, form here is what emerges and evolves amidst the apparent formlessness of the actual world: 'Is it not true that few of our trials—none of those which are most truly trials—seem dignified at the time? If they did, patience would be easier than it is' (ch. 28). Trials within the realm of realism are real trials precisely for not seeming immediately to have the dignity or assurance of that formal title.

Maria Edgeworth's *Helen* has even more far-reaching implications. Her last novel, it is an early nineteenth-century vision of what she believed was to happen to the eighteenth-century moral heritage in the generation that followed. The eighteenth-century figure in the novel is Lady Davenant, a powerful and high-principled intellectual woman, of the school of Johnson and Burke, who, in lieu of love, has devoted her life to her husband's political career to the inadvertent neglect of their daughter. The daughter, Cecilia, finds an alternative home in London's social world of casual appearances, flattery, gossip, and trivial intrigue. There, ironically, her fear of her mother's stern moral law makes her all that her mother would not wish her to be *and* still struggles to prevent her from being. For this is a realist novel, where general thoughts and principles, however absolute, are not abstracted and idealized but embodied and tested in particular human beings, relative to their complications and their inadequacies. Thus contained within the relation between mother and daughter are the novel's own problems about the role of moral didacticism within the narrative lives of a younger generation.

It is Helen, Cecilia's friend since childhood, who is more like a true daughter of Lady Davenant. When Helen finds herself in debt as a result of acquiescing in Cecilia's extravagant tastes, Cecilia turns round in alarm to ask,

'What are you going to do?'

'To tell all my follies to Lady Davenant.'

'Tell your follies to nobody but me,' cried Lady Cecilia. 'I have enough of my own to sympathize with you, but do not go and tell my mother, of all people; she, who has none of her own, how can you expect any mercy?'

'I do not . . .' (ch. 23)

If Lady Davenant will tell me what I ought to do, says Helen, 'I do not care how much I suffer'. That Helen should have to go in confession to the very person whose esteem she would most fear losing; that she should have to look bad in order to get right again: this is what it means to put the claims of classic morality, before those of psychology. 'Do not stop me,' she says to Cecilia who always prefers the strategy of delay; 'It is serious with me now.' In contrast, Cecilia never confesses, but always hides and avoids—in particular, concealing from her jealous husband a past flirtation with a notorious rake which she omitted to mention at the time of their betrothal.

Cecilia is a portent, representing that loss of truth-seeking moral directness which Maria Edgeworth manifestly feared. For increasingly, instead of the old religious forms of outward confession and moral counsel, the realist novel offers internal psychology: the alternative language of indirect secular report, minutely confessing, in the third person rather than the first, the conscious *and* unconscious thoughts of the characters, unbeknownst to themselves. It is what Trollope in *The Claverings* (1867) calls characters being 'so to say, turned inside out before our eyes' (ch. 10). That is what the pure *narrative* ability of the realist novel does, through the stupendous discovery of indirect reported mental speech: it turns the inside of human beings out, in a way that no reader would care or dare to have his or her internal psyche turned into the exposing definiteness of semi-public language. It gives the reader, privately acknowledging relationship with the characters at that deep level of inner being, an alternative to superficial public forms of judgement.

So it was in *Deerbrook*: secrecy in place of confession, a tacit authorial voice in place of direct speech. And thus by the time of *Middlemarch* there is beside the community of the characters, a second community, a tacit society of readers created through the gathering language of George Eliot herself—in that sense of 'we' which comes through sharing recognitions which are not simply private, though found in privacy. In an essay 'The Life of George Eliot' in *Critical Miscellanies* (1886), John Morley wrote that 'In George Eliot a reader with a conscience may be reminded of the saying that when a man opens Tacitus he puts himself in the confessional.' But that confessional exists in place of confession within the novels. Arthur Donnithorne avoids making confession to the Reverend Mr Irwine of the danger of his flirtation with the dairy maid Hetty Sorel —in case he succumbs to it after all (*Adam Bede* (1859), ch. 16). In *Silas Marner* (1861) Godfrey Cass tries to survive by hiding his past:

> The results of confession were not contingent, they were certain . . . He would rather trust to casualties than to his own resolve—rather go on sitting at the feast and sipping the wine he loved, though with the sword hanging over him and terror in his heart. (ch. 3)

'Favourable Chance is the God of all men who follow their own devices instead of obeying a law they believe in' (ch. 9).

Symptomatically, what happened to *Helen* was that it was virtually re-written by Elizabeth Gaskell. In *Wives and Daughters* (1866) the novel now characteristically leaves behind the direct intellectual moralism of the 1830s: there is no Lady Davenant, no explicit voice of 'law', and the world becomes less aristocratic—smaller, softer, more domestic, informally private and contingent. There are still two morally contrasting yet affectionately linked young women— the 'good' little Molly, the 'bad' yet beautiful Cynthia—but the figure of parental authority is now Molly's father, Dr Gibson, a widower who has taken Cynthia's foolish widowed mother to be his second wife for what he thinks is Molly's good. It is a measure of how *implicit* the realist novel has become, when for example in ch. 11 Molly innerly bewails her father's remarriage yet says nothing out loud:

> She was positively unhappy, and her father did not appear to see it; he was absorbed with his new plan and his new wife that was to be.

Yet Mrs Gaskell does not end on that note. Without beginning a new paragraph, she simply goes on fluently to another sentence:

> But he did notice it; and was truly sorry for his little girl; only he thought that there was a greater chance for the future harmony of the household, if he did not lead Molly to define her present feelings by putting them into words.

Mrs Gaskell is not as straightforward as she looks. Reading between these lines means realizing that the two sentences, like the two people, do not exist in dramatically separate spaces but, painfully, both close together and a crucial little distance apart. And still the paragraph does not end:

It was his general plan to repress emotion by not showing the sympathy he felt.

The sentence could have ended on 'by not showing sympathy'. But in this sort of realism, general plans and fixed principles cannot wholly control the particularity of life in time:

Yet, when he had to leave, he took Molly's hand in his, and held it there, in such a different manner to that in which Mrs Kirkpatrick had done; and his voice softened to his child as he bade her good-by, and added the words (most unusual to him),—'God bless you, child!'

The inobtrusive complexity of the shifts ('But he did notice . . . only he thought . . . Yet, when he had to leave') makes the reading of Mrs Gaskell's work as close as she can make it to the reading of real life itself, in its minute passing changes.

In its deep implicitness *Wives and Daughters* offers the greatest test in the reading of a Victorian realist novel. To those who could read Mrs Gaskell, patient of such minutiae as really larger than they were realistically registered as being, it was never the case that her realism was merely unthinking. To a casual reader it might look as though such deceptively fluent work existed below the level of more grandly explicit 'ideas'. But Mrs Gaskell's thinking works in a medium of human embeddedness wherein not just one thought exists at a time, nor even two, but there is the overlapping of three or four or more, until no one simple truth is left, in all the dissolving complexity.

The very syntax of a representative passage from *Sylvia's Lovers* (1863) makes astonishingly clear how thinking within Mrs Gaskell's realism exists not at a level inferior to categorization but beyond it. Sylvia's father has been executed for leading an attack on the press-gang and her mother has lost her mind; out of gratitude for his help Sylvia has married Philip, whom she does not really love. At his shop she now regularly meets Hester who has long loved Philip herself.

But no paraphrase can stand as a substitute for reading, at length and with attention:

> Hester was almost surprised at Sylvia's evident liking for her. By slow degrees Hester was learning to love the woman, whose position as Philip's wife she would have envied so keenly had she not been so truly good and pious. But Sylvia seemed as though she had given Hester her whole affection all at once. Hester could not understand this, while she was touched and melted by the trust it implied. For one thing Sylvia remembered and regretted—her harsh treatment of Hester the rainy, stormy night on which the latter had come to Haytersbank to seek her and her mother, and bring them into Monkshaven to see the imprisoned father and husband. Sylvia had been struck with Hester's patient endurance of her rudeness, a rudeness which she was conscious that she herself should have immediately and vehemently resented. Sylvia did not understand how a totally different character from hers might immediately forgive the anger she could not forget; and because Hester had been so meek at the time, Sylvia, who knew how passing and transitory was her own anger, thought that all was forgotten; while Hester believed that the words, which she herself could not have uttered except under deep provocation, meant much more than they did, and admired and wondered at Sylvia for having so entirely conquered her anger against her. (ch. 30)

This begins with a sentence about Sylvia, then a Hester sentence, then a Sylvia sentence again. But gradually each gets into the other's sentence, and it becomes increasingly clear that the sentences are not simply following upon each other but exist simultaneously, in layer upon layer of imagined reality. The cumulative complexity of this quintessential relativism is mind-spinning—but not to the magisterially calm, almost superhuman novelist so utterly at home in her world. For 'again', says Mrs Gaskell, the two 'different' women were 'divergently affected' by the ever-increasing affection which Sylvia's helpless mother, Bell Robson, has shown Hester ever since Sylvia's wedding day:

> Sylvia, who had always received more love from others than she knew what to do with, had the most entire faith in her own supremacy in her mother's heart, though at times Hester would do certain things more to the poor old woman's satisfaction. Hester, who had craved for the affection which had been withheld from her, and had from that one circumstance become distrustful of her own power of inspiring regard, while she exag-

gerated the delight of being beloved, feared lest Sylvia should become jealous of her mother's open display of great attachment and occasional preference for Hester. But such a thought never entered Sylvia's mind. She was more thankful than she knew how to express towards any one who made her mother happy; as has been already said, the contributing to Bell Robson's pleasures earned Philip more of his wife's smiles than anything else. And Sylvia threw her whole heart into the words and caresses she lavished on Hester whenever poor Mrs Robson spoke of the goodness and kindness of the latter. Hester attributed more virtue to these sweet words and deeds of gratitude than they deserved; they did not imply any victory over evil temptation as they would have done in Hester. (ch. 30)

The intelligent tolerance of the complex coexistence of different existences in the world is not just the novel's humane equivalent to the liberal vision of John Stuart Mill's *On Liberty*. It is closer to the metaphysics of a favourite author of Mrs Gaskell's, John Ruskin, in his account of 'the naturalist ideal': 'The moment that we trust to ourselves, we repeat ourselves, and therefore the moment that we see in a work of any kind whatsoever the expression of infinity, we may be certain that the workman has gone to nature for it' (*Modern Painters*, vol. 1, part 2, sec. 3, ch. 3, para. 22). When immersed thus deeply in its own subject matter, realism becomes a form of mystery even to itself, too various for simple, selective human explanation.

Yet single-minded critics have always tried to argue for Mrs Gaskell's claims by finding her a single idea or theme. Such critics prefer the first, more historical half of *Syliva's Lovers* to the second more personal section, or say that *North and South* is not a mere love story between a northern mill-owner and a southerner-daughter of a clergyman but (for this seems bigger) really a socio-political 'Condition of England' novel. But *North and South* is both at once.[1] Only, it is not the surrounding socio-political language—'I see two classes dependent on each other in every possible way, yet each evidently regarding the interests of the other as opposed to their own' (ch. 15) —but the under-language of intimate human relationship that allows Mrs Gaskell access to her sense of shifting layers and levels, of half-unwilling attractions cutting across the fixity of theoretical principles and social positions. In chapter 24, for example, Margaret

---

[1] See above pp. 49–52.

Hale wants to tell the tough industrialist Thornton that her helping him in the face of a mob was no assent to his social views, and still less 'a personal act between you and me'. He is angry when she thus rejects his love, is bitter too that this very anger at her prejudging him prevents him trying to make himself better understood: 'But for all that—for all his savage words, he could have thrown himself at her feet.' And, likewise, 'when he was gone, she thought she had seen the gleam of unshed tears in his eyes; and that turned her proud dislike into something different and kinder, if nearly as painful'. The novel exists for just such human discrepancies in the excess of life over what, masquerading as thought, often amounts to no more than defence or opinion. The narrated 'thereness' of the life created in these novels solicits an uncategorizable form of attention—attention which does not grasp the explanatory handles of politics, or gender, or religion, or sensation, or science, or national identity. As in *Cousin Phillis* (1865), the situation, developing beyond the notions of simple cause and effect or easy blame, becomes an intermixed happening in its own right, beset by involuntary harm and mutual pain. It is not therefore because Mrs Gaskell died just before its completion that *Wives and Daughters* is like what she says of Trollope's *Framley Parsonage,* a novel that seems as though it need never be conclusive but could go on for ever. It has more to do with that Ruskinian sense of the infinite meaning to be found even in finite lives.[2]

In short then, the most telling difference between *Helen* and *Wives and Daughters* is between what happens to Maria Edgeworth's Cecilia and what does *not* happen to Mrs Gaskell's equivalent in Cynthia.

Cecilia constantly flees the truth, doing and saying anything to deny its external, objective reality. It is only when the game is won, her husband duped into believing in her innocence, and there is now nothing left externally to worry her, that Cecilia suddenly turns round and speaks of her husband in confession to Helen:

'His love for me increased, but it gave me no pleasure; for Helen, now I am going to tell you an extraordinary turn which my mind took, for which I cannot account—I can hardly believe it—it seems out of human nature—

---

[2] See above pp. 149–57 on *Ruth.*

my love for him decreased!—not only because I felt that he would hate me if he discovered my deceit, but because he was lowered in my estimation! . . . I cannot tell you how shocked I was at myself when I felt my love for him decrease every time I saw him. . . . It was a darkness of the mind—a coldness; it was as if the sun had gone out of the universe; it was more—it was worse—as if I was alone in the world.' (*Helen*, ch. 45)

This is the language of unadmitted conscience, coming back to her not out of straightforward belief but rather from what she can 'hardly believe', from her 'shock' at herself. To find the claims of morality re-establishing themselves deep down within the terms of psychology is the terrible triumph of law and truth at this well-nigh apocalyptic ending in *Helen*.

There is no such great moment in the ever ongoing contingencies of *Wives and Daughters*. For Cynthia, who gets by through beauty, wit, and sexual secrecy, lives in improvised fragments—with all the 'glitter of the pieces of a broken mirror'. At one point Cynthia says she cannot live with people who do not think well of her; seventy pages earlier she had said that though she liked to be liked, she did *not* like it when people took liking too far. The connection between these apparent opposites is left implicit, a link to be made by the reader from bits of life unconsciously left behind, as the long Victorian realist novel goes on gradually building up a sense of cumulative familiarity. As with so much in this apparently unshaped novel, one moment recalls another, many pages earlier, which at the time seemed, in passing, to be just below the level of 'significance'. The reader is left to piece together Cynthia's story, to ponder the relation of past to present, like a second novelist remaking the novel or like an analyst forming a case history out of concealed and dispersed hints.

The novel itself remains richly agnostic as to how far any of these links or the explanations inferred from them are actually determining causes. Thus the *truth* about Cynthia is left, as Cynthia herself leaves it, beneath and beside her life, not confessed within it as with Cecilia in *Helen*. That Mrs Gaskell leaves Cynthia free (if that is the word) to carry on and on might have seemed to Maria Edgeworth, in her commitment to explicitness, a lax and casual tolerance as symptomatic as is Cynthia herself. Yet, arguably, that unshaped silent *realist* fate of Cynthia's—the ongoing indefiniteness of continually seeming to get away with her evasions, with nothing out there to stop or hold her—is implicitly *more* terrifying as a life than Cecilia's final breakdown into the confession of truth and the relief of punishment. A serious novelist might well be able to create a deep and serious character, but what Mrs Gaskell does with Cynthia is use all her Tolstoyan resources to create a character who has to remain superficial for deep reasons which she herself cannot afford to take seriously.

But when one thinks of George Eliot's own version of this situation in the depiction of Gwendolen Harleth in *Daniel Deronda*, it becomes clear that what was at stake between Maria Edgeworth and Elizabeth Gaskell is part of the history that also goes into the making of George Eliot. As we shall see, it is through the weighing of the balance between explicit and implicit intelligence, between moral judgement and psychological understanding, that 'George Eliot' comes to be.

II. Trollope and George Eliot

Alongside the mid-nineteenth-century meaning of 'realistic' as 'characterized by artistic or literary realism; representing things as they really are', the *Oxford English Dictionary* also cites a second meaning: 'concerned with, or characterized by, a practical view of life', and gives an example from Sir John Seeley's *Essays and Lectures* (1869) concerning the need to 'be reconciled to life by any plain view of things, by any realistic calculations'. It was this second meaning to 'being realistic' that seemed to Matthew Arnold in *Culture and Anarchy* (1869) so manifestly 'philistine': the robust common sense of the bluffly confident commercial English middle classes, reducing reality to practicality. More than any other novelist, it was Trollope who was accused by his critics in the 1860s and 1870s of making literary realism out of being all too realistic in the second pragmatic sense of the term. From its founding in 1855 *The Saturday Review* held that the realist novel in general and Trollope's work in particular were in danger of being dully mechanical and unimaginative. Of Trollope's novels, one such reviewer wrote, 'It is the literature of the moral and respectable middle-class mind—of people too realistic to be bothered by sentiment, too moral to countenance the sensationalism of crime, and too little spiritual to accept preachments or rhapsody for their daily use' (*The Saturday Review*, 21 September 1867). These are, in every sense, the middling people to whom it is said the prolific Trollope regularly offers his wares.

To Trollope novel-writing was a professional career, just as within the novels themselves, realistic 'to the tendency in all human wishes', the clergy was becoming a profession more often than a calling, and politics a profession more often than a creed (*Barchester Towers* (1857), ch. 1). The case is often as Palliser describes it to Phineas Finn: 'We both went into office early, and the anxiety to do special duties well probably deterred us both from thinking much of the great question. When a man has to be on the alert to keep Ireland quiet, or to prevent peculation in the dockyard, or to raise the revenue while he lowers the taxes, he feels himself to be saved from the necessity of investigating principles' (*The Prime Minister* (1876), ch. 68).

Often in Trollope the great question seems lost, regrettably but also sanely, in the necessities of day-to-day reality. The second-order world that often belongs to realism in the 1860s and 1870s is a realm of experience in which the reader must get used to chastened expectations, non-events instead of dramas, second thoughts rather than ideal feelings. An early neo-Wordsworthian poem, 'Sketches among the Poor', which Elizabeth Gaskell wrote in collaboration with her husband for *Blackwood's Magazine* (January 1837) offers an image of that scene. It tells the story of Mary, an ageing woman who has devoted the whole of her life to the 'cause' of helping others in the local city community but who has constantly looked forward to her 'dream' of going back in the end to the countryside home she left as a young girl. It is the thought of that better, more primary place in her mind that has kept her going in the lesser, secondary one. Yet she never gets to that transcendent realm. The function of her dream, after all, was not that it should be realized but that it should support her continuance in that secondary realm which has become her real home and is the home of realism in the work of Elizabeth Gaskell and Anthony Trollope. The visionary imagination does not exist to transfigure the mundane world but to see within it hidden, belittled, or obscured achievements and sufferings, larger in value than the space that contains them. Mrs Gaskell stays loyal to that small scale: her novellas and short stories of human goodness struggling within the world of experience and disappointment—*Cousin Phillis*, *Cranford*, 'Half a Lifetime Ago', 'The Crooked Branch', 'The Heart of John Middleton', 'The Manchester Marriage'—are like exiled prose versions of Wordsworth's *Lyrical Ballads*, folk tales made out of the important littleness of common life.

In the same way what is impressive about the great representative middle-class novel of the day, *John Halifax Gentleman* (1856) by Mrs Craik (Dinah Mulock) is not what critics now seize upon—the mythic self-made rise of John Halifax from orphan to mill-owner, in the first half of the novel. It is what happens after the achievement, with the *second* generation in the book's *second* half, that makes the novel most moving in its last dozen chapters. One daughter dies, another is wooed by a bad man; one son goes wrong, two of the brothers fall in love with the same girl; while the parents themselves age and decline: 'In the silent watches of the night, heart to heart, husband and wife had taken counsel together' (ch. 34). Nothing—neither economic security nor even a loving home—can prevent an almost biblical continuation of the human story in miniature: 'All parents must feel cruelly a pang like this—the first trouble in which they cannot help their children'; 'For a disaster like this happening in any household—especially a household where love is recognized as a tangible truth . . . makes the family cease to be a family in many things from henceforward' (ch. 33). Here, as also in *Olive* (1850) and *A Life for a Life* (1859), it is love's struggle to save life, in the face of pain, unbelief, or a guilty past, which is the real emotional subject matter. It is not with issues, achievements, or ideals that the mid-century realist novel is most often concerned: for Mrs Craik and Mrs Gaskell as for Wordsworth himself, seeing something at its most humanly humdrum, rather than at its most powerful, yielded a deeper and clearer insight into its basic nature.

Trollope's own career as a novelist really begins with the abandonment of the 'purpose novel' in *The Warden* (1855). As Thackeray had put it in *Punch* (21 August 1847) in his satiric 'Plan for a Prize Novel', 'Unless he writes with a purpose, you know, a novelist in our days is good for nothing'. In *The Warden* the ostensible 'purpose', the social cause in need of reform, is the alleged misuse of the Anglican Church's charitable trusts. The Reverend Septimus Harding has a second post, a sinecure, as warden in charge of an almshouse and its dozen old pensioners. His political opponent is the surgeon John Bull, who is also—and this is fundamental to the cross-connections of life in the realist novel—suitor to Harding's own younger daughter. A reviewer in *The Athenaeum* (27 January 1855) complained that by such means the grave fault of *The Warden* was that 'the right or wrong of the subject' was 'melted down' in the novel. 'Melted down' is a good phrase. For in its effort to bring abstractions down into solution this novel does ask: how will the actual lot of the old bedesmen in Hiram's Hospital 'be improved' by Bull's heavily theoretical campaign? They are promised a little more spending money, which feeds their greed; but they will lose their warden, an old friend who had watched over them for years. The imagined sound levels reflect this disparity of level between general and particular, theory and practice, public and private: 'John Bull sometimes thinks of this, when he is talking loudly of the rights of the bedesmen, whom he has taken under his protection; but he quiets the suggestion within his breast by the high-sounding name of justice' (ch. 4). Yet although Harding feels the attacks personally, he tries to separate the personal relationship with Bold from the public issue. Moreover, the old man then goes on to separate the (to him, new) moral question of the right and wrong of his holding his position as warden, from the political campaign waging around him. Unable to compromise, as is his nervous instinct, he is himself compromised 'between the reformer and the conservative'—between his possible son-in-law John Bull and his actual son-in-law, the formidably reactionary Archdeacon Grantly, married to Harding's elder daughter (ch. 5). In between those pressures of categories and camps—in a place where as Trollope put it, 'the mind of the reader fills up the blanks' (*The Duke's Children*, ch. 9) because there is for Trollope no simple language for individuality—Harding insists upon retaining his little individual space, in Christian conscience. He resigns the wardenship, in an act of belated scrupulous honour not quite distinguishable from newspaper accounts of his surrender, *and* the situation for the old men is predictably only worsened as a result. In this 'melting down' of simple, single, separate issues, the outstanding qualities for good or for bad are likewise characteristically 'diluted and apportioned out in very moderate quantities among two or more, probably among three or four' of Trollope's characters (*The Small House at Allington* (1864), ch. 2). It is as though this little novel, like the later *Miss Mackenzie* (1865), has found the right size for itself, below the level of great claims, in implicit acknowledgement of its limits. As even one of the critics from *The Saturday Review* admitted, 'The world of smallest things is still a serious place to Mr. Trollope' (18 May 1867). The larger novels are not so much bigger than *The Warden* or *Miss Mackenzie* as wider and longer, made up of many such lives.

Even so, the objection remained that Trollope's was the art that the tough, hard, and careworn Victorian world deserved: the mediocre product of material circumstance, rather than Romantic heroism. In an article on George Eliot in his *Essays Theological and Literary* (1871) R. H. Hutton said that Trollope, Thackeray, and Mrs Gaskell made up 'the school of society-novelists' founded by Jane Austen. More like Augustans than Romantics, they did their work from the outside, from the social realm, as though they did not so much create their characters from within, individually, as observe them externally. In a society now offering less room and time than Jane Austen's, Trollope's inner life, like that of his characters, consists in the life of the outer world: the six Barchester novels from 1857 to 1867 and, overlapping them, the six Palliser novels from 1864 to 1880. In contrast with the more Romantic inward work of Charlotte Brontë, wrote Hutton in a review of *Orley Farm* (1862), there is in Trollope 'nothing, apparently, of the agony of meditative travail about his mind . . . No great novelist probably ever drew so little from the resources of his own visionary life,—so much from the impromptu variations of the forms given by experience, as Mr. Trollope' (*The Spectator*, 11 October 1862).

Trollope's men and women, Hutton further noted, 'become to us as the acquaintances we meet every day, neither less distinct nor better known'. But that is precisely the sort of sober, almost anti-literary, realism that Trollope sought. Literature for Trollope could too readily encourage the pretence of effortless verbal access to a steadily existent inner world. But such facility is like the making of moral judgements in the act of reading—all too easy:

People are so much more worldly in practice than they are in theory . . . One girl tells another about how she has changed her mind in love; and the friend sympathizes with the friend, and perhaps applauds. Had the story been told in print, the friend who had listened with equanimity would have read of such vacillation with indignation. . . . Very fine things are written every day about honesty and truth, and men read them with a sort of external conviction that a man, if he be anything of a man at all, is of course honest and true. But . . . internal convictions differ very much from the external convictions. (*The Last Chronicle of Barset* (1867), ch. 56)

We do not even realize that these readerly convictions *are* external; but truly internal convictions are those that come out in relation to what we actually do in real life. Indeed one of the great tests of baffled inwardness in *The Last Chronicle* consists in the taking away of a man's memory, in the face of an accusation of financial irregularity, so that he cannot himself be sure from inside of his own innocence. Josiah Crawley, a proud, disappointed, irascibly half-maddened perpetual curate, puzzles his brain in his efforts 'to create a memory as to the cheque' (ch. 61). It is a more complicated version of a fine short story by Ellen (Mrs Henry) Wood, 'Lease the Pointsman' in which a railwayman causes a fatal accident by forgetting to change the points and yet cannot remember not doing it (*John Ludlow: First Series*, 1874). The shocked mind in such predicaments has to think about itself from *outside in*, as it were.

Real inwardness in Trollope is at best inaccessible, or intermittent, or elusive. That is why he is so interested in the case of Lady Mason in *Orley Farm* who for twenty years has lived with the secret of having forged her dying husband's will in favour of her son by her first marriage. It is that secret which has become her inner life, and equally it is a secret she has had to deny, in order to normalize her existence externally. When she is suddenly threatened with fresh legal inquiries after all that time, she finds herself thinking back over how she has managed the long habitual concealment: 'For years she had slept in that room, if not happily at least tranquilly. It was matter of wonder to her now, as she looked back at her past life, that her guilt had sat so lightly on her shoulders' (ch. 53). In *Cousin Henry* (1879) the protagonist ignores a will which he finds by chance in his library, leaving everything to his cousin; yet he finds himself compulsively staring at the book on the shelves, in which it is hidden, day after day. He does not know that what feels to him like the fear of being found out has now become so irrational and self-revealing, that it must be a displaced and unacknowledged form of inner con-

science. That inability precisely to locate life—to know what is surface and what is depth; or what is really coming from within rather
than without—is what makes life real to Trollope.

Hiding is a normal condition in Trollope; it 'melts down' into
something so normal as often not to know itself as hiding at all.
Lily Dale in *The Small House at Allington* (1864) is the witty single
woman vivaciously defending at one level what is still a damaged
heart at another—like Martha Dunstable in *Doctor Thorne* who can
defend herself by sarcastic intelligence and yet knows that even thus
she is hardly living as she should live; or Lucy Robarts in *Framley
Parsonage*: 'It was evident enough that her misery was real; but yet
she spoke of herself and her sufferings with so much irony, with so
near an approach to joking, that it was very hard to tell how far she
was in earnest' (ch. 26). And still Trollope respects the need to keep
those more superficial levels of life going, not in opposition to the
depths but in half-involuntary protection of them. What interests
Trollope is innerness not as a separate realm—he distrusts that self-
consciousness—but as something merged, hidden, and resurfacing
mysteriously within the outward norms of a creature's continuance.

The Way We Live Now (1875) is bitter enough about a substitute
new world of financial speculations based on nothing more real than
the false credit of reputation and rumour. Yet though Trollope has
all the materials for cynicism, he is not cynical like Thackeray: his
concern is finally the very opposite of Thackeray's interest in
hypocrisy. In writing *The Eustace Diamonds* (1873) Trollope feared
throughout that Lizzie Eustace was but a second-generation version
of the scheming Becky Sharpe in *Vanity Fair* (1848). And indeed
there is nothing in Trollope's novel that matches Thackeray's brilliant external command of the emotional space *between* his characters in key scenes: as when in chapter 53, for example, Rawdon
Crawley returns from his abandonment in prison to find his wife,
Becky, happily entertaining Lord Steyne. But by living through the
sheer length of his novel, in time with his people, Trollope writes
himself *into* his main character as Thackeray never cares to. His own
characters fascinate and even baffle Trollope, in something analogous to the way in which Lizzie's sexual power temporarily overcomes in those whom she targets their sense of her unreality, without
ever permanently obliterating it. Realism in Trollope means that a

character still goes on existing in time, independent of the author, long after a morally placing judgement is delivered in print. Like Cynthia in *Wives and Daughters*, Lizzie carries on and on—but with a shamelessness that is, remarkably, *her* version of what is stoicism in the life of others. Give Trollope long enough time to get used to the unusual, in the attentive length of his books, and he becomes surprisingly and even unpredictably flexible.

Trollope is good at putting moderate, limited people, experimentally, into limitless and extreme situations: that is how in *Orley Farm* and *Cousin Henry* he can use sensationalism of plot and yet remain a realist of character. *The Duke's Children* (1880) is one of the first accounts of what it feels like for a man to be left, not just out of political office, but as a widower with problem-children on the brink of adulthood—the private male exposed at those very points which previously his public concerns had subsumed and his wife had managed. It is not the large obvious challenges that Trollope appreciates so much as those that present themselves off-centre, in mundane surprise, beneath the level of preparation or dignity. As even the austere cleric Mr Puddicombe is finally forced to acknowledge, in the midst of moral grey areas in *Dr Wortle's School* (1881): 'There are few of us not so infirm as sometimes to love best that which is not best' (ch. 23).

Thus, importance arises for Trollope in quietly peculiar places, at unexpected times, in strange sequences. When Palliser's feckless son says of one of his potential scrapes, 'It's just like anything else, if nothing comes of it then it's all right' (*The Duke's Children*, ch. 65), he is unwittingly on the edge of Trollope's ordinary mystery. Why out of the mere process of life does anything become something rather than nothing; why is it sometimes so important when something does take place, and so apparently unimportant when that same thing does not? Of course these questions, just below the level of life's more solid outcomes, are never explicitly asked in Trollope: they are the blanks left for the reader. But they are part of the baffling tautology of contingent existence in Trollope: that some things happen and some do not; that for some people the happening *or* the omission is recognizably important, and for others not at all. For some reason, in their different ways, both Alice Vavasour in *Can You Forgive Her?* (1865) and Lily Dale in *The Small House* and again in

The Last Chronicle of Barset cannot get over the sheer sequence of their lives: because one man came before another, afterwards is never the same as before. Yet other people in these very novels could get out of such patterns, could treat past errors and wounds as matters of chance or as things simply done with.

So immersed, so seemingly formless, and so worldly as not to seem visionary at all, Trollope's imagination is nonetheless a witnessing presence. It becomes most energized, moreover, by the sudden re-emergence of old rites of passage amidst the language of the ordinary informalities. Thus the magnificent Lady Lufton has to face her son's determination to marry lowly Lucy Robarts:

'Dear mother, I will own this, that I should not be happy if I thought you did not love my wife.' These last words he said in a tone of affection that went to his mother's heart, and then he left the room . . .
    She knew she must yield. She did not say so to herself. She did not as yet acknowledge that she must put out her hand to Lucy, calling her by her name as her daughter. She did not absolutely say as much to her own heart—not as yet. But she did begin to bethink herself of Lucy's high qualities, and to declare to herself that the girl, if not fit to be a queen, was at any rate fit to be a woman. . . . The one thing necessary to her daily life was the power of loving those who were near to her. (*Framley Parsonage* (1861), ch. 43)

The apparently small or reluctant concessions of those who are intransigent have more at stake within them, relatively, than the larger movements of freer spirits. Trollope loves working in these back-to-front ways: the dull old conservative become the existential explorer of change. For in the midst of their resistance his characters turn *themselves* around, in spite of what they had taken to be their very principles, and because of the power of the life in front of them. It is part of what Trollope meant by the author and the reader 'living with' the characters, that Lady Lufton should naturally remember that change of hers in *Framley Parsonage* when in *The Last Chronicle of Barset* she gently counsels Archdeacon Grantly, first seen in *The Warden*. Grantly is determined to try to prevent his son's marriage to Grace Crawley, daughter of the clergyman under accusation of theft. Silently Lady Lufton recalls how she too at one time had thought that that marriage of her son's would break her heart. He will cut off his son without a penny, Grantly cries. At once tender and tough, like the eighteenth-century matriarch she is, Lady Lufton replies: 'You, who are so affectionate by nature, would never adhere to it' (*The Last Chronicle of Barset*, ch. 56). On Lady Lufton's advice Grantly goes to see Grace, rather than nourish his wrath by thinking about her:

'If you love him you will not wish to injure him.'
   'I will not injure him. Sir, there is my promise.' And now as she spoke she rose from her chair, and standing close to the archdeacon, laid her hand very lightly on the sleeve of his coat. 'There is my promise. As long as people say that papa stole the money, I will never marry your son. There.' . . .
   He almost relented. His soft heart, which was never very well under his own control, gave way so far that he was nearly moved to tell her that, on his son's behalf, he acquitted her of her promise. What could any man's son do better than have such a woman for his wife? It would have been of no avail had he made her such offer. The pledge she had given had not been wrung from her by his influence . . . 'My dear,' he said, 'if this cloud passes away from you, you shall come to us and be my daughter.' And thus he also pledged himself . . .
   As he walked across to the Court . . . he was lost in surprise at what had occurred. He had gone to the parsonage hating the girl, and despising his son. Now, as he retraced his steps, his feelings were altogether changed. (ch. 57)

It is not pragmatism that induces Grantly suddenly to think of going along with the marriage: 'There was a dash of generosity about the man, in spite of his selfishness.' Yet, on the other hand, he does not quite succumb to his sudden, chivalrous temptation to relent. Indeed his wife later complains, rather sharply, that her husband has simply fallen a little in love with the girl. But not the least of his feelings in relation to Grace Crawley is that sense of 'surprise' at all of them— despite Lady Lufton's own secret insight into the predictability of events. For Grantly has perhaps never felt anything so deeply since he stood at the bed of his dying father, the bishop, at the very beginning of *Barchester Towers*, and 'dared to ask himself whether he really longed for his father's death' that he might succeed him as bishop. 'The proud, wishful, worldy man, sank on his knees by the bedside, and taking the bishop's hand within his own, prayed eagerly that his sins might be forgiven him.' Fallen, occluded, involved in sundry mixed motives and deficiencies, there is even so a sort of natural theology implicitly underpinning Trollope's writing.[3] 'Each created animal must live and gets its food by the gifts which the Creator has given it, let those gifts be as poor as they may' (*He Knew He Was Right* (1869), ch. 47).

We rarely see that theology's bare principles, but they are embodied in the form and come out in the life of the novel. Trollope's is an austere Anglican orthodoxy which does not take human emotions, intentions, responses, or plans to be the reliable measure of things. Untidy inconsistencies do not surprise him. In *He Knew He Was Right*, Nora turns down a marriage proposal from rich Mr Glascock whom she does not love for the sake of Hugh Stanbury whom she does: 'Readers will say that if she loved Hugh Stanbury with all her heart, there could be nothing of regret in her reflections' (ch. 60). But that should not be their internal conviction. The beautiful widow Lady Julia Ongar in *The Claverings* (1867) 'was not heartless because she had once, in one great epoch of her life, betrayed her own heart; nor was she altogether false because she had once lied' (ch. 13). Trollope remains not just sceptical of, but sceptically interested in, the human need to simplify and justify, as an attempt to banish awkwardly hovering uncertainties. The unhappily married Lady Kennedy in *Phineas Finn*, for example, feels an uneasy sense 'that she could not leave her husband without other cause than now existed' (ch. 55). In the midst of an argument with him her own words convey back to her a strong sense of her own wrong, 'or perhaps I should rather say a strong feeling of the necessity of becoming indignant' (ch. 51). In *He Knew He Was Right* the process of disintegration in a marriage begins to assume a life and a momentum of its own, disproportionately far beyond the initial causes: 'When he would say something stronger than he intended, and it would be put to him by his wife, by her father or mother, or by some friend of hers, whether he did believe that she had been untrue to him, he would recoil from the answer which his heart would dictate, lest he should seem to make an acknowledgement that might weaken the ground upon which he stood' (ch. 79). The husband here is not unlike Lady

---

[3] See above pp. 144–9 on realism and religion in Trollope, Mrs Gaskell, and George Eliot.

Kennedy's husband, one of those stern insecure men 'who imagine that lips that have once lied can never tell the truth' (*Phineas Finn*, ch. 52). Robert Kennedy is terrifying because his character is absolutely identical with his religious and moral beliefs: there is no room for movement in him. But in Trollope there is nothing that is simply *one* thing and that thing for ever: that is why Trollope's realism has to be multifarious—not because it is simply liberal and generous and forgiving, but because it struggles to be true to an often uncomfortable, shambling and shifting unfixedness in its vision of the condition of life.

'You cannot always make things fit into one another', says the youthful narrator of Ellen Wood's 'Lease the Pointsman' as he contemplates his feelings for the victims of the railway accident *and* for Lease himself. And yet the realist novelists find a way not only of accepting that thought but of making form out of it. The equivalent form inside Trollope's novels is marriage. Thus Crawley's wife in relation to her husband, while he carries on painfully defying the accusation of theft:

> She knew that he was good and yet weak, that he was afflicted by false pride and supported by true pride, that his intellect was still very bright, yet so dismally obscured on many sides as almost to justify people in saying that he was mad. She knew that he was almost a saint, and yet almost a castaway through vanity and hatred of those above him. But she did not know that he knew all this of himself also. She did not comprehend that he should be hourly telling himself that people were calling him mad and were so calling him with truth. It did not occur to her that he could see her insight into him. (*The Last Chronicle of Barset*, ch. 41)

Less than an absolute or perfect fit, less than completely reciprocal, marriage through all the great twists and turns of this passage remains nonetheless a holding together here, for better and worse.

It is that implicit sense of the formal condition of life, even in its limits and its uncertainties, that calmly sustains both Trollope's interest in and distance from his people. It is not mere coldness that makes him have no such personal investment in their fate as does George Eliot. Because of his formal theology Trollope can be utterly interested in the human realm without being dependent upon good outcomes resulting from it. It is the theology of a fallen world, involved therefore in the austere challenges of the unsatisfactory, the chastening, the disappointing, the incomplete, the residual, and the reluctant as accepted *conditions*. 'Almost', 'quite', and 'nearly', words which offer less than enough, are characteristic Trollopeian phrases. No wonder therefore he is the great novelist of works in series, in those great six-book sequences: there is in him always that belief in continuity which goes on alongside the sense of incompleteness, such that no book has ever to end in a fictively affirmed finale.

In a letter to Trollope, 23 October 1863, George Eliot described his work as like a public garden to which people suppose they go for amusement but, 'whether they think of it or not', find health there as well. Yet for a deeper vision of human life, argued R. H. Hutton, it was George Eliot, rather than Trollope, who put her characters in 'direct contact with the ultimate realities', 'grasping at the truth by which they seek to live'.[4] It is symptomatic of the rich instabilities of the Victorian period that to Hutton, the atheistical George Eliot should seem more truly religious than the orthodox Anglican Anthony Trollope. 'Thus do things change,' said Ludwig Feuerbach in the translation of *The Essence of Christianity* which Marian Evans produced in 1854 before she became 'George Eliot': 'What yesterday was still religion is no longer such to-day; and what to-day is atheism, tomorrow will be religion' (ch. 1, sec. 2).

It was precisely their growing recognition of the relative lack of social purpose for women in Victorian England that put George Eliot's young female protagonists in the vanguard of Victorian metaphysical questioning. To R. H. Hutton it was far easier for a male such as Trollope to find social refuge from the anxieties of individual earnestness. In contrast, in the midst of family complications in *The Mill on the Floss* (1860), Maggie Tulliver must look for 'something' else to give her an alternative sense of being purposefully at 'home' in life.

[4] See David Skilton, *Anthony Trollope and his Contemporaries* (Macmillan, 1996), 109 and ch. 5 throughout. For equivalent, more modern criticisms of the so-called reality of the realist novel as a bourgeois trick see, as representative, Catherine Belsey, *Critical Practice* (Routledge, 1980), esp. 50–1 and 67–84 on false coherence and privileged discourse. But for an account of realism as operating metaphysically between life and literature see J. P. Stern, *On Realism* (Routledge, 1973), esp. chs. 3, 4, and 10.

In books, Maggie found, people were happy and kind, yet 'the world outside the books was not a happy one' (bk. 3, ch. 5). At the least, George Eliot's own books would offer realism, and would struggle inside themselves for a true relation to the world outside which was their subject matter. But finally, realism in George Eliot is the effort to create the book that Maggie Tulliver needed. Thus, inside *The Mill on the Floss*, in one of what George Eliot called her experiments in life, Maggie herself seeks for the clue that will 'link' her life together and give it a language, a syntax, a sense of form and relationship—rather than leave it like a mere list of unhappy bits and pieces:

No dream-world would satisfy her now. She wanted some explanation of this hard, real life: the unhappy-looking father seated at the dull breakfast-table; the childish bewildered mother; the little sordid tasks that filled the hours, or the more oppressive emptiness of weary, joyless leisure; the need of some tender, demonstrative love; the cruel sense that Tom didn't mind what she thought or felt, and that they were no longer playfellows together . . . She wanted some key that would enable her to understand and, in understanding, endure, the heavy weight that had fallen on her young heart. (bk. 4, ch. 3)

Trollope remained sceptical of the power of human thought to stand in place of the creature's doggedly muddling through. But George Eliot was a passionate rationalist. Like Maggie in this, she ardently sought a language of 'explanation' and 'understanding', of links and keys and laws, in the act of finding a form for her novels from within.

To Feuerbach religion was man-made: the invention of God gave a reassuring form and purpose to the multifarious content of human life. But without God, said the High Church novelist Charlotte Yonge writing in *The Monthly Packet* (May 1885), the religious instincts and sentiments of George Eliot's earnest young women, lacking the guiding structure of formal faith, could only be expressed in the yearning of personal feelings. Consequently, argued Charlotte Yonge, Maggie, Dorothea, and Romola might look more earnest and more enthusiastic than truly orthodox believers, but only because George Eliot's were *frustrated* believers.

At the end of *Adam Bede*, it is the Methodist Dinah Morris, the person who most believes in God, who is able to go to the child-murderer Hetty and draw her confession out of her, for the sake of Hetty's peace. But as George Eliot develops onwards from *Adam Bede*, she finds the possibility of direct communication and interference narrowing in the modern secular world. Indirect and often solitary means—writing instead of speaking, reading instead of praying, thinking instead of being counselled—have to serve instead. In the absence of clear new forms of human purpose, Maggie Tulliver is the first of those young women in George Eliot's novels whose half-enlightened emotional struggles, in the words of the 'Prelude' to *Middlemarch*, 'seemed mere inconsistency and formlessness'.

The philosopher Spinoza, whose *Ethics* Marian Evans also translated between the end of 1854 and the beginning of 1856, defined emotion as 'a confused idea'. People suffered and became passive when they could not find the thought hidden confusedly within their feelings; it felt as though a thought were having them, rather than they it. But, for George Eliot, the unresolved predicament of her emotional young women retained within all its suffering and confusion the untransformed preconceptual life stuff of vital need.

It was this pre-linguistic store of unfulfilled experience that music played upon—as though music were a dramatic emotional clue to what true psychic harmony might feel like:

its wondrous harmonies searching the subtlest windings of your soul, the delicate fibres of life where no memory can penetrate, and binding together your whole being past and present in one unspeakable vibration: melting you in one moment with all the tenderness, all the love that has been scattered through the toilsome years

—forming thus one life feeling which blended 'your present joy with past sorrow, and your present sorrow with all your past joy' (*Adam Bede*, ch. 33). Yet for all their romantic music, these young women were 'helped by no coherent social faith and order which could perform the function of knowledge for the ardently willing soul' ('Prelude', *Middlemarch*). Every such young soul seemed left to herself to find, explicitly, what life was *like*, what life was *for*.

Had it not been for the example of Trollope in particular, George Eliot acknowledged, it would have been far harder for her to have had the confidence to make *Middlemarch* as panoramic as it was. Always Victorian critics stressed the 'widening' and 'enlarging' effect of the realist novel, the range of life bringing with it a corresponding extension of 'sympathy' in the reader. But it is not enough for George Eliot to be an immanent realist as Mrs Gaskell and Trollope are, immersed in the multiplicity of an envisioned reality, and content with an implicit language. Characters such as Maggie need for themselves within the novel the equivalent of the deep explicit understanding of life that only George Eliot has from outside and above. In *The Essence of Christianity* Feuerbach offered a useful preliminary distinction between 'life' and 'thought' (ch. 2). 'Life' was the world we lived in, immersed in dependence, but always with the fugitive sense that there was a clearer view to be had of its reality from somewhere above or beyond—whether or not there was anyone or anything out there to do the seeing. 'Thought' was the independent mental effort of the human creature to raise itself to that view of life from outside, while still remaining within it. People in trouble knew the lonely impossibility of trying to think objectively of themselves, while still subjectively remaining what they thought of; yet they needed that extra higher dimension: 'In that hour she repeated what the merciful eyes of solitude have looked on for ages in the spiritual struggles of man . . . she lay on the bare floor and let the night grow cold around her' (*Middlemarch*, ch. 80).

High realism in George Eliot is a product of the effort to sustain existence at both levels: bringing together what it felt like at ground level with some sense of what it all might look like from above. The novel could work at this most easily by splitting the perspective between author above and characters below, employing a language of narration in constant motion inside and out, between the biography and autobiography of its characters. But in George Eliot there is an author who is always drawn back down inside her characters, and there are characters who are frequently struggling on the verge of some semi-transcendent or external view of themselves. In lieu of any coherent social faith and order, 'George Eliot' is the name for the alternative effort to fulfil 'the function of knowledge' for her young strugglers, by finding them a language and not just a music.

Though not the first of the novels, *The Mill on the Floss* (1860) is the starting place from which to see the autobiography not so much

Fig. 11. Frederic Burton, drawing in chalks, *George Eliot*, 1865.
Sensitive as to her personal appearance, she was described by Henry
James, on first meeting her, as 'magnificently ugly . . . this great horse-
faced blue-stocking'. Yet as she began to talk, James found within 'this
vast ugliness' 'a most powerful beauty'—'so that you end, as I ended,
by falling in love with her'.

of Marian Evans as of the process that created 'George Eliot' and culminated in the writing of *Middlemarch* (1872). The first building block in the creation of this code is made up of the simple difference between brother and sister, boy and girl, in both her 'Brother and Sister' sonnets (1874) and *The Mill on the Floss* itself: 'If Tom had told his strongest feeling at that moment, he would have said, "I'd do just the same again." That was his usual mode of viewing his past actions; whereas Maggie was always wishing she had done something different' (bk. 1, ch. 6). Thus, in his encounters with Philip Wakem, Tom simply 'did not see how a bad man's son could be very good' (bk. 2, ch. 3). For him there is only one truth, no conflict, no different levels or considerations, no second thought cutting across the claims of a first. Maggie's is the wider, more sympathetic nature whose very flexibility feels to herself nonetheless like a form of weakness or doubt.

Complexity in George Eliot must feel first of all like a defeat: it checks or baffles first impulses and turns them into second thoughts. As Feuerbach put it: when the pride of the ego first 'stumbles' against the resistance of a 'thou', then 'the consciousness of the world is a humiliating consciousness' (*The Essence of Christianity*, ch. 8). All such corrective moral mutations are characterized initially as painful, not only for the tough like Tom or Adam Bede in learning to be more tender, but also for the tender like Maggie or Romola in having to become more tough: 'The understanding shows us the faults and weaknesses even of our beloved ones; it shows us even our own. It is for this reason that it so often throws us into painful collision with ourselves, with our own hearts' (*The Essence of Christianity*, ch. 2) Those evolutionary shifts—from a first to a second nature, from self to other, from judgement to mitigation, or from affection to knowledge, without the one simply giving way to the other—allowed George Eliot to become a novelist *and* allowed the novelist to see what remains valuable in those who could not make the shift. It was thus essential to George Eliot's purpose that she should split herself to feel for *both* Maggie and Tom whilst simultaneously, superhumanly, seeing the strengths and the weaknesses in each: 'the exhibition of the *right* on both sides being', she wrote to her publisher John Blackwood, 4 April 1861, 'the very soul of my intention in the story'. 'The last refuge of intolerance is in not tolerating the intolerant,' she had said to Sara Hennell, 9 November 1857, 'and I am often in danger of secreting that sort of venom.'

By a similar paradox, the rationalist George Eliot is at her most powerful when the very situations she creates force her language into a sense of reality well-nigh beyond the brink of explanatory reason. As it evolves, the complexity amazes her, as though even the human brain can barely *think out* what human beings themselves just seem able to *do* in ordinary life. So, for example, with Dorothea going to meet her husband, after his consultation with Dr Lydgate as to how long he has to live:

Dorothea had been aware when Lydgate had ridden away, and she had stepped into the garden, with the impulse to go at once to her husband. But she hesitated, fearing to offend him by obtruding herself; for her ardour, continually repulsed, served, with her intense memory, to heighten her dread, as thwarted energy subsides into a shudder; and she wandered slowly round the nearer clump of trees until she saw him advancing. Then she went towards him, and might have represented a heaven-sent angel coming with a promise that the short hours remaining should yet be filled with that faithful love which clings the closer to a comprehended grief. (*Middlemarch*, ch. 42)

From the first impulse to go at once, to the renewed resolve to go after all, Dorothea struggles between her original nature and her acquired experience of rejection—and not just once, but through several waves of alternating feeling. No wonder D. H. Lawrence said of George Eliot's work that all the action was on the *inside*.[5] Even when the action does come out, it comes out as the apparently simple and ordinary 'she went towards him', with no one but the novelist to know all she went through between the first resolve and its renewal. Or what really happened between that renewal and yet another recommitment, in the very face of what she had feared:

His glance in reply to hers was so chill that she felt her timidity increased; yet she turned and passed her hand through his arm.

Yet all her efforts come to the one brief paragraph that follows:

Mr Casaubon kept his hands behind him and allowed her pliant arm to cling with difficulty against his rigid arm.

---

[5] Jessie Chambers ('ET'), *D. H. Lawrence: A Personal Record* (Frank Cass, 1935), 105.

To rescue such things from failure and oblivion requires an alternative language of moral justice, strong enough to deny its being a merely fictional compensation. For one failed act does make a difference, vicariously in the very possibilities of life, to the reader—even though to Dorothea it must remain a failed act. George Eliot builds these self-checking thoughts into her work, always ready as her realism is to turn round upon itself and examine its own real status. Yet finally it is realism in George Eliot that make literature a moral holding ground for meanings that all too often, in a world without the traditional God, would otherwise be unjustly underused or unappreciated, denied, and lost.

That apparently brutal, silent rejection by Casaubon has moreover, simultaneously, its own vulnerable inner story: 'He entered the library and shut himself in, alone with his sorrow.' And as evening deepens into night, Dorothea comes to see that other story too:

The thought with which Dorothea had gone out to meet her husband—her conviction that he had been asking about the possible arrest of all his work, and that the answer must have wrung his heart, could not be long without rising before the image of him, like a shadowy monitor looking at her anger with sad remonstrance. (*Middlemarch*, ch. 42)

Alongside her mental image of her husband, there is 'the thought' of his imminent death and of his own knowledge of it which serves to put that hard image into softer context. She goes out 'with' that thought and it comes back as though of its own accord, 'sad' at what people in trouble can do to each other. Thought is not there in these novels because George Eliot puts it there: heavy-handed, didactic, moralistic, forcing explicitness upon characters and readers alike. Thought exists, substantially if invisibly, as a felt force and a demanding claim in the very air of George Eliot's universe. The more that characters such as Casaubon in *Middlemarch* or Hetty Sorel in *Adam Bede* cannot admit their own thoughts, the more George Eliot's excruciating sensitiveness feels compelled, by the pressure of the reality of those characters in her own imagination, to pick those thoughts up for them. For the thoughts must go somewhere, amidst all the waste of human meaning that realism seeks to rescue in the name of hidden realities. Thoughts as presences, messages, and monitors are 'God' in George Eliot.

It is the sign of Dorothea's movement into a second stage of development that she can begin to imagine beneath the unresponsive appearance of her old scholar-husband 'a sad consciousness in his life which made as great a need on his side as on her own' (ch. 21). For according to Feuerbach thought originally demanded *two* people, in question and answer: 'It is not until man has reached an advanced stage of culture that he can double himself, so as to play the part of another within himself' (*The Essence of Christianity*, ch. 8). To think of two people even if you are one of them, to think of at least two sides to any one person: this was the beginning of the ever-increasing multiplication of complexity which created so many different human centres within the world of *Middlemarch* and so many different cross-cutting thoughts within the novelist's brain. The duty of George Eliot, as novelist, to invent and describe fully those defects of character, which in life itself she would acknowledge in those she loved but wish away, required of her an extraordinary moral stamina, to judge, and an extraordinary susceptibility, to create and to extenuate, which felt like 'hearing the grass grow and the squirrel's heart beat' (*Middlemarch*, ch. 20). Each character, 'each smallest section' of the novel was to have simultaneously 'both its relative and absolute value', in itself and in relation to the whole (*The Saturday Review*, 70 (1886), 725–6). That is the ultimate challenge of George Eliot's intense realism: to be able to bear, through imaginative writing, the spectacle of the whole of ordinary human reality heightened to a degree to which no human being is otherwise biologically adapted.

The authorial pain is registered in depressive mood within the Gothic tale *The Lifted Veil* (1859) where, analogously, the protagonist has a 'super-added consciousness' which allows him an X-ray 'microscopic vision' of 'all the intermediate frivolities, all the suppressed egoism, all the struggling chaos of puerilities' hidden even in the minds of those he loves. In raising herself to super-human demands, by lodging herself with verbal explicitness between her characters in a way that Trollope silently eschewed, George Eliot knew she risked hubris. 'To think is to be God', said Feuerbach (*The Essence of Christianity*, ch. 2), and the omniscient author in George Eliot is not just a literary term but an undertaking on the edge of sanity and the verge of blasphemy. 'I at least have so much to do in unravelling certain human lots, and seeing how they were woven and interwoven,' she writes at the opening of chapter 15 of *Middlemarch*, 'that all the light I can command must be concentrated on this particular web.'

Realism itself to George Eliot risked hubris. She hated writing the beginnings and the conclusions of her books. Partly this was because of the problem of modern formlessness: the life she treats of is essentially that in the middle of affairs, stuck or drifting. But it was also because the boundaries marked by beginnings and endings reminded her of the artificiality of her enterprise. They reminded her that she was writing a book, even while the book was realism's effort to narrow the relation between literature and life, to its nearest possible distance.

But suddenly in the middle of the novels, great visions arise of the structures that lie behind the creation not only of those novels but of human life itself. At one level the following merely arises out of Adam Bede's ashamed antipathy to his own father, whilst also tacitly recalling the family story of Marian Evans and the rejection she suffered from her brother Isaac, when she began her extramarital alliance with George Henry Lewes. But at a higher level, it is another great genetic building block in high realism's formation of a language for human life:

Family likeness has often a deep sadness in it. Nature, that great tragic dramatist, knits us together by bone and muscle, and divides us by the subtler web of our brains; blends yearning and repulsion; and ties us by our heartstrings to the beings that jar us at every movement. We hear a voice with the very cadence of our own uttering the thoughts we despise; we see eyes—ah! so like our mother's—averted from us in cold alienation; and our last darling child startles us with the air and gestures of the sister we parted from in bitterness long years ago. The father to whom we owe our best heritage—the mechanical instinct, the keen sensibility to harmony, the unconscious skill of the modelling hand—galls us, and puts us to shame by his daily errors; the long-lost mother, whose face we begin to see in the glass as our own wrinkles come, once fretted our young souls with her anxious humours and irrational persistence. (*Adam Bede*, ch. 4)

Again, this is not just heavy, leisurely didacticism. It is the sudden linguistic discovery within the novel of the biological ground base that gives human reality, on which the novel itself is modelled, its very form. It only takes another step to reach the vision of that wider human family which is *Middlemarch*—operating like a nineteenth-century version of Edmund Burke's 'great mysterious incorporation of the human race', the whole at any time 'never old, or middle-aged, or young' but 'in a condition of unchangeable constancy', moving on 'through the varied tenour of perpetual decay, fall, renovation, and progression'.[6]

It is the constant interrelation of sameness and difference that is for George Eliot the great mental instrument in the investigation of human reality: 'Knowledge continues to grow by its alternating process of distinction & combination.'[7] In *Middlemarch* the great biological vision in *Adam Bede* is absorbed into the following—as Dr Lydgate urges his wife to help him in the management of their financial difficulties:

'What can *I* do, Tertius?' said Rosamond, turning her eyes on him again. That little speech of four words, like so many others in all languages, is capable by varied vocal inflexions of expressing all states of mind from helpless dimness to exhaustive argumentative perception, from the completest self-devoting fellowship to the most neutral aloofness. Rosamond's thin utterance threw into the words 'What can *I* do?' as much neutrality as they could hold. They fell like a mortal chill on Lydgate's roused tenderness. (ch. 58)

In *Middlemarch* itself, it is Dorothea who is always asking what she can do with her life: 'What is the use of anything I do?' (ch. 42); it is Mrs Bulstrode who stands by her disgraced husband, tacitly asking what she can do for him, in contrast to that 'forsaking which sits at the same board and lies on the same couch with the forsaken soul, withering it the more by unloving proximity' (ch. 74); it is Dr Lydgate himself who feels helplessly obliged to lead the stricken Bulstrode out of the assembly room: 'What could he do? He could not see a man sink close to him for want of help?' (ch. 71). Taking just those four basic little words 'What can I do' is like isolating one representative structure out of which all human diversity is created.

---

[6] Edmund Burke, *Reflections on the Revolution in France* (1790), ed. C. C. O'Brien (Penguin, 1970), 120.

[7] See 'Notes on Form in Art', in Thomas Pinney (ed.), *Essays of George Eliot* (Routledge, 1963), 433, and the opening of ch. 18 ('The Modern Hep! Hep! Hep!') in *The Impressions of Theophrastus Such* (1879).

The basic words are limited, but minute shifts of tone make the meanings and the interpretations almost limitlessly different, creating the experimental *width* of human possibilities across *Middlemarch*. For like Lydgate himself in his scientific research, George Eliot 'wanted to pierce the obscurity of those minute processes which prepare human misery and joy, those invisible thoroughfares which are the first lurking-places of anguish, mania, and crime' (*Middlemarch*, ch. 16). These acts—Rosamond's non-response, Casaubon's rigid arm—may be called 'trivialities', says George Eliot, but it is in these so-called tiny trivialities that in reality 'the seeds of joy are for ever wasted' (*Middlemarch*, ch. 42). George Eliot takes her own microscope to the tiny deep sources of human reality, entering into those molten areas of being where the solid reality of surface words such as 'duty', 'crime', or 'misery' is tested. At that level, says Dorothea in chapter 81, the attraction of a married person to someone other than his or her spouse 'murders our marriage': its real moral name *is* murder, not triviality, though we choose not to hear the grass grow or the squirrel's heartbeat. For if, as Herbert Spencer declared, evolution operates alike in biology and in language, then 'What can I do?' is like a tiny image of the family gene pool that George Eliot spoke of in *Adam Bede*, the simple alphabet out of which human complexity in human characters is generated. 'Nature has her language, and she is not unveracious; but we don't know all the intricacies of her syntax just yet, and in a hasty reading we may happen to extract the very opposite of her real meaning' (*Adam Bede*, ch. 15). That is why to read human life most carefully, George Eliot is what she calls in *Daniel Deronda* 'a wordy thinker' (ch. 13), spelling out deep realities.

But it is not that *Middlemarch* solves the problems of the meaning and purpose of human life. It is rather that the process of questioning creates a force that supports the failure to find the answers. The serious effort at deep metaphysics produces with it, at the very least, a deep psychology and a deep compassion attending it. 'No man is sufficient for the law which moral perfection sets before us; but, for that reason, neither is the law sufficient for man, for the heart' (*The Essence of Christianity*, ch. 3). That is to say, in the face of insufficiency, it is the creation of the sustaining presence of 'George Eliot' herself that is that author's most important contribution to high realism. That intermediate formal presence exists to save the novel from being dismissed as mere fiction, just as surely as it tries to rescue ordinary nineteenth-century life from the imputation of being small and meaningless.

But it is also the case that the ending of *Middlemarch* has to struggle against the disappointment of offering no final goal or destination. Although everything in the writer's career—and in the Victorian period itself—seems to lead to *Middlemarch*, there is another sense in which *Middlemarch* also remains a magnificent by-product of George Eliot's endeavour, making necessary the more flawed and risky writing of *Daniel Deronda* (1876) after it.

'Every man must place before himself a God, *i.e.*, an aim, a purpose', said Feuerbach; 'He who has an aim has a law over him; he does not merely guide himself; he is guided. He who has no aim, has no home, no sanctuary; aimlessness is the greatest unhappiness' (*The Essence of Christianity*, ch. 5). The terror of aimlessness was there from the beginning: in the blankness of the wife of an alcoholic in 'Janet's Repentance' (*Scenes of Clerical Life*, 1858); in the terrible lost wanderings of Hetty Sorel in *Adam Bede*. But it is with *Romola* (1863) that the very denial of aim or thought or law becomes the novel's subject matter.

In the fifteenth-century Florence of *Romola* Tito Melema is George Eliot's early version of modern individualistic man: denying the existence of the moral world that George Eliot's fiction would affirm, in his concern for what is simply pleasant to himself. Again and again, the problem that Tito is to George Eliot forces out of her formulations that go deeper and hold harder than ever before, in an effort to see how far down morality can go within a psychology that denies it. Thus Tito, in denial of the old man who had been as a father to him: 'Am I to spend my life in a wandering search? *I believe he is dead*':

He had chosen his colour in the game, and had given an inevitable bent to his wishes. He had made it impossible that he should not from henceforth desire it to be the truth that his father was dead . . . The contaminating effect of deeds often lies less in the commission than in the consequent adjustment of our desires—the enlistment of our self-interest on the side of falsity. (ch. 9)

This is not just intellectual commentary, it becomes imagination in the form of analysis. For within it there is terrifyingly disclosed within Tito, but unbeknownst to him, a process of gradual, inexorable moral deterioration—'that inexorable law of consequence' which 'acknowledged to be the basis of physical science' is 'still perversely ignored in our social organization, our ethics, and our religion'.[8] The more Tito seeks to evade consequences, the more undeviatingly they track him through his very deviations—here again, in brilliant proposition after proposition, in relation to his wife, Romola:

The terrible resurrection of secret fears, which, if Romola had known them, would have alienated her from him for ever, caused him to feel an alienation already begun between them—caused him to feel a certain repulsion towards a woman from whose mind he was in danger. The feeling had taken hold of him unawares, and he was vexed with himself for behaving in this new cold way to her. (ch. 27)

He was not aware that that very delight in immunity which prompted resolutions not to entangle himself again, was deadening the sensibilities which alone could save him from entanglement. (ch. 18)

It was in one of those apparently 'lawless moments' of his (ch. 13) that Tito, in retreat from the thought of his wife, takes a simple young girl, Tessa, as his mistress:

this creature who was without moral judgment that could condemn him, whose little loving ignorant soul made a world apart, where he might feel in freedom from suspicions and exacting demands, had a new attraction for him now. (ch. 14)

He wanted a little ease, a little repose from self-control . . . he wanted a refuge from a standard disagreeably rigorous, of which he could not make himself independent simply by thinking it folly. (ch. 34)

Refusing to acknowledge abstract concerns as realities, Tito turns them into people instead: morality is only Romola, and Tessa can get him away from her.

In contrast, it is the great religious figure of Savonarola who persuades Romola not to leave her husband, since the breaking of ties means life without law. She returns to Tito, just as Dorothea keeps

[8] Review of Mackay's *The Progress of Intellect* in Pinney (ed.), *Essays of George Eliot*, 31.

returning to Casaubon. But in Dorothea it is done in pity if not love; in Romola—because of what Tito is—it has to be for the sake of the belief, and not for the husband as a person.

Yet Tito's behaviour continues to deteriorate. And at the same time Romola has also to acknowledge flaws within her mentor, Savonarola, which would have been impossible to accept 'if Romola's intellect had been less capable of discerning the complexities in human things' (ch. 52). On both accounts, she is 'thrown back' upon herself in a 'conflict between the demands of an outward law, which she recognized as a widely ramifying obligation, and the demands of inner moral facts which were becoming more and more peremptory' (ch. 56). Tito was the modern man who did not obey the law. Now Romola, in resolving finally to leave Tito, has herself to risk ignoring the outer law. It is done for the sake of something inside her quite different from what lies within Tito, but she cannot yet confidently formulate it as an alternative principle. The problem before her is 'the problem where the sacredness of obligation ended, and the sacredness of rebellion began':

> There had come one of those moments in life when the soul must dare to act on its own warrant, not only without external law to appeal to, but in the face of a law which is not unarmed with Divine lightnings—lightnings that may yet fall if the warrant is false. (ch. 56)

Tito's behaviour not only killed the inner union but then made the external union that remained a set of false duties. Yet though Romola recognizes that the complexity in human things does not make it always possible to fulfil all bonds, she can never fully recover from Tito and be whole again.[9] 'For in strictness there is no replacing of relations: the presence of the new does not nullify the failure and the breach of the old. Life has lost its perfection: it has been maimed' (ch. 69).

The final movement in George Eliot's career lies not with *Middlemarch*'s effort towards bearing that maimedness but with *Daniel Deronda*'s deliberate increase in the realization of it. It is a small,

---

[9] See 'The Antigone and its Moral', *Essays of George Eliot*, 264–5 where it is argued that both Creon and Antigone are conscious that 'in following out one principle, they are laying themselves open to just blame for transgressing another . . . A man must not only dare to be right, he must also dare to be wrong.'

significant measure of the difference that in *Daniel Deronda* the little saint of forbearance in *Middlemarch*, Farebrother the Vicar, is replaced by the corrosively critical musician Klesmer. For *Daniel Deronda* is more a Hebraic book of judgement, in despite of Matthew Arnold's preferred emphasis on Hellenism in *Culture and Anarchy* (1869). Gwendolen Harleth is *Middlemarch*'s Rosamond Vincy, or Cynthia in *Wives and Daughters*, but the representative vain bourgeois girl, now taken much more seriously than she could ever wish to be, under the critical gaze of Deronda himself:

> The darting sense that he was measuring her and looking down on her as an inferior, that he was of different quality from the human dross around her, that he felt himself in a region outside and above her, and was examining her as a specimen of a lower order, roused a tingling resentment which stretched the moment with conflict. (*Daniel Deronda*, ch. 1)

Urgently now, the deep corrosive language that the spectacle of Tito drew out of George Eliot herself is reapplied and spoken directly inside the novel. The indirect procedures of the realist novel are being eschewed: the direct old forms that lay, transmuted, behind it—confession, counsel, protest, judgement, punishment, obedience, prayer, demand—begin to return, freshly alarming, for the sake of a genuine future. Gwendolen is forced to take in the voices of critical thought; thus, Klesmer on her chances of becoming a professional singer:

> For the first time since her consciousness began, she was having a vision of herself on the common level, and had lost the innate sense that there were reasons why she should not be slighted, elbowed, jostled—treated like a passenger with a third-class ticket . . . 'Too old—should have begun seven years ago—you will not, at best, achieve more than mediocrity—-hard, incessant work, uncertain praise—bread coming slowly, scantily, perhaps not at all—mortifications, people no longer feigning not to see your blunders—glaring insignificance'—all these phrases rankled in her. (ch. 23)

There is no mistaking the novel's urgent demand for a fierce adult discipline, an increased consciousness of painful seriousness, even in the face of the lawlessness of Gwendolen's sexual charm.

Before *Daniel Deronda*, George Eliot's fiction had been set in the recent past, the past of the readers' parents or grandparents. The distance gave some relief to the pressures of realism, and it tested the future of old pieties amidst coming changes. But *Daniel Deronda* takes place in the immediate present, a rootless present in danger of forgetting the past and of having no real future. In the few years between the end of *Middlemarch* and the beginning of *Daniel Deronda* it is as though George Eliot sensed that she was living in an English society that was increasingly 'a dwelling-place of lost souls', 'a dead anatomy of culture' (ch. 31). There is no mistaking the change of authorial tone in the face of a sophisticated 'human dross' unwilling and unable to respond to the humanism of George Eliot as anything more than already superannuated and over-earnest. There could be no appeals to the bland worldly Sir Hugo Mallingers or the terminally bored, life-destroying Grandcourts of the world.

'Shall man . . . say, I am an onlooker, ask no choice or purpose of me? That is the blasphemy of this time' (ch. 42). The Jewish visionary Mordecai will not be that onlooker. When Deronda saves Mordecai's sister, Deronda tries to tell Mirah, 'Any other man would have been glad to do what I did', but he in turn is told, 'Saint Anybody is a bad saint to pray to' (ch. 32). Mordecai himself will not say 'If not I, then another', he says 'I': 'an insane exaggeration of his own value . . . many would have counted this' (ch. 38). But there is no polite English-Christian modesty in Mordecai's prophetic belief in himself and in what even in his loneliness he still stands for. He wants to *use* his self, to charge the moment with it, as he says, and to make of Deronda another self to carry on his work towards a new homeland for a race chosen once again to redeem the social world and its values. The huge risk that George Eliot's last novel is committed to taking is like the risk Deronda himself takes in listening to Mordecai though he may be no more than a crank.[10] Every crank has thought he was one of the great misunderstood; every one of the great misunderstood has been put among the cranks: in any one particular case, 'No formulas for thinking will save us' (ch. 41).

In short, *Daniel Deronda* must begin where Romola herself ends—outside the beaten pathways and the accepted languages, for as Mordecai says in a language that bitterly offers an alien challenge to a complacent English audience:

---

[10] On a sometimes characteristic Victorian attempt to minimize risk, see Elaine Freedgood, *Victorian Writing about Risk* (Cambridge University Press, 2000).

'Man finds his pathways: at first they were foot-tracks, as those of the beast in the wilderness; now they are swift and invisible: his thought dives through the ocean, and his wishes thread the air: has he found all the pathways yet? What reaches him, stays with him, rules him: he must accept it, not knowing its pathway.' (ch. 40)

In the dark over-insistent semi-utterances of a Mordecai, whatever reaches or finds readers, readers must make 'stay' with themselves, like content in search of a form in which finally to understand itself.

Deronda is called to the Jews as Fedalma is called to the gypsies in George Eliot's impressive poem *The Spanish Gypsy* (1868): to find within their lost and disinherited memories a people and a faith that links them. But as Mordecai to Deronda, so is Deronda himself—like a middleman, between Hebraic and English cultures—to Gwendolen: a mentor as from 'a region outside and above her'. For her too, even in the English world, the dimensions of reality itself must begin to change. Thus in chapter 28 Gwendolen lies awake in bed on the eve of accepting Grandcourt for a husband, though she had previously promised his mistress that for his mistress's sake and the sake of her children by him, she would do no such thing:

Her state of mind was altogether new: she who had been used to feel sure of herself, and ready to manage others, had just taken a decisive step which she had beforehand thought she would not take—nay, perhaps, was bound not to take. She could not go backward now; she liked a great deal of what lay before her; and there was nothing left for her to like if she went back. But her resolution was dogged by the shadow of that previous resolve which had at first come as the undoubting movement of her whole being.

This is no longer a movement straightforward towards 'what lay before her'. For the complex sentences themselves cannot get away from that previous resolve: she 'had just taken a decisive step which/ she had beforehand thought she would not take'; she 'was appalled at the idea that she was going to do/what she had once started away from with repugnance'. In the midst of those sentences are those missing 'links' Maggie Tulliver needed to make sense of life. But in spite of them Gwendolen is 'on the edge of adopting deliberately, for the rest of her life, what she had rashly said in her bitterness': 'that it did not signify what she did; she had only to amuse herself as best

she could'—the very language of *Romola* is coming back in juxtapositions as terrifying as 'deliberately' with 'rashly'. And now these
thoughts suddenly terrify the person thinking them:

> That lawlessness, that casting away of all care for justification, suddenly
> frightened her; it came to her with the shadowy array of possible calamity
> behind it—calamity which had ceased to be a mere name for her; and all
> the infiltrated influences of disregarded religious teaching, as well as the
> deeper impressions of something awful and inexorable enveloping her,
> seemed to concentrate themselves in the vague conception of avenging
> powers . . . She could bear it no longer, and cried, 'Mamma!'

The future is no longer simply 'before' her: instead, it has 'calamity
behind it'. Her psychological world is turning round upon her,
morally: 'It was new to her that a question of right and wrong in her
conduct should rouse her terror; she had known no compunction
that atoning caresses and presents could not lay to rest.' That is why
she regresses into a child crying for her mother: she wants to go back
to her diminished normality, she wants mechanically to return to her
plan of marrying Grandcourt. But when she does marry him Grandcourt knows that she did so despite her promise to his mistress, and
he makes sure that she finds out he knows. It is intended to make her
feel as corrupt as he is, and it makes their union as terrible as the
long-dead relationship between Mrs Transome and lawyer Jermyn
in *Felix Holt* (1866).

Within that trapped marriage, Deronda keeps offering Gwendolen new ways of thinking. When she speaks of her fear of what she
will do, she is so desperate that Deronda says, 'There is a sort of
remorse before commission, do you understand that?': 'Take your
fear as a safeguard. It is like quickness of hearing. It may make consequences passionately present to you. Try to take hold of your sensibility, and use it as if it were a faculty, like vision' (ch. 36). What is
sought here is an acceleration of evolution, out of the mistakes of the
past before they are made, through the very *fear* of making them. In
the ostensibly comfortable little world of modern England, only
something as ancient as fear can secure real safety, precisely by not
feeling safe. Yet in the same chapter Gwendolen tells Deronda that
she cannot try to make life worthwhile unless she is assured in
advance that it is so: 'What is the good of trying to know more, unless

life were worth more?' But that is her despair, or what the Kierkegaard of *The Sickness unto Death* (1849) would call her despair of despairing, a hopeless, concealed, second-order desperation so characteristic of depressed normality in the nineteenth century. To know in advance of trying is against the book's law of life. The law is closer to Mordecai's risk—that only the future can justify the present's faith in it. I expected someone to come, to follow on from me in my mission, he tells Deronda, and you came. I recognized you when you did not recognize yourself, but you doubt this, as you doubt the idea of predestination itself: 'What are doubts to me? In the hour when you come to me and say, "I reject your soul: I know that I am not a Jew: we have no lot in common"—I shall not doubt. I shall be certain—certain that I have been deluded. That hour will never come!' (ch. 40). There are, concludes Mordecai, two real alternatives: belief and the utter defeat of belief. Anything in between is, like doubt itself, a form of modern non-committed unreality.

In the face of its need for a new collective and a new faith, what is finally terrifying about *Daniel Deronda*, therefore, is the leaving of Gwendolen in that lonely in-between position which, still far short of Mordecai's belief or Deronda's vocation, nonetheless forbids the lost individual's return to unthinking normality. As Deronda leaves for the Middle East, 'The world seemed getting larger round poor Gwendolen, and she more solitary and helpless in the midst':

> That was the sort of crisis which was at this moment beginning in Gwendolen's small life: she was for the first time feeling the pressure of a vast mysterious movement, for the first time being dislodged from her supremacy in her own world, and getting a sense that her horizon was but a dipping onward of an existence with which her own was revolving. (ch. 69)

That after nine hundred pages, this is just a beginning, and a beginning without a clear pathway, is, for George Eliot at least, high realism's final challenge: that humane realism might not suffice if reality as a whole, in people such as Gwendolen, was now becoming increasingly atomized and unreal. Faithfulness to reality might be collusively reductive, if reality as presently understood in the world itself contained no shared faith, no recognized access to dimensions all too easily dismissed as 'emotional' or 'religious'.

10

Lives and Thoughts

Expansion helped to make the Victorian age one of the greatest periods for non-fictional prose. At a time of widening democracy at home and expanding empire overseas, there was increased knowledge and increased curiosity about the ever-burgeoning, diverse subject matter of existence. The climate that produced Victorian realist fiction also produced a non-fictional prose which pursued reality, equivalently, outside the novel. Indeed, discursive prose was the medium through which the Victorians naturally sought to increase the knowledge of human life. Facts, statistics, information, and explanation were all part of the Victorian effort to achieve explicit understanding, in bringing to the forefront of consciousness their own underlying background of social and philosophical changes. That is why non-fictional prose has already figured so largely in the early chapters of this volume, as the medium in which Victorians sought to understand most directly, with the least apparent mediation, their own historical context.

The major public discourses were those of politics and socio-economic concern, history, science, culture, philosophy, and religion. But no realm of discourse was closed to a writer such as John Ruskin:[1] art, history, society, morality, economics, theology—all were sprawlingly intervolved parts of a grand connective project so representative of the Victorian desire for synthesis. To Ruskin the techniques of art were above all human tools, abilities transferable into areas of human life which were themselves not art. Looking at pictures was thus not just to do with learning how to paint but, more than that, with learning how to see. In such a broad context, non-

---

[1] See above, pp. 78–87.

fictional prose seemed the obvious neutral medium, the common meeting ground, for acts of translation between different discourses. So much Victorian writing is committed to what lies outside itself that it is not surprising to find, in the overriding effort to investigate all areas of human concern, a purposeful subordinate prose, relatively unconcerned with its own status, classification, or autonomy.

As so often, it was Thomas Carlyle who first recognized the issue, put the case most forcibly, and then pushed it to extremes. History and the personal form of history which he called biography were, he argued, in the opening of his six-volume *History of Frederick the Great* (1858–65), more truthful than fiction. It was not that their truth was achieved simply by the dry-as-dust research of archives: Carlyle insisted on the necessity of imagination. But the Scottish puritan in him stressed that it was imagination not for purposes of invention but for the re-creation of character and times. Carlyle believed that, by using the human faculties misused in fiction, the writing of history got closer to true reality than fiction could ever do.

Nonetheless, it remained all too easy for the study of history to falsify, indeed to deaden, the experience of the life of the past by the mere use of hindsight: 'For, observe, always one most important element is surreptitiously (we not noticing it) withdrawn from the Past Time: the haggard element of Fear!' (*The French Revolution*, 3 vols. (1837), vol. 3, bk. 2, ch. 4). Instead, by reimagining the past in the living chaos of its present, Carlyle sought to find within the testing ground of history those few individuals who had managed to grasp the true nature of their age at the time, rather than relying upon its artificial forms and formulas.

In the heat of unprecedented revolution, when a whole nation was hurled suddenly beyond known limits, most men's words were poor exponents of their thoughts, and their conscious thoughts poor exponents of the reality of what was happening to them. In the midst of the French Revolution Louis XVI had been as blind as had been Charles I in the English Revolution: both were left stranded with the empty name, the mere theatre and fiction of kingship. The bourgeois semi-revolutionary Girondin party, caught between seeking popularity on the one hand and respectability on the other, were to find that 'the Reality will not translate into their Formula; that they and their Formula are incompatible with the Reality: and, in its dark wrath, the Reality will extinguish it and them!' (*The French Revolu-tion*, vol. 3, bk. 3, ch. 5). Instead, the Revolutionary Government of Robespierre simply threw itself blindly into the whirlpool of forces which it helped to create and which helped to create it. Only Mirabeau and Danton, thought Carlyle, had been as Cromwell had been in the English Revolution—instinctively in touch with the truth of their times, embodying it at a deep level of intuitive being, silently anterior to the noisy distortions of common consciousness. Cromwell 'had *lived* silent; a great unnamed sea of Thought round him all his days; and in his way of life little call to attempt naming or uttering that'. The real intellect of this sort of instinctive knower lay not in 'speaking and logicising' but in the faith and courage of seeing and acting (*On Heroes and Hero-Worship* (1841), lecture 6).

Such were men of what Carlyle called Nature rather than Art, of reality rather than fiction. It is what Carlyle himself aspired to be in the midst of the confused history of England in the 1840s: that is why his prose had to seek to be emphatically non-fictional. For the Carlylean hero can be poet, prophet, king, priest 'according to the kind of world he finds himself born into': they are all 'originally of one stuff', and the mere medium in which they find expression—be it Shakespeare or Cromwell, Muhammad or Burns—hardly matters to Carlyle (*On Heroes and Hero-Worship*, lectures 3 and 2). The powers that go into writing are themselves latter-day versions of what in earlier worlds made the great man a god or a prophet. Originally those powers did not belong to art but to the perception of truth and the undertaking of action: they should not now degener-ate into consciousness, formalism, and artifice. That is why Carlyle's language is so cumulatively cajolling, seeking imaginatively to sum-mon realities direct, virtually regardless of the medium. His *French Revolution* may have been an inspiration for Dickens's fictional *Tale of Two Cities* (1859), but Carlyle's was the extreme version of a non-fictional prose offered as an *alternative* to art—art in realist transla-tion.

I. Life-Writing

Out of a characteristic mixture of confidence and uncertainty, the Victorians seemed to want everything. In their need to understand the processes of human development even from within the midst of its history, they wanted knowledge not only of their own time but of other times: hence George Grote and George Finlay on the history of ancient Greece, and Charles Merivale and John Bury on ancient Rome; Freeman, Stubbs, and Maine on early English history, and Froude, Gardiner, and Macaulay on later periods from the sixteenth century onwards; as well as J. R. Green on English social history, and Buckle, Leslie Stephen, and Lecky on intellectual history in both England and Europe. But the Victorians wanted knowledge not only of different times but of different places and of different people too—as though the whole world of experience were somehow, even confusingly, up for grabs. The literature of travel and of biography are the subject of this section.

First, places. The literature of exploration and travel reflected the way in which the whole world seemed to be opening up through the reach and confidence of the British Empire. The greatest expansion of the Empire only occurred during the last three decades of the Queen's reign, after Disraeli's purchase of the Suez Canal in 1875 and the granting to Victoria of the title empress of India in 1876. Then followed the rapid acquisition of territories in Africa, South-East Asia, and the Pacific. Nonetheless, in the earlier decades of the reign, Britain as the workshop of the world had already developed its interest in expanding trading links. To existing colonies in Australia, Canada, the Caribbean, and the Cape, New Zealand was added in 1840, Hong Kong in 1842, and India in 1858.

As so often, Victorian projects could hold together a wide variety of overlapping interests: the mapping of the world could include the national duties and responsibilities involved in the governmental desire for objective administrative information, the scientists' need for factual data, and the mercantile concern for new sources of supply and new markets—all contained within a spirit of adventure. Under the broad ideal of 'service', a British consul such as Richard Burton or missionaries such as David Livingstone could also be explorers, the scholar Richard Curzon is taken out of the study in the search for ancient manuscripts recounted in *Monasteries of the Levant* (1849), and the military man John Speke became the proud author of the *Discovery of the Source of the Nile* (1835). The very width of its appeal meant that Livingstone's *Missionary Travels* sold 70,000 copies within months of its publication in 1857. Reflecting this diversity of purposes, it became standard practice to assign naturalist observers and recorders to naval surveying expeditions. This system produced the early work of Charles Darwin, Alfred Wallace, and Thomas Huxley, and of the great English traveller in South America, the naturalist Charles Waterton, thus nurturing by pre-professional means the development of professional science.

As a consequence, it is nearly impossible today to read the free-standing journal entries in Charles Darwin's *The Voyage of the Beagle* (1839) save in the light of their contribution to the development of the ideas in *The Origin of Species* twenty years later. Thus 20 February 1835: an earthquake visibly produced within seconds changes usually so imperceptibly gradual as to exceed the lifetime not only of a single man but of many generations—'A bad earthquake at once destroys our oldest associations: the earth, the very emblem of solidity, has moved beneath our feet like a thin crust over a fluid—one second of time has created in the mind a strange idea of insecurity' (*The Voyage of the Beagle*, ch. 14). Suddenly, geography gives way to geology, space goes back in time. The very mission to bring the powers of civilization to bear upon unregulated or unknown primitive wildernesses begins to turn round on itself: 'Nothing is more certain to create astonishment than the first sight in his native haunt of a barbarian—of man in his lowest and most savage state. One's mind hurries back over past centuries, and then asks, could our progenitors have been men like these?' (ch. 21). What the years between 1831 and 1836 on HMS *Beagle*'s voyage around South America offered Darwin was what he later lost inside his study: the sense of the pure naturalness of imagination, taking its place in the midst of the practical life of observation: 'The limit of man's knowledge in any subject possesses a high interest, which is perhaps increased by its close neighbourhood to the realms of imagination' (ch. 13; 30 December 1834). The sight of rows of polypi, each with its own distinct body, yet all acting together as though they were a single mind, provokes the primal thought: 'what is an individual?' (ch. 5).

As the great scholar-adventurer, Richard Burton put it in his *Personal Narrative of a Pilgrimage to Al-Medinah and Mecca* (2 vols., 1855), on riding across the great dangerous open spaces of the desert: 'It is another illustration of the ancient truth that Nature returns to man, however unworthily he has treated her' (vol. 1, ch. 8). That return to nature, that renewed sense of life's inherent risk outside England, was not just a reversion to mere animal existence: life seemed the right way round again, said Burton, when mind followed body instead of leading it—senses, spirits, powers of sight, memory, and imagination all alike invigorated. And yet you knew that when you returned to the tamed comforts of sedentary civilization, you would lose all this in the physical and psychological constrictions of 'artificial life'. A. W. Kinglake, author of *Eothen* (1844), a lively, often humorous personal account of his journey in the Levant, took up his travels precisely in order to get away from the stifling career of a barrister.

It was apt that for writers whose works were focused on the phenomena of contingency, untethered chance should play a major role in creating the literature of exploration. Edward Lane first went to Egypt for the sake of the climate, on account of his poor health: the result was his *Account of the Manners and Customs of the Modern Egyptians* (1836) and his influential translation of *The Thousand and One Nights* (1838–40). The young Austen Layard was supposed to be en route to a job with a friend of the family in Ceylon but, financed instead as an informal observer and agent to the British ambassador in Turkey, became one of the great excavators, the author of *Nineveh and its Remains* (1849) and *Discoveries in the Ruins of Nineveh and Babylon* (1853).

Yet what began with chance became something to do with alternative or lost freedom, with curiosity in the exploration of other ways. Freed from the conventional home-bound assumptions which his travels showed to be no more than relative, Burton above all found in the East a physical mentality which also involved an education in the arts of sexual love wholly lacking in the West (hence in his last years his translation of the *Kama Sutra*). One-half bohemian chancer, the other half of Burton belongs with the inscrutable wise men of the East, the Sufis. For he constantly takes on disguises—in particular in his attempt to be one of the first men of the West to penetrate the holy shrines of Mecca—partly out of the free chameleon delights of risk, but also for the serious impassive purpose of being at once *in* the society and yet not *of* it. And hidden inside the quasi-scientific factuality of the empirical Western ethnographer is a way of seeing also spiritually half-Eastern—a disposition which, almost passive in its detached attention, was implicitly opposed to the perpetual commitment of all physical and mental powers to the demands of the Western work ethic.

In Europe, the opportunity for informal travel was facilitated by the end of the Napoleonic Wars and the development of the steamships and railways. The European tour, which before had been mainly the privilege of the aristocracy, became available by mid-century to the more prosperous middle classes. In 1836 the publisher John Murray began producing a series of handbooks for travellers, the best of which is probably Richard Ford's learned, detailed, but also animatedly anecdotal *Handbook for Travellers in Spain* (1845). Thomas Cook began organizing tours to France, the Rhine, Italy, Switzerland, and the United States in the late 1850s and early 1860s. But it was not merely 'the greater facilities of locomotion' that created what W. H. Davenport Adams in his *Celebrated Women Travellers* (1880) described as the 'great and rapid increase in the number of female travellers': it was a phenomenon due above all, he argued, 'to the greater freedom which women of late years have successfully claimed, and to the consequent development of powers and faculties, their possession of which was long ignored or denied' (pp. 383–4).

It was what Adams called 'the mixed character' of these expeditions that was most striking: for here were Victorian ladies, often spinsters committed to quite conventional proprieties, who nonetheless became amazingly tough and courageous explorers of the wild. Gone was the lady languishing on her sofa, silently oppressed by ideals of domestic devotion or frail femininity. Isabella Bird (1831–1904), a depressive sufferer from spinal injury from an early age, in her forties rode on horseback alone amidst the Rocky Mountains, even through snowstorms (*A Lady's Life in the Rocky Mountains*, 1879). The delight in reading the work of a generation of women born in the 1830s—Isabella Bird, Amelia Edwards in *A Thousand Miles Up the Nile* (1877), Marianne North in her posthumously published *Recollections of a Happy Life* (1892)—comes from their own unfrightened joy in finding a new expanded life, a release into what feels like natural life itself, in the large open spaces of the world. For women who were not hitherto professional writers, the writing itself both resulted from and added to that sense of new vitality. Though theirs was not the discovery of the sources of the Nile, it was discovery and it was exploration—not least of themselves. There is their liberating joy at the sheer size and detail of the landscape— in particular at the 'daily miracles' of sunrise and sunset in the world. And with it there is also a sort of transported domesticity, in the Englishwoman's determined yet courteously flexible capacity to adapt herself to residence in any remote corner of the globe.

It was, said an early reviewer of 'Lady Travellers' in *The Quarterly Review* (June 1845), the absence of ulterior *purpose* in these women's writings that made them so different from the sweeping generalities and preconceived ideas too often enforced on the world by equivalent male authors. Their volumes were often self-edited compendia of journals on location and of letters home: Emily Eden's *Up the Country* (1866), for example, was a collection of letters written from India between 1837 and 1840, when her brother was governor-general. These works were like prose versions of the Victorian sequence poems,[2] they stayed with the absorbing exigencies of the present, often forgetting the past or future back in England, in a continuing journey unshaped and unharassed by the novelistic requirement of narrative outcome. Indeed, the most powerful element in *A Lady's Life in the Rocky Mountains* is what does not happen: the impossible, unfulfilled love affair between plain Isabella Bird and her unlikely soulmate of a mountain guide whose face is one-half beautiful, one-half ravaged by a bear and whose life, equivalently, is partly still heroic and chivalric and partly lost in dissipated ruin.

Interestingly, the finest *domestic* version of the informal spirit expressed in these journals from abroad is to be found hidden in the private incidental diaries of a young man, living the leisured life of

---

[2] See below, pp. 498–512.

a gentleman-curate in Wales and Wiltshire. Though not published until 1938–40, *Kilvert's Diary* was written from 1870 to 1879—significantly, before the man's life was about to take shape. The Rev Francis Kilvert died quite suddenly in 1879, aged 39, a few weeks after he had got married and had given up writing his diary.

What is impressive is how *unexpectedly* memorable and compelling the passing descriptive details of the life of common things turn out to be for the reader. It's a hot day on 10 August 1871:

The sheep grazed in the grassy avenue or lay under the trees grunting and groaning with their bright red bodies panting in the heat and their white foolish curly horned faces stretched out upon the ground. Now and then came up the avenue the tinkle of the wandering bell.

'It's warm,' said I to the stout flushed bearded postman.

'Ah, Sir,' he said, ''tis something more than that.'

Yet nothing more is made of it. The value exists purely *inside* the relished quality of the present moment, postman and sheep flushed alike. A Welsh mountain landscape in mist and sudden sunlight—superior, writes Kilvert, to anything he had seen even among the Alps—goes unexploited and unshared: 'A man came whistling along the road riding upon a cart horse. I would have stopped him and drawn his attention to the mountains but I thought he would probably consider me mad' (14 March 1871). Nor is it just the sensuousness of landscapes that affects him—a beautiful Irish girl lingers temptingly, as she leaves the train: 'A wild reckless feeling came over me. Shall I leave all and follow her? No—Yes—No. At that moment the train moved on' (Wednesday 19 June 1872). Frequently he meets a young woman on what he thinks may turn out to be the most important day of his life—but comically it continually turns out to be 'No'. *Kilvert's Diaries* could not exist as they do without the example of both Wordsworth and John Keble in celebrating the common round of life, or without that particularly sensuous and fleshly version of down-to-earth Protestantism that Kilvert shares with Charles Kingsley. Yet for all these unconscious influences, the diaries retain the freely contingent, episodic, and unharassed quality of a life merely going on in time.

And yet of course Victorian travel- and diary-writing isn't always so provisional and tentative in respect of time, so liberal or impartial in relation to place. Often it is much more publicly assertive and official. Take, for example, the travel diaries that Frances Trollope, mother of the future novelist, wrote up into *Domestic Manners of the Americans* (1832). Her first book, published when she was 53, it was written to salvage something—not least financially—from the family troubles which had sent Mrs Trollope out to America in the first place, leaving her depressive husband and elder sons behind in England. What she saw in America was a new world, with barely a history or a culture—an accelerated version of the Industrial Revolution in England, rapidly taming and exploiting the natural resources of a vast continent, whilst simultaneously seeking to establish a free democracy. Harriet Martineau's *Society in America* (1837), Charles Dickens's *American Notes* (1842), and Matthew Arnold's *Discourses in America* (1885) and *Civilization in the United States* (1888) were products of a similar fascination with what seemed a test case of England's possible future.

But what irritated Mrs Trollope, from her downright English point of view, was that America was neither a primitive nor a cultured society but a semi-educated world dishonestly boasting of its republicanism, its individualistic liberty, and its equality, while at the same time defending black slavery and worshipping the dollar. A book as robustly opinionated as *Domestic Manners of the Americans* requires to be read in two ways. First in its own terms, like a novel, moving across genres: for whatever as social history it lacks in objectivity, it gains in the subjectivity of autobiography—in the expressive portrait of a spirited woman unashamed of her capacity for honest comic dislike. Good as she is, for example, on the vulgarity and sexual hysteria of revivalist meetings, the question of historical accuracy in her targets is not so much the issue, even if it could be reliably determined: what a reader relishes in Fanny Trollope is not fairness, but the thought that *if* these things do imaginably exist as she says they do, then indeed the attitude she has in dismissing them seems a salutary boost to life, in all the bold straightforwardness of early Victorianism. Second, in terms external to itself, such a book can remain valuable not because it is right but because it does not shrink from doing its thinking in the right places. Genuinely opposed to slavery, Mrs Trollope nonetheless dares to report in chapter 16 her impression that slaves at least gave their service with more easy goodwill than ever was given by the whites who doggedly earned proper wages in domestic work. Money-relations were far from producing the equality of which Americans boasted. Yet she adds in a later footnote that, on reflection, the grudging service given by wage earners is not so much inferior to the slave system as the result of the existence of slavery itself, rendering the very idea of domestic service shameful. Even by its roughness, this reproduces the very chronology of thinking, of the experience of first and second thoughts, in areas of genuine social difficulty.

Yet always Victorian travel-writing is at its most impressive when marked by a sense of truly unexpected strangeness, at whatever level it occurs. In Dickens this is at its most melancholy in *Pictures from Italy* (1846) where, unable to speak the language, the writer finds himself in a land that seems to him arrested in its own history, without motion, effort, or advancement—an energetic modernizer caught in the midst of a sort of living death. But when Dickens travels to modern America, what fascinates him in Boston is the particular predicament of a deaf, dumb, and blind girl, living 'in a marble cell, impervious to any ray of light, or particle of sound, with her poor white hand peeping through a chink in the wall, beckoning to some good man for help' (*American Notes*, ch. 3). In *The Englishwoman in America* (1856), Isabella Bird argued that it was the similarity of language that encouraged continual overgeneralized comparisons between America and England (ch. 19), but in *American Notes* it is a specific girl with no communicative language at all who suddenly stirs Dickens's imagination. Off-duty in Boston's impressive school for the blind, the artist in Dickens unconsciously locates an image not only of his own childhood trauma, the boy sent out to work at the blacking warehouse, but of the deepest secret fears within his own fiction: the figure of a trapped inside, unspeakably separated from the world without. Even for writers far inferior to Dickens, travel-writing offered an alternative context for the writing of a more innocent form of autobiography—not by directly looking at the self, but by revealing it through what it sees. That distinction also applies to the literature of biography.

In terms of major biography, the period begins of necessity by looking backwards, with the publication of Lockhart's seven-volume

Memoirs of the Life of Sir Walter Scott (1837–8) the great successor to Boswell's epic *Life of Johnson*. In an early review Carlyle praised Lockhart for his frankness in defying the forces of respectable cant by disclosing Scott's financial imprudence. Scott's dream of establishing a feudal home for himself at Abbotsford had involved him in financial difficulties which eventually led to bankruptcy. For the last six years of his life he struggled desperately against failing powers to earn enough by his writings to settle the losses of his creditors, whilst always fearing the decline in their quality.

It was this struggle against final failure which most moved R. H. Hutton when in his volume on *Sir Walter Scott* in John Morley's 'English Men of Letters' series (1878), he produced what he admitted was virtually an introductory abridgement of Lockhart. Up until the point of bankruptcy Scott was what Hutton in his final chapter called 'a nearly complete natural man, and no more': a naturally gifted craftsman who worked on in silence as to his literary ends, not expecting his work to serve social or political reform. What calamity showed was 'something above nature, something which could endure, though every end in life for which he had fought so boldly should be defeated'. The sheer strain on his mental faculties for the sake of honour made him a lesser writer, but showed him a greater man—and for Hutton it was that very disparity which called for the justice of a final compensatory act of writing, not by Scott, but on Scott's behalf, in the biographical completion of his story. It was the closing failure, not the previous huge successes, 'which made it clear how much greater the man was than his ends, how great was the mind and character which prosperity failed to display'. That is what biography existed for: to register the deep sense of a person as ever implicitly more than the ends he thought he was aiming at, be they the establishment of Abbotsford, or the satisfaction of his debtors. As the man's own writing failed, what the biography helped witness was the greatness transplanted out of the work, out of its art, and seen separately for once in the human force of the life itself.

To Ruskin, who began but never completed his own abridgement of Lockhart's *Life* in *Fors Clavigera* (1871–4, commencing letter 31), Scott was the one writer who had lived a natural human life of body as well as mind, writing in the morning, working for the rest of the day in his woods. People, insisted Ruskin, could not really live only by reading and writing or teaching and learning (letters 58, 93). As part of Victorian realism, it was characteristic of Victorian literary biography to believe that literature was important, precisely because it contained within it all that, in life, was more important than literature itself. Much of the chivalric and feudal spirit of *Fors Clavigera* is thus derived from taking Scott's vision out of his novels and reapplying it within a non-fictional form of expression. For truly to know a fellow creature, said Carlyle in an early essay on 'Biography' (1832), was 'not only to see into him, but even to see out of him, to view the world altogether as he views it'. Novels were imaginary biographies. But like the reader of a novel, the reader of a biography could not only 'theoretically construe' its subject but 'almost practically personate him'—and do so in the service of real life, turning books back into living thoughts and actions (*Critical and Miscellaneous Essays*, 3 vols. (1887), vol. 2, p. 247).

Yet all that followed from this, according to Lytton Strachey, was the standard, respectable Victorian 'Life and Letters', 'those two fat volumes, with which it is our custom to commemorate the dead': 'Who does not know them, with their ill-digested masses of material, their slipshod style, their tone of tedious panegyric, their lamentable lack of selection, of detachment, of design? They are as familiar as the *cortège* of the undertaker' (*Eminent Victorians* (1918), preface). In fact the publication of a 'Life and Letters' often revived contemporary interest. *The Life, Letters and Literary Remains of John Keats* which appeared in two volumes in 1848, edited by Richard Monckton Milnes (1809–85), did much to create Keats's posthumous reputation. But Strachey is thinking of Stanley's biography of Thomas Arnold or John Morley's life of Gladstone. And the accusation is twofold: of biographies bulgingly unselective through lack of artistry; and where selective, selective only through the censorships of piety. With his charges of repression and hypocrisy, it is with Strachey and the generation that followed so reactively upon the last Victorians, that modern suspicion begins: Carlyle may have admired the way in which Lockhart revealed Scott's failings, but why didn't Froude mention Carlyle's own impotence? why didn't Mrs Gaskell reveal Charlotte Brontë's entanglement with a married man abroad? why didn't Forster expose Ellen Ternan, Dickens's young mistress?

But issues of piety and decorum were not simply public fronts or automatic duties. They existed in the tension which biographers experienced between the claims of affectionate loyalty and of critical judgement—all the more so when they were, as so often, the friends or relatives of their own recently deceased subjects. Froude, for example, as Carlyle's trusted friend and disciple, was vilified for what he did reveal of the unhappiness of the Carlyle marriage in his four-volume *Life* (1882, 1884). Yet he did so to complete the frank atonement which Carlyle himself felt he owed his neglected wife Jane, when at the age of 70, shortly after her death, he read his wife's journal. It was an atonement which Carlyle had bequeathed to Froude along with all his and his wife's private papers. And so, in between his volumes on the early and later life of Carlyle, Froude duly published the *Letters and Memorials of Jane Welsh Carlyle* in 1883—a work which shows all the ruefully sharp intelligence of the Victorian witty woman ('I too am here').

The *Life* of the eighteenth-century poet George Crabbe (1834), *The Memorials of Thomas Hood* (1860), and the *Memoir* of Tennyson (1897) were compiled by the poets' children with a tender piety so markedly different from Edmund Gosse's *Father and Son* (1907). The partisan *Letters and Memorials* of Charles Kingsley (1884) was edited by his wife, Mary—ending with one of the most powerful accounts of the deathbed since that of Crabbe. Written or rather edited from the subject's letters and diaries, with as little authorial intrusion as possible, the Victorian 'Life and Letters' sought to present, with appropriate decorum, the private side of a public life, off-duty amidst friends and family, in the attempt to get close to the heart of the subject's inner life.

In literary-historical terms the novel of sensibility is in origin epistolary, as in the eighteenth-century novels of Samuel Richardson: the movement from letters to the novel is part of the history of prose. But these biographies partly reverse that history—particularly when their subject was a creative writer—by turning back from literature to letters and non-literary writings. The courtship correspondence between Robert Browning and Elizabeth Barrett in 1845 and 1846 was not published until 1899 and was not put within a biographical framework. Yet the two-sided reading makes tenderly clear what a vulnerable venture in relationship writing originally is, across the difficulties of distance, in complex dual awareness of both self and recipient, in the movement towards marriage. By the assembly of such letters, Victorian biographies were intended to serve as compensatory, surrogate autobiography, not flattening their subjects into third-person narratives but giving respectful room for something as close as possible to the original. Biography becomes a kind of literary criticism, reassembling the spirit of dead men and women out of their texts and documents. Its generosity of form was intended to allow the picture of a life to compose *itself*, gradually and cumulatively, by the same mysterious connecting force of recognition that, said Newman, fundamentally connected the portrait of a child with the portrait of the adult it grows into, across the many differences that separated the two.

What makes the biographical use of a sequence of letters different from the use of incidental letters and journals in the literature of travel is not only the framing narrative presence of the biographer. It is also the concomitant presence of a second dimension of time which Carlyle rightly associated with the writing of any sort of history: the equivocal advantages and disadvantages of hindsight and retrospect. For it is there—in what Mrs Gaskell calls 'looking back, with the knowledge of what was then the future' (*Life of Charlotte Brontë* (1857), ch. 26)—that the issue of tentative fellow-human delicacy most poignantly arises, especially when the biographer looks back at how a protagonist, now deceased, once looked forward.[3] Or, alternatively, the biographer discloses behind the apparently secure and successful face of the public figure the memory of something far more insecure that nonetheless contributed to the success. That is how it was in John Forster's *Life of Charles Dickens* (3 vols., 1872–4), when Forster for the first time revealed how Charles Dickens had never got over being sent out to work in a bootblacking factory by his parents, at the age of 12. 'I do not write resentfully or angrily: for I know how all these things have worked together to make me what I am.' Nonetheless, Dickens goes on: 'Even now, famous and caressed and happy, I often forget in my dreams that I have a dear wife and children; even that I am a man; and wander desolately back to that time of my life.' Although he only worked in the factory for a

---

[3] See Christopher Ricks, *Essays in Appreciation* (Oxford University Press, 1998), 'Victorian Lives', esp. on Charlotte Brontë's own premonitions of family death and fear of looking forward (118–45).

few months in 1824, for many years after the trauma Dickens could hardly bear to go near the place, could hardly himself believe that he was after all a secure adult and father: 'My old way home by the Borough made me cry, after my eldest child could speak' (*Life*, vol. 1, bk. 1, ch. 2). His parents never afterwards spoke of what they had done, and Dickens in turn never spoke of it to his own family. Instead he used the memory in his writing. It was clear now: the literature did not come out of nowhere, not even out of inventive genius alone. It came from all that Carlyle meant by his key word for anterior, pre-literary reality: silence.

Moreover, when Forster compares the autobiographical fragment which Dickens left him with the use Dickens made of it, several months after its composition, in the writing of *David Copperfield*, he can see that despite the chronological structure of the biography which tells its story, the life of the writer is not a serial process in which the past merely gets left behind: the memory keeps going back, helping to create the works that take the life forward. In these ways the biography of writers offered the later nineteenth century an inner view of people who had found a way to keep *using* their lives and memories. But the more they examine the complex effect of their protagonists' vulnerabilities across time, the more biographers such as Forster, Froude, and Mrs Gaskell are also aware of the paradox which makes the best biographies almost cancel themselves out: namely, that the life which in retrospect the biographers show moving assuredly forwards could not possibly have been lived like that, from within. Writers, in particular, had actually to make, to create, their own way.

So, in her *Life of Charlotte Brontë* Mrs Gaskell tells the story of an elder daughter and elder sister who, with an eccentric widowed father, a dissolute brother and amidst poor family health, had actually to learn how to make the home and family humanly habitable. 'The little Brontës had been brought up motherless; and from knowing nothing of the gaiety and the sportiveness of childhood—from never having experienced caresses or fond attentions themselves—they were ignorant of the very nature of infancy' (ch. 10). When the sisters tried to earn a living away from home as a governess, they were clearly asocial, almost abnormal by nature; they felt lonely and put on protective exteriors. When they thought of taking pupils into their home, there was the shame and danger of the drunken half-maddened Branwell. By an act of will, by using the language of duty, Charlotte Brontë forced herself not only to stay at home and remain single but to become representatively normal—kind and responsible—for the sake of the others. Hence her apologetic preface to her sister Emily's *Wuthering Heights*, for its strange wildness. Hence *Villette*, the story of a spy in a strange society, trying to learn its human ways whilst hiding her own. Only after the death of her sisters—'the two human beings who understood me, and whom I understood'—does Charlotte Brontë make explicit to herself her commitment as a writer and her defiance of the critics: 'The loss of what we possess nearest and dearest to us in this world, produces an effect upon character: we search out what we have yet left that can support, and, when found, we cling to it with a hold of new-strung tenacity' (ch. 18). In contrast, for all the early loss of her mother and the painful remarriage of her father, Mrs Gaskell knew, gratefully, how relatively easy it had been for *her* to normalize herself as wife and mother, and use that experience of everyday normality in her writing.

Thus, what becomes important in reading these biographies is not just the information offered with regard to their subject, but the underlying relationship between biographer and subject, implicated in the very writing of the book. It hurts Forster to witness how, increasingly after the writing of the autobiographical *David Copperfield*, Dickens could never stay inside himself but restlessly used himself up and wore himself out instead.

Likewise, it makes a difference in reading the letters in *The Memorials of Thomas Hood* (2 vols., 1860) that the volume was assembled, fifteen years after their father's death, by Hood's own son and daughter.[4] 'We have thought it best not to omit any of [his] frequent mentions of his children', write the editors, apologetically: to strike out those passages would be to 'fail to show the warmth of his domestic affections' (vol. 2, p. 54). Silently they witness the way their father used jokes and puns, even borrowing from his children a comic childishness, in order to stave off the underlying adult fact of his approaching death. The brother and sister are long since grown

---

[4] See above, pp. 349–50.

up enough to understand more consciously the problems of health and finance that Hood had only half-succeeded in keeping below the surface happiness of family life, as he simultaneously struggled to continue his work as comic author:

> Although Hood's 'Comic Annual', as he himself used to remark with pleasure, was in every house seized upon, and almost worn out by the frequent handling of little fingers, his own children did not enjoy it till the lapse of many years had mercifully softened down some of the sad recollections connected with it. (vol. 2, p. 249)

The use of the third person ('his own children') is not merely formal and stuffy. And, likewise, Hood's own cheery disguises are not hypocrisy and only in part evasion: there is a tacit protective tenderness in and around this book, both past and present, in the father *and* in his grown-up children, which of its nature must half-conceal and half-reveal the truth. It is true that the editors do not admit how, unsurprisingly, the marriage of father and mother had nearly broken down under the strain. But when things are *not* said in the *Memorials*, it is because of that damaged and still vulnerable loving tenderness in the book which is the best defence of piety and delicacy as something other than merely social hypocrisy or repression.

These biographies have genuinely to struggle with the recognition that the lives they describe are not in any sense ideal. In his essays on 'The Lives of the Saints' and Emerson's 'Representative Men' in volume 1 of his *Short Studies on Great Subjects* (4 vols., 1867–83) Froude contrasted the lives of medieval saints with modern biographies. The lives of the saints were all monotonously similar, because they were indeed ideal, because they were meant as heroic 'patterns of a form of human life' which other Christians were to imitate and realize within their own limits. Modern biographies were more varied, more individual, more free, and yet in consequence, though less idealized, were also less exemplary and more ambivalent, because personality was not simply sacrificed to a sense of formal function greater than itself. The difference was a measure of the gains in the freedom of individuality and the losses in certainty of function to be found in the world of the nineteenth century.

The Lives of the Engineers by Samuel Smiles (3 vols., 1861–2) was an attempt to offer exemplary portraits of practical, self-made men—such as James Watt, George Stephenson, Thomas Telford—in terms of the new professions of the Industrial Revolution. Alternatively, A. P. Stanley's *Life and Correspondence of Thomas Arnold* (2 vols., 1844) showed its headmaster-protagonist offering Rugby school as a world against the world, an ethical version of the Empire in which the sixth form in particular served as a model of how to produce moral individuals for sake of the future. The boys were educated to withstand discouragement from the crowd in the outside world by the strength of their inner resources.

Still, for Froude, as for Carlyle, the great examples came from figures of the past. But they, being unequivocal men of action and belief, could hardly be imitated in the modern world and we merely read about them instead. In his *Life of Sterling* (1851) Carlyle had shown that the only place left in the nineteenth century for an educated life which could neither devote itself to religion on the one hand nor commit itself to politics on the other was to be found in the holding ground of literature. The representative figures of the present were the writers and thinkers—precisely for being less single-minded, less involved in the primary immediacy of reality than the heroes of the past, and more aware instead of the myriad of individual differences and of relative points of view involved in the difficulty of making or finding a life.

No biography shows this more than J. W. Cross's *George Eliot's Life* (1885). For the life of George Eliot is a version of what is described in her own 'Prelude' to *Middlemarch*: it marks the endeavour, amidst personal inconsistency, modern formlessness, and the indefiniteness of a woman's position in the world, to find a vocation by which to shape a life. The struggle of Marian Evans (or Mary Ann or Marion—she never could decide on her own name), born 1819, to become George Eliot, born 1856, is the story of how the protagonist could only really develop into a grown-up woman by becoming a writer. Johnny Cross was the man twenty years younger than herself whom George Eliot married after the death of George Henry Lewes. But the three volumes of *George Eliot's Life* offer no intimate revelations: instead, with the least obtrusive editorial presence of all Victorian 'Lives and Letters', the book offers a reading of her letters which leaves the reader free to see the tacit connections in what becomes George Eliot's unconscious autobiography.

The first volume covers the long clumsily frustrated period of humiliated youth between the death of her father and her union with George Henry Lewes, though himself a married man, ending with her becoming a writer. It is the story of someone at once immature *and* advanced for her age, waiting impatiently to become herself, whilst self-consciously trapped in an unlovable moaning for love. Only with age, experience, and the wearying of ego could she give up being the partial, needy, and inchoate Marian and acquire that greater 'freedom of soul' 'to enter into the lives of others' (vol. 3, ch. 17) which was the making of George Eliot. Meantime she just had to hope that the future might redeem the mistakes of the past: 'that the long sad years of youth were worth living for the sake of middle age' (vol. 1, ch. 7).

Yet, by 1859, no sooner is she convinced that *Adam Bede* was a breakthrough 'worth writing, worth living for' than she wonders 'shall I ever write another book as true as *Adam Bede*?' Having redeemed the past, 'the weight of the future presses on me' (vol. 2, ch. 9). Always it is like this, in her second life as 'George Eliot'. In the writing of *The Mill on the Floss*, of *Romola*, of *Middlemarch*, of *Daniel Deronda*, 'the same demon tries to get hold of me' as that which ruined her youth. Beginnings are still difficult, 'that is the history of my life' (vol. 2, ch. 10). In her twenties she had dreams of fame; what upsets her, when she achieves it, is not so much that fame doesn't give her the pleasure she had anticipated, but that it does not even give her confidence.

But this is precisely because George Eliot's strengths as a writer still depended upon of the weaknesses of the woman and her past. She suffers from such double binds: like all the other novels, *Daniel Deronda* is only 'a kind of glass in which I behold my infirmities'. It is with her as she says of the knowledge of consultant physicians, 'the more they have of it, the less absolute—the more tentative—are their procedures' (vol. 3, ch. 17). F. W. H. Myers famously reported that when she was asked from whom she drew the portrait of Casaubon, the old self-doubting failure of a writer in *Middlemarch*, she named no external models but pointed instead to her own heart (*Century Magazine*, November 1881). Throughout Cross's *Life*, the reader finds George Eliot looking back in the journal which is currently under her pen, in order to assure herself that her present depression is not unprecedented, that she felt like this during the writing of the last book and the book before.

At the beginning of her *Autobiography* (1899), a frankly envious Mrs Oliphant complains of George Eliot living safe and sound inside a writer's 'mental greenhouse', without the real burdens of family and children from which Mrs Oliphant suffered. But George Eliot never felt secure, she had always Marian Evans's need for words, writing to herself, writing to others: 'It is an old weakness of mine to have no faith in affection that does not express itself' (*Life*, vol. 1, ch. 7). She could not trust anything if she could not express it; she had what Carlyle called the modern fear that silence was 'nonentity' rather than 'latency' (*On Heroes and Hero-Worship*, lecture 6). In November 1870, in the very midst of writing *Middlemarch*, she still must write to a friend, Barbara Bodichon:

> Lying awake early in the morning, according to a bad practice of mine, I was visited with much compunction and self-disgust that I have ever said a word to you about the faults of a friend whose good qualities are made the more sacred by the endurance his lot has in many ways demanded. I think you may fairly set down a full half of any alleged grievances to my own susceptibility, and other faults of mine which necessarily call forth less agreeable manifestations from others than as many virtues would do, if I had them. . . . I wish to protest against myself, that I may, as much as possible, cut off the temptation to what I should like to purify myself from for the last few remaining years of my life. (*Life*, vol. 3, ch. 16)

Grandly laying down the moral law in *Middlemarch*, she felt she was still behaving poorly, in feeble little ways, herself. In another moment she would rise from bed, and use those very mistakes and those anxieties again in the writing of *Middlemarch*, protesting against herself there too, in that taut to-and-fro relationship—life to art, art to life—which realism constituted. Always the act of writing, especially the writing called realism, was for George Eliot on the verge of hubris: art was trying to be life itself, a human being was writing about other human beings as though she were God. As Thomas Hardy wrote in his notebook, quoting from a lecture by John Morley: 'Success is only the last term of what looked like a series of failures'.[5] George Eliot is the epitome of that democratic

---

[5] *The Literary Notebooks of Thomas Hardy*, ed. Lennart A. Bjork, 2 vols. (Macmillan, 1985), vol. 1, p. 84, entry 839.

humanization of art which makes the biographies of Victorian writers not works of reductive anecdotal interest but a way of thinking about the relation of literature and life.

The third major form of life-writing within the period is the most final: autobiography itself. For if in Victorian biography, the biographer is the presence of the shadow of death, humanly softened, then autobiography is the form that most aspires to the finality of a life summing itself up, even though necessarily written before death itself. As John Foster, a Radical Baptist admired by Marian Evans, put it in his essay 'On a Man's Writing Memoirs of Himself' (1805), autobiography is the human version of God's final judgement: it contains something of the fantastic idea 'of its being possible for a man to live back again to his infancy, through all the scenes of his life, and to give back from his mind and character, at each time and circumstance, as he repassed it, exactly what he took from it, when he was there before' (*Essays in a Series of Letters to a Friend* (1865 edn.), pp. 22–3). That such an end might be achieved only by the help of a magical and religious fiction such as in Dickens's *A Christmas Carol* (1843) is the challenge that the writing of autobiography offers to factual, secular accounts of the world.

It was possible to avoid that challenge. It was also in the nature of the genre, for example, that some memoirs were important not for their own intrinsic merit as writings but simply because they were written by important or significant people, often as the summation of their careers. This is at least partly true even of the autobiographical writings of Charles Darwin or T. H. Huxley. Equally, there are cases where the personality of a scientist, such as Hugh Miller in his beautifully warm *My Schools and Schoolmasters* (1852) or a painter, such as Benjamin Robert Haydon in his frustrated and vainglorious *Autobiography and Memoirs* (1853), is so strongly registered even within their speciality as to make the writing of an autobiography an altogether appropriate expansion outwards. Then again, in the field of autobiographies by working men, for example, some texts are of no more and no less than informative historical value, while others— *The Life of Thomas Cooper written by himself* (1872) or Samuel Bamford's *Early Days* (1848–9)—achieve an independent literary power. That power is perhaps increased by the reader's consciousness that such works are representative of lost or neglected voices: Francis Place, the radical tailor, wrote his autobiography between 1823 and 1835, expecting it would find a publisher after his death; in fact it was only published in 1972.[6] Equally, many of the life stories of professional writers are of interest because of their subordinate relation to the authors' fictional writings or the literary life of the time—for example, the autobiographies of Charlotte Yonge (1877) and Eliza Lynn Linton (*My Literary Life*, 1899), and even perhaps of Anthony Trollope (1883)—while Mrs Oliphant's *Autobiography* is one of the finest works of the century in its own right.

But above all what may restrict Victorian autobiography to a no more than historical value is its tendency to historicize itself. It may easily become, that is to say, a personal version of Carlyle's account of bad history: losing any sense of what the past had felt like at the time, by the act of seeing things only retrospectively in terms of their eventual outcomes. Harriet Martineau's *Autobiography* (1877) is an extreme example. For all the deep pain at her estrangement from her brother James because of religious differences, Harriet Martineau's belief in secular determinism leaves no room even for regret: she did not believe in the possibility of being anything but what she had become.

What equally threatens to flatten out the meaning of Victorian autobiography is the age's temptation to believe in linear progress, leaving the past behind in the wake of ongoing serial success. John Stuart Mill's *Autobiography*—begun in 1853, not completed until 1870, and published only posthumously in 1873—is based upon a philosopher's belief in rational laws and logical sequences, together with a social reformer's conviction that those sequences could be put into practice in order to create a better future. Yet ironically the greatest part of the *Autobiography* is chapter 5, the breakdown of his mental framework. Mill had lived for politics, for social progress; now he asks himself: would he be happy, if his goal of social progress were wholly achieved? What would he live for, if there were no longer a purpose to struggle after? Or did he draw secret comfort from the belief that progress was a process that could never be complete? It was like asking whether the political was sufficient as a way

---

[6] *The Autobiography of Francis Place*, ed. Mary Thale (Cambridge, 1972).

of seeing life and an end in itself. As soon as Mill finds disturbing answers to his questions, the forward movement of his career, of his actual sentences, breaks down. The thinking of the logician now ends only in increasing his realization of the logician's deadlock: 'If I had loved any one sufficiently to make confiding my griefs a necessity, I should not have been in the condition I was.' The very syntax of his being is no longer literally straightforward but turns round upon itself, closer now to the ironic mental shapes of Thomas Hardy: 'To know that a feeling would make me happy if I had it, did not give me the feeling' (Mill, *Autobiography*, ch. 5). Mill's subsequent capacity to get over this breakdown and patch up his life, without a radical change of his principles, leaves the rest of the *Autobiography* oddly disappointing again in its return to normal.

That is why Mill's *Autobiography* is an extreme symbol of how Victorian autobiography as a whole needed to be broken up. Almost by accident, for example, *The Autobiography of Leigh Hunt* becomes a 'life' that actually has to let in real time. The first edition of the *Autobiography* in 1850 ends with chapter 25, the prayer of an ageing, dying man for a better spiritual future for England. But for a revised second edition in 1859, Hunt poignantly added an extra last chapter in the light not only of his own unexpected survival but of the equally unexpected death of his youngest son from consumption. Hunt died later that year.

In the same way, one of the factors that repeatedly helps make the *Autobiography* of Mrs Oliphant so outstanding is that it was begun in 1860, restarted in 1864, and restarted again in 1885, in 1891, and in 1894. The breaks are terrible. In 1860 she lost her husband. In 1864 she lost her eldest child, Maggie: 'I did not know when I wrote the last words that I was coming to lay my sweetest hope, my brightest anticipations for the future . . . in her father's grave.' In 1885 she writes, as though of someone else now, 'Twenty-one years have passed since I wrote what is on the opposite page. I have just been reading it all with tears; sorry, very sorry for that poor soul who has lived through so much since. Twenty one years is a little lifetime.' By 1891 her eldest son is dead and she finds herself writing of his birth in 1856: 'And, best of all, our delightful boy was born. Ah, me! if I had continued this narrative at the time when I broke it off in 1888, I should have told of this event and all its pleasantness, if not with a light heart, yet without the sudden tears that blind me now, so that I cannot see the page.' In 1894 the second son has followed the first: 'I feel that I must try to change the tone of this record. It was written for my boys, for Cecco in particular. Now they will never see it.' By the end she is left alone, writing single-line paragraphs, in bare telegraphese:

And now here I am all alone.
I cannot write any more

Taken to the very verge of the death she is awaiting, this is a *writer's* life, not because she talks about her own books but because, even to the end, there remains a sense of that contingent present in which the act of writing is still being carried out—'when I wrote the last words', 'since I wrote what is on the opposite page', 'if I had continued this narrative', 'And now'.

It is that relative sense of the vulnerable present in which the work is being written which likewise in *Praeterita* (3 vols., 1885–9) saves John Ruskin from the presumptuous responsibility of trying to offer the absolutely final word on his own life. His whole life had been the ever-straining attempt to make his mind contain the universe. But out of the very tiredness and decay of a washed-up 70-year-old man, seeking to avoid violent memories in refuge from a mind nearly wrecked by depression and insanity, there comes a sort of dying grace in the quiet style of composition that remains. Dispersed like travel-writing amongst the great places of his life—Rouen, Geneva, Pisa, and Venice—*Praeterita* is an act of signing-off , as of a man finally disposing of the yellowing journal leaves of his life: 'I recollect that very evening bringing down my big geography book, still most precious to me; (I take it down now, and for the first time put my own initials under my father's name in it)—' (vol. 1, ch. 4, para. 88). It is that quietly witnessing word 'under' which is so telling, just as when Ruskin writes of his being particularly fond as a child of watching his father shave 'and was always allowed to come into his room in the morning (under the one in which I am now writing) to be the motionless witness of that operation' (vol. 1, ch. 2, para. 42). It is not that Ruskin is confidently on top of his life in this book or that, through condescension, the past is utterly beneath him; it is rather that the past is 'under' him, supportively, subconsciously, never fully retrievable and rightly so. Writing lends Ruskin its own time. What can be remembered is not everything—not even perhaps what was most important, in the way that made it important—but simply what happens to be recalled as it comes to mind at the chance moments of writing, at this late stage. It is significant that the composition of *Praeterita* began incidentally in the course of *Fors Clavigera*, that desultory series of letters to the workmen and labourers of Great Britain. For 'Fors' is the power of 'Chance or Fortune' which, taken or rejected by men, 'nails down or fastens their fate for ever', as in 'Clavigera, meaning nail-bearing' (letter 43). The writing is an image of the life: what seems to come by chance becomes inscribed as fate. Like Mrs Oliphant's, Ruskin's is an autobiography produced out of the fate of saddened life-defeat, a sense of failed and still failing powers, and the partiality of lonely weakness. Yet the apparent casualness of the writing of *Praeterita* does honour to the meaning of a life, through acknowledging—even by default—its incapacity completely to contain and summarize it.

The autobiographer cannot do justice to his or her own life in the way that a biographer such as Lockhart could do redemptive justice to the final days of Sir Walter Scott. Ironically then, it is by the partial breakdown of the life form of autobiography—so consciously averted by John Stuart Mill—that Mrs Oliphant and Ruskin succeed. The successive series of events that makes up a life, said the Idealist philosopher F. H. Bradley, 'can not be summed till we are dead, and then, if we have realized it, we, I suppose, do not know it': therefore 'before death, we can not have realized it, because there is always more to come, the series is always incomplete' (*Ethical Studies* (1876), 97). The accounts should never be closed.

The form of the Victorian sequence poem, the sense of the process of living in time as registered in the journals and letters of the literature of travel and of biography, is matched by one other Victorian autobiography—George Borrow's *Lavengro* (1851) and its sequel *The Romany Rye* (1857). Significantly, the volumes follow upon Borrow's travel-writings, *The Zincali* (1841), an account of the gypsies of Spain, and *The Bible in Spain* (1843), the adventures that arose out of Borrow's attempt to circulate the scriptures on behalf of the Bible Society. Like Richard Burton in India and Arabia, George Borrow in his travels round the British Isles seeks to be both scholar-philologist and fighter-wanderer. For formally this is life story as constant movement in exile, without any clear sense of either pilgrim's or Victorian's progress. Hence Borrow's interest in the wandering gypsies who reappear at intervals throughout the books—like the Jews, a lost and alien part of the original world, of its ancient languages, and also somehow of himself.

To his own father, the strange roaming young Borrow seems either stupid or secretive, in comparison with his clever and handsome older brother: 'You are my son, but I know little of your real history, you may know fifty things for what I am aware' (*Lavengro*, ch. 27). Yet Borrow is even to himself rather hidden and lost: a robust devotee of the old-fashioned England of boxing, ale, and horses, Borrow also has recurrent and elusive existential doubts about his own identity and the very existence of the world. There is a conversation with a shepherd at Stonehenge, on how the standing stones got there—Borrow speaking first:

> 'It is impossible there should be a world.'
> 'It a'n't possible there shouldn't be a world.'
> 'Just so.' (ch. 60)

Impossible there should, impossible there shouldn't. In his dual nature, Borrow is a bruiser but one with 'nerves': 'I mean those more secret and mysterious ones in which I have some notion that the mind or soul, call it what you will, has its habitation; how they occasionally tingle and vibrate before any future event closely connected with the future weal or woe of the human being' (ch. 3).

His whole book is elusive rather than familiarising. Often chapters begin afresh not with already-known names but with mysterious pronouns, anonymous participants, free-standing scenes. 'Who is he?' is a key question (ch. 25). Indeed, when connections are made, they are like 'nerves', deep, internal, and almost magical. Thus, the first book that ever awoke the young Borrow's sleeping intelligence and made him want to learn to read was—unsurprisingly in retrospect—Daniel Defoe's *Robinson Crusoe*; years later he takes a book from the hand of an old woman on London bridge, entitled *Moll Flanders*, and reads a sentence here and there: 'Yes, and no mistake!', he says without ever naming the author, '*His* pen, his style, his spirit . . . I covered my face with my hand, and thought of my childhood' (ch. 31). When *Lavengro* does have links to give it form, they seem like links which find Borrow, not that he has made—as though these revelations of memory were signs on the other side of some obscure power of predestination.

Of course, so much in this autobiography is not just reported but recreated that it is impossible to separate memory from fiction in the writing of *Lavengro*. But the effect is not to make its vision of the world fictively more shaped, familiar, or comforting but strangely less so. Thus on the one hand Borrow takes life and death far more seriously and subtly than the gypsies, and yet he also knows he cannot find the satisfaction and relish in life that they do. Who would ever wish to die? says his alternative gypsy 'brother' Jasper Petulengro:

'In sickness, Jasper?'
    'There's the sun and stars, brother.'
    'In blindness, Jasper?'
'There's the wind on the heath, brother; if I could only feel that, I would gladly live for ever.' (ch. 25)

Or again, there is a chance encounter with a man who is scared of being an author because he does not know how much his thoughts are really his own. The same person, back in his youth, when sent the present of a pair of hawks by his uncle, doubted his right to keep them. For although the uncle could reassure him as to their initial provenance, how was the uncle 'to know how the hawks came into the possession of those who sent them to him, and by what right they possessed them or the parents of the hawks'? (ch. 64). These strange digressive and picaresque Wordsworthian encounters do not answer the question how to live or what to do, but serve somehow as other possible parts or versions of Borrow himself. No less for being set amidst ordinary physicality, *Lavengro* is a mystical book, an almost *inarticulately* religious work, culminating in the extraordinary description of an attack of horror in chapter 84:

I could only get rid of it by getting rid of myself . . . I again said the Lord's Prayer, but it was of no use . . . I sat down with my back against a thorn bush; the thorns entered my flesh; and when I felt them, I pressed harder against the bush; I thought the pain of the flesh might in some degree counteract the mental agony; presently I felt them no longer; the power of the mental horror was so great.

The sentences still have an unresolved life and a mysterious imagination within them.

Yet when in this period a formal religious autobiography *is* articulate, what it best articulates is the inability of any explicit account to register the real inner journey of a life.

For who can know himself, and the multitude of subtle influences which act upon him? and who can recollect, at the distance of twenty-five years, all that he once knew about his thoughts and deeds, and that, during a portion of his life, when even at the time his observation, whether of himself or of the external world, was less than before or after, by very reason of the perplexity and dismay which weighed upon him? (John Henry Newman, *Apologia Pro Vita Sua* (1864), pt. 5)

Newman's *Apologia* is, consciously, a defence of his conversion from Protestantism to Roman Catholicism against the imputations of deviousness and betrayal made by the arch-Protestant Charles Kingsley.[7] Outsiders, acting like knowing biographers, might have foreseen for Newman his conversion to Rome; but their 'You will see' and later 'I told you so' is no more than what Newman calls 'an external and common-sense view of what was going on'. The real history was within, taking its own time. Yet what is also remarkable is that the man deep inside that reality could not tell what was really happening at the time. Nor could he ever afterwards locate an explicit point, a simple, dramatic, focal moment at which change definitely took place. He could only eventually recognize that some great change *had already* taken place.

The downright, muscular Christian Kingsley wants an explicit factual answer: why didn't Newman say what he meant, straight and unequivocally, and say it early, instead of hanging on so long in the Church of England, undermining it from within? Newman's is a reply which does not defend himself point by point, but *is* himself. Kingsley 'asks what I *mean*'—and that, says Newman, is not just about words, or specific dates, or particular points of logic, but extends wide and deep to 'that living intelligence, by which I write, and argue, and act' (*Apologia*, pt. 2). He, as a whole, *is* all that he means. This is one of Newman's greatest claims: that what human beings mean, when they really mean it, cannot help but always be,

[7] See above, pp. 99–100, 114–20.

consciously *and* unconsciously, autobiographical. Autobiography is not just a genre, written near the end of a life. The roots of all human expression lie in the autobiographical.

Yet in the *Apologia*, autobiography as such becomes for Newman no more than a secondary account of self. It can easily show the crude sequence of historicized events: then a Protestant, now a Catholic; but it knows it cannot reach down to the micro-reality of all those minute processes that went on inchoately in between the two. It is rather in Newman's great *University Sermons*—preached at the University of Oxford between 1826 and 1843 before his conversion to Rome yet still reprinted with revisionary preface and footnotes by Newman in 1871—that a language is found for those implicit and minute circumstances 'which the mind is quite unable to count up and methodize in argument'—possessed as they are 'of a subtlety and versatility which baffle investigation' (Sermon 13, 'Implicit and Explicit Reason').

Consider, says Newman, when persons 'would trace the history of their own opinions in past years, how baffled they are in the attempt to fix the date of this or that conviction' (Sermon 15, 'The Theory of Developments in Religious Doctrine').

The longer any one has persevered in the practice of virtue, the less likely is he to recollect how he began it; what were his difficulties on starting and how surmounted; by what process one truth led to another; the less likely to elicit justly the real reasons latent in his mind for particular observances or opinions. (Sermon 5, 'Personal Influence, The Means of Propagating the Truth')

Ostensibly impersonal and abstract, the recalling power of the language of these sermons, bare of supporting narrative in time, offers a resonance close to poetry's: words such as 'real' in relation to 'latent' seem to make the mind reach back into its very self. Movements too subtle and gradual for specific narration coalesce into general clusters of meaning whose force is released into memory and emotion by the vocabulary of abstract thought. By this means the language of the *University Sermons* creates, as the *Apologia* largely does not, an imaginative memory of what is too microscopic in the internal processes of mind for the eye of ordinary consciousness to register.

That's why Newman's real autobiography lies not in the *Apologia* but in the more ostensibly impersonal *Essay in Aid of a Grammar of Assent* (1870). For that long philosophical essay takes out of the *Apologia* the most painful problem posed by his opponents: if you were wrong once in believing in the Church of England, how could you ever be sure you were not wrong again in believing in the Church of Rome in its stead? By an act of passionate reason, Newman puts the autobiographical memory of that problem onto a different level, into a different form and genre, without losing the implicit underlying connection. The *Grammar of Assent* is about staying with ourselves through all the stumbling inconsistent efforts to discover what those selves stand for:

It seems to me unphilosophical to speak of trusting ourselves. We are what we are, and we use, not trust our faculties. To debate about trusting in a case like this is parallel to the confusion implied in wishing I had had a choice if I would be created or no, or speculating what I would be like, if I were born of other parents. (pt. 1, ch.3, sect. 4)

Our primary experience cannot be one of uncertainty. We are, instinctively and biologically, naturally believing creatures, to whom the conscious questioning of trust must always come second. Belief is not merely therefore—as the liberal in John Stuart Mill's *On Liberty* might put it—a voluntary extra, personal only as a matter of private choice or opinion. It exists at a deep level where the belief is rooted in the person, the person inextricable from his or her belief. In the same way, 'the life and writings of Cicero or Dr Johnson, of St Jerome or St Chrysostom, leave upon us certain impressions of each of them' (pt. 1, ch. 5, sect. 1), something implicitly *them* even if we cannot make fully explicit all that they resonantly stand for. To bring out and use what we stand for, what within the personal seems implicitly of more-than-personal force, is the human task in Newman.

We only know our experience. 'What belief as such, does imply is, not an intention never to change, but the utter absence of all thought, or expectation, or fear of changing' (*Grammar of Assent*, pt. 2, ch. 6, sect. 2). It is not to say that our beliefs are true just because we believe them, or that uncertainty and change will never come. But the checking and reappraising of beliefs are second-order activities, compared to that intuition of something irreducibly fundamental in us which reason is seeking to redefine or redirect:

If we are never to be certain, after having been once certain wrongly, then we ought never to attempt a proof because we have once made a bad one. Errors in reasoning are lessons and warnings, not to give up reasoning, but to reason with greater caution. It is absurd to break up the whole structure of our knowledge, which is the glory of the human intellect, because the intellect is not infallible in its conclusions. (pt. 2, ch.7, sect. 2/2)

In *An Agnostic's Apology* (1893) Leslie Stephen, a modern rationalist, very plausibly dismissed the *Grammar of Assent* as a psychology of belief, rather than a proof of its objective truth—as if proof could exist. Yet even thus, riskily but in his view inevitably, Newman serves as the great daring bridge between autobiographical life-writing and writing about life itself. For to Newman *real* views are autobiographical not because a person takes hold of ideas in his own particular way, but rather because those ideas have taken hold of the whole person. They are real beliefs and not just personal opinions because they 'are, as it were, part of myself' (*Idea of a University*, (1852, rev. 1859, 1873), pt. 1 'University Teaching', discourse 1, sect. 2). But because of the force with which I hold them or they hold me, they cannot be left merely within myself, they don't feel as though they are merely mine, and they must be launched into the world outside. The autobiographical cannot stay within autobiography.

II. Writings about Life

The New Republic (1877), the brilliantly satirical novel which W. H. Mallock began as an Oxford undergraduate, serves as a flawed model for the difficulty of how to think about Victorian thinkers, in their partly overlapping and yet often conflicting relations. At a house party, hosted by an earnest but rather lost young man modelled on Mallock himself, a variety of thinkers are invited to discuss the Aim of Life. They include Mallock's versions of the critics Matthew Arnold, Walter Pater, and John Ruskin; the Broad Church Jowett and the High Church Tractarian Pusey; and the scientists T. H. Huxley, John Tyndall, and W. K. Clifford; together with a variety of types of women—the society-aristocratic, the sensationalist author, and the genuinely serious. Yet finally, for his attack on the insidious spread of modern atheism even amidst the ostensibly religious, there is only one winner—John Ruskin—if only through his greater sense of privation: 'You have taken my God away from me ... My only consolation is that at least I am inconsolable for His loss' (bk. 5, ch. 1).

What Mallock's novel does not try to offer is what perhaps only the many-sided George Eliot of *Middlemarch* might have been capable of attempting: an imaginative study of intellectual life which moved from mental centre to mental centre, seeking justice to all even in their disagreements with each other, and with an understanding of each that still had relation to some overall whole.

But Mallock's house party is not entirely fictional. He himself contributed to symposia on the fundamental questions assembled by periodicals such as *The Nineteenth Century*, founded in 1877. Is there a soul and does it have an after-life? What are the limits of government? Will a decline in religion lead to a decline in morality? In *The Nineteenth Century* and in the meetings of the Metaphysical Society out of which it arose, it was not just the variety of serious topics which was impressive, but the variety of different points of view assembled together. They included not only men of different faiths, such as Gladstone and Cardinal Manning, but also men of science, reason, and no faith, such as the scientist Huxley, the mathematician Clifford, the philosopher Sidgwick, as well as the follower of Comte, Frederic Harrison. The essential battle-lines were those drawn between religious believers and secularists. But what blurred the distinction was not only the sectarian differences between the religious but the presence in the religious camp of what, to believers even as different as Newman and Ruskin, seemed to be unbelievers, like Harrison with his Religion of Humanity or Matthew Arnold. What further complicated the issue was the attempt by secularists such as John Stuart Mill to define the essential site of battle as political, not religious.

It belongs to just such a climate of debate that certain books were written in direct response to others. James Fitzjames Stephen's *Liberty, Equality, Fraternity* (1873) is a direct counter to John Stuart Mill's *On Liberty* (1858), arguing that force, not freedom, is the essence of life. J. C. Shairp's *Culture and Religion* (1871) is a religious response to the cultural writings of Matthew Arnold. But the conversations and controversies extended further. Critics, reviewers, and commentators, such as R. H. Hutton, John Morley, Henry Sidgwick, or Leslie Stephen, constantly located themselves in the space between Arnold and Newman, or Ruskin and Arnold, or Mill and Newman, bringing one to bear upon the other by implicit or explicit comparison. Even thus through intermediaries as well as direct rebuttals, the great debates—on freedom, liberalism, and democracy; on marriage, tradition, and women's rights; on culture, science, and religion—assembled themselves. They are quarrels and controversies which make plain how misleading it is to speak of 'the Victorians' as an homogeneous entity. Equally, they also show an extraordinary ambition more or less common to all these thinkers. For not only were they writing implicitly *within* the context of social and philosophical changes but also themselves writing explicitly *about* such changes—whilst themselves in part the products of the contemporary situation which they were claiming to examine. It was an extraordinary effort characteristic of a professional class of thinkers—in Coleridge's terms, the 'clerisy'—who, surrounded by the forces of the market, nonetheless were not dependent upon the market for their income; who sought to use their privilege as a form of service; who therefore did their thinking in a form of discursive non-fictional prose which belonged neither to the specialist academic world of the universities nor to the consumerist world of the best-seller, but which sought room for thinkers in the midst of society to get above society by the articulate power of mind.

Yet these Victorian debates on the very aims and principles of life were quite different from Newman's account of what happened when, in the early years of the Church, a powerful new idea created controversy from the moment of appearance:

At first men will not fully realize what it is that moves them, and will express and explain themselves inadequately. There will be a general agitation of thought, and an action of mind upon mind. There will be a time of confusion, when conceptions and misconceptions are in conflict, and it is uncertain whether anything is to come of the idea at all, or which view of it is to get the start of the others. . . . After a while some definite teaching emerges; and as time proceeds, one view will be modified or expanded by another, and then combined with a third; till the idea in which they centre, will be to each mind what at first it was only to all together. (*An*

Essay on the Development of Christian Doctrine (1845), ch. 1, sect. 1)

It is the last clause that is astonishing. For there the participants in the debate are like different thoughts of the same idea, or scattered aspects of the same thought, struggling into existence by the process of collaborative conflict. Only when the idea has finally been honed into clearer realization can each of the parts which helped to form the idea grasp it, individually, as a whole. The idea then brings together those who hold it, creating a coalescing society around itself. But in Victorian England, wrote Carlyle in his essay 'Characteristics' (*The Edinburgh Review*, December 1831), there was no real society because there was no consensus of thought or belief. There was only a noisy hubbub, 'a true Babel-like confusion of tongues'.

That is to say, Victorian controversies did not seem to be about different aspects of the same idea so much as fundamentally different ideas deriving from virtually different worlds. Once those differences were made clear, the similarities and overlaps that also existed across opposing camps served only to make life even more confusing. To Carlyle, to Newman, to Mallock, to the literary critic R. H. Hutton, this near-chaotic plurality was a sign of the weakening of the bonds of belief that held a society in real cohesion. To the modern relativist, principles were merely subjective, private, psychological concerns. As far as Newman was concerned, 'liberalism' meant the illegitimate freedom to deny authority or truth, the modern void that left the individual free to pursue his or her own individual way.

Yet to John Stuart Mill in *On Liberty* liberalism was not indifferent but humanely self-limiting: modestly and carefully it drew boundaries that allowed room in the state for a free diversity of views that was itself a cause for celebration. The liberalism that encouraged individuality of thought was an achievement, when what Mill saw was not a world fragmented by too many differing beliefs but a society increasingly in danger of mass sameness. The long-term disadvantages of having a wise course of action simply *forced* upon the members of a civilized society exceeded the short-term disadvantages of following an unwise course freely. A genuine future for the race could only be created out of what freely emerged from its variety. It was true that modern uniformity did have its good side. It was part of the progress of common enlightenment that the number of doctrines no longer in serious dispute should steadily increase. It was part of the development of democracy, and the opening up of social movement through the rise of trade and commerce, that differences between classes and neighbourhoods should begin to diminish. But the overriding danger lay in the power of social coercion to create mass conformity in the minds of its citizens. Through their very acceptance, beliefs, which were full of meaning and vitality to those who originated them, were always in danger of declining into becoming socially automatic, traditional views unthinkingly accepted at second hand. To Mill it is only free individuals who can generate new thoughts for the future or keep old thoughts truly alive. His kind of thinkers stay alert by imagining the case that could be made out against their own beliefs from the opposite side: thus they individually think out afresh, in the light of opposition, the original living grounds of their thought and, secondly, liberally incorporate such modifications of the original position as the imagination of the alternative point of view provokes.

This was the predicament which, ever since Mill's essays on Bentham and Coleridge, liberals had found most interesting: two clearly opposing voices, each alternately offering a truth which validly criticized the other. Simply taking one side rather than the other was not an option when both sides seemed to hold truth and yet were also in manifest disagreement with each other. To Newman a person who was divided and ambivalent, who wanted to be two different and opposed things, was not yet wholly a person or really themselves. Such were what he called liberals, rather than believers. But Mill prided himself that he could admire two opposing thinkers— and when he did so, he saw in his dual admiration a clue of possible connection, in seeking the best of both. He wanted a form of thinking that augmented and realigned the person who was its thinker, allowing him to have many thoughts rather than one thought and thus to develop more human possibilities in new combinations of person. What Newman was interested in must have seemed to Mill dogmatically one-sided: the finding of one guide, one overall truth, one's own deepest voice or idea, and a whole mental centre. But to such as Newman it was simply not the case that all differences could be reconciled or synthesized.

What was at stake in the debate around liberalism, as Matthew Arnold recognized in *Culture and Anarchy* (1869) and again in *St Paul and Protestantism* (1870), was a new version of the old quarrel between Hebrew monotheism and Greek and Roman polytheism, between a sense of the Many and a commitment to the One. Arnold himself favoured an education in many-sidedness: not one book but many books; not one fixed idea or belief, but the best of many thoughts, taken from many different sources. It was 'criticism' that educated liberalism out of merely 'doing as one likes', as Arnold called it in *Culture and Anarchy*—just as it was 'criticism' that was also to set itself against Carlyle's dogmatic hero-worship. But what in practice Arnold meant by criticism is best shown in a lecture he gave on tour in America in 1883, on one of the favourite writers of his youth, the American prose writer Ralph Waldo Emerson. Now, said Arnold, a youthful personal enthusiasm had to give way to mature critical placing:

It is not always pleasant to ask oneself questions about the friends of one's youth; they cannot always well support it. Carlyle, for instance, in my judgment, cannot well support such a return upon him. Yet we should make the return; we should part with our illusions, we should know the truth. When I come to this country, where Emerson now counts for so much and where such high claims are made for him, I pull myself together, and ask myself what the truth about this object of my youthful admiration is. ('Emerson' in *Complete Prose Works*, vol. 10, pp. 165–86)

The task of criticism is not to swallow the whole of Emerson indiscriminately, but to bear to judge what is relatively weak, inadequate, or faulty, even in an author or work one also largely admires. That capacity for disinterestedness—that mentally rigorous 'return upon oneself' which makes for something freer and larger than the merely personal—is a product of years of reading and thinking and comparing, shaken down into a mature sense of experience so capacious as no longer to be able quite to locate its own specific autobiographical origins. In contrast to the personally over-pressed, the rigidly partial, the dogmatically insular, it is all that Arnold meant by 'culture'.

In Arnold's quasi-theological works *Literature and Dogma* (1873) and *God and the Bible* (1875), the way of Christ himself is found in terms of the 'literary' rather than the 'literal'. In Arnold's

New Testament utterance works less and less by commandment, more and more through metaphor, accent, context, and tone— through specific expressions of Christ's at once so lucid and yet so secret as to defy paraphrase and implicitly require instead the inner way of the spirit, rather than the letter. From the Bible downwards, literary criticism offered a many-sided form of thinking more freely mobile, more attuned to the living shifts and nuances of the specific than the premature over-certainty of the fixed ideas of theology, metaphysics, or social theory. That is why in the subtleties of even a minor work such as *Friendship's Garland* (1871; Arnold's alternative in irony to what Carlyle's *Sartor Resartus* had presented in earnestness), an ear for tone and shift is vital. For with Arnold, writing was to alter the mind of the reader, not simply by the most personally direct and forcible expression of its ideas, but by the very process of thinking and questioning it involved. To Arnold morality itself was not a set of specific rules and prohibitions: it was a complete temper of life in which the whole was more than the sum of its parts. Systems were the result of the harassed Victorian obsession with finding a totally specifiable unity for life.

To Arnold it was the anxious Victorian need for single-minded certainty which ever increasingly in his later years drove Carlyle himself to become a 'moral desperado' (Arnold, letter to Clough, 23 September 1849). Carlyle's *Latter-Day Pamphlets* (1850), for example, are aggressively anti-liberal, offering an energy of Hebraic heat closer to Ruskin's fierceness than to Arnold's Hellenic sweetness and light. Carlyle versus Arnold was like a latter-day version of Luther versus Goethe, the fervent prophet of earnest righteousness opposed by the serene high priest (poet, scientist, and statesman) of culture. Yet, narrow moralistic Hebrew versus flexible intellectual Hellene are no more than the great strategic terms of human history that Arnold initially sets up, not so much for the sake of downright choice but in order to seek orientation between them. By such a measure, Carlyle's pamphlets daringly lose 'balance': they hate the cant 'sympathy' of visitors to the new model prisons, with their show of 'pity' for the interesting-looking prisoners; whilst 'the method of love', it is alleged, makes the lot of the hardened prisoners more comfortable than thousands of starving, law-abiding wretches outside. But what in Carlyle is offered as the simply honest discourse of sincere anger, frustrated amidst mass falsity, becomes a symptom of the very ills it claims to diagnose: to an Arnoldian, Carlyle's overcommitted style—his tone and temper of mind—is distorted by its own vehemence and damaged through the very nature of taking sides.

And yet, to his many opponents on all sides, it was precisely Arnold's refusal to be partisan, and bear its costs in the ongoing process of struggle, that exposed him to the charge of timeless cultural detachment and uncommitted aestheticism. For, in yet another Victorian dialogue, it is just this literary critical strategy of Arnold's which Frederic Harrison dismissed as vague and elusive, in the face of urgent social problems: 'perpetual opening of all questions, and answering of none; infinite possibilities of everything; the becoming of all things, the being nothing'.[8]

It was not that contemporary religious and social pressures had simply been ignored in Arnold: if they had been, it would have been easier to condemn him. Rather they had been acknowledged and accommodated within Arnold's thinking. Yet from two quite different directions, from Henry Sidgwick and from J. C. Shairp, it was precisely the nature of that accommodation that was criticized.

In a review of *Culture and Anarchy* published in *Macmillan's Magazine* (August 1867), Sidgwick argued, as a broadly Millite Utilitarian, that though Arnold spoke in defence of social concern as essential to humanity, in Arnold 'the social impulse springs out of and re-enters into the self-regarding'. The individual development of the self still came first with Arnold. Culture 'is naturally and primarily a study of the individual's perfection'; it is 'only incidentally and secondarily a study of the general perfection of humanity' and that for two reasons, 'one internal, and the other external':

first, because it finds sympathy as one element of the human nature that it desires harmoniously to develop; and secondly, because the development of one individual is bound up by the laws of the universe with the development of at least some other individuals. (*Matthew Arnold: Prose Writings, The Critical Heritage*, pp. 212–13)

By a similar argument, the religious academic J. C. Shairp claimed

---

[8] Frederic Harrison, 'Culture: A Dialogue', *Fortnightly Review* (Nov. 1867), in *Matthew Arnold: Prose Writings, The Critical Heritage*, ed. C. Dawson and J. Pfordresher (Routledge, 1979), 233.

in *Culture and Religion* (1871) that Arnold was using Christ for essentially literary and aesthetic, rather than truly religious, purposes. To Arnold, he said, religion was not so much an end in itself as, covertly, a secondary means towards the higher development of human nature. In dealing between culture and religion, Arnold had placed as primary 'that which is secondary and subordinate, and made that secondary which by right ought to be supreme' (lecture 3). But the order of things mattered and could not simply be shifted around; primary concerns had been transferred into secondary places; what should have been ends in themselves had become means in the service of a vague many-sided development which itself was arguably not so much an end in itself as in lieu of one. In reply to Arnold, Shairp quoted Newman—that those who cultivated virtue for the sake of something other than virtue in the end did not possess virtue at all.

Persons 'evolve', admitted Shairp. They live down certain parts of themselves, take on new thoughts, and by the artifice of thinking recombine the different elements within themselves, legitimating the individualism of this reordering by writing out of it. And yet, Shairp hinted, even through the subsequent complications of their position they can never quite succeed in burying the effect of their starting points. Nor do the secret consequences of not treating first principles as primary simply go away.

In the same spirit R. H. Hutton complained of John Stuart Mill that Mill's was the largest intellect that was ever kept within the limits of a narrow system based on the mere calculation of pleasure and pain: what Mill did, as an act of justification, said Hutton, was enlarge Utilitarianism 'till it was hardly recognisable as Utilitarianism'.[9]

Yet to Mill it was indeed possible to expand the meaning of utility from within. To liberals, the evolving modification of existing structures—the symbiotic relation of ends and means, the shifting of secondary and primary levels—was part of the forward process of human history. Ordinary people forget, said Mill in *Utilitarianism* (1861), that virtue originally existed not for its own sake but for the sake of usefully increasing human happiness. In an essay 'On the

---

[9] *A Victorian Spectator: Uncollected Writings of R. H. Hutton*, ed. R. H. Tener and M. Woodfield (Bristol Press, 1989), 206.

Scientific Basis of Morals' which first appeared in the *Contemporary Review* (September 1875), the atheist W. K. Clifford argued, after Darwin, that individual conscience had simply evolved out of tribal obedience. Thus, ethical maxims appear to be unarguably self-evident and irresistible, only because they are originally acquired from the helpless need for tribal approval, and therefore in the mind of the individual do not rest upon the true reasons for their initial existence. In *Physics and Politics* (1872) Walter Bagehot wrote of the 'two steps' in the development of civilization: first, the enforcement of law and morality, checking the power of individual primitive impulse; second, thereafter, in reverse, the protection and fostering of personal freedom from the tyranny of social custom. In the second stage, the very order of things could mutate.

It was left to James Fitzjames Stephen to retort in the pessimistic realism of his *Liberty, Equality, Fraternity* (1873) that power in the modern world had merely changed its form, not ceased to operate, and that civilized life could easily revert back to chaos and anarchy if this was not clearly understood. The difference between a rough and a civilized society was not, he said, that force is used in the one case and persuasion in another, but that force is (or ought to be) used with greater care in the second. We had not evolved beyond necessities that continued to dog us. Humanism of itself, for all its decency and tolerance, was not sufficient.

W. H. Mallock's own later work, *Is Life Worth Living?* (1879), was a similar attack on the whole liberal-secularist endeavour—in particular in its belief that it could still vaguely retain the most humane or meaningful religious values within what was now an increasingly non-religious context. It was like trying to put old wine into new bottles, he said. A whole series of thinkers—Mill, George Eliot, Huxley, Arnold—were condemned for taking an unsustainable middle position: neither going back to old religious ways, as were Newman and Ruskin, nor forward to the new godless revolution of Nietzsche, but denying the essential conflict by vainly trying to contrive something temporarily adequate in between.

No wonder Carlyle spoke of a confusing Babel of voices, each struggling to neutralize the objections of another by reincorporating them differently within a different framework. As a dizzied Alice said at the table of the Mad Hatter's Tea-Party, you all keep moving

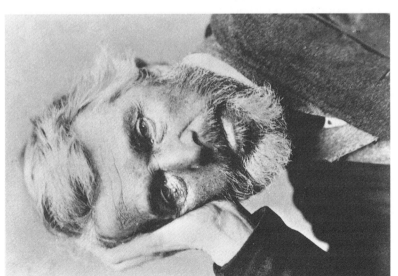

Fig. 12. The faces of Victorian High Seriousness: Elliott and Fry, detail of photograph of Thomas Carlyle, c.1865, aged 70; and Ruskin, *Self-Portrait*, 1874, aged 55 (the left half still so young and light, compared to the dark side of the right).

around (Lewis Carroll, *Alice's Adventures in Wonderland* (1866), ch. 7). So often, significant representative individuals seem to be unstable amalgams of a convergence of influences which they then struggle to include and prioritize in their thinking. For of course it wasn't just liberals who were vulnerable to the charge of contradiction and false coherence. As we have seen, Newman's *Apologia* struggled under just that charge, ironically as a result of Newman finally judging the Church of England itself to be yet another unsatisfactory modern amalgam. Ruskin found himself admitting in a footnote awkwardly placed near the end of the final volume of *Modern Painters* that 'I do not wonder at people sometimes thinking I contradict myself when they come suddenly on any of the scattered passages, in which I was forced to insist on the opposite practical applications of subtle principles' (vol. 5, pt. 9, ch. 7, para. 21). In this pressurized climate it began to feel as though any apparent failure of consistency was a failure of identity itself. To find, in the midst of the model of argument, room in which to pursue a divergent truth; to find further room and time in which, later, to relate that truth to an earlier thought it had differed from: these were tasks which, at once demanding and precluding separate minds, helped lead Ruskin towards the mental breakdowns of his later life, amidst the scattered and fragmented writing of *Fors Clavigera*.

There is no doubt that, in Arnold's terms, Ruskin was a Hebraic figure always starting from one immediate object, one obsession. But remarkably in Ruskin one thing always led him to many things. 'Every action, down even to the drawing of a line or utterance of a syllable' is capable of a higher dignity by the sheer motive involved in doing it and thus can have 'fellowship' with the greater laws of the universe (*The Seven Lamps of Architecture* (1849), introduction). What is more, even what Ruskin found he could *not* do led him admiringly to those, like Turner, who could. This too is what Ruskin calls in volume 5 of *Modern Painters* 'the law of help'. 'Do what you can and confess frankly what you are unable to do,' he urges us magnificently in *The Stones of Venice* (vol. 2, ch. 6, para. 10): 'neither let your effort be shortened for fear of failure, nor your confession silenced for fear of shame.' It is precisely those people who dared start from a strong clear centre within themselves, however flawed or contracted, who were most likely to be drawn into the making of further connections and distinctions, beyond themselves. Inevitably, through all these twists and turns in pursuit of the many in the one, the one through the many, 'the best things shall be seldomest seen in their best form' (para. 11) may even be half-lost in footnotes.

This entanglement was not simply Ruskin's deficiency. It was partly the nemesis of the ambition of so many Victorian thinkers, after the emblematic failure of Coleridge, to contain within their work a whole world-view, when the world itself seemed in confusion. But it was also a problem in the very nature of discursive prose—unshaped, crowded, yet linearly driven—which Newman likewise recognized and suffered from. In the hands of the most powerful thinkers engaged in the most strenuous projects, even non-fictional prose was never the clear, unproblematic medium it appeared to be.

In particular in the *University Sermons* he delivered to theological students, Newman was insistent that words do not have a literal 1:1 relation to the thoughts they represent; that, likewise, thoughts, being immaterial, are not conterminous with the material beginnings and endings of the sentences in which they are lodged. Reason was never sufficient on its own. Even in discursive prose, arguably the most direct form of written language, no sentence could ever be exhaustively explicit or flatly self-explanatory: there was always something implicitly meaningful in the space behind or around it. Alternatively, the thoughts may seem as separate as the sentences that convey them, yet apparently separate propositions are 'ever formed in and round the idea itself (so to speak), and are in fact, one and all, only aspects of it'. Nor was the size of a thought, under pressure of time, necessarily proportionate to the number of sentences used to articulate it. Writing, concluded Newman, 'is the representation of an idea in a medium not native to it' (Sermon 15).

For Newman as for Ruskin, it was precisely the imperfection of the medium that created the most powerful intimations of the meaning, *off* the page, to which it could only approximate on it. The characteristic Newman phrases 'so to speak', or 'as it were', were a sign that the act was always one of partial translation, tacitly calling for imaginative life to fulfil it. That was why discursive writing was still not an autonomous logical system but an act of personal trust, on the

part of the writer, in seeking the recognition of a reader to complete
the act of meaning. Even reading the works of the great was nothing
like directly knowing a great living person (Sermon 5, 'Personal
Influence, The Means of Propagating the Truth'). Words, even the
Biblical Word itself, were dead except in so far as 'transmitted' from
one mind to another. In its mediated struggle for communication
from person to person, writing was a deep, social act, in hope of a
real if invisible society of fellow-believers.

The trust that went into such writing was under strain in a society
without clearly shared beliefs. Rarely in the alien medium of discursive writing could a thought find its own true shape or a syntax
subtle enough to suggest its mental interconnections. To Ruskin, the
often laborious process of discursive prose—its formal syntactic
tendency towards serially pursuing the unfolding of a single explicit
thought at a time—frustratingly precluded that simultaneity of
diverse provisional recognitions of which poetry was capable. Con-
secutiveness was the rule: in discursive prose it was harder to get *out*
of ordinary time; it was impossible to escape the narrow demands of
consecutive logical argument. That is why in that footnote in *Modern Painters*, vol. 5, speaking from the midst of a complex world,
Ruskin refers painfully to '*scattered* passages, in which I was *forced*'
to concentrate upon 'the opposite *practical applications*' of essentially '*subtle* principles'. One moment he seemed to be praising complete 'finish' in a painting; the next he seemed to be disparaging it as
mere polish: it needed extra sentences in the eyeholes between the
two positions to reconcile them—'The clue of connection may in this
case, however, be given in a word. Absolute finish is always right;
finish, inconsistent with prudence and passion, wrong.' Ruskin loved
it when amidst contrasting and diverging thoughts he suddenly
sensed a connection, a law, and found the Many turning back into
the original One—'fitting themselves together in the mind', as he put
it near the end of his footnote, in the very experience of writing. He
loved it too when the painters or poets of great imagination had to
choose, in the thought-crowded midst of their working, between
finishing one conception or partly seizing and suggesting three or
four others.

Particular times in the world, or specific situations within the writing, demanded particular emphases, increasing the risks of trust

involved in the act of communication. Amidst powerful social pressures, with a mind bursting full with considerations, sometimes just one thought—or one side of a thought—had to be carried through, and the others left for another time, place, book, or person. Hence the presence of that word 'forced' again, in the Preface to the first edition of *The Seven Lamps of Architecture* (1849) when Ruskin explains his presumption as an amateur entering the field of architecture: but 'I have suffered too much from the destruction or neglect of the architecture I best loved, and from the erection of that which I cannot love, to reason cautiously', and this therefore is one of those cases 'in which men feel too keenly to be silent, and perhaps too strongly to be wrong; I have been forced into this impertinence'. It is the split-second parenthetic inclusion of that diverging word 'perhaps'—'*perhaps* too strongly to be wrong'—which acknowledges the risk he is also forced into carrying on taking.

Underlying these personal philosophies was the risk that they were overreaching themselves in seeking to become universal philosophies; that the release of the autobiographical from autobiography encouraged a category mistake, symptomatic of the failure of appropriate scales and formal boundaries in Victorian England. It is easy to dismiss a project such as Winwood Reade's in *The Martyrdom of Man* (1872) as characteristically overweening in its post-Christian, Darwinian ambition to achieve a new grand synthesis: 'I shall search out the origin of man, determine his actual condition, speculate upon his future destiny, and discuss the nature of his relations towards that unknown Power of whom he is the offspring and the slave. I shall examine this planet and its contents' (ch. 3). But as he himself explained in *The Outcast* (1875) this was already an age where novelists themselves were 'creating worlds', 'peopling them with animated beings' (letter 2). It was part of the development of the visionary sense that there was indeed a big picture, which we in the middle of ordinary life cannot see:

The earth resembles a picture of which we, like insects which crawl upon its surface, can form but a faint and incoherent idea. We see here and there a glorious flash of colour; we have a dim conception that there is union in all its parts; yet to us, because we are so near, the tints appear to be blurred and confused. But let us expand our wings and flutter off into the air; let us fly some distance backwards into space until we have reached the right point of view. And now the colours blend and harmonize together, and we see that the picture represents One Man.

> The body of a human individual is composed of cell-like bodies . . . Each cell or atom has its own individuality . . . As the atoms are to the human unit, so the human units are to the human whole. There is only one Man upon the earth; what we call men are not individuals but components; what we call death is merely the bursting of a cell. . . . But each atom is conscious of its life; each atom can improve itself in beauty and in strength; each atom can therefore in an infinitesimal degree assist the development of the human mind. (*The Martyrdom of Man*, ch. 4)

Such cosmology was at the height of late Victorian ambition, even at the verge of toppling over. But still elsewhere, in more down-to-earth contexts, questions as to the range, scope, and limits of human purpose had continually to be asked. What was the *right size* of anything? was not just Alice's question in Wonderland.

In an important little review article in *The Westminster Review* (October 1863), for example, S. H. Reynolds offered a contrast between Ruskin and Matthew Arnold, in terms of how each saw his vocation as critic. According to Reynolds, Arnold's sense of 'his proper duty' as literary critic was purely 'to pass judgment upon the literature of each age, viewed in its relation to its own time and circumstance, and to pronounce accordingly upon its "adequacy"'. But Ruskin's aim 'is at once something more and something less than this'. For Ruskin was 'a thorough partisan', and, pushing the personal view to its limits, 'rather perhaps an artist himself than properly a critic'.

Indeed, Ruskin would not have wanted to know exactly what he was—critic, artist, teacher, or even jack of all trades: intensely self-forgetful in his absorption within the intermixture of his concerns, he positioned himself at the interlocking centre of *all* things. His prose was to serve as a medium of translation in which many different realms, subjects, categories could meet. Separation was death. From Ruskin's point of view, what was necessary to bring the disciplines together in mind was the essentially literary language he used for translating Turner from painting to writing in *Modern Painters*. Only a literary language was sufficiently full of resonance, of implicit links and echoes, to move fluently across and between the world's categories. That the language of literature could be the language of *non*-fictional prose was as true to Ruskin as the proposition that the 'artist' was not simply a separate category of human beings. Different not in kind but in degree: artists were not separate, because creativity should not be separate, indeed was available at different levels of human work, however apparently mean. Nor was imagination a separate fiction-making resource but rather what was always necessary to make knowledge itself feel alive rather than become the dry factual residue of experience.

If Reynolds thought that Ruskin was more artist than impartial critic, that was because Ruskin did not believe in the disinterested impartiality, the harmonious impersonality, beloved of Matthew Arnold. For Arnold, culture was the critical study of and search for perfection, and the Greeks were the great classical model of high symmetry, of harmonious perfection, and formal wholeness. For Ruskin, perfection was an intimation and oneness an intuition, neither of them ever a completed achievement. '*The demand for perfection*', he insisted in the great chapter 'The Nature of Gothic' in the second volume of *The Stones of Venice* (1853), '*is always a sign of a misunderstanding of the ends of art.*' It was the Gothic not the Greek or the Renaissance mentality that best understood 'that imperfection is in some sort essential to all that we know of life' (ch. 6, para. 23). What came out of messiness was life itself.

That is why Ruskin, along with A. W. N. Pugin (1812–52),[10] disliked the clean, proud neo-classical architecture of Victorian England. For them, it was the essentially secular architecture of too many industrial, commercial, and municipal buildings—monuments to the spirit of capitalism and competitive civic pride to be found in the new cities. What was expressed in the new Houses of Parliament (begun in 1837 but not completed until 1867) or in Liverpool's St George's Hall (1841–56) was an attitude of imperialism, founded on the model of that other empire, ancient Rome, with its monolithic forces of administration. To Ruskin and Pugin, it was the values of pagan Rome which had formed the basis of Renaissance design, with its impersonally simplified, classical symmetries. What they preferred was the way of life embodied in the religious architecture of the

---

[10] On Pugin and the contrast between neo-classical and Gothic architecture, see below, pp. 549–51.

Gothic age in Northern Europe from the twelfth to the sixteenth century. Gothic was a humble art in the service of God not Man; it allowed for individual creativeness, and was as generous and divergent in its detailing as Nature itself; it was a local art, the building materials a product of the vicinity in which the edifice was raised. That was the spirit of feudal medievalism, interrupted by the Renaissance, which Ruskin celebrated in *The Stones of Venice*, inspiring the Victorian Gothic revival in architecture and the Pre-Raphaelite Brotherhood in painting. To Ruskin it was the loss of that spirit in architecture, and the loss of the society that had upheld it, which had forced lonely, individual artists such as Turner to try to recover some equivalent value, in their own way, in painting.

But in his essay 'The Literary Influence of Academies' (1864), Arnold's complaint was precisely that Ruskin himself lacked 'architectonicé', that his work was all in scattered and crowded pieces, and that it showed a flawed 'provinciality' rather than a classical urbanity in its lack of balance and its verbal over-insistencies. Indeed in the ever-shifting places around the debating table, Arnold set Newman against Ruskin, as an example of true urbanity in prose. Yet, in contrast to Arnold's Enlightenment confidence, Ruskin's point was itself theologically orthodox: imperfection was the result of the Fall. 'Nothing that lives is, or can be, rigidly perfect . . . To banish imperfection is to destroy expression, to check exertion, to paralyse vitality' (*The Stones of Venice*, vol. 2, ch. 6, para. 25). The very life, the natural expressiveness of work depended upon *not* making the workman into a servile tool of overall perfection—that was the road to mechanization—but on first getting the individual creative man out of him, in all his honest inadequacies, and on risking the personal at whatever cost to the smooth design of the whole. Even the genius of Ruskin's Turner, in refusing easy formal success, aimed for the point at which failure itself revealed what was beyond him: we should never prefer 'the perfectness of the lower nature to the imperfection of the higher' (para. 11).

R. H. Hutton said that the books of John Stuart Mill had no personal style, but offered instead a persuasive strategy of apparently impersonal, calm, and evenly flowing reasoning, 'and the less closely they are associated with his name and personality, the more do they seem to partake of the impersonal intelligence of the age, and the more readily do they pass into the very essence of what is called the Time-Spirit' (*A Victorian Spectator*, p. 231). In contrast, there is an honest generosity in Ruskin's openly offering of himself as personal, not perfect; in his being as much himself as he possibly could; in the use of both his gifts and his failings, without certainty as to the difference: 'The finer the nature, the more flaws it will show through the clearness of it' (*The Stones of Venice*, vol. 2, ch. 6, para. 11). All his works are a mixture of essay and lay-sermon, of attempt and injunction, which finally in *Fors Clavigera* he enclosed within the form of letters to 'the working men of Great Britain', if not in the present, at least of the future. '*Fors is a letter*, and written as a letter should be written, frankly, and as the mood, or topic, chances' (letter 81). The letter-mode kept a lonely, weakened Ruskin going, across a realm of wide-ranging and subtly connected interests, without the demands of a stricter form. It was his last-ditch attempt to close the gap between his increasingly private world of art and the outside realm of modern economics, seeking, even by means of personal tone and form, to extend the human relations of literature into the resistant working world beyond it.

'Do what you can and confess frankly what you are unable to do.' The risk of personal belief is all the more intensified when a single person or a handful of creative individuals have to stand in place of the good society and have to represent in themselves something of the lost universal framework of faith and understanding which earlier ages had embodied impersonally in Church and State. Seen as parts of a complex dialogue, so many of the participants in the great Victorian debates seem like endless mutual correctives to each other, the split-off pieces of some grand elusive whole for which they would not stop searching.

But Ruskin and Newman did not want to be what ironically they were becoming: the eccentric or original individuals defended in John Stuart Mill's *On Liberty*. That was why Newman joined the Roman Catholic Church, the repository of the framework and community of earlier ages. Alone, even the individual believer, Newman acknowledges, may experience 'that strange and painful feeling of unreality . . . from time to time . . . as if religion were wiped out from the world' through 'the temporary obscuration of some master vision' (*University Sermons*, Sermon 15). That was why dogma was necessary to give permanence to what in the individual could only be evanescent in feeling. Obedience to the authority of dogma sustained the individual between and through all the comings and goings of the personal vision. But for Newman there is no implicit peace in individualism: intellectual anxiety 'shows itself in our running back in our minds to the arguments on which we came to believe, in not letting our conclusions alone, in going over and strengthening the evidence, and, as it were, getting it by heart . . . as if to reassure ourselves' (*Grammar of Assent*, ch. 6, sect. 2). 'A literary religion', concluded Newman, 'is so little to be depended upon; it looks well in fair weather; but its doctrines are opinions' (ch. 4, sect. 3). It was to Newman a literary religion that Matthew Arnold offered when in 'The Study of Poetry' (1880; in *Complete Prose Works*, vol. 9, pp. 161–88) he claimed that religion had originally materialized itself in the 'fact', that facts were now failing in the light of new secular knowledge, and that only poetry—in its widest possible meaning—could keep alive the 'idea' instead.

Yet the coming and going of thoughts, the creative forgetting and remembering of them under the pen, constituted the very dynamic of Ruskin's writing. That *was* his literary religion. Characteristically Ruskin would begin his work from a strong feeling, an intuition like that he felt about the primacy of Turner at a raw age somewhere between 13 and 17. He would then messily immerse himself in his scattered material, so as to try to exclude nothing, having faith almost to forget his initial intuition unless and until his material brought it back to him again. Hence Ruskin's manic-depressive tendency—the impatience of his imagination, eschewing perfect finish; the incessant worry about keeping up a constant rhythm of work; the sporadic anxiety, shown in the impressive travel diaries, not to lose the future memory of what was presently before his eyes. Hence too the scrupulous fear of his own Romanticism—in, say, his strictures against 'the pathetic fallacy' in *Modern Painters* (vol. 3, ch. 13)—lest his work should be all too subjective in projectively creating meanings rather than finding them.

Ruskin was individual, exceptional, and yet, even in extremity, extraordinarily representative of the tensions of his age. He thought he had lost his faith in 1858; it took him years to discover that what he had lost was his faith in Evangelical Protestantism: he was a God-intoxicated man without a formal religion. Always, therefore, there was for him the risk that the thoughts that had seemed found or given, in the interior emotional experience of thinking, were in fact self-consciously willed or personally invented—and that itself was not just Ruskin's anxiety but a buried Victorian apprehension which could only be properly articulated in the fiction of the age. *Wilfrid Cumbermede* (1872), for example, a novel by Ruskin's friend George MacDonald, is about that fear of an unconscious wish to be deceived.[11]

But above all, there remained for Ruskin the recurrent fear of 'literary religion': the fear lest, in the modern world, art of itself could neither replace religion nor overcome society, nor even perhaps hold on at all to its risky place in between the two.

Yet the holding on was essential, in whatever diverging ways it was managed. At times it seemed that important thoughts, felt needs, and intuitive half-beliefs could hardly *be* thought within the increasingly materialistic framework of Victorian England. What broke through this constrictive mentality was the unpredictability of art, of individual writers and artists. Handfuls of creative individuals, often working outside the structures or vocabularies of the present, kept sporadically alive the feel of lost, unknown, or unadmitted ways of being which other handfuls of individuals could emotionally recognize in their work. Hence, the need for the language of literary culture as a language of dynamic memory, and not just dead history or flat ideology. It was not the least of the role of the writers of non-fictional discursive prose to try to consolidate those artistic insights and openings and, working within their spirit and resonance, translate them into forms that made them last longer or go further within the discourse of the non-artistic world.

[11] See above, p. 160.

11

Poetry

I. The Form in Difficulties

It was no more than a phrase in a letter to Arthur Hugh Clough in February 1849, but in declaring his age to be fundamentally 'unpoetical'—'not unprofound, not ungrand, not unmoving:—but *unpoetical*'—Matthew Arnold was to clinch the terms of much contemporary and future estimate. Victorian poetry was a poetry made self-consciously weak in an age that, because of vast social and economic changes, seemed ever increasingly in literary terms the age of the novel. The mid-century crisis of poetic confidence marked the point at which, in the history of English culture, poetry first began to lose its nerve and its place. 'Show me the books . . . The books! The books!' cries the ruined protagonist in the nightmare of Tennyson's 'Sea Dreams' (1860), knowing that the books are no longer biblical or literary but accountancy's.

Yet never before had the times had to seem propitious in order for there to be a strong poetry. It was its own consciousness of its social and historical situation that helped internally to weaken Victorian poetry. Swamped by the thought of its questionable relevance within a new mass industrial and democratic society, poetry became self-consciously peripheral. When in a letter of 23 September 1849 Arnold listed to Clough all the difficulties of the age, the culmination lay in 'the sickening consciousness' of those difficulties.

John Stuart Mill's *Autobiography* (1873) describes the sort of pressure that literary culture was under in the period 1810–40, as a result of the rise of Benthamite Utilitarianism in response to the social and economic upheaval caused by rapid industrialization.

With only a few absolute adherents, it was a philosophy that none-theless managed to sustain a strong attack upon the luxury of Romantic individualism, in defence of the increased material happi-ness of the greatest possible number in society. Thus of his Bentham-ite father James Mill (1773–1836), Mill writes in chapter 2:

> For passionate emotions of all sorts, and for everything which has been said or written in exaltation of them, he professed the greatest contempt. He regarded them as a form of madness. 'The intense' was with him a bye-word of scornful disapprobation. He regarded as an aberration of the moral standard of modern times, compared with that of the ancients, the great stress laid upon feeling. Feelings as such, he considered to be no proper subjects of praise or blame.

The failure of the idealist poet in Shelley's *Alastor, or The Spirit of Solitude* (1816) was a portent here. Early responses to Shelley's poem rehearse Victorian resistance to 'the morbid ascendancy of the imagination' which in its 'utter uselessness' incapacitated the mind 'for bestowing an adequate attention on the real objects of this work-day life' (*The Eclectic Review*, October 1816). It is a dismissal very similar to John Stuart Mill's own disquiet over Browning's *Pauline* (1833) which, with *Paracelsus* (1835) and *Sordello* (1840), is Browning's version of the *Alastor* problem. Such criticism defined the 'real' in terms of the external world and, making acceptance of such realism a social and moral duty, effectively severed the inter-relation between inner and outer worlds, putting the former in service to the latter. The effect of conceiving the relation between the mind and the world to be fundamentally dualistic was to leave poetry vulnerable to charges of solipsism. That is why in his Preface to *Philip Van Artevelde* (1834) the poet Sir Henry Taylor sought a return to a neoclassical version of poetry, as a language of expanded reason. What Romantic poets such as Shelley had done, argued Taylor, was to 'unrealize' objects, 'until they shall have been so decomposed from their natural order and coherency as to be brought before the reader in the likeness of a phantasma or a vision'. To Taylor, Shelleyan poetry too often bordered upon madness and anarchy, since, in inventing rather than finding meaning, it did not acknowledge how non-referential it really was.

The raw question—What had been the practical *usefulness* of

Romantic feeling?—became compelling, given the new responsibilities devolving upon an intelligent middle class for the government of the country. Beneath the emotive Romantic vocabulary of 'life' or 'spirit' or 'nature' or 'intuition', the Utilitarian rationalist detected the particular vested interests of a certain class and a certain culture defending its privileged mystique. The Benthamite attack was not just on poetry but on the deceptive nature of all human language: rhetoric in general produced a fictional language system that took over reality even while it claimed to be representing it. Government, law, material welfare, political economy, and the balancing of rival interests were concerns which (as John Stuart Mill put it in his own essay on 'Bentham' in 1838) could not afford to be 'left in the dominion of vague feeling or inexplicable internal conviction' but were to be 'made a matter of reason and calculation' (*Collected Works*, vol. 10, p. 111). To Bentham there were no levels of quality, only measurable quantities of pleasure or pain: poetry, said Bentham, gave about the same amount of pleasure as the child's game of push-pin and accordingly could be calculated to be just about as important. What Utilitarianism claimed to offer, in the name of a true politics, was an analytically scientific language, in which words would stand more nearly for the real things of world.

In reply, noted John Stuart Mill, literary men and women defended themselves against the Utilitarians in the terms that Macaulay had employed against Mill's father: 'Utility was denounced as cold calculation; political economy as hard-hearted; anti-population doctrines as repulsive to the natural feelings of mankind. We retorted by the word "sentimentality" which, along with "declamations" and "vague generalities" served us as common terms of opprobrium' (*Autobiography*, ch. 4). All too easily, under the pressure of antagonism, literature was being forced into a half-misshapen moral justification of itself as the realm of personal feeling and intangible spiritual value. But, with the tangible social changes and miseries of the nation increasingly difficult to ignore or to answer, such a defence left literary men and women of the second and third quarters of the century unable guiltlessly to resist the criticisms made against feeling. 'What helps it', says Matthew Arnold, that Byron bore 'the pageant of his bleeding heart' throughout Europe? 'What boots it, Shelley, that the breeze | Carried thy lovely wail away?' ('Stanzas from the Grande Chartreuse'). However much Arnold might set his poetry against Utilitarianism, this was his poetic version of utilitarian questions. In the face of accusations of lyric elitism, this, like Tennyson's 'The Palace of Art', is a poetry about poetry's deficiencies, battening upon its own self-doubts in a version of that entangled self-division which Hegel in the *Phenomenology of Mind* (1807) called 'Unhappy Consciousness'.

An elegiac pining *against* pining is a characteristic of much Victorian lyric verse. 'The nobleness of grief is gone,' cries Arnold, 'Ah, leave us not the fret alone!' ('Stanzas from the Grande Chartreuse'). It was that plaintive note of loss which provoked charges of melancholy and morbidity, passivity and other-worldly yearning—charges tendentiously summed up in the word often used to dismiss such poetry in a world of hard masculine realities: 'feminine'. It is characteristic of the period, in all its extension and blurring of meanings, that certain categories, such as male–female, initially established as definitive should begin to float free of their immediate referents, in search of the bounds of significance.

Indeed, the very tone of such poetry also seems related to the Victorian cult of death: the ritualization of loss, as witnessed in deathbed scenes, elaborate funerals, mourning dress, and piously inscribed gravestones, in reaction against the secular fear of extinction. As in Tennyson's *In Memoriam* itself (1850), this feeling of death-in-life extended beyond the terms of personal mourning: it brought together in a strange but powerful amalgam both a religious sense of loss and a sense of the loss of religion.

Thus made to stand for more than itself, poetry in particular was trapped by the very terms of its own defence. Thought for *thought's* sake, claimed G. H. Lewes, was science, but thought for *feeling's* sake, and feeling for feeling's sake, was poetry. The novel, said John Stuart Mill, gave a true picture of *life*, whereas the truth of poetry was to paint the human *soul* truly. In these mutually weakening alternatives, 'soul' was separated from 'life', just as 'feeling' was split off from 'thought', and a powerful lyricism seemed to have no power to reach current political realities.[1]

---

[1] G. H. Lewes, 'Hegel's Aesthetics: Philosophy of Art', *British and Foreign Review* (March 1842); J. S. Mill, 'What is Poetry?', *The Monthly Repository* (Jan. 1833).

Without a social mission, the problem for poetry became a religious problem, within a material world. Yet poetry was increasingly explained in psychological terms, as the product of emotional associations in persons possessed of a sensitivity greater in degree than that of ordinary people, though not different in kind. In his essay on Tennyson in *The Westminster Review* (January 1831), W. J. Fox argued that there was nothing mysterious in the power of producing poetry: it came out of the subjective force of emotional associations, as external objects and places triggered sudden links with inner feelings and latent memories. Modern psychology, wrote Fox, gave a poet such as Tennyson new access to that inner world, even through the medium of its response to the world outside. Indeed, John Stuart Mill expressed gratitude to Wordsworth, as the poet of unpoetical natures, for depicting not merely the scenes of outward beauty but the states of feeling that responded to those scenes. Wordsworth's poetry had helped Mill over the nervous breakdown he suffered in his early twenties. Yet to Mill what Wordsworth stood for was not poetry as a form of philosophical thought or social action, so much as therapy for Mill's initial miscalculation in not giving more allowance to the necessary luxury of feeling, within the inner realm of the individual's private life.

The domain appropriate to poetry seemed to be shrinking. 'In the old times', Arthur Hallam had written in a review of the *Poems: Chiefly Lyrical* of his friend Tennyson, 'the poetic impulse went along with the general impulse of the nation', but not so in these days:

hence the melancholy which so evidently characterizes the spirit of modern poetry; hence that return of the mind upon itself and the habit of seeking relief in idiosyncracies rather than community of interest. ('On Some of the Characteristics of Modern Poetry', *The Englishman's Magazine*, August 1831)

Without confidence in a shared sense of common belief, and unsure of their readers, poets turned back in upon themselves in their uncertainty—to what Matthew Arnold in the 'Preface to the First Edition' of his *Poems* (1853) was to call 'the dialogue of the mind with itself'. Poetry had become a prisoner of the swings of its own history, in particular of the passional reaction of the Romantics against the 'over-civilized condition of thought' of their Augustan predecessors. As a result the whole mental system no longer worked harmoniously—in the division of faculties, Tennyson was, like Keats and Shelley, a poet of 'sensation' rather than 'reflection':

> Those different powers of poetic disposition, the energies of Sensitive, of Reflective, of Passionate Emotion, which in former times were inter-mingled, and derived from mutual support an extensive empire over the feelings of men, were now restrained within separate spheres of agency. (Hallam, 'On Some of the Characteristics of Modern Poetry')

In that competitive separation, 'there arose a violent and unusual action in the several component functions, each for itself, all striving to reproduce the regular power which the whole had once enjoyed'. The elegiac feeling of loss was made to include the loss of feeling, and even the loss of access to other functions besides feeling.

To Gerard Manley Hopkins, in a critique self-banished to the realm of private notes and letters, too much Victorian poetry was what he called Parnassian. On Mount Parnassus, sacred to Apollo and the Muses, Poetry bore a capital 'P': by the middle of the nine-teenth century, however, it had degenerated into becoming a ready-made lyric language, of lofty diction and heavy lamenting tones, which made the production of a poem possible without its first hav-ing to earn its individual right to existence. In the original creative poetry of a Shakespeare, wrote Hopkins in a letter to A. W. M. Baillie, 10 September 1864, 'every fresh beauty could not in any way be predicted or accounted for by what one has already read'. But 'it is the mark of Parnassian that one could conceive oneself writing it if one were the poet'; 'in Parnassian pieces you feel that if you were the poet you could have gone on as he has done'. Hopkins picks out as a representative example a ringing phrase from Tennyson's 'Enoch Arden'

> the glows
> And glories of the broad belt of the world

This was Tennyson being all too predictably Tennysonian, said Hopkins. It was a post-Romantic poetry sealed in a dreamily self-protective withdrawal from the unpoetic world outside.

Hopkins's diagnosis offers a vital mental tool for critical discrimi-nation. And yet, wrongly applied, the charge of Parnassianism can make it too easy to dismiss much Victorian poetry, even as it half-dismissed itself. It was not that 'the poetic impulse' was simply in rural retreat from 'the general impulse of the nation': rather, in its very indirections and dislocations, poetry was *more* affected by the state of the nation than any other art form. For so far from being merely 'unpoetical', it is the Victorian period that produces the first fully felt contrast between the language of the realist novel and the language of poetry. And in that contest with the novel, so structured and so worldly, poetry feels more strange, more disturbing, more uncertain than perhaps it had ever felt before. Indeed, the challenge of that difference throws into the reader's immediate experience one of the most disquieting forms of the question (John Stuart Mill's question, in the title of one of his essays)—'What *is* Poetry?' Whilst the realist novel sought to close the gap between art and life to its closest possible distance, the place of poetry was left as art's problem.

Thus, whatever the experiments in human psychology that went on *within* the novel, the novel itself remained for the most part formally content with the establishment of realism: it was in poetry that self-conscious experimentation went on, as between its own history and the ongoing history of the outside world poetry struggled to find a justified place for the mind's free inventive creativity. Consequently, a Victorian reader, turning to poetry from the reassuring grounding and the contextual security of the realist novel, might suddenly find this unlocated voice coming out of the midst of its own reality, starting as it were from out of nowhere:

> Gr-r-r—there go, my heart's abhorrence!
>   Water your damned flower-pots, do!
> If hate killed men, Brother Lawrence,
>   God's blood, would not mine kill you!
> What? Your myrtle-bush wants trimming?
>   Oh, that rose has prior claims—
> Needs its leaden vase filled brimming?
>   Hell dry you up with its flames. . . .

The critic R. H. Hutton writes of this opening to the 'Soliloquy of the Spanish Cloister':

Mr Browning rushes upon you with a sort of intellectual douche, half stuns you with the abruptness of the shock, repeats the application in a multitude of swift various jets from unexpected points of the compass, and leaves you at last giddy and wondering where you are, but with a vague sense that, were you but properly prepared beforehand, you would discern a real unity and power. (*Essays Theological and Literary* (1871), vol. 2, ch. 4)

Something had happened to agitate the very pace and reliability of mentality. Browning offers no gentle introduction to this dramatic monologue, no sense of where it is coming from, only the challenge to meaning of a racily demotic colloquialism implicitly demanding that, as Hutton again puts it:

the whole must be fairly grasped before any of the 'component parts' are intelligible; the component parts, indeed, being little more than diminutive wholes, too diminutive to be clearly legible until you have seen the whole, whence you go back to the component parts again with a key to their meaning that at last gradually deciphers them.

Readers have to wait almost until the end of the poem before they can tell where it begins from—a monk seeking the damnation of a colleague. Time no longer reads straightforwardly; a steady orientating centre often seems elusive or even missing. The strange artful poetry of this disembodied voice, displaced from its own context and transposed into print, is like a violent, teasing satire played upon the reassuring mediation and extension of sympathy that was offered in the reading of so-called realist novels.

For this is the great Victorian discovery of the dramatic monologue in which character is taken off the physical stage and, instead of being set within the alternative context of the novel, is released into the air of poetic voice. If the early Victorian reader expected poetry to be essentially lyric expressionism—'feeling', as John Stuart Mill put it in 'What is Poetry?', 'confessing itself to itself, in moments of solitude'—then this was almost anti-poetry. For here authors could free themselves from the direct all-confessing 'I' of Romantic self-expression, precisely by creating a context for the 'I' that was implicitly social rather than solitary. In dramatic monologues such as 'My Last Duchess' or 'Porphyria's Lover' the person to whom the words are addressed is missing, and the reader overhears the speaker instead at one remove—as though there were some ironic critique silently waiting to be collusively assembled between author and reader, some second unwritten poem disturbingly hidden behind the first.[2] Steady confidence in the direct relation of language to the world outside or to the self inside was under test here. Subjectivity is rendered a disturbingly exposed textual object before the reader's eyes—as open to critical scrutiny as even the texts of the Bible now were.[3] Indeed, Browning's 'Essay on Shelley' (1852) is an account of just that shift from the visionary expressiveness of Romantic subjectivity, found in Browning's own early work, to a more 'objective poetry' recording life's phenomena as from the outside.

So often the protagonists of the dramatic monologue seem, even dimly to themselves, to be somehow acting: they are so conscious of being seen from without that they ever verge on an uncomfortably false yet realistic inauthenticity. And yet in the very process of talk their tone stumbles unpredictably between a brash social self and something really more vulnerable buried beneath it. Browning's 'Bishop Blougram's Apology' (1855) is the greatest example of that shifting quickness. For in the midst of an apparently worldly defence of religion against an accusatory non-believer, the canny Bishop finds himself in suddenly authentic relation to his own faith and doubt—'With me faith means perpetual unbelief | Kept quiet like the snake 'neath Michael's foot | Who stands calm just because he feels it writhe'. At once he backs off again, to offer snuff—'Or, if that's too ambitious,—here's my box -'—only then to use the snuff as a quirky metaphor for the spice that doubt gives to faith. The reader has to stay alert to these sudden unsignalled shifts and changes in time, without any constant moral reassurance as to the essential status of the speaker. 'To read poems', wrote George Eliot in a review of Browning's work in *The Westminster Review* (January 1856), 'is often a substitute for thought; fine-sounding conventional phrases and the sing-song of verse demand no co-operation in the reader; they glide over the mind.' But by making artifice a disturbing

---

[2] On the double poem see E. D. H. Johnson on the 'dark companion' to the apparent meaning in *The Alien Vision of Victorian Poetry* (Princeton University Press, 1952), 217 and Isobel Armstrong, *Victorian Poetry: Poetry, Poetics and Politics* (Routledge, 1993), esp. the intro.

[3] See above, pp. 109–12.

presence in the poetry through the oscillating self-consciousness of character, reader and writer alike, Browning prevents the drowsy passivity of easy reading. Things move so fast in so much Victorian poetic experimentation. 'I must not think,' writes Browning in *Pauline*, 'lest this new impulse die | In which I trust; I have no confidence: | So I will sing on fast.'

But it is not just Browning's abrupt poetry that seems able to start anywhere and come out of nowhere, giving no clear indication of quite where or why it exists, or what its force really stands for. Hallam had insisted that, in the absence of securely shared values, it was characteristic of modern poetry as a whole that reading it required exertion in order to find its subjective orientation: to understand and follow the poem, the reader had to try '*to start from the same point*, i.e. clearly to apprehend that leading sentiment of the poet's mind' ('On Some of the Characteristics of Modern Poetry'). To R. H. Hutton Tennyson was far more the quintessential type of the lyric poet than the restless Browning since in Tennyson's brooding poetry the mind more often falls 'under the dominion of a single sentiment'. But even with Tennyson the mind does not always know quite what or where that predominant emotion really is, or how to stop it expanding to envelope and take over the whole world. It is easy to get *into* the helplessly spreading depressive monomania of Tennyson's 'Mariana', but, as the struggle in 'The Two Voices' shows, not so easy to get out of it again—what started as lyric and as mood seems not to want to remain so defined. The reader of Tennyson nearly always feels strange and displaced:

> Below the thunders of the upper deep;
> Far, far beneath in the abysmal sea,
> His ancient, dreamless, uninvaded sleep
> The Kraken sleepeth: faintest sunlights flee
> About his shadowy sides . . .
>
> ('The Kraken')

> There would be neither moon nor star;
> But the wave would make music above us afar—
> Low thunder and light in the magic night—
> Neither moon nor star.
>
> ('The Merman')

In *Biographia Literaria* (1817) Coleridge had said that Wordsworth's poetry was 'like a green field reflected in a clear and transparent lake' (ch. 22). But in Wordsworth the poetry always allows the mental reflection to be checked alongside the field itself, and there is always that interchange between art and the life which is its subject matter; in Tennyson the green field itself is gone, the external half of life is available only on reflection within some strange shadowy sonic inner or under world, like

> some dead lake
> That holds the shadow of a lark
> Hung in the shadow of a heaven
>
> (*In Memoriam*, 16)

In 'The Kraken' whatever it is that lies ancient, monstrous, and unconscious in the nightmare depths below expires when it reaches surface life at the end of the poem. For Tennyson here, it seems that the deepest thing dies when it is recognized in life, and its death is strangely not resolvable into a single feeling of either disappointment or relief. All this leaves the reader unsure of the place, the purpose, and even the rationalizable feelings of such poetry. For poems such as 'The Lady of Shalott' and 'The Kraken', or Christina Rossetti's 'Goblin Market', are like elusive parables or riddling myths, not so far away from the nonsense verse of Lewis Carroll and Edward Lear[4] as they may at first seem. In an age obsessed with the need for translation (between secular and religious, between past and modern, between art and the life outside it), such poems seem to mean unsettlingly more than they say and yet will not let the meaning quite out of themselves. What is the right context or appropriate generic framework in which to read such poems? what are they *there for*? Such poems genuinely embody the difficulties for poetry itself in the period, while also tacitly turning the difficulties of meaning back round upon their reader.

The disturbing disparity between what is so lucidly said within a poem and what on the other side it might truly mean is central to Tennyson. As the poet and critic Edward Dowden put it in a letter 15 March 1874:

---

[4] See above, pp. 344, 350–1.

Now the fact that Tennyson has a style . . . is a great fact. For what we call style, must mean a set of sensations and feelings (i.e. matter) too fine and delicate to be expressed or seized save in this way inapprehensible by the intellect. In fact, manner is matter of a fine kind, and to have enriched the world with a style is to have opened a new set of human organs to new sources of feeling. (*Fragments of Old Letters: E.D to E.D.W 1869–1892* (1914), p. 85)

So it is in a song suddenly intruding upon the narrative of *The Princess* (1847):

> The splendour falls on castle walls
> And snowy summits old in story:
> The long light shakes across the lakes,
> And the wild cataract leaps in glory.
> Blow, bugle, blow, set the wild echoes flying,
> Blow, bugle; answer, echoes, dying, dying, dying.

> (3. 348–53)

In 'Blow, bugle, blow', although the *grammar* is imperative, the *mood* of helplessness is far from it, and the distance between the two is as much part of the meaning as anything else. For it is not so much the loud crying sounds and the grand old sensations that interest Tennyson but the weaker inner echoes of them—the secret and inexpressible feelings which those feelings give him, even as they die away within. In his poem 'Why should I say I see the things I see not', Arthur Hugh Clough speaks of two utterly different musics known to men: one 'loud and bold and coarse' like public noise in the social dance, the other 'soft and low', near-silent, hard to hear, and yet easy to forget. Hopkins had detected the parody of a grand style in Tennyson's Parnassianism. But tacitly Tennyson can find the poetry of the soft and ghostly even *within* the loud Parnassian cries of lament. Behind the voice of the Lotos-Eaters, luxuriating in ease, is the echoing memory of the past pain of the life which seeks that oblivion; the more the protagonist in *Maud* finds himself loving the young woman, the more he expresses it through hatred of the brother who keeps them apart—one feeling thus disturbingly serving its opposite.

Often the ostensible language exists, back to front, for the sake of a silenced opposite within, which produces it. Indeed, the secret inner echo in Tennyson is at once so near and yet so far from the terms that loudly summon it that only a strange form of modified repetition registers an effect 'too fine and delicate to be expressed or seized save in this way inapprehensible by the intellect'. Thus: 'O breaking heart that will not break', 'That which we are, we are', 'O grief, can grief be changed to less | O last regret, regret can die.'[5] A word or sentence may be so repeated in Tennyson, noted W. J. Fox in one of the earliest reviews, that the same sound nonetheless 'conveys a different meaning or shade of meaning, excites a varied kind of emotion, and is involuntarily uttered in a different tone' (*The Westminster Review*, January 1831). So it is with King Arthur's repetition of 'The old order changeth, yielding place to new' in *The Idylls of the King*—spoken with such different tacit feelings at the end of his reign as compared with its beginning. There are, said Hallam, 'innumerable shades of fine emotion in the human heart' which only tone, and not the understanding, can register. The different meaning of the same sound sinking in constitutes the unplaceable 'shade' of something different—'the law within the law' ('The Two Voices')—which to the prosaic mind appears merely the same. It is not merely a matter of Tennyson's fine ear but repetition 'till the word we know so well | Becomes a wonder and we know not why' ('Lancelot and Elaine', 1021–2). Poetry here is that which comes, audibly but invisibly, from somewhere different than it seems to:

> The first gray streak of earliest summer-dawn,
> The last long stripe of waning crimson gloom,
> As if the late and early were but one . . .
> ('The Ancient Sage')

Hallam himself recognized these strangely mingled connections of life and death, first and last, pleasure and pain, past and present in the sensations of Tennyson's mind: even when he brings back the very feel of childhood, he does so paradoxically with 'a latent knowledge, which heightens the pleasure, that to our change from really childish thought we owe the capacities by which we enjoy the recollection' ('On Some of the Characteristics of Modern Poetry').

---

[5] From 'The Ballad of Oriana', 'Ulysses', and *In Memoriam*, 78 respectively.

Thus, in a remarkable review of Tennyson's *Poems* (2 vols., 1842),
John Sterling had spoken not so much of an unpoetical or prosaic age
but, more accurately, an age inchoately massing itself, through a
multiplicity of sensations, towards the very verge of utterance:

> Even our magazine stanzas, album sonnets, and rhymes in corners of
> newspapers aim at the forms of emotion, and use some of the words in
> which men of genius have symbolized profound thoughts. The whole,
> indeed, is generally a lump of blunder and imbecility, but in the midst there
> is often some turn of cadence, some attempt at an epithet of more
> significance and beauty than perhaps a much finer mind would have hit on
> a hundred years ago. The crowds of stammering children are yet the off-
> spring of an age that would fain teach them—if it knew how—a richer,
> clearer language than they can learn to speak. (*The Quarterly Review*,
> September 1842)

For Sterling, the problem that the age passed on to its art was a
problem of framework and form. The times were not as in Chaucer's
day when men had lived 'within the range marked out by custom':
modern England was notoriously confused, crowded, and incoherent, and it did not help that everyone said so, so repeatedly. We
found ourselves in a land of ever-increasing means without clear
ends, 'our overwrought materialism fevered by its own excess into
spiritual dreams'. Awash with sensations, mental associations were
nightmarishly rapid, randomly particular in their passage through
the impressed brain—like the molten 'atom-streams' in Tennyson's
'Lucretius', continuously flying apart and clashing together again
to 'make | Another and another frame of things | For ever'. 'Facts',
said Sterling, were not yet developed into 'thoughts', as philosophy
desires. In 'an age so diversified and as yet so unshapely', he concluded, anyone who 'draws forth any graceful and expressive forms',
who can turn 'into fixed beauty any part of the shifting and mingled
matter of our time' is 'well entitled to high praise'. So Dora Greenwell, for example, finds in 'The Railway Station' 'e'en now' an
under-song of humanity's meetings and partings. For just occasionally amidst a mass of content, says Sterling, an odd cadence or epithet
offered a passing clue towards a new framework of understanding.
And so it is ever increasingly after *Poems* (1842) in the strange
experiments of Tennyson—in that wide variety of voices from the

'Northern Farmer' dialect-poems, to the feminism of *The Princess*, to *Maud* above all:

> And the wheels go over my head,
> And my bones are shaken with pain,
> For into a shallow grave they are thrust,
> Only a yard beneath the street,
> And the hoofs of the horses beat, beat,
> The hoofs of the horses beat,
> Beat into my scalp and brain,
> With never an end to the stream of passing feet,
> Driving, hurrying, marrying, burying,
> Clamour and rumble, and ringing and clatter
>
> (*Maud* (1855), 2. 5)

In the preconceptual rhythmic sensations of Tennyson[6] it *still* seems stylistically astonishing and disturbing, and not just politically correct, to find the matter of new economic concerns within the old inherited lyricism of Parnassus. We talk of the Crimea, says the love-frenzied narrator of *Maud*, but what of the disguised civil war that goes on at home in the name of peaceful competitive trading? Is it only madness that brings love and politics together in a poem? Or, in the case of Clough's 'Amours de Voyage', what is it that links Claude's denial of both the revolutionary excitement of Rome in 1848 and the charms of a young English woman tourist? By a strange new realism, the poetry reproduces, with honest unease, a disorientating sense of incongruously confused categories and languages and voices: politics and poetry, morality and commerce, the energies of erotic love unsure of their source or their place:

> There the passions cramped no longer shall have scope and
>   breathing space;
> I will take some savage woman, she shall rear my dusky race.
>
> Iron jointed, supple-sinewed, they shall dive, and they shall run,
> Catch the wild goat by the hair, and hurl their lances in the sun
>
> .   .   .   .

---

[6] For a good account of issues at stake in rhythm and metre, see Yopie Prins, 'Victorian Meters', in Joseph Bristow (ed.), *The Cambridge Companion to Victorian Poetry* (Cambridge University Press), 89–113.

Fool, again the dream, the fancy! but I *know* my words are wild

('Locksley Hall', 1842)

If to find a new form is for Sterling the straight way to success, then demonstrably *not* to find it—'I *know* the words are wild'—is the strange, reversed, and roundabout route that was available to Tennyson. So Browning too in 'An Epistle of Karshish' can recover the meaning of Christ and the raising of Lazarus outside in, back to front, through the incredulous eyes of an Arab physician.

It is Walter Bagehot who best describes the variety of strategies in Victorian poetry and the difficulties implicitly necessitating their adoption. In an essay on 'Wordsworth, Tennyson and Browning' in *The National Review* (November 1864), Bagehot defined each poet respectively in terms of the categories Pure, Ornate, and Grotesque art.

Bagehot takes from Matthew Arnold's idea of 'the grand style' his account of Pure art as a classical ideal: an art calmly representing its object as perfectly as possible by the minimal possible means. In Milton and Wordsworth the ideal universal type is described chastely, 'in its simplicity', as if at the very beginning of things, without incidental detail or unnecessary clutter.

Ornate art, in contrast, works 'not by choice and selection but by accumulation and aggregation': it is the over-rich product of the psychology of associationism, gathering anxiously round its imperfect object 'every associated thought that can be connected with it' till 'nothing is described as it is' and 'everything has about it an atmosphere of *something else*'. Oppressively it offers too much, in fragments, to satisfy, and yet it cannot do with less, as its content struggles to compensate for its lack of form. Arising out of a later, more secondary phase of civilization than Pure art, Ornate art lacks final definition because of its nervously hidden wants. Thus Tennyson's 'Tears, idle tears' arise out of the incongruity of 'looking on the happy Autumn fields' and 'thinking of the days that are no more'. Above all, where Pure art can speak out what it has to say plainly and simply, 'and cannot hesitate', Ornate art deals with 'half belief', in 'an atmosphere of indistinct illusion and of moving shadow'. This then, says Bagehot, is the ornamental art of Tennyson, achieving only a second-order grandeur by clothing its wavering objects in what Hopkins would have called the disguise of a dreamy Parnassian richness. Yet 'all experience', says Tennyson's Ulysses

> is an arch wherethrough
> Gleams that untravelled world, whose margin fades
> For ever and for ever when I move.

And 'unto dying eyes', says the singer of 'Tears, idle tears',

> The casement slowly grows a glimmering square;
> So sad, so strange, the days that are no more

The glimmering square, the gleam through the arch—indistinct, hesitant, *half*-believing—are Ornate art almost transcending itself in the glimpse of a completion still only half-achieved on *this* side of the grave. The great image here, of poetic persistence of experience even amidst shadowy incompletion, strangeness, and difficulty, is Tennyson's refusal in *In Memoriam* to leave off mourning the death of Hallam, despite both his own self-doubts and the reproaches even of friends such as the poet Edward FitzGerald.

We need 'types', insists Bagehot, as we need genres in art or classifications in science—to provide a general background of understanding against which to make out specific variations. Otherwise, for example, we meet particular human beings and find that they do not mean anything to us: we do not understand them or know what to make of them, and so we forget them: 'for they *hitched* on to nothing, and we could not classify them'. But when we see 'the *type* of the genus', then 'the inferior specimens are explained by the perfect embodiment; the approximations are definable when we know the ideal to which they draw near'. Yet the third category of art in which Bagehot is interested is, in its strangeness and its disorderliness, the most characteristic of the Victorian period. It is the Grotesque or 'the type *in difficulties*'.

'That type of Perfect in his mind | In Nature can he nowhere find' ('The Two Voices'). The very idea of 'type' was itself in difficulties by the second quarter of the nineteenth century. Increased numbers, increased pace, increased crowding vertiginously disrupted the perceptual and moral sense of framework, scale, and perspective. Random associationism seemed a more appropriate model of mind in such contingent circumstances than Romantic idealism. The novel constantly confronted the blank or giddy sense of the collision of particular human beings, who made little of each other for want of anything but the most crude material measures of human classification. Biblical typology had always served to point towards a providentially assured future: now, traditional models, functions or vocations, were backward-looking, and in danger of being replaced by classification in terms of economics, profession, and class. By the second half of the century, with evolutionary theory, even species were no longer considered as fixed and absolute. The grotesque, says Bagehot, 'deals, to use the language of science, not with normal types but with abnormal specimens; to use the language of old philosophy, not with what nature is striving to be, but with what by some lapse she has happened to become'.

Here Bagehot was influenced by Ruskin. For in the third volume of *The Stones of Venice* (1853) Ruskin discussed the Grotesque as the impure phenomenon of artists forced to 'play' with their 'terror'. A claustrophobic sense of social imprisonment, of unrealizable models of feeling and being, could be released only in the overreaction of a symptomatically extreme excitement. A distorted intensity was produced, ranging from strange perverse humour and uneasy vulgar caricature to bitter quirkiness and pathological satire; from wildly extravagant fantasy to a decadent and diseased imaginativeness. Ruskin's literary examples were the humorists Thomas Hood ('Miss Kilmansegg and Her Precious Leg') and Lewis Carroll—and in particular amongst the novelists Charles Dickens, and amongst the poets Robert Browning. The Grotesque is thus the type of art in which type itself fails, the sense of a normative ideal is lost, and a radical sense of incongruity and displacement takes over.

Yet there still existed poetry which sought to locate itself within the great type images—in particular of pure love. The ancient chivalric 'type' of marriage, for example, is represented by Coventry Patmore's *The Angel in the House*, where within the formal pattern of courtship there is always *room* for the vulnerable young lovers to get themselves innerly used to inhabiting their new condition. Thus the newly weds are shy and delighted, in gentle comedy:

> So we two wore our strange estate:
> Familiar, unaffected, free,
> We talk'd, until the dusk grew late,
> Of this and that; but, after tea,
> As doubtful if a lot so sweet
> As ours was ours in very sooth,
> Like children, to promote conceit,
> We feign'd that it was not the truth;
> And she assumed the maiden coy,
> And I adored remorseless charms,
> And then we clapp'd our hands for joy,
> And ran into each other's arms.
>
> (bk. 2, canto 12, 'Husband and Wife')

'The quality of all emotion which is not ignoble is to boast of its allegiance to law', wrote Patmore in his influential 'Essay on English Metrical Law' (1857). And the law here is figured by both the type of marriage and the bounds of rhyme:

> They live by law, not like the fool,
> But like the bard, who freely sings
> In strictest bonds of rhyme and rule,
> And finds in them, not bonds, but wings.
>
> (bk. 1, canto 10, 'The Joyful Wisdom')

It is itself a marriage reached between 'the law of the verse and the freedom of the language':

> I vow'd unvarying faith, and she,
> To whom in full I pay that vow,
> Rewards me with variety
> Which men who change can never know.
>
> (bk. 2, canto 11, 'Constancy Rewarded')

'The language should always seem to *feel*, though not to *suffer from*, the bonds of verse', said Patmore, thus forming a thoroughgoing union of emotion with poetic technique, of corporeal metrics with spiritual content, of freedom and formal commitment.[7]

It is no wonder that the Patmore of fine later lyrics on the death of his first wife ('Departure') and the state of himself and his young son in bereavement ('The Toys') should also have been an admirer of the learned Dorsetshire dialect poet and country parson William Barnes. So too were the great philologist Max Muller and the innovative poet Gerard Manley Hopkins, as well as Thomas Hardy. For Barnes as for Patmore, family feelings are pieties: not just personal emotions but great rhythmic types, estates, and sacraments of being personally lived out. Barnes's tenderly specific lyrics on the courtship of his wife, their marriage, her early death, his widowerhood with five children form one of the great exemplary narratives of traditional goodness in the century, as rooted in tradition as the dialect in which they are for the most part written. For Barnes loved using the language's primary roots. To him, the earthy rural dialect was not a corruption of that 'proper' standard English which was increasingly insisted upon in the bourgeois manuals of 'correct' usage; it was the direct physical offspring of an earlier Anglo-Saxon tongue unobscured by later abstract Latinate overlays. Instead of 'dejected', Barnes wrote 'cast down'; instead of being 'imposed upon', 'put upon'; for 'opposed to', 'set against'. Yet it was the use of dialect, defending the very tone of the emotion within a felt tradition, which also contributed to the critical neglect of Barnes's poems, as belonging to rural backwaters. But 'Walken Hwome at Night', 'The Hedger', 'When We That Now Ha' Childern Wer Childern', 'The Turnstile', 'The Rwose in the Dark', 'The Vierzide Chairs', 'The Wife A-Lost', 'Leaves A-Vallen', 'Joy Passing By', 'Jay A-Pass'd', and many more poems written in the early 1860s go on in their provincial way, making the quiet claims of memory:

> An' often, at the evenen-tide
> I still so saunter out, wi' tears,
> Down drough the orcha'd, where my ears
> Do miass the vaïces gone.
>
> (The Vaïces that Be Gone)

---

[7] See Eric Griffiths, *The Printed Voice of Victorian Poetry* (Clarendon Press, 1989), ch. 3.

Yet Patmore, who converted to Catholicism after the death of his first wife, described his own age as one of 'unnatural divorce of sense and sound'. And it is something like divorce, in every sense, that produces the contrasting grotesque reality of George Meredith's *Modern Love* (1862) which, on its publication, Meredith himself described in a letter to Augustus Jessopp of 20 September 1862 as 'a dissection of the sentimental passion of these days'.

Modern Love is the story of a marriage continuing amidst marital infidelities, with a romantic language which fits ill, indeed surreally, with the horrors it describes. But it is precisely that sense of ill-fittingness—including the extension of the traditional fourteen-line sonnet into sixteen lines—which Meredith is after. 'See that I am drawn to her even now', says the cuckolded husband—only to fear that where he kisses, her lover has kissed before (Sonnet 3). Yet still she plays the hostess, I the host, and the guests (including her secret lover) are happy:

> They see no ghost.
> With sparkling surface-eyes we play the ball:
> It is in truth a most contagious game:
> HIDING THE SKELETON, shall be its name.
> Such play as this, the devil might appal!
> But here's the greater wonder; in that we
> Enamoured of an acting nought can tire,
> Each other, like true hypocrites, admire.

(Sonnet 17)

This is the work of a 'discord-loving clown', a state of affairs so painfully ludicrous as not to be able to be expressed by the normal tone and language of Arnoldian high seriousness. To see this verse as against the work of Patmore and Barnes is to recognize the grotesque.

'Good elements hidden in horrid accompaniments', wrote Bagehot, 'are the special theme of grotesque art.' *Modern Love* insists that the modern way is ever tending towards the failure of the old types and forms, in both literature and the world. It leaves behind Meredith's own beautiful version of Patmore, the earlier idyllic poem of pastoral courtship 'Love in the Valley', written in 1852 but still revised, despite *Modern Love*, in 1878:

for she is what my heart first awaking
Whispered the world was; morning light is she.

Yet the bitter implication of *Modern Love* is that historically, social-ly, the future of marriage and of love itself is fatally determined, the more so as the nineteenth century nears its evening. Bagehot himself feared that a society that had lost its sense of norms would grow (grotesquely) used to the grotesque life—even as in *Modern Love* the couple carry on playing the game and admire each other bitterly for so doing, share moments of renewed sexual alliance, and yet have each their own alternative partners. Browning in particular had become conditioned to the grotesque, said Bagehot, just as soldiers become habituated to warfare, until, no longer sick-ened by the smell of blood, they actually gain an appetite for slaugh-ter: 'It is a principle that if we put down a healthy instinctive aversion, nature avenges herself by creating an unhealthy insane attraction' ('Wordsworth, Tennyson and Browning'). So, for exam-ple, a couple in Browning's 'The Statue and the Bust' do not commit adultery but in delaying, die unfulfilled: one of the poem's voices speaks from the moral norm, 'But delay was best I For their end was a crime'; but there is another voice which says:

—Oh, a crime will do
As well, I reply, to serve for a test

As a virtue golden through and through

There's a sort of half-terrible, half-marvellous, rough courage in this second impure and anti-melancholic voice, practically committed to living out the instinct for life—be it crime or in virtue, in war or peace, in sanity or madness: 'Let a man contend to the uttermost I For his life's set prize, be it what it will!' For Browning, at once so neurotic and so robust, always accepts the grotesquely abnormal, and with the impressive second-order crudeness of Victorian will-power, lives it out because it has now to be *made* normal, individual-istically. That is the meaning of 'Childe Roland to the Dark Tower Came', still going through with the absurd old quest he has wearily almost given up on:

For, what with my whole world-wide wandering,
What with my search drawn out thro' years, my hope
Dwindled into a ghost not fit to cope

> With that obstreperous joy success would bring,—
> I hardly tried now to rebuke the spring
> My heart made, finding failure in its scope.

In all its twists and turns, this is the impure Browning version of Tennyson's 'Ulysses', the Grotesque semi-sceptic and the heroic Parnassian stoic unexpectedly close to each other.

It is a resemblance representative of a broader general truth about Victorian poetry. For what unites Browning and Tennyson despite their differences is the larger fact that the Grotesque itself is only an extreme example of what Victorian poetry is in general: the type in difficulties amidst the strange unplaceable phenomena of experience. In the liminal hesitancies of so much Victorian poetry—at doorways, in catches of breath at line-endings even—there is a difficult negotiation for the desired, elusive, reluctant or half-lost typefeeling to inhabit the poem's own situation:

> Shall I never miss
> Home-talk and blessing and the common kiss
> That comes to each in turn, nor count it strange,
> When I look up, to drop on a new range
> Of walls and floors . . .
>
>   (Elizabeth Barrett Browning, *Sonnets from*
>   *the Portuguese*, 35)

For this is writing that manifests the need to turn apparent disability

> for, heart, thou shalt find her—
> Next time, herself!—not the trouble behind her.
>   (Browning, 'Love in a Life')

into a sufficient subject: 'Still the same chance! she goes out as I enter'. Thus in Clough's 'Amours de Voyage' and Meredith's *Modern Love*, the poems seem implicitly to cry out over their own travesties of experience, Is this what is really meant by 'Love'? Is this meant to be 'Marriage'? For the motive behind those long Victorian poetic sequences—in particular, in the continuous process of losing and finding within *In Memoriam*—lies in the often unavailing need, through each successive lyric attempt, to refind the type, the form, the way. As Tennyson knew from his reading of Lyell, and as *The*

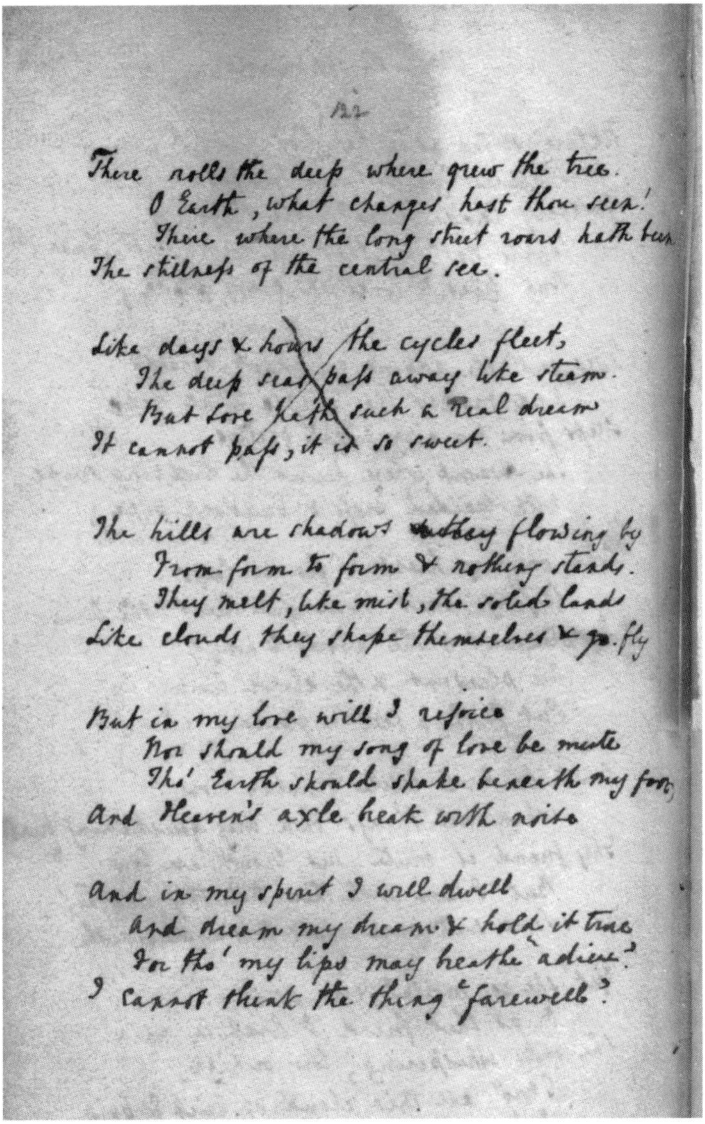

122

There rolls the deep where grew the tree.
O Earth, what changes hast thou seen!
There where the long street roars hath been
The stillness of the central sea.

Like days & hours the cycles fleet,
The deep seas pass away like steam.
But love hath such a real dream
It cannot pass, it is so sweet.

The hills are shadows as they flowing by
From form to form & nothing stands.
They melt, like mist, the solid lands
Like clouds they shape themselves & go. fly

But in my love will I rejoice
Nor should my song of love be mute
Tho' Earth should shake beneath my foot
And Heaven's axle heak with noise

And in my spirit I will dwell
And dream my dream & hold it true
For tho' my lips may breathe adieu?
I cannot think the thing "farewell"?

Fig. 13. Tennyson, *In Memoriam* 123, Trinity Manuscript, *c.*1842, one of the sections on evolution, and at that stage of composition the last poem in the manuscript sequence, characteristically ending, nonetheless, with 'I cannot think the thing "farewell".'

Vestiges of Creation and Darwin were later to confirm,[8] 'A thousand types are gone' (*In Memoriam*, 56).

With so much variety, experimentation, and strategic indirection, there can be no straightforward literary history of Victorian poetry—not even in chronological terms when the premature death of the second-generation Romantics left their successors stranded in a time lag; when 1850 saw the publication of *The Prelude*, posthumously, alongside *In Memoriam*, two long poems of memory actually separated by nearly fifty years; when Keats's letters to Fanny Brawne only appeared publicly for the first time in 1878; and when the first generation of Tennyson and Browning outlasted their own second-generation successors Arnold and Clough. Yet the sheer variety of differing voices is itself an expression of 'the type in difficulties', even though across those shared difficulties the poets could often hardly speak to each other—as the correspondence between Arnold and Clough makes clear.

The language of communication was itself in difficulties, when the poets were meant to be the great defenders of language.[9] The American man of letters Ralph Waldo Emerson spoke of language as 'fossil poetry' and, quoting him, R. C. Trench went on to describe many a single word as 'itself a concentrated poem' with a story to tell us (*The Study of Words* (1851), lecture 1). Yet how far these deep historic meanings could survive in contemporary society was like another of evolution's tests. As the writers of nonsense verse in their playful scepticism well knew, language was not of itself a necessary guarantee of meaning, let alone truth:

for language, though indispensable as an instrument of thought, lends itself with equal facility to every combination, and thus furnishes no criterion by which we can judge between sense and nonsense—between the conceivable and the inconceivable. A round square or a bilinear figure, is, as a form of speech, quite as possible as a straight line or an equilateral triangle. The mere juxtaposition of the words does not indicate the possibility or the impossibility of the corresponding conception. (H. L. Mansel, *Metaphysics* (1860), pp. 187–8)

It is Clough who most overtly represents the mid-century conscious-

[8]   See above, pp. 61–7.
[9]   See Dennis Taylor, *Hardy's Literary Language and Victorian Philology* (Clarendon Press, 1993).

ness of what is often suppressed even by the very use of language itself. And it is, likewise, Clough who is most politically conscious of the dangers of infection by a mass language—the language of newspapers, of political slogans, of conventional pieties—acting as an automatic replacement for thought. The Victorian poet could take the well-worn word 'Duty' and then find the word turn under his very pen from its religious and ethical meaning to its now social and political register, as Clough sees in this short poem:

> DUTY—that's to say complying
> With whate'er's expected here
>
> ('Duty')

'The noted phrase of the prayer-book, | *Doing our duty in that state of life to which God has called us*':

> Seems to me always to mean, when the little rich boys say it
> .   .   .   .
> Eat, drink, and never mind others.
>
> (*The Bothie of Tober-Na-Vuolich*, 2. 203–7)

But in the face of words that offer either bluff confidence or hidden evasion, it was the real duty of the poet, Clough believed, to be hesitant, even at the cost of seeming weak—

> I tremble for something factitious,
> Some malpractice of heart and illegitimate process;
> We are so prone to these things with our terrible notions of duty.
>
> ('Amours de Voyage', 2. 11)

—scrupulously hesitant in order not to foreclose the complex relation between using words, making sense, and finding truth and meaning:

> Hints haunt me ever of a More beyond:
> I am rebuked by a sense of the incomplete,
> Of a completion over-soon assumed,
> Of adding up too soon.
>
> ('Dipsychus', scene 11)

To Matthew Arnold, Clough was risking the very ruin of poetry by such dissection. Yet the disturbing consciousness that Clough dares to represent so fully in himself was nothing less than what was present intermittently and at different levels in all the age's poets.

Thus amidst all the diversity, there was one truth which, as Matthew Arnold claimed, stood out above all: that modern times found themselves fundamentally unsynchronized

> with an immense system of institutions, established facts, accredited dogmas, customs, rules, which have come to them from times not modern. In this system life has to be carried forward, yet they have a sense that this system is not of their own creation, that it by no means corresponds exactly with the wants of their actual life, that, for them, it is customary, not rational. The awakening of this sense is the awakening of the modern spirit. ('On the Modern Element in Literature' (1869), in *Complete Prose Works*, vol. 1, pp. 18–37)

The internally felt 'want of correspondence'—that sense of a gap between meaning and language, between mind and the terms inside which it had to work, even within itself; the lack of true verbal fit too with the surrounding social world; the unease as to what in the way of the inarticulate, the tacit, the anomalous, or the unspeakable was going unexpressed or being fenced off even in the very act of using language—all this was what the poets, in so many strange forms, most vulnerably registered in their intimate relation to the available language:

> And long we try in vain to speak and act
> Our hidden self, and what we say and do
> Is eloquent, is well—but 'tis not true!
>
> (Arnold, 'The Buried Life')

II. Long Poems and Sequence Poems

To Matthew Arnold poems such as his own *Empedocles on Etna*[10] were long but long in an inadequate way: 'in which the suffering finds no vent in action; in which a continuous state of mental distress is prolonged, unrelieved by incident, hope, or resistance; in which there is everything to be endured, nothing to be done' ('Preface to the First Edition' of *Poems*, 1853).

[10] See above, pp. 76–8, 96.

Arnold believed in a poetry that was not small, occasional, or transient, that was not passively at the mercy of recent history, but which created through itself a dimension steadily *above* the world and outside time, 'becoming a complete *magister vitae* [teacher of life] as the poetry of the ancients did' ('The Study of Poetry' (1880), in *Complete Prose Works*, vol. 9, pp. 161–88). If poetry was again to become that director of life, it had like the poetry of the ancients to include 'religion with poetry, instead of existing as poetry only, and leaving religious wants to be supplied by the Christian religion, as a power existing independent of the poetic power' (letter to Clough, 28 October 1852).

But to Arnold the poetry of Keats and Shelley, of Browning, Tennyson, and Clough had no such mastery, no form, no 'architectonicé': alike it lost itself 'in parts and episodes and ornamental work', it did not 'press forwards to the whole' (letter to Clough, 28 October 1852), for it had no 'Idea of the world in order not to be prevailed over by the world's multitudinousness' and so only replicated that multitudinousness (letter to Clough, September 1848 or 1849). In Arnold's great poem 'The Buried Life' the failure of poetry in the nineteenth century is seen within the broader perspective of the general failure of human expression and self-understanding. Indeed, for Arnold, as for Sterling and Bagehot, the age's inability to create and sustain a great epic poem was not just poetry's problem but a failure of form symptomatic of the very structurelessness of modern existence where 'each half-lives a hundred different lives' ('The Scholar Gypsy'). So much of Arnold's own poetic work takes that failure of utterance as its subject matter, the lyrics reading like broken epics, in which rarely and only briefly

> A bolt is shot back somewhere in our breast,
> And a lost pulse of feeling stirs again.

> ('The Buried Life')

As 'the Sea of Faith' goes out and Arnold is left hearing 'its melancholy, long withdrawing roar' ('Dover Beach'), the lyrics become residual fragments washed up on dry land:

> Silent, while years engrave the brow;
> Silent—the best are silent now.

> ('Stanzas from the Grande Chartreuse')

Just above the level of silence, these are austerely quiet neoclassical elegies caught, nonetheless, in the act of romantically lamenting a lost greatness of order and style and stature: 'A great human action of a thousand years ago is more interesting . . . than a small human action of to-day' ('Preface to the First Edition' of *Poems*, 1853). The novel dealt in the small human actions of today, whilst meanwhile the poetry of Arnold's 'Rugby Chapel' must tell of the loss of a father's large sense of quest and goal: 'We, we only are left', 'We bring | Only ourselves'.

In direct contemporary contrast with Arnold's sense of the diminished possibility of epic, there is, however, in 1856 this voice in the midst of a poem occupying nine books, each of about 1,200 lines:

> The critics say that epics have died out
> With Agamemnon and the goat-nursed gods;
> I'll not believe it . . .

> (*Aurora Leigh*, 5. 139–41)

'Every age', writes Elizabeth Barrett Browning, appears to souls who live in it 'most unheroic'. The critics, commentators, and poets have talked themselves into calling our age 'an age of mere transition':

> meaning nought
> Except that what succeeds must shame it quite
> If God please. That's wrong thinking, to my mind,
> And wrong thoughts make poor poems.

> (*Aurora Leigh*, 5. 163–6)

Committed to living neither in the future nor in the past but in the present, *Aurora Leigh*, said Hippolyte Taine, was 'a system of notation . . . created from instant to instant, out of anything and everything'.[11] It is the voice of a woman who has won her present liveliness by making herself an enemy to the stubbornly retarding tendency of her own unhappiness. Miseries strike, she says, and we want to say a permanent 'farewell Life!':

> And so, as froward babes, we hide our eyes
> And think all ended.—Then Life calls to us

---

[11] *Notes on England* (1871), trans. W. F. Rae (1872), ch. 8 ('The English Mind').

And what all too often do we then do, but resist or resent that call: why?

> because we are more ashamed
> To own our compensations than our griefs
> (*Aurora Leigh*, 1. 672–3, 677–8)

Compensations are better than griefs, though not so heroic looking. In the poem's narrative it is brave success, not gloomy failure, that is celebrated and coaxed out of guilt and remorse. Wry intelligent wit—the short-circuiting insouciant voice of Byron's *Don Juan* made female—is here the salutary light enemy of heavy elegiac melancholy. It makes satire not cynical or bitter but a sharp instrument of survival and liberation. The moralistic Evangelical aunt with whom the poem's protagonist is forced to reside,

> had lived, we'll say,
> A harmless life, she called a virtuous life,
> A quiet life, which was not life at all
> (But that, she had not lived enough to know)
> (*Aurora Leigh*, 1. 287–90)

A poem *is* a person to Elizabeth Barrett Browning, and both poem and person first of all need inner *life* ahead of anything else:

> What form is best for poems? Let me think
> Of forms less, and the external. Trust the spirit,
> As sovran nature does, to make the form;
> For otherwise we only imprison spirit
> And not embody. Inward evermore
> To outward—so in life, and so in art
> Which still is life.
> (*Aurora Leigh*, 5. 223–9)

Romantic self-expression is not a mere commonplace to the woman of the later nineteenth century but as new as she is: it is a capacity that, for example, Dora Greenwell simply admired in her two sonnets to Elizabeth Barrett Browning and in 'The Singer': 'These are not only Songs they sing | They are the Singer's Life'. In *Aurora Leigh* there is, beyond momentary song, the sustained breakthrough of a freshly freed voice, delighting in the undeniable realities of the present, the particular, the informal. It is a voice unashamed of being Romantically resistant to the very idea of predetermining genres, of conventional forms, fixed hierarchies and set attitudes—including, remarkably, her own. For not only does she challenge the male cousin, the would-be political reformer and social statistician, who

> lives by diagrams,
> And crosses out the spontaneities
> Of all his individual, personal life
> With formal universals.
>
> (3. 744–7)

No less surely does she also combat the need for general systems on her own side: too often a woman in this age

> fears
> To let the perfect action take her part,
> And rest there: she must prove what she can do
> Before she does it, prate of woman's rights,
> Of woman's mission, woman's function. . .
>
> (8. 816–22)

The poem is itself like someone making a new and specifically individual start to life, opening up closed roads, and securing an authentic preliminary basis, however flawed, partial, and vulnerable to criticism:

> Poems are
> Men, if true poems—and who dares exclaim
> At any man's door, 'Here, 'tis understood
> The thunder fell last week and killed a wife
> And scared a sickly husband—what of that?
> Get up, be merry, shout and clap your hands,
> Because a cheerful genius suits the times—'?
> None says so to the man, and why indeed
> Should any to the poem?
>
> (3. 90–8)

Aurora Leigh is at its most vital when, in the very act of its writing, it opens up the autobiography of life *within* art. 'The world of books is still the world' (bk. 1. 748).

But the choice represented by the contrast between Matthew

Arnold and Elizabeth Barrett Browning was one that Arnold had already expressed in his own stark terms at the end of his 'Preface to the First Edition' of *Poems* (1853):

Two kinds of *dilettanti*, says Goethe, there are in poetry: he who neglects the indispensable mechanical part, and thinks he has done enough if he shows spirituality and feeling; and he who seeks to arrive at poetry merely by mechanism, in which he can acquire an artisan's readiness, and is without soul and matter. And he adds, that the first does most harm to art, and the last to himself. If we must be *dilettanti*: if it is impossible for us, under the circumstances amidst which we live, to think clearly, to feel nobly, and to delineate firmly: if we cannot attain to the mastery of the great artists;— let us, at least, have so much respect for our art as to prefer it to ourselves. Let us not bewilder our successors; let us transmit to them the practice of poetry, with its boundaries and wholesome regulative laws, under which excellent works may again, perhaps, at some future time, be produced.

Aurora Leigh has no successor in Victorian poetic writing. Arnold's choice was for art, for the conservation of poetry through transmittable lyric echoes of a lost grand style which, even without a present goal, at least held onto the past while awaiting a future. Yet if that was Arnold's critical preference between the two poles of Classic Art and Expressive Self, his poetic achievement was to make the choice of the one pole (classicism) include within itself the experience of the loss of the other. The calm clarity of the static opposites within Arnold's verse prevents his poetry restlessly falling apart even if it keeps it also locked and truncated:

> Ah! two desires toss about
> The poet's feverish blood.
> One drives him to the world without,
> And one to solitude.
>
> ('In Memory of the Author of
> "Obermann"')

The borrowing of this second-order lucidity is a form-preserving means of being able to speak of the self's predicament, without actually taking the poetry down into that disordered space between the alternatives, as Arnold accused Clough's verse of doing.

If to Arnold epic was the great lost form, to other poets the continuous long poem still remained a possibility, even in the religious
or post-religious challenge of creating a cosmogony for the modern
world. The long verse dramas of the 'Spasmodic' school, for
example—so-called for their violent celebration of Keatsian excess
and Faustian excitement—were dismissed by Arnold as characteristically post-Romantic: fragmentary, overwrought, fantastic, wanting in sanity. Yet Philip Bailey's *Festus* (1839), Alexander Smith's
Life Drama (1853), and Sidney Dobell's *Balder* (1854) arose out of
that desire to live many lives pressed into one great life, which is so
powerfully expressed in Dobell's fine lyric 'Perhaps':

> Ten heads and twenty hearts! so that this me,
> Having more room and verge, and striking less
> The cage that galls us into consciousness,
> Might drown the rings and ripples of to be
> In the smooth deep of being . . .

Then again, in the midst of failure, the Chartist poet Thomas
Cooper published in 1845 a ten-book epic in Spenserian stanzas *The
Purgatory of Suicides: A Prison Rhyme*, an analysis of political
despair which brings together, in a debate within purgatory, figures
as historically diverse as Judas and Empedocles and Castlereagh.
A far more conservative world-view is found in Tennyson's *Idylls of
the King*, one of the period's Arthurian imitations prompted by the
republication of Malory's *Morte D'Arthur* in 1816, and assembled
over a period of twenty-eight years from 1857. It is an attempt to re-
create, as parable, the whole separate world of the Round Table in
an England and a poem alike held together only by internal laws
of loyalty, character, and conscience. Alternatively, from the quite
different perspective of fifteenth-century Spain, George Eliot's *The
Spanish Gypsy* (1868) offers a modern Darwinian version of the elemental conflicts of ancient Greek tragedy, the protagonists almost
physically divided between the rival demands of hereditary claims
and individual need: between the deep memory of race, family, home,
on the one hand, and the compelling love of an outsider, on the other.
Fedalma is the Spanish Gypsy, a beautiful foundling who, raised a
Spaniard and due to marry a Spanish nobleman, discovers she is after
all the daughter of the Gypsies' leader. The poem's Jews, Christians,

and Moors may all now mock the Gypsy outcasts, but long ago they too, she knows,

> Were slaves, lost, wandering, sunk beneath a curse,
> Till Moses, Christ and Mahomet were born,
> Till beings lonely in their greatness lived,
> And lived to save their people.

(bk. 1)

It is the call of the Gypsies which provides the imaginative spur to begin again the story of the old myths, in the midst of contemporary conflicts, and this prompts a whole series of astonishing thoughts— 'Feeling and action flowing into one | . . . as full vowelled words | Are new impregnate with the master's thought': 'But is it what we love, or how we love, | That makes life good?' (bk. 1).

There is no shortage of variety in these attempts at creating other worlds through a power of imagination which, undermined in the present, so often seeks a future even through the past or the distant. Though no more than four hundred lines long in its final version, Edward FitzGerald's *Rubaiyat of Omar Khayyam* (first published 1859, revised in its three subsequent editions) offered a sceptical hedonistic Persian alternative to both the ascetic stoicism of Arnold's own *Empedocles on Etna* and the sorrowing Christianity of Tennyson's *In Memoriam*. 'Make Game of that which makes as much of Thee' (1859, stanza 45); fill the cup and drink, for wine is all the meaning of the universe:

> And fear not lest Existence closing your
> Account, and mine, should know the like no more;
>   The Eternal Sáki from that Bowl has poured
> Millions of Bubbles like us, and will pour.

(1889, stanza 46)

Admired by Swinburne and Dante Gabriel Rossetti for offering a way of thinking outside the conventions, the *Rubaiyat* should be read alongside Richard Burton's neglected, one-thousand-line poem *The Kasidah* (supposed written 1843–4 but not published until 1880). Pretending to be a translation of the wisdom of the Sufi master Haji, it accepts virtually all the sceptical propositions on offer in the Victorian age: that our idea of a personal God laying down

reward or punishment hereafter is man-made; that no organized religion has the truth; that man, though large in his own eyes, is tiny and
ignorant within the great universe; that there is no clear distinction
between right and wrong; that everything has evolved out of matter.
But though Burton, posing as his own editor, admits that the poem is
'destructive in appearance', it uses these thoughts to break down
pride and fear and certainty, he says, and by creating a state of
unknowing becomes 'essentially reconstructive'. The idealist Zealot
may cry out against the 'matter-mongers' of science who reduce all to
molecules and protoplasm, but the mystic Sufi master replies in calm
acceptance of evolution:

> Vain cavil! all that is hath come
> Either by Miracle or by Law; -
> Why waste on this your hate and fear,
> Why waste on that your love and awe?
>
> Why heap such hatred on a word,
> Why 'Prototype' to type assign?
> Why upon matter spirit mass?
> Wants an appendix your design?
>
> Is not the highest honour his
> Who from the worst hath drawn the best?
>
> (bk. 7, stanzas 16–18)

Why these names, these fears? what need for forms and categories
amidst continually transforming process? This essentially *religious*
scepticism, forming its questions so teasingly on the ever-shifting
boundary between faith and unbelief, is poetry not so much for any
brilliance of diction or invention, but because it holds to the belief
that what is crucial is not the literal meaning of the thoughts so much
as the *way* in which they are held—the tacit context or the emergent
form through which those thoughts are moved into their right perspective.

Yet the period's two most significantly contrasting efforts at the long
poem are those of William Morris and Robert Browning.

William Morris's compendium of tales *The Earthly Paradise*
(1868–70) extends into the confidence of full-blown verse narrative
the work that Morris had done in his impressive dramatic lyrics of

1858: the snapshots of Arthurian legend and medieval history in 'The Defence of Guenevere', 'The Haystack in the Floods', and 'Sir Peter Harpdon's End'. Arising out of Morris's retelling of the journeyings of Jason and the Argonauts in his seventeen-book *The Life and Death of Jason* (1867), *The Earthly Paradise* was published in four parts and three volumes and consists of over 45,000 lines of verse. One of the longest poems in the language, it consists of twenty-four stories told within the framework of a larger, failed narrative. That narrative is the story of a band of fourteenth-century wanderers who set out on an odyssey in search of a paradise upon earth, but now disappointed and wearied old men, take a last refuge in 'some Western land'. To pass the time that remains, two tales are told each month—one by the wanderers, one by their hosts—from March onwards, with each month introduced by a poem describing its nature. The recounting of these ancient stories, usually of struggling defeat or painful loss, is thus set within a second framework: the great repetitive cycle of the seasonal year, moving out of winter and back into it again, like the archetypal life story through which the wanderers have passed repeatedly. In that context it does not seem to matter that the tales or the thoughts accompanying them are not wholly new. For Morris had created a framework of tradition in which the great human thoughts came round again and again in a deeper sense of that word 'original'.

The famous opening lines of Morris's Apology ('The idle singer of an empty day') and Prologue ('Forget six counties overhung with smoke . . .') have served only to convince critics that *The Earthly Paradise* may be safely dismissed as a loose profusion of classical and medieval escapism. Yet the whole point of the poem is that there is *no* earthly paradise, and there can be no escape—not even from the repressed but painfully continuing hope of that paradise. Even when in their first youthful voyage the wanderers first imagined they had sighted Paradise, the feeling was well-nigh unbearable:

> Then might be seen how hard is this world's lot
> When such a marvel was our grief forgot,
> And what a thing the world's joy is to bear
> When on our hearts the broken bonds of care
> Had left such scars, no man of us could say
> The burning words upon his lips that lay;

> Since trained to hide the depths of misery,
> Amidst that joy no more our tongues were free.
>
> (Prologue)

Like a simple founding text describing the very fall from simplicity, the poem offers its readers a sort of anonymous genetic memory. For so long have human beings had to 'train' themselves to endure disappointment—without even admitting it to *be* disappointment—that they have almost forgotten their latent hope, so vulnerably released here by the sight of something apparently too good to be true. 'What hour is this | That brings so fair a thing to crown my bliss', says one protagonist, poignantly adding to his beloved: 'How shall I know that such a thing is true, | Unless some pain yet fall on thee and me' ('Bellerophon in Lycia').

And as it is with hope and joy, so is it again and again with the bitter-sweet life-force of sexual love in Morris:

> they, by whom all close
> Her body passed, must tremble, and be fain
> To think of common things to dull the pain
> Of longing, as her lovely majesty
> Too sweet and strange for earth, brushed swiftly by.
>
> ('The Story of Rhodope')

In tales of sexual complication and betrayal, such as 'The Lovers of Gudrun', *The Earthly Paradise* shows the pain of the simple man who has lost simplicity and must feel at least two things now when the integrity of his whole life depended upon feeling one. Erotic love may be 'a trap baited well | With some first minutes of unheard-of bliss', but 'How shall I hate my love?':

> Yea, the end is hell and death,
> The midmost hid, yet the beginning Love.
> Ah me! despite the worst Love threateneth,
> Still would I cling on . . .
>
> ('The Hill of Venus')

It is bad enough that there is no paradise ever to be found on earth; it is worse that, instead, there is always, recurrently, the unlosable feeling of the loss of it. And yet Morris's protagonists 'cling on' to the sadness even in hope itself and cannot but go on from the lost begin-

ning through the veiled midmost to the foreknown end. Narrative
here is not just a frame but a commitment.

Emotionally driven onward by events swiftly passing by, the
narratives in *The Earthly Paradise* are to be read fast and at length,
till the reader becomes so accustomed to the slightly archaic diction
and syntax as hardly to notice them at all, save as providing a sort
of large, anonymous, neutral time and place for poetry to work in.
'So let me sing of names remembered | Because they, living not, can
ne'er be dead | Or long time take their memories quite away' ('An
Apology'). As Morris recognizes, the tales achieve a strange resonant
effect upon the mortals who listen to them—as thus the bitter-sweet
sense of coming round, for the ageing wanderers, after the end of
'The Death of Paris':

> And thoughts uncertain, hard to grasp, did flit
> 'Twixt the beginning and the end of it —
> And to their ancient eyes it well might seem
> Lay tale in tale, as dream within a dream;
> Untold now the beginning, and the end
> Not to be heard by those whose feet should wend
> Long ere that tide through the dim ways of death . . .

Just below the level of normal consciousness, these stories, like little
life forms in the middle of things, suggest the larger life epic outside
them, awakening the listener to intimations of the greater beginning
and the greater end. In themselves they remain nonetheless contained
within a stoic solidity of life, close to the primal simplicity of the Ice-
landic sagas which Morris translated: 'no word is wasted in the
process of giving the detail. There is nothing didactic and nothing
rhetorical in these stories; the reader is left to make his own commentary on the events' (*The Saga Library*, 5 vols. (1891–5), vol. 1,
preface).

Thus, amidst a surrounding silence, the detail exists to hold emotion spare and tight inside the physical condition of the dying Paris:

> And in their midst a litter did they bear
> Whereon lay one with linen wrapped around,
> Whose wan face turned into the fresher air
> As though a little pleasure he had found
> Amidst of pain . . .
>
> ('The Death of Paris')

Feeling here is not individually introspective as it is in Tennyson or Browning; feeling in Morris is physical, it is a life's inner register of the outside world, which human beings must still inhabit. *The Earthly Paradise* is a version of what in *News from Nowhere* (1891) leads a young woman to dismiss nineteenth-century individualism, with its overconscious interest in self and its concerns with identity. For in 'The Death of Paris' or 'The Son of Croesus', Morris remains stoically committed to individual feeling being wholly channelled into a world of work and tasks, of effort, action, and acceptance, where realities are confronted as external necessities.

The spareness of physical detail is exactly matched with the bleakness of that condition. So in 'The Love of Alcestis', Alcestis is granted the power to save the life of her husband Admetus, but on condition she loses not only her own life but thereafter the love of Admetus himself, shamed by her sacrifice on his behalf. At least if he had simply died and I lived, cries Alcestis, 'I had not lost him . . . | For still was he in me'. Yet in full knowledge, she still makes the bare sacrifice and departs:

> Her lonely shadow even now did pass
> Along the changeless fields, oft looking back,
> As though it yet had thought of some great lack.

Then Admetus himself, finding the price of his life to be loss of love for her who saved it, ironically 'fell wondering if his life were gain'. And now there is no one left to say if it had been worth the sacrifice. 'The reader is left to make his own commentary on the events.' Before the advent of Thomas Hardy, *The Earthly Paradise* is the most unflinchingly painful work of the century—the work of a determinedly simple man committed to single-minded action in what he nonetheless knows to be a world of complexity.

Browning offered, in contrast, what H. B. Forman writing in the *London Quarterly Review* (July 1869) called 'the Epic of Psychology'. In an age of evolutionary theory, it seemed plausible that, like species, genre itself should be capable of modification, and the modern variant of epic was of the inner not the outer world. 'So find, so fill full, so appropriate forms', says Browning himself near the beginning of his epic—seeking imaginatively to melt the external hardness of the past into something now more fluid.

Browning's *The Ring and the Book* was issued in monthly parts between November 1868 and February 1869. Set in late Renaissance Florence, where the aristocrat Guido is suspected of killing his young wife, it tells the same story of murder ten times over, from within different subjective points of view. Employing the form of the trial in law, with witnesses each in turn giving their relative testimonies as in Wilkie Collins's *The Woman in White* (1860), it is the long poem turned into an experimental novel in verse. But where *Aurora Leigh* has a definite trust in narrative—the story of Aurora, her cousin, and the fallen Marion Erle—the structure of *The Ring and the Book* is created precisely by the suspension of any belief that a story can ever be fully known or truthfully told. That is why in *The Speaker* (January 1891) Henry James famously defined Browning's 'modernness' in terms of 'the all-touching, all-trying spirit of his work, permeated with accumulations and playing with knowledge'.

It is that fluid 'playing' with knowledge which characterizes Browning's mobile capacity to step outside any situation or any point of view, even when seemingly in its very midst. This externalizing capacity, which enabled Browning to create his dramatic monologues, is often in the ten extended dramatic monologues of *The Ring and the Book* on the very verge of alienated disgust. Untethered from a sure relation to truth, belief, and even trust in narrative, 'modernness' in Browning makes for the bitter human game in which anything is plausible, everything fluid, and nothing wholly trustworthy.

It is not only that in book 5 a guilty man can speak as though he were innocent. But, once Guido is condemned in book 11, even an innocent man, found guilty, could only speak thereafter with a criminalized consciousness, knowing he sounded guilty. Guido is not an innocent man—but he can still know what it is like to feel like one, as he calls out to his judges:

> You understand me and forgive, sweet Sirs?
> I blame you, tear my hair and tell my woe—
> All's but a flourish, figure of rhetoric!
> One must try each expedient to save life.

> (11. 849–52)

This strange, stranded, and sarcastic tone exists in place of the simpler, straighter personal expressiveness of *Aurora Leigh* or even *The Earthly Paradise*. For there is hardly any space left to Guido between authority's assumption that he will always be lying and his own consciousness of that unvarying reception. Worse, there is no longer any room for a distinction between his own manipulation of rhetoric and any genuine pain he may nonetheless be feeling even in so doing. And this society which judges me, Guido cries, is itself corrupt. That too has in it an aspect which separately is true—the society *is* corrupt—albeit pronounced so by a person who is false. It is that ever-shifting clash of different levels of consideration, that disturbing dichotomy

> the dangerous edge of things,
> The honest thief, the tender murderer,
> The superstitious atheist . . .
>   .   .   .   .   .
>   one step aside,
> They're classed and done with.

('Bishop Blougram's Apology')

—which characteristically had fascinated Browning in the moment-by-moment shifts of balance in the dramatic monologue.

Hence the twists and turns of Guido's multiple defences of himself. For here I stand, he says, an old aristocratic husband alleged to have murdered a low-born but beautiful young wife: look at the society that judges me; consider what that wife and her handsome young priestly protector may have got up to; add too the connivance of her grey-haired parents who tricked me into marrying for wealth. Then, wasn't my interpretation plausible?

> Reject the plausible they do, these fools,
> Who never even make pretence to show
> One point beyond its plausibility
> In favour of the best belief they hold!
> 'Saint Somebody-or-other raised the dead:'
> Did he? How do you come to know as much?
>   .   .   .   .   .
> Tell them my story—'plausible but false!'
> False to be sure! What else can story be
> That runs—a young wife tired of an old spouse,

Found a priest whom she fled away with,—both
Took their full pleasure in the two-days' flight,
Which a grey-headed greyer-hearted pair,
(Whose best boast was, their life had been a lie)
Helped for the love they bore all liars. Oh,
Here incredulity begins! Indeed?
Allow then, were no one point strictly true,
There's that i' the tale might seem like truth at least
To the unlucky husband,—jaundiced patch, —
Jealousy maddens people, why not him?
Say he was maddened, so, forgivable!
Humanity pleads that though the wife were true,
The priest true, and the pair of liars true,
They might seem false to one man in the world!

(11. 862–7, 873–89)

'False to be sure!' Yet the reader of the young priest's own account in book 6 cannot help pick up strong involuntary hints of sexual attraction sublimated into religious devotion ('Man and priest . . . | How mingling each its multifarious wires | Now heaven, now earth, now heaven and earth at once', bk. 1. 1017–19), even whilst the reader *also* shares Caponsacchi's disgust at the vulgar reception his tale of innocence received amongst his fellow clergy:

The titter stifled in the hollow palm
Which rubbed the eyebrow and caressed the nose,
When I first told my tale; they meant, you know,
'The sly one, all this we are bound to believe!
Well, he can say no other than what he says.
We have been young, too . . .'

(6. 16–21)

'Play' originates in that grotesque half-disgusted fascination of seeing it both ways or many ways, the narrative breaking into various plausible aspects of itself. Despite the dying Pope's best theoretic efforts in book 10, there is no straightforward, sincere, unmixed, or unambiguous way in *The Ring and the Book*.

Both physically, and in the demands it makes upon the reader, *The Ring and The Book* is undoubtedly a formidable long poem. But some contemporary reviewers—John Rickards Mozley, Alfred Austin—thought that it was really the analytic expansion of something essentially smaller.[12] 'Permeated with accumulations', as Henry James put it, with one book not so much following and consolidating upon one another as starting again from a different angle or point in time, *The Ring and the Book* is not so much an epic as a super-enlarged example of the Victorian sequence poem, which issued out of the dramatic monologue. For like an extended dramatic monologue attentive to its own movements, the sequence poem lives tonally moment by moment, no sooner content with a conclusion or attitude than finding it go false or flat or partial, and forced into further reappraisals.

The great examples of the Victorian sequence poem are Elizabeth Barrett Browning's *Sonnets from the Portuguese* (forty-five sonnets privately printed in 1847 and finally published in 1850); Arthur Hugh Clough's 'Amours de Voyage' (five cantos of verse epistles, 1858); George Meredith's *Modern Love* (fifty extended 'sonnets' of sixteen lines, 1862); Christina Rossetti's 'Monna Innominata: A Sonnet of Sonnets' (1881) and 'Later Life' (a twenty-eight sonnet sequence, 1881); Dante Gabriel Rossetti's 'The House of Life' (written throughout his life from 1848, published as fifty sonnets in 1870 and expanded into 101 sonnets by 1881); and, of course, Tennyson's *In Memoriam* (composed from 1833, 131 lyrics published 1850). As assembled continuities, rather than continuous long narratives, they are the Victorian solution to the problems of referential framework and poetic form. The gaps, the uncertain silences, the temporal lapses or changes implicit in the spaces in between the individual poems create a tacit, inferable, and extended context in time. This tentative structure, created even as it goes along, allows the component poems severally a temporary autonomy—in *Sonnets from the Portuguese* 'A place to stand and love in for a day' (Sonnet 22)—while also involving them in the interrogation of their own possible links and changes. Experience is never wholly finished or complete in these self-reappraising sequences: 'In things long past new features now can trace' ('The House of Life', 80. 'From Dawn to Noon').

It is a new Victorian discovery in these poems that time is no longer an abstract or optional element but intrinsic to the very nature of experience. In the sequence poem it is not the case that time exists in thought—that is only fully possible in the immaterial world, after death, in Newman's *Dream of Gerontius* (1868), where 'intervals in their succession | Are measured by the living thought alone' and every one 'is standard of his own chronology'. On the contrary, thought now exists in time—in the present instant of consciously provisional writing, where the present itself will not stay still or distinct but is so often looking before or after:

> I wish I could remember that first day,
>   First hour, first moment of your meeting me,
>   If bright or dim the season, it might be
> Summer or Winter for aught I can say;
> So unrecorded did it slip away,
>   So blind was I to see or to foresee.
>
>   ('Monna Innominata', 2)

'It seemed to mean so little, meant so much': the structuring and restructuring of experience goes on in experience's very midst, as the sequence unfolds, changing the very meaning of past or future in the internal search for form and unity:

> What words are these have fallen from me?
>   Can calm despair and wild unrest
>   Be tenants of a single breast,
> Or sorrow such a changeling be?
>
>   (*In Memoriam*, 16)

What is being questioned, in the alternation of feelings, is the very status and meaning of what is so easily dismissed as 'mood'.

More bitterly, Meredith's cuckolded husband finds that 'the mad Past, on which my foot is based' will not remain past or solid, but through the discovery of a long-standing but hitherto unsuspected infidelity, is now made vulnerable to reappraisals that seem to reach further and further backwards: 'But where began the change?' (*Modern Love*, 12, 10).

The present itself may seem merely washed up, the result of a past's future that never came to be:

> The hour which might have been yet might not be,
>   Which man's and woman's heart conceived and bore

> Yet whereof life was barren,—on what shore
> Bides it the breaking of Time's weary sea?
>
> ('The House of Life', 55. 'Stillborn Love')

Or even more ironically, the present may feel not so much present as belated:

> Oh, wisdom never comes when it is gold,
> And the great price we pay for it full worth:
> We have it only when we are half earth.
> Little avails that coinage to the old!
>
> (*Modern Love*, 4)

As the individual poems cumulatively make, or fail to find, within themselves a journey towards some resolving unity or terminus, the form becomes the subject matter, the subject matter becomes the form. So, in the courtship described in *Sonnets from the Portuguese*, the woman at one point asks her beloved to 'call me by my pet-name'—the name to which she responded as a child, to run to the loving face which called her. Now 'catch the early love up in the late':

> Yes, call me by that name,—and I, in truth,
> With the same heart, will answer and not wait.
>
> (Sonnet 33)

But the very next sonnet picks up those last words:

> With the same heart, I said, I'll answer thee
> As those, when thou shalt call me by my name—
> Lo, the vain promise! is the same, the same,
> Perplexed and ruffled by life's strategy?
>
> (Sonnet 34)

Yet the very difference—the sense of breach in the passage from childhood to adult love, and the half-defeated desire to pass over it— is itself part of what maintains the sequence.

The poets had found in these loose verse sequences a form which could be sustained or retrieved over decades, as the sequence gradually developed a life of its own:

> As growth of form or momentary glance
> In a child's features will recall to mind

The father's with the mother's face combin'd,—
Sweet interchange that memories still enhance:
And yet, as childhood's years and youth's advance,
    The gradual mouldings leave one stamp behind,
    Till in the blended likeness now we find
A separate man or woman's countenance:-

So in the Song, the singer's Joy and Pain,
    Its very parents, evermore expand . . .
        ('The House of Life', 60. 'Transfigured Life')

Whenever he found a blank space in the sequence, said Tennyson of the composition of *In Memoriam*, he inserted a poem. Writing one poem required him to write another, by opening up resonant spaces or disturbing holes, leaving room for inference, silence, and anomaly. In thus keeping the poet in the thick of an ongoing imagined life, the verse sequence was a project that made the continuous writing of poetry *called for*, even through its very interruptions and discontinuities. Moreover, the poet did not have to keep pressing forward, but as with Tennyson in the composition of *Maud*, could turn back and fill out more of the middle of the sequence, coming at the thing from as many different angles as there are different possible lives:

What man has bent o'er his son's sleep, to brood
How that face shall watch his when cold it lies?—
Or thought, as his own mother kissed his eyes,
Of what her kiss was when his father wooed?
        ('The House of Life', 63. 'Inclusiveness')

And all the time within those opening spaces of possibility the poems themselves had to weigh the mixture of invention and memory, of opportunism and necessity involved in their existence; had to question to what degree the author of one was still in some sense the same person as the author of another. The individual lyrics become like the lost days of my life which, says Dante Gabriel Rossetti, will gather before me after death, as 'Might-have-been', 'No-more', 'Too-late', 'He, or I?':

Each one a murdered self, with low last breath.
'I am thyself,—what hast thou done to me?'
        ('The House of Life', 86. 'Lost Days')

Yet sometimes in these exploratory poems, amidst circumstances so intimate as to affect tone and inflection almost from minute to minute, the poets suddenly find the guidance of what seems to be their own most genuine voice. Browning finds access to that deep, straight personal voice for a moment in the wonderful poem 'One Word More' reached at the very end of *Men and Women* (1855)— not so much a sequence poem as a collection of fifty portraits in verse. It is the voice of which *In Memoriam* or *Sonnets from the Portuguese* are in search and which 'Amours de Voyage' and *Modern Love* believe to be either non-existent or forever lost. For these are poems written to someone absent or distant, and their writers become versions of that someone, listening to themselves in the lonely dark, trying to make out the meaning of their own tones. Thus Clough's Claude in those verse epistles of his in which writing becomes a nineteenth-century secular rendering of prayer:

> Yes, it relieves me to write, though I do not send, and the chance that
> Takes may destroy my fragments. But as men pray, without asking
> Whether One really exist to hear or do anything for them,—
> Simply impelled by the need of the moment to turn to a Being . . .
>
> ('Amours de Voyage', 5. 5)

The new challenge for this Victorian form is that one voice has to speak, over time, for two lives and not just one. The great Romantic inheritance declared that knowledge came only through identity, through individual experience. But what gradually takes over from that is a voice that begins as a feminized consciousness, conscious of self *and* other—as in the complex self-reflexive shifts of Caroline Norton's sonnet sequence of 1840. Do not be kind to me, she says, as though I were a grieving child: 'This dressing pity in the garb of Love, | This effort of the heart to *seem* the same' alike

> Remind me more, by their most vain deceit,
> Of the dear loss of all which thou dost counterfeit.
>
> (Sonnet 4)

Or again: I do not fear slander, she says in Sonnet 5, because I know I am 'thy choice'; what I do fear is the effect of the slanderers upon you—'howe'er thy soul may strive | Against the weakness of that inward pain'—and thence the effect, through you, back upon me: 'Therefore I sometimes weep'. So many Victorian sequence poems thus begin with the surrender of solitary singleness, amidst feelings testingly compounded of ardour and reluctance at once:

> Nevermore
> Alone upon the threshold of my door
> Of individual life, I shall command
> The uses of my soul, nor lift my hand
> Serenely in the sunshine as before,
> Thy touch upon the palm.
>
> (*Sonnets from the Portuguese*, 6)

'Nevermore | Alone'. At this threshold, it is not merely that the course of a life is no longer to be in the hands of the one person leading it—if ever it was. It is now not even to be in the hands of two people together, instead. 'Not like to like, but like in difference' as the Prince puts in Tennyson's *The Princess* (8. 262). For marriage in *Sonnets from the Portuguese* is the pledge of each partner to a form of life which, for all its apparent conventionality, must develop in time beyond the control of either separately or both together. As such, the testing of permanent love within the Victorian sequence poem is an intimate working model for the reconciliation of independence and communality in the wider forms of human association.[13] That is why, in its complex time movements, *Sonnets from the Portuguese* constitutes as a whole the woman's efforts to *prepare* her emotions for a knowing commitment of life, in the present, to an unknown future, lasting unto death.

For before marriage is entered upon, the form must seem arbitrary, always open to argument and to doubts both particular and general. The intellectual bachelor Claude in Clough's 'Amours de Voyage' maintains that marriages are formed out of the mere 'juxtaposition' of two needy people: a mixture of chance proximity with biological need, a refuge from fear of transience and loneliness. But these motivations are hidden under the social-religious fiction that marriages are ideal affinities somehow 'made in heaven' (3.6).

---

[13] On the poetic use of marriage as a primary analogy for the balance of liberty and law in public and political society, see Matthew Reynolds, *The Realms of Verse: English Poetry in a Time of Nation-Building* (Oxford University Press, 2001), 44–72.

'Where does Circumstance end, and Providence where begins it?'
(*The Bothie of Tober-Na-Vuolich*, 9. 49).

Yet after the marriage has begun, as the hesitant Claude well
knows, what before was intellectually arbitrary becomes a now
irrevocable part of experience. It sickeningly galls Meredith—'I get a
glimpse of hell in this mild guess' (*Modern Love*, 22)—that the mere
accident of choice and luck is itself sufficient to turn into the lasting
ruin of a life. He may warn, from a bitter distance—

> Prepare,
> You lovers, to know Love a thing of moods:
> Not like hard life, of laws.

> (*Modern Love*, 10)

—but there could be no preparation for Meredith's husband as there
was for Elizabeth Barrett, and he remains caught in a terrible lawlessness, the recidivist formlessness of a marriage living on, with a
perverse sexuality, *after* its own end:

> a changed eye finds such familiar sights
> More keenly tempting than new loveliness

> (*Modern Love*, 5)

Moreover, as the protagonist takes a mistress, to match his wife's
having taken a lover, what these symmetries enact is not so much
formlessness, as a chaotic *anti*-form.

In such ways, so many of these sequence poems seem to take up
their positions in tacit debate with each other, especially over matters
of love or death. If the religious movement of *In Memoriam* is from
death to renewed life, the erotic direction of 'The House of Life' is all
the other way, from life to death. And just as surely as 'The House
of Life' reads like Dante Gabriel Rossetti's erotic challenge to his
sister's sense of a barren existence going nowhere in 'Later Life', so
'Later Life' itself, together with 'Monna Innominata', is Christina
Rossetti's critical religious alternative to the achieved love-happiness
of *Sonnets from the Portuguese*. In turn, the vision in Elizabeth
Barrett Browning's courtship poems—and the tradition embodied
in the marital poems of Coventry Patmore and the family poems of
William Barnes—is very much what is rejected in both 'Amours de
Voyage' and *Modern Love*.

One group of voices offered a particular challenge. In the 1870s, Meredith, Morris, Dante Gabriel Rossetti, and Swinburne were fairly indiscriminately classed together as in the avant-garde of anti-conventionalism. Known loosely—with the painters Holman Hunt, Millais, and Burne-Jones—as the Pre-Raphaelite Brotherhood, they were also called the 'Fleshly School of Poetry'—not least because of rumours and sexual scandals connecting the four writers. The Fleshly School was a phrase coined by the minor poet Robert Buchanan in a deeply conservative review of Rossetti's fifth edition of *Poems* (*Contemporary Review*, October 1871) which complained of a 'decadent' programme committed, in effect, to beauty in art and sex in life. Buchanan quotes Rossetti's extraordinary sonnet 'Nuptial Sleep':

> At length their long kiss severed, with sweet smart:
>   And as the last slow sudden drops are shed
>   From sparkling eaves when all the storm has fled,
> So singly flagged the pulses of each heart.
> Their bosoms sundered, with the opening start
>   Of married flowers to either side outspread
>   From their knit stem; yet still their mouths, burnt red,
> Fawned on each other where they lay apart.
> Sleep sank them lower than the tide of dreams,
>   And their dreams watched them sink, and slid away.
> Slowly their souls swam up again, through gleams
>   Of watered light and dull drowned waifs of day;
> Till from some wonder of new woods and streams
>   He woke, and wondered more: for there she lay.

Buchanan then comments: 'Here is a full-grown man, presumably intelligent and cultivated, putting on record for other full-grown men to read, the most secret mysteries of sexual connection, and that with so sickening a desire to reproduce the sensual mood, so careful a choice of epithet to convey mere animal sensations, that we merely shudder at the shameless nakedness.' This, together with 'Jenny', a poem spoken over a sleeping prostitute, was an expansion, said Buchanan, of the worst of both Tennyson and Browning—the sensualism of 'Merlin and Vivian' (from the *Idylls of the King*), the hysteria of Maud, the racy soliloquies of the grotesque—creating a poetry of hyper-sensations. 'Nuptial Sleep' was a poem that Rossetti was later to omit from 'The House of Life' sequence. But he still contested Buchanan's central proposition—that the fleshly school had pledged itself 'to extol fleshliness as the distinct and supreme end of poetic and pictorial art; to aver that poetic expression is greater than poetic thought, and by inference that the body is greater than the soul, and sound superior to sense'. If body seemed greater than soul, responded Rossetti, it was only because of the soul's own commitment thereto:

> Lady, I fain would tell how evermore
> Thy soul I know not from thy body, nor
> Thee from myself, neither our love from God
>
> ('The House of Life', 5. 'Heart's Hope')

Rossetti claimed to borrow from his namesake Dante a passionate refusal to separate spiritual and physical. Yet 'The House of Life' remains the great erotic, not theological, sequence of the Victorian age precisely because in Rossetti, as Buchanan half-recognized, the whole late Romantic mind becomes sexualized. This was not a rational world, it was not an ethical world, it was not a world in which space was mapped out externally in terms of normal orthodox perspectives. Rather, it was a world in which Rossetti was sensuously immersed and surrounded, as in the strange underwater perspectives of 'Nuptial Sleep': a man absorbed in a woman 'whose voice . . . Is like a hand laid softly on the soul; | Whose hand is like a sweet voice' ('The House of Life', 26. 'Mid-Rapture'). 'The House of Life', with all its signs, memories, and ghosts, its dreams and nightmares, becomes Rossetti's private cosmological world, claustrophobically packed like the walls of Rossetti's own rooms with pictures and mirrors:

> What glory of change by nature's hand amass'd
> Can vie with all those moods of varying grace
> Which o'er one loveliest woman's form and face
> Within this hour, within this room, have pass'd?
>
> ('The House of Life', 17. 'Beauty's Pageant')

The normal boundaries of reality are broken down: 'Not in thy body is thy life at all | But in this lady's lips and hands and eyes' ('The House of Life', 36. 'Life-in-Love'). In an orgasmic intermixture, different parts of the beloved offer, almost simultaneously, different feelings—cheeks, arms, eyes: pity, refuge, fear. 'To be all this 'neath one soft bosom's swell': yet how strange, writes the poet, that the woman can simply *be* what the man can hardly *know*, save 'as a sacred secret' ('The House of Life', 56. 'True Woman'). For always what is felt in *his* body seems to come from *hers*: hence the constant urge to bring the two together. For the lyrics, constantly spent and constantly renewed, are like kisses 'led | Back to her mouth which answers there for all' ('The House of Life', 21. 'Love-Sweetness'), until the erotic impulse must burst under the strain, in a desperately self-consuming death. Rossetti puts body *in* mind in ways that mind itself can then hardly articulate. 'And as she kissed, her mouth became her soul' ('The House of Life', 45. 'Secret Parting'). In Swinburne's *Poems and Ballads*, first series (1866), the eroticism is flagrantly opposed to Christian love—Venus against Christ:

> Lo, she was thus when her clear limbs enticed
> All lips that now grow sad with kissing Christ
>
> ('Laus Veneris')

> Wilt thou yet take all, Galilean? But these thou shalt not take,
> The laurel, the palms and the paean, the breasts of the nymphs in
> the brake;
> Breasts more soft than a dove's, that tremble with tenderer breath
> . . . .
> Thou hast conquered, O pale Galilean; the world has grown grey
> from thy breath
>
> ('Hymn to Proserpine')

But Dante Gabriel Rossetti does not so much take away the Christian form as translate its loving language back inside the sensuous content of a life. Soul is poured into mouth, as the lovers try to pour themselves into one another, in a commitment not to the forms of marriage and religion but to the fate of love and sex. For forms will not hold together long enough in this intense world. In the poem's desperation for continually fulfilled content, personifications such as 'Love's Hour' stand, 'with bodiless form', ''til she and I shall meet', yearningly waiting to be sexually incarnated and consummatingly filled by the lovers themselves ('The Stream's Secret').

Rossetti cannot be, as Browning or Clough or Meredith are in their differing ways, an ironist or sceptic; emotionally he has to seek to be a believer. For him it is not love as a social ethic that can replace religion: what alone has the intensity and beauty to take over from religion is love as sex. Thus poetry in Rossetti becomes the doomed attempt of erotic lyric to sustain epic. As more nakedly in Swinburne's 'Dolores', it is like running a race against a future that is already there, urgently seeking its own transformation: 'Ah, feed me and fill me with pleasure, | Ere pain comes in turn', 'There have been and there yet shall be sorrows | That smite not and bite not in play'.

Thus, it is not just that the debate that goes on within and between the Victorian sequence poems is simply the result of a variety of different individual views held at a time of transition. In their very attempt to sustain themselves beyond mere opinion, within time, these views themselves constitute the embodied traditions and counter-traditions—the competing thoughts *and* the spaces for further thought between them—which were to form the mental range and complex of human response for the next hundred years.

For the Victorian sequence poem made form a problem of belief, at the level of intimate risk and trust: belief as to what if anything in human life could lastingly sustain itself and hold a life together in time; as to what, if all these things failed, might have to serve as a structure of emotional expectation instead. That is why, finally, the greatest sequence poem is the long poem which experiences the problem of faith most deeply: *In Memoriam*.

Like a series of entries in a poetic diary, *In Memoriam* has no beginning, no shape: it exists, in stranded and disoriented lyrics, *after* an ending—the sudden early death in Vienna of Arthur Hallam, Tennyson's best friend, of a brain haemorrhage. Its subject is not there. Instead there is the left-over feeling that Hallam's life was at once finite *and* incomplete. That paradox bequeathes the poet an emotional condition of mourning which goes on precisely because the very object of that feeling no longer does, and which continues, moreover, for years after the initial loss. In persevering in that state, there is no definite line between faithful love and morbid self-indulgence, nor is it clear to what degree the whole process is or is not voluntary, or whether its cessation will be anything other than arbitrary. The end of mourning is not like the end of the life it mourns: it is not an event; nor is there any external measure as to how long is a sufficient time to mourn. For the way to recovery cannot be planned: to a man of Tennyson's honesty, the capacity to foresee a conventional religious resolution threatens to preclude that solution as an authentically rediscovered possibility. This is a situation in which familiar, commonplace, and apparently realistic thoughts appear turned outside-inwards into things now disturbing and distant and unreal:

> One writes, that 'Other friends remain,'
> That 'Loss is common to the race'—
> And common is the commonplace,
> And vacant chaff well meant for grain.

> (*In Memoriam*, 6)

In revulsion against the public language of the outside world, Tennyson has instead to employ in his poem the widest possible variety of different moods, voices, and forms of relation. The religious is made strange again by being experienced through the realm of the supernatural or even the blasphemous. The relationship with Hallam becomes expressed through male–female terms. Anything and everything is tried. In the absence of firm starting or ending points—and amidst the poem's resistance to that unrelenting Victorian pressure towards any semblance of progress—individual poems or individual stanzas or even individual lines offer temporary holding points, however apparently ill-fitting in relation to a possible whole. Without knowing what to do with it, Tennyson can still find room in his world for an uncertain thought, too emotionally desirable not to be doubted, yet too doubted to be a sure belief—

> The wish, that of the living whole
> No life may fail beyond the grave

—and, having got the thought out to *be* thought, he can then produce a delayed syntax which questions, without repression, in what framework to place that thought and where if at all to go with it:

> Derives it not from what we have
> The likest God within the soul?

> Are God and Nature then at strife . . . ?

> (*In Memoriam*, 55)

Equally, amidst the depressing fear of almost literally dead ends, some words temporarily allow a thought to go forward, experimentally:

> My own dim life should teach me this,
>   That life shall live for evermore,
>   Else earth is darkness at the core,
> And dust and ashes all that is.

> (*In Memoriam*, 34)

Thus 'should' here enables 'shall' and yet remains still doubtfully behind it, surfacing again in that fearful 'else', as the range of possible attitudes and direction remains held in solution, ready to turn both the syntax and the feeling a different way at the very next turn of line.

A telling contrast here, in the poetic deliberations about death, would be with the poetry of Emily Brontë in the late 1830s and early 1840s. Her lyrics are so self-absorbed that they are the extreme example of the difficulty of knowing where Victorian poetry comes from. In a characteristically haunting lyric, a voice like a spirit's simply says to some equally unknown hearer: 'I'll come when thou art saddest'. It is not just that behind many of these poems is the barely recoverable fantasy world, named Gondal, which Emily Brontë had invented in childhood with her sister Anne. The lyrics, emptied of all immediately recognizable context, seem to exist absolutely independent of each other. Instead of being part of a continuous sequence-poem like *In Memoriam*, each isolated lyric is true only to itself for the absolute time it takes. For what prevents these poems becoming a sequence is a particular notion of self, separate both from the world and from time, each poem absolutely centred upon its own speaker. As it is said in a poem attributed to either Emily or Charlotte Brontë, 'The earth that wakes *one* human heart to feeling | Can centre both the worlds of Heaven and Hell' ('Often rebuked, yet always back returning'). That centre is the self's 'God within my breast' in poems such as 'No coward soul is mine' or 'To Imagination' or 'Cold in the earth'—a pre-Victorian Romantic self, braced by the force of will shown by the protagonists in Byron's plays:

> And am I wrong to worship where
> Faith cannot doubt nor Hope despair

Since my own soul can grant my prayer?

('O thy bright eyes must answer now')

It is a self whose deep inner mystic resources are bared by its very closeness to finding death: 'That I could never dream, till Earth was lost to me. | Then dawns the Invisible' ('The Prisoner').

In Memoriam is nothing like so confident: even though it begins to lead to a different dimension of being, the poem finds its own strangeness, its very separateness from the world disturbing. For fear of personal hubris, Tennyson had to half-hide from himself the Idealist recognition[14] that, at some level, his mind was made greater than anything it witnessed, including its own experience of worry and pain and sorrow. The language had to raise itself upon itself—'like a finer light in light' (91), 'A higher height, a deeper deep' (63)—working its way 'through darkness up to God' (55), until 'honest doubt' changes its own nature to become a lower version of 'faith' (96). Yet even thus from below Tennyson still continues to set his normal human consciousness to track the intuitions of that greater, stranger mind of his. The lamed, slower mind, dogged in its honest doubtfulness, always seeks to bring back to this world something from the accelerated work of the Romantic, poetic, idealist, or religious consciousness:

> I stretch lame hands of faith, and grope,
> And gather dust and chaff, and call
> To what I feel is Lord of all,
> And faintly trust the larger hope.

(*In Memoriam*, 55)

Tennyson existed so often in two minds. The lesser and more frightened mind says 'faintly', while the other says 'larger'. But it is the very experience of faintness which creates the imaginative apprehension: what is seen so dimly, at such a distance, must in itself be very large indeed, if it can be made out at all from here. That is why the more normal, personal, and lesser mind can still do well in adding 'trust' to what otherwise only feels like 'hope'. It is also why Tennyson on finishing *In Memoriam* could feel that the poem was more optimistic than he ordinarily found himself to be.

---

[14] See above, pp. 177–9, 184.

Yet the chastening achievement of *In Memoriam* is not that it discovers something newer or better than the Judaeo-Christian faith, but that it renews trust in that faith by finding it again, irreducibly primal and pristine, within a strangely different perspective:

> Then was I as a child that cries,
>   But crying, knows his father near;
>
> And what I am beheld again
>   What is, and no man understands
>
>   (*In Memoriam*, 124)

As, by a sort of brail, 'what I am' is drawn towards 'what is', the poem's anxiety concerning personal extinction is itself absorbed into something more than personal, which can only be addressed as 'That which':

> That which we dare invoke to bless;
>   Our dearest faith; our ghastliest doubt;
>   He, They, One, All; within, without;
> The Power in darkness whom we guess.
>
>   (*In Memoriam*, 124)

III. From May to September: Poetry and Belief

A poem by George Barlow (1847–1913), 'To September', is a representative later nineteenth-century answer to Wordsworth's 'To May'. For Wordsworth, 'in that happier day', 'Knew not that ere his century's close | Dark doubt so deadly would arise':

> But in this later darker day
>   Despair has found us out.
>
> We realise that we may be,
>   We human sufferers, quite alone:
>   Created by no conscious will,
>   Doomed to live on and suffer still,
>   Without a heavenly eye to see
>   Or ear to hear us groan.

After Darwin,[15] 'Dark September suits us best'.

---

[15] See above, pp. 74–8.

The great September poems of the period—rural and urban respectively—are George Meredith's 'The Woods of Westermain' (1883) and James Thomson's *The City of Dreadful Night* (1880)— the publication of *The City of Dreadful Night* winning Thomson Meredith's friendship. Both poems are radically post-Darwinian and thus inevitably anti-Wordsworthian in their denial of a supportive natural universe.

'The Woods of Westermain' takes its origin from poem 30 in the sequence of *Modern Love*: 'What are we first? First animals; and next | Intelligences at a leap'. There the speaker uses a scientific language to distance himself from the failure of his marriage by attributing human infidelity to love's being incompletely evolved out of the still tenacious biology of animal sexuality. But now the Woods become a phantasmagorial landscape, encapturing the very energies of creation, in which an old human language of love and honour struggles for survival with the language of pre-moral natural forces. 'Enter these enchanted woods, | You who dare.'

With extraordinarily wild and swift verbal power, the poem fights to stabilize its own energies, even as the human dimension within it struggles to transmute the forces out of which it has arisen: 'Growths of what they step on, these; | With the roots the grace of trees', 'Love, the great volcano, flings | Fires of lower Earth to sky'. The aim is to fight fire with fire, violently to overcome violence itself in the universe: 'Scaring fear till fear escapes'. The very consciousness of transience is used to defeat transience within the precincts of the human mind: 'Even as dewlight off the rose | In the mind a jewel sows' (3).

The poem forges its own language as it goes along, a language for what wasn't language in the first place. It struggles against a dragon which turns out to be called the Self, at its most primordial and destructive; it seeks to create mental roses. But it rises only to fall, settles only to suffer throwbacks. For Evolution is not settled and completed here but is fighting itself out all over again—wild against tame, light against dark, progress against regression—before our very eyes and virtually within and behind them:

> You must love the light so well
> That no darkness will seem fell.
> .   .   .   .   .

> Then you touch the nerve of Change
> Then of Earth you have the clue;
> Then her two-sexed meanings melt
> Through you, wed the thought and felt.
>
> .　　.　　.　　.　　.　　.
>
> Change is on the wing to bud
> Rose in brain from rose in blood.
> Wisdom throbbing shall you see
> Central in complexity.　　　　　(4)

Nothing is quite clear or safe in this poem: the reader too has to live dangerously, going along with unresolved present difficulties, in tense trust of future clarifications. Even so does the poem itself, like the humans within it, seek to embody into meaning the very process that makes it.

Only gradually do pieces of the poem begin to chime or clash together—the reader listening to the heartbeats of the poem, to find the meaning of its ever-changing preconceptual rhythms:

> Mind of man and bent of brute.
> Hear that song; both wild and ruled.
> Hear it: is it wail or mirth?
> Ordered, bubbled, quite unschooled?
> None, and all . . .　　　　　(4)

Half of the poem wants to pump its wild beat through the blood, into the brain, up into a finally calming spirit: 'Blood and brain and spirit, three | . . . Join for true felicity'. But the other regressive and vengeful half of the poem seeks its life in breaking down that transmutation of itself. Terrifyingly, both halves—Earth's 'two-sexed meanings'—are nonetheless part of the same self-struggling process in this universe. And it stands on a knife's edge whether human beings can overcome or are overcome by those base forces within them, out of which they have evolved. Every second in the poem the balance seems to shift alarmingly, ending closer to the threat of chaos and extinction than to settlement. For in 'The Woods of Westermain' the dynamic of constant momentary change and oscillating uncertainty that lay behind the Victorian discovery of the dramatic monologue and the sequence poem is now finally and dramatically registered as fundamentally cosmological.

In *The City of Dreadful Night* the Victorian age is much closer to extinction. The poem is far more overdetermined than 'The Woods of Westermain', lacking the terrible vitality of the fight, and much closer to death. It uses the language of Dante's *Inferno*—'they leave all hope behind who enter here'—only to abolish the very idea of Heaven and Hell, leaving life as a hell-on-earth instead. For this is a language not only consciously nearing the end of the century but almost at the end of its line, wearing out its own meanings and traditions.

A last-ditch sermon thus offers only bitterly ironic 'good tidings': 'There is no God' (14). There is no meaning, nothing:

> When Faith and Love and Hope are dead indeed,
> Can Life still live? By what doth it proceed?
>
> (2)

It merely proceeds, whilst human beings desperately try to continue to read into it feeling or meaning or order. One terrible brief vision reveals a city chokingly polluted by feelings which human beings cannot help still feeling because they are the very air they breath. They are inhaled and exhaled continuously, until the poem itself can no longer breathe as Wordsworth had breathed his poetry in the Lakes:

> So that no man there breathes earth's simple breath,
> As if alone on mountains or wide seas . . .

The poem breaks down into gasps of delirium, nightmarish images arising out of a post-religious hangover. Even when the creatures of the city throw off the pains of hope, they do not walk more upright and unburdened, but become more bowed, collapsing in upon themselves (6). They have nothing inside them any more, not even—says Thomson—'reticence' (7): they just cry, make noise, repetitively and meaninglessly. In *The City of Dreadful Night* it is by now long after May and well beyond September—as if to say, by a species of historical determinism, that December is where the nineteenth century is finally and inevitably headed. In this way Thomson poses the great challenge which any study of Victorian England must meet in the end: does not its bitter late-century outcome 'in this later darker day' act as a final judgement upon Victorian literature's earlier achievements, rendering them temporary compromises, showing them coming ever-increasingly apart?

But this was a question which had already posed itself many times throughout the post-Romantic century. Did May have to be left behind, was the movement to a dark December inevitable? Indeed, in the face of a deep personal sense of 'something that is gone', it had been Wordsworth's own question in the great 'Ode: Intimations of Immortality':

> Whither is fled the visionary gleam?
> Where is it now, the glory and the dream?

When Wordsworth wrote that ode in 1807, said Gerard Manley Hopkins in a letter to R. W. Dixon, 23 October 1886, human nature within the man had seen something, had 'got a shock', and had been 'in a tremble ever since'. And still, near the century's end, 'the tremble from it is spreading'. It was as though all that Romanticism stood for in the way of belief was saying to Victorianism in the poem:

> O joy! that in our embers
> Is something that doth live.

Yet the question for the rest of this chapter is: after Wordsworth, *did* something in the way of belief still remain alive in the embers? To Matthew Arnold it was the inability of the Victorian poets, himself included, to build on the precarious flawed legacy left by Wordsworth which was the most powerful evidence of a failure of religious unity at the heart of later nineteenth-century poetry. The tacit past presence of Wordsworth made Arnold himself feel all the more painfully the alien gulf he now had to register between man and the universe, in poems such as 'Resignation', 'The Youth of Nature', and *Empedocles on Etna*. But 'Man must begin, know this, where Nature ends', wrote Arnold ('In Harmony with Nature')—and begin again where Wordsworth, and the vision of Nature he had cherished, ended.

In Walter Pater's eyes, Wordsworth, like Coleridge, stood for the last, ancient sense of the permanent—the unified form, the absolute whole—which was passing out of view in a world now dominated by a sense of transience. Writing in 1866 in a review of 'Coleridge's

Writings' which was later reprinted in his *Appreciations*, Pater said that modern thought was distinguished from ancient 'by its cultivation of the "relative" spirit in place of the "absolute" ':

Ancient philosophy sought to arrest every object in an eternal outline, to fix thought in a necessary formula, and types of life in a classification by 'kinds' or *genera*. To the modern spirit nothing is, or can be rightly known except relatively under conditions.

The sciences of observation 'reveal types of life evanescing into each other by inexpressible refinements of change', not 'the truth of eternal outlines effected once for all' but 'a world of fine gradations and subtly linked conditions, shifting intricately as we ourselves change'.

> The hills are shadows, and they flow
> From form to form, and nothing stands;
> They melt like mist, the solid lands,
> Like clouds they shape themselves and go.
>
> (*In Memoriam*, 123)

It was Tennyson who, in bereavement, had to meet the challenge of the broken epic of faith and memory and rewrite the Wordsworthian long poem as *In Memoriam*. And as the philosopher Henry Sidgwick told Tennyson's son Hallam, *In Memoriam* had explicitly to confront the challenges of science as *The Excursion* and *The Prelude* had not.

Yet, as Clough saw, it was not only scientific but also socio-economic change which made all that Wordsworth represented seem outdated to a new generation. In an age plunged into the political urgencies of industrial and urban crisis, Wordsworth lived on in what in his 'Lecture on the Poetry of Wordsworth' Clough called a spirit of rural 'withdrawal and seclusion' far removed from 'the actual world'—a semi-recluse in the Lake District, surviving the other great Romantic poets by nearly thirty years, until his death in 1850. Yet this was precisely the time when Clough himself was concerned to turn poetry away from pastoral idyll and create an essentially political verse as real in relation to modern life—'the actual, palpable things with which our every-day life is concerned'—as was Dickens's *Bleak House* or Thackeray's *Vanity Fair*. Characteristically in *The Bothie* Clough writes both with and without irony of a version of that aspiration in Philip Hewson, privileged Oxford undergraduate on vacation in rural Scotland, yet would-be poet of democratic realism and Chartist sympathizer, who seeks marriage to a real woman of the lower classes, not a false leisured lady from a higher station. If poetry was not to come to a dead end, thought Clough, it had to start again, lower down, shedding its grandiloquence.

For this is how the shock wave from the 'Immortality Ode' was still spreading: in the experimentalism of poets in search of a poetry of belief—or of alternatives to belief—after Wordsworth. The crucial contrasts here are between the innovators Clough, Hopkins himself, and Swinburne.

Where Wordsworth in the *Lyrical Ballads* could claim to be bringing poetry back from an artificial diction to start it again closer to nature, Clough's attempted restart was precisely to do with the absence of such natural beliefs or beliefs in the natural. In the attempt to make a new start, experimenting with a wide variety of languages, high and low, 'Dipsychus', for example, reads like a fast first draft for a poem, its very subject matter the unformed period *before* a self-divided young man gets started in the world. Like *Aurora Leigh* it takes inspiration from the Byron of *Don Juan*—an ostensibly loose, fresh, improvised alternative verse, offering qualities which Elizabeth Barrett Browning had admired in *The Bothie*. Yet 'Dipsychus' is like a challenging opposite to *Aurora Leigh* in its equivocal spirit of sceptical freedom. A Byronic Spirit talking to the young man of sexual initiation says, 'I know it's mainly your temptation | To think the thing a revelation' and goes on, half-devil, half-therapist, merely to conclude: 'I tell you plainly that it brings | Some ease' (scene 3). What's the fuss, where's the poetry in that? Yet the Romantic-minded youth, half-suspecting that the Spirit's voice is also his own, cannot command decisiveness either way:

> 'Tis gone, the fierce, inordinate desire,
> The burning thirst for Action—utterly;
> Gone, like a ship that passes in the night
> On the high seas; gone yet will come again.
> Gone, yet expresses something that exists.

(scene 12)

To Matthew Arnold, such verse was not a new beginning but a poetry that kept *un*making itself in its comings and goings, reversing the very direction of thinking, back and back, aspect by aspect. Yet the movement in grammatical tense, across the lines, from 'gone yet *will* come again' to 'Gone, yet expresses something that *exists*' establishes what intelligence is in Clough: the refusal to live unthinkingly at the mercy of time and mood. Yet in another minute he will be questioning whether, conversely, it is right to use such intelligence precisely to compel himself to live more in the present and take opportunity as it comes: 'Must I then do violence to myself | And push on nature, force desire . . .?' In this way 'Dipsychus' and 'Amours de Voyage' are equivocal refusals of narrative, opting out of the Victorian sequence poem even from within it.

In Clough's underdetermined world, no one thought can remain indefeasibly sufficient or decisive even for the moment. Action, courage, heroism, unshakable faith—in politics or religion or love: these are suspected of being Romantic fictions or religious illusions which cannot be accepted until *after* they are tested. Belief would make all the difference—'for we should so, if only we thought that we could so' ('Dipsychus', scene 5). But to desire belief for the extra ability and confidence it will give is still only to know its absence—and then to fear lest a subconscious will should fictitiously create what it wants. Instead of belief within this not-quite-*post*-Christian poet, there is a respect for the sense of an unattainable truth: a scrupulous regard for those extra unsettling thoughts which he will not repress, even though they undermine present certainties by going round the back of the easier line previously taken:

> Oh, and of course you will say, 'When the time comes, you
> will be ready.'
> Ah, but before it comes, am I to presume it will be so?
>
> ('Amours de Voyage', 2. 4)

Poetic lineation exists in place of simply going along with things. Yet there is also in Clough a feline tone—'Ah, but *before* it comes . . .'—which seems to tease the reader's anxieties as to settled meaning, in being itself highly finished and polished and yet providing *less* than a reader expected. The hovering tone of irony deliberately repels easy sympathy just as surely as Browning's dramatic monologues disappoint the reader's expectation of pure emotional identification. It is the voice of an anti-Parnassian poetry which is floatingly provisional, not yet definite; which, in the equivocal extra freedom given by the act of writing, refuses to take up any position forced upon it and yet is simultaneously suspicious of its own temptation to non-commitment.

Clough stopped writing poetry in 1850: 'Dipsychus' was never published in his lifetime, 'Amours de Voyage' was published only in a journal in America. But it is characteristic of the ambivalence in and around Clough that it is impossible to decide how far his coming to a premature dead-end as a poet was the result of a society's hostility, ironically represented even in the adverse criticisms of Matthew Arnold; or whether, as Arnold argued, it was because Clough's thinking and poetry really could lead nowhere. But, for all their differences, the radically sceptical Clough and the lyrically stoical Arnold were alike in one devastating respect that speaks much for the general difficulty of writing poetry in the later half of the century. Save for 'Thyrsis', his elegy on the death of Clough (1866), Arnold also stopped writing major poetry by 1855 when he was still only 33, and turned to education and literary criticism instead. Both men were thus consciously failed poets, poets whose work seemed even to themselves foreshortened and incomplete, and whose very ability to write, almost as a consequence, ran out long before the end of their lives.

Clough had been a product of the pressures of Thomas Arnold at Rugby and the Tractarian Movement of Newman and W. G. Ward at Oxford in the 1830s and 1840s. He could not join these believers but neither could he easily turn away from them, without offering an argument as strenuous as that of the believers themselves. That is why his is a conscientious agnosticism held uneasily in between the surety of religious faith and the relaxation of post-religious unbelief. But a later post-Wordsworthian poetic experimenter was a less ambiguous product of the Oxford Movement in its second wave. Opposed to any sort of 'half-way house' (the title of a poem written the year before his conversion from Anglicanism and a bitter phrase of Newman's in his *Apologia*), Gerard Manley Hopkins was received into Catholicism by Newman himself in 1866, gave up the writing of poetry for seven years after becoming a Jesuit in 1868, and was ordained priest in 1877. Only when his superior suggested that he write an elegy for the five German Franciscan nuns drowned in a shipwreck did he find in the composition of 'The Wreck of the Deutschland' in 1876 a language that did not seem incompatible with his religious vocation. More or less unpublished during his lifetime, no poetry looks (in his word) more 'odd', less orthodox Victorian, than does Hopkins's, with its self-immolating stresses and its implosive condensations. It looked like a language of his own—'All things counter, original, spare, strange' ('Pied Beauty')—a language 'charged' electrically with an intense sense of the creation re-creating itself afresh:

> Falcon, in his riding
> Of the rolling level underneath him steady air, and striding
> High there . . .

('The Windhover')

'My heart in hiding | Stirred for a bird,—the achieve of, the mastery of the thing!' Amidst all that is 'seared with trade; bleared, smeared with toil | And wears man's smudge', there lives again as there lived for Wordsworth 'the dearest freshness deep down things' ('God's Grandeur').

Yet if Hopkins's purpose was to create his own poetic energy system and language structure, he did so within a thoroughly Victorian context. The very particularity of Hopkins's vision—the sense of 'thisness' which he took from the medieval Schoolman Duns Scotus—is the extreme version of that Victorian abandonment of type, of form, of reliable generality which occurred when an ordered framework gave way to an exhaustive, swamping sense of structureless facts and phenomena called 'the real'. The prolonged and hallucinatory intensity of aesthetic detail recorded in the Pre-Raphaelite paintings of Millais or Holman Hunt was a related development—so disturbingly close was the appreciation of sensuous beauty to Hopkins's own religious transmutation of the same into an act of worship. And yet it was Ruskin, and Ruskin's link with Wordsworth, rather than the Pre-Raphaelites themselves, who early directed Hopkins's religious sense of beauty. And it was Newman who in his *Essay in Aid of a Grammar of Assent* (1870) had taught Hopkins that primary experience was of individual things, and that generalization was a secondary and notional grid of abstractions.

At Oxford, moreover, there was not only the influence of Newman, Liddell, and Pusey. Hopkins had as tutors both the religious Idealist philosopher T. H. Green and the aesthetic relativist Walter Pater and therefore knew at first hand what was at stake between the rival claims of what Pater called the Absolute and the Relative. With Pater—above all, in the 'Conclusion' to *The Renaissance* (1873)—particularity reached atomic level: the continuous action of the elements of which we are composed extended on every side beyond us, said Pater, threatening to flood the stability of personal identity. In place of the past history of dogmatism and fixed principles, Pater offered art and culture, the grasp of momentary beauty and individual creative style.

Yet, although Pater remained a friend, increasingly Hopkins knew that he wanted to resist Pater's philosophy of flux, in its flight of ever-vanishing impressions. As he was to put it in the fourth stanza of 'The Wreck of the Deutschland', Hopkins felt like sand in an hourglass, 'at the wall | Fast' but drifting away from underneath. He knew that he could not resist flux without entering flux. That is why Hopkins created in his poetry an essentially blind acoustic universe, one word flowing into another in strains on the very verge of hypersensitive nonsense verse: 'womb-of-all, home-of-all, hearse-of-all night', 'dis-remembering, dismembering' ('Spelt from Sibyl's Leaves'). What Hopkins wanted was to invent an inextricable medium, offering no escape into secondary paraphrase, riskily seeking to create itself even as it stutteringly went along

> But how shall I . . . make me room there:
> Reach me a . . .
>
> ('The Wreck of the Deutschland', 28)

Where prose makes mundane sense too completely, swallowing the traces of its own effort, Hopkins out of the midst of dark despair in 'Carrion Comfort' can barely manage 'Can something'—but it is the 'achieve' of the thing ('The Windhover').

Nature, said Hopkins in a youthful essay, is not a string along which all the evolutionary differences arbitrarily fade in and out of each other: the chords and points of change, he argued, are

Fig. 14. The claustrophobic hyper-reality of W. Holman Hunt's
The Lady of Shalott, 1857, based on Tennyson's poem of 1832:
'And moving thro' a mirror clear | That hangs before her all the year, |
Shadows of the world appear.'

mathematically fixed in advance—but only at definite distances, when the precise conditions are fulfilled, will the developing principle act.[16] In the dark, Hopkins's improvised poetry, working itself along its lines and often failing, sometimes suddenly finds the precise condition of a thought breaking through and coming to itself—the stress point at which a distinct thing suddenly emerges and realizes itself:

> finds tongue to fling out broad its name;
> Each mortal thing does one thing and the same:
> Deals out that being indoors each one dwells;
> Selves—goes itself; *myself* it speaks and spells,
> Crying *What I do is me: for that I came.*
>
> ('As kingfishers catch fire')

This is what Hopkins means by what he called the principles of inscape and instress in his verse: respectively, original form and animating energy coming together *in* the 'achieve' or the 'doing' of the verse. The word and its stress become no longer separable from each other, as the rhythm becomes the very incarnation of mind: 'What I do is me.' For Hopkins identity is not a Victorian social construct or a product of post-Romantic self-consciousness but what poetry suddenly finds *given* in all its distinct particularity: it is the immediate felt realization of a created thing, inseparable from the very 'taste' of experience (*Sermons and Devotional Writings*, p. 123).

What Hopkins sought in poetry was a primary process of utterance in which, as far as humanly possible, he could not predetermine outcomes, or surrender intellect to common assumptions and categories; but instead would have to feel and hear his way through, word by word, to a salvation or a damnation which were terrifyingly close to each other. Always Hopkins sought his own equivalent of the 'magical change' in rhythm he found in the 'Immortality Ode' when Wordsworth turned from the line on custom, 'Heavy as frost, and deep almost as life', to the fresh time signature, 'O joy! That in our embers I Is something that doth live'.[17] It comes most powerfully

---

[16] *The Journals and Papers of Gerard Manley Hopkins*, ed. Humphry House and Graham Storey (Oxford University Press, 1959), 120: 'The Probable Future of Metaphysics'.

[17] See Geoffrey Hill, 'Redeeming the Time' and also 'Poetry as "Menace" or "Atonement"' in *The Lords of Limit* (Andre Deutsch, 1984); also John Coulson, *Religion and Imagination* (Clarendon Press, 1981).

of all in the split-second realization found within the last four words
of 'Carrion Comfort'—

> That night, that year
> Of now done darkness I wretch lay wrestling with (my God!)
> my God.

—turning from expletive into grace. There the momentary and the
eternal fuse in that almost unbelievable consummation of belief
which for Hopkins was the guarantee of truth.

It is only when, sporadically, Hopkins's high-risk poetry fails that
it seems no more than a style of his own devising, a self-generating
aesthetic. Yet what in Hopkins meant failure was in Pater the only
thing left for the artist. For style in Pater is art's final defence against
the envelopment of personality by 'the real'. In a world without
trustworthy external meanings, without ordering frameworks that
stand for anything more than collusive social habit, Pater's style
becomes the means of personally filtering and mastering reality,
enabling the subjective to express and externalize itself. Against the
bombardment of impressions and objects, the literary artist, says
Pater, 'is really vindicating his liberty in the making of a vocabulary,
an entire system of composition, for himself, his own true manner'
('Style'). 'What is lost in precision of form is gained in intricacy of
expression' ('Coleridge's Writings'). Without forms that could truthfully support the individual's relation to the universal or the traditional, there remained only the human content which the individual
creates and defends from within, as a last stronghold.

There, in the end of any representational aspiration, is the death of
nineteenth-century realism. And it is Swinburne who celebrates that
death along with many other endings, actual or desired: the end
of Christianity, the end of marriage, the end of imperial monarchy,
the end of bourgeois moral complacency, the end of the political
tyranny of law as power. His is the coming of the increasingly *post*-
Victorian poet of the 1890s onwards. For Swinburne despised that
mid-Victorian vacillation of Tennyson, Arnold, and Clough which
he said was built half of doubts and half of dreams; instead, like
Pater, praising Dante Gabriel Rossetti for breaking with 'the semi-
Christianity of "In Memoriam" and the demi-semi-Christianity of

"Dipsychus"' (*Essays and Studies* (1875), pp. 80–1).

So much of Swinburne's own verse gives up on living between two worlds and begins instead from the sensation of living *afterwards*. When customary human emotions are beginning to end, what is offered is a return to the bare present of a new pagan world:

> We are not sure of sorrow
>   And joy was never sure;
> Today will die tomorrow;
>   Time stoops to no man's lure
> .   .   .   .   .   .
>
> From too much love of living,
>   From hope and fear set free,
> We thank with brief thanksgiving
>   Whatever gods may be
> That no life lives for ever
> That dead men rise up never;
> That even the weariest river
>   Winds somewhere safe to sea.
>
> ('The Garden of Proserpine')

Using variants of the dramatic monologue as a release from norms, Swinburne goes past the old Christianized feelings, even by experimentally wearying of them. 'We thank': but whom? and for what? And if thanks, then deadpan thanks that are very, very 'brief'. Not wanting to go on being tossed to and fro between the old halves of hope and fear, Swinburne takes terminal human emotions and re-cycles them:

> Where the dead red leaves of the years lie rotten,
>   The cold old crimes and the deeds thrown by,
> The misconceived and the misbegotten,
>   I would find a sin to do ere I die.
>
> ('The Triumph of Time')

Excited by not knowing whether this is decadence or innovation, the poet reactively *uses* his despair to try to live desperately beyond it. It is Swinburne's demonic mirror image of Hopkins's 'can something'.

> I could hurt thee—but pain would delight thee;
>   Or caress thee—but love would repel
>
> ('Dolores')

Emotions have now gone beyond the rules that used to accompany them: they intermix and evolve by their own logic, a logic of sexual desire, to produce new secondary characteristics of loving fear, hating love that defy the so-called 'natural' order they have left behind. Thus

> The delight that consumes the desire,
> The desire that outruns the delight
>
> ('Dolores')

finds a solution only in the choice between

> A strong desire begot on great despair,
> A great despair cast out by strong desire.
>
> ('Hermaphroditus')

Such mentally dizzying effects take place at the very bounds of Swinburne's style. They are the infinitely proliferating variations that can go on anew within what from of old remains nonetheless finite and closed. Swinburne loves these internally self-rearranging lists in 'the making of man': 'Night, the shadow of light, I And life, the shadow of death' (Chorus, *Atalanta in Calydon*); 'The live wave's love for the shore I The shore's for the wave as it dies' ('Triads'). 'The message' of night to day, of day to night, of April to May, of May to June, is sent on and on, in the beautiful quasi-sexual dying of one thing into another, and yet is never explicitly told or released. For as the words are passed on from line to line, there is no progress, no end point, but endless recycling and deferral:

> Outside of all the worlds and ages,
> There where the fool is as the sage is,
>   There where the slayer is clean of blood,
> No end, no passage, no beginning,
> There where the sinner leaves off sinning,
>   There where the good man is not good.
>
> There is not one thing with another
>
> ('Ilicet')

Swinburne said of Blake that to him 'all symbolic things were literal, all literal things symbolic' (*William Blake: A Critical Essay* (1868; 1906 edn., p. 45). There are no clear distinctions left in Swinburne, no world outside against which to establish them. As Pater put it in his own version of 'Wordsworth' (1874), this is art because it abolishes the idea of means to an end and instead makes means and ends identified. It is like Pater's famous account of music in which 'it is impossible to distinguish the form from the substance or matter, the subject from the expression' ('Style'). For there is form here, but form as circle, form as the chess game of 'Stage Love', in a world-view whose meaning exists only in the increasingly self-referential patterns of its own structured continuance—no more, no less. 'If any reader could extract from any poem a positive spiritual medicine— if he could swallow a sonnet like a moral prescription,' wrote Swinburne, 'then clearly the poet supplying these intellectual drugs would be a bad artist'—no artist but a tradesman in second-hand morality ('Charles Baudelaire: Les Fleurs du Mal', *The Spectator*, 6 September 1862). That is why Swinburne admired Blake rather than Wordsworth, for refusing, as Swinburne saw it, to sell his meanings to the world.

By art for art's sake, Pater meant all that in the way of creativity no longer had a name or a purpose or a place in the world, save now through art. But Swinburne's version of aestheticism is to bring into being a world-view which exists unyieldingly only in its own terms, like an ever-self-rhyming poem which the strange incantatory magic of his poetry makes it impossible simply to dismiss. And any protesting emotional content—which a writer such as Thomas Hardy could not have helped registering, against the form in which he found himself—is superseded and abolished, because the form and the content have eerily become one.

Thomas Hardy belongs to the conclusion of this history. What is more, he reaches beyond it, in particular in the 'Poems of 1912–1913' on the death of his wife and the end of their unhappy marriage —a sequence that reads like a latter-day clash between the goodness of the Wessex poetry of William Barnes, which Hardy himself edited, and the bitterness of George Meredith's *Modern Love* which Hardy, like Swinburne, defended against adverse reviews. For Hardy is the strugglingly self-divided embodiment of the question of May to September, unwilling to leave behind what he nonetheless also feels forced on past. His are the winter words of a writer still not knowing which way to turn:

> So unrefreshed from foregone weariness
> So overburdened by foreseen distress
>
> (Sonnet 4)

> I am sick of where I am and where I am not,
>   I am sick of foresight and memory
>
> (Sonnet 17)

Yet though these are indeed September words—'So late in Autumn one forgets the Spring, | Forgets the Summer' (Sonnet 18)—they are *not*, of course, Hardy's:

> We lack, yet cannot fix upon the lack:
>   Not this, nor that; yet somewhat, certainly.
> We see the thing we do not yearn to see
> Around us: and what see we glancing back?
> Lost hopes that leave our hearts upon the rack,
>   Hopes that were never ours yet seemed to be
>
> (Sonnet 6)

Rather, they are taken from Christina Rossetti's sonnet sequence 'Later Life' written around 1880.[18]

The poem 'Memory'—so much more marked by Tractarian reserve[19] than anything that could have been written by Hopkins—early sealed Christina Rossetti's decision to remain single and celibate ('None know the choice I made and broke my heart'). 'Later Life' is the product of a now middle-aged woman, left with a self which even to itself is essentially secondary, the very obstacle to all it would need in order to transcend itself ('Who Shall Deliver Me?'). It is a sequence without outward events, since while the form of the Victorian sequence poem is about living in time, the subject matter of 'Later Life' is the emotional impossibility of so doing. 'When I was young I deemed that sweets are sweet' ('Later Life', 12): but it turns out that sweets are not really sweet, that spring is not really spring for long, that hopes that were never ours yet seemed to be, and that all too much is, like the scenes in her memory, 'so out of reach while quite within my reach' ('Later Life' 17). In a world that is fallen and

---

[18] Respectively sonnets 4, 17, and 6.
[19] See above, p. 115.

secondary, where language does not tell the truth, life is not *life* and does not keep its apparent promise.

What is more, 'Later Life' was written at the time when Christina Rossetti was nursing her brother, Dante Gabriel, through the terrible physical and mental decay of his final years. It is in part her continuing answer to what she knew of the fleshly school of poetry, even near its end. 'Shame', she writes in sonnet 13, is 'a shadow cast by sin' yet itself may be a grace: 'One virtue pent within an evil place.' It is part of the fallen way which began in Eden when 'man deemed poison sweet for her sweet sake'—and, oddly but powerfully in Christina Rossetti, we do not so much repent of that (it is far, far too late) as carry it through and live by it still:

> Did Adam love his Eve from first to last?
> I think so; as we love who works us ill,
> And wounds us to the quick, yet loves us still.
>
> ('Later Life', 15)

This is the alternative to Swinburne's version of sweet poison, to Swinburne's sense of living through and beyond past emotions; and it remains historically possible as a position so long as someone, believing it, can make it so.

Extraordinarily then, life appears as painful for Christina Rossetti as for Thomas Hardy—and painful moreover in what seem remarkably similar ways—not because Christina Rossetti, like Thomas Hardy, did not believe in God but even while, and even because, she did. Implicitly, Hardy's one intellectual certainty—his recognition that a post-Darwinian universe made a radical historical difference to the sense that human beings had of their place in the cosmos— is denied by Christina Rossetti. 'Cobwebs' is Christina Rossetti's imagination of an afterlife at the very end of time, and it is a poem bleakly dominated by the words 'no', 'neither', and 'nor', ending 'No future hope, no fear for evermore'. To find earthly life unsatisfactory, to have a religious vision that proves it more so, and yet never to be able to get any nearer to what that vision still leaves so removed and distant makes Christina Rossetti like a blinded person: 'And still we peer beyond with craving face' ('Later Life', 23). This is poetry powerful enough to make a position—often unsympathetic to modern-day readers, except as a psychological case study—become more than an external matter of curious religious history but an imaginative challenge to easy secular preconceptions.

So many of Christina Rossetti's lyrics are static but in 'Later Life' that sense of being blocked is painful not just because it is always there but because it keeps returning. That equivocal movement in 'Later Life' is just sufficient finally to release the writing of Christina Rossetti's greatest poem. 'An Old-World Thicket' is a 180–line journey through the wood that in Dante, at the opening of *Inferno*, is entered midway through a life. The balked midway position of 'Later Life' is now held more fluidly in confusion between sleep and waking, within a landscape which is itself imaginative. The poem's speaker is left searching for an orientating clue: she looks for similes to describe the beauty of the birds she hears on first entry and has to conclude, 'Like anything they seemed, and everything'. It is like a widened and actualized version of the search for a language in 'Later Life': 'Something this foggy day, a something which I Is neither of this fog nor of today' ('Later Life', 17).

Yet though the poem is a journey, it is not that the speaker actually moves during the course of the poem. Instead, time moves from the morning to the evening of life. And because for much of the poem the speaker has her eyes closed, her movements are deeply and involuntarily inner. 'Alas, I had no shutter to mine ear.' The language becomes that of a genuine poetry because it begins to struggle blindly towards something just beyond itself: 'Without, within me music seemed to be; I Something not music, yet most musical' ('An Old-World Thicket').

But it is the reason for the closing of her eyes that is decisive. For it marks yet another late-century break with Wordsworth and with what Wordsworth stood for. The very sweetness of the sight of natural beauty 'moved me to despair':

> Stung me to anger by its mere content,
> Made me all lonely on that way I went . . .
> .   .   .   .
> For all that was but showed what all was not,
>   But gave clear proof of what might never be;
>   Making more destitute my poverty,
>   And yet more blank my lot,
>   And me much sadder . . .

By its very contrast, nature reminds the now lonely speaker of 'each sore defeat of my defeated life'. Separation is the law here. Half a lifetime's endurance of a limited spiritual vision, too great to be dismissed, too remote to be embraced, finally must admit its attendant anger and despair.

Thus, closing her eyes, she then hears instead a universal cry of lamentation coming it seems from all creation groaning—a cry far from the voice of Nature in *The Prelude*, closer to Paul's Epistle to the Romans or the Fall in *Paradise Lost*. Though it is partly coming from inside herself, it is still a cry that she does not want to hear, any more than she wanted to see the earlier perfection.

It is then that a further, final change occurs. As evening falls, as a harmony begins to descend, the speaker hears the gentle yet persistent sound of a bell and the bleatings of a flock of sheep and, opening her eyes again, looks up. The setting sun, before so high, has stooped to earth, the flock comes home led by a patriarchal ram, nature takes its radiance now from the light of heaven, and differences grow subdued: inspired by the spirit of Dante, the religious symbols are held so beautifully incarnate within the literal vision here, that they restore to Christina Rossetti the Christianized version of Wordsworth that Wordsworth made of himself in the later years of his life. The gently setting sun shines full on the faces of the flock in some of the finest explicitly Christian poetry since Milton's 'Lycidas':

> Mild face by face, and woolly breast by breast,
>   Patient, sun brightened too,
> Still journeying toward the sunset and their rest.
>
> ('An Old-World Thicket')

For here, near the very end of the day, the speaker sees not less but more through the sun's 'slow | Warm, dying loveliness brought near and low': dying—that most powerful of Victorian concerns, at the very boundary-point between the secular and religious—in this context is no longer a painful or pessimistic word.[20]

---

[20] Thus the double vision of even the celebrated Brighton preacher Frederick W. Robertson (1816–53): 'Talk as we will of immortality, there is an obstinate feeling that we cannot master, that we end in death; and *that* may be felt together with the firmest belief of resurrection. Brethren, our faith tells us one thing, and our sensations tell us another. When we die, we are surrendering in truth all that with which we have associated existence' (quoted in Michael Wheeler, *Death and the Future Life in Victorian Literature and Theology* (Cambridge University Press, 1990), 27).

In the movement from May to September then, 'An Old-World Thicket' is not only an alternative to *The City of Dreadful Night* as a version of Dante, it is also a counter-vision to 'The Woods of Westermain'. No period has been more anxiously obsessed with its own historical position than was the Victorian age. At the very heart of a poetry such as Arnold's is the still to him strange and disturbing recognition that to be born fifty years earlier or later changes the very nature and possibility of belief. Yet the literary history of the period is not as historically determined as was sometimes thought or feared even at the time. On the contrary, its literary history remains precarious, as precarious as the age itself, sited between past and future: for it depends upon the beliefs maintained or lost by individuals, often at great cost either way; upon the creative power and skill with which those thoughts and feelings are able to be invested and made existent; and finally upon the subsequent value that is granted or denied that achievement. In an age of so many competing, inchoate, or recovered frameworks of belief, of so many standpoints and changes of view at the very origin of powerful feelings over a century later, the perspective of the Victorian years can shift, and shift again, within seconds of imaginative reading.

Conclusion

The story of the period 1830–1880 has two alternative endings, one characterized in the novels of George Meredith (1828–1909), the other culminating in the novels of Thomas Hardy (1840–1928).

Meredith began writing fiction at the same time as George Eliot, in the late 1850s, but lived on for twenty-nine years after her death in 1880. Everything in Meredith points towards the literature of the 1890s: the politicized reaction of father against son and of woman against man; the destabilizing power of sexual disturbance; the growth of stylistic experimentalism in the abandonment of universal readability; the disdain of popular pressure amongst the reading public—the 'porkers', the 'moral contingent' as Meredith called them; the fracturing of both religious belief and humanist confidence involved in the intelligent assumption of a cool, external, ironic viewpoint;—in short, that sense of living on *after* the passing of something now seen to have been too innocent or crude or earnest or moralistic in the decades preceding. Of the ordeal of sexual love Hot Blood feels, 'It is a divinity! All that is worth living for in the world', but Cold Blood replies, 'It is a name men and women are much in the habit of employing to sanctify their appetites' (*The Ordeal of Richard Feverel* (1859), ch. 21). Beneath all the human twittering, it is Darwinian sexual selection that holds sway: 'You spread a handsomer tail than your fellows, you dress a finer top-knot, you pipe a newer note, have a longer stride; she reviews you in competition and selects you' (*The Egoist* (1879), ch. 5).

Yet in Meredith even Cold Blood's externalizing language of science all too often comes from within—the words of cool reason a mask for heated fear, a distancing defence against pain. And our own inner language is equally duplicitous: its real, hidden directives begin just where the words of self-deceptive consciousness leave off, giving way to a series of unspoken inner dots or dashes:

> The dash is a haven reached that would not be greeted if it stood out in words. Could we live with ourselves letting our animal do our thinking for us legibly? We live with ourselves agreeably so long as his projects are phrased in his primitive tongue, even though we have clearly apprehended what he means, and though we sufficiently well understand the whither of our destination under his guidance. (*The Tragic Comedians* (1880), ch. 11)

That is where Darwinism led Meredith—to something terrifyingly simple (unconscious pride, vanity, fear, sexual need, power, 'our animal') still left silently at the heart of a mentally evolved complexity: 'the civilized Egoist, primitive still, as sure as man has teeth, but developed in his manner of using them' (*The Egoist*, ch. 39). Like a challenge in sophisticated burlesque to the deep sense of human meaning revealed in the complex language of George Eliot, the mandarin intricacy of Meredith's own narrative style has behind its brilliant metaphors that secret of an undermining simplicity, absorbed into complicated hybrid versions of itself within the modern world. As Meredith put it in his Blue Notebook, 'To know ourselves is more a matter of will than of insight'. His is not a language of belief, directly summoning primary realities; through its powers of sceptical disbelief, it evokes instead a renewed sense of the inner twisted slipperiness of meaning, miming the delusive fictions and obfuscatory games played out in the human world, in evasion of the will-to-truth. This is the work of what Meredith in his *Essay on Comedy* (1877) calls the Comic Spirit. It sees, for example, a young woman using with 'tender cruelty' the adoring lover she *can* have, in hidden relation to the adored beloved who is unobtainable and, cutting through all sentiment, recognizes that 'she to him was what she sought for in another':

> Anatomy is the title for the operation, because the probing of herself in another, with the liberty to cease probing as soon as it hurt her, allowed her while unhurt to feel that she prosecuted her researches in a dead body. The moment her strong susceptibility to the likeness shrank under a stroke of pain, she abstained from carving, and simultaneously conscious that he lived, she was kind to him. (*The Tragic Comedians*, ch. 5)

It happens all the time in the necessary economy of the social world—this 'manner' of using and discarding others—as people pass on along their paths: 'This can be done when love is gone. It is done more or less at any meeting of men and men; and men and women who love not are perpetually doing it, unconsciously or sensibly' (*The Amazing Marriage* (1895), ch. 44). *The Amazing Marriage* is itself the dark, ironic story of an aristocrat who struggles to repent of his desertion of his lower-born wife, only to find that the woman, grown independent in her bitter suffering, will not now accept him back after all.

'[W]hen love is gone.' Meredith's is the genius of essentially negative complications and negative emotions: a woman, Clara Middleton, in the hands of the egoist, Sir Willoughby Patterne—

> With a frigidity that astonished her, she marvelled at the act of kissing, and at the obligation it forced upon the inanimate person to be an accomplice. . . . He fondled her hand, and to that she grew accustomed; her hand was at a distance. And what is a hand? Leaving it where it was, she treated it as a link between herself and dutiful goodness. (*The Egoist*, ch. 7)

—while meanwhile the man, thinking himself so loved and admired, is seen from an increasingly critical distance, his words merely overheard. Even Laetitia Dale, the single woman taken for granted for simply loving the egoist from the first, begins to be 'strangely swayed by Clara'—in tart comedy which undoes the emotional suppression of intelligence: 'ideas of Sir Willoughby that she had never before imagined herself to entertain, had been sown in her, she thought; not asking herself whether the searchingness of the young lady had struck them and bidden them rise from where they lay embedded' (ch. 24). Sir Willoughby himself tries to fight off these doubts both from inside and out:

> Within the shadow of his presence he compressed opinion, as a strong frost binds the springs of the earth, but beyond it his shivering sensitiveness ran about in dread of a stripping in a wintry atmosphere. This was the ground of his hatred of the world; it was an appalling fear on behalf of his naked eidolon, the tender infant Self swaddled in his name before the world (*The Egoist*, ch. 29)

This is the opposite of George Eliot's searing yet compassionate treatment of Casaubon in *Middlemarch*: here Meredith's readers *are* the critical world beyond his influence that Sir Willoughby fears; and if even so they do identify with Sir Willoughby, it is an imaginative identification that breeds not sympathy but its own fear in turn.

The cool, merciless, externalizing Comic Spirit that presides over these novels is carefully distinguished from the rival spirits of satire and of humour on either side of itself. The laughter of satire, says Meredith in his *Essay on Comedy*, is a moralist's blow on the back or the face, while the laughter of comedy is more elusively 'impersonal and of unrivalled politeness, nearer a smile'. It laughs 'through the mind', he says, whilst with the humourists it is rather 'the feelings' which are primary. It must be Dickens's comedy of love that Meredith is thinking of when he dismisses humour as sentimental, an unpaid-for comfort. Take a ridiculous person: 'If you laugh all round him, tumble him, roll him about, deal him a smack, and drop a tear on him, own his likeness to you, and yours to your neighbour, spare him as little as you shun, pity him as much as you expose, it is a spirit of Humour that is moving you.' In Dickens there is always sufficient belief for this kind of rescue work. Even in *Dombey and Son* (1848) there is a deeply instinctive Christian spirit in him that recognizes how the 'enforced distortions' of a fallen world make it 'natural to be unnatural' (ch. 47), and can recover even from the emphatically fallen world living memories of that pre-lapsarian nature of humanity. But in Dickens it is a rough, demotic, disguised spirit, finding good and high things in strange and low places. And to Meredith the broad traditional Dickensian gusto of, for example, Douglas Jerrold's *Mrs Caudle's Curtain Lectures* (1845)—so forcibly delivered in the marital bed to a husband forbidden to sleep—would have grown to seem merely vulgar.

Comedy in Meredith's hands is refined—refining itself even into pain at times, but aristocratic and secular in spirit, dependent upon a shared sense of high civilization 'where women are on the road to an equal footing with men'. When the witty adventuress Diana finally, almost grudgingly, accepts marriage to her prosaic good and loving man—the prudent investor she has teased by suggesting for his new country estate the title 'The Funds' or 'Capital Towers' or 'Dividend Manor'—she takes him with 'Banality thy name is marriage' on her tongue; while in her heart 'she was not enamoured: she could say it to herself. She had, however, been surprised, both by the man and her unprotesting submission; surprised and warmed, unaccountably warmed' (*Diana of the Crossways* (1885), ch. 43). It is that surprise which adds some colour—not merely rose-tinted—to what is otherwise, she says, the sanction of 'grey-toned reason'.

At that point Meredith is close to Jane Austen. Yet for the most part, and not least in his opposition to Dickens, he descends from Thackeray in taking an externalized viewpoint—but a Thackeray now without the robust eighteenth-century tradition recalled, for example, in Thackeray's own *English Humourists of the Eighteenth Century* (1853). Instead, Meredith is on his way towards the aristocratic rational liberalism of the civilized world of Bloomsbury— admired as he was by Leonard and Virginia Woolf and E. M. Forster. The great rational comic example for Meredith here is Molière, and it is Meredith who marks the shift from the German philosophic contribution to English literature from Carlyle to George Eliot, to the more aesthetic French influence, beginning with Matthew Arnold's 'Literary Influence of Academies' (1864). It is symptomatic that in his *Notes on England* (1862), the French man of letters Hippolyte Taine complained of the Protestant aesthetic of the men of the north: even John Ruskin, the greatest art critic in England, could not praise the pleasure of beauty of itself until he moralized and spiritualized it.

It is to a civilized Francophile rationality that Meredith's Comic Spirit appeals in its sensitiveness to the slightest movement away from a classically poised standard: 'A lover pretending too much by one foot's length of pretence, will have that foot caught in her trap' (*The Egoist*, 'Prelude'). Equally, it is only small gains won by highly cultivated reason that Meredith thinks possible in human life, gains at once so simple and so complex as, for example, the achievement of 'respect' in *The Amazing Marriage*. And when a happy resolution does come in, for example, *Evan Harrington* (1861), it is not so much through wholehearted human triumph as the coolly observed recognition that 'good and evil work together in this world . . . The Two Generals were quite antagonistic, but no two, in perfect ignorance of one another's proceedings, ever worked so harmoniously toward the main result' (ch. 29). In the sheer skill of his novelistic designs Meredith himself is never in such perfect ignorance. Yet it is of course the irrationality on every side of that small central area of reason in him which captures Meredith's imagination—as surely in the depiction of those maddened fathers and husbands, as in the much more wildly involved immediacy of the poetry of *Modern Love* and 'The Woods of Westermain'.[1]

What Meredith inherits and passes on is a hybrid world, a Darwinian amalgam of reason and unreason. It is the world of late Victorian male feminism, as in George Gissing and Mark Rutherford, existing alongside deep sexual unease. It is the politically realigned order in which patriotic aristocrat turns left-wing radical as a result of the sort of story told in *Beauchamp's Career* (1876)—how a man 'loved his country, and for another and a broader love, growing out of his first passion, fought it' (ch. 4), because he only owes a duty to his class 'as long as he sees his class doing its duty to the country' (ch. 16).

As earlier in the case of Bulwer-Lytton,[2] the consequence of such amalgams is a series of experimental mutations at disturbingly interconnected levels of politics, marriage, class, and literary genre, in the search for the very form of contemporary reality. At times the novels shift almost feverishly from one mode to another, sensing gaps and inauthenticities in the midst of expression, because something is wrong in the very shape and structure of things. Thus, in *Beauchamp's Career* the woman who most loves Beauchamp is on the opposite side of the political divide; in *The Amazing Marriage* the husband finds only in Catholicism the impersonal forms for that complete confession to a priest which he cannot bring himself to make to his wronged wife in the full complexity of the human medium; in *The Ordeal of Richard Feverel* the father tries to eradicate human failings (in particular, the sexual forces from which he himself had suffered in the desertion of his wife) by imposing, to disastrous effect, a scientific 'system' of education upon the son.

In all this kaleidoscopic instability around the very forms of reality, Meredith was himself, as Oscar Wilde put it in 'The Decay of Lying' (1889), like Richard Feverel 'a child of realism who is not on speaking terms with his father'. By the time he writes *The Tragic Comedians*, Meredith's version of tragicomedy—tragedy dissolved into comedy—is the only thing like a genre left to describe how the two simple wishes of protagonists seeking to marry despite their society still cannot make 'one will'. The would-be hero, the great

[1] See above, pp. 476–8, 499–500, 504, 513–14.   [2] See above, pp. 272–89.

radical reformer of society, cannot get the young aristocratic girl who loves him to hold out against her own family: 'Great enemies, great undertakings, would have revived him as they had always revived and fortified. But here was a stolid small obstacle, scarce assailable on its own level': 'He gnawed the paradox, that it was huge because it was petty' (ch. 9).

It is always finally like that in Meredith's modern post-Darwinian world—a petty hugeness. Human beings are so absurdly negligible in the face of the universe, they are like the working-class urchin saved from drowning at the expense of the life of yet another failed hero, in the bitter last words of *Beauchamp's Career*: insignificant bits of 'mudbank life'.

It is there that Hardy offers the alternative ending—but not because he opposes the bleakest version of the Darwinian world-view. On the contrary:

April 7 1889. A woeful fact—that the human race is too extremely developed for its corporeal conditions, the nerves being evolved to activity abnormal in such an environment. Even the higher animals are in excess in this respect. It may be questioned if Nature, or what we call Nature, so far back as when she crossed the line from invertebrates to vertebrates, did not exceed her mission. This planet does not supply the materials for happiness to higher existences. Other planets may, though one can hardly see how. (F. E. Hardy, *The Life of Thomas Hardy*)

Human beings are the accidental results of *over*-evolution, ironically conscious and emotional products of a universe which is itself both mindless and uncaring: 'The emotions have no place in a world of defect, and it is a cruel injustice that they should have developed in it' (*The Life of Thomas Hardy*, 9 May 1881). It is unjust that our very strengths of feeling are our vulnerabilities, that our hopes and morality and ideals, for being unrealizable, themselves cause us fear, disappointment, suffering, and pain. And perhaps the worst feeling is that there is no one—no god, nothing—that is actively being unjust in all this: it is another of those ironic achievements which only rebound back upon them, that human beings create their own sense of injustice, for the sense of justice is created precisely through its being found wanting. It is almost literally unspeakable to Hardy that, biologically, emotionally, even linguistically, we are condemned to treat as essential what is in itself accidental. And so we keep on seeking and making meanings, as though through some self-generating meaning-making machine constructed by a writer such as Lewis Carroll.

So many Victorian poets, in particular, seem on the verge of this recognition: that their words are not actually naming anything, are not really referring outwards at all, as the realist novelists could more easily assume, but are turning back round upon themselves in a cocoon of melancholy. To Tennyson or to Arnold, it can seem as though human resources—the thoughts, the feelings, the very language of individual expression framed in 'matter-moulded forms of speech' (*In Memoriam*, 95)—are no more than the gesturings of thick and stumbling fingers failing, for want of some imagined microsurgery, to reach meanings that are too minute, evasive, or alien to be grasped or else (as Clough most of all suspected) are simply factitious and non-existent after all. All this Hardy himself might describe as merely the biggest of what he wryly calls 'life's little ironies' (the title of a collection of short stories published in 1894). But in place of God, the guarantor of meaning in the universe, Hardy has only the metaphysical language of 'planets' and 'what we call, Nature', of a sort of space fiction, with human beings left to occupy the space between earth and sky:

To persons standing alone on a hill during a clear midnight such as this, the roll of the world eastward is almost a palpable movement. . . . The poetry of motion is a phrase much in use, and to enjoy the epic form of that gratification it is necessary to stand on a hill at a small hour of the night, and, having first expanded with a sense of difference from the mass of civilized mankind, who are dreamwrapt and disregardful of all such proceedings at this time, long and quietly watch your stately progress through the stars. After such a nocturnal reconnoitre it is hard to get back to earth, and to believe that the consciousness of such majestic speeding is derived from a tiny human frame. (*Far from the Madding Crowd* (1874), ch. 2)

In Hardy that epic Romantic poetry of motion, such as Wordsworth celebrated in the felt roll of the universe, is always dragged back down to earth, to prosaic stories and mundane identities, by a law as universal as gravity itself. It is the law of the Darwinian world order that the consciousness of the universe comes from only a small disinherited part of it, belittled even by its own capacity to register hugeness: 'Law has produced in man a child who cannot but constantly reproach its parent for doing much and yet not all' (*The Life of Thomas Hardy*, 9 May 1881). Because it is so awesomely hard 'to believe' the irony that 'the consciousness of such majestic speeding' could be merely 'derived from a tiny human frame', Hardy is left with the problem of belief as an emotion rooted in the very biology of his being.

Because of the power of this emotion, the overwhelming sense of cosmic irony cannot finally produce in Hardy Meredith's detached Comic Spirit, tempted as he is by that attitude. Hardy's young Jude can hardly get over the simple fact that to protect the crops he must stop the birds eating the seeds: 'Events did not rhyme quite as he had thought. Nature's logic was too horrid for him to care for. That mercy towards one set of creatures was cruelty towards another sickened his sense of harmony.' And yet he does get over it, and almost immediately so, by refusing adult consciousness: 'Then, like the natural boy, he forgot his despondency, and sprang up' (*Jude the Obscure* (1895), Part First, ch. 2). If being 'the *natural* boy' is a way of forgetting Nature's horrid logic, it is Hardy's shuddering adult thought that even our escapes are part of our imprisonment. No human being can fully bear a felt consciousness of the human situation. And yet no human being can for ever evade it.

That is why it is the Tragic, not the Comic, Spirit which is Hardy's. In *Middlemarch* George Eliot argued that if realism could indeed penetrate the normal tragedies that go on in concealment within ordinary life, we could not bear it, it would be like 'hearing the grass grow and the squirrel's heart beat' (ch. 20): that *is* what it is like in Hardy's super-sensitivity—'All around you there seemed to be something glaring, garish, rattling, and the noises and glares hit upon the little cell called your life, and shook it, and warped it' (*Jude the Obscure*, Part First, ch. 2). George Eliot believed that the spectacle of human beings in trouble produced in those who witness or read of it a secondary compassion, a seed of kindness, which may grow into being increasingly primary in the long future. It is a belief, felt in the emotion of compassion itself, which derives from Wordsworth:

Sorrow that is not sorrow, but delight,
And miserable love, that is not pain
To hear of, for the glory that redounds
Therefrom to human kind, and what we are.
(*The Prelude* (1850), 13. 246–9)

But in Hardy vicarious sympathy is just another part of fiction: pain
is the law of the universe in *Jude* and to register that pain in others
serves only to redouble the sense of human trouble.

Yet still, as by a biological law, Hardy's people cannot live for long
by taking the view from outside; moments of detachment only
increase the pains and bafflements of involvement. 'Upon her sensations the whole world depended to Tess; through her existence all her
fellow-creatures existed, to her. The universe itself only came into
being for Tess on the particular day in the particular year in which
she was born' (*Tess of the d'Urbervilles* (1891), ch. 25). Even when
his characters begin to learn of the biological law that compels the
little human cells to have feelings, still, they have to live from within
them, to keep on feeling those emotions subjectively, in the instinctive life and belief of individual feeling. That is why, by a species of
obstinate recuperation within the natural organism, the still youthful Tess cannot help hoping again, rallying, after the initial sexual
ruin of her life. That is why the ageing Michael Henchard still cannot
strategically withdraw or give up on life but has to keep returning to
it, even if it only means the repetition of mistakes and rejections in
relation to his quasi-daughter: 'The remembrance would continually
revive in him . . . To make one more attempt to be near her: to go
back; to see her, to plead his cause, to endeavour strenuously to hold
his own in her love; it was worth the risk of repulse, ay, of life itself'
(*The Mayor of Casterbridge* (1886), ch. 44). In *The Egoist* the primitive in man still keeps reaching forward, reasserting and blending
itself into strange modern configurations of itself; but in Henchard
the man is rooted in the primitive, his emotional energy is always in
living memory of it, it keeps coming back unrefined.

As a reader of manuscripts for Chapman and Hall, Meredith in
1869 was the first established literary figure to offer encouragement
to the aspiring Hardy. Significantly the manuscript Meredith read
was *The Poor Man and the Lady*, sensitive as were both men to

cross-class complexities. But Hardy himself was always more rooted than was Meredith in both his own past and the traditions of his provincial Wessex upbringing. Meredith evolved. Born the son of a tailor, turned urbane cosmopolitan, haunted by a disastrous semi-bohemian marriage, Meredith is always about leaving things behind, artistically getting outside and recombining them—the autobiographical *Evan Harrington* being a conscious model for George Gissing's significantly entitled *Born in Exile* (1892), just as *The Ordeal of Richard Feverel* had an influence upon James Joyce's *Portrait of the Artist as a Young Man* (1916). But Hardy is not, like Meredith or James or Joyce or Woolf, 'the artist' finding refuge in his art; he is rather the final representative of that quintessential Victorian phenomenon: the figure with religious feelings who is left without a religion. For Hardy nothing—no artistic invention, no secular humanism, no politics, not even the changes he sought in the social structure—could finally replace the old religious feelings: he never gets over them, they remain nagging as memory, as pained need, as lost questionings. *Jude the Obscure* ends with Jude repeating the great ancient cries of Job: 'Let the day perish wherein I was born . . . Wherefore is light given to him that is in misery, and life unto the bitter in soul?' (Part Sixth, ch. 11).

In Hardy human self-reflection will not suffice: it is not so much autonomous as lonely. The evolution of the impersonal view, the seeing of our selves as though from outside them, can never be fully sustained. Tess recalls all the important dates of her life as they come to pass in the revolution of each calendar year—and then she suddenly finds a view from outside herself

She suddenly thought one afternoon, when looking in the glass at her fairness, that there was yet another date, of greater importance to her than those; that of her own death, when all these charms would have disappeared; of a day which lay sly and unseen among all the other days of the year, giving no sign or sound when she annually passed over it; but not the less surely there. (*Tess of the d'Urbervilles*, ch. 15)

The view from outside finally means death to the individual: it is only from the inside that she can live. 'What's the use of learning that I am one of a long row only . . . The best is not to remember that your nature and your past doings have been just like thousands' and thousands', and your coming life and doings'll be like thousands' and thousands'' (*Tess of the d'Urbervilles*, ch. 19). In Hardy that external view of a life and the inevitable foreknowledge of its place within the common end of mortality can never replace the experience of still going through it to the end. That is why Hardy's novels remain formally old-fashioned in being linearly tied to time, story, consequence, outcome, and finally death itself, the only real ending left to Hardy in place of an afterlife.

Henchard in particular, as the man who is his own worst enemy, never stops, never sidesteps but takes his life all the way through to its very death by dint of that power in himself which is killing him. It is the paradox left even in his final will—

> & that no man remember me.
> To this I put my name.
> MICHAEL HENCHARD
>
> (*The Mayor of Casterbridge*, ch. 45)

—what is human in him inescapably leaving a memory even in the attempt to erase it. Similarly *Jude the Obscure* is a novel that tears itself apart—between spirit and flesh, theory and practice, man and woman, in defiance of the artistic creation of any fictive order when no *real* order exists in the world. It is the end of the road for Hardy as a novelist, the accidental human hybrid at the extreme edge of the Wessex map, with nowhere to go.

In that sense Hardy is the real ending for Victorianism. After Hardy's tragic novels, it is as though nothing is left—save a few small survivors. And at least in that ending, Hardy seems to be saying to the 1890s, there is nothing that can simply go on deteriorating, decadently metamorphosing even after everything is really over. This is the worst.

For Hardy takes what W. H. Mallock took to be the greatest out of all the multitude of Victorian questions, in the light of the decline of Christianity, the fundamental question facing secularization: Is life worth living? Not life supported any longer by the idea of an after life, not life 'accidentally' as it happens to turn out by good luck or bad luck for one particular individual, but life 'essentially' in itself, in this world, without God-given meanings or values: whether, that is to say, 'life has some deep inherent worth of its own, beyond what it can acquire or lose by the caprice of circumstance' (W. H. Mallock, *Is Life Worth Living?* (1879), ch. 1). Like John Stuart Mill in the midst of the breakdown he recalls in his *Autobiography* (1873)—'I felt that the flaw in my life must be a flaw in life itself' (ch. 5)—Hardy is on the verge of answering 'no', with all the pained reluctance that makes that answer in its struggle with itself a death sentence. And still with Carlyle's 'everlasting no' almost upon their lips, Hardy's protagonists continue to live out their life-force. For in Hardy even that 'no' is broken-heartedly loyal, as Meredith's negative emotions cannot be, to the human ideals and the religious needs it finds so utterly defeated. Life, in the loss or failure of these things, is not worth living. Hardy is always potentially Victorian humanism's great nemesis, not least because emotionally he himself did not want it to fail and still found it doing so. Yet still, any replacement for the old faiths, any high human seriousness must meet the challenges embodied in someone such as Thomas Hardy if it is indeed truly to make life worth living.

In the face of the absolute No of later nineteenth-century pessimists, it was very much in defence of all that George Eliot meant to him that the philosopher James Sully offered a reply in his book *Pessimism* (1877). 'We have resolved to measure the value of the world by human feeling' (p. 398); and yet that resolve, argues Sully, depends upon something unreliable, changeable and, above all, relative: 'there is a constant tendency to measure the dimensions of any given feeling not from an absolute zero-point, but from the point of our most frequent, customary and habitual emotional states' (p. 276). We are not capable of absolutes and finalities. 'Is he worth living for?' Dorothea finds herself forced into asking of Casaubon in *Middlemarch* (ch. 42): 'And just as clearly in the miserable light she saw her own and her husband's solitude—how they walked apart so that she was obliged to survey him. If he had drawn her towards him, she would never have surveyed him—never have said "Is he worth living for?" but would have felt him simply a part of her own life.' Always in her work George Eliot was fighting the coming shadow of Thomas Hardy—of all that he stood for in terrible answers to vital questions—even before it finally loomed. It is the attempted but anticlimactic 'Finale' of *Middlemarch*, and the way that novel cannot have a real ending in its commitment to continuance, that Hardy is challenging at the apocalyptic close of his own works.

Yet simultaneously it is as though, in their different ways, Scott Holland, Adam Seth, and Winwood Reade[3] are saying to Hardy what William James says in his review of *Is Life Worth Living?* in *Essays in Popular Philosophy* (1897). For there James considers those products of apparent over-evolution—human consciousness and human emotion—and questions whether they are as accidental, ironic, disinherited, and redundant as they must sometimes seem. 'If you surrender to the nightmare view,' James argues, 'your mistrust of life has removed whatever worth your own enduring existence might have given to it.' Our own reactions to the world, he goes on, are part of the final equation, even when they feel excluded from it: 'small as they are in bulk, they are integral parts of the whole thing, and necessarily help to determine the definition. They may even be the decisive elements' (ch. 2). Human intervention may not be merely arbitrary, uncalled-for, fictive, and redundant, papering the cracks or filling the void; it may be the freedom of human consciousness to solve for itself the problems it sees, to give form and expression to the universe out of which it has evolved. It is a Victorian version of Pascal's wager, a risk as to which it is. Part of Hardy votes no, while, not least in the poetry, he still acts as though yes:

> So fair a fancy few would weave
>   In these years! Yet, I feel,
> If someone said on Christmas Eve,
>   'Come; see the oxen kneel
>
> In the lonely barton by yonder coomb
>   Our childhood used to know,'
> I would go with him in the gloom
>   Hoping it might be so.
>
> ('The Oxen', 1915)

At the very least in Hardy, the human emotions, like the memory of Henchard, revive in the midst of their own defeat and persist even in suffering through to their very end, 'Hoping it might be so'. With a mixture of what must have seemed to Hardy stubborn commitment and biological determinism, belief in individual inward

---

[3] See above, pp. 101–2; 143–6; 96–7; 449–50, respectively.

existence, however useless, remains powerful in Hardy. 'Did you ever find | The thought "What profit" move me much?' ('Your Last Drive', 1912). And in that there also remains in Hardy a still abiding tribute to the commitment to the human throughout Victorian literature. It is a commitment to some sense—in Tennyson's *In Memoriam*, in Elizabeth Barrett Browning's *Aurora Leigh*, and in all that thinking within the terms of the human which characterizes the realist novel—that the personal, inward, and individual holds within itself something implicitly richer and more complex in experience than any explicit idea or system or policy can ever fully represent. And still in the early years of the twentieth century Hardy writes a poetry which, defended only by rhyme, is nonetheless no more and no less than the content of personal experience—without a modernist mythology or a religion or an ideology to protect or elevate it. As George MacDonald's Hugh Sutherland puts it, after telling his anxious young pupil a story about how patience, acceptance, and adaptability go on in the growth of seeds: 'There seemed to himself to be more in his parable than he had any right to invent. But is it not so with all stories that are rightly rooted in the human?' (*David Elginbrod* (1863), vol. 1, ch. 4).

It is true that in Victorian literature that human surplus or residue of meaning is often not sufficient to itself and feels like a content still in search of a form to justify or appease it. But culminating in *Middlemarch*, the realist novel has just sufficient form to hold onto that content, without a fuller framework of purpose or belief, and keep in trust a holding ground or reservoir of all that human complexity—like rich, raw material—which the efforts of the future must emerge out of and seek to satisfy. In Trollope, in Mrs Gaskell, in George Eliot, the realist novel says that still a life can and must go on being led, empirically, going along in ordinary time, whatever the problems, conscious and unconscious, around or beneath it. There were always signs that gains were temporary, that problems must return, that the work of a generation might be overtaken in a moment: witness the troubles of the second generation in Dinah Craik's *John Halifax Gentleman* (1856) or the sudden unexpected destruction of the great city at the close of George MacDonald's *The Princess and Curdie* (1882).

But, crucially in the nineteenth century, it is literature that recovers and preserves the memory which history may dissolve into outcomes. What inspires that literary perseverance is the Victorian experience of plenitude expressed first of all and most of all in Dickens—in that extreme, almost apocalyptic life-sense of an overbrimming world, full of unpredictable and unordered human variety, emerging at one moment close to feelings of paradise, at another on the verge of final damnation. It is the sense of a life-force which is never written off. And with it goes a recurrently stubborn belief implicit in the act of realist writing: that everything written stands for something that exists, independent of the writing of it. The existence of 'George Eliot', in *Middlemarch*, is the greatest Victorian invention in this respect. For however much its author had been a godless freethinker, rational and relativistic, 'George Eliot' signifies that there *is* a view to be had of this thing called life we live within, from outside or from above it—whether there is or is not anything or anyone there to do the viewing. It is an impossible view for a human being to take up in place of God, and even its version of the absolute must remain relative; yet it is not merely a fiction, it is the metaphysical impossibility that art exists to allow: an image of truth never to be fully known by anyone, yet present in the very sense of being dependent human creatures held here below. Victorian agnosticism is the refusal to believe that truth is a post-religious ghost, an empty signifier without any possible referent. It is there, in the space that George Eliot imaginatively occupies, even with consciously relative inadequacy.

The period 1830–80 had everything, held as though in one great conversation of voices. As Alexander Bain put it in proclaiming the law of relativity in the revised edition of *Senses and the Intellect* (1874) and in his *Logic* (1870), everything must be twofold, every affirmation contains the opposite or negation of itself, everything is answered by everything else. The age was Comic, the age was Tragic. 'It was the best of times, it was the worst of times, it was the age of wisdom, it was the age of foolishness, it was the epoch of belief, it was the epoch of incredulity, it was the season of Light, it was the season of Darkness, it was the spring of hope, it was the winter of despair, we had everything before us, we had nothing before us' (Dickens, *A Tale of Two Cities* (1859), ch. 1). It often feels as though the title of the book A. W. N. Pugin first published in 1836 and revised in 1841 clamours to be the title of the age itself: *Contrasts*. For in Pugin there is one great contrast which contains within it all the others: the difference in the whole inherent order of life revealed by a comparison between the architecture created in times of faith and the modern architecture of an age of unbelief.

And yet always amidst the noise of large contrasts there is a quieter, more sceptical Dickens who is suspicious of every age's consciousness of itself and knows that the real issues are always working themselves out, confusedly, in the area that exists *between* the extreme superlatives. Increasingly throughout the 1850s, 1860s, and 1870s, after the extreme volatility of the earlier decades, that is where the writers have to do their work: in the midst of life, in the melting pot of all human elements and concerns, with almost everything between the old world and the new held in solution. In particular, the writers of non-fictional prose are harassed on every side: Arnold, trying simultaneously to defend seriousness whilst attacking the philistine version; Ruskin, the puritan man of art, opposing the aesthetes who separate art from religion and the puritans who separate religion from art. These are writers who are indeed the symptomatic middlemen, beset by the need to establish an explicit position through making distinctions and mounting arguments; who forgo, through a sense of social duty, the power of art to create work which can speak for itself implicitly, whether heard or not. All the genres, all the responses, all the possible languages and ways of being are called for in what feels like a struggle to make the great final choices about the future of human life.

Nonetheless, this variety and plurality is not simply to be celebrated by semi-detached modern readers, when it was itself a symptom and problem to many who lived within it. It wasn't simply that these Victorians, poor souls, were struggling in the confused aftermath of a religious hangover to learn about matters of democracy, relativism, irresolvable indeterminacy, and the secular diversity of multiple values which we enlightened moderns now so easily can accept. It is the tense co-presence of the religious and the secular, the claims for both the one and the many, the moral struggle between the need for groundedness and the relish of chance, which generates the whole background of seriousness out of which choices and resolutions come, making them original again. A liberal such as John Morley

KINGS CROSS BATTLE BRIDGE
S Geary Arch⁻

CONTRASTED CROSSES

CHICHESTER CROSS

Fig. 15. A. W. N. Pugin, 'Contrasted Crosses', 1841: The modern utilitarian world of Kings Cross Battle Bridge in contrast with the beauty of the medieval piety of Chichester Cross.

considered it a public duty to respect the existence of different and even opposing points of view in a modern society, without one's ceasing to hold one's own convictions to the uttermost. This was how John Stuart Mill had squared the sense of a fundamental human sameness, in the collective sharing of common characteristics and basic needs, with the recognition of the development of complex individual differences: he did it by appeal for a joint commitment to both public tolerance and private liberty in each and every person.

From the fictional perspective of the omniscient narrator, novelists themselves managed that toleration of a wide range of diversity. For the Victorian novel is the product of a relative world in which people are conscious of themselves in two-way terms as at once individual and social, subjects within themselves and yet objects to others—as everyone else is. But still, for all this liberal humanitarian achievement, it worried Morley that tolerance could encourage a kind of mild, distant indifference:

> People are too willing to look on collections of mutually hostile opinions with the same kind of curiosity which they bestow on a collection of mutually hostile beasts in a menagerie.

If these people were 'truly alive' to the inexpressible magnitude of the subjects involved, 'this light-hearted neutrality' would be 'unendurable'. Is there a God? And if not God, what? As it is, in answer,

> They speak as if they affirmed, and they act as if they denied, and in their hearts they cherish a slovenly sort of suspicion that we can neither deny nor affirm. It may be said that this comes to much the same thing as if they had formally decided in the last or neutral sense. It is not so. This illegitimate union of three contradictories fritters character away, breaks it up into discordant parts. (*On Compromise* (1874), ch. 3)

Dickens or Thackeray? Charlotte Yonge or George Eliot? George Eliot or Thomas Hardy? Mill on Bentham and Coleridge: but also Mill versus Newman; Tennyson versus Browning; Arnold versus Clough. Is the answer always, both?—or that the question shouldn't arise, because of the nature of simply separate viewpoints, discourses, and categories? There is, manifestly, something wrong with the painful pressure to make over-decisive choices, taking sides between often mutually weakening alternatives in a suppression of painful doubt. But equally, in the face of significantly opposed view-points, each offering a separately compelling imaginative vision in relation to vital problems, there is something too aesthetically dis-tant from either in simply seeking, somehow, to appreciate both. What does the reader do with all these individualistic differences, if not merely accept them in the way that Morley deplored: the tourist-mentality staring in at the collection in history's human zoo?

To Arnold it meant seeking more than one book, more than one hero, more even than merely two conflicting thoughts, but three, four, and more until the pattern was too wide and deep for mere party-prejudice. Yet Arnold's critics were always asking whether all this width of culture in him ever shook down into anything real, active, or useful? What is at stake here is another of those great, chal-lenging, half-admitted Victorian fears: the fear lest reading—at the very heart of the hopes of George Eliot, Matthew Arnold, and John Ruskin—may be only a form of pick-and-mix liberal tolerance, or what Newman dismissed in his *Essay in Aid of a Grammar of Assent* (1870) as 'a literary religion', a notional education in place of belief, which does not hold up in the foul weather of life outside (ch. 4, sect. 3).

In the face of such powerful difficulties, there is a clue to be found in the actual act of reading Victorian novels. It has to do with those moments of unexpected generosity, particularly in Dickens: when in *David Copperfield* the self-pitying Mrs Gummidge becomes at once utterly resolute in the terrible loss of Little Em'ly; or the hitherto laughable Sir Leicester Dedlock suddenly becomes the genuinely noble emotional centre of *Bleak House*; or at the very ending of *Our Mutual Friend* the feeble Twemlow defiantly supports the marriage of Eugene to a female waterman he insists upon calling 'a lady'; or when, most dramatically at the end of *A Tale of Two Cities*, Sidney Carton sacrifices his worse self for the sake of his likeness to Charles Darney. It is then that people in these novels find themselves going beyond themselves in ways that also shake the reader's habitual orderings and prejudices—as at the end of Mrs Oliphant's great novel *Hester* (1883) when the elderly, disappointed Catherine Vernon finally sees that Hester, whom she has always instinctively opposed, is like a younger version of herself. At such points—in the very process of the transformation of the whole within the part—the reader feels that almost all the people in the novel are surprisingly, potentially valuable, making their contribution to the overall. This is like the spirit of the synthesis which the Victorians so often sought, the holism they so often continued to believe in after Coleridge, without their ever quite seeing what could hold it all together or how it could be done.

But what if the realist novel did have a bearing upon reality? For as it is with characters in those novels, so it is also with thoughts in the Victorian world: so often in Victorian literature one thing turns into another, almost its opposite—the unconscious found in the midst of the voluntary, absolutes turning relative, secularization unexpectedly offering new opportunities for religious concern. Or again: as it is with a novel's characters, or with the differing elements of a Turner composition in the eyes of Ruskin, so it may be with the authors who compel bafflingly different, seemingly competing assents or create powerfully disturbing disagreements—they really do belong together in the human picture. The intuitive belief that the variety of books and writers which affect a reader strongly must somehow finally fit together—as in a novel before the eyes of the missing God—may not be a long-past Victorian delusion, but the great Victorian challenge that remains for those who use their literature in relation to their lives.

Author Bibliographies

AINSWORTH, WILLIAM HARRISON (1805–1882)

The son of a Manchester solicitor, he himself abandoned the study of law in London to write novels, *Sir John Chiverton* (1826), and his first spectacular success, *Rookwood* (1834). Its climactic account of Turpin's ride to York was written quickly, 'a hundred novel pages in less than twenty-four hours' as Ainsworth was prone to boast. Walter Scott had died two years previously, and Ainsworth claimed to be his successor though he shifted the historical novel from character and idea to event and scenery, with his interest in the rogue's tale *Jack Sheppard* (1839) or the life story of a building, *The Tower of London* (1840) and *Old Saint Paul's* (1841), their popularity enhanced by Cruikshank's illustrations. He edited and founded magazines in order to serialize his work, *Bentley's Miscellany* (1840), *Ainsworth's Magazine* (1842), and *The New Monthly Magazine* (1853). Declining readership in later years diminished the sums he could command but he remained prolific, writing twenty-five novels between 1860 and 1882.

There are occasional modern reprints of the popular titles, including *Rookwood* and *Jack Sheppard* in the collection of Newgate novels edited, with a useful introduction, by Juliet John (1998). S. M. Ellis, *W. H. Ainsworth and his Friends*, 2 vols. (1911) has a bibliography and there is a modern monography in Twayne's English Authors, 138, by G. J. Worth (1972). Discussion of his contribution to fashionable genres is to be found in K. Hollingsworth, *The Newgate Novel, 1830–1847* (1963) and A. Sanders, *The Victorian Historical Novel, 1840–1880* (1978).

ARNOLD, MATTHEW (1822–1888)

Born on Christmas Eve, he was educated at Rugby, the son of its Broad Church reforming headmaster Dr Thomas Arnold, and at Winchester. At Oxford, he was coached by A. H. Clough, a former Rugbeian, and won the premier prize for poetry. He published his first collection of verse, *The Strayed Reveller and Other Poems*, in 1849 after he became secretary to the Whig statesman Lord Lansdowne. From him he accepted the post of inspector of schools in 1851 and married shortly after. His subsequent literary career was both varied and inherently consistent. Most of his greatest poetry was written in the decade following *Empedocles on Etna, and Other Poems* (1852), in *Poems* (1853), *Poems, Second Series* (1855), *Merope, a Tragedy* (1858), and *New Poems* (1867). He was elected professor of poetry at Oxford in 1857, holding the position for ten years, the lectures being published as *On Translating Homer* (1861) and *On the Study of Celtic Literature* (1867) where he argued for a Celtic presence in English poetry. Many of his poems expressed anxiety about writing poetry in unpropitious times or concerned other writers, and the 1853 volume appeared with an important critical preface. This anticipated the more extended literary essays collected in *Essays in Criticism*, series 1 (1865) and 2 (1888). His continuing professional duties as inspector of schools led him to the studies *Popular Education in France* (1861) and *Schools on the Continent* (1868), and his sense that Britain was resistant to intellectual issues taken seriously in other European countries inspired *Culture and Anarchy* (1869) and *Friendship's Garland* (1871). Fundamental to this critique of contemporary culture was his belief that it failed to redefine its religious objectives, and he offered preliminary reassessments in *St Paul and Protestantism* (1870), *Literature and Dogma* (1873), and *God and the Bible* (1875). His fastidious diagnosis of British hyperactivity, its mixture of cultural grossness with moral simplification, raised outraged opposition which he also rather enjoyed and cultivated, though it limited his effectiveness.

The standard edition of the poems is the *Longman's Annotated Edition by Kenneth Allott, revised by Miriam Allott (1979). The prose work is collected in *The Complete Prose Works of Matthew Arnold* in 11 vols. by R. H. Super (University of Michigan, 1960–77). *The Letters of Matthew Arnold to Arthur Hugh Clough*, ed. H. F. Lowry (Oxford University Press, 1932) are important; an edition of the *Letters* is in progress complete up to 1884 so far in 5 vols., ed. Cecil Y. Lang (University of Virginia, 1996–). There is an Oxford Authors selection of Arnold's prose and poetry edited by Miriam Allott and R. H. Super (1986). The most helpful biography based on original research is by Park Honan (1981); there is also Ian Hamilton's *A Gift Imprisoned: The Poetic Life of Matthew Arnold* (1988). Stefan Collini's brief introduction *Arnold* (1988) in the Oxford Past Masters series is a useful starting place. David De Laura in *Hebrew and Hellene* (1969) places Arnold in relation to Newman and Pater. H. W. Fulweiler, *Letters from the Darkling Plain* (1972) compares Arnold and Hopkins. Ruth apRoberts discusses the development of Arnold's religious ideas in *Arnold and God* (1983). In Routledge's Critical

Heritage series Carl Dawson on the poetry (1973) and Dawson and John Pfordresher (1979) on the prose provide a fine selection of contemporary reviews: see also Sidney Coulling, *Matthew Arnold and his Critics* (1974).

BAGEHOT, WALTER (1826–1877)

The son of a Unitarian father and a Church of England mother, he was educated in Bristol and at University College, London, where he graduated with prizes in mathematics and moral philosophy. Called to the Bar in 1852, instead he joined his father's bank but also began contributing literary essays to *The Prospective Review* and, after 1855, *The National Review*, which he co-edited with R. H. Hutton who was to collect his friend's critical writings in *Literary Studies* (2 vols., 1879). Always interested in how actual practice embodied unconscious ideas, he claimed to study 'the man behind the writing'. His political views developed from his editorship of *The Economist*, a Liberal journal, from 1860 to his death, marrying the proprietor's daughter in 1858. It was the inexplicitness of the British political system that he observed in *The English Constitution* (1867), though the union of executive and legislature through the identification of the cabinet with parliament was a typically Burkean perception. In 1872 he developed his trust in evolution along Darwinian lines in *Physics and Politics*, arguing for the place of competition and progression in international affairs, and also wrote a notable account of the money market in *Lombard Street* (1873).

*The Collected Works have been edited under the supervision of Norman St John-Stevas (author of the modern standard life, 1959), 11 vols. (The Economist, 1965–78). There is a usefully polemical essay by C. H. Sisson, *The Case of Walter Bagehot* (1972) and a good chapter in Gertrude Himmelfarb, *Victorian Minds* (1962).

BARNES, WILLIAM (1801–1886)

The son of a tenant farmer at Rushay in Dorset, his penmanship at the local school recommended him to a place in a solicitor's office in Sturminster. He taught himself to engrave, began to learn languages, and from 1820 wrote poems that appeared in the local papers. In 1823 he became master of a small school at Mere in Wiltshire, married in 1827, and took on boarders before moving the successful establishment to Dorchester in 1835. From 1833 he was writing verse in the Dorset dialect not out of scholarly interest but, as he said to Hardy, because 'he could not help it'. In 1838 he enrolled on the books of St John's College, Cambridge as a part-time student (a 'ten-years' man') intending to take holy orders, was ordained in 1847, and took his BD in 1850. Much archaeological and philological writing appeared in various London journals in the interval and in 1844, prefaced by a dissertation on their language, *Poems of Rural Life in the Dorset Dialect*, subsequent volumes being *Hwomely Rhymes* (1859) and *Poems, Third Collection* (1862), the whole series being collected in a single volume in 1879. He resigned the curacy he held at Whitcomb in Dorset in 1852 to pursue his language studies, publishing *A Philological Grammar* (1854) and *Tiw: Or, a View of the Roots and Stems of the English as a Teutonic Tongue* (1862). In 1862 he was inducted into the rectory of Came where he served as the very model of a country parson for the rest of his days. His beloved wife, Julia died in 1852, leaving him with two sons and three daughters. There are good accounts of Barnes in both Kilvert's *Diary* (entry for 'May Eve 1874') and in the diary of the Irish poet William Allingham (1824–89) describing his meeting with Tennyson (31 October 1865).

The standard modern edition is *Poems*, ed. Bernard Jones, 2 vols. (Centaur Press, 1962), though there is a useful Penguin selection by Andrew Motion (1994). There is a critical biography by William Turner Levy, *Barnes: The Man and his Poems* (1960), but Giles Dugdale's *William Barnes of Dorset* (1953) still holds the reader's attention. His friend Thomas Hardy's memoir and reviews are reprinted in *Hardy: Personal Writings*, ed. Harold Orel (1967) and Philip Larkin has written on the poetry in *Required Writing* (1983).

BORROW, GEORGE [HENRY] (1803–1881)

He was born in Norfolk, the son of a Cornish recruiting sergeant and an actress, travelling as a boy all over the British Isles wherever his father's occupation led the family. He received unwillingly a belated education at the grammar school when they settled at Norwich in 1816 and was articled to a solicitor in 1819. By 1820 he was ready to surrender this position having fallen in with John Thurtell, a Welsh pugilist and ostler, later hanged for murder. William Taylor, the reprobate Norwich radical, introduced him to German literature and thought, and Borrow discovered his remarkable facility for languages. As a boy he had already mingled with gypsy groups, and after the failure of his attempt to make a literary career in London in 1824 he probably lived the vagrant life described in his later works. In 1833 he began work for the British and Foreign Bible Society, recommended by both his command of languages and the Skeppers, pious Norwich Unitarians, whose daughter Mary he was later to marry. After two years in Russia (1833–5), and four in Portugal and Spain, he returned to England, married, and for the rest of his life lived quietly on his wife's estate near Lowestoft. Only in 1841 did he start to write. *The Zincali, or the Gypsies in Spain* was followed by *The Bible in Spain* (1843), part autobiography, part scholarly treatise, and largely wild adventure story. His subsequent reputation derives from the fictionalized accounts of his earlier life, *Lavengro* (1851) and *The Romany Rye* (1857). *Wild Wales* (1862) was the result of his command of the Welsh language.

The collected works were edited by H. G. Wright (6 vols., 1928). There are modern biographies by Michael Collie, *George Borrow, Eccentric* (1982) and David Williams, *A World of his Own* (1982).

BRADDON, MARY ELIZABETH (1835–1915)

The daughter of a spendthrift solicitor who wrote sporting books, she was brought up by her Irish mother who left her husband when Mary was 4. She received good schooling and wrote from early years, but money was short and she briefly went on the stage in 1857 to help support the family. In 1860 she met a publisher, John Maxwell, whose wife was confined in an asylum, eventually had seven children by him, and married him only in 1874 with attendant scandal. *Lady Audley's Secret* which she wrote for Maxwell in 1862 established the popularity of the sensation novel and made her own fortune and that of the publisher Tinsley. *Aurora Floyd* (1863) was followed by an exuberant succession of plays, poems, annuals, the editing of journals, and a varied series of novels that by 1911 numbered upwards of eighty works. She sustained her popularity as 'Queen of the Circulating Library' until late in her life, and despite her notoriety became an admired part of London literary life.

The major novels are available in *Oxford World's Classics, while the Sensation Press is publishing some lesser-known works. R. L. Wolff, *Sensational Victorian: The Life and Fiction of Mary Elizabeth Braddon* (1979) combines criticism with biography. Useful criticisms include: Elaine Showalter, *A Literature of their Own* (rev. edn., 1982) and 'Family Secrets and Domestic Subversion', in A. S. Wohl (ed.), *The Victorian Family: Structure and Stresses* (1978), and Winifred Hughes, *The Maniac in the Cellar* (1980).

BRONTË, ANNE (Acton Bell) (1820–1849); CHARLOTTE (Currer Bell) (1816–1855); EMILY (Ellis Bell) (1818–1848)

Their father Patrick Brunty, born in Ireland in 1777, started work as a labourer but opened a school at the age of 16 and attracted the attention of the local vicar who supported him through St John's College, Cambridge: he graduated and was ordained in 1806. He married a Cornishwoman, Maria Branwell, with strong Methodist connections in 1812 and accepted the perpetual curacy of Haworth the year Anne was born. He published poems in 1811 and 1813 and two religious stories by 1818. After his wife's death in 1821, his sternly Evangelical sister-in-law, Elizabeth, acted as housekeeper for him and his six children. Charlotte and Emily both suffered privations at a boarding school for the daughters of the clergy at Cowan Bridge in 1824 and when the two elder sisters returned home to die in 1825, Charlotte and Emily were withdrawn from it. Thereafter they were taught at home, partly by their aunt. The isolation and intensity of family feeling encouraged the children early to write, along with brother Branwell (1817–48), a series of romances, including a serial epic originally about Glasstown which became for Emily and Anne, Gondal and for Charlotte and Branwell, Angria. In 1831 Charlotte, followed by her two sisters, received more formal education at Roe Head school, where she briefly also taught in 1835, before leaving home to become a governess in 1839, an unhappy experience. Ambitious to establish a school of their own, Charlotte and Emily entered a school in Brussels in 1842 to learn French where Charlotte fell hopelessly in love with the married proprietor, M. Heger. Deeply homesick, Emily stayed for only six months but Charlotte returned to Belgium in 1843. By 1844, however, the school ambition had been dropped. Meanwhile, Anne, at whatever cost to herself, maintained her job as a governess, the second posting with a family called Robinson near York (1840–5), only leaving because of some entanglement between the lady of the house and Branwell who had joined her as tutor in 1843. All the family had written verse, often as part of the romances of Gondal and Angria, and in 1846 the three sisters published *Poems* by 'Currer, Ellis and Acton Bell', without any financial success. In 1847, however, Emily's *Wuthering Heights* and Anne's *Agnes Grey* were published together under the original pseudonyms. It was only when Currer Bell's *Jane Eyre* appeared later that year that the whole family suddenly achieved attention, not wholly favourable. As a result Anne brought out *The Tenant of Wildfell Hall* in 1848 but in this year also Emily died of consumption and Anne followed her in 1849. Branwell, having failed as a portrait artist and poet, drank and drugged himself to death, amidst family discord, in 1848. Charlotte lived on with her fierce and reclusive old father and a succession of curates, bringing out *Shirley* in 1849 and *Villette* in 1853. Marrying Arthur Nicholls, another of the curates, in 1854, she died six months into her pregnancy. Her father shared the parsonage with Mr Nicholls until his own death in 1861.

Penguin Classics and *Oxford World's Classics reprint all the major novels. The standard edition of the novels is published by the Clarendon Press under the general editorship of Ian Jack, with individual volumes by Herbert Rosengarten and Margaret Smith, but the World's Classics volumes use the same text. There are separate editions of the poems, Charlotte's by T. J. Winnifrith (Shakespeare Head Press and Basil Blackwell, 1984), Emily's by Derek Roper and Edward Chitham (Clarendon Press, 1995), and Anne's by Edward Chittam (Macmillan, 1979). There is an ongoing edition of Charlotte's letters edited by Margaret Smith, so far in two volumes up to 1851 (Clarendon Press, 1995, 2000). The most famous biography by Charlotte's friend Elizabeth Gaskell attempted to save her subject from notoriety but itself contributed to the mythology already growing round the family: it appeared in 1857 the year that Charlotte's first novel, *The Professor*, was also first published. There are scholarly biographies of Emily and Anne by Edward Chittam (1987 and 1991 respectively) and of Charlotte by Rebecca Fraser (1988); but also see Juliet Barker's monumental *The Brontës* (1994). Miriam Allott's Critical Heritage volume (1974) collects contemporary and later Victorian reviews. Much modern criticism recognizes the feminist typology of their work, deriving from Elaine Showalter's *A Literature of their Own* (rev. edn., 1982) and Sandra M. Gilbert and Susan Gubar's *The Madwoman in the Attic* (1979); for example, Stevie Davies's *Emily Brontë: The Artist as a Free Woman* (1983). Sally Shuttleworth's *Charlotte Brontë and Victorian Psychology* (1996) establishes a valuable context, and Robert Liddell, *Twin Spirits* (1990) studies the surprising relation between the novels of Anne, the most orthodox of the sisters, and *Wuthering Heights*. There are useful chapters in William Myers, *The Presence of Persons* (1998), and Marianne Thormählen offers a change of emphasis in *The Brontës and Religion* (2000).

BROWNING, ELIZABETH BARRETT (1806–1861)

The eldest of twelve children of Edward Moulton-Barrett whose income derived from Jamaican plantations, she had an idyllic childhood at Hope End in Herefordshire. Classical scholarship and intellectual curiosity were fostered at home, and her poems *The Battle of Marathon* (1820) and *An*

Essay on Mind (1826) were published anonymously by her father. Misfortunes gradually encroached. In 1827 she received a permanent though mysterious injury, probably spinal, in a riding accident; in 1828 her mother Mary (née Graham-Clarke) died; in 1832 the family had to leave Hope End when the abolition of slavery affected their finances; and in 1840 an adored brother drowned just after they had had a passing quarrel.

These circumstances depressed a temperament always liable to extreme swings of mood, yet her public reputation rose steadily with the publication of each volume of poems, *The Seraphim and Other Poems* (1838) and, especially, *Poems* (1844). In 1850 there were demands that she be made Poet Laureate in succession to Wordsworth. Her overprotective father exaggerated her dependence on him, but she never lost her keen interest in contemporary affairs and 'The Cry of the Children' (1844) responded to the mood of anxiety about child labour. When the mutual admiration between her and Robert Browning led to a secret marriage and elopement in 1846, the sense of release was mixed with pain at the lasting estrangement from her father and some of her siblings. Married life in Italy—Pisa and then from 1848 Florence—brought a new robustness and passion to the poetry, *Sonnets from the Portuguese* being printed in a new two-volume *Poems* in 1850. She survived four miscarriages as well as the birth of her only child, Robert, in 1849 and wrote confidently about contemporary issues, including Italian independence, in *Casa Guidi Windows* (1851) and *Aurora Leigh* (1856) where they were unified by her interest, as she put it, in 'opposing the practical and ideal lifes [*sic*]'. She died in Browning's arms.

There is no complete modern edition of the poems and readers must use *The Complete Works*, 6 vols., ed. Charlotte Porter and Helen A. Clarke (Crowell, New York, 1900), though *Aurora Leigh* has been edited by Kerry McSweeney for *World's Classics* (1993) and by Margaret Reynolds for Ohio University Press (1992) and Norton (1996); *Casa Guidi Windows* by Julia Markus (Browning Institute 1977); and there is a good selection of poems edited by Margaret Forster (Chatto and Windus, 1988). Her letters are to be included in *The Brownings' Correspondence*, ed. Philip Kelley and Ronald Hudson (Wedgestone Press and Athlone, 1984–), and her *Letters to Mary Russell Mitford*, ed. Meredith B. Raymond and Mary Rose Sullivan are in 3 vols. (Wedgestone Press, 1983). The best modern biography is Angela Leighton's *Elizabeth Barrett Browning* (1986) (also see her *Victorian Women Poets: Writing Against the Heart*, 1992), which may be supplemented by Daniel Karlin's *The Courtship of Robert Browning and Elizabeth Barrett* (1987). Dorothy Mermin argues for the innovation of the poetry in *Elizabeth Barrett*

Browning (1989) and in a book of the same title Marjorie Stone (1995) offers strongly feminist readings, while the emphasis in Linda M. Lewis's *Elizabeth Barrett Browning's Spiritual Progress* (1998) is on the poet 'face to face with God'.

BROWNING, ROBERT (1812–1889)

The son of a banker, with an eclectic scholar's library of six thousand volumes, and of a mother of firm Congregationalist faith, he was educated chiefly at home though briefly enrolled (1828) at the new University of London. His first published poem *Pauline* (1833), in the style of Shelley, was followed by *Paracelsus* (1835), in celebration of a Carlylean prophet figure, which brought him friendship with Macready, the actor. He began a series of verse plays with *Strafford* (1837), written for Macready, and this interest in the stage may have persisted because of the failure of his long poem *Sordello* (1840) which won notoriety for being supposedly incomprehensible. It was to be the shorter dramatic monologues on which his reputation was to rest, *Dramatic Lyrics* (1842) and *Dramatic Romances* (1845). In the 1852 preface to a collection of (spurious) Shelley letters, he argued that the subjective visions of the Romantics had to be replaced by a new objectivity. His secret marriage to Elizabeth Moulton-Barrett and their elopement to Italy proved happy and close, despite disagreements over her enthusiasm for Napoleon III and American spiritualism, and in Florence he produced his single greatest collection of poems *Men and Women* (1855). George Eliot in her review of it claimed 'Fra Lippo Lippi' superior to any mere essay on 'realism in art'. His growing reputation was confirmed by *Dramatis Personae* (1864). After the death of Elizabeth in 1861 he returned to England and became a convivial figure in literary and artistic circles, especially after the success of the extravagantly extended sequence of dramatic monologues, *The Ring and the Book* (1868–9). Lionized as an intellectual by such figures as Benjamin Jowett, Master of Balliol, his later poems proved no less demanding in their condensed, esoterically allusive style: *Fifine at the Fair* (1872), *Red Cotton Nightcap Country* (1873), *La Saisiaz* (1878), *Ferishtah's Fancies* (1884). He returned in later years to Italy and died in Venice on the day his last collection, *Asolando*, appeared in print.

There are many modern editions with competing claims. *The Complete Works* ed. Roma A King Jr, Morse Peckham, Park Honan, and Gordon Pitts (University of Ohio, 1969–) is nearing completion, in 16 vols. so far; and the Clarendon Press Browning is still in progress under the general editorship of Ian Jack (1983–), reaching *The Ring and the Book* with vols. 7–8, ed. S. Hawlin and T. Burnett (1998, 2001). Longman's Annotated Poets have an edition in 2 vols., so far, by John Woolford and Daniel Karlin (1991) and *Penguin have *Robert Browning: The Poems*, 2 vols., ed. John Pettigrew and Thomas J.Collins (1981). *The Letters of Robert Browning and Elizabeth Barrett 1845–6*, ed. E. Kentner, 2 vols. (Harvard University Press, 1969) will eventually be included in the huge Wedgestone Press edition of *The Brownings Correspondence*. Clyde de L. Ryals, *The Life of Robert Browning: A Critical Biography* (1993) is the most helpful study, while for information about the poems W. C. De Vane's *A Browning Handbook* (2nd edn., 1955) is still useful. Modern criticism of the poems really started with Robert Langbaum's *Poetry of Experience* (1957); but see also Isobel Armstrong, *Victorian Poetry: Poetry, Poetics and Politics* (1993); Daniel Karlin, *Browning's Hatreds* (1993); and, on the effect of his early reading upon his poetic style, Donald S. Hair, *Robert Browning's Language* (1999). On the dramatic monologue Ralph W. Rader, 'The Dramatic Monologue and Related Lyric Forms', *Critical Inquiry*, 3 (1976), 1311–51, is impressive.

BULWER-LYTTON, EDWARD [George, Earle Lytton] (later Lord) (1803–1873)

His father, a Bulwer, died when he was 4, and he was brought up by his mother, a Lytton, overprotected and precociously educated, producing his first Byronic verse in 1820, *Ismael*. He went up to Cambridge, first Trinity, and then Trinity Hall after a disagreement, wrote poetry, dressed as a dandy, flirted with Byron's old flame Caroline Lamb, but still managed to graduate in 1826. He married Rosina Wheeler in 1827, with disastrous results not only because the marriage collapsed in acrimony (see her novel *Cheveley*, 1839) but because his mother cut off his allowance, and the role of outcast he had been playing now became more real, as he had to write for an income. *Pelham* (1828) established his success a society novelist, but *Paul Clifford* (1830) and *Eugene Aram* (1832) both expressed sympathy for criminal outsiders and, while useful financially, brought critical attacks and the dislike of Thackeray, for example. Though he wrote with a studied aristocratic carelessness, his desire to manage the relationship of Liberal change with a Tory sense of continuity inspired historical novels such as *Rienzi* (1835), *The Last of the Barons* (1843), and *Harold* (1848). He had become a Liberal MP in 1832, Member for Lincoln until 1841. He was writing successful plays, *Money* (1840), and in the long poem *The New Timon* (1846) tried to extend Byronic satire into Victorian contexts.

In 1843 he inherited the family estate at Knebworth after his mother's death, and returned to the Commons in 1852 now as a Disraelian Tory, serving as Secretary for the Colonies (1858–9). Though *The Caxtons* (1849) was a domestic novel, his later works were marked by an interest in the occult, the short story *The Haunted and the Haunters* (1859), *A Strange Story* (1862), and *The Coming Race* (1871), proto-science fiction. He was made a baron in 1866.

There are no modern editions of his novels, though *The Coming Race* is sometimes reprinted (e.g. Wesleyan University Press, forthcoming). The *Collected Edition in 39 vols. (Knebworth Edition, Routledge, 1873–7) is incomplete. Andrew Sanders, *The Victorian Historical Novel* (1978) has a chapter on Lytton and E. M. Eigner, *The Metaphysical Novel in England and America* (1978) is good on the occult novels.

BURTON, SIR RICHARD [FRANCIS] (1821–1890)

Born at Torquay, the son of an army officer, he was often resident abroad with his family as a boy and restlessly left Oxford without graduating to join the Indian army (1842). He served with Napier but lived among the local Muslim people as one of themselves, and described his experience in *Scinde, or the Unhappy Valley* (1851). His flamboyant eccentricity intensified his resistance to what he saw as the restrictive norms of his time and class. He modelled his writing on the adventurous style of Elizabethan prose in the record of his journey in disguise to the cities forbidden to Western infidels in *The Personal Narrative of a Pilgrimage to Al-Medinah and Mecca* (1855). From the Arabian peninsula he went on to Somalia and thence inland with the explorer John Hanning Speke, discovering Uganda and Lake Tanganyika, as recounted in *First Footsteps in East Africa* (1856) and *The Lake Regions of Central Africa* (1859). He claimed to have learned thirty languages and he certainly fought in the Crimea, but above all he endlessly travelled, to Salt Lake City, to South America, as described in *Explorations of the Highlands of Brazil* (1869), and served as British consul in Damascus (1869–71) and at Trieste until his death. There is a one-thousand-line poem *The Kasidah* (supposed written 1843–4 but not published until 1880), which pretended to be a translation of the wisdom of the Sufi master Haji. His delight in erotic literature, shared with Swinburne and Richard Monckton Milnes, both of whom he knew, produced defiantly unexpurgated translations of *The Arabian Nights* (1885–8), *The Kama Sutra* (1883), and *The Perfumed Garden* (1886), published in private editions.

There are very few modern editions, except of the translations. The *Life* by his wife Isabel (née Arundell) has to be corrected by more modern studies, for example, Byron Farwell, *Burton* (1963).

CARLYLE, THOMAS (1795–1881)

The eldest son of a prosperous stonemason and farmer, he grew up in Ecclefechan on the Scottish borders in a strict and devout household, destined for the Church when he went up to Edinburgh University in 1809. Drifting away from orthodoxy under the influence of Scottish Enlightenment ideas, he taught mathematics at his old school in Annan from 1814, but returned to Edinburgh to study German, and in 1821 underwent a spiritual and mental crisis which remained a critical moment for the rest of his life. His life of Schiller (1823–4 in *The London Magazine*) was followed by a translation of Goethe's *Wilhelm Meister* (1824–7). He himself attributed the indigestion, from which he suffered from the days of privation in 1819 onwards, to the violence and anger of his writing, 'a rat . . . gnawing at the pit of his stomach', though it was sustained by his secularized Calvinism. That personal voice found expression in the essays he wrote for the *Edinburgh Review*, 'Signs of the Times' (1829) and 'Characteristics' (1831), and in the sense of national turbulence expressed in *Chartism* (1839). He had married Jane Welsh in 1825, the daughter of a small laird and herself a remarkable woman, as the letters and journals published after her death at Carlyle's insistence (3 vols., 1883) amply demonstrate. After the publication of *Sartor Resartus* in *Fraser's* (1833–4), they settled in London in Cheyne Row, Chelsea, since Edinburgh had lost some of its old literary pre-eminence. His belief in the turbulent way in which the spirit moved in human affairs led him to his study of *The French Revolution* (3 vols., 1837) and of the transformative individual in *On Heroes and Hero-Worship* (1841; originally lectures). Though J. S. Mill was a close friend (in whose house a maid in error lit a fire with the first draft of the book on the French Revolution, necessitating a complete rewrite), they came to represent opposed accounts of the age, with Carlyle's faith in the creative individual growing into a rejection of contemporary trust in committees and collective action. It was a smallish step from *Past and Present* (1843) to his edition of Cromwell's *Letters and Speeches* (1845) and *The History of . . . Frederick the Great* (6 vols., 1858–65). His increasingly bleak diagnoses were expressed in *The Life of John Sterling* (1851), *Latter Day Pamphlets* (1850), and 'Shooting Niagara and After', his extreme diatribe against the Second Reform Act in *Macmillan's Magazine* (1867). He survived into old age as a kind of public monument.

The *Collected Works* in the Centenary Edition, ed. H. D. Traill, 30 vols. (1896–9) is standard, but there is a Penguin selection edited by Alan Shelston (1971). There are modern *Oxford World's Classics editions of *Sartor Resartus*, ed. Kerry McSweeney and Peter Sabor (1987), and of *The French Revolution*, ed. K. J. Fielding and David Sorensen (1989). The irreplaceable but controversial biography is by J. A. Froude, 4 vols. (1882–4), but there is also F. Kaplan, *Thomas Carlyle* (1983), and A. F. Le Quesne's helpful introduction, *Carlyle* (1982). J.Clubbe (ed.), *Carlyle and his Contemporaries* (1976) is a useful collection, and Rosemary Ashton, *The German Idea: Four English Writers and the Reception of German Thought, 1800–1860* (1980) provides a necessary intellectual context. B. V. Qualls, *The Secular Pilgrims of Victorian Fiction: The Novel as Book of Life* (1982) has a valuable chapter on *Sartor*, and see also G. B. Tennyson, *Sartor Called Resartus* (1965) on the genesis and structure of the work. J. D. Rosenberg, *Carlyle and the Burden of History* (1985) writes about the relation of past to present, while Chris Vanden Bossche, *Carlyle and the Search for Authority* (1990) is valuable in all areas. On the relationship with his talented but neglected wife, see Rosemary Ashton's scholarly work *Thomas and Jane Carlyle* (2002).

CARROLL, LEWIS [Charles Lutwidge Dodgson] (1832–1898)

The third of eleven children of a clergyman, he was educated largely at home and grew up diffident and a stammerer. At Christ Church, Oxford, he was happy and remained there to lecture in mathematics after graduation in 1855. Regulations required him to be ordained but he never proceeded beyond deacon's orders (1861). Overcoming his shyness only in the company of little girls, he was valued by them and their parents as entertainer and storyteller. 'Alice's Adventures Underground', written out to please Alice Liddell, daughter of the dean of Christ Church, became *Alice's Adventures in Wonderland* (1865) after approval by the children of George MacDonald. Its success prompted *Through the Looking-Glass and What Alice Found There* (1871) which is more influenced by Dodgson's professional skills in mathematical logic. The gift for verse which the books display found more extended expression in *The Hunting of the Snark* (1876). A devotee of all sorts of games and puzzles, he was also a skilled photographer from 1856 onwards. His income from his children's books was large enough by 1881 to allow him to resign his lectureship and devote his attention to what he intended to be a more serious book for older children, *Sylvie and Bruno* (1889) and *Sylvie and Bruno Concluded* (1893). His final book, however, was *Symbolic Logic* (1896).

The most useful edition of the Alice books is still *The Annotated Alice*, ed. Martin Gardner (Penguin, 1965). There is a facsimile of *Alice's Adventures Under Ground*, the original unpublished version of *Alice* (Macmillan, 1886). **The Complete Works of Lewis Carroll* were edited by Alexander Woollcott for Nonesuch (1939). *The Letters* have been edited by M. N. Cohen and R. L. Green, 2 vols. (Macmillan, 1979) and the *Diaries* by R. L. Green (Cassell, 1953). Morton N. Cohen's *Lewis Carroll: A Biography* (1995) is the standard life. William Empson's chapter on Alice in *Some Versions of Pastoral* (1935) remains a classic. Jean-Jacques Lecercle has written on *The Philosophy of Nonsense* (1994).

CLOUGH, ARTHUR HUGH (1819–1861)

The second son of a Liverpool cotton broker who in 1822 emigrated to Charleston, South Carolina, Arthur was thrown early upon his own resources when sent back to England to enter Rugby school in 1829. The favourite pupil of Dr Arnold and friend of his son Matthew, the relationship continued later at Oxford where he had won a Balliol scholarship in 1837. The rational theology of Dr Arnold now had to contend with his admiration for Newman, though his politics remained radical. Despite surprisingly graduating in 1841 with only second-class honours, he was elected a fellow of Oriel in 1842, Oxford's intellectual centre. Without his family, he regularly led reading parties during the vacations, travelled in Italy in 1843 and 1846, and went to Paris in May 1848 with Emerson to see the revolution in action. Late that year he resigned his fellowship, unable to accept the religious regulations of Oxford. *The Bothie of Toberna-Vuolich* (1848; originally *Fuosich*, in Gaelic a lewd pun) fictionalized the reading party of 1840. In Italy in 1849 he witnessed the suppression of Mazzini's Roman Republic and wrote 'Amours de Voyage' though it was only published in 1858, serially in America in the Boston *Atlantic Monthly*. Still more radical in its rejection of credal religion, 'Dipsychus' was written during a visit to Venice in 1850, though it picks up a phrase from an Easter poem written in April of the previous year, 'Christ is not risen'. In 1852 he had to resign the chair of English at University College, London, held for only fourteen months, after disputes over his religious opinions, though he made friends with Carlyle and Bagehot. He sailed to Boston, in the same ship as Thackeray, but returned when, like Matthew Arnold, he was offered a post as examiner in the Education Office. In 1854 he married Blanche Smith, revised Dryden's *Plutarch*, but wrote no more poems until 1861 when he composed a series of rather depersonalized narratives, *Mari Magno*. He died in Florence after a bout of maleria contracted after holidaying in the Pyrenees with the Tennysons.

The standard text is *The Poems*, ed. F. L. Mulhauser (2nd edn., Clarendon Press, 1974), but there is an annotated *Selected Poems* (without the *Bothie*), ed. J. P. Phelan (Longman, 1995) and a Penguin selection, ed. Jim McCue (1991). *The Correspondence of Arthur Hugh Clough* was also edited by F. L. Mulhauser, 2 vols. (Clarendon Press, 1957). Essential for studying his developing views of poetry's function is *Selected Prose Works*, ed. Buckner B. Trawick (University of Alabama, 1964), based on the *Prose Remains*, ed. by Mrs Clough (1869). *The Oxford Diaries*, ed. Anthony Kenny (Clarendon Press, 1990) display the religious struggles in that period of his life: see also Kenny's comparison with Hopkins in *God and Two Poets* (1988). The most sympathetic biography is Katharine Chorley, *Arthur Hugh Clough: The Uncommitted Mind* (1962); R. K. Biswas, *Arthur Hugh Clough: Towards a Reconsideration* (1972) is a mine of detailed knowledge. John Goode, 'Amours de Voyage: The Aqueous Poem', in Isobel Armstrong (ed.), *The Major Victorian Poets: Reconsiderations* (1969) has been influential. W. David Shaw, *The Lucid Veil: Poetic Thought in the Victorian Age* (1987) provides a philosophical context for the poetry (see also Michael Thorpe's fine volume on the reviews of Clough in Routledge's Critical Heritage series, 1972); Patricia Ball offers an alternative context in *The Heart's Genius: The Victorian Poetry of Relationships* (1976).

COLLINS, [WILLIAM] WILKIE (1824–1889)

A Londoner, son of William Collins RA, the portrait and landscape artist, he grew up in a household that was devoutly High Church, disorganized, and constantly on the move, resident in France and Italy, 1836–8. After five years working for a tea-merchant, he was admitted to Lincoln's Inn in 1846 and called to the Bar in 1851, but in the mean time he had acted on stage, had written in 1848 a memoir of his father, who had died the year before, and also an unpublished novel set in Tahiti, and had met Charles Dickens. He subsequently lived by writing. Several of his later novels were also written as plays and in the preface to his first characteristic work, *Basil* (1852), he called novel and play 'twin-sisters in the family of Fiction'. His first great success, *The Woman in White*, written for Dickens's journal *All the Year Round* (1859–60), drew partly on a contemporary French scandal and partly on first impressions of the woman who became his mistress, Caroline Graves. He gave up journalism to concentrate on the novel, *No Name* (1862), *Armadale* (1864–6), and *The Moonstone* (1868), for example. Prescribed laudanum for the pains of gout in 1862, he became increasingly dependent on it and in that year met and lived with Martha

Rudd who was to bear him three children, with Caroline eventually acting as housekeeper. The later novels never recovered his earlier popularity but often contain sympathetic portraits of curiously disadvantaged and non-conformist figures in *Poor Miss Finch* (1872), *The Law and the Lady* (1875), and *The Evil Genius* (1886).

   *Penguin Classics and Oxford World's Classics reprint all the major novels. William M. Clarke, *The Secret Life of Wilkie Collins* (1988) and Catherine Peters, *The King of Inventors* (1991) have added to our knowledge of his complicated personal affairs. Current critical attention exploits the accessibility of his novels to different kinds of specialized interest, the psycho-medical in Jenny Bourne Taylor, *In the Secret Theatre of Home* (1988) and Winifred Hughes, *The Maniac in the Cellar* (1980); the political implications in Nicholas Rance, *Wilkie Collins and other Sensation Novelists* (1991); the detective theme in Ronald R. Thomas, 'Detection in the Victorian Novel', in Deidre David (ed.), *The Victorian Novel* (2001); and feminist readings in Tamar Heller, *Dead Secrets: Wilkie Collins and the Female Gothic* (1992) which should be compared with Alison Milbank, *Daughters of the House* (1992). Sue Lonoff, *Wilkie Collins and his Victorian Readers* (1982) valuably compares contemporary with modern interpretations.

DARWIN, CHARLES [Robert] (1809–1882)

The grandson of Erasmus Darwin, the scientific poet, and by his mother of Josiah Wedgwood, he was educated at Shrewsbury School and went first to Edinburgh University (1825) but, discovering his unsuitability to study medicine, transferred to Christ's College, Cambridge (1928), intending to enter the Church. Attracted to the study of natural history, he was recommended by J. S. Henslow as official naturalist to sail with Captain Fitzroy on HMS *Beagle* during its surveying expedition to South America, 1831–6. On his return he published his *Journal of Researches* (1839) and in 1842 developed the theory on the formation of coral reefs which corrected the arguments of Sir Charles Lyell and was his first major discovery. In 1839 he married his cousin, Emma Wedgwood, and in 1842 moved to Down in Kent where he lived quietly as a family man for the rest of his life, regularly contributing papers to the scientific journals. Though he had accepted the usual view that the species were fixed by Creation, in 1837 he began a notebook on the transmutation of species starting with his observations on the Galapagos Islands. His thesis was still in draft when in 1858 he received a manuscript from Alfred Russel Wallace which contained the same argument, that creatures with advantageous mutations were selected by their environments for survival; though Darwin saw evolution as neutral, where both Wallace and Herbert Spencer valued it as inevitable progress. The whole first edition of *On the Origin of Species* (1859) sold out on the day of publication. *The Descent of Man* (1871) extended the original theory to human development, and the argument against the special status of man was completed by *The Expression of Emotions in Man and Animals* (1872). Thereafter he worked on less controversial subjects, the strength of hybrid plants (1876) and the contribution of worms to soil fertility (1881). His *Autobiography* appeared posthumously (1887).

The first edition of the *Origin* appears in *Penguin Classics, the second edition in Oxford World's Classics, and Penguin also publish an edition of *The Voyage of the Beagle*. The *Autobiography*, along with T. H. Huxley's, is edited by G. de Beer (Oxford University Press, 1974). The *Correspondence* is being edited by F. Burckhardt, S. Smith, et al. (Cambridge University Press, 1985–). There is a useful biography, *Darwin* by Adrian Desmond and James Moore (1991). For the context of debate see Tess Cosslett's excellent anthology *Science and Religion in the Nineteenth Century* (1984) and the illuminating essays of Robert M. Young collected in *Darwin's Metaphor* (1985). Daniel Dennett's *Darwin's Dangerous Idea* (1995) is provoking. For the literary consequences of his work, Gillian Beer, *Darwin's Plots* (1983) and George Levine, *Darwin and the Naturalists* (1988) are essential reading. A. Ellegard, *Darwin and the General Reader* (1990) offers a useful account of the reception of the theory in the periodicals 1859–72.

DICKENS, CHARLES [John Huffam] (1812–1870)

His father, John, was a clerk in the Navy Pay Office, moving from Portsea where Charles, the second child, was born, to Chatham (1817) and thence (1822) to London. It was less poverty than bad management that led John to imprisonment for bankruptcy in 1824 and Charles to be sent to work in a factory producing shoeblacking. The dread that life had ended in menial occupation before it had properly begun remained with him always and was deepened by his memory of the apparent lack of concern of both his father and his mother, Elizabeth. A small legacy saved the situation, and Charles attended Wellington House Academy by midsummer 1824. By 1827, however, family exigencies demanded that he be articled as a solicitor's clerk in Gray's Inn. He learned shorthand and became, as his father now was, a reporter, first at Doctor's Commons, where much of the business concerned wills, and in 1831–2 of parliamentary debates. He started producing descriptive pieces and short stories in 1833, and married

Catherine Hogarth, daughter of the editor of *The Morning Chronicle* in 1835. The death in his arms of his idolized sister-in-law, Mary, aged 17 in 1837 was another of those events that for ever marked his world of feelings. His articles were collected in 1836 as *Sketches by Boz* (originally his own pet name as a child for a younger brother) and the same year began the serial publication in monthly parts of *Pickwick Papers* which made his reputation by the time it finished in 1837. Meanwhile, he edited *Bentley's Miscellany* (1836), a monthly paper, and contributed *Oliver Twist* to it from 1837, overlapping eventually with *Nicholas Nickleby*, also published in monthly parts from April 1838. Driven on by fear and ambition, quarrelling with various publishers over terms, when *Master Humphrey's Clock* (1840–1) faltered, he was afraid for his hold on his readers and modified the format to be a frame for the next two novels, *The Old Curiosity Shop* and *Barnaby Rudge*. His visit to America was intended as a break from this frantic activity, but though *A Christmas Carol* (1843) on his return was successful, he had trouble with *Martin Chuzzlewit* (1843–4) and again changed publishers. Supposedly resting in Switzerland, he started *Dombey and Son* (1846–8), the first novel which he planned part by part. Back in England, a public figure much engaged in charitable projects and fund-raising, he serialized *David Copperfield* (1849–50) which confirmed the new depth and seriousness of his work, and was followed by the Carlylean fury of *Bleak House* (1852–3). His continued liking for the dash and contemporaneity of journalism had produced a steady flow of articles and in 1850 he started the weekly *Household Words* where he serialized *Hard Times* in 1854. After another quarrel with the publishers, he reinvented it as *All the Year Round* in 1859. Moving into ever-larger houses, partly to accommodate a family of nine children by 1852, he was also finding his marriage increasingly unhappy and separated from Catherine in 1858. Involved with his own theatrical troupe, which led in 1854 to the start of the public readings of his novels, he met in 1857 a young actress Ellen Ternan with whom his continuing relationship remains open to interpretation. *Little Dorrit* (1855–7) in its monthly parts brought him the largest income of his career, though it was his own weekly which saw the publication of *The Tale of Two Cities* (1859) and *Great Expectations* (1860–1). After completing *Our Mutual Friend* in twenty parts (1864–5), he planned further reading tours in America (1867–8) and England, when in 1869 he introduced 'Sikes and Nancy', a performance of such intensity that it dangerously increased his exhaustion. *The Mystery of Edwin Drood* (1870) was left incomplete by his death from a stroke.

Most of the novels have appeared in Clarendon Press editions with the texts reprinted in *Oxford World's Classics, along with details of the working notes where appropriate; there are also good Penguin editions. The magisterial Pilgrim edition of *The Letters*, ed. M. House, G. Storey, K. Tillotson, et al., from the Clarendon Press (1974–) is ongoing, as in Michael Slater's impeccable edition of *Dickens' Journalism* (Dent, 1994–). The official *Life* by Dickens's long-time friend John Forster (3 vols., 1872–4) is a mine of information but needs supplementing by Peter Ackroyd's *Dickens* (1990) and Grahame Smith, *Charles Dickens: A Literary Life* (1996). Paul Davis's *Penguin Dickens Companion* (1999) is admirable, and Paul Schlicke (ed.), *Oxford Reader's Companion to Dickens* (1999) offers a wealth of material. Stephen Wall's *Penguin Critical Anthology* (1970) is excellent, and among older critics notable are Edmund Wilson, 'Dickens: the Two Scrooges', in *The Wound and the Bow* (1941); F. R. Leavis on *Little Dorrit* in his and Q. D. Leavis's *Dickens the Novelist* (1970); Gabriel Pearson on *The Old Curiosity Shop*, in J. Gross and Pearson (eds.), *Dickens in the Twentieth Century* (1962); and Garrett Stewart, *Dickens and the Trials of the Imagination* (1974). Recent criticism has tended to examine specialized aspects of the work: particular points in the career as in Kathryn Chittick, *Dickens and the 1830s* (1990); the representation of structures of power as in D. A. Miller, *The Novel and the Police* (1988); narrative design such as Peter Brooks on *Great Expectations* in *Reading for the Plot* (2nd edn., 1992); or feminist readings like Kate Flint's *Dickens* (1986). Dennis Walder, *Dickens and Religion* (1981) points in a direction as yet little discussed.

DISRAELI, BENJAMIN [1st Earl of Beaconsfield] (1804–1881)

Son of a Jewish literary antiquarian, he was baptized (1817) and attended local schools before entering Lincoln's Inn in 1825. He preferred writing to the law, however, and published *Vivian Gray* (1826–7) anonymously with great success and *The Young Duke* (1831). He travelled in Spain, Italy, the Levant, and Egypt (1828–31), and the combination of exotic settings, political discussion, and dandified wit gave popularity to *Contarini Fleming* (1832) and *Alroy* (1833). His paternalist ideas were more formally expressed in *A Vindication of the English Constitution* (1835). In 1837 he entered practical politics as Conservative MP for Maidstone and in 1847 for Buckinghamshire. He married the widow Mrs Wyndham Lewis in 1839, an heiress and great support throughout his career, and bought an estate at Hughenden. His finest novels were written when he was at odds with his party leader, Sir Robert Peel, over the Corn Laws: *Coningsby* (1844), *Sybil* (1845), and *Tancred* (1847). As leader of the

Young England grouping, with its romantic vision of medieval feudalism, he claimed it was through novels he could best influence public opinion. Thereafter his public career took priority, though he published a biography of Lord George Bentinck in 1852. He was chancellor of the exchequer three times (1852, 1858–9, and 1866–7), and prime minister twice (1868 and 1874–80). In the only significant later novel *Lothair* (1870), he was again concerned with political responsibility in an industrialized society, finding it in the idea of religious duty. He was raised to the peerage in 1876.

There was a full reprint of the novels and tales (the Brackenham edition) ed. P. Guedella in 12 vols. (1926–7). Modern editions of *Sybil* are published by *Penguin and Oxford World's Classics, and *Coningsby* is in *Penguin. Robert Blake's *Disraeli* (1966) is the definitive modern biography. D. R. Schwarz, *Disraeli's Fiction* (1979) surveys the whole range of his work.

Dodgson, Charles Lutwidge. See CARROLL, LEWIS.

ELIOT, GEORGE, née Mary Anne [Marian] Evans (1819–1880)

She was born outside Nuneaton in Warwickshire, where her father was land agent for a nearby estate, and grew up close to her father but hero-worshipping her elder brother, Isaac. Her mother, Robert Evans's second wife, died in 1836, the year after Mary Anne left school in Coventry where her father moved in 1841, and she became in effect housekeeper with responsibilities deepened by her Evangelical seriousness. She studied German with Charles and Cara Bray in 1842 and under their influence converted to a religion without God which alienated her from her father. Typically, after refusing to attend church, she returned to it shortly after, as an expression of love for her earthly father rather than an act of faith. Encouraged by Charles Hennell, a relation of the Brays, she devoted two years to the translation of D. F. Strauss's *Life of Jesus* (1846). Supported by a small legacy after her father's death in 1849, she went to London and from 1851 worked as unpaid assistant to John Chapman, a married man with whom she became romantically involved, but in practice was editor of *The Westminster Review*. At the centre of a group of intellectual men, after an unhappy relationship with Herbert Spencer, she met George Henry Lewes in 1852 and, trapped as he was in an unrewarding marriage, she lived with him from 1854 as effectively his wife. That year she published a translation of Feuerbach, *The Essence of Christianity* which gave formulation to her Wordsworthian belief in the mind's religious identity. The intricate and lucid style of her review articles for the *Westminster*, the renewed intellectual confidence following the translation, and Lewes's encouragement, which her frail self-belief always needed, propelled her into imaginative writing. 'The Sad Fortunes of the Rev. Amos Barton' (1857) was followed by two more stories to make *Scenes of Clerical Life* (1858), when she first used her pseudonym. Her publisher, Blackwood, became another of her needed supports and brought out *Adam Bede* (1859), *The Mill on the Floss* (1860), and *Silas Marner* (1861). Her novels were based on increasing levels of research to guarantee, partly in her own mind, the sense of dealing with realities, and *Romola* (1863) which appeared in the *Cornhill* involved detailed enquiry into life in fifteenth-century Florence. In 1866, at the time of agitation for the Second Reform Bill, she published *Felix Holt, The Radical*, a study of events surrounding the First Reform Bill and a defence of education for the would-be new voters. Estranged from her brother Isaac by her relations with Lewes, she commemorated her childhood feelings not only in *Adam Bede* and *The Mill on the Floss* but in the sonnet sequence 'Brother and Sister' (1869). Her poems, especially *The Spanish Gypsy* (1868) and 'Armgart' (1871), are often starker expressions of thoughts and feelings embedded more deeply in the novels. *Middlemarch* appeared in eight sections over 1871–2, as close as she came to the serial publication favoured by Dickens, and this novel developed her interest in 1830 as the foundation point for the present age. *Daniel Deronda* (1876) was published in the same way and, despite criticism of the ever-increasing intellectual complexity of her work, continued to bring in a large income which allowed the Leweses to entertain other writers and thinkers in a succession of grand houses. Both of them were in weak health, saddened by the death of two of Lewes's sons, when Lewes died in 1878. Although she later married her young legal adviser J. W. Cross in 1880, and saw Lewes's *Problems of Life and Mind* through the press, she was broken by her loss. When it was almost too late to bring comfort, her marriage restored a slight communication with Isaac, but she died in December of that year of a kidney disorder.

Penguin Classics and *Oxford World Classics reprint all the major novels, with the latter adopting the text of the standard Clarendon Press editions. J. W. Cross's *Life* (1885) must be supplemented by Gordon Haight's standard *George Eliot: A Biography* (1968), though Ruby Redinger's *George Eliot: The Emergent Self* (1975) is outstanding on the process of her becoming 'George Eliot'. Gordon Haight has edited the *Letters* in a magisterial 9-vol. edition (Yale University Press, 1954–74); Rosemarie Bodenheimer's *The Real Life of Mary Ann Evans* (1994) is an account of these letters in relation to the fiction. The *Essays*, best edited by T. Pinney (Routledge, 1963), are available in Penguin and World's Classics selections. The *Journals* have been edited by Margaret Harris and Judith Johnson (Cambridge University Press, 1998). The notebooks have also been published: *Quarry for 'Middlemarch'*, ed. Anna T. Kitchel (1950); *George Eliot's Middlemarch Notebooks*, ed. John Clark Pratt and Victor A. Neufeldt (1979); *George Eliot: A Writer's Notebook 1854–1879*, ed. Joseph Wisenfarth (1981); and *George Eliot's 'Daniel Deronda' Notebooks*, ed. Jane Irwin (1996). The *Collected Poems* are edited, albeit perfunctorily, by Lucien Jenkins (Skoob Books, 1989). The translations of Strauss, Feuerbach, and also Spinoza's *Ethics* have been published respectively by SCM Press (1973), Harper & Row (1957), and Salzburg Studies in English Literature (ed. T. Deegan, 1981). John Rignall (ed.), *Oxford Reader's Companion to George Eliot* (2000) is most useful, and Graham Handley's *State of the Art: George Eliot, a Guide through the Critical Maze* (1990) redeems its promise. Valuable studies include David Carroll, *George Eliot and the Conflict of Interpretations* (1992); U. C. Knoepflmacher, *Religious Humanism and the Victorian Novel* (1965); Sally Shuttleworth, *George Eliot and Nineteenth-Century Science* (1984); together with Gillian Beer, *Darwin's Plots* (1983); and William Myers, *The Teaching of George Eliot* (1984). For a good introduction to the technical means of the conveying of mentality, see Derek Oldfield, 'The Language of the Novel', in Barbara Hardy (ed.), *Middlemarch: Critical Approaches to the Novel* (1967).

FitzGerald, Edward (1809–1883)

Seventh of eight children of a landowning father, John Purcell, and an immensely rich Irish mother, Mary Frances FitzGerald, whose surname the family adopted, though she largely ignored her children, he was educated at Bury St Edmunds and, from 1826, Trinity College, Cambridge, befriending Thackeray and the Tennysons. He entered into lively correspondence with his friends, including Carlyle, usually from various locations in his native Suffolk, where he enjoyed boating above all. He published nothing until 1849 and then only a brief memoir of his father-in-law, the Quaker poet Bernard Barton. In *Euphranor: A Dialogue on Youth* (1851) he argued for the importance of physical exercise as part of education. Under the tuition of E. B. Cowell of Ipswich he was studying Spanish and Persian, but used his knowledge to compose free paraphrases rather than translations, first of *Six Dramas of Calderón* (1853) and then of *Salamán and Absál* (1856), a mystical love song by the fifteenth-century

Iranian poet Jámi. He collected manuscripts in order to render the quatrains (Rubaiyat) of Omar Khayyam, a twelfth-century Iranian astronomer, ordering them into a continuous poem in 1859. The first edition was remaindered but then caught the attention of Swinburne and D. G. Rossetti: becoming widely read, it was revised in 1868, 1872, and 1879. In 1856–7 he abridged but never published one of the greatest of Islamic poems, *The Bird Parliament* of Attar.

Most of his work was first collected by W. Aldis Wright in *Letters and Literary Remains*, 3 vols. (1889); *The Letters*, ed. A. M and A. B. Terhune, 4 vols. (Princeton UP, 1980) adds further material. There is a critical edition of the *Rubaiyat* by Christopher Decklin (University of Virginia, 1997) and a generous selection by Joanna Richardson for the Reynard Library (1962). The standard life is Robert Bernard Martin, *With Friends Possessed* (1985).

FROUDE, JAMES ANTHONY (1818–1894)

Son of the Archdeacon of Totnes, he joined his elder brother by fifteen years, Richard Hurrell (1803–36), at Oriel College, Oxford in 1835 and was taken to be part of the group around Newman. After graduation in 1842 he was offered a fellowship at Exeter College and took deacon's orders (1844). At the same time, he was reading Carlyle and German theology, and his growing religious doubts were intensified by his (increasingly incredulous) work on the life of St Neot for Newman's *Lives of the English Saints* (1844–5). His revulsion at Newman's conversion to Roman Catholicism was reflected in *Shadows of the Clouds* published anonymously in 1847, but it was the scandal created by *The Nemesis of Faith* (1849), publicly burnt by William Sewell after a lecture in Exeter College hall, which led Froude to resign his fellowship. The same year he married Charlotte, sister-in-law of Charles Kingsley, a constant friend who introduced him to the London literary scene. Thereafter he wrote essays for the *Westminster* and *Fraser's*, and worked at his *History of England*, from the fall of Wolsey to the defeat of the Armada, 12 vols. (1856–70). He was editor of *Fraser's Magazine* (1860–74) and completed his classic biography of Carlyle in 1884. He throve on controversy, and the partisan Protestant sympathies developed in the earlier history supported his defence of eighteenth-century British policy in Ireland in a later work (1872–4). In 1892 he returned to Oxford as Regius professor of history.

His review essays were collected as *Short Studies on Great Subjects*, 4 vols. (1867–83). *The Nemesis of Faith* has been reprinted by Libris (1988) with a useful introduction by Rosemary Ashton. The original biography was written by Herbert Paul (1907) but there is a more recent life and study of his work by Waldo Hilary Dunn, 2 vols. (1961, 1963).

GASKELL, ELIZABETH CLEGHORN (née Stevenson) (1810–1865)

Her mother died thirteen months after her birth, and her father, William, who been a Unitarian minister but was then a Treasury official and radical writer, sent her from London to be reared by her maternal aunt, a widow, in Knutsford, Cheshire, in genteel poverty. She was well educated in local schools and at Stratford-on-Avon, with a good knowledge of classical and modern languages. In 1832 she married the Revd William Gaskell, assistant minister at Cross Street Unitarian chapel in nearby Manchester. After some early essays she only turned to writing in 1845 after the death of her baby son from scarlet fever. *Mary Barton* (1848), her account of industrial poverty and class antipathies in contemporary Manchester, was an international success and a scandal to many local manufacturers, including W. R. Greg. But its social analysis concealed a deeper concern with submerged feelings overcoming limited circumstances, the subject that became evident in *Cranford* (published in *Household Words*, 1851–3) and still more in *Ruth* (1853), culminating in the union of social and personal in her second Manchester novel, *North and South* (1855). When her friend Charlotte Brontë died in 1855, old Mr Brontë and Mr Nicholls asked her to write *The Life* (1857), and she returned from a visit to Rome, following publication, to discover herself facing libel proceedings arising from it. She was unusual for her times in writing so many short stories—collected in *Round the Sofa* (1859), *Right at Last* (1861), and *My Lady Ludlow* (1861)—many of them with their origins in family tales, localities she knew, and her own experience, such that Dickens called her his Scheherazade. She was also working on a historical novel set in Whitby during the war with France, *Sylvia's Lovers* (1863). She published a novella *Cousin Phillis* (1864) while working on what turned out to be her final novel *Wives and Daughters*, appearing in the *Cornhill* and almost completed when she died suddenly in the house she had bought and furnished secretly ready for William's retirement.

The novels are collected in the Knutsford Edition, ed. A. W. Ward, 8 vols. (1906), but all the major books are available in *Penguin and Oxford World's Classics. *The Letters*, ed. J. A. V. Chapple and Arthur Pollard (Manchester University Press, 1966) with *Further Letters*, ed. J. Chapple and A. Shelston (Manchester University Press, 2000), are the best introduction to the life, together with Jenny Uglow's critically acute *Elizabeth Gaskell: A Habit of Stories* (1993). Angus Easson, *Elizabeth Gaskell* (1979) provides knowledgeable contexts; Hilary M. Schor, *Scheherazade in the Market Place* (1992) discusses the economics of publication; Josie Billington, 'Watching a Writer Write', in P. Davis (ed.), *Real Voices on Reading* (1997) is excellent on manuscript revisions of *Wives and Daughters*; and Patricia Ingram's *The Language of Gender and Class* (1996) defines her particular interests.

GILBERT, SIR WILLIAM SCHWENCK (1836–1911)

The son of William Gilbert of independent means and Liberal politics, and from 1858 a popular novelist, he graduated from King's College, London (1855), joined and left the Civil Service, and, though called to the Bar in 1864, turned instead to light journalism. He published comic verse in *Fun* magazine under his childhood's pet name, Bab, collected as *Bab Ballads* in 1869. In 1866 at the suggestion of T. W. Robertson, he started writing for the theatre burlesques that were a success (*Dulcarama, or the Little Duck and the Great Quack*, 1866) and serious plays that flopped. In 1870 he met Arthur Sullivan, the composer, and together they collaborated in fourteen comic opera that made their fortune—their first real success being *Trial by Jury* (1875), where the charm of the music partly disguises the acuteness with which contemporary customs and ideas were mocked. *Princess Ida* (written in 1870 though not performed until 1875) was based on Tennyson's *The Princess*. It was over the division of the spoils that the partnership eventually broke. Gilbert continued to write topical plays, as in *The Hooligan* (1911). He died trying to rescue a girl from drowning in his own swimming-pool.

The plays have often been reprinted in four volumes, and the operas in two volumes, by *Penguin, and there is a collection of five plays edited by George Rowell (Cambridge University Press, 1982). *Bab Ballads* has been edited by James Ellis (Harvard University Press, 1970). There is a modern biography by Jane Stedman, *W. S. Gilbert: A Classic Victorian and his Theatre* (1996). *W. S. Gilbert: A Century of Scholarship and Commentary*, ed. J. B. Jones (1970) is a collection of useful essays.

GREEN, THOMAS HILL (1836–1882)

A rector's son educated at Rugby and Balliol College, Oxford, where he became fellow in 1860 and tutor in 1866, gaining the Whyte's chair in moral philosophy in 1878. His critique of empirical philosophy was formulated in introductions to a new edition of Hume's *Treatise* (1874–8). His version of Hegel, 'the real world is esentially a spiritual world', was modified by practical and social ethics, as witnessed by his report on middle-class schooling, 1865–6. His influence was powerful beyond a purely academic audience, on Mrs Humphry Ward and George Eliot, for example.

His lectures were collected and published posthumously: *Prolegomena to Ethics*, by A. C. Bradley in 1883, and the other works by R. L. Nettleship, 3 vols. (1885–8). M. Richter, *The Politics of Conscience: Green and his Age* (1964) demonstrates his influence, and there is an excellent essay by Geoffrey Hill in *The Lords of Limit* (1984).

HARDY, THOMAS (1840–1928)

Born in the remote hamlet of Higher Bockhampton in Dorset, the son of a small-time builder. After education in the school at Dorchester, he was apprenticed to a local architect (1856) and made friends with William Barnes and Horace Moule who encouraged his continuing self-education. In 1862 he went to London and found employment with Sir Arthur Blomfield, the noted neo-Gothic architect, reading widely, attending evening classes at King's College, visiting theatres, falling in love, but returning to Dorchester in 1867, when his health collapsed. He had been writing largely poems, though he had a short story in *Chambers's Journal* (1865), but his first novel *The Poor Man and the Lady* (lost) was rejected in 1868, and the advice of Meredith as reader that he attend to plot led to *Desperate Remedies* (1871), a sensation novel. He found his true voice in *Under the Greenwood Tree* (1872), with its few characters breeding misunderstanding in a confined environment, a situation complicated by class differences in *A Pair of Blue Eyes* (1873). The Dorchester architects specialized in church restoration, a business ironical to Hardy, who had surrendered his religious beliefs partly under the influence of Darwinian biology, without losing the love of religious rites and habits of thought. It was when he was sent to St Juliot in Cornwall in 1872 that he met Emma Gifford whom he married in 1874, the year in which *Far from the Madding Crowd* was published anonymously, but with great success, in the *Cornhill*. The main line of his fiction witnessed a steady darkening of tone, perhaps partly connected with Moule's suicide and the deterioration of his own marriage, seen first in *The Return of the Native* (1878), and in his last tragic novels, *The Mayor of Casterbridge* (1886), *The Wood-landers* (1887), *Tess of the d'Urbervilles* (1891), and *Jude the Obscure* (1895). It was not only the critique of marriage, and the sexual freedom of these works, that led them to be, while widely read, the objects of some-times violent attack, but even more their grim sense of destructive energies at work in life itself. *The Trumpet Major* (1880) was his first attempt to relate the intimately provincial to the European struggle with Napoleon; *The Dynasts* (1904–8) was a vast Napoleonic verse drama. Hostile criti-cism led him to concentrate his attention on the poetry he had always seen as his primary interest, culminating in his poems on the death of Emma in 1912.

All the main fiction is reprinted by Macmillan, *Penguin, and Oxford World's Classics, but often with considerable textual differences. *The Complete Poetical Works* are edited by S. Hynes, 5 vols. (Clarendon Press, 1982–95). The best introduction to his mind is probably in the *Life* by F. E. Hardy, his second wife, but really written by himself (first published in two volumes 1928, 1930; in one volume 1962; and edited by Michael Millgate, removing F. E.'s alterations, 1985). Millgate has written the standard modern life, *Thomas Hardy: A Biography* (1982). *The Literary Notebooks*, ed. L. Björk, 2 vols. (Macmillan, 1985) are valuable, as is *Thomas Hardy's Personal Writings*, ed. H. Orel (Macmillan, 1967). Modern criticism includes John Bayley, *An Essay on Hardy* (1978); Philip Davis in *Memory and Writing* (1983); J. Hillis Miller, *Thomas Hardy: Distance and Desire* (1970) and *Fiction and Repetition* (1982); Penny Boumelha, *Thomas Hardy and Women* (1982); and Dennis Taylor, *Hardy's Literary Language and Victorian Philology* (1993).

HOOD, THOMAS (1799–1845)

The son of a London bookseller, educated at local schools, he suffered from ill health throughout his life and seems to have begun writing while convalescing with relations in Dundee, 1815–18. On his return to London he became sub-editor at *The London Magazine* (1821–3): always poor, he made a living out of hack-work and comic poems and tales, editing *The Gem*, an annual (from 1829), *The Comic Annual* (1830), *The New Monthly Magazine* (from August 1841), and *Hood's Magazine* (1844). His most famous poem in defence of social compassion, 'The Song of the Shirt', appeared in *Punch* (Christmas 1843). A Civil List pension in 1844 arrived when he was already fatally ill of tuberculosis.

The collected works edited by his son came eventually to ten volumes (1869–73), and the son and daughter produced a classic biography in the form of a collection of his letters, *Memorials of Thomas Hood*, 2 vols. (1860). *Poems Comic and Serious* is edited by Peter Thorogood (Bramber Press, 1995) and there is a selection by John Clubbe (Harvard University Press, 1970), who also wrote *Victorian Forerunner* (1968).

HOPKINS, GERARD MANLEY (1844–1889)

The son of cultivated, prosperous, and High Church parents, living in outer London, he was educated at Highgate School where he was taught by R. W. Dixon, later an important correspondent, and at Balliol College, Oxford, from 1863. He was influenced by Ruskin's belief in the value of close observation of nature into keeping a series of journals to record moments of particularized contemplation as a form of devotion. In 1866 he converted to Catholicism and, on deciding to enter the Jesuit order in pursuit of yet stricter discipline, burnt his early poems (1868) though copies of the best of them had been sent to his friend, Robert Bridges. The journals persisted, but he did not write poetry again until 1876 when, with the permission of his superior, he produced 'The Wreck of the Deutschland', in memory of the shipwreck and drowning of five Franciscan nuns the previous year. The places he had trained and served in—Stonyhurst (1870–3), St Beuno's in North Wales (1874–7)—influenced his later work, including his knowledge of Welsh poetry. A series of sonnets, influenced by theories of inscape and sprung rhythm he had already worked out, followed his ordination and ministry in Oxford and Liverpool (1880–1), none of them composed for publication. He was oppressed by the squalor of his parishes and by his sense of failure as a preacher, but was no less so in Dublin, where, appointed to the chair of Greek and Latin at University College (1884–9), he was unhappy at Irish nationalism and the administrative duties of office. He died of typhoid. No attempt at coherent publication was made until Bridges' edition of 1918, and the journals have been still later discoveries.

The Poetical Works, ed. Norman H. Mackenzie (Clarendon Press, 1990) is now the standard edition. Also important are *The Journals and Papers*, ed. Humphrey House and Graham Storey (Oxford University Press, 1959); *The Sermons and Devotional Writings*, ed. Christopher Devlin (Oxford University Press, 1959); and the *Correspondence to R. W. Dixon* and *Correspondence to Robert Bridges* (Oxford University Press, 1955) with *Further Letters* (Oxford University Press, 1956) all edited by C. C. Abbott. Norman White, *Hopkins: A Literary Biography*

(1992) offers a more scholarly distance than does the psychological interpretation of Robert Bernard Martin's *G. M. Hopkins: A Very Private Life*
(1991). Walter J. Ong, *Hopkins: The Self and God* (1986) is theologically
sympathetic, but see also Margaret Johnson, *Gerard Manley Hopkins and
Tractarian Poetry* (1997) and J. Hillis Miller, *The Disappearance of God*
(1975). Gillian Beer offers a scientific context in 'Helmholtz, Tyndall,
Gerard Manley Hopkins', in *Open Fields* (1996) as does Daniel Brown,
Hopkins's Idealism: Philosophy, Physics, Poetry (1997).

HUTTON, RICHARD HOLT (1826–1897)

The son of a Unitarian minister, he was moved with the family from Leeds
to London in 1835 and educated at University College School and the
College itself, where he graduated BA in 1845 and MA 1849, with a gold
medal in philosophy. He studied subsequently in Heidelberg and Berlin,
intending to enter the ministry like his father, but instead became editor of
the Unitarian journal *The Inquirer* in 1851 and married. His theology was
in process of change, and objections to his opinions by readers might have
led to his dismissal had not ill health forced his resignation. In 1853,
returning from Barbados in improved vigour, though his wife had died
there, he met F. D. Maurice and, convinced by him of the divinity of
Christ, gradually assumed a Church of England position, completed by
his *Incarnation and Principles of Evidence* (1862). After co-editing *The
National Review* with Bagehot 1855–64, he accepted another shared
editorship at *The Spectator*, where he stayed till shortly before his death.
His politics were Liberal, as shown in his political writings for *The Pall
Mall Gazette*, collected in 1866 as *Studies in Parliament*. His literary interests lay with the Romantics and he wrote a monograph on Scott (1878).
With a strong interest in both Newman (on whom he wrote a monograph
in 1891) and the predicament of contemporary agnosticism, he grew
increasingly critical of the growth of secularism and scientific triumphal-
ism. His collections—*Essays Theological and Literary* (1871), *Essays on
Some of the Modern Guides of English Thought in Matters of Faith*
(1887), which was particularly impressive on George Eliot, and *Criticisms
and Contemporary Thought and Thinkers* (1894)—show him to be one of
the age's outstanding critics and reviewers.

   Though his essays are often reprinted in the Critical Heritage series in
relation to specific authors such as George Eliot or Trollope, a new selection of his essays is badly needed, to supplement *A Victorian Spectator*, ed.
R. H. Tener and M. Woodfield (Bristol Press, 1989). Malcolm Woodfield,
R. H. Hutton: Critic and Theologian (1986) is valuable.

HUXLEY, THOMAS HENRY (1825–1895)

The son of an Ealing schoolmaster, he studied medicine at London University and Charing Cross Hospital (MB 1845). Sailing in 1848 as assistant surgeon on a ship surveying the Great Barrier Reef in Australia, he was able to do scientific work on jellyfish, and was made fellow of the Royal Society in 1851. He became a lecturer at the Royal School of Mines in 1854 and married the following year, making a wider name for himself for popularizing science by lectures to the public. He continued his research into the morphology of marine and terrestrial creatures, and it was this knowledge of biology which immediately persuaded him of the truth of Darwin's thesis in 1859. He tirelessly devoted his energies to spreading the gospel of evolution by natural selection: naturally belligerent and known as Darwin's Bulldog, he wrote of 'the satisfaction of throwing down a triumphant fallacy', claiming 'the first great commandment of science consecrated doubt'. He claimed the term 'agnostic' to describe his position, and became a national figure, served on various royal commissions, and becoming president of the Royal Society, 1883–5. The long sequence of lectures and papers were finally published as *Collected Essays*, 9 vols. (1893–4). In the Romanes lecture on *Evolution and Ethics* (1893), he argued that natural process carries no moral ends and that human morality derives from the struggle of consciousness with necessity.

His son, Leonard Huxley, produced the *Life and Letters*, 2 vols. (1900), but the standard modern biography is Adrian Desmond's two volumes: *Huxley: The Devil's Disciple* (1994) and *Huxley: Evolution's High Priest* (1997).

KINGSLEY, CHARLES (1819–1875)

The son of a clergyman and raised on the Devon coast, it was there he learned to love the sea. When his father moved to a Chelsea parish, Charles attended King's College, London and then Magdalene College, Cambridge (1838). Echoes of the Oxford Movement moved him to gloomy doubt which he resisted by sporting activities, rowing, boxing, and fishing, and by his love for Frances Grenfell whom he met in 1839 and married in 1844. After scraping a first-class degree in 1842, he was ordained, and served the parish of Eversley in Hampshire on the edge of Windsor Forest, first as curate, and from 1844 as rector. His verse play, *The Saint's Tragedy* (1848), uses the life of St Elizabeth of Hungary to express his distrust of the ascetic tradition within Christianity and drew him to the attention of F. D. Maurice. Under the influence of Maurice's Christian Socialist group, he wrote *Yeast* (serialized in *Fraser's Magazine* (July–December 1848), published separately 1851) and *Alton Locke* (1850). In particular, he pamphleteered against the sweatshops of the tailoring trade under the pseudonym 'Parson Lot' and was temporarily banned by the Bishop of London from preaching radicalism in the capital, though *Two Years Ago* (1857) returns to social issues. He saw his own times as a struggle between modernizers and reactionaries whom he largely identified with the Catholic revival. He fought for his cause not only in his historical novels, *Hypatia* (1853) about the early Church and *Westward Ho!* (1855) set in Elizabethan England, but also in his public quarrel with Newman. Belligerent, he was also subject to fits of melancholy and had a constant stammer. One of the few clergymen to welcome Darwin's *Origin of Species*, science was for him the language of a revised natural theology not only in *Glaucus, or the Wonders of the Shore* (1855) but in his tale for children, *The Water Babies* (1863). He held the Regius chair of modern history at Cambridge (1860–9) where he tutored the future Edward VII, and eventually became royal chaplain, 1873–5. He battled on in lectures and tracts on behalf of progressive causes, especially education and sanitation, as well as ideas of racial superiority. His younger brother, the black sheep of the family, Henry Kingsley (1830–76), also wrote novels, including *Geoffrey Hamlyn* (1859), an Australian story, and *Ravenshoe* (1861) on a Protestant in a Catholic family.

Letters and Memoirs was written by his wife, 2 vols. (1876) and needs supplementing by R. B. Martin, *The Dust of Combat* (1959) and Susan Chitty, *The Beast and the Monk* (1975) on his religio-sexual nature. On the Protestant concern with the body, see David Alderson, *Mansex fine* (1998). B. Colloms, *Charles Kingsley* (1975) concentrates on the work as reformer, and Sheila Smith, *The Other Nation* (1980) offers a context for 'Condition of England' novels in general.

LEAR, EDWARD (1812–1888)

The youngest son of a family of fifteen surviving children of a stockbroker, his father's bankruptcy forced him into learning his trade as a hack draughtsman at the age of 15, but his gifts turned him into a noted illustrator and artist. While working for the Earl of Derby at Knowsley Hall (1831–5), he wrote limericks to entertain the children of the house which acquired such a reputation that he published them in 1846 as *A Book of Nonsense* under the pseudonym Down Derry Down. In succeeding editions the volume was enlarged mainly with lyrics and narrative poems (1861, 1863). Social awkwardness and self-consciousness about his appearance (a large bulbous body and nose), which he constantly parodied in the drawings in his book, made him happier to be a solitary traveller, producing accounts illustrated with delicate prints, *Journals of a Landscape Painter in Albania* (1851) and *Views in the Seven Ioanian Islands* (1863). In 1870 he settled in San Remo, keeping in contact with a large circle of friends by writing, according to Holman Hunt, 'as many as thirty letters before breakfast'. Ruskin placed him at the top of a list of contemporary writers in the *Pall Mall Gazette* in 1886.

The collected verses and tales have been often reprinted as *The Nonsense Omnibus*, but Vivian Noakes's edition of *The Complete Verse and Other Nonsense* for Penguin (2001) is definitive. *The Selected Letters*, ed. Vivian Noakes (Oxford University Press, 1988) also supplements Noakes's biography, *Edward Lear: The Life of a Wanderer* (1968). Thomas Byrom considers the drawings alongside the verse in *Nonsense and Wonder* (1977).

LEWES, GEORGE HENRY (1817–1878)

Born into a family literary and theatrical in background, he was educated spasmodically at schools in London, where he was born, Jersey, and France. He tried out law, commerce, and medicine, travelled in Germany, but remained true to journalism. From around 1840 he was writing reviews for journals like the *Westminster*, including essays on Hegel and aesthetics, which were admired by J. S. Mill, and much dramatic criticism, later collected (*On Actors and the Art of Acting*, 1875). He himself made a brief appearance on the stage, wrote plays and two novels, *Ranthorpe* (1847) and *Rose, Blanche and Violet* (1848). He made his serious name with his *Biographical History of Philosophy*, 4 vols. (1845–6) which predicts the end of mythologies and the triumph of Comte's positivism. It had an influence in its day second only to J. S. Mill's *Logic*, according to Beatrice Webb. A member of Leigh Hunt's radical circle, he later co-edited *The Leader* with Thornton, Hunt's son (1851–4). He had married Agnes Jervis in 1841 and they lived communally with Thornton and his own family in the so-called Phalanstery, Fourier's term for group living. In 1851 when Agnes was expecting a third child by Thornton, to be attributed to Lewes's paternity, the relationship broke down and he met Marian Evans in 1852. Divorce was not possible, since he had condoned the adultery, and his virtual marriage to 'George Eliot' had therefore to remain unofficial. His activity as business manager for his 'wife's' career stimulated his own writing, which, after the success of his *Life and Works of Goethe*, 2 vols. (1855), became increasingly scientific: *Seaside Studies* (1858); *The*

Physiology of Common Life, 2 vols. (1859–60); and his last great work, *The Problems of Life and Mind*, 5 vols. (1874–9). His interest in literature was affected by George Eliot's career and he produced a defence of realism in *The Principles of Success in Literature* (1865). When he died, his last work was completed by Marian Evans herself.

Ranthorpe, ed. B. Smalley was reprinted by Ohio University Press (1974). *The Life of Goethe* long survived as an old Everyman. Rosemary Ashton has edited *Versatile Victorian: Selected Critical Writings* (Bristol Press, 1992) and also written the standard modern life (1991). Rick Rylance, *Psychological Theory and British Culture 1850–1880* (2000) makes the strongest possible case for him (ch. 7).

MACAULAY, THOMAS BABINGTON, LORD (1800–1859)

Son of the prosperous philanthropist Zachary, he grew up in the heart of the Clapham Sect, the reformist group of humanitarian Evangelicals, including William Wilberforce and John Venn, who prefigured many of the preferences and beliefs of the early Victorian period. Called to the Bar after graduating at Trinity College, Cambridge (1824), he published an essay on Milton in the Whig journal *The Edinburgh Review* (1825) which was admired and became the first in a series. His public career flourished between Parliament (Liberal MP, 1830, 1831, 1839–47, 1852–6) and the Civil Service, particularly in India (1834–8) where he reformed education policy. Famous as a public speaker, it was the rhetorical capacity to articulate accepted ideas which ensured the success of *Essays Critical and Historical* (1843), 'a key to half the prejudices of our age' as Lord Acton called them. *Lays of Ancient Rome* (1842) honoured the heroes and critical events of an earlier empire. *The History of England* (vols. 1–2, 1849; vols. 3–4, 1855), which earned him a barony (1857), owed its immense commercial success to brilliant storytelling of a steady progress towards the achievements of the present, though he had only reached 1697 when he died.

The Complete Works were edited by his sister, Lady Trevelyan (8 vols., 1866), and his nephew, Sir George Trevelyan, wrote one of the great biographies of the period (2 vols., 1876). The *Essays* and *History* were available in the old Everyman library, and Hugh Trevor-Roper produced an abridged edition of the *History* for Penguin (1979). The *Letters*, ed. Thomas Pinney, are in six volumes (Cambridge University Press, 1974–81). Jane Millgate in *Macaulay* (1973) and George Levine in *The Boundaries of Fiction* (1968) address the literary issues, while J. W. Burrow's *A Liberal Descent* (1981) and John Clive's *Thomas Babington Macaulay:*

The Shaping of the Historian (1976) consider the intellectual basis of the Whig interpretation.

MACDONALD, GEORGE (1824–1905)

Born near Huntly in what was then the remote Buchan peninsula, his father a farmer descended from Culloden survivors and his mother also of Highland stock, the local scenery and family stories provided image and character for his later novels. From 1840 to 1845 he studied at Aberdeen University, winning prizes in the natural sciences and privately reading much German romantic literature. He went to London, intending to tutor while he looked around, but instead entered college to train for the Congregational ministry and became pastor in Arundel in 1850. Married in 1851 and starting a family that was eventually to number eleven children, he was forced out of his ministry for lack of stern theological precision in 1853, and began a writing career with a long verse play *Within and Without* (1855), which attracted the attention of Tennyson, and the prose romance *Phantastes* (1858). The fantastic stories influenced by *Undine* and Novalis often had to be disguised as children's stories, *At the Back of the North Wind* (1871) and *The Princess and the Goblin* (1872), while his novels are apparently realistic tales of Scottish life, *David Elginbrod* (1863), *Alec Forbes of Howglen* (1865), and *Robert Falconer* (1868). Their dream-like intensity and the intimacy of their spiritual search make the two strands of his fiction in fact alike. He found a small and devoted readership, who also supported his lectures and sermons, influenced as they were by the broad theology of the day (as in *Wilfrid Cumbermede*, 1872). In considerable poverty, he still entertained at his London home friends who included Browning, the Tennysons, Arnold, Ruskin, Morris, and Burne-Jones, He was granted a Civil List pension in 1877 by special request of the Queen, but years of privation had weakened fragile health and from the 1880s he lived largely in Italy. He worked seven years on *Lilith* (1895), his final work, which expresses the heart of his distinctive point of view.

Admired by C. S. Lewis, Tolkien, and Auden, his work has now been extensively reprinted by *Johanessen (Whitehorn, California). *The Complete Fairytales*, ed. U. C. Knoepflmacher, is published by Penguin (2000) and *The Princess and the Goblin* in Puffin Classics (1966). There are lives by his son Greville (1924) and W. Raeper (1987). Studies include D. Robb, *George MacDonald* (1988); R. L. Wolff, *The Golden Key* (1961); and Stephen Prickett, *Victorian Fantasy* (1979).

MALLOCK, WILLIAM HURRELL (1849–1923)

Son of a country clergyman and of the sister of the Froude brothers, educated at Balliol College, Oxford, he was secure from the need to earn his living and could afford to maintain a critical relation to the intellectual compromises of the day. *The New Republic* (1871), started as an undergraduate, is a Peacockian debate about religious belief and its substitutes, between slightly disguised versions of leading Victorian thinkers. In *The New Paul and Virginia* (1878) he continues to ask what, without God, provides a basis for life-choices by placing his figures on a desert island. The sequence was completed by *Is Life Worth Living?* (1879) in which human values are to be found only within a defined religious belief. He continued to write novels of ideas but critical now of political, rather than of theological or ethical, liberalism, as in *The Old Order Changes* (1886) and *The Individualist* (1899). He converted to Catholicism on his deathbed.

*The New Republic (Leicester University Press, 1975) has a useful introduction by John Lucas, editor of the illuminating *Literature and Politics in the Nineteenth Century* (1971).

MARTINEAU, HARRIET (1802–1876)

Daughter of a Norwich cloth-manufacturer and sister of the Revd Professor James Martineau, Unitarian minister and scholar, she passed an unhappy childhood, physically weak and deaf. In her twenties she wrote articles on religion and women's issues for the Unitarian *Monthly Repository*, and began to write professionally to help to support the family, following the failure of the family firm in 1829. Moving to London in 1832, her interest in Utilitarian economics led her to write a successful series of popularizing and didactic tales, *Illustrations of Political Economy* (9 vols., 1832–4). After travelling to America 1834–6, she published *Society in America* (1837) and then her novel *Deerbrook* (1839). By then she had lost her faith and turned to a stern rationalism (tempered by an interest in mesmerism, to the influence of which she attributed a miraculous cure from serious illness). The publication of *Letters on the Laws of Man's Nature and Development* (1851) with H. G. Atkinson, a work of atheistical determinism, caused a final breach with her brother. In 1845 she retired to the Lake District, where she produced an abridged translation of Comte's *Philosophie positive* (2 vols., 1853) and wrote articles in support of divorce reform and the repeal of the Contagious Diseases Acts, as well as her candid *Autobiography* which was published posthumously in 1877.

Both *Deerbrook* and the *Autobiography* have been reprinted by
*Virago (1983). There is a *Selected Letters*, edited by Valerie Sanders
(Oxford, 1990) who has also written *Harriet Martineau and the Victorian
Novel* (1986). R. B. Webb's *Harriet Martineau: A Radical Victorian*
(1960) is the standard biography, placing the life in the context of Victori-
an radicalism.

MASSEY, GERALD (1828–1907)

Born in a stone hut on the canal near Tring, Hertfordshire, his parents
both illiterate and his father a canal boatman, he worked from the age of
8 but read whatever he could. He worked as an errand boy in London from
the age of 15, read Tom Paine, and was inspired first by Chartism and then
by Christian Socialism. He began writing verse, started up a working
men's newspaper, and published *Poems and Chansons* in the revolutionary year of 1848. *The Ballad of Babe Christabel with Other Lyrical Poems*
(1854), including a biographical sketch, made him as famous as the
other main working-class poet Ebenezer Elliott, the Yorkshire Corn-Law
Rhymer, and admired by Tennyson, Ruskin, and, as an example of the
self-made man, Samuel Smiles. He was an assistant to the radical publisher
John Chapman (and may have been the model for George Eliot's *Felix
Holt* as a result of that connection). Subsequently losing several jobs on
account of his politics, he worked as a journalist, moving to Edinburgh in
1854. Eventually he found a patron in Lady Marian Alford, received
a Civil List pension in 1863, and turned to more mystical writing and
lecturing.

There is no modern edition to supersede *Complete Poetical Works*
(Boston 1857, 1861), with a biographical sketch by Samuel Smiles. David
Shaw's *Gerald Massey: Chartist, Poet, Radical and Freethinker* was
published in 1955. Martha Vicinus, *The Industrial Muse* (1974) remains
a seminal work.

MAYHEW, HENRY (1812–1887)

One of seventeen children of a London solicitor, he ran away to sea from
Westminster School in 1825 but on his return was nevertheless articled to
his father. He turned instead to popular journalism and literature, writing
farces, starting with *The Wandering Minstrel* (1834), and founding a
predecessor of *Punch*, *Figaro in London* (1831–9) and in 1832 *The Thief*,
a miscellany magazine. In 1841 he was one of the founding contributors to
Punch itself and married a daughter of his colleague, Douglas Jerrold, in

1844. Financial difficulties made him turn to popular fiction which he continued to write until 1870, often collaborating with his brother Augustus. His fame rests on the series of eighty-two articles, written in sympathy with the submerged poor, which started in the *Morning Chronicle* in 1849 and were first collected in 1852, *London Labour and the London Poor*, eventually reaching four volumes (1862, 1865). He lived in Germany in 1862, preparatory to writing a life of Luther of which only *The Boyhood* appeared in 1865, whereas his gifts as a sociological observer led to the far livelier *German Life and Manners in Saxony* (1864).

There is a *Penguin selection from *London Labour and the London Poor*, ed. V. E. Neuburg (1985). **The Unknown Mayhew: Selections from The Morning Chronicle* ed. E. P. Thompson and Eileen Yeo (Penguin, 1984) contains good introductory essays; see also E. P.Thompson, 'The Political Education of Henry Mayhew', *Victorian Studies*, 11/1 (1967), 41–62. The standard biography is Anne Humpherys, *Travels into the Poor Man's Country* (1977).

MEREDITH, GEORGE (1828–1909)

He was the son of a naval tailor in Portsmouth and a mother who died when he was 5. The business had declined since his grandfather's days and the father migrated to London and then to South Africa, leaving his son to be cared for by his four sisters, all of whom in social terms had married well. George was educated locally and in Germany (1842–4). Articled to a London solicitor, he supported himself precariously by journalism and some published verse. In 1849 he met and married the widowed daughter of the satirical novelist Thomas Love Peacock, seven years older than himself, but in 1855 Mary Ellen left son and husband to elope with Henry Wallis, the Pre-Raphaelite painter, who had been using Meredith as his model in *The Death of Chatterton*. She was later deserted by her lover and died wretchedly in 1861. The experience lies behind the sonnet sequence *Modern Love* (1862). Meredith wrote both poetry and prose fiction through his life, *Poems* (1851) being followed by *The Shaving of Shagpat* (1855), *The Ordeal of Richard Feverel* (1859), and the more popular, semi-autobiographical *Evan Harrington* (1860). He depended on newspaper articles when he remarried in 1864, and on the income for being literary adviser to Chapman and Hall, with whom he turned down Mrs Henry Wood's *East Lynne* and Samuel Butler's *Erewhon* but gave help to Hardy and Gissing. *Harry Richmond*, another of his more popular novels, appeared in the *Cornhill* (1871), while *Beauchamp's Career* (1875) concerned itself with the idealism of radical politics; but it was *The Egoist*

(1879) which confirmed his critical reputation. Later poems like *Ballads and Poems of Tragic Life* (1887) appeared alongside novels analysing the situation of the 'new woman', *Diana of the Crossways* (1885) and *One of our Conquerors* (1891). From 1885 he was progressively disabled by a spinal complaint.

Most of the major novels appear in Penguin or *Oxford World's Classics, though later novels such as *The Tragic Comedians* and *The Amazing Marriage* are currently out of print: together with the 'Essay on Comedy' (1877), they are to be found in the *Memorial edition of the *Works*, 27 vols. (1910). **The Poems of George Meredith*, edited by Phyllis Bartlett, 2 vols. (Yale University Press, 1978) is the standard edition. **The Letters* are edited by C. L. Clive, 3 vols. (Clarendon Press, 1970) who has written a biography, *The Ordeal of George Meredith* (1953). Virginia Woolf's 'On Re-Reading Meredith' (*Collected Essays*, 4 vols. (Chatto and Windus, 1967), vol. 1) remains important. Gillian Beer's *Meredith: A Change of Masks* (1970) is still a useful guide to six of the novels, while J. Moses, *The Novelist as Comedian* (1983) defends him as proto-modernist. Carol Bernstein offers a reading of the poetry in *Precarious Enlightenment* (1979).

MILL, JOHN STUART (1806–1873)

The precocious son of James Mill, the Utilitarian economist, he was famously subjected to an austere programme of education at home, starting Greek at the age of 3. His youth was passed in a ferment of activity, being involved in the formation of the Utilitarian Society in 1823 (the year he joined his father in the East India Company office); *The Westminster Review*, the organ of intellectual radicalism, in 1824; and the London Debating Society in 1825, when he also edited works by Bentham. In 1826–7 he suffered a mental and emotional crisis, the discovery of Wordsworth helping to modify his narrow rationalism, though depression recurred in 1836, following his father's death. In 1830 he fell in love with Harriet Taylor, wife of a friend, whom he was only able to marry after John Taylor's death in 1851. The conflict in his mind between system and impulse found expression in essays on Bentham (1838) and Coleridge (1840) and in the modification of Utilitarianism finally formulated in a work with that title in 1863. In 1843 the *System of Logic* attempted to establish a general basis of thought and method for scientific theory, and this attempt to rethink what lay behind the issues of the day led to *Principles of Political Economy* (1848), which addresses the conditions of the new industrial proletariat. His later works were much influenced by his wife's thought, though she died in 1858, most clearly *The Subjection of Women* (1869) but also the increased interest in the individual in *On Liberty* (1859) and *Considerations on Representative Government* (1860). He retired when the East India Company was dissolved in 1859 and entered the Commons as Independent MP for Westminster, 1865–8. His *Autobiography* appeared posthumously.

The **Collected Works* has been appearing under the general editorship of J. M. Robson (University of Toronto, 1963–) and includes the correspondence. **The Autobiography* has been edited to restore earlier suppressed passages by Jack Stillinger (Oxford University Press, 1969). Selected works are available as Penguins and Oxford World's Classics. Michael Packe has written a life (1954) and there is a good brief introduction by William Thomas, *Mill* (1985), as well as Alan Ryan's *The Philosophy of John Stuart Mill* (2nd edn., 1987). Of special interest to students of literature is Fred Berger, *Happiness, Justice and Freedom* (1985).

MORRIS, WILLIAM (1834–1896)

The son of a rich stockbroker, he spent an idyllic childhood, with games of medieval make-believe, in a big house on the edge of Epping Forest. After attending Marlborough College, one of the new public schools (1848–52), he entered Exeter College, Oxford (1853), where he formed a lifelong friendship with the Pre-Raphaelite painter Edward Burne-Jones and was influenced by Ruskin's *Stones of Venice*, in his interest in medieval society and culture as a basis for a critique of his own times. Believing architecture would be the way to express his ideas, he was briefly articled (1856) to George Street in whose office he met Philip Webb. A collection of poems, *The Defence of Guenevere* (1858), was his first notable work, expressive of dreads and misgivings he had recurrently felt since childhood. After he married Jane Burden in 1859, the Red House was designed for them by Webb, and his interest in its furnishing led to the setting up of the firm of Morris, Marshall, Faulkner and Co., which included Webb, Burne-Jones, Ford Madox Brown, and D. G. Rossetti, with the intention to transform the standards of British design. It was the start of the Arts and Crafts movement, in protest against mass production. The ideas are also apparent in the poetry; where contemporaries largely wrote short poems about the interior life, Morris produced extended narratives in sparely archaic, often rhymed lines, about active life and the suffering, stoically endured, which was produced by passion, *The Life and Death of Jason* (1867) and *The Earthly Paradise* (1868–70). Whilst living with Morris, Rossetti had a love affair with Jane, much to Morris's pain. He leased Kelmscott Manor in Oxfordshire in 1871 and escaped to Iceland. He had already translated sagas and in 1876 wrote *The Story of Sigurd the Volsung and the Fall of the Niblungs*. His restless energies were meanwhile devoted to reviving hand-printing at the Kelmscott press and weaving carpets using natural dyes. His quiescent political radicalism, roused by the 1878 massacres in Bulgaria, flared into a passionate socialism, reading Marx and joining the Social Democratic Federation in 1883 and the Socialist League in 1884. *A Dream of John Ball* (1888) and *News from Nowhere* (1890) were followed by heroic prose-romances, showing 'the melting of the individual into the society of the tribes', *The Roots of the Mountains* (1890), *The Wood Beyond the World* (1894), and *The Sundering Flood* (1897).

The **Collected Works*, edited by May Morris, is in 24 vols. (Longmans, Green, 1910–15). *The Earthly Paradise* has recently been edited by F. S. Boos in 2 vols. (Routledge, 2003). For biographies see J. W. Mackail, 2 vols. (1899), E. P. Thompson, *William Morris: Romantic to Revolutionary* (1955), and Fiona MacCarthy, *William Morris* (1994). Useful criticism includes Amanda Hodgson, *The Romances of William Morris* (1987) and *Against the Age*, by Peter Faulkner (editor of the Critical Heritage volume, 1973).

NEWMAN, JOHN HENRY (1801–1890)

The son of an Evangelical banker, he was educated at Trinity College, Oxford, and, despite a poor degree, his acknowledged abilities secured him a fellowship at Oriel (1822) and then, after having been ordained in 1824, the charge of St Mary's, the university church, in 1828. His afternoon sermons, in which his later ideas were first adumbrated, attracted large congregations. After a visit to Italy, where he continued to write the poems collected in *Lyra Apostolica* (1836) with Hurrell Froude, Keble, and Pusey (all Oriel Fellows), he became the moving spirit of the Oxford Movement. In the attempt to restore vitality to the idea of the Church as a mystical body (as against the individualism of Evangelicals), he started a series of *Tracts for the Times* (hence Tractarianism) in 1833 which, despite his suspicion of Rome, moved in a steadily Catholic direction. They culminated in Tract 90 (1841), which argued that the Church's apparently Protestant formulary, the Thirty-Nine Articles, was actually open to Catholic interpretation. He was placed under an episcopal ban, resigned his living in 1843, and was received into the Roman Catholic Church in 1845. He was commissioned to establish Oratory churches, the first of them in Birmingham where he thereafter lived. The first fruit of his new position was his *Essay on the Development of Christian Doctrine* (1845), and when he was personally vilified by Kingsley, he responded with an account of his personal development, drawing on the same ideas of the evolution of belief, in *Apologia Pro Vita Sua* (1864). Made rector of the newly established Catholic University in Dublin (1851–8), he produced *The Idea of a University* (1852; rev. 1859, 1873). His most generally philosophical study of the way in which decisions are reached, *An Essay in Aid of a Grammar of Assent* (1870), was his final word, in effect, on how his conversion had happened. He continued to write poetry and the account in *The Dream of Gerontius* (1866) of the transition of the soul to God through death involves an imagery that affects all his work, not least his most famous poem, 'Lead, kindly light'. There are also two austere novels, *Loss and Gain* (1848) and *Callista* (1856). He was made a cardinal in 1879 by the scholarly Leo XIII.

There is no modern collected edition since the Longman edition in 41 vols. (1908–18), but there are separate editions of **The Idea of a University*, ed. I. T. Ker (Clarendon Press, 1976); **The Grammar of Assent* by the same editor (Clarendon Press, 1985); *An Essay on the Development of Christian Doctrine* (University of Notre Dame Press, 1989); **The University Sermons*, ed. D. M. MacKinnon and J. D. Holmes (SPCK, 1970); and the **Apologia*, ed. Martin Svaglic (Clarendon Press, 1967). **Loss and Gain* is published by Oxford World's Classics. *The Letters and Diaries*, ed. C. S. Dessain, T. Gornall, and I. T. Ker, occupy 31 vols. (Clarendon Press, 1961–78). I. T. Ker has written *John Henry Newman: A Biography* (1988). J. Coulson and A. M. Allchin (eds.), *The Rediscovery of Newman* (1967) is invaluable, as is John Coulson's *Religion and Imagination* (1981).

OLIPHANT, MRS [Margaret Oliphant, née Wilson] (1828–1897)

Born in Scotland, the daughter of Francis Wilson, a customs and excise official, and of Margaret Oliphant, a clever, rather sarcastically spoken mother, her first novel, *Margaret Maitland* (1849), expressed strong Scottish Free Church opinions. In 1852 she married her cousin, Francis Oliphant, a stained-glass designer, and she supplemented the family income by continuing to write. In 1859, however, her husband died suddenly of consumption, leaving his wife in poverty, with two children and a third on the way. She had now to write in order to live and was already engaged on a two-volume life of the Scottish religious leader Edward Irving (1862), scarcely likely to be remunerative. Success came with 'The Chronicles of Carlingford', seven novels (1863–76), effectively beginning with *Salem Chapel*, serialized anonymously in *Blackwood's Magazine*. As told in her posthumously published *Autobiography*, her life became a struggle of hard work and pain, with the death of her surviving daughter in 1864, her adoption of three of her brother's children, and the eventual loss of the two sons (1890 and 1894) to whom she had devoted her life. She wrote up to three novels a year, leaving over one hundred works, novels, criticism, biography, histories, and many articles for the reviews and journals. Her later fiction, in particular *Hester* (1883) and *Kirsteen* (1890), shows an increase in her dry-eyed penetration of self-delusion and unsentimental intelligence; while her later ghost stories, *A Beleaguered City* (1880) and 'Stories of the Seen and the Unseen' (from 1885 on), are actually a complex mixture of realism and religious vision.

The *Autobiography and Letters* was edited by Mrs H. Coghill (1899) and has been reprinted by the University Presses of both Leicester and Chicago: there is a fine modern edition of the *Autobiography* by Elisabeth Jay (Oxford University Press, 1990) who has written the biographical *Mrs Oliphant: A Fiction to Herself* (1995). 'The Chronicles of Carlingford' were reprinted by *Virago (1984 onwards) as was *Hester* (1984). *Miss Marjoribanks* is currently available in Penguin. *A Beleaguered City* appeared in *Oxford World's Classics in 1988, and there is a *Selected Short Stories of the Supernatural*, ed. Margaret K. Gray (Scottish Academic Press, 1985). R. C. Terry, *Victorian Popular Fiction* (1983) considers her status in her own day, while Valentine Cunningham's valuable *Everywhere Spoken Against* (1975) provides the context of religious dissent.

PATER, WALTER [Horatio] (1839–1894)

Shy and withdrawn as a child (he lost his father, a doctor, when he was 4), he only shone when in the sixth form at King's School, Canterbury. This slow development was repeated at Oxford, where he won a scholarship in 1858 graduating with a second-class degree in 1862, but valuing two vacation visits to Germany and entry to a postgraduate society of which T. H. Green was a member. He gained a fellowship at Brasenose in 1864. The influence of Ruskin's *Modern Painters*, Jowett's Platonism, Hegelianism, a first heady visit to Italy in 1865, and the aestheticism of Swinburne were all apparent in the series of articles written largely for *The Fortnightly Review*, collected in 1873 as *Studies in the History of the Renaissance*. Twelve years passed before his second book, the semi-novel *Marius the Epicurean: His Sensations and Ideas* (1885; rev. 1888 and 1892), a fastidious version of life under an ancient social system with a religion in its final stage of sophisticated decline, as much late Victorian Britain as Antonine Rome. He spent increasing time in London and Italy, writing a collection of fictional lives to characterize historical moments, *Imaginary Portraits* (1887), and works of impressionist criticism, *Appreciations* (1889) and *Plato and Platonism* (1893).

The *Renaissance* has been edited by Donald L. Hill (University Of California Press, 1980) and is in Oxford World's Classics. A good selection from his essays is *Walter Pater: Essays on Literature and Art*, edited by Jenny Uglow for Everyman (1991) which must be supplemented, however, by the important essays in *Appreciations* (1889). Denis Donoghue, *Walter Pater: Lover of Strange Souls* (1995) is the best modern life. Anthony Ward, *Walter Pater: The Idea in Nature* (1966), Wolfgang Iser, *Walter Pater: The Aesthetic Moment* (1987), and Elinor Shaffer, *Walter Pater and the Culture of the Fin-de-Siècle* (1995) all witness to his influence as a hinge figure in later Victorian culture.

PATMORE, COVENTRY [Kersey Dighton] (1823–1896)

Son of Peter George Patmore, a journalist and friend of Lamb and Hazlitt, who lost the family capital in the railway collapse of 1846, Coventry had to find employment in the Printed Book department of the British Museum. In 1847 he married Emily Andrews, daughter of a Congregationalist minister who once tutored Ruskin. His *Poems* (1844) attracted the notice of the young Pre-Raphaelites, and he contributed to the short-lived *Germ* (1850). The happiness of his domestic life led to the fictionalized semi-narrative sequence, *The Angel in the House* (1854 and 1856), continued in *Faithful for Ever* (1860) and *The Victories of Love* (1862), written in sorrow while his wife was dying of consumption. On a visit to Rome in 1864 he met Marianne Byles, a Catholic, and married her, having converted to her religion. Returning to poetry in *The Unknown Eros* (1877), he uses human as a metaphor for divine love and experiments with freer verse forms, though his study of prosody in the preface to *Amelia* (1878) was criticized by his friend Tennyson. The objections of Hopkins to poems on the Virgin led him to destroy them, publishing no more except *The Rod, The Root and the Flower* (1895), a series of devotions. He married a third time in 1880.

There has been no collected edition since that of F. Page (Clarendon Press, 1949). J. C. Reid, *The Mind and Art of Coventry Patmore* (1957) offers biography, and Eric Griffiths writes powerfully on *The Angel in the House*, in contrast to Hardy's 'Poems of 1912–1913', in *The Printed Voice of Victorian Poetry* (1989).

ROBERTSON, THOMAS WILLIAM (1829–1871)

The eldest of twenty-two children of an acting family, managing the Lincoln 'circuit', he had a desultory education while helping out with various stage tasks, including acting. After the disbanding of his father's company in 1848, he went to London, writing and adapting plays but also producing stories, poems, and reviews, suffering all the rigours of the early Victorian Grub Street. He married an actress, Elizabeth Burton, in 1856 and they appeared on stage together all over the British Isles, while Robertson continued to write, finding success with *David Garrick* (1864). The strict stage directions and demand for realistic settings in *Society* (1865) helped to alter the amateurishly improvisation of his father's days and led to the immense success of *Caste* (1867). His final play, *War* (1871), an allusion to the Franco-Prussian conflict, failed while he lay dying; he commented, 'I shan't trouble them again'.

  *Plays, ed. William Tydeman (Cambridge University Press, 1982) is a generous selection. George Rowell's *The Victorian Theatre: A Survey* (1967) describes the conditions for which Robertson wrote, and there is a combined life and literary study in M. Savin, *Robertson: his Plays and Stage Craft* (1950).

ROSSETTI, CHRISTINA [Georgina] (1830–1894)

Born of an Italian father, a Carbonari refugee from Naples, and a half-Italian mother, sister of Byron's doctor John Polidori, she grew up in London in bohemian poverty, even though her father held the chair of Italian at King's College, and with her mother's High Church piety. At the age of 2, her obstinacy made her father compare her with the House of Lords rejecting the Reform Bill, but with maturity she kept a check on her inherent obduracy and temper. By the age of 12, she was writing poems, contributing to her brother's *The Germ* in 1850. She was engaged briefly to the minor painter James Collinson in 1848 after he had reverted to the Church of England, but separated from him, with some pain, when he returned to his adopted Catholicism. She was sought in marriage by Charles Cayley in 1862, but devoted herself to the care of her mother and aunts, especially after her loved sister, Maria, entered a religious order in 1873, and also to social work at St Mary Magdalene Penitentiary. Her first collection, *Goblin Market and Other Poems* (1862), was an instant success and was followed by *The Prince's Progress* two years later, but thereafter poems appeared separately in religious journals, adding to the constantly expanding *Poems* collected in 1875. In 1870 she nearly died of

Graves's disease which disfigured her appearance, increasing her reserve. She was, nevertheless, involved in causes such as anti-vivisection agitation but also devotional studies, resulting in 1892 in her long commentary on the book of Revelation. She nursed her brother Dante Gabriel through his protracted collapses and death in 1882, and her mother through her last illness in 1886. She herself died in great pain of cancer.

The standard edition is *Complete Poems*, ed. R. W. Crump, 3 vols. (Louisiana State University Press, 1979–90), which is the text for the Penguin edition (2001). The letters are being edited by Anthony H. Harrison, 3 vols. (University Press of Virginia, 1997–). The story *Maude*, ed. Elaine Showalter and Penny Mahon (1993) is also included in Jan Marsh's useful collection of poetry and prose (Everyman, Dent, 1994), and the best modern biography, *Christina Rossetti: A Literary Biography*, comes from the same hand (1994). There is a varied collection of essays, in David A. Kent (ed.), *The Achievement of Christina Rossetti* (1987), and both Dolores Rosenblum, *Christina Rossetti: The Poetry of Endurance* (1983) and Anthony H. Harrison, *Christina Rossetti in Context* (1988) study the poetry by reference to the life.

ROSSETTI, DANTE GABRIEL (1828–1882)

Elder brother of Christina, he painted and wrote verse from an early age. He joined the Royal Academy School in 1844, along with Holman Hunt and Millais, with whom he founded the Pre-Raphaelite Brotherhood, a name adopted in 1848 to express their preference for the clarity of colour and passive purity of image in painters before the time of Raphael (1483–1520). They were later joined by William Morris and Burne-Jones (1857). He had already begun the translation of Dante's *Vita Nuova*, as well as the composition of the sonnets that eventually grew into his constantly developing sequence 'The House of Life', and published 'The Blessed Damozel' in *The Germ* (1850). His painting *Christ in the House of his Parents* (1850) was attacked by Dickens as 'mean, odious, revolting and repulsive', though Ruskin was a stout defender of the Pre-Raphaelite Brotherhood, paying for Dante Gabriel's translation, *Early Italian Poets* (1861). The unstable union of spiritual aspiration with sensual realism resulted in the watercolour *Found*, the image of a penitent magdalen, at the same time as he wrote the monologue concerning a prostitute, 'Jenny'. In 1860 he married Elizabeth Siddal, his model and mistress, and when she died in 1862 of a laudanum overdose, he buried with her the manuscript of his poems, exhuming it in 1869 for the edition of 1870. He shared a house with Swinburne and Meredith, but his increasing dissipation and addiction, the attack on his poetry by Robert Buchanan (1871), the separation from Morris over his affair with Jane Morris, led to despair and paranoia. His last years also produced some of the best poems, ballads influenced by Poe, his severely realistic account of a journey to Belgium, and the scrupulous revision of 'The House of Life' for the edition of 1881. He died by the sea in Kent, under the care of Christina.

The Complete Poetical Works, edited by his brother W. M., 2nd edn., 2 vols. (1911) is still the fullest collection, though *Dante Gabriel Rossetti: Collected Writings*, ed. Jan Marsh (Dent, 1999) is a good modern edition. *The Letters*, ed. O. Doughty and J. R. Wahl, 4 vols. (Clarendon Press, 1965–7) needs supplementing with *Dante Gabriel Rossetti and Jane Morris: Their Correspondence*, ed. J. Bryson (Clarendon Press, 1976). There is a critical biography by Robert M. Cooper, *Lost on Both Sides* (1970). Joan Rees, *The Poems of Dante Gabriel Rossetti: Modes of Self Expression* (1981) examines the poetry, as does Jerome McGann in *Dante Gabriel Rossetti and the Game that Must Be Lost* (2000), with relation to both the paintings and modernism.

RUSKIN, JOHN (1819–1900)

The only child of a prosperous London wine merchant and a strict Evangelical mother, he was overprotected by his parents, educated at home, and accompanied by his mother, and at weekends by his father, when he entered Christ Church, Oxford in 1837, where he was dogged by ill health. His parents had hoped he might take holy orders, but he had already found his vocation when he published *The Poetry of Architecture* (1838) and written *The King of the Golden River* (not published until 1851): both works reflect the family travels in France and the Alps and reveal the moral identity of his aesthetics. His enthusiasm for Turner's late paintings, at the time much criticized, and his belief in the ennobling of the mind by the visual sublime, led to the first volume of *Modern Painters* (1843). Succeeding volumes (1846, 1851, 1856, 1860) turned into an encyclopaedia, in which human perception was wedded to the natural world. His evolving belief that art, and especially architecture, express the total way of life of historical societies found statement in *The Stones of Venice*, 3 vols. (1851–3) and *Seven Lamps of Architecture* (1849). His marriage to Euphemia (Effie) Gray was annulled amid scandal in 1855 and she married Ruskin's former friend, Millais. Ruskin returned to his parents' house to attack, with increased bitterness, 'the deforming mechanism' of modern urban society in *Unto This Last* (1860–2) and *Munera Pulveris* (1862–3), provoking such adverse reaction that the magazines in which they were published—the *Cornhill* and *Fraser's* respectively—had to suspend publication. In *Sesame and Lilies* (1865) he turned polemically to defend the private sanctities of the home, in opposition to the competitive individualism of the day. His father died in 1864 and the fortune he inherited was spent on public works, while he lived on the income from his books. In 1871 he initiated the guild of St George, to engage the different social classes in establishing schools, farms, and communal trade—from which followed his letters to the working men of Britain, *Fors Clavigera* (1871–84). In 1866 he had proposed to the 18-year-old Rose La Touche, whom he had loved since she was 9, but the disapproval of her Evangelical parents ended in her madness and death in 1875. Appointed Slade professor of fine art at Oxford in 1869, he founded a drawing school there the following year, but he resigned the chair in 1878, ostensibly because of criticism of the politics of his lectures. But in the same year he had lost a libel suit brought against him by Whistler, whose paintings he thought not honest work, and, close to collapse, he suffered a first bout of madness. In the intermission of his illness, 1883–5, he resumed his chair and wrote *Praeterita* (1885), his autobiography, which the intervention of madness preventing his completing.

*The Works, ed. E. T. Cook and Alexander Wedderburn, 39 vols. (1903–12) is probably the best early edition bestowed on any Victorian writer; there are selections by Clive Wilmer, *Unto This Last and Other Writings* (Penguin, 1985), and of significant chapters in *Modern Painters* and *The Stones of Venice* in *Selected Writings* ed. P. Davis (Everyman, 1995), while Dinah Birch has admirably edited a selection of *Fors* for Edinburgh University Press (2000). *The Diaries* have been edited by Joan Evans and John Howard, 3 vols. (Clarendon Press, 1956–9). Tim Hilton's two-volume *John Ruskin* (1985, 2000) is a very detailed biography, where John Batchelor's *John Ruskin: No Wealth But Life* (2000) is more succinct. The best introduction remains J. D. Rosenberg, *The Darkening Glass* (1961). Accounts of the theory behind Ruskin's aesthetic are offered in Robert Hewison, *John Ruskin and the Argument of the Eye* (1976) and Jay Fellowes, *The Failing Distance* (1978). Michael Wheeler pursues the religious concerns in *Ruskin's God* (1999) as does Peter Fuller's *Theoria* (1988). Tony Tanner, *Venice Desired* (1992) on Ruskin's Venice and John Unrau, *Looking at Architecture with John Ruskin* (1978) are important studies.

SPENCER, HERBERT (1820–1903)

The only surviving child of a radically minded Derbyshire schoolteacher, his own education was rather neglected and he is a supreme example of the Victorian autodidact. He worked as a civil engineer on the railways, and then briefly edited *The Pilot*, the journal of the universal suffrage movement, though readers objected to his anti-religious views, before becoming sub-editor at *The Economist* 1848–53. Through John Chapman of the *Westminster*, he met Marian Evans and G. H. Lewes, and also Huxley and Tyndall, who in due course came to see him as the theorist needed by the new science. The extreme individualism of *Social Statics* (1851) proved popular, and in 1852 he published his first thoughts on 'the development hypothesis' (as he termed evolution) for Lewes's *The Leader*. *Principles of Psychology* (1855, subsequently revised) found fewer readers, partly because of Spencer's besetting weakness, his refusal to take other people's ideas seriously. Sustained mental concentration brought on the first of several breakdowns, but in 1857, reading through his published papers in sequence, he became conscious of a unity of theme. The first volume of the 'Synthetic Philosophy' now planned, *First Principles* (1862), followed by *The Principles of Biology*, *The Principles of Psychology*, *The Principles of Sociology*, and *The Principles of Ethics*, offered a unified naturalistic explanation of all phenomena on the basis of evolution, which he believed to be a new system of thought. *Education* (1861), a plea for schooling in the sciences, proved popular, as did his *Study of Sociology* (1873), especially in America. Much read in developing countries like India and Japan, his last years of ill health were occupied in bitter defensiveness about his increasing neglect at home. His *Autobiography* appeared posthumously in 1904.

The Life and Letters was compiled by his assistant D. Duncan (1908). W. H. Hudson, *Herbert Spencer* (1908) offers a still accessible introduction; R. C. K. Ensor, *Some Reflections on Spencer's Doctrine* (1946) addresses Spencer's ideas as a whole; and J. D. Y. Peel's *Herbert Spencer* (1971) is particularly valuable on 'the evolution of a sociologist'.

SWINBURNE, ALGERNON CHARLES (1837–1909)

The eldest son of aristocratic, rich, and devoutly High Church parents, the physically tiny and frail Algernon began his rebellious career at Eton, where the regime of flogging his aberrant behaviour seems to have become more pleasure than punishment. At Balliol College, Oxford, in 1856, whilst befriending Ruskin, Burne-Jones, Morris, and Rossetti, he maintained a stance of militant atheism and democratic republicanism. When he went to live in London in 1861, he was still being supported by his father, the admiral, who paid for the publication of the first volumes of poetry. *Atalanta in Calydon* (1865), a classical drama, and *Poems and Ballads*, first series (1866) were admired for their rhythmic dexterity, their learning and flow of images, as much as they were execrated for their sexual adventurousness and transformation of pain to aesthetic ends. A dazzling talker, he became an alcoholic, self-consumingly fixated on drugs and prostitutes, and was only rescued from total collapse in 1879 by his friend, Theodore Watts-Dunton. But the poetry continued to flow, *Songs before Sunrise* (1871), *Poems and Ballads*, second series (1878), *Tristram of Lyonesse* (1882), *Poems and Ballads*, third series (1889). His critical study of Blake (1868) and his articles on Elizabethan dramatists for the *Encyclopaedia Britannica* as well as his book on *Chapman* (1875) were influential in helping to change critical assessments.

The Complete Works, ed. E. Gosse and T. Wise, 20 vols. (1925–7) must be consulted, although selections, as that by the Carcanet Press (ed. L. M. Findlay, 1982), or the Penguin *Poems and Ballads and Atalanta in Calydon* (ed. K. Haynes) are available. See also the selection *Swinburne as Critic*, ed. C. K. Hyder (Routledge, 1972). *The Swinburne Letters*, ed. Cecil Y. Lang, 6 vols. (Yale University Press, 1959–62) gives some impression of the vitality of conversation. Rikky Rooksby, *A. C. Swinburne: a Poet's Life* (1997) is the most useful biography, and Rooksby and Nicholas Shrimpton's collection of essays *The Whole Music of Passion* (1993) is helpful. See also Jerome J. MacGann, *Swinburne: An Experiment in Criticism* (1972) and the context provided by Patricia Clements, *Baudelaire and the English Tradition* (1985).

TENNYSON, ALFRED [Lord] (1809–1892)

The fourth of twelve children of the rector of Somersby in a remote part of Lincolnshire, he was educated at Louth Grammar School and at home, and went up to Trinity College, Cambridge in 1827. Earlier that year he had collaborated with his brother Charles (1808–78), who throughout his life wrote sonnets, in producing *Poems by Two Brothers*. His release from the crowded rectory and his father's increasing mental instability, partly caused by brooding on his disinheritance of the family estates, gave his university friendships a special intensity, especially with Arthur Henry Hallam whom he met in 1829 and who introduced him to the Apostles, the exclusive undergraduate debating society. He published *Poems, Chiefly*

Lyrical in 1830, but misfortunes now accumulated: his father died in 1831 and he had to return home without taking his degree; his brother Edward was declared insane in 1832; and, most of all, Hallam, on whose support he depended and who was engaged to his sister Emily, died suddenly in Vienna of a brain haemorrhage in November 1833. The *Poems* of 1830 and 1832–3, moreover, had received harsh reviews, and Tennyson now lived with the family in Epping Forest (1837), cut off from society, breaking his engagement to Emily Sellwood (1840) because of his financial insecurity, made worse when with the rest of his family he lost his money by a bad investment (1843). His acute depressive state of mind did not prevent him from producing *Poems* in two volumes in 1842 and *The Princess*, his version of *Love's Labours Lost*, in 1847, and he was granted a Civil List pension in 1845. Growing recognition was completed by the publication of *In Memoriam* (1850), the sequence of elegies he had been secretly writing for Hallam since 1833. He married Emily immediately after and was appointed Poet Laureate in succession to Wordsworth later that year. Thereafter, especially following the move to the Isle of Wight in 1853, his life was one of domestic quiet and public honour, though the fears of his earlier experience lie behind *Maud* (1855) and maybe *Enoch Arden* (1864). In the long series of narratives *The Idylls of the King* (1859–74), he turns the King Arthur of national epic into a study of personal motive and character. A series of verse plays, starting with *Queen Mary* (1875), were successfully brought to the stage, and in 1883 he accepted a barony (having twice rejected a baronetcy). He went on writing to the end, *Demeter* in 1889 for example, and when he died, another volume was ready for publication, *The Death of Oenone*, 1892.

The great standard edition is **Poems*, ed. Christopher Ricks, 3 vols. (2nd edn. 1987), and there are informative editions of *In Memoriam* by Susan Shatto and Marion Shaw (Clarendon Press, 1982) and by Susan Shatto of *Maud* (Athlone, 1986). *The Letters* have been edited by Cecil Y. Lang and Edgar F. Shannon Jr, 3 vols. (Clarendon Press, 1982–90). His son's biography, *A Memoir* by Hallam Tennyson, 2 vols. (1897), is a mine of information but needs supplementing by Robert Bernard Martin, *Tennyson, The Unquiet Heart* (1980) and by the life of *Emily Tennyson* by Ann Thwaite (1996). John Jump (ed.), *Tennyson: The Critical Heritage* (1967) is excellent, as is Isobel Armstrong, *Victorian Scrutinies: Reviews of Poetry 1830–1870* (1972). Joseph Gerhard, *Tennyson and the Text* (1992) examines his habits of revision, but see also Christopher Ricks, 'Tennyson's Methods of Composition', *Proceedings of the British Academy*, 57 (1966–7), 209–30. Herbert F. Tucker, *Tennyson and the Doom of Romanticism* (1988) considers his immediate antecedents, while

Tennyson: A Critical Reader, ed. Rebecca Stott (1996) contains a selection of theoretical readings.

THACKERAY, WILLIAM MAKEPEACE (1811–1863)

His father, who died in 1816, was in the Indian Civil Service, and in 1817 Thackeray was sent back to England, to be rejoined by his mother, who had remarried, in 1820. He was educated at Charterhouse, where he wrote comic verse, and at Trinity College, Cambridge, leaving in 1830 without a degree. He had inherited a considerable fortune from his father and travelled in France and Germany, but returned to try the law in 1831, though he had thought seriously of developing his natural talent as an artist. He bought a paper, *The National Standard*, which collapsed after a year, leaving him poorer but with friends in the business. He became a gambler, and in 1834 went to Paris to try his hand as an artist. In 1836 he married an Irish girl, Isabella Shawe, and now had to write to support his family, his first success being *The Yellowplush Papers* for *Fraser's* (1837–8), a below-stairs comic satire. After the birth of three daughters, the first of whom died in infancy, his wife lapsed into insanity and he took her to be cared for by her family in Ireland. His first substantial novel, *Barry Lyndon* (1844) was written alongside largely humourous journalism, notably in sketches for *Punch* (1846–7) which became *The Book of Snobs* (1848). His growing success encouraged him to write a novel in monthly parts, like Dickens, and in January 1847 *Vanity Fair* (1848) began to appear, followed immediately in 1848–50 by the partly autobiographical *Pendennis*, interrupted by a near-fatal illness which left him permanently weakened. *Henry Esmond* (1852), set up in an eighteenth-century typeface by his printers, expressed his interest in the England of Addison and Fielding as freer in manners than his own day, which he regarded with a radical Whig disdain. *The Newcomes* (1853–5), a novel of family rivalry and vendetta, was illustrated by Doyle, replacing for once his own hand, but *The Virginians* (1857–9), a sequel to *Esmond*, where he resumed the illustrations, proved less popular. Ill health and hopeless love for a friend's wife intensified his growing melancholy, but his editorship of *The Cornhill Magazine* from 1859 helped his finances and he wrote essays for it (*The Roundabout Papers*, 1863) and serialized *Philip* (1861–2). He died shortly after moving to a new residence designed by himself in the Queen Anne style he loved.

All the major novels are reprinted by Penguin and *Oxford World's Classics, the latter often with original illustrations. *The Letters* were edited in 4 vols. by Gordon N. Ray (Harvard University Press, 1945–6) who wrote a two-volume biography (1955, 1958) which should be supplemented by D. J. Taylor's *Thackeray* (1999). John Sutherland, *Thackeray at Work* (1974) is concerned with the process of composition, and P. L. Shillingburg, *Pegasus in Harness* (1992) examines the relation with the Victorian publishing world. *Thackeray: The Critical Heritage*, ed. G. Tillotson and D. Hawes (Routledge, 1968) is excellent in reprinting contemporary reviews. Robert A. Colby, *Thackeray's Canvass of Humanity* (1979) offers the contemporary context, and Catherine Peters, *Thackeray's Universe* (1987) provides a useful introduction.

THOMSON, JAMES BYSSHE VANOLIS (1834–1882)

Born at Port Glasgow to a poor merchant-seaman's family which moved to London in 1842, he became an army teacher in Ireland in 1852 until discharged for drunkenness. Back in London, he lodged for a time with Charles Bradlaugh, the atheist and republican MP, whom he had met in the army, and published poems, essays, and translations of Leopardi in Bradlaugh's weekly, *The National Reformer*. Despite recurrent attempts to find a career, as inspector of mines in Colorado in 1872 for example, or reporter on the Spanish civil war in 1873, he sank into melancholic alcoholism. *The City of Dreadful Night* in *The National Reformer* (1874) proved popular, despite its combination of democratic ardour with bleak disbelief in human progress, and he received encouragement from Meredith. He ended miserably, thrown out of his one-room lodgings and dying in hospital of exposure and malnutrition.

*Poems and Some Letters, ed. Anne Ridler (Centaur Press, 1963) may be supplemented by William David Schaefer's prose selection, *The Speedy Extinction of Evil and Misery* (University of California, 1967). The same scholar has a study *James Thomson (B.V.): Beyond 'The City'* (1965) in which he argues for the development of his ideas independent of his life. There are studies by Kenneth Hugh Byron, *The Pessimism of James Thomson (B.V.) in Relation to his Times* (1965) and Tom Leonard, *Places of the Mind* (1993).

TROLLOPE, ANTHONY (1815–1882)

He was the son of a depressive and incompetent barrister and of an energetic mother, Fanny, mordant commentator on America and popular novelist. The total failure of the farm his father attempted in Harrow, and his mother's absence in America in 1827, setting up a store in Cincinnati, meant that the neglected Trollope found his schooldays, first as a day-boy at Harrow and later at Winchester, a humiliating disaster. Nor did prospects improve when he entered the Post Office as a clerk in 1834. After a serious illness, in 1840 he took the position of surveyor for the Royal Mail in Ireland, a post no one else wanted, and proved an enterprising and inventive administrator. As a result of this change of fortune, he married in 1844, took to fox-hunting, and started to write novels, though at first without much notice, *The Macdermots of Ballycloran* (1847) and *The Kellys and the O'Kellys* (1848). Back in England, travelling in the West Country to organize improved mail deliveries, he invented Barsetshire and published *The Warden* (1855). Five further novels set in that county dominated by the clergy and parish gentry—*Barchester Towers* (1857), *Doctor Thorne* (1858), *Framley Parsonage* (1860–1), *The Small House at Allington* (1862–4), and, greatest of all, *The Last Chronicle of Barset* (1866–7)—were interspersed with a stream of novels of varied situation and character. *The Three Clerks* (1857) was partly autobiographical, *Castle Richmond* (1860) has the Irish famine for background, and *Orley Farm* (1861–2) typically finds understanding for a mother who forges a will for her son's sake. In 1864 *Can You Forgive Her?* began what was to become a second sequence of novels with a background of politics: *Phineas Finn* (1867–9), *The Eustace Diamonds* (1871–3), *Phineas Redux* (1873–4), *The Prime Minister* (1875–6), and *The Duke's Children* (1879–80). After leaving the Post Office in 1867, he travelled in Australia and New Zealand and wrote accounts of them, returning to fight an unsuccessful election as a Liberal, an experience reflected in *Ralph, the Heir* (1871). His misgivings about political and cultural change are reflected in the melancholy of *He Knew He Was Right* (1868–9) and culminated in *The Way We Live Now* (1874), and his readership declined. He was firmly unromantic about writing as an occupation, as he records in the posthumously published *Autobiography*, yet many of his late novels, *Cousin Henry* (1879) or *Mr Scarborough's Family* (1883), for example, have been subsequently revalued.

There are scholarly editions of the novels published by the Trollope Society and most of the fiction appears in *Penguin and Oxford World's Classics. There are many fine modern biographies, by R. H. Super, R. Mullen, and N. J. Hall (editor of *The Letters*, 2 vols., Stanford University Press, 1983), but the most sympathetic is *Trollope* by Victoria Glendinning (1992). Asa Briggs is good on Trollope and Bagehot in *Victorian People* (rev. edn., 1970) and Robin Gilmour's *The Idea of the Gentleman in Victorian Fiction* (1981) has proved influential. Stephen Wall, *Trollope and Character* (1988) and David Skilton, *Anthony Trollope and his Contemporaries* (2nd edn., 1996) are both excellent.

WARD, MRS HUMPHRY [Mary Augusta, née Arnold] (1851–1920)

She grew up in a household disturbed by the religious intensities of the time. Her father, Thomas Arnold, son of the headmaster of Rugby, had emigrated to Tasmania to farm, but changed to school administration and then had to surrender his post, when Tractarianism led him into the Catholic Church. Returning to Britain in 1856, he taught at Newman's Catholic University in Dublin while the, eventually, eight children and their mother (a devout Protestant) lived usually at the old Arnold home, Fox Howe, in the Lake District. In 1865, her father returned to the Church of England and accepted a post at Oxford, where Mary read deeply, making herself by the 1870s an authority on early Spanish church history and mingling with Pater, Mark Pattison, and T. H. Green, all influences on her thought. She married a don at Brasenose in 1872, had three children by him, and became secretary to the Oxford Association for the Education of Women whose aim was to open the university's doors. In 1876 her father's return to Catholicism broke up his marriage and probably influenced Mary's growing agnosticism. The family's move to London, when Ward became a leader-writer for *The Times* in 1881, further opened her to current trends. Her translation in 1885 of the *Journal intime* of the Swiss devout doubter Amiel brought her to write a novel, *Miss Bretherton*, in 1884, which failed, before she produced her vindication of radicalized religious agnosticism, *Robert Elsmere* (1888). With the proceeds of its enormous success, she helped open a centre in Bloomsbury in 1890 for the instruction of working people, called University Hall. Her belief in a practical religion lay behind *The History of David Grieve* (1892), *Marcella* (1894), and its sequel *Sir George Tressady* (1896) which address a variety of social issues. A more personal anguish over the divisions caused by religious disagreements found expression in the impressive *Helbeck of Bannisdale* (1898), writing to her father in Ireland that she had revised it 'for your dear sake'. A member of one of the great intellectual clans, she had the confidence to cultivate a stubborn independence of mind, leading the Women's Anti-Suffrage League, for example, in 1908. *A Writer's Recollections* (1918) is an interesting account of her intellectual life and milieu.

There are modern editions of *Robert Elsmere* in Oxford World's Classics and *Helbeck of Bannisdale* in Penguin, and others in Garland reprints. The standard modern life is J. A. Sutherland, *Mrs Humphry Ward: Eminent Victorian, Pre-Eminent Edwardian* (1990). W. S. Peterson's *Victorian Heretic* (1976) describes in detail the theological issues at stake in *Robert Elsmere*.

YONGE, CHARLOTTE [Mary] (1823–1901)

The only daughter of a country gentleman with a small estate in Hampshire, she was educated at home with a command of languages, ancient and modern. The family was devout and much influenced by John Keble, who arrived in 1835 to be vicar of the united parish of Hursley. His rejection of ambition, his care for the parish, and use of the income from his writing to restore the parish church, on the lines suggested by her father, influenced her youthful admiration for lives of dedication and conscience. Though she had only one brother, regular holidays with a huge family of cousins supplied the interest in sibling relationships in her later fiction. Keble encouraged her to use the gift for narrative, apparent in her Sunday school teaching, more widely in the service of religion, but warned her against preaching, overseeing her work until his death in 1866. Her first novel, *Abbey Church, or Self Control and Self-Conceit* (1844), typifies her later work in the discrimination of subtitle and in the subject itself, the opening of a restored church. Anonymously published, the early works sold well, and *The Heir of Redcliffe* (1853), which drew on the enthusiasm for medieval chivalry inspired by Kenelm Digby's *The Broadstone of Honour* (1822), was admired by Tennyson, Rossetti, and Morris, going through twenty-two editions by 1876. All the proceeds went to the mission fund. Her experience was narrow, teaching in the village school, moving to a nearby cottage when her brother married in 1862; but the tempering of romantic idealism by severe analysis of character, and her understanding of social problems, housing, education, drunkenness, gave her constantly varied subjects for the stream of over a hundred and fifty books, half of them novels, she had completed by her death. In 1857 she became editor of *The Monthly Packet*, a church magazine for the young, and retained the post for thirty-nine years, writing many children's books, in addition to the fiction on which her reputation rested, *Heartsease* (1854), *The Daisy Chain* (1856), *Hopes and Fears* (1860), *The Clever Woman of the Family* (1865).

There are reprints of ** The Heir of Redcliffe* in Oxford World's Classics and of *The Daisy Chain* and *The Clever Woman of the Family* by Virago. The official *Life and Letters* was prepared by C. R. Coleridge (1903) but should be supplemented by *A Chaplet for Charlotte Yonge*, ed. M. Laski (1965). R. L. Woolf, *Gains and Losses* (1977) provides a religious context, as does Elisabeth Jay, *Faith and Doubt in Victorian Britain* (1986) and Barbara Dennis, *Charlotte Yonge, Novelist of the Oxford Movement* (1992). Mark Girouard's *The Return to Camelot: Chivalry and the English Gentleman* (1981) offers another ideal.

Suggestions for Further Reading

The *Nineteenth Century* volume (2000) in the *Short Oxford History of the British Isles* is a clear and useful starting point, in particular the essays by its editor, Colin Matthew. The best full-length introduction to the general history remains Asa Briggs, *The Age of Improvement 1783–1867* (corrected edn., 1979) and, with special reference to the mid-Victorian generation, W. L. Burn, *The Age of Equipoise* (1964). G. M. Young, *Portrait of an Age* (2nd edn., 1953) is still important. E. A. Wrigley's *People, Cities and Wealth* (1987) and *Continuity, Chance and Change* (1988) subtly describe the transforming power of the Industrial Revolution, and Harold Perkin, *The Origins of Modern English Society 1780–1880* (1969) is genuinely stimulating on the evolving structures of society, as is Patrick Joyce in his account of the self and the social in *Democratic Subjects* (1994). On the social history, J. F. C. Harrison, *Early Victorian Britain 1832–1851* (1971) and Geoffrey Best, *Mid-Victorian Britain 1851–1870* (1971) offer good, detailed introductions, while J. A. Auerbach offers the best account of *The Great Exhibition of 1851* (1999). On class issues, L. Davidoff and C. Hall, *Family Fortunes: Men and Women of the English Middle-Class, 1780–1850* (1987); Patrick Joyce, *Visions of the People* (1991); and David Cannadine, *The Decline and Fall of the British Aristocracy* (1990) and *Class in Britain* (1998) are all properly provoking. H. J. Dyos and Michael Wolff, *The Victorian City: Images and Realities*, 2 vols. (1973) is a pioneering work, usefully supplemented by A. S. Wohl, *Endangered Lives* (1983), on issues of public health. G. E. Mingay (ed.), *The Victorian Countryside* 2 vols. (1981) completes the national picture. Gertrude Himmelfarb, *The Idea of Poverty in the Early Industrial Age* (1984) is a work by an always interestingly controversial (and conservative-minded) scholar of the period; but see also G. R. Searle's impressive *Morality and the Market in Victorian Britain* (1998) on the relation of capitalism and Christianity.

On areas of personal feeling see A. S. Wohl (ed.), *The Victorian Family* (1978); Peter Gay, *The Bourgeois Experience*, 2 vols. (1984–6); Michael Mason, *The Making of Victorian Sexuality* (1994) and *The Making of Victorian Sexual Attitudes* (1995); and Stephen Marcus, *The Other Victorians: A Study of Sexuality and Pornography in Mid-Victorian England* (1966). Mary Poovey in *Uneven Development* (1988) offers a feminist account of the ideological dependence on gender-difference in Victorian England.

The standard authority on Victorian religion is Owen Chadwick's two-volume *The Victorian Church* (1966–70), but the really stimulating work in this area lies in Boyd Hilton, *The Age of Atonement: The Influence of Evangelicalism on Social and Economic Thought 1785–1865* (1988) and with relation to European-wide problems of secularization, culminating in the nineteenth century, Alasdair MacIntyre's classic *After Virtue* (1981). With particular reference to Newman, John Coulson, *Religion and Imagination* (1981) shows why literary students should be interested in the language of religion. Stephen Gill, *Wordsworth and the Victorians* (1998) examines one important source of non-dogmatic religion.

On the relation of religion to scientific developments, see F. M. Turner, *Between Science and Religion* (1974); Tess Cosslett's selection, *Science and Religion in the Nineteenth Century* (1984); and Laura Otis's *Literature and Science in the Nineteenth Century* (2002). The major works on the Darwinian Revolution are R. M. Young, *Darwin's Metaphor: Nature's Place in Victorian Culture* (1985); Gillian Beer, *Darwin's Plots* (1983); and J. W. Burrow, *Evolution and Society* (1966), usefully supplemented at the level of general thought by T. S. Kuhn, *The Structure of Scientific Revolutions* (1962). On matters of mind and brain, R. M. Young, *Mind, Brain and Adaptation in the Nineteenth Century* (1970) and Rick Rylance, *Psychological Theory and British Culture 1850–1880* (2000) are both stimulating, and Janet Oppenheim's *'Shattered Nerves': Doctors, Patients and Depression in Victorian England* (1991) is a mine of information.

On Victorian intellectual life itself, see Stefan Collini, *Public Moralists: Political Thought and Intellectual Life in Britain 1850–1913* (1991) and T. W. Heyck, *The Transformation of Intellectual Life in Victorian England* (1982). Walter Houghton, *The Victorian Frame of Mind, 1830–1870* (1957) is still useful as a compendium, though rather schematic.

The individual feel of the pressure of the great questions is best registered by reading contemporary European texts, such as Nietzsche's *Untimely Meditations* (written between 1873 and 1876) and Kierkegaard's *Fear and Trembling* (1843) or *The Suffering unto Death* (1849) in the context marked out by W. H. Mallock, *Is Life Worth Living?* (1879) or by Alasdair MacIntyre in chapter 1 of *Three Rival Versions of Moral Enquiry* (1990). There MacIntyre examines late nineteenth-century efforts at a comprehensive, encyclopaedic synthesis, in contrast to those thinkers (like Kierkegaard or Newman) who claim there can be no translation of religious into secular discourse. For a usefully provocative attack on the search for absolutes see, however, Christopher Herbert's *Victorian Relativity: Radical Thought and Scientific Discovery* (2001), most profitably considered perhaps in relation to William James, 'What Pragmatism Means' in *Pragmatism* (1907), on which Thomas Hardy commented, apropos of the dictum 'Truth is what will work', 'A worse corruption of language was never perpetrated'. Elaine Freedgood, *Victorian Writing about Risk: Imagining a Safe England in a Dangerous World* (2000) opens up the area of chance, anxiety, and belief described in her subtitle, though safety is not always the issue.

The relation of these serious moral and religious concerns to literature may be bridged through the use of J. P. Stern's shamefully underrated work *On Realism* (1973); Michael Wheeler, *Death and the Future Life in Victorian Literature and Theology* (1990); J. Hillis Miller, *The Disappearance of God: Five Nineteenth-Century Writers* (1965); Hilary Fraser, *Beauty and Belief* (1986); or, more indirectly, Isaiah Berlin's classic essay on Tolstoy and the novel, *The Hedgehog and the Fox* (1953). William James's chapter on 'The Divided Self' in *The Varieties of Religious Experience* (1902) is a potentially stimulating introduction to the predicament of writers such as A. H. Clough.

On the novel, politicized readings are offered by Georg Lukács in his classic *Studies in European Realism* (1964) and, more recently, in Nancy Armstrong, *Desire and Domestic Fiction* (1987), at the personal level, and Catherine Gallagher, *The Industrial Reformation of English Fiction 1832–1867* (1985), on the impact of industrialism (but also see Martin J. Weiner, *English Culture and the Decline of the Industrial Spirit 1850–1980* (1992) for a polemical defence of the industrial spirit). J. Hillis Miller's *The Form of Victorian Fiction* (1968) defines the novel formally 'as a structure of interpenetrating minds', while George Levine, *The Realistic Imagination* (1981) has vital things to say on realism's relation to faith, in its attempt to use a language to get beyond language and 'discover some non-verbal truth out there'. E. D. Ermarth has two interesting books—*Realism and Consensus* (1983) and *The English Novel in History 1840–1895* (1997)—which depict the (to her regrettable) mid-century refusal to take the final step to utter pluralism. On the other hand, Barbara Hardy's *Forms of Feeling in Victorian Fiction* (1985) remains a salutary reminder of the role of emotion, as does, more generally, Fred Kaplan, *Sacred Tears* (1987). On the crucial technique of conveying indirect mental speech, see Dorrit Cohn, *Transparent Minds: Narrative Modes for Presenting Consciousness in Fiction* (1978). Ashgate is bringing out a series, *Chartist Fictions* (ed. Ian Haywood, 1999, 2001), which reprints radical narratives from Chartist newspapers. The best anthology of Victorian criticism of the novel taken from the periodicals is J. C. Olmstead's three-volume *A Victorian Art of Fiction* (1979). John Sutherland's *Longman Companion to Victorian Fiction* (1988) is always a valuable guide to novels and novelists, though a reader should be alert to occasionally idiosyncratic plot summaries.

Matthew Reynolds's excellent *The Realms of Verse: English Poetry in a Time of Nation-Building* (2001) offers an interesting challenge to Isobel Armstrong's influential *Victorian Poetry: Poetry, Poetics and Politics* (1993). Eric Griffiths, *The Printed Voice of Victorian Poetry* (1989) gets to the very feel of the poets, in particular Browning, Tennyson, and Hopkins, while his essay 'Tennyson's Idle Tears' in P. A. W. Collins (ed.), *Tennyson: Seven Essays* (1992) provides important thoughts in relation to the philosophy of Kant. See also on the relation of poetry and philosophy, W. David Shaw, *The Lucid Veil* (1987); also valuable is his book on *Victorians and Mystery* (1990). The best collection of Victorian criticism of poetry is Isobel Armstrong, *Victorian Scrutinies* (1972). There are many anthologies of Victorian verse—Valentine Cunningham's selection for Blackwell (2000); T. J Collins and V. J. Rundle's Broadview Anthology (1999); Daniel Karlin's *Penguin Book of Victorian Verse* (1997); and Christopher Ricks's *New Oxford Book of Victorian Verse* (1987), all of which contain notable minor poets (Cosmo Monkhouse, William Allingham, C. S. Calverley) and the first two of which include contemporary prose writings on poetry. Isobel Armstrong and Joseph Bristow's *Nineteenth-Century Women Poets* (1996), like Angela Leighton and Margaret Reynolds's *Victorian Women Poets* (1995), significantly adds more voices to the canon, with important figures such as Dora Greenwell, as does Brian Maidment's *The Poorhouse Fugitives* (1987), a useful collection of working-class or self-taught poets, on whom further information can be found in Owen Ashton and Stephen Roberts, *The Victorian Working-Class Writer* (1999) and Martha Vicinus's seminal *The Industrial Muse* (1974).

For the theatre, see M. R. Booth, *Theatre in the Victorian Age* (1991); A. Nicoll, *A History of Late Nineteenth-Century English Drama 1850–1900*, 2 vols. (1946); and, on the growth of women writing in this sphere too, Tracy C. Davis and Ellen Donkin (eds.), *Women and Playwriting in Nineteenth-Century Britain* (1999). Interest in performance is reviving: see, for example, G. Taylor, *Players and Performance in the Victorian Theatre* (1989); Gail Marshall, *Actresses on the Victorian Stage* (1998); and Kerry Powell, *Women and Victorian Theatre* (1997). Peter Bailey, *Popular Culture and Performance in the Victorian City* (1998) is particularly good on music hall.

On life-writing, A. O. J. Cockshut, *Truth to Life* (1974) is still useful, Christopher Ricks is excellent on 'Victorian Lives' in *Essays in Appreciation* (1998), and G. P. Landow has edited a useful collection, *Approaches to Victorian Autobiography* (1979). David Vincent's *Bread, Knowledge and Freedom* (1981) is the standard work on working-class autobiography. Valerie Sanders writes on *The Private Lives of Victorian Women* (1989), a theme she pursues powerfully in *Eve's Renegades* (1996). J. W. Burrow's *A Liberal Descent* (1981) is an important work on Victorian historians, while S. Collini, D.Winch, and J. W. Burrow's *The Noble Science of Politics* (1983) is indispensable on political writings. Hilary Fraser's *English Prose of the Nineteenth Century* (1997), with Daniel Brown, in the Longman Literature in English Series, is a particularly good survey, with a most useful bibliography.

On publishing, John Sutherland's *Victorian Novels and Publishers* (1976) and *Victorian Fiction: Writers, Publishers, Readers* (1995) are seminal and should be supplemented by R. D. Altick's classic *The English Common Reader: A Social History of the Mass Reading Public 1800–1900* (1957); Simon Eliot, *Some Patterns and Trends in British Publishing 1800–1919* (1994); A. C. Dooley, *Author and Printer in Victorian England* (1992); and Kate Flint, *The Woman Reader 1837–1914* (1993). J. Shattock and Michael Wolff edit a good collection of introductory essays on *The Victorian Periodical Press* (1982), as do L. Brake, A. Jones, and L. Madden, *Investigating Victorian Journalism* (1990).

On literacy and education begin with John Hurt, *Education in Evolution* (1971), then at its various levels, see David Vincent, *Literacy and Popular Culture: England 1750–1914* (1989); J. F. C. Harrison, *Learning and Living* (1961); Gillian Sutherland, *Elementary Education in the Nineteenth Century* (1971); T. W. Bamford, *The Rise of the Public Schools* (1967); M. Sanderson, *The Universities in the 19th Century* (1975); Sheldon Rothblatt, *The Revolution of the Dons, Cambridge and Society in Victorian England* (1968); M. G. Brock and M. C. Curthoys (eds.), *The History of the University of Oxford*, vols. 6–7 (1997, 2000); C. Harvie, *The Lights of Liberalism: University Liberals and the Challenge of Democracy 1860–86* (1976); and Noel Annan's influential 'The Intellectual Aristocracy', in J. H. Plumb (ed.), *Studies in Social History* (1955). Richard Jenkyns, *The Victorians and Ancient Greece* (1980) is a valuable study of Hellenism in Victorian education and culture. For studies of the reading habits of the working classes, see, in addition to Altick's *The English Common Reader*, Louis James's *Fiction for the Working Man, 1830–1850* (1963) and Jonathan Rose's lively *The Intellectual Life of the British Working Classes* (2001). John Burnett, David Vincent, and

David Mayall have edited a three-volume, annotated bibliography, *The Autobiography of the Working Class* (1984–9), containing nearly two thousand documents, published and unpublished, from nineteenth- and twentieth-century Britain.

The standard bibliography for the period is *The Cambridge Bibliography of English Literature*, Volume 4. *1800–1900*, 3rd edn., ed. Joanne Shattock (1999), though in a few cases (e.g. Sir Richard Burton) the equivalent third volume in F. W. Bateson's *Cambridge Bibliography* (1940) is still necessary. For discovering the authors of periodical reviews, see the superb *Wellesley Index to Victorian Periodicals*, ed. W.E. Houghton et al., 5 vols. (Toronto, 1966–89). The Victorian Database Online offers 'all things Victorian', 1945 to 2000 (www.victoriandatabase.com).

Index

Bold references indicate author-bibliographies, italic references, illustrations.